Diskette Offer

There are many useful and interesting programs contained in this book. If you're like me, you probably would like to use them, but hate typing them into the computer. When I key in routines from a book it always seems that I type something wrong and spend hours trying to get the program to work. This is especially true for Windows programs, which tend to be long. For this reason, I am offering the source code on diskette for all the example programs contained in this book for $24.95. Just fill in the order blank on the next page and mail it, along with your payment, to the address shown. Or, if you're in a hurry, just call (217) 586-4021 (the number of my consulting office) and place your order by telephone. (Visa and Mastercard accepted.) You may also fax your order to (217) 586-4997.

Please send me _____ copies, at $24.95 each, of the programs in the *Osborne Windows Programming Series, Volume 3: Special Purpose API Functions* on an IBM-compatible diskette.

Foreign orders only: Checks must be drawn on a U.S. bank and please add $5 shipping and handling.

_____

Name

_____

Address

_____   _____   _____

City   State   Zip

_____

Telephone

Diskette size (check one):   5 1/4" _____ 3 1/2" _____

Method of payment: Check _____ Visa _____ MC _____

Credit card number: _____

Expiration date: _____

Signature: _____

Send to:
   Herbert Schildt
   398 County Rd 2500 N
   Mahomet, IL 61853

   or phone: (217) 586-4021
   FAX: (217) 586-4997

This offer subject to change or cancellation at any time.

Please allow 3 to 6 weeks for delivery.
Osborne McGraw-Hill assumes NO responsibility for this offer. This is solely an offer of Herbert Schildt, and not of Osborne McGraw-Hill.

Herbert Schildt, Chris Pappas, William Murray, III

Osborne Windows Programming Series, Vol. 3: Special Purpose API Functions

Osborne McGraw-Hill

Berkeley New York St. Louis San Francisco Auckland Bogotá Hamburg London Madrid Mexico City
Milan Montreal New Delhi Panama City Paris São Paulo Singapore Sydney Tokyo Toronto

Publisher	Osborne **McGraw-Hill**
Lawrence Levitsky	2600 Tenth Street
	Berkeley, California 94710
Acquisitions Editor	U.S.A.
Jeffrey Pepper	

Project Editor
Mark Karmendy

For information on software, translations, or book distributors outside of the U.S.A., please write to Osborne **McGraw-Hill** at the above address.

Computer Designer
Peter F. Hancik

Osborne Windows Programming Series, Vol. 3: Special Purpose API Functions

1234567890 DOC 9987654

Cover Design
Compass Marketing

ISBN 0-07-881992-X

Contents at a Glance

Contents

21 MULTIMEDIA WAVE FUNCTIONS 337

22 MULTIMEDIA FILE I/O 369

23   OBJECT LINKING AND EMBEDDING (OLE)   389

26 PRINTING 469

27   PROCESSES AND THREADS   513

28 REGIONS 551

A Complete Programming Example,   566

29 REGISTRATION 571

Preface

This is Volume 3 of the *Osborne Windows Programming Series*. It describes the special purpose Application Programming Interface (API) functions. The special purpose API functions are those that provide support for various specialized subsystems contained in Windows. These subsystems include such things as synchronization, pipes, Dynamic Data Exchange (DDE), Object Linking and Embedding (OLE), Windows NT's security system, and others.

By any standard, Windows is a complicated operating system to write programs for. It contains numerous subsystems and it can sometimes make what seems to be the simplest task extraordinarily complex. Two of the factors that contribute to Windows' complexity are the richness and size of its API. However, this book simplifies the API by organizing it into subsystems.

Unlike other references that simply present an alphabetical listing of the API functions, this book (and its companion, Volume 2) present the API functions by category. Here, the API functions are discussed subsystem-by-subsystem, with each chapter describing all functions related to its particular area. Also, at the end of many chapters is a complete program that illustrates how the subsystem is actually used.

16-bit Windows, Windows NT, and Win32

As you probabaly know, there are currently two general versions of Windows. The first is the traditional, 16-bit Windows. This is the version of Windows that is currently in the widest use. 16-bit Windows run on top of DOS and is largely restricted by its use of the DOS system architecture. The second version of Windows is Windows NT. Windows NT is a stand-alone operating system that does not require DOS. It uses the Win32 API library, which is an expanded version of the standard API, and utilizes full 32-bit addressing. To further complicate things, it is actually possible to create applications compatible with 16-bit Windows that use the Win32 library. As Windows evolves, it is expected that the Win32 library will become the standard API.

Since both the standard API and the new Win32 library are used and will continue to be important, both are fully covered in this book. Thus, this reference will not be out-of-date for quite some time.

In addition to coverage of the Win32 library, Windows NT/Win32 conversion notes are included throughout the book, which explain specific differences between 16-bit Windows and Windows NT/Win32.

What Programming Tools You will Need

The code examples in this book were written, compiled, and tested using the Microsoft C/C++ compiler, version 7, and with Borland C/C++, version 3.1 and 4.0. You will need either of these compilers or another C/C++ compiler that is designed to produce Windows compatible object code. (The Windows NT examples were compiled using the Microsoft Windows NT developers kit C/C++ compiler.)

Don't Forget Volume Two

While this book is complete within itself, you will also want to have Volume 2 in this series: *The General Purpose API Functions*. The general purpose API functions are those that are used by every Windows application and form the backbone of your development efforts. Volume 2 also uses the subsystem-by-subsystem organization that helps make the API accessible.

Together, Volumes 2 and 3 include coverage of the entire API, including both the 16-bit API and the new Win32 API.

Conventions

Most of the conventions used in this book are self-explanatory. However, a few short comments are in order. First, parameter names reflect the variety of styles in current use. While most Windows programmers have adopted the general form of the Microsoft naming convention (which uses type-specific prefix codes), few follow it precisely or consistently. Also, several variants of the Microsoft naming convention have emerged. We decided to reflect the variety of naming styles in this book. For the most part, parameter names use the

Microsoft prefix recommendations, but we have also included examples of alternative styles that we have seen.

Second, when a function is specific to Win32, that is, when it is not part of the 16-bit Windows API, it will have this symbol next to it in the left margin:

Third, the Win32 library **typedef**s most pointer types into names such as **LPPOINT**. However, in the 16-bit API, this type is generally specified as **POINT FAR ***. When one of these types appears in a function prototype and that function is included in both the 16-bit and the Win32 library, the 16-bit type declaration is used. Our reason for this is easy to understand: the prototype is accurate for both libraries.

Finally, some functions have slight differences between their 16-bit and 32-bit versions. When this is case, the specific differences are noted.

Herbert Schildt
Chris Pappas
William Murray

Chapter 1

Atoms

T H I S chapter describes those functions that manage atoms. An atom is a unique value that identifies a string. Thus, you can use atoms to quickly refer to and manage certain commonly used strings. Atoms are unsigned integer values.

There are two types of atoms: local and global. *Local* atoms have their scope confined to your program. *Global* atoms may be accessed by any application currently executing. Global atoms are one way that processes may communicate with each other.

ATOM AddAtom(LPCSTR *lpszString*)

AddAtom() adds the string pointed to by *lpszString* to an application's local atom table. It returns a unique atom that identifies that string. The function returns zero if an error occurs.

If the specified string is already in the atom table, then that string's reference count is increased by one. Reference counts are maintained to prevent a call to **DeleteAtom()** from removing a string that is still needed for some other use.

RELATED FUNCTION

DeleteAtom()

ATOM DeleteAtom(ATOM *atom*)

DeleteAtom() decreases the specified local atom's reference count by one and, if the count is zero, removes the string associated with the specified atom from that process's local atom table. It returns zero if the atom is removed, or non-zero otherwise. (Zero is only returned if the atom is actually deleted, not if its reference count is simply reduced.)

The atom to delete is passed in *atom*.

USAGE

The following fragment shows how to add and then delete an atom.

```
ATOM a1;

a1 = AddAtom("My Atom");

/* ... */

if(DeleteAtom(a1))
  MessageBox(hwnd, "Cannot delete", "Atom", MB_OK);
else
  MessageBox(hwnd, "Deleted", "Atom", MB_OK);
```

RELATED FUNCTIONS

AddAtom()
FindAtom()

ATOM FindAtom(LPCSTR *lpszString*)

FindAtom() returns the local atom associated with the specified string. That is, it searches the atom table for the specified string and, if found, returns the atom linked to it. It returns zero if the string is not found.

The string to search for is pointed to by *lpszString*.

RELATED FUNCTION

AddAtom()
DeleteAtom()

HLOCAL GetAtomHandle(ATOM *atom*)

GetAtomHandle() is obsolete for all versions of Windows since 3.0. It returns a handle to the specified atom.

UINT GetAtomName(ATOM *atom*, LPSTR *lpszString*, int *nSize*)

GetAtomName() copies the string associated with the local atom specified by *atom* into the character array pointed to by *lpszString*. It returns the length of the string, or zero if the atom is not found.

The size of the array pointed to by *lpszString* must be passed in *nSize*.

USAGE

The following fragment adds a string to the atom table and then retrieves it using **GetAtomName()**.

```
ATOM a1;

/* ... */

a1 = AddAtom("My Atom");
/* ... */
if(GetAtomName(a1, str, sizeof(str)))
  MessageBox(hwnd, str, "Atom Name", MB_OK);
```

RELATED FUNCTION

AddAtom()

ATOM GlobalAddAtom(LPCSTR *lpszString*)

GlobalAddAtom() adds a string to the global atom table. It returns a unique atom that identifies that string. The function returns zero if an error occurs.

If the specified string is already in the global atom table, then that string's reference count is increased by one. Reference counts are maintained to prevent a call to **GlobalDeleteAtom()** from removing a string that is still needed for some other use.

USAGE

Unlike local atoms, global atoms are not automatically removed when an application terminates. Therefore, your application must delete all global atoms before termination.

RELATED FUNCTION

GlobalDeleteAtom()

ATOM GlobalDeleteAtom(ATOM *atom*)

GlobalDeleteAtom() decreases the specified global atom's reference count by one and, if the count is zero, removes the string associated with the specified atom from the global atom table. It returns zero if the atom is removed, or non-zero otherwise. (Zero is only returned if the atom is actually deleted, not if its reference count is simply reduced.)

The atom to delete is passed in *atom*.

USAGE

The following fragment shows how to add and then delete an atom.

```
ATOM a1;

a1 = GlobalAddAtom("My Atom");

/* ... */

if(GlobalDeleteAtom(a1))
  MessageBox(hwnd, "Cannot delete", "Atom", MB_OK);
else
  MessageBox(hwnd, "Deleted", "Atom", MB_OK);
```

RELATED FUNCTIONS

GlobalAddAtom()
GlobalFindAtom()

ATOM GlobalFindAtom(LPCSTR *lpszString*)

GlobalFindAtom() returns the global atom associated with the specified string. That is, it searches the global atom table for the specified string and, if found, returns the atom linked to it. It returns zero if the string is not found.

The string to search for is pointed to by *lpszString*.

RELATED FUNCTIONS

GlobalAddAtom()
GlobalDeleteAtom()

UINT GlobalGetAtomName(ATOM *atom,*
LPSTR *lpszString,* int *nSize*)

GlobalGetAtomName() copies the string associated with the global atom specified by *atom* into the character array pointed to by *lpszString*. It returns the length of the string, or zero if the atom is not found.

The size of the array pointed to by *lpszString* must be passed in *nSize*.

USAGE

The following fragment adds a string to the atom table and then retrieves it using **GlobalGetAtomName()**.

```
ATOM a1;

/* ... */

a1 = GlobalAddAtom("My Atom");
/* ... */
if(GlobalGetAtomName(a1, str, sizeof(str)))
  MessageBox(hwnd, str, "Atom Name", MB_OK);
```

RELATED FUNCTION

GlobalAddAtom()

BOOL InitAtomTable(int *nSize*)

InitAtomTable() initializes the local atom table and sets its size to *nSize*.

Since the atom table is accessed using hashing, the size of the table must be a prime number.

USAGE

The local atom table is automatically initialized when your application begins. It can hold 37 atoms. You only need to call **InitAtomTable()** if you need to create a larger atom table.

Since **InitAtomTable()** establishes the atom table, it must be called before you put any atoms into the table.

RELATED FUNCTION

AddAtom()

LPCSTR MAKEINTATOM(WORD *wValue*)

MAKEINTATOM() is a macro that creates a string that corresponds to the integer specified in *wValue*. It returns a pointer to this string. You can use this pointer in a call to **AddAtom()** to add the string to the local atom table. (You can add the string to the global atom table by calling **GlobalAddAtom()**.)

A Complete Programming Example

Here is an example program that demonstrates several atom functions.

```
/*
   Demonstrate atoms.
*/

#include <windows.h>
#include <string.h>

LONG FAR PASCAL WndProc(HWND, UINT, WPARAM, LPARAM);

char szProgName[] = "ProgName"; /* name of window class */

ATOM a1, a2;
char str[255];

int PASCAL WinMain(HINSTANCE hInst, HINSTANCE hPreInst,
                   LPSTR lpszCmdLine, int nCmdShow)
{
```

```
HWND hWnd;
MSG lpMsg;
WNDCLASS wcApp;

if (!hPreInst) { /* if no previous instance */
  wcApp.lpszClassName = szProgName; /* window class name */
  wcApp.hInstance     = hInst; /* handle to this instance */
  wcApp.lpfnWndProc   = WndProc; /* window function */
  wcApp.hCursor       = LoadCursor(NULL, IDC_ARROW);
  wcApp.hIcon         = LoadIcon(NULL, IDI_APPLICATION);
  wcApp.lpszMenuName  = NULL;

  /* make the background of window white */
  wcApp.hbrBackground = GetStockObject(WHITE_BRUSH);
  wcApp.style         = 0; /* use default window style */
  wcApp.cbClsExtra    = 0; /* no extra info */
  wcApp.cbWndExtra    = 0; /* no extra info */

  /* register the window class */
  if (!RegisterClass (&wcApp))
    return FALSE;
}

/* Now that window has been registered, a window
   can be created. */
hWnd = CreateWindow(
  szProgName,
  "Demonstrate Atoms",
  WS_OVERLAPPEDWINDOW,
  CW_USEDEFAULT,
  CW_USEDEFAULT,
  CW_USEDEFAULT,
  CW_USEDEFAULT,
  (HWND)NULL,
  (HMENU) NULL,
  (HANDLE)hInst,
  (LPSTR)NULL
);

/* Display the Window. */
ShowWindow(hWnd, nCmdShow);
UpdateWindow(hWnd);

/* Create the message loop. */
```

```
  while (GetMessage(&lpMsg, NULL, 0, 0)) {
    TranslateMessage(&lpMsg); /* allow use of keyboard */
    DispatchMessage(&lpMsg); /* return control to Windows */
  }
  return(lpMsg.wParam);
}


/* Window Function. */
LONG FAR PASCAL WndProc(HWND hWnd, UINT messg,
                        WPARAM wParam, LPARAM lParam)
{
  HDC hdc;
  PAINTSTRUCT ps;

  switch (messg) {
    case WM_CREATE:
      /* define two atoms */
      a1 = AddAtom("This is a sample string. ");
      a2 = AddAtom("This is another sample string.");
      break;
    case WM_PAINT: /* process a paint request */
      hdc = BeginPaint(hWnd, &ps); /* get DC */

      /* display atomic strings */
      GetAtomName(a1, str, sizeof(str));
      TextOut(hdc, 1, 1, str, strlen(str));

      GetAtomName(a2, str, sizeof(str));
      TextOut(hdc, 1, 20, str, strlen(str));

      EndPaint(hWnd, &ps);
      break;
    case WM_DESTROY: /* terminate the program */
      /* remove the atoms */
      DeleteAtom(a1);
      DeleteAtom(a2);
      PostQuitMessage(0);
      break;
    /* Let Windows process any messages not specified in
       the preceding cases. */
    default:
      return(DefWindowProc(hWnd, messg, wParam, lParam));
  }
  return(0L);
}
```

Chapter 2

Communications Functions

H E functions described in this chapter manage and configure communications devices (ports). You will use these functions to set and examine various options associated with these devices.

For 16-bit Windows, communications devices are opened using **OpenComm()** *and are referred to by the ID value returned by this function. However, for Windows NT/Win32, communications devices are opened using* **CreateFile()** *and are referred to by the handle returned by* **CreateFile()**.

int BuildCommDCB(LPCSTR *lpszMODE,*
DCB FAR *★lpCtrlBlock*)

BuildCommDCB() converts a MODE-style serial port configuration command into a **DCB** (Device Control Block) structure. (MODE is the DOS-style command that configures, among other things, the serial port.) The function returns non-zero if successful, and zero otherwise.

The return type for **BuildCommDCB()** *for Windows NT/Win32 is* **BOOL** *instead of* **int**.

The MODE-style command is contained in the string pointed to by *lpszMODE*. This command is converted into a form usable by a **DCB** structure, and the result is copied into the structure pointed to by *lpCtrlBlock*.

The **DCB** structure defined for 16-bit Windows differs significantly from the one defined by Windows NT/Win32. The 16-bit Windows **DCB** structure is defined like this:

```
typedef struct tagDCB
{
  BYTE Id;
  UINT BaudRate;
  BYTE ByteSize;
  BYTE Parity;
  BYTE StopBits;
  UINT RlsTimeout;
  UINT CtsTimeout;
  UINT DsrTimeout;

  UINT fBinary :1;
  UINT fRtsDisable :1;
  UINT fParity :1;
  UINT fOutxCtsFlow :1;
  UINT fOutxDsrFlow :1;
  UINT fDummy :2;
  UINT fDtrDisable :1;

  UINT fOutX :1;
  UINT fInX :1;
  UINT fPeChar :1;
  UINT fNull :1;
  UINT fChEvt :1;
  UINT fDtrflow :1;
  UINT fRtsflow :1;
  UINT fDummy2 :1;

  char XonChar;
  char XoffChar;
  UINT XonLim;
  UINT XoffLim;
  char PeChar;
  char EofChar;
  char EvtChar;
  UINT TxDelay;
} DCB;
```

Here, **Id** is the value that identifies the device and is set by the device driver.

BaudRate specifies the baud rate. If the high-order byte is 255, then the low-order value determines the baud rate, using one of the following self-explanatory values:

CBR_110
CBR_300
CBR_600
CBR_1200
CBR_2400
CBR_4800
CBR_9600
CBR_14400
CBR_19200
CBR_38400
CBR_56000
CBR_128000
CBR_256000

ByteSize specifies the number of data bits and must be between 4 and 8, inclusive. **Parity** specifies the parity. This value must be one of the following: **EVENPARITY, ODDPARITY, NOPARITY,** or **MARKPARITY**. **StopBits** sets the number of stop bits, which must be either **ONESTOPBIT, ONE5STOPBITS** (1.5 stop bits), or **TWOSTOPBITS**.

The carrier-detect timeout is set by **RlsTimeout**. This value is in milliseconds. The clear-to-send timeout is set by **CtsTimeout**. This value is also in milliseconds. The data-set-ready timeout is specified, in milliseconds, by **DsrTimeout**.

The next 15 members are bit fields, which have the following effects when set:

Member	Effect
fBinary	Binary communications. EOF is not recognized as signaling the end of the data (that is, EOF is simply another binary value).
fRtsDisable	Request-to-send is disabled.
fParity	Parity checking is used.
fOutxCtsFlow	Clear-to-send is used.
fOutxDsrFlow	Data-set-ready is used.
fDummy	Not used.
fDtrDisable	Data-terminal-ready is not used.
fOutX	XON/XOFF protocol is used for output.
fInX	XON/XOFF protocol is used for input.
fPeChar	Replace parity errors with the character specified in PeChar.
fNull	Discard null characters.
fChEvt	When a character is received that matches the one specified in EvtChar, signal an event.
fDtrFlow	Data-terminal-ready is used for input.
fRtsFlow	Ready-to-send is used for input.
fDummy2	Not used.

XonChar contains the character that represents XON. XoffChar contains the character that represents XOFF. XonLim specifies the minimum number of characters that may be in the input queue before an XON signal is sent. XoffLim specifies the maximum number of characters that may be in the input queue before an XOFF signal is sent.

The character specified by PeChar is substituted for characters damaged by parity errors if the fPeChar flag is set.

The character specified by EofChar is the EOF character. The character specified in EvtChar causes an event signal when received if fChEvt is set.

TxDelay is not used.

For Windows NT/Win32, the DCB structure is defined like this:

```
typedef struct _DCB {
  DWORD DCBlength;
  DWORD BaudRate;
  DWORD fBinary: 1;
  DWORD fParity: 1;
  DWORD fOutxCtsFlow:1;
  DWORD fOutxDsrFlow:1;
  DWORD fDtrControl:2;
  DWORD fDsrSensitivity:1;
  DWORD fTXContinueOnXoff: 1;
  DWORD fOutX: 1;
  DWORD fInX: 1;
  DWORD fErrorChar: 1;
  DWORD fNull: 1;
  DWORD fRtsControl:2;
  DWORD fAbortOnError:1;
  DWORD fDummy2:17;
  WORD wReserved;
  WORD XonLim;
  WORD XoffLim;
  BYTE ByteSize;
  BYTE Parity;
  BYTE StopBits;
  char XonChar;
  char XoffChar;
  char ErrorChar;
  char EofChar;
  char EvtChar;
} DCB;
```

Here, DCBlength specifies the size, in bytes, of the DCB structure.

BaudRate specifies the baud rate. If the high-order byte is 255, then the low-order value determines the baud rate, using one of these self-explanatory values:

CBR_110
CBR_300
CBR_600
CBR_1200
CBR_2400
CBR_4800
CBR_9600
CBR_14400
CBR_19200
CBR_38400
CBR_56000
CBR_128000
CBR_256000

The next 14 members are bit fields, which have the following effects when set:

Member	Effect
fBinary	Binary communications. This must always be set for Windows NT/Win32.
fParity	Parity checking is used.
fOutxCtsFlow	Clear-to-send is used.
fOutxDsrFlow	Data-set-ready is used.
fDtrControl	Data-terminal-ready. Must be either: DTR_CONTROL_DISABLE DTR_CONTROL_ENABLE DTR_CONTROL_HANDSHAKE
fDsrSensitivity	Driver uses data-set-ready signal.
fTXContinueOnXoff	Transmission continues even though an XOFF signal has been sent.
fOutX	XON/XOFF protocol is used for output.
fInX	XON/XOFF protocol is used for input.
fErrorChar	Replace parity errors with the character specified in ErrorChar.
fNull	Discard null characters.
fRtsControl	Specify request-to-send protocol. It must be either: RTS_CONTROL_DISABLE RTS_CONTROL_ENABLE RTS_CONTROL_HANDSHAKE RTS_CONTROL_TOGGLE
fAbortOnError	Communications stop if an error occurs.
fDummy2	Not used.

The **wReserved** member is reserved for future use and must be set to zero.

XonLim specifies the minimum number of characters that may be in the input queue before an XON signal is sent. **XoffLim** specifies the maximum number of characters that may be in the input queue before an XOFF signal is sent.

ByteSize specifies the number of data bits and must be between 4 and 8, inclusive. **Parity** specifies the parity. This value must be one of the following: **EVENPARITY**, **ODDPARITY**, **NOPARITY**, or **MARKPARITY**. **StopBits** sets the number of stop bits, which must be either **ONESTOPBIT**, **ONE5STOPBITS** (1.5 stop bits), or **TWOSTOPBITS**.

XonChar contains the character that represents XON. **XoffChar** contains the character that represents XOFF.

The character specified by **ErrorChar** is substituted for characters damaged by parity errors if the **fErrorChar** flag is set.

The character specified by **EofChar** is the EOF character. The character specified in **EvtChar** causes an event signal when received.

USAGE

The following builds a **DCB** structure that sets the second serial port to 1200 baud using even parity, 7 data bits, and 2 stop bits.

```
DCB com2dcb;

BuildCommDCB("COM2:1200,e,7,2", &com2dcb);
```

RELATED FUNCTION

SetCommState()

int ClearCommBreak(int *Device*)

ClearCommBreak() restarts communications for the specified device. It returns zero if successful, and –1 if an error occurs.

The ID of the device to restart is specified in *Device*.

ClearCommBreak() is called to restart communications after being halted by a call to **SetCommBreak()**.

NOTE

For Windows NT/Win32, the prototype for **ClearCommBreak()** is

BOOL ClearCommBreak(HANDLE hDevice)

The function returns non-zero if successful, and zero on failure. In this case, the handle to the device is passed in hDevice.

RELATED FUNCTION

SetCommBreak()

BOOL ClearCommError(HANDLE *hDevice,*
LPDWORD *lpdwErr,*
LPCOMSTAT *lpStatus*)

ClearCommError() clears a communications error and allows further communication to take place. It also obtains error and status information about the specified device. This function should be called only after a communications error has occurred. It returns non-zero if successful, and zero if an error occurs.

The handle to the device that experienced the error is passed in *hDevice.*

The variable pointed to by *lpdwErr* will receive a value that describes the error that occurred. It will be a combination of the values described in the following table.

Value	Error
CE_BREAK	Break occurred
CE_DNS	Device not selected
CE_FRAME	Framing error
CE_IOE	I/O error
CE_MODE	Invalid device mode
CE_OOP	Out of paper
CE_OVERRUN	Buffer overrun
CE_PTO	Timeout on a parallel port
CE_RXOVER	Input buffer overrun
CE_RXPARITY	Input parity error
CE_TXFULL	Output buffer full

The **COMSTAT** structure pointed to by *lpStatus* receives information about the specified device. The **COMSTAT** structure is defined like this:

```
typedef struct _COMSTAT {
  DWORD fCtsHold : 1;
  DWORD fDsrHold : 1;
  DWORD fRlsdHold : 1;
  DWORD fXoffHold : 1;
  DWORD fXoffSent : 1;
  DWORD fEof : 1;
  DWORD fTxim : 1;
  DWORD fReserved : 25;
  DWORD cbInQue;
  DWORD cbOutQue;
} COMSTAT;
```

Here, **fCtsHold** is set if the device is waiting for a clear-to-send signal. **fDsrHold** is set if the device is waiting for a data-set-ready signal. **fRlsdHold** is set if the device is waiting for a receive-line-signal-detect signal. **fXoffHold** is set if the device is waiting for an XON signal because an XOFF had been received. **fXoffSent** will be true if an XOFF character was transmitted. **fEof** is set if an EOF character has been received. **fTxim** is set if there is a character waiting to be transmitted.

cbInQue contains the number of characters currently in the input queue. **cbOutQue** contains the number of characters currently in the output queue.

USAGE

The *lpStatus* parameter may be NULL if no status information is required.

RELATED FUNCTIONS

ClearCommBreak()
SetCommBreak()

int CloseComm(int *Device*)

CloseComm() closes a communications device opened using **OpenComm()**. It returns zero if successful, and negative on failure.

NOTE

This function is not applicable to Windows NT/Win32.

The device to close is specified by *Device*.

RELATED FUNCTION

OpenComm()

BOOL EnableCommNotification(int *Device*, HWND *hWnd*, int *nNumBytes*, int *nQueueSize*)

EnableCommNotification() determines whether or not the **WM_COMMNOTIFY** message is sent to the specified window. It returns non-zero if successful, and zero if an error occurs.

NOTE

This function is not available when using Windows NT/Win32.

The device is specified by *Device*, which is the value returned by **Open-Comm()**. The handle of the affected window is specified by *hWnd*. The number of bytes that must be in the application's input queue before a notification message is sent is specified in *nNumBytes*. The minimum number of bytes that can remain in the output queue before a notification message is sent is specified in *nQueueSize*.

RELATED FUNCTION

OpenComm()

LONG EscapeCommFunction(int *Device*, int *Code*)

EscapeCommFunction() causes the device specified by *Device* to execute the function passed in *Code*. The function returns zero if successful, and negative otherwise.

NOTE *This function description is for 16-bit Windows only.*

The operation for the communications device to execute is passed in *Code* and must be one of these values:

Macro	Function
CLRDTR	Reset data-terminal-ready.
CLRRTS	Reset request-to-send.
GETMAXCOM	Obtain the number of serial ports in the system.
GETMAXLPT	Obtain the number of parallel ports in the system.
RESETDEV	Reset a printer connected to a parallel port. (This function is ignored for serial ports.)
SETDTR	Transmit data-terminal-ready.
SETRTS	Transmit request-to-send.
SETXOFF	Simulate receipt of an XOFF.
SETXON	Simulate receipt of an XON.

USAGE

EscapeCommFunction() is used to cause a communications port to execute an extended function. It is possible that additional extended functions will be supported in the future.

RELATED FUNCTION

EscapeCommFunction() (Win32 version)

BOOL EscapeCommFunction(HANDLE *hDevice,* DWORD *Code)*

EscapeCommFunction() causes the device specified by *hDevice* to execute the function passed in *Code*. The function returns true if successful, and false otherwise.

NOTE

This function description is for Windows NT/Win32 only.

The handle passed in *hDevice* is obtained via a call to **CreateFile()**.

The function for the communications device to execute is passed in *Code* and must be one of these values:

Macro	Function
CLRBREAK	Same as calling **ClearCommBreak()**
CLRDTR	Reset data-terminal-ready
CLRRTS	Reset request-to-send
SETBREAK	Same as calling **SetCommBreak()**
SETDTR	Transmit data-terminal-ready
SETRTS	Transmit request-to-send
SETXOFF	Simulate receipt of an XOFF
SETXON	Simulate receipt of an XON

USAGE

EscapeCommFunction() is used to cause a communications port to execute an extended function. It is possible that additional extended functions will be supported in the future.

RELATED FUNCTION

EscapeCommFunction() (16-bit Windows version)

int GetCommError(int *Device*, **COMSTAT FAR** **lpErr*)

GetCommError() obtains error information about the specified communications device. It returns the error value, which will be one or more of these values:

Value	Error
CE_BREAK	Break occurred
CE_CTSTO	Clear-to-send timeout
CE_DNS	Device not selected
CE_DSRTO	Data-set-ready timeout
CE_FRAME	Framing error
CE_IOE	I/O error

CE_MODE	Invalid device mode
CE_OOP	Out of paper
CE_OVERRUN	Buffer overrun
CE_PTO	Timeout on a parallel port
CE_RLSDTO	Receive-line-signal-detect timeout
CE_RXOVER	Input buffer overrun
CE_RXPARITY	Input parity error
CE_TXFULL	Output buffer full

NOTE

This function is obsolete for Windows NT/Win32 and is no longer supported.

The device identifier is passed in *Device*.

On return, the **COMSTAT** structure pointed to by *lpErr* will contain information about the device. For 16-bit Windows, **COMSTAT** is defined like this:

```
typedef struct tagCOMSTAT
{
  BYTE status;
  UINT cbInQue;
  UINT cbOutQue;
} COMSTAT;
```

Here, **status** contains the status of the device. It will be one or more of these values:

Value	Status
CSTF_CTSHOLD	Waiting for clear-to-send
CSTF_DSRHOLD	Waiting for data-set-ready
CSTF_EOF	EOF received
CSTF_RLSDHOLD	Waiting for receive-line-signal-detect
CSTF_TXIM	Character ready to send
CSTF_XOFFHOLD	Waiting because XOFF received
CSTF_XOFFSENT	XOFF transmitted

cbInQue and **cbOutQue** contain the number of characters in the input and output queues.

USAGE

The *lpErr* parameter may be NULL if no status information is desired.

RELATED FUNCTION

ClearCommError()

UINT GetCommEventMask(int *Device*, int *Events*)

NOTE

This function is available only for 16-bit Windows. For Windows NT/Win32, use **Get-CommMask()**.

GetCommEventMask() returns the current device event control word. It also resets the control word.

The device affected is specified in *Device*.

The return value indicates what events have occurred. It will be one or more of these values:

Value	Event
EV_BREAK	Break
EV_CTS	Clear-to-send
EV_CTSS	Change in status of clear-to-send
EV_DSR	Data-set-ready
EV_ERR	Error
EV_PERR	Printer error
EV_RING	Ring indicator
EV_RLSD	Receive-line-signal-detect
EV_RLSDS	Change in receive-line-signal-detect
EV_RXCHAR	Character received
EV_RXFLAG	Event character received
EV_TXEMPTY	Transmit buffer empty

RELATED FUNCTION

SetCommEventState()

BOOL GetCommMask(HANDLE *hDevice,*
LPDWORD *lpdwMask*)

GetCommMask() obtains the event mask for the specified device. It returns non-zero if successful, and zero on failure.

The handle to the device is passed in *hDevice.*

The variable pointed to by *lpdwMask* will receive the event mask. It will contain one or more of these values:

Value	Event
EV_BREAK	Break on input
EV_CTS	Change in clear-to-send
EV_DSR	Change in data-set-ready
EV_ERR	Framing, parity, or buffer overrun occurred
EV_RING	Ring detected
EV_RLSD	Change in receive-line-signal-detect
EV_RXCHAR	Character received
EV_RXFLAG	Event character received
EV_TXEMPTY	Output buffer empty

USAGE

The following fragment determines if a character was received.

```
DWORD value;

/* ... */

GetCommMask(hDevice, &value);

if(value & EV_RXCHAR) /* character received */
```

RELATED FUNCTIONS

GetCommModemStatus()
SetCommMask()

BOOL GetCommModemStatus(HANDLE *hDevice*, LPDWORD *lpdwStatus*)

GetCommModemStatus() obtains status information about the specified modem. It returns non-zero if successful, and zero otherwise.

The handle to the modem port is passed in *hDevice*.

The variable pointed to by *lpdwStatus* will receive the modem status. It will contain one or more of these values:

Value	Meaning
MS_CTS_ON	Modem is clear-to-send
MS_DSR_ON	Modem shows data-set-ready
MS_RING_ON	Modem ring indicator is on
MS_RLSD_ON	Modem receive-line-signal-detect is on

RELATED FUNCTION

GetCommMask()

BOOL GetCommProperties(HANDLE *hDevice*, LPCOMMPROP *lpProperties*)

GetCommProperties() obtains the capabilities associated with the specified device. It returns non-zero if successful, and zero on failure.

The handle of the device is passed in *hDevice*.

On return, the **COMMPROP** structure pointed to by *lpProperties* will contain information about the configuration of the specified device. **COMMPROP** is defined like this:

```
typedef struct _COMMPROP {
  WORD wPacketLength;
  WORD wPacketVersion;
  DWORD dwServiceMask;
  DWORD dwReserved1;
  DWORD dwMaxTxQueue;
  DWORD dwMaxRxQueue;
  DWORD dwMaxBaud;
```

```
  DWORD dwProvSubType;
  DWORD dwProvCapabilities;
  DWORD dwSettableParams;
  DWORD dwSettableBaud;
  WORD  wSettableData;
  WORD  wSettableStopParity;
  DWORD dwCurrentTxQueue;
  DWORD dwCurrentRxQueue;
  DWORD dwProvSpec1;
  DWORD dwProvSpec2;
  WCHAR wcProvChar[1];
} COMMPROP;
```

Here, **wPacketLength** contains the size of the data packet. **wPacketVersion** contains the version number of the **COMMPROP** structure. **dwServiceMask** contains the value **SP_SERIALCOMM**.

dwMaxTxQueue contains the size of the output buffer. **dwMaxRxQueue** contains the size of the input buffer.

dwMaxBaud contains the fastest baud at which the device can transfer data. The permissible values are shown here:

BAUD_075	BAUD_1200	BAUD_14400
BAUD_110	BAUD_1800	BAUD_19200
BAUD_134_5	BAUD_2400	BAUD_38400
BAUD_150	BAUD_4800	BAUD_56K
BAUD_300	BAUD_7200	BAUD_128K
BAUD_600	BAUD_9600	BAUD_USER (user defined)

dwProvSubType contains the type of port or device. It will be one of these values:

PST_RS232	PST_NETWORK_BRIDGE
PST_RS422	PST_PARALLELPORT
PST_RS423	PST_SCANNER
PST_RS449	PST_TCPIP_TELNET
PST_FAX	PST_UNSPECIFIED
PST_LAT	PST_X25

dwProvCapabilities tells what capabilities the device has. It will be one or more of the following values:

Value	Capability
PCF_DTRDSR	Data-terminal-ready and data-set-ready
PCF_INTTIMEOUTS	Interval timeouts
PCF_PARITY_CHECK	Parity checking
PCF_RLSD	Receive-line-signal-detect
PCF_RTSCTS	Request-to-send and clear-to-send
PCF_SETXCHAR	XON/XOFF under program control
PCF_SPECIALCHARS	Special characters
PCF_TOTALTIMEOUTS	Total timeouts
PCF_XONXOFF	XON/XOFF protocol
PCF_16BITMODE	16-bit operation

dwSettableParams contains the device settings that can be changed under program control. It will contain one or more of these values:

```
SP_BAUD
SP_DATABITS
SP_HANDSHAKING
SP_PARITY
SP_PARITY_CHECK
SP_RLSD
SP_STOPBITS
```

dwSettableBaud contains a combination of allowable baud rates. (The baud values macros are the same as shown earlier.)

wSettableData contains the number of data bits. It will be one of these self-explanatory values: **DATABITS_5**, **DATABITS_6**, **DATABITS_7**, **DATABITS_8**, or **DATABITS_16**.

wSettableStopParity contains the number of stop bits and parity setting. It will contain one value from each column shown here:

STOPBITS_10	PARITY_EVEN
STOPBITS_15	PARITY_ODD
STOPBITS_20	PARITY_MARK
	PARITY_NONE
	PARITY_SPACE

The stop bit values specify 1, 1.5, and 2 stop bits, respectively.

dwCurrentTxQueue contains the size of the device driver's output queue.

dwCurrentRxQueue contains the size of the device driver's input queue.

dwProvSpec1, **dwProvSpec2**, and **wcProvChar** are used by the device driver and not by your program.

RELATED FUNCTION

SetCommState()

int GetCommState(int *Device*, DCB FAR ★ *lpCtrlBlock*)

GetCommState() obtains the control block associated with *Device*. The control block contains the current settings associated with the specified communications device. The function returns zero if successful, or negative on failure.

The device is specified by *Device*.

NOTE

For Windows NT/Win32, **GetCommState()** *has this prototype:*

BOOL GetCommState(HANDLE hDevice, LPDCB lpCtrlBlock)

It returns non-zero if successful, and zero on failure. Notice that a handle (rather than an ID value) to the device is passed as the first parameter.

Information about the device is returned in the **DCB** structure pointed to by *lpCtrlBlock*. The **DCB** structure is described under **BuildCommDCB()**.

RELATED FUNCTIONS

BuildCommDCB()
SetCommState()

Win32
only

BOOL GetCommTimeouts(HANDLE *hDevice*, LPCOMMTIMEOUTS *lpTmOut*)

GetCommTimeouts() obtains information about the timeout settings for the specified communications device. It returns non-zero if successful, and zero on failure.

The handle to the device is passed in *hDevice*.

The timeout information is returned in the **COMMTIMEOUTS** structure pointed to by *lpTmOut*. **COMMTIMEOUTS** is defined like this:

```
typedef struct _COMMTIMEOUTS {
  DWORD ReadIntervalTimeout;
  DWORD ReadTotalTimeoutMultiplier;
  DWORD ReadTotalTimeoutConstant;
  DWORD WriteTotalTimeoutMultiplier;
  DWORD WriteTotalTimeoutConstant;
} COMMTIMEOUTS;
```

Here, **ReadIntervalTimeout** contains the maximum number of milliseconds that can elapse between characters when inputting data. **ReadTotalTimeoutMultiplier** contains the number of milliseconds, which is multiplied by the number of characters input, to compute the total timeout when inputting data. **ReadTotalTimeoutConstant** contains the number of milliseconds to add to the total timeout when inputting data.

WriteTotalTimeoutMultiplier contains the number of milliseconds, which is multiplied by the number of characters output, to compute the total timeout when outputting data. **WriteTotalTimeoutConstant** contains the number of milliseconds to add to the total timeout when outputting data.

USAGE

Any or all of the fields in **COMMTIMEOUTS** may be zero. A zero indicates that the timeout is unused.

RELATED FUNCTION

SetCommTimeouts()

---

int OpenComm(LPCSTR *lpszName*, UINT *InQSize*, UINT *OutQSize*)

OpenComm() opens a communications device. It returns the identifier attached to that device, or a negative value if an error occurs.

NOTE *This function is obsolete and not supported for Windows NT/Win32. Use* **CreateFile()** *instead.*

The name of the device is specified in *lpszName*, which must be either "COM#" or "LPT#", where # is the number of the serial or parallel port, respectively.

The sizes of the input and output queues are specified in *InQSize* and *OutQSize*. For parallel ports, these values are ignored.

USAGE

If the device cannot be opened, the return value may be one of the following values.

Value	Error
IE_HARDWARE	Hardware not available
IE_MEMORY	Queue size too big
IE_OPEN	Device is already open

This fragment opens LPT1:

```
id = OpenComm("LPT1", 1, 1);
```

RELATED FUNCTION

CloseComm()
CreateFile()

BOOL PurgeComm(HANDLE *hDevice*, DWORD *dwWhat*)

PurgeComm() does one or more of the following: removes all characters from the input buffer, removes all characters from the output buffer, cancels an input operation, or cancels an output operation. It returns non-zero if successful, and zero otherwise.

The handle to the device affected is passed in *hDevice*.

What operation takes place is determined by the value of *dwWhat*, which may be any combination of the following values.

Value	Effect
PURGE_RXABORT	Cancel a pending read operation.
PURGE_RXCLEAR	Discard all characters in the input buffer.
PURGE_TXABORT	Cancel a pending output operation.
PURGE_TXCLEAR	Discard all characters in the output buffer.

RELATED FUNCTIONS

FlushFileBuffers()
SetCommState()

int SetCommBreak(int *Device*)

SetCommBreak() halts communication and puts the specified device into a "break" state. This state continues until a call to **ClearCommBreak()** is executed. The function returns zero if successful, and negative on failure.

The ID of the device affected is specified in *Device*.

NOTE

For Windows NT/Win32, **SetCommBreak()** *has this prototype:*

BOOL SetCommBreak(HANDLE hDevice)

In this case, it returns non-zero if successful, and zero on failure. Also, notice that the handle to the device is passed in hDevice.

RELATED FUNCTION

ClearCommBreak()

UINT FAR *SetCommEventMask(int *Device*, UINT *Events*)

SetCommEventMask() sets the state of a device event control word. It returns a pointer to the control word, or NULL if an error occurs.

This function is available only for 16-bit Windows. For Windows NT/Win32, use **SetCommMask()**.

The device affected is specified in *Device*.

The events to set are specified in *Events,* which can be any of these values:

Value	Event
EV_BREAK	Break
EV_CTS	Clear-to-send
EV_CTSS	Change in status of clear-to-send
EV_DSR	Data-set-ready
EV_ERR	Error
EV_PERR	Printer error
EV_RING	Ring indicator
EV_RLSD	Receive-line-signal-detect
EV_RLSDS	Change in receive-line-signal-detect
EV_RXCHAR	Character received
EV_RXFLAG	Event character received
EV_TXEMPTY	Transmit buffer empty

RELATED FUNCTION

GetCommEventState()

BOOL SetCommMask(HANDLE *hDevice,* DWORD *lpdwMask)*

SetCommMask() sets the event mask for the specified device. The event mask determines what events the device will respond to. It returns non-zero if successful, and zero on failure.

The handle to the device is passed in *hDevice*.

The value specified by *lpdwMask* determines what events are enabled. It must contain zero (to disable all events) or one or more of these values:

Value	Event
EV_BREAK	Break on input
EV_CTS	Change in clear-to-send

EV_DSR	Change in data-set-ready
EV_ERR	Framing, parity, or buffer overrun occurred
EV_RING	Ring detected
EV_RLSD	Change in receive-line-signal-detect
EV_RXCHAR	Character received
EV_RXFLAG	Event character received
EV_TXEMPTY	Output buffer empty

USAGE

The following fragment causes the device to monitor clear-to-send.

```
SetCommMask(hDevice, EV_CTS);
```

RELATED FUNCTION

GetCommMask()

int SetCommState(const DCB FAR ★ *lpCtrlBlock*)

SetCommState() sets a communications device's control block. This causes the device to be completely reinitialized, but any pending characters in the input or output buffers are not lost. The function returns zero if successful, or negative on failure.

The device control block for the desired device is in the **DCB** structure pointed to by *lpCtrlBlock*.

For Windows NT/Win32, **SetCommState()** *has this prototype:*

BOOL SetCommState(HANDLE hDevice, LPDCB lpCtrlBlock)

It returns non-zero if successful, and zero on failure.

For 16-bit Windows, the device is specified in the **Id** member of the **DCB** structure. For Windows NT/Win32, the device is specified in *hDevice*.

The **DCB** structure is described under **BuildCommDCB()**.

RELATED FUNCTIONS

BuildCommDCB()
GetCommState()

BOOL SetCommTimeouts(HANDLE *hDevice,*
LPCOMMTIMEOUTS *lpTmOut*)

SetCommTimeouts() sets timeout information for the specified communications device. It returns non-zero if successful, and zero on failure.

The handle to the device is passed in *hDevice*.

The timeout information is passed in the **COMMTIMEOUTS** structure pointed to by *lpTmOut*. **COMMTIMEOUTS** is defined like this:

```
typedef struct _COMMTIMEOUTS {
  DWORD ReadIntervalTimeout;
  DWORD ReadTotalTimeoutMultiplier;
  DWORD ReadTotalTimeoutConstant;
  DWORD WriteTotalTimeoutMultiplier;
  DWORD WriteTotalTimeoutConstant;
} COMMTIMEOUTS;
```

Here, **ReadIntervalTimeout** contains the maximum number of milliseconds that can elapse between characters when inputting data. **ReadTotalTimeoutMultiplier** contains the number of milliseconds, which is multiplied by the number of characters input, to compute the total timeout when inputting data. **ReadTotalTimeoutConstant** contains the number of milliseconds to add to the total timeout when inputting data.

WriteTotalTimeoutMultiplier contains the number of milliseconds, which is multiplied by the number of characters output, to compute the total timeout when outputting data. **WriteTotalTimeoutConstant** contains the number of milliseconds to add to the total timeout when outputting data.

USAGE

Any or all of the fields in **COMMTIMEOUTS** may be zero. A zero indicates that the timeout is unused.

RELATED FUNCTION

GetCommTimeouts()

BOOL SetupComm(HANDLE *hDevice,*
DWORD *dwInQSize,*
DWORD *dwOutQSize*)

SetupComm() sets the queue sizes of the specified device. It returns non-zero if successful, and zero on failure.

The handle to the specified device is passed in *hDevice.*

The sizes of the input and output queues are passed in *dwInQSize* and *dwOutQSize.*

USAGE

This function should be called immediately after the device handle is obtained through a call to **CreateFile()**. If this function is not called, default settings are used.

RELATED FUNCTIONS

SetCommMask()
SetCommState()

int TransmitCommChar(int *Device,* char *Ch*)

TransmitCommChar() outputs a character to the specified device. Specifically, the character is transmitted as soon as possible, bypassing any characters waiting in the output queue. It returns zero if successful, and negative on failure. (The function will fail if the character cannot be transmitted.)

The ID of the device to which the character is sent is specified by *Device.*

The character is passed in *Ch.*

NOTE

For Windows NT/Win32, **TransmitCommChar()** *has this prototype:*

BOOL TransmitCommChar(HANDLE hDevice, *char* Ch)

It returns non-zero if successful, and zero on failure. The device handle is specified in hDevice.

USAGE

This function will fail if the previous character output by it has not been transmitted.

This statement outputs a Ctrl-Z:

```
TransmitCommChar(Device, (char) 26);
```

RELATED FUNCTIONS

SetCommMask()
WaitCommEvent()

BOOL WaitCommEvent(HANDLE *hDevice,*
LPDWORD *lpEvent,*
LPOVERLAPPED *lpOverlap*)

WaitCommEvent() waits for a communications event to occur. (It does not return until one does.) It returns non-zero if successful, and zero on failure.

The handle to the device in question is specified by *hDevice*.

On return, the variable pointed to by *lpEvent* will contain the event that occurred. It will be one of these values:

Value	Event
EV_BREAK	Break
EV_CTS	Clear-to-send
EV_DSR	Data-set-ready
EV_ERR	Error
EV_RING	Ring indicator
EV_RLSD	Receive-line-signal-detect
EV_RXCHAR	Character received
EV_RXFLAG	Event character received
EV_TXEMPTY	Transmit buffer empty

The *lpOverlap* parameter points to an **OVERLAPPED** structure. If overlapped I/O is not needed, then this value should be NULL. The **OVERLAPPED** structure is defined like this:

```
typedef struct _OVERLAPPED {
  DWORD Internal; /* reserved */
  DWORD InternalHigh; /* reserved */
  DWORD Offset; /* low word of starting location */
  DWORD OffsetHigh; /* high word of starting location */
  HANDLE hEvent; /* event to signal */
} OVERLAPPED;
```

USAGE

The only events that will occur (and, thus, cause **GetCommEvent()** to return) are those that have been defined in the device's event mask. This mask can be set by calling **SetCommMask()** or obtained by calling **GetCommMask()**.

RELATED FUNCTION

SetCommMask()

A Complete Programming Example

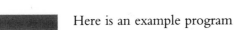

Here is an example program that demonstrates several communications functions.

```
/*
  Demonstrate communications functions.
*/

#include <windows.h>
#include <string.h>

LONG FAR PASCAL WndProc(HWND, UINT, WPARAM, LPARAM);

char szProgName[] = "ProgName"; /* name of window class */

int com;
char str[255];
```

```
int PASCAL WinMain(HINSTANCE hInst, HINSTANCE hPreInst,
                   LPSTR lpszCmdLine, int nCmdShow)
{
  HWND hWnd;
  MSG lpMsg;
  WNDCLASS wcApp;

  if (!hPreInst) { /* if no previous instance */
    wcApp.lpszClassName = szProgName; /* window class name */
    wcApp.hInstance     = hInst; /* handle to this instance */
    wcApp.lpfnWndProc   = WndProc; /* window function */
    wcApp.hCursor       = LoadCursor(NULL, IDC_ARROW);
    wcApp.hIcon         = LoadIcon(NULL, IDI_APPLICATION);
    wcApp.lpszMenuName  = NULL;

    /* make the background of window white */
    wcApp.hbrBackground = GetStockObject(WHITE_BRUSH);
    wcApp.style         = 0; /* use default window style */
    wcApp.cbClsExtra    = 0; /* no extra info */
    wcApp.cbWndExtra    = 0; /* no extra info */

    /* register the window class */
    if (!RegisterClass (&wcApp))
      return FALSE;
  }

  /* Now that window has been registered, a window
     can be created. */
  hWnd = CreateWindow(
    szProgName,
    "Demonstrate Communications Functions",
    WS_OVERLAPPEDWINDOW,
    CW_USEDEFAULT,
    CW_USEDEFAULT,
    CW_USEDEFAULT,
    CW_USEDEFAULT,
    (HWND)NULL,
    (HMENU) NULL,
    (HANDLE)hInst,
    (LPSTR)NULL
  );

  /* Display the Window. */
```

```
      ShowWindow(hWnd, nCmdShow);
      UpdateWindow(hWnd);

      /* Create the message loop. */
      while (GetMessage(&lpMsg, NULL, 0, 0)) {
        TranslateMessage(&lpMsg); /* allow use of keyboard */
        DispatchMessage(&lpMsg); /* return control to Windows */
      }
      return(lpMsg.wParam);
    }

    /* Window Function. */
    LONG FAR PASCAL WndProc(HWND hWnd, UINT messg,
                            WPARAM wParam, LPARAM lParam)
    {
      DCB dcb;

      switch (messg) {
        case WM_CREATE:
         /* display data bits and stop bits for COM1 */
          com = OpenComm("COM1", 1, 1);
          GetCommState(com, &dcb);
          sprintf(str, "Data bits: %d\nStop bits: %d",
                  dcb.ByteSize, dcb.StopBits);
          MessageBox(hWnd, str, "", MB_OK);
          CloseComm(com);
          break;
        case WM_DESTROY: /* terminate the program */
          PostQuitMessage(0);
          break;
        /* Let Windows process any messages not specified in
           the preceding cases. */
        default:
          return(DefWindowProc(hWnd, messg, wParam, lParam));
      }
      return(0L);
    }
```

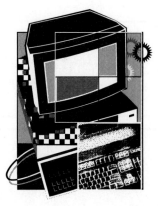

Chapter 3

Debugging Support

T H E functions described in this chapter support program debugging. These functions are primarily for developers of debuggers and are not generally used by application programmers.

CAUTION

Many of the functions described here must not be called by an application unless it is being debugged. That is, versions of your program designated for general distribution will not normally call these functions.

Win32 only

BOOL ContinueDebugEvent(DWORD *dwProcID,*
DWORD *dwThreadID,*
DWORD *dwHow)*

ContinueDebugEvent() continues execution of a thread that was halted because of a debugging event (generally, a breakpoint). It returns non–zero if successful, and zero otherwise.

The process ID is passed in *dwProcID,* and the thread ID is passed in *dwThreadID.*

How execution of the thread is continued is determined by *dwHow.* It must be one of these values: **DBG_CONTINUE** or **DBG_EXCEP-TION_NOT_HANDLED**. In both cases, execution of the thread is resumed. The difference between them is only significant if the thread stopped because of an **EXCEPTION_DEBUG_EVENT**. In this case, **DBG_CONTINUE** stops exception processing, but **DBG_EXCEPTION_NOT_HANDLED** does not.

RELATED FUNCTION

DebugBreak()

BOOL DebugActiveProcess(DWORD *dwProcID*)

DebugActiveProcess() attaches the debugger that calls this function to the specified process. After the attachment has been made, all debugging events are passed to the debugger. It returns non-zero if successful, and zero on failure.

The process to debug is specified in *dwProcID*.

RELATED FUNCTION

WaitForDebugEvent()

void DebugBreak(void)

DebugBreak() executes a breakpoint, sending a break signal to the debugger attached to the process. If no debugger exists, then default processing will occur, with possibly unpredictable results.

USAGE

Setting a breakpoint causes the current thread to stop and turns control over to a debugger. Generally, the stopped thread can be resumed later. Breakpoints are useful for examining the operation of a program when it would otherwise be difficult to do so.

RELATED FUNCTION

DebugActiveProcess()

void FAR DebugOutput(UINT *Message,*
LPCSTR *lpszFormat, ...)*

DebugOutput() displays output on the debugging terminal.

The value of *Message* identifies the type of message. It must be one of these values: **DBF_TRACE** (no error), **DBF_WARNING** (possible error), **DBF_ERROR** (error returned by API function), or **DBF_FATAL** (terminal error).

DebugOutput() can write formatted data. It uses the same format codes as **printf()**.

RELATED FUNCTION

OutputDebugString()

void FatalAppExit(UINT *Reserved*, LPCSTR *lpszMessage*)

FatalAppExit() displays a message box containing the string pointed to by *lpszMessage* and then immediately terminates the calling program. Control will then pass back to the debugger.

Reserved must have the value zero.

USAGE

FatalAppExit() is an emergency means of returning control to a debugger. It does not perform an orderly shutdown of the calling program. It is not intended for normal program termination.

RELATED FUNCTION

FatalExit()

void FatalExit(int *nCode*)

FatalExit() immediately terminates the calling program and control passes back to the debugger.

nCode contains a code that identifies the error that caused termination.

For 16-bit Windows, you will be given a choice of aborting the program completely, returning to the debugger, or ignoring the problem and continuing execution. For Windows NT/Win32, execution passes directly to the debugger.

USAGE

FatalExit() is an emergency means of returning control to a debugger. It does not perform an orderly shutdown of the calling program. It is not intended for normal program termination.

RELATED FUNCTION

FatalAppExit()

BOOL GetThreadContext(HANDLE *hThread,* LPCONTEXT *lpContext*)

GetThreadContext() obtains the context for the thread identified by *hThread.* It returns non-zero if successful, and zero on failure.

hThread is the handle to the thread, which must have **THREAD_GET_CONTEXT** access rights.

The thread context will be put into the **CONTEXT** structure pointed to by *lpContext.* The **CONTEXT** structure describes a register map of a call frame, which may change with new versions of Windows NT/Win32 or for new processors. For an explanation of this structure, examine its definition (and the associated comments) in the WINNT.H header file.

RELATED FUNCTION

SetThreadContext()

void OutputDebugString(LPCSTR *lpszMessage*)

OutputDebugString() outputs the specified string on the debugging terminal.

RELATED FUNCTION

DebugOutput()

BOOL ReadProcessMemory(HANDLE *hProc,*
LPVOID *lpFrom,*
LPVOID *lpBuf,*
DWORD *dwNum,*
LPDWORD *lpdwNumRead*)

ReadProcessMemory() copies a region of memory from the specified process. It returns non-zero if successful, and zero on failure.

The handle of the process from which memory will be copied is passed in *hProc.*

The starting address of the memory to copy is passed in *lpFrom.* The address of the buffer that will receive the memory is passed in *lpBuf.* (Make sure that this buffer is large enough to hold all the memory that you want to copy.)

The number of bytes to copy is passed in *dwNum,* and the number of bytes actually copied is returned in the variable pointed to by *lpdwNumRead.* (This parameter can be NULL if it is not needed.)

USAGE

The handle passed in *hProc* must have **PROCESS_VM_READ** access privileges.

RELATED FUNCTION

WriteProcessMemory()

BOOL SetThreadContext(HANDLE *hThread,*
LPCONTEXT *lpContext*)

SetThreadContext() sets the thread identified by *hThread* to the context specified by *lpContext.* It returns non-zero if successful, and zero on failure.

hThread is the handle to the thread, which must have **THREAD_SET_CONTEXT** access rights.

The context to set is specified in the **CONTEXT** structure pointed to by *lpContext.* The **CONTEXT** structure describes a register map of a call frame, which may change with new versions of Windows NT/Win32 or for new processors. For an explanation of this structure, examine its definition (and the associated comments) in the WINNT.H header file.

RELATED FUNCTION

GetThreadContext()

BOOL WaitForDebugEvent(LPDEBUG_EVENT *lpEvent,* DWORD *dwTimeOut*)

WaitForDebugEvent() waits until a debugging event (typically caused by a breakpoint being encountered in the monitored process) occurs. It returns non-zero if successful, and zero on failure.

The number of milliseconds to wait for a debugging event to occur is specified in *dwTimeOut*. To wait forever, use the value **INFINITE**.

On return, the **DEBUG_EVENT** structure pointed to by *lpEvent* will contain debugging information related to the monitored program. The **DEBUG_EVENT** structure is defined like this:

```
typedef struct _DEBUG_EVENT {
  DWORD dwDebugEventCode;
  DWORD dwProcessId;
  DWORD dwThreadId;
  union {
    EXCEPTION_DEBUG_INFO Exception;
    CREATE_THREAD_DEBUG_INFO CreateThread;
    CREATE_PROCESS_DEBUG_INFO CreateProcessInfo;
    EXIT_THREAD_DEBUG_INFO ExitThread;
    EXIT_PROCESS_DEBUG_INFO ExitProcess;
    LOAD_DLL_DEBUG_INFO LoadDll;
    UNLOAD_DLL_DEBUG_INFO UnloadDll;
    OUTPUT_DEBUG_STRING_INFO DebugString;
    RIP_INFO RipInfo;
  } u;
} DEBUG_EVENT;
```

Here, **dwDebugEventCode** contains the type of debugging event that occurred. It will be one of these values:

CREATE_PROCESS_DEBUG_EVENT
CREATE_THREAD_DEBUG_EVENT
EXCEPTION_DEBUG_EVENT
EXIT_PROCESS_DEBUG_EVENT
EXIT_THREAD_DEBUG_EVENT
LOAD_DLL_DEBUG_EVENT
OUTPUT_DEBUG_STRING_EVENT
RIP_EVENT (internal error)
UNLOAD_DLL_DEBUG_EVENT

dwProcessId and **dwThreadId** identify the process and thread that generated the event.

Depending upon the type of event, the union **u** will contain one of the following structures:

CREATE_PROCESS_DEBUG_INFO
CREATE_THREAD_DEBUG_INFO
EXCEPTION_DEBUG_INFO
EXIT_PROCESS_DEBUG_INFO
EXIT_THREAD_DEBUG_INFO
LOAD_DLL_DEBUG_INFO
OUTPUT_DEBUG_STRING_INFO
RIP_INFO
UNLOAD_DLL_DEBUG_INFO

These structures are shown in the following code, and the meaning of their fields is given in the comments.

```
typedef struct _CREATE_PROCESS_DEBUG_INFO {
  HANDLE hFile; /* handle of process image file */
  HANDLE hProcess; /* handle of process */
  HANDLE hThread; /* handle of thread */
  LPVOID lpBaseOfImage; /* entry address of process */
  DWORD dwDebugInfoFileOffset; /* offset into hFile at which
                                  debugging info is found */
  DWORD nDebugInfoSize; /* size of debugging info file */
  LPVOID lpThreadLocalBase; /* address of thread data */
  LPTHREAD_START_ROUTINE lpStartAddress; /* address of thread
                                            entry point */
  LPVOID lpImageName; /* name of image file -- optional */
  WORD fUnicode; /* non-zero if filename is Unicode, zero if
```

```
                          filename is ANSI */
} CREATE_PROCESS_DEBUG_INFO;

typedef struct _CREATE_THREAD_DEBUG_INFO {
  HANDLE hThread; /* handle of thread */
  LPVOID lpThreadLocalBase; /* address of thread data */
  LPTHREAD_START_ROUTINE lpStartAddress; /* address of thread
                                            entry point */
} CREATE_THREAD_DEBUG_INFO;

typedef struct _EXCEPTION_DEBUG_INFO {
  EXCEPTION_RECORD ExceptionRecord; /* exception info,
                                       described below */
  DWORD dwFirstChance; /* non-zero if first time exception is
                          encountered, zero otherwise */
} EXCEPTION_DEBUG_INFO;

typedef struct _EXIT_PROCESS_DEBUG_INFO {
  DWORD dwExitCode; /* exit code */
} EXIT_PROCESS_DEBUG_INFO;

typedef struct _EXIT_THREAD_DEBUG_INFO {
  DWORD dwExitCode; /* exit code */
} EXIT_THREAD_DEBUG_INFO;

typedef struct _LOAD_DLL_DEBUG_INFO {
  HANDLE hFile; /* handle of DLL */
  LPVOID lpBaseOfDll; /* base address of DLL */
  DWORD dwDebugInfoFileOffset; /* offset into debugging info
                                  in file associated with hFile */
  DWORD nDebugInfoSize; /* size of file associated with hFile */
  LPVOID lpImageName; /* name of image file -- optional */
  WORD fUnicode; /* non-zero if filename is Unicode, zero if
                    filename is ANSI */
} LOAD_DLL_DEBUG_INFO;

typedef struct _OUTPUT_DEBUG_STRING_INFO {
  LPSTR lpDebugStringData; /* Debugging string */
  WORD fUnicode; /* non-zero if string is in Unicode,
                    zero if ANSI */
  WORD nDebugStringLength; /* length of string */
} OUTPUT_DEBUG_STRING_INFO;

typedef struct _RIP_INFO {
```

```
    DWORD dwError; /* error code */
    DWORD dwType; /* one of the following values:
                       SLE_ERROR (fatal error),
                       SLE_MINORERROR (nonfatal error),
                       SLE_WARNING (nonfatal warning), or
                       0 (no additional information)
                   */
} RIP_INFO;

typedef struct _UNLOAD_DLL_DEBUG_INFO {
  LPVOID lpBaseOfDll; /* base address of DLL */
} UNLOAD_DLL_DEBUG_INFO;
```

The **EXCEPTION_DEBUG_INFO** structure contains an **EXCEP-TION_RECORD** structure, which is defined like this:

```
typedef struct _EXCEPTION_RECORD {
  DWORD ExceptionCode; /* exception code */
  DWORD ExceptionFlags; /* zero if process can be
                            continued, non-zero otherwise */
  struct _EXCEPTION_RECORD *ExceptionRecord; /* next
                                                exception */
  PVOID ExceptionAddress; /* address of at which the
                             exception was activated */
  DWORD NumberParameters; /* number of entries in the
                             ExceptionInformation array */

  /* additional information related to the exception */
  DWORD ExceptionInformation[EXCEPTION_MAXIMUM_PARAMETERS];
} EXCEPTION_RECORD;
```

USAGE

As mentioned at the start of this chapter, the debugging functions are intended for those programmers developing debuggers. Specifically, **Wait-ForDebugEvent()** is not for normal program usage.

RELATED FUNCTIONS

ContinueDebugEvent()
DebugBreak()

BOOL WriteProcessMemory(HANDLE *hProc*,
LPVOID *lpFrom*,
LPVOID *lpBuf*,
DWORD *dwNum*,
LPDWORD *lpdwNumWritten*)

WriteProcessMemory() copies data to a region of memory in the specified process. It returns non-zero if successful, and zero on failure.

The handle of the process to which information will be written is passed in *hProc*.

The starting address at which data will be written is passed in *lpFrom*. The address of the buffer that contains the data to write is passed in *lpBuf*.

The number of bytes to write is passed in *dwNum*, and the number of bytes actually written is returned in the variable pointed to by *lpdwNumWritten*. (This parameter can be NULL if it is not needed.)

USAGE

The handle passed in *hProc* must have **PROCESS_VM_WRITE** and **PROCESS_VM_OPERATION** access privileges.

RELATED FUNCTION

ReadProcessMemory()

Chapter 4

Dropped File Functions

H E functions described in this chapter support Windows' drag, drop interface. The drag, drop interface allows a file to be dragged from the File Manager to your program. For example, if your application is a text editor, using the drag, drop interface, you could allow the user to drag a file from the File Manager to the text editor. The dropped file could then be edited.

You must include the header file SHELLAPI.H to use the drag, drop functions.

void DragAcceptFiles(HWND *hWnd,* BOOL *Status*)

DragAcceptFile() determines whether the specified window accepts dropped files.

The handle to the window affected is passed in *hWnd*.

If *Status* is non-zero, then the window will accept dropped files. This will cause the window to receive a **WM_DROPFILES** message when a file is dropped into the window. If *Status* is zero, then the window will not accept dropped files.

RELATED FUNCTION

DragQuery()

void DragFinish(HDROP *hDragDrop*)

DragFinish() frees a dropped file handle (and the memory associated with it).

The handle specified in *hDragDrop* is obtained from *wParam* when a **WM_DROPFILES** message is received.

RELATED FUNCTION

DragAcceptFiles()

UINT DragQueryFile(HDROP *hDragDrop,* UINT *Index,* LPSTR *lpszFilename,* UINT *Size*)

DragQueryFile() obtains the name of a file that has been dropped. The function returns the length of the filename, or other results, as described in the following discussion.

The handle of the dropped file is passed in *hDragDrop.* (This handle is acquired from *wParam* when a **WM_DROPFILES** message is received.)

The index of the file to find the name of is passed in *Index.* File indexes begin with zero. If this parameter is –1, then the function returns the total number of dropped files.

The filename is copied in the character array pointed to by *lpszFilename.* (If this parameter is NULL, then the length of the filename is returned.)

The size of the array receiving the filename is passed in *Size.*

USAGE

In essence, you will use **DragQueryFile()** to obtain the names of the files that have been dragged to your application.

RELATED FUNCTION

DragQueryPoint()

BOOL DragQueryPoint(HDROP *hDragDrop,* POINT FAR **lpPoint*)

DragQueryPoint() obtains the coordinates at which the file is dropped. If the file is dropped within the client area of the window, then it returns non–zero. If the file is dropped outside the client area, zero is returned.

The handle of the dropped file is passed in *hDragDrop*. This handle is obtained from *wParam* when a **WM_DROPFILES** message is received.

On return, the location at which the file is dropped is contained in the **POINT** structure pointed to by *lpPoint*. **POINT** is defined like this:

```
typedef struct tagPOINT
{
  int x;
  int y;
} POINT;
```

NOTE

For Windows NT/Win32, the members of **POINT** are **LONG**.

RELATED FUNCTION

DragDropFile()

A Complete Programming Example

Here is an example program that demonstrates the drag, drop functions. To try the program, follow the instructions in the comments.

```
/*
   Demonstrate drag, drop functions.

   To use: Execute this program. Then, using the File Manager,
           drag a file from the file list to the window created
           by this program and drop it there. This program will
           then report the name of the file you dragged and the
           location at which it was dropped.
*/

#include <windows.h>
#include <shellapi.h>
#include <stdio.h>
#include <string.h>

LONG FAR PASCAL WndProc(HWND, UINT, WPARAM, LPARAM);
```

```c
char szProgName[] = "ProgName"; /* name of window class */

int PASCAL WinMain(HINSTANCE hInst, HINSTANCE hPreInst,
                   LPSTR lpszCmdLine, int nCmdShow)
{
  HWND hWnd;
  MSG lpMsg;
  WNDCLASS wcApp;

  if (!hPreInst) { /* if no previous instance */
    wcApp.lpszClassName = szProgName; /* window class name */
    wcApp.hInstance     = hInst; /* handle to this instance */
    wcApp.lpfnWndProc   = WndProc; /* window function */
    wcApp.hCursor       = LoadCursor(NULL, IDC_ARROW);
    wcApp.hIcon         = LoadIcon(NULL, IDI_APPLICATION);
    wcApp.lpszMenuName  = NULL;

    /* make the background of window white */
    wcApp.hbrBackground = GetStockObject(WHITE_BRUSH);
    wcApp.style         = 0; /* use default window style */
    wcApp.cbClsExtra    = 0; /* no extra info */
    wcApp.cbWndExtra    = 0; /* no extra info */

    /* register the window class */
    if (!RegisterClass (&wcApp))
      return FALSE;
  }

  /* Now that window has been registered, a window
     can be created. */
  hWnd = CreateWindow(
    szProgName,
    "Demonstrate Drag Drop Functions",
    WS_OVERLAPPEDWINDOW,
    CW_USEDEFAULT,
    CW_USEDEFAULT,
    CW_USEDEFAULT,
    CW_USEDEFAULT,
    (HWND)NULL,
    (HMENU) NULL,
    (HANDLE)hInst,
    (LPSTR)NULL
  );
```

```
    /* Display the Window. */
    ShowWindow(hWnd, nCmdShow);
    UpdateWindow(hWnd);

    /* Create the message loop. */
    while (GetMessage(&lpMsg, NULL, 0, 0)) {
      TranslateMessage(&lpMsg); /* allow use of keyboard */
      DispatchMessage(&lpMsg); /* return control to Windows */
    }
    return(lpMsg.wParam);
}

/* Window Function. */
LONG FAR PASCAL WndProc(HWND hWnd, UINT messg,
                        WPARAM wParam, LPARAM lParam)
{
  DCB dcb;
  POINT pt;
  char str[255];
  char fname[255];

  switch (messg) {
    case WM_CREATE:
      /* enable dropped file messages */
      DragAcceptFiles(hWnd, 1);
      break;
    case WM_DROPFILES: /* process dropped file messages */
      DragQueryFile(wParam, 0, fname, sizeof(fname));
      DragQueryPoint(wParam, &pt);
      sprintf(str, " dropped at %d %d", pt.x, pt.y);
      strcat(fname, str);
      MessageBox(hWnd, fname,
                 "Filename and Location of Drop", MB_OK);
      DragFinish(wParam);
      break;
    case WM_DESTROY: /* terminate the program */
      PostQuitMessage(0);
      break;
    /* Let Windows process any messages not specified in
       the preceding cases. */
    default:
      return(DefWindowProc(hWnd, messg, wParam, lParam));
  }
  return(0L);
}
```

Chapter 5

Dynamic Data Exchange

T H E functions in this chapter support Windows' Dynamic Data Exchange (DDE) system. DDE allows Windows applications to exchange data with each other. That is, DDE is a form of interprocess communication.

There are several terms related to DDE that need to be defined. A dynamic data interchange consists of a *conversation* in which two processes send messages to each other. The process that originates the conversation is called the *client*. The process that the client "talks to" is the *server*. Typically, but not always, the server contains information that the client wants. However, DDE data flow can be bidirectional. DDE data is identified using three strings that identify the *application*, the *topic,* and the *item.*

Many functions require a conversation handle. This handle is passed to the program when its DDE callback function is called.

To use most DDE functions, your application must include DDEML.H. A complete DDE programming example is shown at the end of this chapter.

BOOL DdeAbandonTransaction(DWORD *InstID,*
HCONV *hConversation,*
DWORD *TransID)*

DdeAbandonTransaction() aborts an asynchronous DDE transaction. It returns non-zero if successful, and zero on failure.

The instance identifier, obtained by calling **DdeInitialize()**, is passed in *InstID.*

The handle to the conversation that began the transaction is passed in *hConversation.* This parameter may be NULL, in which case all transactions are discontinued.

TransID specifies which transaction will be aborted. If NULL, then all transactions related to the conversation specified by *hConversation* are discontinued.

RELATED FUNCTION

DdeInitialize()

BYTE FAR *DdeAccessData(HDDEDATA *hData,*
DWORD FAR *lpdwData)

DdeAccessData() returns a pointer to the start of a global DDE memory object. It returns NULL if the function fails.

The handle to the DDE object is passed in *hData*.

On return, *lpdwData* will contain the number of bytes in the object. If your application does not need this information, this parameter may be NULL.

USAGE

When your application is done accessing the global DDE memory object, it may call **DdeUnaccessData()** to release it.

RELATED FUNCTION

DdeUnaccessData()

HDDEDATA DdeAddData(HDDEDATA *hData,*
void FAR *lpInfo,*
DWORD *dwSize,*
DWORD *dwOffset)*

DdeAddData() adds data to a global DDE object, thus creating a new object. The function returns a handle to the new object. On failure, the function returns NULL.

The handle to the existing object is passed in *hData*.

The information to add to the object is pointed to by *lpInfo*. The size of this data, in bytes, is passed in *dwSize*.

The new data is added to the existing object at the offset (in bytes from the start of the object) passed in *dwOffset*.

USAGE

The handle returned by **DdeAddData()** will generally differ from the one that is passed in *hData* because the addition of new data will require that a larger memory object be allocated to accommodate the new information. Thus, it is necessary to use the new handle in subsequent operations.

RELATED FUNCTIONS

DdeUnaccessData()

HDDEDATA DdeClientTransaction(void FAR *lpData, DWORD *dwSize*, HCONV *hConversation*, HSZ *hszString*, UINT *CBFormat*, UINT *TransType*, DWORD *dwTimeout*, DWORD FAR *lpResult*)

DdeClientTransaction() initiates a DDE transaction. This function is called by the client process. For synchronous transactions, the function returns a handle to the data passed to the client from the server. For asynchronous transactions, non-zero is returned if successful. In both cases, zero is returned if an error occurs.

The data that will be passed to the server is pointed to by *lpData*. This parameter can be NULL if no data is passed to the server. The size of this data, in bytes, is specified in *dwSize*.

The handle of the DDE conversation is passed in *hConversation*.

hszString is the handle to the string that identifies the data being requested.

CBFormat identifies the format of the data. It must be in one of the standard Clipboard formats. (See Volume 2, Chapter 5 for details on the Clipboard.)

TransType specifies the type of the transfer. It must be one of the following values.

Value	Format
XTYP_ADVSTART	Start advise loop.
XTYP_ADVSTART | XTYPF_NODATA	Start advise loop and notify only.
XTYP_ADVSTART | XTYP_ACKREQ	Start advise loop. Server waits for acknowledgment between transmission of each piece of data.
XTYP_ADVSTOP	Stop advise loop.
XTYP_EXECUTE	Execution request.
XTYP_POKE	Poke data. (*Poked data* is data that is transferred but not requested.)
XTYP_REQUEST	Request a transaction.

dwTimeout specifies, in milliseconds, how long the client will wait for a response. For asynchronous transfers, specify **TIMEOUT_ASYNC**.

On return, *lpResult* will contain the result of the transaction. For synchronous transactions, this parameter may be NULL. For asynchronous transactions, *lpResult* will contain an identifier that can be used in a call to **DdeAbandon-Transaction()** if it is necessary to abort the transaction.

RELATED FUNCTION

DdeAbandonTransaction()
DdeConnect()

int DdeCmpStringHandles(HSZ *hString1*, HSZ *hString2*)

DdeCmpStringHandles() compares the strings associated with the specified string handles. It returns zero if the strings are the same, negative if the string associated with *hString1* is less than the one associated with *hString2*, and positive if *hString1* is greater than *hString2*.

USAGE

The string comparison is not case-sensitive. Also, either or both handles may be zero. If both are zero, then **DdeCmpStringHandles()** returns zero. If only one is zero, then the one that is zero will compare as less than the other one.

RELATED FUNCTION

DdeCreateStringHandle()

HCONV DdeConnect(DWORD *InstID,*
HSZ *hServiceName,*
HSZ *hTopicName,*
CONVCONTEXT FAR ★ *lpContext)*

DdeConnect() initiates a conversation between the client (the calling process) and a server. It returns a handle to the conversation, or NULL if it fails to make a connection.

InstID is the instance identifier that is returned by **DdeInitialize()**.

The service name is specified by the string handle *hServiceName.* The name of the desired topic is specified by the string handle *hTopicName.*

lpContext is a pointer to a **CONVCONTEXT** structure that defines the conversation context, or NULL, in which case the default context is used. **CONVCONTEXT** is defined like this:

```
typedef struct tagCONVCONTEXT
{
  UINT cb;
  UINT wFlags;
  UINT wCountryID;
  int iCodePage;
  DWORD dwLangID;
  DWORD dwSecurity;
} CONVCONTEXT;
```

Here, **cb** specifies the size of the **CONVCONTEXT** structure. **wFlags** is reserved for future use. **wCountryID** specifies the country code. **iCodePage** specifies the code page. **dwLangID** specifies the language. **dwSecurity** specifies a security code that is defined by the application.

NOTE

In Windows NT/Win32, the **CONVCONTEXT** *includes the following additional member:*

```
SECURITY_QUALITY_OF_SERVICE qos;
```

This member is related to the Windows NT/Win32 security system and governs how the server may impersonate the client. (Impersonation allows the server to temporarily gain the security rights of the client.)

USAGE

If *hServiceName* is NULL, then any available server is used. If *hTopicName* is NULL, then any topic is used.

Typically, *lpContext* is specified as NULL, and the system defaults governing conversations are used.

RELATED FUNCTIONS

DdeConnectList()
DdeDisconnect()

HCONVLIST DdeConnectList (DWORD *InstID,*
HSZ *hServiceName,*
HSZ *hTopicName,*
HCONVLIST *hCList,*
CONVCONTEXT FAR **lpContext*)

DdeConnectList() initiates a conversation between the client (the calling process) and all servers that respond to the specified service and topic names. It returns a handle to the conversation list, or NULL if it fails to make a connection.

InstID is the instance identifier that is returned by **DdeInitialize()**.

The service name is specified by the string handle *hServiceName*. The name of the desired topic is specified by the string handle *hTopicName*.

To form a new list, *hCList* must be NULL. However, it can be the handle of a previously obtained list. In this case, Windows will remove those handles that have been terminated or that do not apply to the currently specified service and name.

lpContext is a pointer to a **CONVCONTEXT** structure that defines the conversation context, or NULL, in which case the default context is used. **CONVCONTEXT** is defined like this:

```
typedef struct tagCONVCONTEXT
{
  UINT cb;
  UINT wFlags;
  UINT wCountryID;
  int iCodePage;
  DWORD dwLangID;
  DWORD dwSecurity;
} CONVCONTEXT;
```

Here, **cb** specifies the size of the **CONVCONTEXT** structure. **wFlags** is reserved for future use. **wCountryID** specifies the country code. **iCodePage** specifies the code page. **dwLangID** specifies the language. **dwSecurity** specifies a security code that is defined by the application.

In Windows NT/Win32, the **CONVCONTEXT** *includes the following additional member:*

```
SECURITY_QUALITY_OF_SERVICE qos;
```

This member is related to the Windows NT/Win32 security system and governs how the server may impersonate the client. (Impersonation allows the server to temporarily gain the security rights of the client.)

USAGE

If *hServerName* is NULL, then any available server is used. If *hTopicName* is NULL, then any topic is used.

Typically, *lpContext* is specified as NULL, and the system defaults governing conversations are used.

The handle returned by **DdeConnectList()** must be freed by calling **DdeDisconnectList()**.

RELATED FUNCTIONS

DdeConnect()
DdeDisconnectList()

HDDEDATA DdeCreateDataHandle(DWORD *InstID*,
void FAR **lpSource*,
DWORD *dwSize*,
DWORD *dwOffset*,
HSZ *hItem*,
UINT *CBFormat*,
UINT *How*)

DdeCreateDataHandle() constructs a DDE-compatible global memory object that contains the data pointed to by *lpSource*. It returns a handle to the object if successful, and NULL on failure.

InstID is the instance identifier that is returned by **DdeInitialize()**.

lpSource points to the data that will be copied into the global memory object. The number of bytes of data to copy is passed in *dwSize*. The point in *lpSource* at which to start copying data is passed in *dwOffset*. To start at the beginning, this value must be zero.

The handle to the name of the data is passed in *hItem*.

CBFormat identifies the format of the data. It must be in one of the standard Clipboard formats. (See Volume 2, Chapter 5 for details on the Clipboard.)

How determines how the object is created. If you want the calling process (which is the server) to own the handle, then pass **HDATA_APPOWNED** in this parameter. Otherwise, this parameter can be zero, in which case the handle is not owned by the server. If the server owns the handle, it must be released by calling **DdeFreeDataHandle()**.

RELATED FUNCTIONS

DdeGetData()
DdeFreeDataHandle()

HSZ DdeCreateStringHandle(DWORD *InstID*, LPCSTR *lpszString*, int *CodePage*)

DdeCreateStringHandle() returns a handle to the specified string. If an error occurs, it returns NULL.

InstID is the instance identifier that is returned by **DdeInitialize()**.

lpszString is a pointer to the string that will have the handle associated with it.

The *CodePage* parameter specifies the code page used by the string. This parameter should either be **CP_WINANSI** (for normal characters provided by the default code page) or any other valid code page value. When using Windows NT/Win32, this parameter may also be **CP_WINUNICODE**, which specifies the Unicode code page.

USAGE

String handles have some important properties. First, when you create a string handle, the case of the string is not significant. Second, string handles are global resources in the sense that when one application creates a handle to a string and then another application creates a handle to the same string, both handles will be the same. Finally, you must free string handles, using **DdeFreeStringHandle()**, when they are no longer needed.

The following fragment creates a string handle to the string "My String".

```
HSZ hStr;
hStr = DdeCreateStringHandle(InstID, "My String", CP_WINANSI);
```

RELATED FUNCTIONS

DdeCmpStringHandles()
DdeFreeStringHandle()
DdeKeepStringHandle()

BOOL DdeDisconnect(HCONV *hConversation*)

DdeDisconnect() ends a DDE conversation. It returns non-zero if successful, and zero on failure.

The handle of the conversation to disconnect is passed in *hConversation*.

RELATED FUNCTIONS

DdeConnect()
DdeDisconnectList()

BOOL DdeDisconnectList(HCONVLIST *hConversation*)

DdeDisconnectList() ends all DDE conversations in the specified list. It returns non-zero if successful, and zero on failure.

The handle of the conversation list to disconnect is passed in *hConversation*.

USAGE

The conversation list handle passed to **DdeDisconnectList()** is invalid after the call.

RELATED FUNCTIONS

DdeConnectList()
DdeDisconnect()

BOOL DdeEnableCallback(DWORD *InstID*,
HCONV *hConversation*,
UINT *Action*)

DdeEnableCallback() determines whether conversation transactions are sent to the process that calls the function. It returns non-zero if successful, and zero on failure.

InstID is the instance identifier that is returned by **DdeInitialize()**.

The handle to the conversation that will be affected is passed in *hConversation*.

Whether transactions are enabled or disabled is determined by the value of *Action,* which must be one of these values: **EC_ENABLEALL** (allow all transactions), **EC_ENABLEONE** (allow one transaction), or **EC_DISABLE** (block transactions).

USAGE

DdeEnableCallback() can be called by either the client or the server.

Blocked transactions are held in the transaction queue and may be retrieved by re-enabling transactions. If transactions are blocked too long, some may be lost.

RELATED FUNCTION

DdeConnect()

BOOL DdeFreeDataHandle(HDDEDATA *hData*)

DdeFreeDataHandle() releases the global memory object associated with the specified handle. It returns non-zero if successful, and zero on failure.

The handle to the object to free is passed in *hData*.

USAGE

Since a DDE data object is a global entity, you must not free it until it is no longer needed by either the application that created it or an application that it was passed to. However, all global objects must be released at some point after they are no longer needed.

RELATED FUNCTIONS

DdeCreateDataHandle()
DdeFreeStringHandle()

BOOL DdeFreeStringHandle(DWORD *InstID,* HSZ *hString*)

DdeFreeStringHandle() frees a string handle. It returns non-zero if successful, and zero on failure.

InstID is the instance identifier that is returned by **DdeInitialize()**.

The handle to the string to be freed, created by calling **DdeCreateString-Handle()**, is passed in *hString*.

RELATED FUNCTIONS

DdeCreateStringHandle()
DdeFreeDataHandle()

DWORD DdeGetData(HDDEDATA *hData,*
void FAR *★lpTarget,*
DWORD *dwSize,*
DWORD *dwOffset*)

DdeGetData() obtains data from a global memory object. It returns the number of bytes transferred.

The handle to the data object is passed in *hData*.

The data will be copied from the object into the buffer pointed to by *lpTarget*. This buffer must be large enough to hold the data being copied. This parameter can be NULL. If it is, then the function returns the buffer size required to hold the data.

dwSize specifies the number of bytes of data to copy, which must not exceed the size of the buffer pointed to by *lpTarget*.

The point at which to start reading data from within the global data object is passed in *dwOffset*. To start at the beginning, use zero.

USAGE

The following fragment copies 200 bytes of data from the specified global memory object.

```
char buf[200];

if(DdeGetData(hData, buf, sizeof(buf), 0)!=sizeof(buf))
  MessageBox(hWnd, "Data transfer error.", "", MB_OK);
```

RELATED FUNCTION

DdeAccessData()

UINT DdeGetLastError(DWORD *InstID*)

DdeGetLastError() returns the last DDE error.

InstID is the instance identifier that is returned by **DdeInitialize()**.

USAGE

DdeGetLastError() also clears the last error from the system. The following is a list of possible DDE errors.

Value	Error
DMLERR_ADVACKTIMEOUT	Request for advise transaction timeout.
DMLERR_BUSY	Busy.
DMLERR_DATAACKTIMEOUT	Request for data transaction timeout.
DMLERR_DLL_NOT_INITIALIZED	**DdeInitialize()** not called.
DMLERR_DDL_USAGE	Application not permitted to perform DDE transactions.
DMLERR_EXECACKTIMEOUT	Execution request timeout.
DMLERR_INVALIDPARAMETER	Invalid parameter.
DMLERR_LOW_MEMORY	Insufficient memory.
DMLERR_MEMORY_ERROR	Out of memory.
DMLERR_NO_CONV_ESTABLISHED	No conversation established.
DMLERR_NOTPROCESSED	Transaction not processed.
DMLERR_POKEACKTIMEOUT	Request for poke transaction timeout.
DMLERR_POSTMSG_FAILED	DDEML call to **PostMessage()** results in error.
DMLERR_REENTRANCY	Second synchronous transaction initiated before first has completed.
DMLERR_SERVER_DIED	Server terminated.
DMLERR_SYS_ERROR	DDEML internal error.
DMLERR_UNADVACKTIMEOUT	Request to end advise transaction timeout.
DMLERR_UNFOUND_QUEUE_ID	Invalid transaction ID.

RELATED FUNCTION

DdeInitialize()

BOOL DdeImpersonateClient(HCONV *hConversation*)

DdeImpersonateClient() allows a server to impersonate the client. It returns non-zero if successful, and zero on failure.

In a secure system, it may be necessary for a server to impersonate a client. Impersonation allows the server to have the same security attributes as the client, which may be needed to achieve access to certain data. Impersonation and **DdeImpersonateClient()** only apply to secure systems.

The handle of the conversation is passed in *hConversation*.

RELATED FUNCTIONS

For more information about the Windows NT/Win32 security system, refer to Chapter 32.

UINT DdeInitialize(DWORD FAR *lpInstID, PFNCALLBACK pfnCallback, DWORD dwFlags, DWORD dwNotUsed)

DdeInitialize() initializes the DDE activity and registers the calling process with the DDE library.

Before the call, the variable pointed to by *lpInstID* must contain the value 0L. On return, it will contain the instance identifier for the calling application. This value is used in many other DDE function calls and must be preserved.

pfnCallback points to the function that will be called by the system when DDE transactions are passed. (See "Usage," for details.)

The value of *dwFlags* determines precisely what **DdeInitialize()** does and what transactions it will process. It can be any valid combination of the following values.

Value	Effect
APPCLASS_MONITOR	Register as DDE monitor.
APPCLASS_STANDARD	Register as DDE standard application.
APPCMD_CLIENTONLY	Register as client only.
APPCMD_FILTERINITS	Suppress use of XTYP_CONNECT and XTYP_WILDCONNECT transactions.
CBF_FAIL_ALLSVRXACTIONS	Client receives no server transactions.
CBF_FAIL_ADVISES	Callback function receives no XTYP_ADVSTART or XTYP_ADVSTOP transactions.
CBF_FAIL_CONNECTIONS	Callback function receives no XTYP_CONNECT or XTYP_WILDCONNECT transactions.
CBF_FAIL_EXECUTES	Callback function receives no XTYP_EXECUTE transactions.
CBF_FAIL_POKES	Callback function receives no XTYP_POKE transactions.
CBF_FAIL_REQUESTS	Callback function receives no XTYP_REQUEST transactions.

Value	Effect
CBF_FAIL_SELFCONNECTIONS	Callback function receives no XTYP_CONNECT transactions from the client to itself.
CBF_SKIP_ALLNOTIFICATIONS	Callback function receives no notifications.
CBF_SKIP_CONNECT_CONFIRMS	Callback function receives no XTYP_CONNECT_CONFIRM notifications.
CBF_SKIP_DISCONNECTS	Callback function receives no XTYP_DISCONNECT notification.
CBF_SKIP_REGISTRATIONS	Callback function receives no XTYP_REGISTER notification.
CBF_SKIP_UNREGISTRATIONS	Callback function receives no XTYP_UNREGISTER notification.

The following values only apply if **APPCLASS_MONITOR** is also specified. They are used to create DDE monitor applications.

MF_CALLBACKS	Notify when a transaction occurs.
MF_CONV	Notify when a conversation is begun.
MF_ERRORS	Notify when an error occurs.
MF_HSZ_INFO	Notify when a string handle is created or freed.
MF_LINKS	Notify when an advise loop is started or stopped.
MF_POSTMSGS	Notify when a DDE message is posted.
MF_SENDMSGS	Notify when a callback function sends a DDE message.

The *dwNotUsed* parameter must be set to 0L prior to the call. **DdeInitialize()** returns one of the following:

Value	Error
DMLERR_DDL_USAGE	Application not permitted to perform DDE transactions.
DMLERR_INVALIDPARAMETER	Invalid parameter.
DMLERR_NO_ERROR	Success.
DMLERR_SYS_ERROR	DDEML internal error.

USAGE

A callback function that is called when DDE transactions occur must exist within any application that wants to use Dynamic Data Exchange. This function must have the following prototype:

HDDEDATA CALLBACK DdeCBack(UINT *TransType,*

UINT *CBFormat,*

HCONV *hConversation,*

HSZ *hString1,*

HSZ *hString2,*

HDDEDATA *hData,*

DWORD *dwData1,*

DWORD *dwData2);*

Of course, the name of the function is arbitrary.

Each time the DDE callback function is called, *TransType* will contain the type of transaction. Each transaction belongs to a transaction class, which is identified by one of these values: **XCLASS_BOOL**, **XCLASS_DATA**, **XCLASS_FLAGS**, or **XCLASS_NOTIFICATION**. The transactions associated with each class are described in the following paragraphs.

If the class is **XCLASS_BOOL**, then the function must return zero or non-zero. The transaction types belonging to this class are **XTYP_ADVSTART** and **XTYP_CONNECT**.

If the class is **XCLASS_DATA**, then the function must return a handle to DDE data. The transaction types belonging to this class are **XTYP_ADVREQ**, **XTYP_REQUEST**, and **XTYP_WILDCONNECT**.

If the class is **XCLASS_FLAGS**, then the function must return **DDE_FACK** (acknowledge), **DDE_FBUSY** (busy, can't process now), or **DDE_FNOTPROCESSED** (did not process). The transaction types belonging to this class are **XTYP_ADVDATA**, **XTYP_EXECUTE**, and **XTYP_POKE**.

If the class is **XCLASS_NOTIFICATION**, the return value is ignored. The transaction types belonging to this class are **XTYP_ADVSTOP**, **XTYP_CONNECT_CONFIRM**, **XTYP_DISCONNECT**, **XTYP_ERROR**, **XTYP_MONITOR**, **XTYP_REGISTER**, **XTYP_XACT_COMPLETE**, and **XTYP_UNREGISTER**.

CBFormat identifies the format of the data. It must be in one of the standard Clipboard formats. (See Volume 2, Chapter 5 for details on the Clipboard.)

The handle of the conversation is passed in *hConversation*. *hString1* and *hString2* contain information related to the transaction. *hData* is the handle to the data associated with the transaction. *dwData1* and *dwData2* contain data related to the transaction.

As stated, *TransType* contains the type of transaction passed to the DDE callback function. The following table describes the contents of the other parameters for each transaction type that it receives.

Message	Parameters
XTYP_ADVDATA	CBFormat: Format of data. hConversation: Handle of conversation. hString1: Topic. hString2: Item. hData: Handle to data. dwData1: Unused. dwData2: Unused.
XTYP_ADVREQ	CBFormat: Format of data. hConversation: Handle of conversation. hString1: Topic. hString2: Item. hData: Unused. dwData1: Low-order word contains the number of ADVREQ transactions still to be processed. This value is zero if the current transaction is the last one. dwData2: Unused.
XTYP_ADVSTOP	CBFormat: Format of data. hConversation: Handle of conversation. hString1: Topic. hString2: Item. hData: Unused. dwData1: Unused. dwData2: Unused.
XTYP_ADVSTART	CBFormat: Format of data. hConversation: Handle of conversation. hString1: Topic. hString2: Item. hData: Unused. dwData1: Unused. dwData2: Unused.
XTYP_CONNECT	CBFormat: Unused. hConversation: Unused. hString1: Topic. hString2: Item. hData: Unused. dwData1: Pointer to CONVCONTEXT structure. dwData2: 1 if client and server are the same instance, and 0 if not.
XTYP_CONNECT_CON-FIRM	CBFormat: Unused. hConversation: Handle to conversation. hString1: Topic. hString2: Item. hData: Unused. dwData1: Unused. dwData2: 1 if client and server are the same instance, and 0 if not.

Message	Parameters
XTYP_DISCONNECT	CBFormat: Unused. hConversation: Handle of conversation. hString1: Unused. hString2: Unused. hData: Unused. dwData1: Unused. dwData2: 1 if client and server are the same instance, and 0 if not.
XTYP_ERROR	CBFormat: Unused. hConversation: Handle of conversation, or NULL if the error is not related to a conversation. hString1: Unused. hString2: Unused. hData: Unused. dwData1: Low-order word contains error. dwData2: Unused.
XTYP_EXECUTE	CBFormat: Unused. hConversation: Handle of conversation. hString1: Topic. hString2: Unused. hData: Command to execute. dwData1: Unused. dwData2: Unused.
XTYP_MONITOR	CBFormat: Unused. hConversation: Unused. hString1: Unused. hString2: Unused. hData: Data about DDE event. dwData1: Unused. dwData2: DDE event that took place.
XTYP_POKE	CBFormat: Format of data. hConversation: Handle of conversation. hString1: Topic. hString2: Item. hData: Handle of data. dwData1: Unused. dwData2: Unused.
XTYP_REGISTER	CBFormat: Unused. hConversation: Unused. hString1: Service being registered. hString2: Instance-specific service name. hData: Unused. dwData1: Unused. dwData2: Unused.
XTYP_REQUEST	CBFormat: Format of data. hConversation: Handle of conversation. hString1: Topic. hString2: Item. hData: Unused. dwData1: Unused. dwData2: Unused.

Message	Parameters
XTYP_UNREGISTER	CBFormat: Unused. hConversation: Unused. hString1: Service name to remove. hString2: Instance-specific service name. hData: Unused. dwData1: Unused. dwData2: Unused.
XTYP_WILDCONNECT	CBFormat: Unused. hConversation: Unused. hString1: Topic. hString2: Item. hData: Unused. dwData1: Pointer to a CONVCONTEXT structure. dwData2: 1 if client and server are the same instance, and 0 if not.
XTYP_XACT_COMPLETE	CBFormat: Format of data. hConversation: Handle of conversation. hString1: Topic. hString2: Item. hData: Handle of data. dwData1: Transaction ID. dwData2: Status flags.

RELATED FUNCTIONS

DdeConnect()
DdeConnectList()

BOOL DdeKeepStringHandle(DWORD *InstID*, HSZ *hString*)

DdeKeepStringHandle() allows a string handle passed to a DDE callback function to be saved and remain valid even after the callback function returns. Without this function, string handles are deleted when the callback function terminates.

InstID is the instance identifier that is returned by **DdeInitialize()**.
hString is the handle of the string to keep.

USAGE

Technically, a call to **DdeKeepStringHandle()** increments a usage count associated with the string handle. No string handle is deleted until its usage count is zero.

RELATED FUNCTIONS

DdeCreateStringHandle()
DdeFreeStringHandle()

HDDEDATA DdeNameService(DWORD *InstID*,
HSZ *hService*,
HSZ *hNotUsed*,
UINT *Flags*)

DdeNameService() registers the names of the services related to a server. (It can also remove a service name.) It returns non-zero if successful, and zero on failure. (Despite its return type declaration, **DdeNameService()** does *not* return a handle!)

InstID is the instance identifier that is returned by **DdeInitialize()**.

The handle to the service name to be registered is passed in *hService*.

hNotUsed is reserved and should be NULL.

Flags determines the specific operation of **DdeNameService()**. It can be one of these values: **DNS_REGISTER** (register name), **DNS_UNREGIS-TER** (remove name), **DNS_FILTERON** (turn on filtering), or **DNS_FIL-TEROFF** (turn off name filtering). If name filtering is on, then the server will not receive **XTYP_CONNECT** transactions for services it does not provide. (This is the default.)

USAGE

If *hService* is NULL and *Flags* is **DNS_UNREGISTER**, then all service names are removed.

The following fragment registers the service name "Wage".

```
HSZ hWage;

/* make a string handle */
hWage = DdeCreateStringHandle(InstID, "Wage", CP_WINANSI);

/* register it */
DdeNameService(InstID, hWage, NULL, DNS_REGISTER);
```

RELATED FUNCTIONS

DdeConnect()
DdeInitialize()

BOOL DdePostAdvise(DWORD *InstID,*
HSZ *hTopic,*
HSZ *hItem*)

A server calls **DdePostAdvise()** to post an **XTYP_ADVREQ** to all clients that have an advise loop on the specified topic and/or item. The function returns non-zero if successful, and zero on failure.

InstID is the instance identifier that is returned by **DdeInitialize()**.

hTopic is the handle of the topic name. *hItem* is the handle of the item name. To advise for all topics, specify *hTopic* as NULL. To advise for all items, specify *hItem* as NULL.

USAGE

DdePostAdvise() is used to update clients to changes in the data that they have requested.

RELATED FUNCTIONS

DdeAccessData()
DdeGetData()

UINT DdeQueryConvInfo(HCONV *hConversation,*
DWORD *TransID,*
CONVINFO FAR *lpConvInfo)

DdeQueryConvInfo() obtains information about a DDE transaction. It returns the number of bytes copied into the structure pointed to by *lpConvInfo*, or zero on failure.

hConversation specifies the handle of the conversation.

TransID is the ID of the transaction.

lpConvInfo is a pointer to a **CONVINFO** structure that will, upon return, contain the state of the conversation and current transaction. **CONVINFO** is defined like this:

```
typedef struct tagCONVINFO
{
  DWORD cb;
  DWORD hUser;
  HCONV hConvPartner;
```

```
    HSZ hszSvcPartner;
    HSZ hszServiceReq;
    HSZ hszTopic;
    HSZ hszItem;
    UINT wFmt;
    UINT wType;
    UINT wStatus;
    UINT wConvst;
    UINT wLastError;
    HCONVLIST hConvList;
    CONVCONTEXT ConvCtxt;
} CONVINFO;
```

Here, **cb** contains the size of the **CONVINFO** structure. **hUser** is the identifier of user-defined data. **hConvPartner** is the handle of the partner application (client or server). **hszSvcPartner** is the handle of the name of the partner. (The term "partner" here has no special significance. It simply refers to the other half of the DDE connection.) **hszServiceReq** is the handle of the service name. **hszTopic** is the handle of the topic requested. **hszItem** is the handle of the item requested. **wFmt** contains the format of the data. It will be one of the standard Clipboard formats. **wType** contains the type of the transaction. It will be one of these values:

Value	Transaction Type
XTYP_ADVDATA	Client receives advise data.
XTYP_ADVREQ	Client requests advise data.
XTYP_ADVSTART	Client requests that server start an advise loop.
XTYP_ADVSTOP	Stop an advise loop.
XTYP_CONNECT	Client requires a conversation.
XTYP_CONNECT_CONFIRM	Confirm establishment of conversation.
XTYP_DISCONNECT	End conversation.
XTYP_ERROR	Error.
XTYP_EXECUTE	Instruct server to execute a command.
XTYP_MONITOR	Notify DDE monitor that a transaction is occurring.
XTYP_POKE	Client sending data to server.
XTYP_REGISTER	Register a service name.
XTYP_REQUEST	Client requests data from server.
XTYP_UNREGISTER	Remove a service name.
XTYP_WILDCONNECT	Establish multiple conversations with a single client.

Value	Transaction Type
XTYP_XACT_COMPLETE	Asynchronous transaction is done.

The current state of the conversation is contained in **wStatus** and **wConvst**. The various status values for **wStatus** begin with **ST**, and the values for **wConvst** begin with **XST**. (Examine the DDEML.H header file for a list and description.) **wLastError** contains the error code for the last DDE transaction error, if there is one.

If a conversation list is active, then **hConvList** contains the handle of that list. Otherwise, this member is NULL.

The context of the conversation is specified in **ConvCtxt**. (For a description of the **CONVCONTEXT** structure, see **DdeConnect()**.)

RELATED FUNCTIONS

DdeInitialize()
DdeConnect()

HCONV DdeQueryNextServer(HCONVLIST *hConvList*, HCONV *hPreConv*)

DdeQueryNextServer() returns the next conversation handle in a conversation list. It returns NULL on failure or if no more handles exist.

hConvList is the handle to the conversation list in question.

hPreConv is the handle to the conversation previously obtained. To obtain the first handle, use NULL for this parameter.

RELATED FUNCTION

DdeConnectList()

DWORD DdeQueryString(DWORD *InstID*, HSZ *hString*, LPSTR *lpszTarget*, DWORD *dwSize*, int *CodePage*)

DdeQueryString() copies the string associated with the specified string handle. It returns the length of the string, or NULL on failure.

InstID is the instance identifier that is returned by **DdeInitialize()**.

hString specifies the handle of the string that will be copied. *lpszTarget* is a pointer to a character array into which the string will be copied. The size of the array is passed in *dwSize*.

The code page is passed in *CodePage*. This value should be **CP_WINANSI** or another valid code page.

USAGE

If *lpszTarget* is NULL, then the function returns the length of the string associated with the specified handle.

RELATED FUNCTION

DdeCreateStringHandle()

HCONV DdeReconnect(HCONV *hConversation*)

DdeReconnect() reestablishes a conversation with a server. If successful, it returns a handle to the conversation, or NULL on failure.

hConversation specifies the handle of a conversation to reconnect.

USAGE

Generally, a client will use **DdeReconnect()** to attempt to reestablish a conversation with a server that has disconnected, perhaps unexpectedly. If the reconnection is made, Windows will try to reset all conversation parameters to their state before the disconnection occurred.

RELATED FUNCTIONS

DdeConnect()
DdeConnectList()

BOOL DdeSetQualityOfService(HWND *hClient,*
CONST SECURITY_QUALITY_OF_SERVICE
PSECURITY_QUALITY_OF_SERVICE *lpPreQos*)

DdeSetQualityOfService() sets the quality of service that the next conversation will have. It returns non-zero if successful, and zero otherwise. The quality of service determines how a server will impersonate a client.

The window handle of the application that initiates DDE activity is passed in *hClient.*

lpNewQos is a pointer to a **SECURITY_QUALITY_OF_SERVICE** structure that defines the impersonation desired. On return, the structure pointed to by *lpPreQos* will contain the old quality settings. (This parameter may be NULL if this information is not needed.) **SECURITY_QUALITY_OF_SERVICE** is defined like this:

```
typedef struct _SECURITY_QUALITY_OF_SERVICE
{
  DWORD Length;
  SECURITY_IMPERSONATION_LEVEL ImpersonationLevel;
  SECURITY_CONTEXT_TRACKING_MODE ContextTrackingMode;
  BOOLEAN EffectiveOnly;
} SECURITY_QUALITY_OF_SERVICE;
```

Here, **Length** contains the size of the **SECURITY_QUALITY_OF_SERVICE** structure. **ImpersonationLevel** determines the specific nature of the impersonation. It must be one of these values: **SecurityAnonymous** (client is not impersonated), **SecurityIdentification** (server knows client's ID but cannot access secure data), or **SecurityImpersonation** (server impersonates client and has access to all data).

ContextTrackingMode determines if the server will be updated about changes in the client's security status. If this is the case, then this field will be **SECURITY_DYNAMIC_TRACKING**. Otherwise, the server will only know about the client's security status at the time the connection is established. In this case, **ContextTrackingMode** must be **SECURITY_STATIC_TRACKING**.

If **EffectiveOnly** is non-zero, then the server may affect aspects of the client's security context. Otherwise, the client's security context may not be affected.

RELATED FUNCTION

DdeImpersonateClient()

BOOL DdeSetUserHandle(HCONV *hConversation,*
DWORD *dwTransID,*
DWORD *dwAppValue*)

DdeSetUserHandle() links a value with a conversation handle and transaction ID. It returns non-zero if successful, and zero on failure.

hConversation specifies the handle of the conversation, and *dwTransID* specifies the transaction.

The value, which is defined by you, is passed in *dwAppValue.*

USAGE

The value linked by **DdeSetUserHandle()** can be obtained later by calling **DdeQueryConvInfo()**. The user handle is a means by which you can identify specific transactions, if necessary.

RELATED FUNCTION

DdeQueryConvInfo()

BOOL DdeUnaccessData(HDDEDATA *hData*)

DdeUnaccessData() frees the global data object specified by *hData.* It returns non-zero if successful, and zero otherwise.

USAGE

This function is frequently used to free a data handle that was obtained using **DdeAccessData()**.

RELATED FUNCTIONS

DdeAccessData()
DdeCreateDataHandle()

BOOL DdeUninitialize(DWORD *InstID*)

DdeUninitialize() ends all DDE activity relative to the calling process. Specifically, it terminates all conversations and frees all DDE resources allocated to it. It returns non-zero if successful, and zero on failure.

InstID is the instance identifier that is returned by **DdeInitialize()**.

USAGE

An application should call **DdeUninitialize()** when it has completed its DDE-related activity.

RELATED FUNCTION

DdeInitialize()

A Complete Programming Example

The following DDE skeleton programs demonstrate several DDE fundamentals. The programs are very simple. The server registers itself and waits for the client to request data. The client requests data from the server and displays that data. To use the programs, execute the server side first and then execute the client. To quit, terminate the client and then terminate the server. (Note: the server is executed as a minimized task.)

Here is the client side:

```
/*
   Client side of DDE demonstration programs.
*/

#include <windows.h>
#include <ddeml.h>
#include <stdio.h>
#include <string.h>

#define SIZE 10

LONG FAR PASCAL WndProc(HWND, UINT, WPARAM, LPARAM);
HDDEDATA CALLBACK DdeCBack(UINT TType, UINT CBFmt,
                     HCONV hCon, HSZ hStr1, HSZ hStr2,
```

```
                HDDEDATA hData, DWORD dwD1, DWORD dwD2);

char szProgName[] = "ProgName"; /* name of window class */

HINSTANCE hThisInst;
HWND hWnd;
DWORD InstID;
HCONV hConv;

char ServerName[] = "SERVER";
char TopicName[] = "DATA";

int PASCAL WinMain(HINSTANCE hInst, HINSTANCE hPreInst,
                   LPSTR lpszCmdLine, int nCmdShow)
{
  MSG lpMsg;
  WNDCLASS wcApp;

  if (!hPreInst) { /* if no previous instance */
    wcApp.lpszClassName = szProgName; /* window class name */
    wcApp.hInstance     = hInst; /* handle to this instance */
    wcApp.lpfnWndProc   = WndProc; /* window function */
    wcApp.hCursor       = LoadCursor(NULL, IDC_ARROW);
    wcApp.hIcon         = LoadIcon(NULL, IDI_APPLICATION);
    wcApp.lpszMenuName  = NULL;

    /* make the background of window white */
    wcApp.hbrBackground = GetStockObject(WHITE_BRUSH);
    wcApp.style         = 0; /* use default window style */
    wcApp.cbClsExtra    = 0; /* no extra info */
    wcApp.cbWndExtra    = 0; /* no extra info */

    /* register the window class */
    if (!RegisterClass (&wcApp))
      return FALSE;
  }

  /* Now that window has been registered, a window
     can be created. */
  hWnd = CreateWindow(
    szProgName,
    "DDE Client",
    WS_OVERLAPPEDWINDOW,
    CW_USEDEFAULT,
```

```
        CW_USEDEFAULT,
        CW_USEDEFAULT,
        CW_USEDEFAULT,
        (HWND)NULL,
        (HMENU) NULL,
        (HANDLE)hInst,
        (LPSTR)NULL
      );

      hThisInst = hInst; /* save instance handle */

      /* Display the Window. */
      ShowWindow(hWnd, nCmdShow);
      UpdateWindow(hWnd);

      /* Create the message loop. */
      while (GetMessage(&lpMsg, NULL, 0, 0)) {
        TranslateMessage(&lpMsg); /* allow use of keyboard */
        DispatchMessage(&lpMsg); /* return control to Windows */
      }
      DdeUninitialize(InstID);
      return(lpMsg.wParam);
    }

    /* Window Function. */
    LONG FAR PASCAL WndProc(HWND hWnd, UINT messg,
                            WPARAM wParam, LPARAM lParam)
    {
      FARPROC CBFunc;
      HSZ server, topic;
      HDDEDATA hd;
      char str[255];

      switch (messg) {
        case WM_CREATE:
          CBFunc = MakeProcInstance((FARPROC) DdeCBack, hThisInst);
          if(DdeInitialize(&InstID, (PFNCALLBACK) CBFunc,
                           APPCLASS_STANDARD | APPCMD_CLIENTONLY,
          0L)) {
            MessageBox(hWnd, "Error", "", MB_OK);
            return 0L;
          }
          server = DdeCreateStringHandle(InstID, ServerName, 0);
          topic = DdeCreateStringHandle(InstID, TopicName, 0);
```

```
        hConv = DdeConnect(InstID, server, topic, NULL);
        hd = DdeClientTransaction(NULL, 0, hConv, topic, CF_TEXT,
                            XTYP_REQUEST, 100, NULL);
        if(hd) DdeGetData(hd, str, SIZE, 0);
        MessageBox(hWnd, str, "Data Received", MB_OK);
        break;
      case WM_DESTROY: /* terminate the program */
        DdeFreeStringHandle(InstID, server);
        DdeFreeStringHandle(InstID, topic);
        DdeNameService(InstID, server, NULL, DNS_UNREGISTER);
        DdeDisconnect(hConv);
        PostQuitMessage(0);
        break;
      /* Let Windows process any messages not specified in
         the preceding cases. */
      default:
        return(DefWindowProc(hWnd, messg, wParam, lParam));
  }
  return(0L);
}


/* Client side DDE callback skeleton. */
HDDEDATA CALLBACK DdeCBack(UINT TType, UINT CBFmt,
                  HCONV hCon, HSZ hStr1, HSZ hStr2,
                  HDDEDATA hData, DWORD dwD1, DWORD dwD2)

{

  switch(TType) {
    case XTYP_DISCONNECT:
      MessageBox(hWnd, "Client received XTYP_DISCONNECT",
                "", MB_OK);
      return NULL;
  }
  return NULL;
}
```

Here is the server side:

```
/*
  Server side of DDE demonstration.
*/

#include <windows.h>
#include <ddeml.h>
```

```c
#include <stdio.h>
#include <string.h>

#define SIZE 10

LONG FAR PASCAL WndProc(HWND, UINT, WPARAM, LPARAM);
HDDEDATA CALLBACK DdeCBack(UINT TType, UINT CBFmt,
                HCONV hCon, HSZ hStr1, HSZ hStr2,
                HDDEDATA hData, DWORD dwD1, DWORD dwD2);

char szProgName[] = "ProgName"; /* name of window class */

HINSTANCE hThisInst;
HWND hWnd;
DWORD InstID;
HCONV hConv;
HSZ server, topic;

char str[SIZE] = "123456789";

char ServerName[] = "SERVER";
char TopicName[] = "DATA";

int PASCAL WinMain(HINSTANCE hInst, HINSTANCE hPreInst,
                LPSTR lpszCmdLine, int nCmdShow)
{
  MSG lpMsg;
  WNDCLASS wcApp;

  if (!hPreInst) { /* if no previous instance */
    wcApp.lpszClassName = szProgName; /* window class name */
    wcApp.hInstance     = hInst; /* handle to this instance */
    wcApp.lpfnWndProc   = WndProc; /* window function */
    wcApp.hCursor       = LoadCursor(NULL, IDC_ARROW);
    wcApp.hIcon         = LoadIcon(NULL, IDI_APPLICATION);
    wcApp.lpszMenuName  = NULL;

    /* make the background of window white */
    wcApp.hbrBackground = GetStockObject(WHITE_BRUSH);
    wcApp.style         = 0; /* use default window style */
    wcApp.cbClsExtra    = 0; /* no extra info */
    wcApp.cbWndExtra    = 0; /* no extra info */

    /* register the window class */
```

```
    if (!RegisterClass (&wcApp))
      return FALSE;
  }

  /* Now that window has been registered, a window
     can be created. */
  hWnd = CreateWindow(
    szProgName,
    "DDE Server",
    WS_OVERLAPPEDWINDOW,
    CW_USEDEFAULT,
    CW_USEDEFAULT,
    CW_USEDEFAULT,
    CW_USEDEFAULT,
    (HWND)NULL,
    (HMENU) NULL,
    (HANDLE)hInst,
    (LPSTR)NULL
  );

  hThisInst = hInst; /* save instance handle */

  /* Display the Window. */
  ShowWindow(hWnd, SW_SHOWMINIMIZED);
  UpdateWindow(hWnd);

  /* Create the message loop. */
  while (GetMessage(&lpMsg, NULL, 0, 0)) {
    TranslateMessage(&lpMsg); /* allow use of keyboard */
    DispatchMessage(&lpMsg); /* return control to Windows */
  }
  DdeUninitialize(InstID);
  return(lpMsg.wParam);
}

/* Window Function. */
LONG FAR PASCAL WndProc(HWND hWnd, UINT messg,
                        WPARAM wParam, LPARAM lParam)
{
  FARPROC CBFunc;

  switch (messg) {
    case WM_CREATE:
      CBFunc = MakeProcInstance((FARPROC) DdeCBack,
                                hThisInst);
```

```
          if(DdeInitialize(&InstID, (PFNCALLBACK) CBFunc,
                       APPCLASS_STANDARD, 0L)) {
            MessageBox(hWnd, "Error", "", MB_OK);
            return 0L;
          }
          server = DdeCreateStringHandle(InstID, ServerName, 0);
          topic = DdeCreateStringHandle(InstID, TopicName, 0);
          DdeNameService(InstID, server, NULL, DNS_REGISTER);
          break;
        case WM_DESTROY: /* terminate the program */
          DdeFreeStringHandle(InstID, server);
          DdeFreeStringHandle(InstID, topic);
          DdeNameService(InstID, server, NULL, DNS_UNREGISTER);
          DdeDisconnect(hConv);
          PostQuitMessage(0);
          break;
        /* Let Windows process any messages not specified in
           the preceding cases. */
        default:
          return(DefWindowProc(hWnd, messg, wParam, lParam));
    }
    return(0L);
}


/* Server side DDE callback skeleton. */
HDDEDATA CALLBACK DdeCBack(UINT TType, UINT CBFmt,
                   HCONV hCon, HSZ hStr1, HSZ hStr2,
                   HDDEDATA hData, DWORD dwD1, DWORD dwD2)
{
    switch(TType) {
      case XTYP_CONNECT:
        MessageBox(hWnd, "Server received XTYP_CONNECT", "",
                   MB_OK);
        return 1;
      case XTYP_REQUEST: /* data request */
        /* see if data requested is available */


        if(!DdeCmpStringHandles(topic, hStr1))
          /* requested data is available */
          return DdeCreateDataHandle(InstID, str, SIZE, 0,
               hStr2, CF_TEXT, 0);
        else
          return NULL;
```

```
    case XTYP_DISCONNECT:
      MessageBox(hWnd, "Sever received XTYP_DISCONNECT",
                "", MB_OK);
      return 1;
  }
  return NULL;
}
```

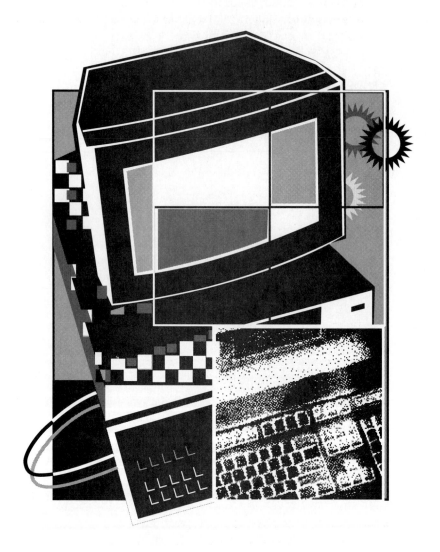

Chapter 6

Environmental Access

t H E functions described here allow access to the computing environment. Items available to your program include the environmental strings, the command line parameters, and the initial window specifications. A complete program is presented at the end of this chapter that illustrates several of the environmental functions.

Win32 only

LPSTR GetCommandLine(void)

GetCommandLine() returns a pointer to the command line used to execute the program.

USAGE

The following fragment displays the command line.

```
char *p;

p = GetCommandLine();
MessageBox(hWnd, p, "Command Line", MB_OK);
```

RELATED FUNCTION

GetEnvironmentStrings()

LPSTR GetDOSEnvironment(void)

GetDOSEnvironment() returns a pointer to a character array containing the environmental strings for the calling program.

This function is obsolete for Windows NT/Win32 and is not available for that environment.

USAGE

The environmental array may contain more than one string. Each environmental string is null terminated. The environmental string list will end with a null string.

The following fragment displays the first environmental string.

```
char FAR *p;

p = GetDOSEnvironment();
MessageBox(hWnd, p, "Environment", MB_OK);
```

RELATED FUNCTION

GetEnvironmentStrings()

LPVOID GetEnvironmentStrings(void)

GetEnvironmentStrings() returns a pointer to an array containing the environmental strings for the calling program.

USAGE

The environmental array may contain more than one string. Each environmental string is null terminated. The environmental string list will end with a null string.

The following fragment displays the first environmental string.

```
char *p;

p = GetEnvironmentStrings();
MessageBox(hWnd, p, "Environment", MB_OK);
```

RELATED FUNCTION

GetDOSEnvironment()

DWORD GetEnvironmentVariable(LPSTR *lpszVarName,*
LPSTR *lpszData,*
DWORD *dwSize)*

GetEnvironmentVariable() obtains the data associated with an environmental variable. It returns the number of bytes copied into *lpszData* if successful, or zero if an error occurs.

lpszVarName is a pointer to the environmental variable. The data associated with this variable is copied into the character array pointed to by *lpszData*. The size of the array pointed to by *lpszData* is passed in *dwSize.*

USAGE

The following fragment obtains the current PATH specification.

```
char envar[255];

GetEnvironmentVariable("PATH", envar, sizeof(envar));
MessageBox(hWnd, envar, "Current Path", MB_OK);
```

RELATED FUNCTION

SetEnvironmentVariable()

void GetStartupInfo(LPSTARTUPINFO *lpInfo)*

GetStartupInfo() obtains the properties associated with the main window of the program that calls this function.

The information is returned in a **STARTUPINFO** structure pointed to by *lpInfo.* **STARTUPINFO** is defined like this:

```
typedef struct _STARTUPINFO {
  DWORD cb;
```

```
    LPSTR lpReserved;
    LPSTR lpDesktop;
    LPSTR lpTitle;
    DWORD dwX;
    DWORD dwY;
    DWORD dwXSize;
    DWORD dwYSize;
    DWORD dwXCountChars;
    DWORD dwYCountChars;
    DWORD dwFillAttribute;
    DWORD dwFlags;
    WORD wShowWindow;
    WORD cbReserved2;
    LPBYTE lpReserved2;
    HANDLE hStdInput;
    HANDLE hStdOutput;
    HANDLE hStdError;
} STARTUPINFO;
```

Here, **cb** contains the size of the **STARTUPINFO** structure, and **lpReserved** is reserved.

lpDesktop points to the name of the desktop. It will be NULL if the default desktop is used. **lpTitle** relates only to console programs and points to the name displayed in the console's title bar. This member will be NULL if no console title exists or if the program is not a console program.

dwX and **dwY** contain the location (in pixels) of the upper-left corner of the window in screen-relative coordinates. **dwXSize** and **dwYsize** contain the X and Y dimensions, in pixels, of the window.

dwXCountChars and **dwYCountChars** relate only to console windows. They contain the number of columns and rows in the screen buffer.

dwFillAttribute relates only to console windows. It specifies the character and background colors for text output.

wShowWindow specifies how the window was initially shown.

cbReserved2 and **lpReserved2** are reserved.

The standard handles are contained in **hStdInput**, **hStdOutput**, and **hStdError**.

dwFlags contains one or more of the following values.

Value	Effect
STARTF_FORCEOFFFEEDBACK	Cursor feedback is off.
STARTF_FORCEONFEEDBACK	Cursor feedback is on.
STARTF_SCREENSAVER	The application is a screen saver.

STARTF_USECOUNTCHARS	dwXCountChars and dwYCountChars are used.
STARTF_USEFILLATTRIBUTE	dwFillAttribute is used.
STARTF_USEPOSITION	dwX and dwY are used.
STARTF_USESHOWWINDOW	wShowWindow is used.
STARTF_USESIZE	dwXSize and dwYSize are used.
STARTF_USESTDHANDLES	hStdInput, hStdOutput, and hStdError are used.

If the **USE** flags are not present, then the associated member(s) is ignored.

RELATED FUNCTION

GetEnvironmentStrings()

DWORD GetVersion(void)

GetVersion() returns the version of Windows and DOS (if applicable) currently running.

For 16-bit Windows, in the return value, the low-order word contains the Windows version and the high-order word contains the DOS version number. For Windows, the low-order byte contains the major revision number and the high-order byte contains the minor revision number. For DOS, the higher-order byte contains the major version number and the low-order byte contains the minor revision number.

For Windows NT/Win32, in the return value, the low-order word contains the Windows version and the high-order word contains a value that identifies the platform. The Windows version number is encoded like this: the low-order byte contains the major revision and the high-order contains the minor revision. The high-order word of the return value will be zero if the platform is Windows NT. It will be 1 if it is 16-bit Windows.

USAGE

The following fragment displays the current Windows version.

```
unsigned ver;
char str[255];

/* ... */

ver = LOWORD(GetVersion());
sprintf(str, "%d.%d", LOBYTE(ver), HIBYTE(ver));
MessageBox(hwnd, str, "Windows Version", MB_OK);
```

CHAPTER 6

ENVIRONMENTAL ACCESS

105

RELATED FUNCTIONS

GetDOSEnvironment()
GetEnvironmentStrings()

BOOL SetEnvironmentVariable(LPSTR *lpszVarName*, LPSTR *lpszData*)

SetEnvironmentVariable() sets the data associated with an environmental variable. It returns non–zero if successful, and zero otherwise.

lpszVarName is a pointer to the environmental variable to set. The string to assign to this variable is copied from the string pointed to by *lpszData*. If *lpszData* is NULL, then the specified environmental variable is removed.

RELATED FUNCTION

GetEnvironmentVariable()

A Complete Programming Example

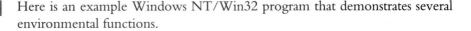

Here is an example Windows NT/Win32 program that demonstrates several environmental functions.

```
/* Demonstrate Environmental Functions */

#include <windows.h>
#include <string.h>
#include <stdio.h>

LRESULT CALLBACK WindowFunc(HWND, UINT, WPARAM, LPARAM);

char szWinName[] = "MyWin"; /* name of window class */

int WINAPI WinMain(HINSTANCE hThisInst, HINSTANCE hPrevInst,
                   LPSTR lpszArgs, int nWinMode)
{
  HWND hwnd;
  MSG msg;
```

```
WNDCLASS wcl;

/* Define a window class. */
wcl.hInstance = hThisInst; /* handle to this instance */
wcl.lpszClassName = szWinName; /* window class name */
wcl.lpfnWndProc = WindowFunc; /* window function */
wcl.style = 0; /* default style */

wcl.hIcon = LoadIcon(NULL, IDI_APPLICATION);
wcl.hCursor = LoadCursor(NULL, IDC_ARROW);
wcl.lpszMenuName = NULL;

wcl.cbClsExtra = 0;
wcl.cbWndExtra = 0;

/* Make the window light gray. */
wcl.hbrBackground = GetStockObject(LTGRAY_BRUSH);

/* Register the window class. */
if(!RegisterClass (&wcl)) return 0;

/* Now that a window class has been registered, a window
   can be created. */
hwnd = CreateWindow(
  szWinName, /* name of window class */
  "Environmental Functions", /* title */
  WS_OVERLAPPEDWINDOW, /* window style - normal */
  CW_USEDEFAULT, /* X coordinate - let Windows decide */
  CW_USEDEFAULT, /* Y coordinate - let Windows decide */
  CW_USEDEFAULT, /* width - let Windows decide */
  CW_USEDEFAULT, /* height - let Windows decide */
  NULL, /* handle of parent window - there isn't one */
  NULL, /* no menu */
  hThisInst, /* handle of this instance of the program */
  NULL /* no additional arguments */
);

/* Display the window minimized. */
ShowWindow(hwnd, SW_SHOWMINIMIZED);
UpdateWindow(hwnd);

/* Create the message loop. */
while(GetMessage(&msg, NULL, 0, 0))
{
```

```
      TranslateMessage(&msg);
      DispatchMessage(&msg);
   }
   return msg.wParam;
}


/* This function is called by Windows NT and is passed
   messages from the message queue.
*/
LRESULT CALLBACK WindowFunc(HWND hwnd, UINT message, WPARAM
wParam,
                  LPARAM lParam)
{
   unsigned ver;
   char *p;
   char envar[255], str[255];

   switch(message) {
     case WM_CREATE:
       p = GetCommandLine();
       MessageBox(hwnd, p, "Command Line", MB_OK);

       p = GetEnvironmentStrings();
       MessageBox(hwnd, p, "Environment", MB_OK);

       GetEnvironmentVariable("PATH", envar, sizeof(envar));
       MessageBox(hwnd, envar, "Path", MB_OK);

       ver = LOWORD(GetVersion());
       sprintf(str, "%d.%d", LOBYTE(ver), HIBYTE(ver));
       MessageBox(hwnd, str, "Windows Version", MB_OK);

       break;
     case WM_DESTROY: /* terminate the program */
       PostQuitMessage(0);
       break;
     default:
       /* Let Windows NT process any messages not specified in
          the preceding switch statement. */
       return DefWindowProc(hwnd, message, wParam, lParam);
   }
   return 0;
}
```

Chapter 7

Error-Related Functions

T H E functions in this chapter obtain error information, set the error mode, or otherwise respond to errors. A complete program is presented at the end of this chapter that demonstrates several of the error-related functions.

BOOL Beep(DWORD *dwHertz,* DWORD *dwLength*)

Beep() sounds the bell. It returns non-zero if successful, and zero otherwise. This function is typically used to alert the user to an error condition.

The frequency of the tone is specified by *dwHertz*.

The number of milliseconds that the tone is sounded is passed in *dwLength*.

USAGE

This statement sounds a 1,000Hz tone for 100 milliseconds:

```
Beep(1000, 100);
```

RELATED FUNCTIONS

See Volume 2, Chapter 28 for other sound-related functions.

BOOL ExitWindows(DWORD *dwRestart,* UINT *NotUsed*)

ExitWindows() terminates Windows. It returns zero on failure. If successful, there is no return value.

For 16-bit Windows: the value passed in *dwRestart* must be one of these values: **EW_REBOOTSYSTEM**, **EW_RESTARTWINDOWS**, or zero. If **EW_REBOOTSYSTEM** is specified, then the computer is rebooted. If **EW_RESTARTWINDOWS** is specified, then Windows is restarted. If zero is specified, then Windows is terminated and DOS resumes control.

For Windows NT: *dwRestart* must be zero. A call to **ExitWindows()** logs off the user.

NotUsed is reserved and must be zero.

USAGE

The following statement terminates Windows.

```
ExitWindows(0, 0);
```

RELATED FUNCTIONS

ExitWindowsExec()
ExitWindowsEx()

BOOL ExitWindowsEx(UINT *How*, DWORD *NotUsed*)

ExitWindowsEx() terminates Windows NT. It returns non-zero if successful, and zero otherwise. (In some cases the calling process is terminated before a return value can be obtained.)

Precisely what **ExitWindowsEx()** does is determined by the value of *How*, which must be one or more of these values: **EWX_FORCE** (forces termination of all processes), **EWX_LOGOFF** (logs off), **EWX_REBOOT** (reboots the computer), or **EWX_SHUTDOWN** (terminates Windows NT).

NotUsed is reserved.

Some security-related constraints may affect system shutdown. Refer to Chapter 32 in this volume for details.

RELATED FUNCTION

ExitWindows()

BOOL ExitWindowsExec(LPCSTR *lpszCommand*, LPCSTR *lpszParams*)

ExitWindowsExec() executes a DOS program. It terminates Windows, runs the DOS command, and then restarts Windows. The function returns zero on failure. (No return value is available if the function succeeds.)

This function is not available in Windows NT.

The name of the file that contains the DOS program to execute must be contained in the string pointed to by *lpszCommand*. This string may include a full drive and path specification. The command must not exceed 128 bytes in length.

Parameters to pass to the command are in the string pointed to by *lpszParams*. This string must not exceed 127 bytes in length. If there are no parameters, this value may be NULL.

RELATED FUNCTION

ExitWindows()

BOOL FlashWindow(HWND *hWnd*, BOOL *How*)

FlashWindow() reverses the state of the specified window's title bar. If called repeatedly, it causes the title bar to "flash." Flashing a window is the proper means by which an application notifies the user that it requires attention. The function returns non-zero if the title bar was highlighted prior to the call, and zero if it was not.

The handle of the window to flash is passed in *hWnd*.

If *How* is non-zero, then the window is flashed. If *How* is zero, then the window is returned to its original state prior to flashing.

USAGE

Each call to **FlashWindow()** flashes the window only once. Therefore, to flash repeatedly, you must call **FlashWindow()** several times. You will also need to have some sort of delay between calls. If you don't, you will not see the window flash. (Delays can be generated using a timer, a delay loop, or, if you are using Windows NT or Win32, the **Sleep()** function.)

The following fragment flashes the window.

```
int i;
unsigned long d;

for(i=0; i<10; i++) {
```

```
    FlashWindow(hWnd, 1);
    for(d=0; d<100000; d++) ; /* delay */
}
```

RELATED FUNCTIONS

Beep()
Sleep()

DWORD GetLastError(void)

GetLastError() returns the code for the last error set by an API function or by a call to **SetLastError()**.

USAGE

Error codes are thread-relative. That is, the last error of one thread is separate from and does not overwrite the last error of another thread.

A list of the error code macros is found in WINDOWS.H (or its support header files).

RELATED FUNCTION

SetLastError()

UINT SetErrorMode(UINT *Mode*)

SetErrorMode() determines how errors are handled. It returns the previous error mode.

The value of *Mode* determines how errors are processed. It must be one or more of the following values: **SEM_FAILCRITICALERRORS**, **SEM_NOGPFAULTERRORBOX**, or **SEM_NOOPENFILEERROR-BOX**. Each is explained in the following paragraphs.

If **SEM_FAILCRITICALERRORS** is specified, then the standard critical-error message box is not displayed and critical errors must be processed by your program. Generally, you will not want to specify this mode because critical errors usually cannot be correctly handled by your program.

If **SEM_NOGPFAULTERRORBOX** is specified, then the standard general-protection-fault message box is not displayed and GPF errors must be processed by your program. This mode only applies to debuggers and should not be used by normal programs.

If **SEM_NOOPENFILEERRORBOX** is specified, then the standard file-not-found error box is not displayed and your program must process this error.

When opening user-specified files, use the Open common dialog box rather than managing this within your program.

USAGE

Most applications will never need to change the default error mode. This function exists mostly to accommodate special situations.

RELATED FUNCTION

SetLastError()

void **SetLastError(DWORD** *dwErr***)**

SetLastError() sets the current error code.

The error code is specified in *dwErr*.

USAGE

Error codes are thread-relative. That is, the last error of one thread is separate from and does not overwrite the last error of another thread.

A list of the error code macros is found in WINDOWS.H (or its support header files).

RELATED FUNCTION

GetLastError()

void SetLastErrorEx(DWORD *dwErr,* DWORD *dwType*)

SetLastErrorEx() sets the current error code and type.

The error code is specified in *dwErr.*

The type of the error is passed in *dwType.* It will be one of these values: **SLE_ERROR** (fatal error), **SLE_MINORERROR** (nonfatal error), **SLE_WARNING** (possible error), or zero, if no type information is relevant.

USAGE

Error codes are thread-relative. That is, the last error of one thread is separate from and does not overwrite the last error of another thread.

A list of the error code macros is found in WINDOWS.H (or its support header files).

RELATED FUNCTION

SetLastError()

A Complete Programming Example

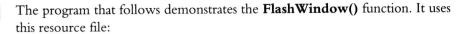

The program that follows demonstrates the **FlashWindow()** function. It uses this resource file:

```
#include <windows.h>
#include "example.h"

MYMENU MENU
{
  POPUP "Menu"
  {
    MENUITEM "Flash", ID_FLASH
    MENUITEM "Flash Once", ID_FLASHONCE
  }
}


MYMENU ACCELERATORS
{
```

```
   VK_F1, ID_FLASH, VIRTKEY
   VK_F2, ID_FLASHONCE, VIRTKEY
}
```

The header file EXAMPLE.H is defined like this:

```
#define ID_FLASH  200
#define ID_FLASHONCE 201
```

The flash-window program is shown here.

```
/*
  Flash the window.
*/

#include <windows.h>
#include "example.h"

LONG FAR PASCAL WndProc(HWND, UINT, WPARAM, LPARAM);

char szProgName[] = "ProgName"; /* name of window class */
char szApplName[] = "MYMENU"; /* name of main menu */

int PASCAL WinMain(HINSTANCE hInst, HINSTANCE hPreInst,
                   LPSTR lpszCmdLine, int nCmdShow)
{
  HWND hWnd;
  MSG lpMsg;
  WNDCLASS wcApp;
  HACCEL hAccel;

  if (!hPreInst) { /* if no previous instance */
    wcApp.lpszClassName = szProgName; /* window class name */
    wcApp.hInstance     = hInst; /* handle to this instance */
    wcApp.lpfnWndProc   = WndProc; /* window function */
    wcApp.hCursor       = LoadCursor(NULL, IDC_ARROW);
    wcApp.hIcon         = LoadIcon(NULL, IDI_APPLICATION);
    wcApp.lpszMenuName  = szApplName; /* main menu */

    /* make the background of window white */
    wcApp.hbrBackground = GetStockObject(WHITE_BRUSH);
    wcApp.style         = 0; /* use default window style */
    wcApp.cbClsExtra    = 0; /* no extra info */
```

```
  wcApp.cbWndExtra    = 0; /* no extra info */

  /* register the window class */
  if (!RegisterClass (&wcApp))
    return FALSE;
}


/* Now that window has been registered, a window
   can be created. */
hWnd = CreateWindow(
  szProgName,
  "Flash the Window",
  WS_OVERLAPPEDWINDOW,
  CW_USEDEFAULT,
  CW_USEDEFAULT,
  CW_USEDEFAULT,
  CW_USEDEFAULT,
  (HWND)NULL,
  (HMENU) NULL,
  (HANDLE)hInst,
  (LPSTR)NULL
);

hAccel = LoadAccelerators(hInst, "MYMENU");

/* Display the Window. */
ShowWindow(hWnd, nCmdShow);
UpdateWindow(hWnd);

/* Create the message loop. */
while (GetMessage(&lpMsg, NULL, 0, 0)) {
  if(!TranslateAccelerator(hWnd, hAccel, &lpMsg)) {
    TranslateMessage(&lpMsg); /* allow use of keyboard */
    DispatchMessage(&lpMsg); /* return control to Windows */
  }
}
return(lpMsg.wParam);
}


/* Window Function. */
LONG FAR PASCAL WndProc(HWND hWnd, UINT messg,
                        WPARAM wParam, LPARAM lParam)
{
  int i;
```

```
unsigned long d;

switch (messg) {
  case WM_COMMAND:
    switch(LOWORD(wParam)) {
      case ID_FLASH: /* flash window several times */
        FlashWindow(hWnd, 1);
        for(i=0; i<10; i++) {
          FlashWindow(hWnd, 1);
          for(d=0; d<100000; d++) ; /* delay */
        }
        FlashWindow(hWnd, 0);
        break;
      case ID_FLASHONCE: /* flash window once */
        FlashWindow(hWnd, 1);
        break;
    }
    break;
  case WM_DESTROY: /* terminate the program */
    PostQuitMessage(0);
    break;
  /* Let Windows process any messages not specified in
     the preceding cases. */
  default:
    return(DefWindowProc(hWnd, messg, wParam, lParam));
}
return(0L);
}
```

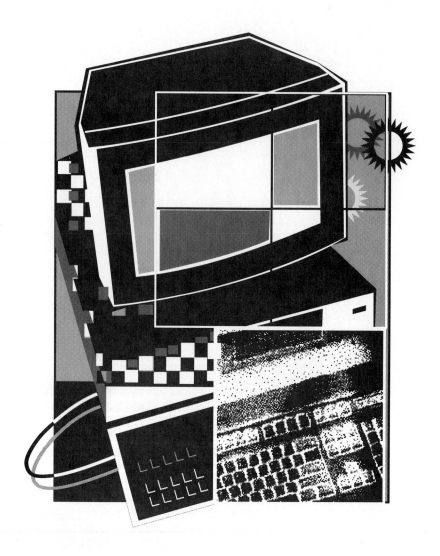

Chapter 8

Event Logs

U S I N G Windows NT, it is possible to record various program-related events in a log that is managed by Windows NT. Later, you can retrieve one or more events. You can also view the contents of an event log using the standard Windows NT Event Viewer accessory. Event logs are especially useful for debugging or for monitoring program performance. However, an event log is not designed for normal data storage or retrieval.

Event logs are contained in files not directly accessible by your program using the normal file management functions. Instead, event logs are accessed via the functions described in this chapter or by using the Event Viewer.

BOOL BackupEventLog(HANDLE *hLog*, LPSTR *lpszFilename*)

BackupEventLog() copies the current contents of the event log into the specified file. It returns non-zero if successful, and zero otherwise.

The handle of the event log to back up is passed in *hLog*.

The name of the file that will receive the copy of the event log is pointed to by *lpszFilename*.

USAGE

The backup file created by **BackupEventLog()** is in ASCII.

The following fragment copies the event log associated with **hEvent** into "MYLOG.EVT".

```
BackupEventLog(hEvent, "MYLOG.EVT");
```

RELATED FUNCTIONS

OpenEventLog()
RegisterEvent()

BOOL ClearEventLog(HANDLE *hLog,* LPSTR *lpszFilename*)

ClearEventLog() erases the contents of the specified event log. Before doing so, however, it copies the log to the specified file. The function returns non-zero if successful, and zero on failure.

The handle to the event log to clear is passed in *hLog.*

The name of the file into which the log will be copied is pointed to by *lpszFilename.* If you don't want a copy of the log, specify NULL for this parameter.

RELATED FUNCTIONS

BackupEventLog()
CloseEventLog()

BOOL CloseEventLog(HANDLE *hLog*)

CloseEventLog() closes the specified log. It returns non-zero if successful, and zero otherwise.

The handle of the log to close is passed in *hLog.*

RELATED FUNCTION

ClearEventLog()

BOOL DeregisterEventSource(HANDLE *hLog*)

DeregisterEventSource() deactivates the specified event log handle. It returns non-zero if successful, and zero on failure.

The handle to close is specified by *hLog.*

USAGE

After calling **DeregisterEventSource()**, *hLog* may no longer be used.

RELATED FUNCTION

RegisterEventSource()

BOOL GetNumberOfEventLogRecords(HANDLE *hLog*, PDWORD *pdwRecs*)

GetNumberOfEventLogRecords() obtains the number of event records in the specified log file. It returns non-zero if successful, and zero on failure.

The handle to the event log file is passed in *hLog*.

On return, the number of records in that file are in the variable pointed to by *pdwRecs*.

RELATED FUNCTIONS

GetOldestEventLogRecord()
ReadEventLog()

BOOL GetOldestEventLogRecord(HANDLE *hLog*, PDWORD *pdwRecord*)

GetOldestEventLogRecord() obtains the number of the oldest event record in the specified log file. It returns non-zero if successful, and zero on failure.

The handle to the event log file is passed in *hLog*.

On return, the number of the oldest record in that file is in the variable pointed to by *pdwRecord*.

RELATED FUNCTIONS

GetNumberOfEventLogRecords()
ReadEventLog()

HANDLE OpenBackupEventLog(LPSTR *lpszServerName,*
LPSTR *lpszFilename*)

OpenBackupEventLog() returns the handle to the specified backup event log. On failure, it returns NULL.

If a network server is being used, its name must be pointed to by *lpszServerName.* If not, then this parameter must be NULL.

The name of the backup file is pointed to by *lpszFilename.*

RELATED FUNCTION

BackupEventLog()

HANDLE OpenEventLog(LPSTR *lpszServerName,*
LPSTR *lpszSourceName*)

OpenEventLog() returns a handle to an event log. It returns NULL if an error occurs.

If a network server is being used, its name must be pointed to by *lpszServerName.* If not, then this parameter must be NULL.

The name of the source that the handle refers to must be pointed to by *lpszSourceName.* This must be a name that is registered in the log. (See **RegisterEventSource()**.) If the specified name is not found, then the standard name "Application" is used.

USAGE

The following fragment obtains a handle to the event log. The log is local and the source name is "MyApp".

```
HANDLE hEvent;

hEvent = OpenEventLog(NULL, "MyApp");
```

RELATED FUNCTIONS

RegisterEventSource()
ReadEvent()
ReportEvent()

BOOL ReadEventLog(HANDLE *hLog,* DWORD *dwHow,* DWORD *dwRecord,* LPVOID *lpBuf,* DWORD *dwBufSize,* DWORD **pdwNumRead,* DWORD **pdwSize*)

ReadEventLog() reads one (or more) event records from the specified event log. It returns non-zero if successful, and zero otherwise.

The handle of the event log is specified in *hLog.*

How the log will be read is determined by the value of *dwHow,* which must be one of these values: **EVENTLOG_SEEK_READ** (read file randomly) or **EVENTLOG_SEQUENTIAL_READ** (read file sequentially). In either case, you will need to OR one of these values with one of the following direction flags: **EVENTLOG_BACKWARDS_READ** (read file backwards) or **EVENTLOG_FORWARDS_READ** (read file forwards).

The record at which to begin reading is passed in *dwRecord.*

The event records will be read into the buffer pointed to by *lpBuf.* (The format of an event record is described under "Usage.")

dwBufSize specifies the maximum number of bytes to read. **ReadEventLog()** will read as many whole records as is possible so long as the buffer is not overrun.

The number of bytes actually read will be returned in the variable pointed to by *pdwNumRead.*

On return, if the specified buffer is too small, then the variable pointed to by *pdwSize* will contain the minimum buffer size.

USAGE

Event records are based upon the **EVENTLOGRECORD** structure, which is defined like this:

```
typedef struct _EVENTLOGRECORD {
  DWORD Length;
  DWORD Reserved;
  DWORD RecordNumber;
  DWORD TimeGenerated;
  DWORD TimeWritten;
  DWORD EventID;
  WORD EventType;
  WORD NumStrings;
  WORD EventCategory;
  WORD ReservedFlags;
  DWORD ClosingRecordNumber;
  DWORD StringOffset;
  DWORD UserSidLength;
  DWORD UserSidOffset;
  DWORD DataLength;
  DWORD DataOffset;
  /* Event dependent info follows in this order:
    Source Name
    Computer Name
    User Security ID
    Strings
    Data
  */
} EVENTLOGRECORD;
```

Here, **Length** is the size of the record and **RecordNumber** is the number of the record.

The time, in seconds since January 1, 1970, that the record was generated is stored in **TimeGenerated**. The time, again in seconds from January 1, 1970, that the record was actually written is stored in **TimeWritten**.

EventID contains the identifier of the event. **EventType** contains the type of the event. It will be one of these values: **EVENTLOG_AUDIT_FAILURE, EVENTLOG_AUDIT_SUCCESS, EVENTLOG_ERROR_TYPE, EVENTLOG_INFORMATION_TYPE,** or **EVENTLOG_WARNING_TYPE**.

NumStrings contains the number of user-defined strings at the location specified by **StringOffset**.

EventCategory is a user-specific category code.

UserSidLength contains the length of the user's security identifier. **UserSidOffset** contains the offset in the record at which the user's security identifier will be found.

DataLength contains the size in bytes of additional data in the record. **DataOffset** contains the offset in the record at which this data will be found.

The source name and the computer name identify the source and the computer.

Reserved, **ReservedFlags**, and **ClosingRecordNumber** are reserved.

RELATED FUNCTION

ReportEvent()

HANDLE RegisterEventSource(LPSTR *lpszServerName*, LPSTR *lpszSourceName*)

RegisterEventSource() registers an event source and returns a handle to it. It returns NULL on failure.

If a network server is being used, its name must be pointed to by *lpszServerName*. If not, then this parameter must be NULL.

lpszSourceName is the user-defined name of the event source. This may be a name that is in the system registry under the heading "EventLog". It may also be a name that is not in the system registry. If this is the case, then the standard "Application" log file is used. In either case, the source name is still registered.

USAGE

The handle returned by **RegisterEventSource()** is used in calls to **ReportEvent()**. To close this handle, call **DeregisterEventSource()**.

RELATED FUNCTIONS

DeregisterEventSource()
ReportEvent()

BOOL ReportEvent(HANDLE *hLog,* **WORD** *wType,*
 WORD *wCategory,* **DWORD** *dwID,*
 PSID *pSecurityID,* **WORD** *wNumStr,*
 DWORD *dwDataSize,*
 LPSTR ★*lpszStrings,* **LPVOID** *lpData***)**

ReportEvent() adds a record to the specified event log. It returns non-zero if successful, and zero on failure.

The handle to the event log is passed in *hLog.* This handle must have been obtained through a call to **RegisterEventSource()**.

wType specifies the type of the event. It will be one of these values: **EVENTLOG_AUDIT_FAILURE, EVENTLOG_AUDIT_SUCCESS, EVENTLOG_ERROR_TYPE, EVENTLOG_INFORMATION_TYPE,** or **EVENTLOG_WARNING_TYPE.**

wCategory contains a user-defined value that specifies the category of the event.

An event identifier value is passed in *dwID.*

The user's security ID must be pointed to by *pSecurityID.* This value can be NULL if security is not implemented.

lpszStrings points to a character array that contains user-defined null-terminated strings (or NULL if no strings are present). The *wNumStr* parameter specifies the number of strings. The strings are added to the end of the event record.

lpData is a pointer to data that is added to the event record. The size, in bytes, of this data is specified by *dwDataSize.* The data is added to the end of the event record.

RELATED FUNCTION

RegisterEventSource()

A Complete Programming Example

Here is a complete program that demonstrates several event logging functions. The program registers the source "MYAPP", writes two reports from that

source, copies the log to "mylog.evt", and then deregisters that source. To view
the reports, use the Event Viewer accessory provided by Windows NT.

```c
/*

    Demonstrate Event Logging

   This is a Windows NT program.
*/

#include <windows.h>
#include <string.h>
#include <stdio.h>

LRESULT CALLBACK WindowFunc(HWND, UINT, WPARAM, LPARAM);

char szWinName[] = "MyWin"; /* name of window class */

HANDLE hEvent;
char str[255];

int WINAPI WinMain(HINSTANCE hThisInst, HINSTANCE hPrevInst,
                   LPSTR lpszArgs, int nWinMode)
{
  HWND hwnd;
  MSG msg;
  WNDCLASS wcl;

  /* Define a window class. */
  wcl.hInstance = hThisInst; /* handle to this instance */
  wcl.lpszClassName = szWinName; /* window class name */
  wcl.lpfnWndProc = WindowFunc; /* window function */
  wcl.style = 0; /* default style */

  wcl.hIcon = LoadIcon(NULL, IDI_APPLICATION); /* icon style */
  wcl.hCursor = LoadCursor(NULL, IDC_ARROW); /* cursor style */
  wcl.lpszMenuName = NULL; /* no menu */

  wcl.cbClsExtra = 0;
  wcl.cbWndExtra = 0;

  /* Make the window light gray. */
  wcl.hbrBackground = GetStockObject(LTGRAY_BRUSH);

  /* Register the window class. */
```

```
if(!RegisterClass (&wcl)) return 0;

/* Now that a window class has been registered, a window
   can be created. */
hwnd = CreateWindow(
  szWinName, /* name of window class */
  "Event Logging", /* title */
  WS_OVERLAPPEDWINDOW, /* window style - normal */
  CW_USEDEFAULT, /* X coordinate - let Windows decide */
  CW_USEDEFAULT, /* Y coordinate - let Windows decide */
  CW_USEDEFAULT, /* width - let Windows decide */
  CW_USEDEFAULT, /* height - let Windows decide */
  NULL, /* handle of parent window - there isn't one */
  NULL, /* no menu */
  hThisInst, /* handle of this instance of the program */
  NULL /* no additional arguments */
);

/* Display the window. */
ShowWindow(hwnd, SW_SHOWMINIMIZED);
UpdateWindow(hwnd);

/* register the source */
hEvent = RegisterEventSource(NULL, "MYAPP");
if(!hEvent) MessageBox(hwnd, "Cannot Register",
                       "Error", MB_OK);

/* report 2 events */
if(!ReportEvent(hEvent, EVENTLOG_INFORMATION_TYPE,
                1, 1, NULL, 0, 0, NULL, NULL))
   MessageBox(hwnd, "Report Error", "Error", MB_OK);

if(!ReportEvent(hEvent, EVENTLOG_INFORMATION_TYPE,
                1, 2, NULL, 0, 0, NULL, NULL))
   MessageBox(hwnd, "Report Error", "Error", MB_OK);

/* Save Event Log */
BackupEventLog(hEvent, "mylog.evt");

DeregisterEventSource(hEvent);

/* Create the message loop. */
while(GetMessage(&msg, NULL, 0, 0))
{
```

```
      TranslateMessage(&msg); /* allow use of keyboard */
      DispatchMessage(&msg); /* return control to Windows */
   }
   return msg.wParam;
}


/* This function is called by Windows NT and is passed
   messages from the message queue.
*/
LRESULT CALLBACK WindowFunc(HWND hwnd, UINT message,
                            WPARAM wParam, LPARAM lParam)
{
  switch(message) {
    case WM_DESTROY: /* terminate the program */
      PostQuitMessage(0);
      break;
    default:
      /* Let Windows NT process any messages not specified in
         the preceding switch statement. */
      return DefWindowProc(hwnd, message, wParam, lParam);
  }
  return 0;
}
```

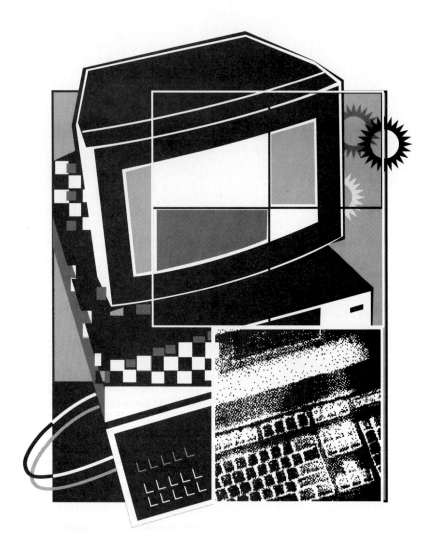

Chapter 9

Exception Handling

T H E functions described in this chapter support structured exception handling under Windows NT/Win32. An exception is an unintended program event that may be caused by hardware or software failure. That is, an exception is, essentially, an error that occurs at runtime.

A complete programming example is included at the end of this chapter that demonstrates exception handling.

Structured exception handling relies upon special compiler features, such as nonstandard keywords or nonstandard preprocessor directives. The example shown in this chapter uses the Microsoft convention, which defines three nonstandard keywords: **try,** **except,** *and* **finally.** *Other compilers may implement structured exception handling differently. Only the exception handling functions are described in this chapter—no explanation of the additional keywords is given. (Consult your user manuals for details.) However, the following shows the general form of these keywords:*

```
try {
  /* protected statements */
}
except (Filter Expression) {
  /* here is the exception handling code */
}
try {
  /* protected statements */
}
finally {
  /* here is the finally code */
}
```

BOOL AbnormalTermination(void)

AbnormalTermination() returns non-zero if a **try** block terminated normally, and zero if it did not. This function must be called from within the **finally** block. If a **try** block is left using a **break**, **continue**, **goto**, or **return**, an abnormal termination occurs.

NOTE

This function has nothing to do with the termination of your program.

USAGE

AbnormalTermination() is used to confirm that a **try** block does not terminate abnormally. It does not, in itself, raise an exception.

RELATED FUNCTION

RaiseException()

DWORD GetExceptionCode(void)

GetExceptionCode() returns a value that indicates what type of exception occurred.

USAGE

GetExceptionCode() must either be part of the filter expression or called from within the **except** block.

The exception code values are defined in WINBASE.H and all begin with the prefix EXCEPTION. Refer to this file for a description of the codes relevant to your compiler and hardware environment.

RELATED FUNCTION

GetExceptionInformation()

LPEXCEPTION_POINTERS GetExceptionInformation(void)

GetExceptionInformation() returns information about the state of the computer when the exception occurred and about the exception itself.

The return value is a pointer to an **EXCEPTION_POINTERS** structure, which is defined like this:

```
typedef struct _EXCEPTION_POINTERS {
  PEXCEPTION_RECORD ExceptionRecord;
  PCONTEXT ContextRecord;
} EXCEPTION_POINTERS;
```

The **CONTEXT** structure, which describes the state of the computer, is machine-dependent. (Its definition can be found in WINBASE.H.) The **EXCEPTION_RECORD** structure is defined like this:

```
typedef struct _EXCEPTION_RECORD {
  DWORD ExceptionCode;
  DWORD ExceptionFlags;
  struct _EXCEPTION_RECORD *ExceptionRecord;
  PVOID ExceptionAddress;
  DWORD NumberParameters;
  DWORD ExceptionInformation[EXCEPTION_MAXIMUM_PARAMETERS];
} EXCEPTION_RECORD;
```

Here, **ExceptionCode** contains a code that determines what exception occurred. The exception code values are defined in WINBASE.H and all begin with the prefix EXCEPTION. Refer to this file for a description of the codes relevant to your compiler and hardware environment.

ExceptionFlags will be zero if your program may continue execution, or **EXCEPTION_NONCONTINUABLE** if the exception is fatal.

ExceptionRecord points to the next exception record in the chain, or NULL if no other exceptions occurred.

The address at which the exception took place is pointed to by **ExceptionAddress**.

Additional information about the exception is contained in the **ExceptionInformation** array. (Generally, extra information is only available when an exception is generated through a call to **RaiseException()**.) The number of values in this array (if any) is specified in **NumberParameters**. (Consult your compiler manual for details about additional information associated with exceptions.)

USAGE

You may only call **GetExceptionInformation()** from within the filter expression.

RELATED FUNCTIONS

GetExceptionCode()
RaiseException()

void RaiseException(DWORD *dwCode*, DWORD *dwFlags*, DWORD *dwNumArgs*, LPDWORD *lpdwArgs*)

RaiseException() generates an exception. Generally, exceptions are caused by hardware or software failure not intended by the programmer. However, **RaiseException()** deliberately generates an exception.

The exception code is specified in *dwCode*. You may use any value you like, but the 28th bit is reserved and will be zeroed.

dwFlags must be zero if your program may continue execution after processing the exception, or **EXCEPTION_NONCONTINUABLE** if the exception is fatal.

lpdwArgs points to an array of optional arguments that will be passed to the exception handler. If no additional information beyond the exception code is required, then this parameter must be NULL. The number of elements in this array is passed in *dwNumArgs*.

RELATED FUNCTIONS

GetExceptionCode()
GetExceptionInformation()

LPTOP_LEVEL_EXCEPTION_FILTER
SetUnhandledExceptionFilter
(LPTOP_LEVEL_EXCEPTION_FILTER *lpFunc*)

SetUnhandledExceptionFilter() specifies a new top level exception filter function that is called when an exception occurs that is not handled by any other exception handler. It returns the address of the old unhandled exception filter.

The filter function pointed to by *lpFunc* must have the following prototype:

LONG *UnhandledFilter*(LPEXCEPTION_POINTERS *lpException*);

The **LPEXCEPTION_POINTERS** structure is discussed under **GetExceptionInformation()**. The return value of the function must be either **EXCEPTION_CONTINUE_EXECUTION** (continue execution), **EXCEPTION_CONTINUE_SEARCH** (pass exception to debugger), or **EXCEPTION_EXECUTE_HANDLER** (execute exception handler). Of course, the name of the function is arbitrary.

RELATED FUNCTION

UnhandledExceptionFilter()

LONG UnhandledExceptionFilter
(LPEXCEPTION_POINTERS *lpException*)

UnhandledExceptionFilter() processes unhandled exceptions. It may be called only from within the **except** filter expression.

lpException must point to an **EXCEPTION_POINTERS** structure that is obtained through a call to **GetExceptionInformation()**. (The **LPEXCEPTION_POINTERS** structure is discussed under **GetExceptionInformation()**.)

The return value of the function will be either **EXCEPTION_CONTINUE_SEARCH** (exception passed to debugger) or **EXCEPTION_EXECUTE_HANDLER** (execute exception handler).

NOTE

Both **UnhandledExceptionFilter()** *and* **SetUnhandledExceptionFilter()** *are special-purpose functions that you are not likely to need in your day-to-day programming.*

RELATED FUNCTION

SetUnhandledExceptionFilter()

A Complete Programming Example

Here is a complete program that demonstrates exception handling. Try removing various comments to see the effects.

```c
/*
  Demonstrate Exception Handling
*/

#include <windows.h>
#include <string.h>
#include <stdio.h>

LRESULT CALLBACK WindowFunc(HWND, UINT, WPARAM, LPARAM);

char szWinName[] = "MyWin"; /* name of window class */

int WINAPI WinMain(HINSTANCE hThisInst, HINSTANCE hPrevInst,
                   LPSTR lpszArgs, int nWinMode)
{
  HWND hwnd;
  MSG msg;
  WNDCLASS wcl;

  /* Define a window class. */
  wcl.hInstance = hThisInst; /* handle to this instance */
  wcl.lpszClassName = szWinName; /* window class name */
  wcl.lpfnWndProc = WindowFunc; /* window function */
  wcl.style = 0; /* default style */

  wcl.hIcon = LoadIcon(NULL, IDI_APPLICATION); /* icon style */
  wcl.hCursor = LoadCursor(NULL, IDC_ARROW); /* cursor style
```

```
*/
  wcl.lpszMenuName = NULL; /* no menu */

  wcl.cbClsExtra = 0;
  wcl.cbWndExtra = 0;

  /* Make the window light gray. */
  wcl.hbrBackground = GetStockObject(LTGRAY_BRUSH);

  /* Register the window class. */
  if(!RegisterClass (&wcl)) return 0;

  /* Now that a window class has been registered, a window
     can be created. */
  hwnd = CreateWindow(
    szWinName, /* name of window class */
    "Exceptions", /* title */
    WS_OVERLAPPEDWINDOW, /* window style - normal */
    CW_USEDEFAULT, /* X coordinate - let Windows decide */
    CW_USEDEFAULT, /* Y coordinate - let Windows decide */
    CW_USEDEFAULT, /* width - let Windows decide */
    CW_USEDEFAULT, /* height - let Windows decide */
    NULL, /* handle of parent window - there isn't one */
    NULL, /* no menu */
    hThisInst, /* handle of this instance of the program */
    NULL /* no additional arguments */
  );

  /* Display the window. */
  ShowWindow(hwnd, nWinMode);
  UpdateWindow(hwnd);

  try {
/*
    Enable this statement to generate an exception:

    RaiseException(0, 0, 0, NULL);
*/

/*    Enable this statement to see an example of abnormal
      termination.

      goto done;
*/
```

```
  }
  finally {
    if(AbnormalTermination())
      MessageBox(hwnd, "Abnormally", "Finally", MB_OK);
    else
      MessageBox(hwnd, "Normally", "Finally", MB_OK);
  }

/* Enable this statement to see an example of abnormal

   termination.

   done:
*/


  /* Create the message loop. */
  while(GetMessage(&msg, NULL, 0, 0))
  {
    TranslateMessage(&msg); /* allow use of keyboard */
    DispatchMessage(&msg); /* return control to Windows */
  }
  return msg.wParam;
}

/* This function is called by Windows NT and is passed
   messages from the message queue.
*/
LRESULT CALLBACK WindowFunc(HWND hwnd, UINT message,
                            WPARAM wParam, LPARAM lParam)
{
  switch(message) {
    case WM_DESTROY: /* terminate the program */
      PostQuitMessage(0);
      break;
    default:
      /* Let Windows NT process any messages not specified in
         the preceding switch statement. */
      return DefWindowProc(hwnd, message, wParam, lParam);
  }
  return 0;
}
```

Chapter 10

Handle Duplication

H E function described in this chapter duplicates a handle. This function, added to Windows NT/Win32, allows two processes to have access to the same handle. It may also be used to duplicate a handle within the same process.

BOOL DuplicateHandle(HANDLE *hOrigProc,*
                 HANDLE *hOrigHandle,*
                 HANDLE *hToProc,*
                 LPHANDLE *hNewHandle,*
                 DWORD *dwAccessMode,*
                 BOOL *Inheritance,*
                 DWORD *dwHow)*

DuplicateHandle() creates a copy of a handle. Any type of handle may be duplicated. It returns non-zero if successful, and zero otherwise.

The handle of the process containing the original handle that will be duplicated is passed in *hOrigProc*. The handle to be duplicated is passed in *hOrigHandle*. The process in which the duplicate handle will be created is specified by *hToProc*. (The two processes may be the same, if desired.) The new handle is pointed to by *hNewHandle*.

The duplicate handle can have either the same or a different access mode as the original handle. To specify a different access mode, pass the appropriate flags in the *dwAccessMode* parameter. What access modes apply are determined by the type of handle being duplicated. (See function descriptions related to the type of handle being duplicated for appropriate access mode values.)

If *Inheritance* is non-zero, the new handle can be inherited. If *Inheritance* is zero, the duplicate handle cannot be inherited.

If *dwHow* is **DUPLICATE_CLOSE_SOURCE**, then the *hOrigHandle* is closed. If *dwHow* is **DUPLICATE_SAME_ACCESS**, then the new handle will have the same access mode and rights as the original handle. Using this value causes any values passed in *dwAccessMode* to be ignored. *dwHow* may also be zero if neither of the preceding actions is desired.

USAGE

The handle of the current process can be obtained by calling **GetCurrentProcess()**.

DuplicateHandle() is a special-use function that is not required in normal, day-to-day programming.

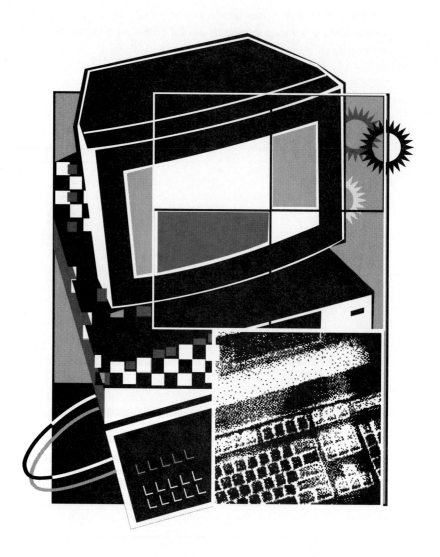

Chapter 11

Hook Functions

WINDOWS allows your program to monitor, filter, or, in some cases, modify messages. To accomplish this, your program must insert a function into Windows' message management system. The point at which your function enters the message chain is called a *hook*. (Put differently, your program *hooks* a function into the message chain.) The functions described in this chapter support and manage hook functions. A complete programming example is shown at the end of this chapter.

NOTE

The general form of a hook function is described under **SetWindowsHookEx()**.

BOOL CallMsgFilter(MSG FAR *lpMess, int *Value*)

CallMsgFilter() sends a message and a value to the hook function that processes all messages. It returns zero if further processing is required, and non-zero if not.

The message is pointed to by *lpMess*. It points to a standard Windows **MSG** message structure, which is defined like this:

```
typedef struct tagMSG
{
  HWND hwnd; /* window receiving message */
  UINT message; /* message */
  WPARAM wParam; /* message-dependent info */
  LPARAM lParam; /* message-dependent info */
  DWORD time; /* time message was posted */
  POINT pt; /* location of mouse cursor */
} MSG;
```

Value may be used for any purpose your program requires.

USAGE

The hook function called by **CallMsgFilter()** is the one installed as either a **WH_MSGFILTER** or a **WH_SYSMSGFILTER** by the **SetWindows-HookEx()** function. These hook functions receive all dialog and menu messages.

The following fragment passes a message to the current hook message function.

```
MSG msg;

/* ... */

CallMsgFilter(&msg, 0);
```

RELATED FUNCTION

SetWindowsHookEx()

LRESULT CallNextHookEx(HHOOK *hHookFunc*,
int *nValue*, **WPARAM** *wParam*,
LPARAM *lParam*)

CallNextHookEx() calls the next hook function in the chain. (The next hook function is the one that was installed prior to the one that calls this function.) Its return value depends upon the message and how that message is finally processed.

The handle of the current hook function is passed in *hHookFunc*.

nValue is a value that is passed to the next hook function and may be used for any purpose by your program.

wParam and *lParam* are additional message-related information.

NOTE

CallNextHookEx() *replaces the obsolete* **DefHookProc()** *function, which was used prior to Windows version 3.1.*

USAGE

The following hook function skeleton calls the next hook function in the chain.

```
/* A hook function skeleton. */
LRESULT CALLBACK MyHook(int val, WPARAM wParam, LPARAM lParam)
{
   /* ... do other processing here ... */
   return CallNextHookEx(hHook, val, wParam, lParam);
}
```

RELATED FUNCTION

SetWindowsHookEx()

HHOOK SetWindowsHook(int *ID,*
HOOKPROC *HookFunc*)

SetWindowsHook() adds a hook function to the chain. However, this function is obsolete except for versions of Windows predating 3.1. Instead, use **SetWindowsHookEx()**. The first two parameters of **SetWindows-HookEx()** are the same as the two parameters of **SetWindowsHook()**.

HHOOK SetWindowsHookEx(int *ID,*
HOOKPROC *HookFunc,*
HINSTANCE *hInst,*
HTASK *hTask*)

SetWindowsHookEx() adds a hook function to the chain. It returns a handle to the hook, or NULL if an error occurs.

The ID of the hook that the specified function will monitor is specified by *ID.* It must be one of these values:

Value	Processes
WH_CALLWNDPROC	Messages sent to your program's window procedure.
WH_CBT	Window commands, such as sizing or moving.
WH_DEBUG	All messages—used for debugging.
WH_GETMESSAGE	Messages obtained by **GetMessage()**.

Value	Processes
WH_HARDWARE	Hardware-based messages obtained by **Getmessage()** or **PeekMessage()**. (Not available for Windows NT/Win32.)
WH_JOURNALPLAYBACK	Plays back mouse or keyboard messages.
WH_JOURNALRECORD	Records mouse or keyboard messages and removes them from the message queue.
WH_KEYBOARD	Keyboard messages.
WH_MOUSE	Mouse messages.
WH_MSGFILTER	Dialog, menu, or message box messages.
WH_SYSMSGFILTER	Global (system-wide) version of WH_MSGFILTER.

Of these, the **WH_JOURNALRECORD**, **WH_JOURNALPLAY-BACK**, and **WH_SYSMSGFILTER** are always global. The others may be global or local to a specific application. A system hook function impacts all programs running in the system and should be used sparingly, if at all.

HookFunc is a pointer to the hook function that will be installed. For 16-bit Windows, this must be a procedure-instance pointer. For Windows NT/Win32, it is a normal pointer. The general form of a hook function is shown under "Usage."

The instance handle of the module in which the hook function is defined is passed in *hInst*.

hTask specifies the task the hook function is for. For a global hook function, specify *hTask* as NULL. A task handle can be obtained by calling **GetCurrentTask()** or **GetWindowTask()**.

NOTE

In Windows NT/Win32, the fourth parameter (hTask) is of type **DWORD** *and specifies the thread ID for which the hook function will be installed. If this parameter is zero, then the hook function is for all threads (in which case, the hook function must be in a DLL). Also, hInst must be NULL if the hook function is defined within the calling process's code.*

USAGE

You must unhook all hook functions before your program terminates by calling **UnhookWindowsHookEx()**.

All hook functions must have this prototype (of course, the function name will differ and is arbitrary):

LRESULT CALLBACK *hookfunc*(int *Value*, WPARAM *wParam*,
LPARAM *lParam*);

In general, the function must return non-zero if it handles the message, and zero if not. Within the body of a hook function, you will generally need to call **CallNextHookEx()** to execute the next hook function in the chain and then return its value.

The contents of *Value*, *wParam*, and *lParam* will depend upon the type of hook function that you have created. The following table describes these parameters for each type of hook function.

Hook type: WH_CALLWNDPROC

Value:	If negative, pass this message to next hook function in the chain.
wParam:	Non-zero message is sent by the application that contains the hook function.
lParam:	Pointer to the following message data, in the order and type specified: LPARAM WPARAM UINT HWND

Hook type: WH_CBT

Value:	A value that identifies the window activity. It will be one of the values shown below.
wParam and lParam:	Depends upon *Value,* as shown here: HCBT_ACTIVE: wParam is the handle of the window that will be activated, and lParam contains a pointer to a CBT_ACTIVATESTRUCT structure. HCBT_CLICKSKIPPED: wParam is the mouse message that was removed, and lParam contains a pointer to a MOUSEHOOKSTRUCT structure. HCBT_CREATEWND: wParam is the handle of the window that will be created, and lParam contains a pointer to a CBT_CREATEWND structure. HDCT_DESTROYWND: wParam is the handle of the window that will be destroyed, and lParam is not used (and is 0).

Hook type: WH_CBT (continued)

HCBT_KEYSKIPPED: wParam is the virtual key code of the key that was removed, and lParam contains the key state.

HCBT_MINMAX: wParam is the handle of the window to be minimized or maximized, and lParam contains an SW constant that determines how the window will be minimized or maximized.

HCBT_MOVESIZE: wParam is the handle of the window that will be moved or resized, and lParam contains a pointer to the window's coordinates described by a RECT structure.

HCBT_QS: Neither wParam nor lParam is used. This value is used when a WM_QUEUESYNC message is received.

HCBT_SETFOCUS: wParam is the handle of the window that is obtaining input focus, and LOWORD(lParam) contains the handle of the window that lost focus.

HCBT_SYSCOMMAND: wParam is a system command. Generally, lParam is not used. However, if wParam contains SC_HOTKEY, then LOWORD(lParam) is the handle of the window that is being switched to. If a system menu command is selected using the mouse, then LOWORD(lParam) is the mouse's x coordinate and HIWORD(lParam) is the mouse's y coordinate.

Hook type: WH_DEBUG

Value:	If negative, pass this message to next hook function in the chain.
wParam:	Handle of the process that installed the function.
lParam:	A pointer to a DEBUGHOOKINFO structure.

Hook type: WH_GETMESSAGE

Value:	If negative, pass this message to next hook function in the chain.
wParam:	NULL.
lParam:	A pointer to a MSG structure.

Hook type: WH_HARDWARE

Value:	If negative, pass this message to next hook function in the chain.
wParam:	NULL.
lParam:	A pointer to a HARDWAREHOOKSTRUCT structure.

Hook type: WH_JOURNALPLAYBACK

Value:	If negative, pass this message to next hook function in the chain.

Hook type: WH_JOURNALPLAYBACK (continued)

wParam:	NULL.
lParam:	A pointer to an EVENTMSG structure.

Hook type: WH_JOURNALRECORD

Value:	If negative, pass this message to next hook function in the chain.
wParam:	NULL.
lParam:	A pointer to an MSG structure.

Hook type: WH_KEYBOARD

Value:	If negative, pass this message to next hook function in the chain.
wParam:	Contains the virtual key code.
lParam:	Contains key state information (see WM_CHAR message for details).

Hook type: WH_MOUSE

Value:	If negative, pass this message to next hook function in the chain.
wParam:	Contains the mouse message.
lParam:	A pointer to a MOUSEHOOKSTRUCT structure.

Hook type: WH_MSGFILTER

Value:	MSG_DIALOGBOX if dialog box message. MSG_MENU if menu message. (Otherwise, if negative, pass this message to next hook function in the chain.)
wParam:	NULL.
lParam:	A pointer to an MSG structure.

Hook type: WH_SYSMSGFILTER

Value:	MSG_DIALOGBOX if dialog box message. MSG_MENU if menu message. (Otherwise, if negative, pass this message to next hook function in the chain.)
wParam:	NULL.
lParam:	A pointer to an MSG structure.

For an example of a hook function, refer to the complete program example at the end of this chapter.

RELATED FUNCTION

UnhookWindowsHookEx()

BOOL UnhookWindowsHook(int *ID,* HOOKPROC *hookProc*)

UnhookWindowsHook() removes a hook function. It returns non-zero if successful, and zero on failure.

The hook identifier is passed in *ID*. The procedure-instance of the hook function is passed in *hookProc*.

NOTE

This function is obsolete. Use **UnhookWindowsHookEx()** *instead.*

BOOL UnhookWindowsHookEx(HHOOK *hHook*)

UnhookWindowsHookEx() removes a hook function. It returns non-zero if successful, and zero otherwise.

The handle to the function to remove is passed in *hHook*.

USAGE

All hook functions should be removed before your application terminates. The following fragment unhooks a function.

```
UnhookwindowsHookEx(hHook);
```

RELATED FUNCTION

SetWindowsHookEx()

A Complete Programming Example

The following program demonstrates the use of a hook function. The hook function, when inserted in the message chain, simply discards minimize and maximize messages. You may install and remove the hook function using the menu.

The header file EXAMPLE.H, used by the program, is shown here:

```
#define ID_INSTALL 200
#define ID_REMOVE 201
```

The following resource file is required.

```
#include <windows.h>
#include "example.h"

MYMENU MENU
{
  POPUP "Menu"
  {
    MENUITEM "Install Hook", ID_INSTALL
    MENUITEM "Remove Hook", ID_REMOVE
  }
}

MYMENU ACCELERATORS
{
  VK_F1, ID_INSTALL, VIRTKEY
  VK_F2, ID_REMOVE, VIRTKEY
}
```

Here is the program that demonstrates a hook function.

```
/*
  Use a hook function.
*/

#include <windows.h>
#include "example.h"

LONG FAR PASCAL WndProc(HWND, UINT, WPARAM, LPARAM);
LRESULT CALLBACK MyHook(int val, WPARAM wParam, LPARAM lParam);

char szProgName[] = "ProgName"; /* name of window class */
char szApplName[] = "MYMENU"; /* name of main menu */
```

```
HINSTANCE hInstance;
HHOOK hHook;

int ishooked = 0; /* indicates if hook function is installed */

int PASCAL WinMain(HINSTANCE hInst, HINSTANCE hPreInst,
                   LPSTR lpszCmdLine, int nCmdShow)
{
  HWND hWnd;
  MSG lpMsg;
  WNDCLASS wcApp;
  HACCEL hAccel;

  if (!hPreInst) { /* if no previous instance */
    wcApp.lpszClassName = szProgName; /* window class name */
    wcApp.hInstance     = hInst; /* handle to this instance */
    wcApp.lpfnWndProc   = WndProc; /* window function */
    wcApp.hCursor       = LoadCursor(NULL, IDC_ARROW);
    wcApp.hIcon         = LoadIcon(NULL, IDI_APPLICATION);
    wcApp.lpszMenuName  = szApplName; /* main menu */

    /* make the background of window white */
    wcApp.hbrBackground = GetStockObject(WHITE_BRUSH);
    wcApp.style         = 0; /* use default window style */
    wcApp.cbClsExtra    = 0; /* no extra info */
    wcApp.cbWndExtra    = 0; /* no extra info */

    /* register the window class */
    if (!RegisterClass (&wcApp))
      return FALSE;
  }

  /* Now that window has been registered, a window
     can be created. */
  hWnd = CreateWindow(
    szProgName,
    "Use a Hook Function",
    WS_OVERLAPPEDWINDOW,
    CW_USEDEFAULT,
    CW_USEDEFAULT,
    CW_USEDEFAULT,
    CW_USEDEFAULT,
```

```
                (HWND)NULL,
                (HMENU)NULL,
                (HANDLE)hInst,
                (LPSTR)NULL
        );

        hAccel = LoadAccelerators(hInst, "MYMENU");
        hInstance = hInst;

        /* Display the Window. */
        ShowWindow(hWnd, nCmdShow);
        UpdateWindow(hWnd);

        /* Create the message loop. */
        while (GetMessage(&lpMsg, NULL, 0, 0)) {
          if(!TranslateAccelerator(hWnd, hAccel, &lpMsg)) {
            TranslateMessage(&lpMsg); /* allow use of keyboard */
            DispatchMessage(&lpMsg); /* return control to Windows */
          }
        }
        return(lpMsg.wParam);
}

/* Window Function. */
LONG FAR PASCAL WndProc(HWND hWnd, UINT messg,
                        WPARAM wParam, LPARAM lParam)
{
  int i;
  unsigned long d;
  FARPROC hookfunc;

  switch (messg) {
    case WM_COMMAND:
      switch(LOWORD(wParam)) {
        case ID_INSTALL: /* install MinMax filter */
          hookfunc = MakeProcInstance((FARPROC) MyHook,
                                       hInstance);
          hHook = SetWindowsHookEx(WH_CBT, hookfunc,
                                   hInstance,
                                   GetCurrentTask());
          ishooked = 1;
          break;
```

```
      case ID_REMOVE: /* remove filter */
        ishooked = 0;
        UnhookWindowsHookEx(hHook);
        break;
    }
    break;
  case WM_DESTROY: /* terminate the program */
    /* unhook if necessary */
    if(ishooked) UnhookWindowsHookEx(hHook);
    PostQuitMessage(0);
    break;
  /* Let Windows process any messages not specified in
     the preceding cases. */
  default:
    return(DefWindowProc(hWnd, messg, wParam, lParam));
  }
  return(0L);
}


/* A hook function skeleton. */
LRESULT CALLBACK MyHook(int val, WPARAM wParam, LPARAM lParam)
{
  /* Do whatever you like here.  The following is only
     for demonstration. */

  /* cause minimize or maximize messages to be skipped */
  if(val==HCBT_MINMAX) return 1L;

  else return 0L; /* process other messages */
  /* or return CallNextHookEx() */
}
```

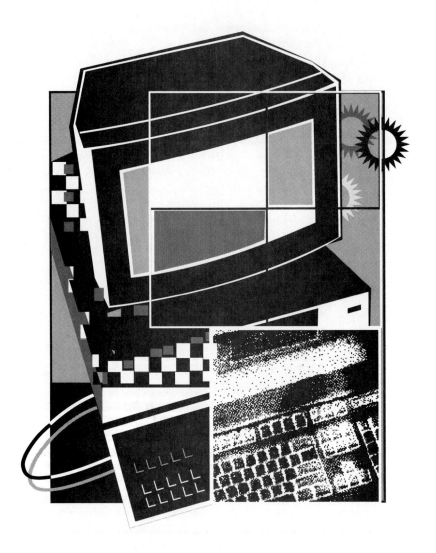

Chapter 12

Initialization File Functions

s you know, Windows, and many Windows applications, use .INI files for support. In this chapter, the functions that manage .INI files are discussed. A complete program example is included at the end of this chapter, which demonstrates several of these functions.

.INI files are assumed to have the following format:

```
[heading name1]
item1=value1
item2=value2
item3=value3
    ...
itemN=valueN

[heading name2]
    ...
```

Here, *heading name* is the name of a heading and *item* is the name of an entry under that heading. The value associated with each item is specified by *value*.

.INI files are ASCII text files. However, .INI files are not case-sensitive, and the INI functions described here are also not case-sensitive. Therefore, you must not attempt to rely upon case to differentiate between two entries in an initialization file.

NOTE

Windows NT/Win32 adds a system registry that holds initialization information. The system registry supersedes the older .INI files. However, .INI files are still supported for backward compatibility with 16-bit Windows.

BOOL CloseProfileUserMapping(void)

CloseProfileUserMapping() closes all initialization file mapping handles. The function returns non-zero if successful, and zero otherwise.

See Chapter 29 later in this book for details on the Windows registry.

UINT GetPrivateProfileInt(LPCSTR *lpszHeading,*
LPCSTR *lpszItemName,*
int *NotFound,*
LPCSTR *lpszFileName*)

GetPrivateProfileInt() searches an .INI file and returns the integer value associated with an item under the specified heading. The name of the heading is pointed to by *lpszHeading*. The name of the desired item that is under that heading is pointed to by *lpszItemName*. The name of the initialization file is pointed to by *lpszFileName*.

If the specified item is found, then the value associated with it is returned. If the item is not found, then the value passed in *NotFound* is returned. If the value found is not an unsigned integer, then zero is returned.

USAGE

The most common use of **GetPrivateProfileInt()** is to obtain the configuration values contained within an application's .INI file.

.INI files are in ASCII. Thus, numeric data is stored in string form. **GetPrivateProfileInt()** *automatically converts a numeric string into an integer quantity.*

The following fragment obtains the number of concurrent users that an application called "MYNET" can have.

```
unsigned int users;
users = GetPrivateProfileInt("NumUsers", "Users",
                        0, "MYNET.INI");
```

RELATED FUNCTION

GetPrivateProfileString()

DWORD GetPrivateProfileSection(LPCSTR *lpszHeading,*
LPSTR *lpszResult,*
DWORD *Size,*
LPCSTR *lpszFileName*)

GetPrivateProfileSection() copies all items and values in the specified .INI file that are under the specified heading into the specified character array. The function returns the number of characters copied.

The name of the heading is pointed to by *lpszHeading*.

The character array that will receive the null-terminated information is pointed to by *lpszResult*. The size of this array is passed in *Size*.

The name of the .INI file is pointed to by *lpszFileName*.

USAGE

In general, Windows NT/Win32 programs use the Windows registry rather than .INI files to store configuration information about applications. Therefore, this function is primarily included to provide backward compatibility with older applications.

RELATED FUNCTION

WritePrivateProfileSection()

int GetPrivateProfileString(LPCSTR *lpszHeading,*
LPCSTR *lpszItemName,*
LPCSTR *lpszNotFound,*
LPSTR *lpszResult,*
int *Size,*
LPCSTR *lpszFileName*)

GetPrivateProfileString() obtains a string value (associated with the specified item) from an .INI file. The name of the heading that the specified item is under is pointed to by *lpszHeading*. The name of the desired item is pointed to by *lpszItemName*. If this parameter is NULL, then all strings under the heading are obtained.

The string is copied into the character array pointed to by *lpszResult*. The size of this array is passed in *Size*. If the specified item is not found, then the string pointed to by *lpszNotFound* is copied into *lpszResult*.

The name of the initialization file is pointed to by *lpszFileName*.

Whether the function is successful or not, the number of characters copied into *lpszResult* is returned.

USAGE

The most common use of **GetPrivateProfileString()** is to obtain the configuration strings contained within an application's .INI file.

The following fragment obtains the string associated with *MonthName* defined by the .INI file for an application called "CALENDAR".

```
char month[40];

GetPrivateProfileString("DateParms", "MonthName", "None",
                        month, sizeof(month), "CALENDAR.INI");
```

RELATED FUNCTION

GetPrivateProfileInt()

UINT GetProfileInt(LPCSTR *lpszHeading,*
LPCSTR *lpszItemName,*
int *NotFound*)

GetProfileInt() searches the WIN.INI file and returns the integer value associated with an item under the specified heading. The name of the heading is pointed to by *lpszHeading*. The name of the desired item that is under that heading is pointed to by *lpszItemName*.

If the specified item is found, then the value associated with it is returned. If the item is not found, then the value passed in *NotFound* is returned. If the value found is not an unsigned integer, then zero is returned.

USAGE

The WIN.INI file is in ASCII. Thus, numeric data is stored in string form. **GetProfileInt()** *automatically converts a numeric string into an integer quantity.*

RELATED FUNCTION

GetProfileString()

DWORD GetProfileSection(LPCSTR *lpszHeading,* LPSTR *lpszResult,* DWORD *Size*)

GetProfileSection() copies all items and values in WIN.INI that are under the specified heading into the specified character array. The function returns the number of characters copied.

The name of the heading is in the string pointed to by *lpszHeading.*

The character array that will receive the null-terminated information is pointed to by *lpszResult.* The size of this array is passed in *Size.*

USAGE

In general, Windows NT/Win32 programs use the Windows registry rather than .INI files to store configuration information about applications. Therefore, this function is primarily included to provide backward compatibility with older applications.

RELATED FUNCTION

WriteProfileSection()

int GetProfileString(LPCSTR *lpszHeading,*
LPCSTR *lpszItemName,*
LPCSTR *lpszNotFound,*
LPSTR *lpszResult,* int *Size*)

GetProfileString() obtains a string value (associated with the specified item) from the WIN.INI file. The name of the heading that the specified item is under is pointed to by *lpszHeading*. The name of the desired item is pointed to by *lpszItemName*. If this parameter is NULL, then all strings under the heading are obtained.

The string is copied into the character array pointed to by *lpszResult*. The size of this array is passed in *Size*. If the specified item is not found, then the string pointed to by *lpszNotFound* is copied into *lpszResult*.

Whether the function is successful or not, the number of characters copied into *lpszResult* is returned.

RELATED FUNCTION

GetProfileInt()

BOOL OpenProfileUserMapping(void)

OpenProfileUserMapping() opens the user key in the system registry. This key is used for initialization file mapping. The function returns non-zero if successful, and zero otherwise.

This function is used by programs that must impersonate other programs. See Chapter 29 later in this book for details on the Windows registry.

RELATED FUNCTION

CloseProfileUserMapping()

BOOL WritePrivateProfileSection(LPCSTR *lpszHeading,*
LPCSTR *lpszInfo,*
LPCSTR *lpszFileName*)

WritePrivateProfileSection() writes information to the specified .INI file under the specified heading. The function returns non-zero if successful, and zero on failure.

The name of the heading is pointed to by *lpszHeading.*

The character array that contains the information is pointed to by *lpszInfo.* This array must consist of one or more null-terminated strings. The last string must end with two null characters. (That is, the last string in the list must be null.)

The name of the .INI file is pointed to by *lpszFileName.* If the file does not exist, it is created. If no path is specified, then the file is created in the WINDOWS directory.

USAGE

Any preexisting information under the specified heading is lost.
The new information must be in this form:

item=value

Initialization files are not case-sensitive.

In general, Windows NT/Win32 programs use the Windows registry rather than .INI files to store configuration information about applications. Therefore, this function is primarily included to provide backward compatibility with older applications.

RELATED FUNCTION

GetPrivateProfileSection()

BOOL WritePrivateProfileString(LPCSTR *lpszHeading,*
LPCSTR *lpszItemName,*
LPCSTR *lpszString,*
LPCSTR *lpszFileName*)

WritePrivateProfileString() writes a string to an .INI file. The function returns non-zero if successful, and zero on failure.

The name of the heading that the string will be written under is pointed to by *lpszHeading.*

Strings are stored in .INI files in association with an item name using this format:

   item=string

The name of the item that is associated with the string is pointed to by *lpszItemName.* If this parameter is NULL, then all strings under the heading are removed. If the specified item already exists, the new string will replace the existing string. That is, any preexisting string associated with *lpszItemName* is lost. If the item does not exist, a new entry in the .INI file is created.

The string is copied from the character array pointed to by *lpszString.* If this parameter is NULL, the associated item is removed.

The name of the initialization file is pointed to by *lpszFileName.* If the file does not exist it is created. If no path is specified, then the file is created in the WINDOWS directory.

USAGE

The most common use of **WritePrivateProfileString()** is to create or update the configuration strings contained within an application's .INI file.

The following fragment writes the string associated with *MonthName* defined by the .INI file for an application called "CALENDAR".

```
char month[40];

WritePrivateProfileString("DateParms", "MonthName",
                "JULY", "CALENDAR.INI");
```

RELATED FUNCTION

GetPrivateProfileString()

BOOL WriteProfileSection(LPCSTR *lpszHeading,*
LPCSTR *lpszInfo)*

WriteProfileSection() writes information to the WIN.INI file under the specified heading. The function returns non-zero if successful, and zero on failure.

The name of the heading is in the string pointed to by *lpszHeading.*

The character array that contains the information is pointed to by *lpszInfo.* This array must consist of one or more null-terminated strings. The last string must end with two null characters. (That is, the last string in the list must be null.)

USAGE

Any preexisting information under the specified heading is lost.
The new information must be in this form:

item=value

In general, Windows NT/Win32 programs use the Windows registry rather than .INI files to store configuration information about applications. Therefore, this function is primarily included to provide backward compatibility with older applications.

RELATED FUNCTIONS

GetProfileSection()
WritePrivateProfileSection()

BOOL WriteProfileString(LPCSTR *lpszHeading,*
LPCSTR *lpszItemName,*
LPCSTR *lpszString)*

WriteProfileString() writes a string to the WIN.INI file. The function returns non-zero if successful, and zero on failure.

The name of the heading that the string will be written under is pointed to by *lpszHeading*.

Strings are stored in .INI files in association with an item name using this format:

item=string

The name of the item that is associated with the string is pointed to by *lpszItemName*. If this parameter is NULL, then all strings under the heading are removed. If the specified item already exists, the new string will replace the existing string. That is, any preexisting string associated with *lpszItemName* is lost. If the item does not exist, a new entry in the .INI file is created.

The string is copied from the character array pointed to by *lpszString*. If this parameter is NULL, the associated item is removed.

USAGE

The most common use of **WriteProfileString()** is to update the configuration strings contained within the WIN.INI file. However, be careful when changing WIN.INI since it contains several important settings used by Windows.

RELATED FUNCTIONS

GetProfileString()
WritePrivateProfileString()

A Complete Programming Example

The following program demonstrates the use of .INI files. It creates (if necessary) an .INI file and it reads the contents of that file.

The header file EXAMPLE.H, used by the program, is shown here:

```
#define ID_CREATEINI 200
#define ID_READINI 201
```

The following resource file is required.

```
#include <windows.h>
#include "example.h"

MYMENU MENU
{
  POPUP "Menu"
  {
    MENUITEM "Create INI File", ID_CREATEINI
    MENUITEM "Read INI File", ID_READINI
  }
}


MYMENU ACCELERATORS
{
  VK_F1, ID_CREATEINI, VIRTKEY
  VK_F2, ID_READINI, VIRTKEY
}
```

Here is the program that demonstrates the initialization functions.

```
/*
  Use INI files.
*/


#include <windows.h>
#include "example.h"

LONG FAR PASCAL WndProc(HWND, UINT, WPARAM, LPARAM);

char szProgName[] = "ProgName"; /* name of window class */
char szApplName[] = "MYMENU"; /* name of main menu */

char str[255];

int PASCAL WinMain(HINSTANCE hInst, HINSTANCE hPreInst,
                   LPSTR lpszCmdLine, int nCmdShow)
{
  HWND hWnd;
  MSG lpMsg;
  WNDCLASS wcApp;
  HACCEL hAccel;
```

```
if (!hPreInst) { /* if no previous instance */
  wcApp.lpszClassName = szProgName; /* window class name */
  wcApp.hInstance     = hInst; /* handle to this instance */
  wcApp.lpfnWndProc   = WndProc; /* window function */
  wcApp.hCursor       = LoadCursor(NULL, IDC_ARROW);
  wcApp.hIcon         = LoadIcon(NULL, IDI_APPLICATION);
  wcApp.lpszMenuName  = szApplName; /* main menu */

  /* make the background of window white */
  wcApp.hbrBackground = GetStockObject(WHITE_BRUSH);
  wcApp.style         = 0; /* use default window style */
  wcApp.cbClsExtra    = 0; /* no extra info */
  wcApp.cbWndExtra    = 0; /* no extra info */

  /* register the window class */
  if (!RegisterClass (&wcApp))
    return FALSE;
}

/* Now that window has been registered, a window
   can be created. */
hWnd = CreateWindow(
  szProgName,
  "Use INI Files",
  WS_OVERLAPPEDWINDOW,
  CW_USEDEFAULT,
  CW_USEDEFAULT,
  CW_USEDEFAULT,
  CW_USEDEFAULT,
  (HWND)NULL,
  (HMENU) NULL,
  (HANDLE)hInst,
  (LPSTR)NULL
);

hAccel = LoadAccelerators(hInst, "MYMENU");

/* Display the Window. */
ShowWindow(hWnd, nCmdShow);
UpdateWindow(hWnd);

/* Create the message loop. */
while (GetMessage(&lpMsg, NULL, 0, 0)) {
```

```
         if(!TranslateAccelerator(hWnd, hAccel, &lpMsg)) {
           TranslateMessage(&lpMsg); /* allow use of keyboard */
           DispatchMessage(&lpMsg); /* return control to Windows */
         }
      }
   return(lpMsg.wParam);
}

/* Window Function. */
LONG FAR PASCAL WndProc(HWND hWnd, UINT messg,
                        WPARAM wParam, LPARAM lParam)
{
   int i;
   unsigned long d;

   switch (messg) {
     case WM_COMMAND:
       switch(LOWORD(wParam)) {
         case ID_CREATEINI: /* Write INI file */
           /* initialize (if necessary) APP.INI */
           WritePrivateProfileString("INITEST",  "Coords",
               "1, 1, 100, 100", "INIAPP.INI");
           WritePrivateProfileString("INITEST",  "BufSize",
               "1024", "INIAPP.INI");
           WritePrivateProfileString("INITEST",  "LastFile",
               "MyFile.dat", "INIAPP.INI");
           break;
         case ID_READINI: /* read INI file */
           GetPrivateProfileString("INITEST", "Coords",
               "NOTFOUND", str, sizeof(str), "INIAPP.INI");
           MessageBox(hWnd, str, "Coordinates", MB_OK);

           GetPrivateProfileString("INITEST", "BufSize",
               "NOTFOUND", str, sizeof(str), "INIAPP.INI");
           MessageBox(hWnd, str, "Buffer Size", MB_OK);

           GetPrivateProfileString("INITEST", "LastFile",
               "NOTFOUND", str, sizeof(str), "INIAPP.INI");
           MessageBox(hWnd, str, "Last File Edited", MB_OK);

           GetPrivateProfileString("INITEST", "won't find",
               "NOTFOUND", str, sizeof(str), "INIAPP.INI");
           MessageBox(hWnd, str, "Won't Find", MB_OK);
           break;
```

```
      }
      break;
   case WM_DESTROY: /* terminate the program */
      PostQuitMessage(0);
      break;
   /* Let Windows process any messages not specified in
      the preceding cases. */
   default:
      return(DefWindowProc(hWnd, messg, wParam, lParam));
  }
  return(0L);
}
```

The .INI file produced by the preceding program looks like this:

```
[INITEST]
Coords=1, 1, 100, 100
BufSize=1024
LastFile=MyFile.dat
```

Chapter 13

Installation and Compression

Functions

T H E functions described in this chapter manage file installation and compression. Since files prepared for distribution are often compressed and require installation, these two subsystems are discussed together. A complete program is presented at the end of this chapter that demonstrates file compression.

The compression functions require that the header file LZEXPAND.H be included in your program. The compressed file functions are designed to operate on files compressed by (or compatible with) the Microsoft COMPRESS.EXE utility.

The installation functions require that the header file VER.H be included in your program.

NOTE

Many compression functions begin with the prefix LZ, which stands for the Lempel-Ziv compression algorithm used by these functions.

LONG CopyLZFile(HFILE *hFrom*, HFILE *hTo*)

CopyLZFile() is used to copy multiple compressed files. It must be used as part of an **LZStart(), CopyLZFile(), LZDone()** sequence. It returns the size of the output file if successful or a negative value if an error occurs.

The handle of the source file is passed in *hFrom* and the handle of the output file is passed in *hTo*.

NOTE

CopyLZFile() *is obsolete in Windows NT/Win32. Use* **LZCopy()** *instead.*

USAGE

For the greatest portability, use **LZCopy()** instead of the **LZStart()**, **CopyLZFile()**, **LZDone()** sequence.

RELATED FUNCTIONS

LZCopy()
LZDone()
LZStart()

int GetExpandedName(LPCSTR *lpszCompFile,* LPSTR *lpszOrigFile*)

GetExpandedName() obtains the original uncompressed filename associated with a compressed file. The function returns 1 if successful, and negative on failure.

The name of the compressed file is pointed to by *lpszCompFile.*

The original filename will be copied into the array pointed to by *lpszOrigFile.*

USAGE

This function is for use on files compressed using the standard COMPRESS utility with the /R option.

RELATED FUNCTION

LZOpenFile()

BOOL GetFileResource(LPCSTR *lpszFileName,* LPCSTR *lpszType,* LPCSTR *lpszID,* DWORD *dwFileOffset,* DWORD *dwSize,* void FAR **lpBuf*)

GetFileResource() obtains a resource from an installation file. It returns non-zero if successful, and zero on failure.

The name of the file that contains the resource is pointed to by *lpszFileName*. The type of the resource is pointed to by *lpszType*. The ID of the resource is pointed to by *lpszID*.

dwFileOffset determines where in the file the resource will be found. To search the file for the specified resource, specify *dwFileOffset* as NULL.

lpBuf is a pointer to the array into which the resource is copied. The size of this array is passed in *dwSize*.

USAGE

The size of the resource, and therefore the minimum size required for the array pointed to by *lpBuf,* may be obtained by calling **GetFileResourceSize()**.

The value **VS_FILE_INFO** is often passed in the *lpszType* parameter, and **VS_VERSION_INFO** is generally passed in *lpszID*.

RELATED FUNCTION

GetFileResourceSize()

DWORD GetFileResourceSize(LPCSTR *lpszFileName,*
LPCSTR *lpszType,*
LPCSTR *lpszID,*
DWORD FAR **lpOffset*)

GetFileResourceSize() returns the size of a resource in an installation file. It returns NULL on failure.

The name of the file that contains the resource is pointed to by *lpszFileName*. The type of the resource is pointed to by *lpszType*. The ID of the resource is pointed to by *lpszID*.

On return, *lpOffset* is a pointer to a variable that contains the offset of the specified resource within the file. (The value can be used as the *dwFileOffset* parameter in **GetFileResource().**)

USAGE

The value **VS_FILE_INFO** is often passed in the *lpszType* parameter, and **VS_VERSION_INFO** is generally passed in *lpszID*.

RELATED FUNCTION

GetFileResource()

BOOL GetFileVersionInfo(LPCSTR *lpszFileName,* DWORD *dwVersionID,* DWORD *dwSize,* void FAR *★lpInfo*)

It is possible to embed version control information in a file. If this is the case, you can use **GetFileVersionInfo()** to obtain the version control information contained in a file. The function returns non–zero if successful, and zero on failure.

The name of the file is pointed to by *lpszFileName.* The handle of the version information is passed in *dwVersionID.* The array into which the version information will be copied is pointed to by *lpInfo.* The size of this array is passed in *dwSize.*

USAGE

The value passed in *dwVersionID* is generally obtained by calling **Get-FileVersionInfoSize()**. Also, if *dwVersionID* is NULL, then the file is searched for its version control information.

File version control data is organized as described by a **VERSIONINFO** resource statement. (See Volume 1, Appendix A.)

NOTE

The dwVersionID *is not used by the Win32 version of this function.*

RELATED FUNCTION

GetFileVersionInfoSize()

DWORD GetFileVersionInfoSize(LPCSTR *lpszFileName,* DWORD FAR *★lpdwVersionID*)

GetFileVersionInfoSize() performs two functions. First, it returns the size of the version information contained in a file. Second, it obtains the identifier associated with that version information. This handle is used by **GetFileVersionInfo()** to actually read the information. The function returns NULL if an error occurs.

The name of the file is pointed to by *lpszFileName*.

The handle associated with the version information is assigned to the variable pointed to by *lpdwVersionID*.

USAGE

The following fragment illustrates how **GetFileVersionInfo()** and **GetFileVersionInfoSize()** work together.

```
char ver[255];
unsigned long id, size;

size = GetFileVersionInfoSize("myfile.exe", &id);
if(size < sizeof(ver)
 GetFileVersionInfo("myfile.exe", id, size, ver);
```

RELATED FUNCTION

GetFileVersionInfo()

---

void LZClose(HFILE *hFile*)

LZClose() closes the specified file. The handle to the file is passed in *hFile*. This handle must have been opened using **LZOpenFile()**.

In Windows NT/Win32, hFile *is an INT value.*

RELATED FUNCTION

LZOpenFile()

LONG LZCopy(HFILE *hSource,* HFILE *hTarget*)

LZCopy() copies the compressed file specified by *hSource* to the file specified by *hTarget*. The destination file will be decompressed, but the original file will remain compressed. The function returns the size of the target file, or negative if an error occurs.

USAGE

Technically, **LZCopy()** can also be used to copy an uncompressed file (in which case the source and target files will be identical after the copy), but this is not the purpose for which this function was designed.

The handle passed in *hSource* is generally obtained through a call to **LZOpen-File()**.

RELATED FUNCTIONS

CopyLZFile()
LZOpenFile()

void LZDone(void)

LZDone() is called to conclude a series of file copies that was begun with a call to **LZStart()**.

LZDone() *is obsolete and should not be used by Windows NT/Win32 programs.*

RELATED FUNCTION

LZStart()

HFILE LZInit(HFILE *hFile*)

LZInit() initializes the necessary internal data structures required for file decompression. It returns a file handle, as described below. A negative value is returned if an error occurs.

The handle of the original file is passed in *hFile*.

If the file specified by *hFile* is not compressed, then *hFile* is returned. If the file specified by *hFile* is compressed, then the handle returned is to a new file.

NOTE

In Windows NT/Win32, hFile *is an INT value. It also returns an INT value.*

USAGE

If you will be using a compressed file opened for input using **LZOpenFile()**, you will not need to call **LZInit()**.

RELATED FUNCTION

LZRead()

HFILE LZOpenFile(LPCSTR *lpszFileName,* OFSTRUCT FAR *★lpInfo,* UINT *Mode)*

LZOpenFile() opens a compressed file and returns a handle to it. On failure, it returns a negative value.

The name of the file to open is pointed to by *lpszFileName. lpInfo* is a pointer to an **OFSTRUCT** into which file information is copied. (This structure is mostly for internal use.) The value of *Mode* determines how the file is opened. It may be one or more of the following values:

Macro	Mode
OF_CANCEL	Causes a Cancel button to be included in the dialog box that is displayed if an attempt is made to open a nonexistent file.
OF_CREATE	Creates a new file, erasing any preexisting file by the same name.
OF_DELETE	Erases the specified file.
OF_EXIST	Determines if the file exists.
OF_PARSE	Obtains file information but does not actually open the file.
OF_PROMPT	Displays a dialog box if an attempt is made to open a nonexistent file.
OF_READ	Opens the file for input. Also, all necessary decompression initialization is performed. (**LZInit()** need not be called separately.)
OF_READWRITE	Opens the file for input/output.
OF_REOPEN	Reopens the file.
OF_SHARE_DENY_NONE	Allows all sharing.
OF_SHARE_DENY_READ	Does not allow read sharing.
OF_SHARE_DENY_WRITE	Does not allow write sharing.
OF_SHARE_EXCLUSIVE	Allows no sharing.
OF_WRITE	Opens the file for output.

USAGE

Technically, **LZOpenFile()** will open any type of file, but it is designed to open a compressed file.

If the file is compressed and **OF_READ** *is the specified mode, then all necessary initialization is performed and there is no need to call* **LZInit()**.

RELATED FUNCTIONS

LZClose()
LZInit()

int LZRead(HFILE *hFile,* **void FAR** *★lpBuf,*
int *NumToRead*)

LZRead() inputs information from the specified compressed file. It returns the number of bytes read. If an error occurs, the return value will be negative.

The handle of the file is passed in *hFile*. The file must have been opened for input operations.

The information read from the file is put into the buffer pointed to by *lpBuf*. The number of bytes to read is passed in *NumToRead*. The information is decompressed in the process. Therefore, the information in the buffer will be decompressed, and the number of bytes to read is in terms of decompressed data.

USAGE

You can use **LZRead()** to access data in a compressed file without actually decompressing the file. (This is the most efficient way to read small portions of a compressed file.)

Technically, **LZRead()** will read any type of file, but it is designed to read a compressed file.

RELATED FUNCTIONS

LZOpenFile()
LZSeek()

LONG LZSeek(HFILE *hFile,* long *Offset,* int *Origin*)

LZSeek() sets the file-position indicator (file pointer) associated with the specified compressed file according to the values of *Offset* and *Origin*. It returns the number of bytes the new file position is from the start of the file, or a negative value on failure.

The handle of the file to affect is passed in *hFile*.

The new location of the file pointer is set by moving the file pointer *Offset* bytes from the specified origin. The value of *Origin* must be either 0, 1, or 2, with 0 being the start of the file, 1 the current position, and 2 the end of the file. Thus, to move the file pointer to the location 100 bytes from the start of the file, *Offset* will be 100 and *Origin* will be 0.

USAGE

Technically, **LZSeek()** will work with any type of file, but it is expressly designed to operate on a compressed file.

The following fragment moves the file pointer 200 bytes from its current location.

```
LZSeek(hFile, 200, 1);
```

RELATED FUNCTIONS

LZOpenFile()
LZRead()

---

int LZStart(void)

LZStart() initiates an **LZStart(), CopyLZFile(), LZDone()** sequence. This sequence is only needed when copying multiple files.

NOTE

This function is obsolete and should not be used by Windows NT/Win32 programs.

RELATED FUNCTIONS

CopyLZFile()
LZCopy()
LZDone()

UINT VerFindFile(UINT *Mode,* LPCSTR *lpszFileName,*
            LPCSTR *lpszWindowsDir,*
            LPCSTR *lpszApplicationDir,*
            LPSTR *lpszCurrentDir,*
            UINT FAR *lpCurDirSize,*
            LPSTR *lpszTargetDir,*
            UINT FAR *lpTargDirSize)

VerFindFile() obtains the directory into which the specified file should be installed. It does not actually install the file, however. The function returns zero if successful, and an error code on failure.

Currently, the value of *Mode* must be **VFFF_ISSHAREDFILE**.

The name of the file that will be installed (by a different function) is pointed to by *lpszFileName*.

The paths to the Windows directory and the application directory (into which related files are being installed) are pointed to by *lpszWindowsDir* and *lpszApplicationDir,* respectively.

On return, the character array pointed to by *lpszCurrentDir* will contain the path to the current version of the file (that is, the version of the file that is being superseded). This string will not be longer than **_MAX_PATH**. The size of the array pointed to by *lpszCurrentDir* is passed in *lpCurDirSize.*

On return, the character array pointed to by *lpszTargetDir* will contain the path to the current recommended directory into which the file should be installed. This string will not be longer than **_MAX_PATH**. The size of the array pointed to by *lpszTargetDir* is passed in *lpTargDirSize.*

USAGE

The following error return values are possible. If the current version of the file is not in the recommended directory, then **VFF_CURNEDEST** is returned. If the file is currently being used, **VFF_FILEINUSE** is returned. If the size of one (or both) arrays that receive path strings is not large enough, **VFF_BUFFTOOSMALL** is returned.

RELATED FUNCTION

VerInstallFile()

DWORD VerInstallFile(UINT *Mode,*

          LPCSTR *lpszFileName,*

          LPCSTR *lpszInstalledName,*

          LPCSTR *lpszFromDir,*

          LPCSTR *lpszToDir,*

          LPCSTR *lpszCurrentDir,*

          LPSTR *lpszTempName,*

          UINT FAR **lpTempNameSize***)**

VerInstallFile() installs the specified file. It returns one of the values described below.

Currently, the value of *Mode* must be **VIFF_FORCEINSTALL** (ignore version number mismatches) or **VIFF_DONTDELETEOLD** (leave old version of file, if possible).

The name of the file to install is pointed to by *lpszFileName*. The installed version of the file will be given the name pointed to by *lpszInstalledName*.

The directory containing the file to install is pointed to by *lpszFromDir*, and the directory into which the file will be installed is pointed to by *lpszToDir*.

If a prior version of the file exists, the path to the directory that contains it must be pointed to by *lpszCurrentDir*. If there is no current version (or if you choose to ignore it), then this parameter must be NULL.

lpszTempName points to an array that, upon return, will contain the temporary name of the installed file. This string will be no longer than **_MAX_PATH**. The size of the array pointed to by *lpszTempName* is passed in *lpTempNameSize*.

USAGE

The directory names pointed to by *lpszToDir* and *lpszCurrentDir* are commonly obtained by calling **VerFindFile()**.

If an error occurs, the value returned by **VerInstallFile()** may be any valid combination of the following values.

Macro	Error
VIF_ACCESSVIOLATION	Access violation.
VIF_BUFFTOOSMALL	Size of *lpszTempName* is too small.
VIF_CANNOTCREATE	Temporary file cannot be created.
VIF_CANNOTDELETE	Current version of the file being installed cannot be erased.
VIF_CANNOTREADDST	Destination file or directory cannot be read.
VIF_CANNOTREADSRC	Source file or directory cannot be read.
VIF_CANNOTRENAME	Temporary file cannot be renamed.
VIF_DIFFCODEPG	Required code page is not available.
VIF_DIFFLANG	New version of file uses different language code than original version.
VIF_DIFFTYPE	New version of file is of different type than current version.
VIF_FILEINUSE	Original file is currently being used and cannot be overwritten or erased.
VIF_MISMATCH	New version of file is different than current version.
VIF_OUTOFMEMORY	Out of memory.
VIF_OUTOFSPACE	Out of disk space.
VIF_SHARINGVIOLATION	Sharing violation.
VIF_SRCOLD	New version of file is older than current version.
VIF_TEMPFILE	Temporary file has not been deleted. This implies that another type of error has also occurred.
VIF_WRITEPROT	Current version of file is write-protected.

VerInstallFile() uses a temporary file during installation, which is renamed to the proper installed name when installation is complete.

RELATED FUNCTIONS

VerFindFile()
VerLanguageName()

UINT VerLanguageName(UINT *LangID,* LPSTR *lpszLangStr,* UINT *Size*)

VerLanguageName() converts a language code into its string equivalent. The function returns the length of the converted code if successful, or zero on failure.

The language code to be converted is passed in *LangID*. The character array that will, upon return, contain the string equivalent is pointed to by *lpszLangStr*. The size of that array is passed in *Size*.

USAGE

For the currently supported language codes, see **VERSIONINFO** in Volume 1, Appendix A.

RELATED FUNCTION

VerQueryValue()

BOOL VerQueryValue(const void FAR *lpResource,* LPCSTR *lpszValue,* void FAR * FAR *lplpVerPointer,* UINT FAR *lpSize*)

VerQueryValue() obtains specific items from within a version resource. It returns non-zero if successful, and zero on failure.

NOTE

Before **VerQueryValue()** *can be used, you must obtain a resource using* **GetFileVersionInfo()**.

The version resource is a string pointed to by *lpResource*.

The specific item to obtain from within the resource string is pointed to by *lpszValue*. Items within the version resource are separated by a backslash. The form of the information is determined by the **VERSIONINFO** resource statement. (See Volume 1, Appendix A.) There are only three value strings that may be used for *lpszValue*: a backslash, which refers to the version information; **\VarFileInfo\Translation**, which refers to the translation table; and **\StringFileInfo**, which refers to language.

On return, the pointer pointed to by *lplpVerPointer* will point to the desired information. The length of this information, in bytes, will be assigned to the variable pointed to by *lpSize*.

RELATED FUNCTIONS

GetFileVersionInfo()
VerLanguageName()

A Complete Programming Example

The following program reads and displays a line from a compressed text file. The file must have been compressed using COMPRESS.EXE.

```
/*
  Using the Data Compression Functions

  To use this program, first create a compressed
  text file (using COMPRESS.EXE) called COMPTEST.
*/

#include <windows.h>
#include <lzexpand.h>

LONG FAR PASCAL WndProc(HWND, UINT, WPARAM, LPARAM);
```

```
char szProgName[] = "ProgName"; /* name of window class */
char str[80], mess[] = "Decompressed Data";

int PASCAL WinMain(HINSTANCE hInst, HINSTANCE hPreInst,
                   LPSTR lpszCmdLine, int nCmdShow)
{
  MSG lpMsg;
  WNDCLASS wcApp;
  HWND hWnd;

  if (!hPreInst) { /* if no previous instance */
    wcApp.lpszClassName = szProgName; /* window class name */
    wcApp.hInstance     = hInst; /* handle to this instance */
    wcApp.lpfnWndProc   = WndProc; /* window function */
    wcApp.hCursor       = LoadCursor(NULL, IDC_ARROW);
    wcApp.hIcon         = LoadIcon(NULL, IDI_APPLICATION);
    wcApp.lpszMenuName  = NULL;

    /* make the background of window white */
    wcApp.hbrBackground = GetStockObject(WHITE_BRUSH);
    wcApp.style         = 0; /* use default window style */
    wcApp.cbClsExtra    = 0; /* no extra info */
    wcApp.cbWndExtra    = 0; /* no extra info */

    /* register the window class */
    if (!RegisterClass (&wcApp))
      return FALSE;
  }

  /* Now that window has been registered, a window
     can be created. */
  hWnd = CreateWindow(
    szProgName,
    "Read a Compressed File",
    WS_OVERLAPPEDWINDOW,
    CW_USEDEFAULT,
    CW_USEDEFAULT,
    CW_USEDEFAULT,
    CW_USEDEFAULT,
    (HWND) NULL,
    (HMENU) NULL,
    (HANDLE) hInst,
    (LPSTR) NULL
  );
```

```
    /* Display the Window. */
    ShowWindow(hWnd, nCmdShow);
    UpdateWindow(hWnd);

    /* Create the message loop. */
    while (GetMessage(&lpMsg, NULL, 0, 0)) {
      TranslateMessage(&lpMsg); /* allow use of keyboard */
      DispatchMessage(&lpMsg); /* return control to Windows */
    }
    return(lpMsg.wParam);
}

/* Window Function. */
LONG FAR PASCAL WndProc(HWND hWnd, UINT messg,
                        WPARAM wParam, LPARAM lParam)
{
  HFILE hFile;
  OFSTRUCT ofInfo;
  HDC hdc;
  PAINTSTRUCT ps;

  switch (messg) {
    case WM_CREATE:
      /* open compressed file */
      hFile = LZOpenFile("COMPTEST", &ofInfo, OF_READ);

      /* if file is open, read a line of data */
      if(hFile>=0) {
        LZRead(hFile, str, sizeof(str)-1);
        LZClose(hFile);
      }
      else {
        MessageBox(hWnd, "Cannot Open File", "Error", MB_OK);
        PostQuitMessage(0);
      }
      break;
    case WM_PAINT:
      hdc = BeginPaint(hWnd, &ps);
      TextOut(hdc, 1, 1, mess, strlen(mess));

      /* display a line of decompressed text from the file */
      TextOut(hdc, 1, 20, str, strlen(str));
```

```
            EndPaint(hWnd, &ps);
            break;
        case WM_DESTROY: /* terminate the program */
            PostQuitMessage(0);
            break;
        /* Let Windows process any messages not specified in
           the preceding cases. */
        default:
            return(DefWindowProc(hWnd, messg, wParam, lParam));
    }
    return(0L);
}
```

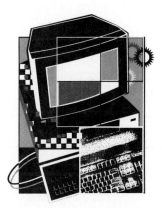

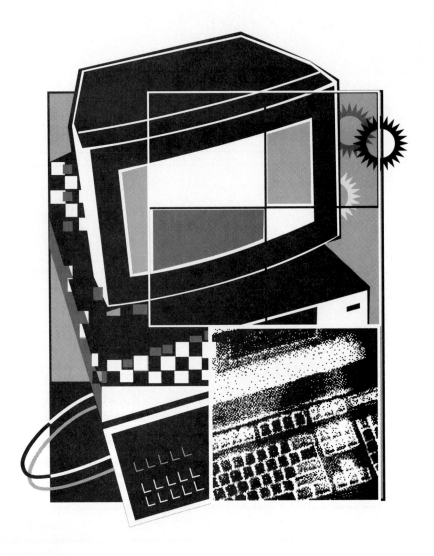

Chapter 14

Mapped Files

file that is copied into the virtual address space of an application is called a *mapped file*. Further, the process of doing this is called *file mapping*. An instance of a mapped file is called a *file view*. Once a file has been mapped by one application, another process can access that image. Thus, file mapping is one way that two processes can share information.

The functions in this chapter describe file mapping. A complete program example is presented at the end of this chapter that demonstrates several of the file mapping functions.

Mapped files relate only to Windows NT/Win32 and do not apply to 16-bit Windows.

HANDLE CreateFileMapping(HANDLE *hFile,*
            LPSECURITY_ATTRIBUTES *lpSecurity,*
            DWORD *dwAccess,*
            DWORD *dwLowWordSize,*
            DWORD *dwHighWordSize,*
            LPSTR *lpszMapName***)**

CreateFileMapping() creates a file-mapping object and returns a handle to it. It returns NULL if an error occurs.

The handle of the file that will be mapped is passed in *hFile*.

The mapped file object will have the security attributes pointed to by *lpSecurity*. (See Chapter 25 for information on the **SECURITY_ATTRIBUTES** structure.) If this parameter is NULL, then default security attributes are used. (If your application does not use security, then specify NULL.)

How the mapped object may be accessed is determined by the value of *dwAccess,* which may be one of these values: **PAGE_READONLY** (read-only access), **PAGE_READWRITE** (read/write access,) or **PAGE_WRITE-COPY** (copy on write access).

The maximum size of the mapped object is a 64-bit value that is passed using a combination of *dwLowWordSize* and *dwHighWordSize.* As the names imply, the high-order part of the maximum size is passed in *dwHighWordSize,* and the low-order part of the maximum size is passed in *dwLowWordSize.* If both parameters are zero, the entire file is mapped.

The name of the mapped-file object is pointed to by *lpszMapName.* For an unnamed object, use NULL for this parameter. If the specified object does not exist, it is created. If a mapped-file object by the specified name already exists, then a handle to that object will be returned.

RELATED FUNCTIONS

MapViewOfFile()
OpenFileMapping()

BOOL FlushViewOfFile(LPVOID *lpStart,* DWORD *dwSize*)

FlushViewOfFile() writes the specified portion of a mapped file memory image to disk. It returns non-zero if successful, and zero on failure.

The address of the beginning of the region to write is passed in *lpStart.* The number of bytes to write, beginning at that address, is passed in *dwSize.*

RELATED FUNCTION

UnmapViewOfFile()

LPVOID MapViewOfFile(HANDLE *hMap,*
         DWORD *dwAccess,*
         DWORD *dwLowWordSize,*
         DWORD *dwHighWordSize,*
         DWORD *dwSize)*

MapViewOfFile() maps a file view. The file that is mapped is loaded into the memory space of the application that uses this function and is accessible to that application. The function returns the address of the beginning of the view, or NULL on failure. Mapping a view is one way that processes can share data.

The handle of the mapped file is passed in *hMap.*

How the file view can be accessed is determined by the value of *dwAccess,* which must be one of these values:

Value	Access Permitted
FILE_MAP_ALL_ACCESS	Read/write
FILE_MAP_COPY	Copy on write
FILE_MAP_READ	Read-only
FILE_MAP_WRITE	Read/write

The point in the file at which file mapping will begin is specified by a 64-bit value that is passed using a combination of *dwLowWordSize* and *dwHighWord-Size.* As the names imply, the high-order part of the starting location is passed in *dwHighWordSize,* and the low-order part of the starting location is passed in *dwLowWordSize.*

The number of bytes from the file to map into memory is specified by *dwSize.* To map the entire file, use zero for this parameter.

RELATED FUNCTIONS

MapViewOfFileEx()
UnmapViewOfFile()

LPVOID MapViewOfFileEx(HANDLE *hMap,*
DWORD *dwAccess,*
DWORD *dwLowWordSize,*
DWORD *dwHighWordSize,*
DWORD *dwSize,*
LPVOID *lpStart*)

MapViewOfFileEx() is an enhanced version of **MapViewOfFile()**. It maps a file view into a specific location within the memory space of the application that uses this function. Once mapped, the file view is accessible to that application. The function returns the address of the beginning of the view, or NULL on failure. Mapping a view is one way that processes can share data.

The handle of the mapped file is passed in *hMap.*

How the file view can be accessed is determined by the value of *dwAccess,* which must be one of these values:

Value	Access Permitted
FILE_MAP_ALL_ACCESS	Read/write
FILE_MAP_COPY	Copy on write
FILE_MAP_READ	Read-only
FILE_MAP_WRITE	Read/write

The point in the file at which file mapping will begin is specified by a 64-bit value that is passed using a combination of *dwLowWordSize* and *dwHighWord-Size.* As the names imply, the high-order part of the starting location is passed in *dwHighWordSize,* and the low-order part of the starting location is passed in *dwLowWordSize.*

The number of bytes from the file to map into memory is specified by *dwSize.* To map the entire file, use zero for this parameter.

The beginning memory address at which the file will be mapped is passed in *lpStart.* This address should be on an even 64K boundary. (However, the address is rounded down, if necessary, to a 64K boundary, by the function.)

USAGE

The address passed in *lpStart* is typically that of a shared region of memory, which is accessed by two or more processes so that data may be shared. If there is not sufficient memory at this location, an error will occur.

RELATED FUNCTIONS

MapViewOfFile()
UnmapViewOfFile()

HANDLE OpenFileMapping(DWORD *dwMode,*
BOOL *Inherit,*
LPSTR *lpszMapName*)

OpenFileMapping() opens the specified file mapping object and returns a handle to it. The function returns NULL if an error occurs.

The name of the object is pointed to by *lpszMapName*.

The desired access mode is passed in *dwMode*. It must be one of these values:

Value	Access Permitted
FILE_MAP_ALL_ACCESS	Read/write
FILE_MAP_COPY	Copy on write
FILE_MAP_READ	Read-only
FILE_MAP_WRITE	Read/write

If the handle may be inherited, *Inherit* must be non-zero. If *Inherit* is zero, no inheritance is allowed.

RELATED FUNCTION

CreateFileMapping()

BOOL UnmapViewOfFile(LPVOID *lpStart*)

UnmapViewOfFile() removes a mapped file view and writes any modified regions to disk. It returns non-zero if successful, and zero on failure.

The starting address of the file view is passed in *lpStart*.

USAGE

The address specified in *lpStart* is obtained when the file view is created using either **MapViewOfFile()** or **MapViewOfFileEx()**.

RELATED FUNCTIONS

MapViewOfFile()
MapViewOfFileEx()

A Complete Programming Example

Here is a complete Windows NT example that illustrates several file-mapping functions. Remember, the main use of file mapping is to allow shared data between processes. As such, you might want to create two versions of this program and experiment with sharing information between them.

```
/*
  Demonstrate Mapped Files
*/

#include <windows.h>
#include <io.h>

LRESULT CALLBACK WindowFunc(HWND, UINT, WPARAM, LPARAM);

char szWinName[] = "MyWin"; /* name of window class */

int hFile;
HANDLE hMap;
OFSTRUCT of;

char *view;

int WINAPI WinMain(HINSTANCE hThisInst, HINSTANCE hPrevInst,
                   LPSTR lpszArgs, int nWinMode)
{
  HWND hwnd;
  MSG msg;
  WNDCLASS wcl;

  /* Define a window class. */
  wcl.hInstance = hThisInst; /* handle to this instance */
  wcl.lpszClassName = szWinName; /* window class name */
  wcl.lpfnWndProc = WindowFunc; /* window function */
  wcl.style = 0; /* default style */
```

```
wcl.hIcon = LoadIcon(NULL, IDI_APPLICATION); /* icon style */
wcl.hCursor = LoadCursor(NULL, IDC_ARROW); /* cursor style */
wcl.lpszMenuName = NULL; /* no menu */

wcl.cbClsExtra = 0;
wcl.cbWndExtra = 0;

/* Make the window light gray. */
wcl.hbrBackground = GetStockObject(LTGRAY_BRUSH);

/* Register the window class. */
if(!RegisterClass (&wcl)) return 0;

/* Now that a window class has been registered, a window
   can be created. */
hwnd = CreateWindow(
  szWinName, /* name of window class */
  "File Mapping",
  WS_OVERLAPPEDWINDOW, /* window style - normal */
  CW_USEDEFAULT, /* X coordinate - let Windows decide */
  CW_USEDEFAULT, /* Y coordinate - let Windows decide */
  CW_USEDEFAULT, /* width - let Windows decide */
  CW_USEDEFAULT, /* height - let Windows decide */
  NULL, /* handle of parent window - there isn't one */
  NULL, /* no menu */
  hThisInst, /* handle of this instance of the program */
  NULL /* no additional arguments */
);

/* Display the window. */
ShowWindow(hwnd, nWinMode);
UpdateWindow(hwnd);

/* Create the message loop. */
while(GetMessage(&msg, NULL, 0, 0))
{
  TranslateMessage(&msg); /* allow use of keyboard */
  DispatchMessage(&msg); /* return control to Windows */
}
return msg.wParam;
}
```

```
/* This function is called by Windows NT and is passed
   messages from the message queue.
*/
LRESULT CALLBACK WindowFunc(HWND hwnd, UINT message,
                            WPARAM wParam, LPARAM lParam)
{
  PAINTSTRUCT paintstruct;
  HDC hdc;

  switch(message) {
    case WM_CREATE: /* create a mapped file and view */
      hFile = OpenFile("TEST.TXT", &of, OF_READ);
      if(hFile==HFILE_ERROR) {
        MessageBox(hwnd, "Cannot Open File", "ERROR", MB_OK);
        PostQuitMessage(0);
      }
      hMap = CreateFileMapping((HANDLE) hFile,
                               (LPSECURITY_ATTRIBUTES) NULL,
                               PAGE_READONLY,
                               0, 0, "MapObj");
      view = MapViewOfFile(hMap, FILE_MAP_READ, 0, 0, 0);
      break;
    case WM_PAINT: /* display part of the file view */
      hdc = BeginPaint(hwnd, &paintstruct); /* get DC */
      TextOut(hdc, 1, 1, view, 80); /* output view */
      EndPaint(hwnd, &paintstruct); /* release DC */
      break;
    case WM_DESTROY: /* terminate the program */
      UnmapViewOfFile(view);
      close(hFile);
      PostQuitMessage(0);
      break;
    default:
      /* Let Windows NT process any messages not specified in
         the preceding switch statement. */
      return DefWindowProc(hwnd, message, wParam, lParam);
  }
  return 0;
}
```

Chapter 15

MDI Functions

m

D I (Multiple Document Interface) functions allow your applications to use multiple documents. While a full description of the MDI interface and its use is beyond the scope of this book, the following terms will help you understand the MDI function descriptions contained in this chapter. An MDI application's top level window is called a *frame window*. The frame window (and its client area) is not actually used for output. Instead, the frame contains one or more *MDI client windows* that are used to display documents. The client windows are child windows of the frame. A client window belongs to the **MDICLIENT** class.

HWND CreateMDIWindow(LPSTR *lpszClass,*
LPSTR *lpszTitle,*
DWORD *dwHow,* int *nX,*
int *nY,* int *nWidth,*
int *nHeight,* HWND *hParent,*
HINSTANCE *hInst,*
LPARAM *lParam)*

CreateMDIWindow() creates an MDI window and returns a handle to it. If an error occurs, NULL is returned.

The MDI window will be constructed as specified by the class name pointed to by *lpszClass.* This class must have been previously registered.

The title of the MDI window is pointed to by *lpszTitle.*

How the window is actually constructed is determined by the value (or values) passed in *dwHow.* This can be any valid combination of the following values: **WS_HSCROLL** (horizontal scroll bar), **WS_MAXIMIZE** (show maximized), **WS_MINIMIZE** (show minimized), and **WS_VSCROLL** (vertical scroll bar).

Technically, if the class used to create the MDI window includes the style specifier **MDIS_ALLCHILDSTYLES**, then you can use any window style. However, MDI windows will generally only require the four styles just described.

The initial location at which the MDI window is displayed is passed in *nX* and *nY*. If you don't care where the window is displayed, let Windows decide by specifying **CW_USEDEFAULT** for these values.

nWidth and *nHeight* determine the initial dimensions of the window. These, too, can be left up to Windows by specifying **CW_USEDEFAULT**.

hParent is the handle of the client window that will own the MDI window. *hInst* is the handle of the application that calls **CreateMDIWindow()**.

Any application-dependent information required to create the window can be passed in *lParam*.

RELATED FUNCTION

DefMDIChildProc()

LRESULT DefMDIChildProc(HWND *hWnd*, UINT *Msg*, WPARAM *wParam*, LPARAM *lParam*)

When an MDI child window receives a message that it does not, itself, wish to process, it should call **DefMDIChildProc()** to handle the message. The function returns the result of the message.

The handle of the window is passed in *hWnd*. The message and its associated information are passed in *Msg, wParam,* and *lParam*. All of these parameters are passed to the MDI child window when it receives a message. You simply pass them along for default processing when you call **DefMDIChildProc()**.

USAGE

An MDI child window must *not* attempt to call **DefWindowProc()** to provide default processing.

RELATED FUNCTIONS

DefFrameProc() (See Volume 2)
TranslateMDISysAccel()

BOOL TranslateMDISysAccel(HWND *hWnd,* MSG FAR **lpMsg*)

TranslateMDISysAccel() translates system menu accelerator keys for an MDI child window. It returns non-zero if it translates a key, and zero if it does not.

REMEMBER

Not translating a message is not an error. It simply means that the message was not an accelerator key.

The handle of the MDI window is passed in *hWnd*. The message to translate is pointed to by *lpMsg*.

USAGE

Only two messages are affected by **TranslateMDISysAccel()**: **WM_KEYDOWN** and **WM_KEYUP**. Both are translated into **WM_SYSCOMMAND** messages.

RELATED FUNCTIONS

CreateMDIWindow()
DefMDIChildProc()

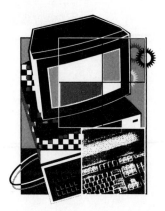

Chapter 16

Memory Allocation and

Management

215

t H E functions in this chapter perform memory allocation and management. A complete programming example is presented at the end of this chapter that demonstrates several memory management functions.

HANDLE GetProcessHeap(void)

GetProcessHeap() returns a handle to the heap associated with the application. It returns NULL on failure.

RELATED FUNCTIONS

HeapAlloc
HeapReAlloc()

HGLOBAL GlobalAlloc(UINT *How,* DWORD *dwSize*)

GlobalAlloc() allocates memory from the global heap and returns a handle to it. It returns NULL if the memory cannot be allocated.

The number of bytes to allocate is passed in *dwSize.* If this amount of memory is unavailable, then the function fails.

Precisely how memory is allocated from the global heap is determined by the value of *How,* which must be a valid combination of the following:

Macro	Effect
GHND	Memory is moveable and initialized to zero.
GMEM_DDESHARE	Memory is sharable.
GMEM_DISCARDABLE	Memory is discardable.
GMEM_FIXED	Memory is not moveable.
GMEM_LOWER	Memory is not bank-switched (this value is ignored because it is obsolete).
GMEM_MOVEABLE	Memory is moveable.

Macro	Effect
GMEM_NOCOMPACT	Memory may not be compacted or removed.
GMEM_NODISCARD	Memory may not be discarded.
GMEM_NOTIFY	A notification function is called when the memory is discarded.
GMEM_NOT_BANKED	Memory is not bank-switched (this value is ignored because it is obsolete).
GMEM_SHARE	Memory is sharable.
GMEM_ZEROINIT	Memory is initialized to zero.
GPTR	Memory is not moveable and is initialized to zero.

USAGE

The memory allocated by **GlobalAlloc()** becomes a global memory object. The distinction between global and local heaps only relates to 16-bit Windows. For Windows NT/Win32, there is no difference.

RELATED FUNCTIONS

GlobalFree()
LocalAlloc()

DWORD GlobalCompact(DWORD *dwSize)*

GlobalCompact() defragments the global heap by compacting all moveable objects. It will also remove discardable objects, if necessary. The function attempts to create as much free memory as specified by *dwSize*. It returns the size of the largest object that can be allocated.

NOTE

This function is not supported by Windows NT/Win32.

USAGE

To find out the size of the largest object that can be allocated if all discardable objects are removed and the heap is compacted, specify zero for *dwSize*.

If the requested amount of memory cannot be obtained, the function still compacts the heap.

RELATED FUNCTION

GlobalFree()

HGLOBAL GlobalDiscard(HGLOBAL *hMemory*)

GlobalDiscard() discards the global memory associated with the specified handle. If successful, it returns the handle to the object that was discarded. If the function fails, NULL is returned.

USAGE

The memory being discarded must have been allocated using either **GlobalAlloc()** or **GlobalReAlloc()**. Further, the **GMEM_DISCARDABLE** attribute must have been specified when the memory was allocated.

A discarded object is different from a freed object. A discarded object's handle is still valid and may be used in a call to **GlobalReAlloc()**.

RELATED FUNCTION

GlobalFree()
GlobalReAlloc()

DWORD GlobalDosAlloc(DWORD *dwSize*)

GlobalDosAlloc() allocates memory from the first megabyte of RAM in the system. (The first megabyte is where DOS runs.) It returns the segment of the allocated memory in the high-order word, and the offset value in the low-order word. It returns zero if the allocation request cannot be granted.

The amount of memory to allocate is specified by *dwSize*.

For Windows NT/Win32, this function is obsolete and not supported.

RELATED FUNCTION

GlobalDosFree()

UINT GlobalDosFree(UINT *Mem*)

GlobalDosFree() frees the memory associated with the *Mem*. The function returns zero if successful, or *Mem* on failure.

The value passed in *Mem* is the value obtained from **GlobalDosAlloc()**. This function may only be used to free memory allocated using **GlobalDosAlloc()**.

NOTE

For Windows NT/Win32, this function is obsolete and not supported.

RELATED FUNCTION

GlobalDosAlloc()

UINT GlobalFlags(HGLOBAL *hObj*)

GlobalFlags() returns various attributes associated with the specified global memory object.

The handle to the object is passed in *hObj*.

The return value is encoded as follows. The object's lock count is contained in the low-order byte. The high-order byte contains one or more of these values: **GMEM_DDESHARE** (object may be shared), **GMEM_DIS-CARDABLE** (object may be discarded), or **GMEM_DISCARDED** (object has been discarded).

RELATED FUNCTION

GlobalAlloc()
GlobalFree()
GlobalLock()

HGLOBAL GlobalFree(HGLOBAL *hObj*)

GlobalFree() releases the memory associated with the specified object. It returns NULL if successful, or *hObj* if the object cannot be freed.

The handle of the object to free is passed in *hObj*.

USAGE

This function destroys the specified handle, and it cannot be used to reallocate memory. Also, once an object has been freed, do not try to free it again. A runtime error will almost certainly result.

RELATED FUNCTIONS

GlobalAlloc()
GlobalReAlloc()

void FAR *GlobalLock(HGLOBAL *hObj*)

GlobalLock() locks the specified object. If that object has already been locked, then its lock count is incremented. This function applies only to moveable objects.

The handle of the object to lock is passed in *hObj*.

GlobalLock() returns the address of the start of the object if successful, and NULL on failure.

USAGE

A global memory object must be locked before it can be used by your program. Thus, **GlobalLock()** is the way that your program obtains a pointer to a global memory object.

A locked object (even a discardable one) will not be removed or relocated until its lock count drops to zero.

This fragment allocates a moveable global object and then locks it:

```
HGLOBAL hObj;
char *p;
hObj = GlobalAlloc(GMEM_MOVEABLE, 100);
p = (char *) GlobalLock(hObj);
```

RELATED FUNCTION

GlobalAlloc()

void GlobalMemoryStatus(LPMEMORYSTATUS *lpStatus*)

GlobalMemoryStatus() obtains the current status of memory.

lpStatus points to a **MEMORYSTATUS** structure which, upon return, will contain the current memory status. **MEMORYSTATUS** is defined like this:

```
typedef struct _MEMORYSTATUS {
  DWORD dwLength;
  DWORD dwMemoryLoad;
  DWORD dwTotalPhys;
  DWORD dwAvailPhys;
  DWORD dwTotalPageFile;
  DWORD dwAvailPageFile;
  DWORD dwTotalVirtual;
  DWORD dwAvailVirtual;
} MEMORYSTATUS;
```

Here, **dwLength** contains the size of the **MEMORYSTATUS** structure, and **dwMemoryLoad** contains the percentage of memory in use, represented as a value between 0 and 100.

The total amount of memory is contained in **dwTotalPhys**. The amount of available memory is in **dwAvailPhy**s. The number of bytes that a page file can hold is contained in **dwTotalPageFile**. The amount of page file storage available is contained in **dwAvailPageFile**.

The amount of virtual memory is contained in **dwTotalVirtual**. The amount of available virtual memory is in **dwAvailVirtual**.

USAGE

The following example reports the amount of currently available free memory.

```
MEMORYSTATUS memstat1;
char str[80];

GlobalMemoryStatus(&memstat);
sprintf(str, "Available: %lu", memstat.dwAvailPhys);
MessageBox(hWnd, str, "Memory", MB_OK);
```

RELATED FUNCTIONS

GlobalAlloc()
GlobalSize()

void GlobalNotify(GNOTIFYPROC *lpFunc*)

GlobalNotify() installs a callback function that is called whenever a global memory object is being discarded and that object was allocated with the **GMEM_NOTIFY** attribute.

NOTE

This function applies to 16-bit Windows only. It is not supported by Windows NT/Win32.

The address of the notification function is passed in *lpFunc*. The notification callback function must have this prototype:

BOOL CALLBACK NotifyFunc(HGLOBAL *hObj*)

Here, *hObj* will be the handle to the object in the process of being discarded. The function must return non-zero if the object should actually be discarded, and zero if not. This function must be in a fixed code segment of a DLL.

RELATED FUNCTION

GlobalAlloc()

HGLOBAL GlobalReAlloc(HGLOBAL *hObj,*   DWORD *dwSize,*   UINT *How*)

GlobalReAlloc() reallocates (changes the size of) a piece of dynamically allocated memory. (This memory must have been allocated initially by calling **GlobalAlloc()**.) The function returns a handle to the memory if successful, or NULL on failure.

The handle to the memory to reallocate is passed in *hObj*. Remember, the handle returned by **GlobalReAlloc()** may be different from *hObj*.

The amount of memory that you want to allocate is passed in *dwSize*. This value may be larger or smaller than what is currently allocated.

How the memory is actually allocated is determined by *How,* which may be any valid combination of the following values.

Value	Effect
GMEM_DISCARDABLE	Memory is discardable.
GMEM_MOVEABLE	Memory is moveable.
GMEM_NOCOMPACT	Memory may not be compacted or removed.
GMEM_NODISCARD	Memory may not be discarded.
GMEM_ZEROINIT	Memory is initialized to zero.

If **GMEM_MODIFY** is included, then the memory object's size is not affected but its attributes are changed. This value can only be used in conjunction with **GMEM_DISCARDABLE** and **GMEM_MOVEABLE**.

USAGE

The following fragment reallocates the memory associated with *hMem*.

```
hMem = GlobalReAlloc(hMem, 100, GMEM_DISCARDABLE);
```

RELATED FUNCTION

GlobalAlloc()

DWORD GlobalSize(HGLOBAL *hObj*)

GlobalSize() returns the size of the memory associated with the handle passed in *hObj*. It returns zero on error or if the memory has been discarded.

RELATED FUNCTION

GlobalAlloc()

BOOL GlobalUnlock(HGLOBAL *hObj*)

GlobalUnlock() decrements the lock count associated with the specified memory. It returns zero if, after decrementing, the lock count is zero (that is, the memory is fully unlocked). It returns non-zero otherwise.

The handle of the memory to unlock is passed in *hObj*.

USAGE

The following fragment fully unlocks the object associated with *hObj*. (This type of procedure could be used to fully unlock an object when the program is being reset, for example.)

```
while(GlobalUnlock(hObj)) ;
```

RELATED FUNCTION

GlobalLock()

LPVOID HeapAlloc(HANDLE *hHeap*, DWORD *dwHow*, DWORD *dwSize*)

HeapAlloc() allocates memory from the heap and returns a pointer to it. (Note that this function returns a pointer to the memory, not a handle to it.) If the allocation request cannot be fulfilled, then NULL is returned. Therefore, be sure to check the return value before using the function.

The handle of the heap to allocate the memory from is passed in *hHeap*.

The amount of memory to allocate is passed in *dwSize*.

How the memory is allocated is determined by the value of *dwHow*, which can be any valid combination of the following values: **HEAP_GENER-ATE_EXCEPTIONS** (raise exception if memory cannot be allocated), **HEAP_NO_SERIALIZE** (heap accesses are not serialized), or **HEAP_ZERO_MEMORY** (initialize memory to zero).

USAGE

The heap handle passed in *hHeap* is obtained using the **HeapCreate()** function.

Memory allocated using this function is not moveable.

If the **HEAP_GENERATE_EXCEPTIONS** flag is set, then on failure, one of these exceptions will be raised: **STATUS_NO_MEMORY** or **STATUS_ACCESS_VIOLATION**.

The following fragment allocates 2,000 bytes of memory from the heap.

```
char *p;
/* .. */
p = (char *) HeapAlloc(hHeap, HEAP_ZERO_MEMORY, 2000);
```

RELATED FUNCTIONS

HeapCreate()
HeapFree()
HeapReAlloc()

HANDLE HeapCreate(DWORD *dwHow,*
DWORD *dwInitSize,*
DWORD *dwMaxSize*)

HeapCreate() creates a local heap and returns a handle to it. It returns NULL on failure.

How the heap is allocated is determined by the value of *dwHow*. It can be one or both of these values (or zero if neither apply): **HEAP_GENER-ATE_EXCEPTIONS** (raise exception if memory cannot be allocated) or **HEAP_NO_SERIALIZE** (heap accesses are not serialized). If **HEAP_NO_SERIALIZE** is specified, two or more threads may access the heap at the same time. However, this situation is seldom acceptable (it generally causes the heap to be corrupted).

The heap is allocated from the calling process's virtual address space. The value passed in *dwMaxSize* specifies the maximum size of the heap that is allocated from the virtual address space. The value of *dwInitSize* determines how much of that virtual memory is mapped to physical memory. If memory allocation requests exhaust what is currently available, then more of the heap is created in physical memory.

USAGE

Some of the heap is always consumed by the overhead associated with heap maintenance. Thus, you will not be able to allocate every byte of memory in the heap.

Local heaps are private to the creating process and do not conflict with other heaps in the system.

RELATED FUNCTIONS

HeapAlloc()
HeapDestroy()
HeapSize()

BOOL HeapDestroy(HANDLE *hHeap*)

HeapDestroy() destroys the heap specified by *hHeap*. It returns non-zero if successful, and zero on failure.

hHeap is the handle of the heap. This handle must have been created by **HeapCreate()**.

RELATED FUNCTION

HeapCreate()

BOOL HeapFree(HANDLE *hHeap*, DWORD *dwHow*, LPVOID *lpP*)

HeapFree() frees memory previously allocated from the specified heap. It returns non-zero if successful, and zero on failure.

The handle to the heap from which the memory was allocated is passed in *hHeap*.

At the time of this writing, *dwHow* must be either zero or **HEAP_NO_SE-RIALIZE**. Specifying the latter allows other threads to access the heap while the specified memory is being freed.

The memory being released is pointed to by *lpP*.

USAGE

The following fragment illustrates **HeapFree()**.

```
char *p;
p = (char *) HeapAlloc(hHeap, HEAP_ZERO_MEMORY, 100);
/* ... */
HeapFree(hHeap, 0, p);
```

RELATED FUNCTIONS

HeapAlloc()
HeapCreate()

LPVOID HeapReAlloc(HANDLE *hHeap*,
DWORD *dwHow*,
LPVOID *lpP*,
DWORD *dwSize*)

HeapReAlloc() reallocates (changes the size of) a piece of dynamically allocated memory. (This memory must have been allocated initially by calling **HeapAlloc()**.) The function returns a pointer to the memory if successful, or NULL on failure.

The handle of the heap from which the memory was originally allocated (and from which it will be reallocated) is passed in *hHeap*.

How the memory will be reallocated is determined by the value of *dwHow*, which may be any valid combination of the following values (or zero if none apply).

Macro	Effect
HEAP_GENERATE_EXCEPTIONS	Raises exception if memory cannot be allocated.
HEAP_NO_SERIALIZE	Allows two or more threads to access the heap at the same time.
HEAP_REALLOC_IN_PLACE_ONLY	Does not move existing memory. If a memory increase cannot be accommodated, then **HeapReAlloc()** fails.
HEAP_ZERO_MEMORY	Initializes the additional memory to zero.

NOTE

If **HEAP_ZERO_MEMORY** *is specified, only the new memory is affected. The contents of the original memory are not changed.*

---

lpP points to the currently allocated memory that will be changed.

The amount of memory that you want to allocate is passed in *dwSize*. This value may be larger or smaller than what is currently allocated.

RELATED FUNCTIONS

HeapAlloc()
HeapCreate()

DWORD HeapSize(HANDLE *hHeap*, DWORD *dwHow*, LPVOID *lpP*)

HeapSize() returns the size of an object that has been allocated from a heap. If an error occurs, zero is returned.

The handle of the heap from which the memory was allocated is passed in *hHeap*.

At the time of this writing, *dwHow* must be either zero or **HEAP_NO_SE-RIALIZE**. Specifying the latter allows other threads to access the heap while the specified memory is being checked.

lpP is a pointer to the allocated memory whose size you want to obtain. This pointer must have been obtained originally through a call to **HeapAlloc()**.

USAGE

The following fragment displays the size of a heap object.

```
unsigned long size;
char str[255];
size = HeapSize(hHeap, 0, MyObj);
sprintf(str, "%lu", size);
MessageBox(hWnd, str, "Object Size", MB_OK);
```

RELATED FUNCTIONS

HeapAlloc()
HeapCreate()
HeapReAlloc()

BOOL IsBadCodePtr(FARPROC *lpP*)

IsBadCodePtr() returns non-zero if *lpP* points to non-executable code (that is, the code is "bad"). It returns zero if the code is executable.

RELATED FUNCTION

Other **IsBad...** functions

BOOL IsBadHugeReadPtr(const void _huge *lpP, DWORD dwSize)

IsBadHugeReadPtr() returns non-zero if *lpP* points to non-readable memory (that is, the memory is "bad"). It returns zero if the memory is readable.
dwSize specifies the amount of memory to check.

RELATED FUNCTION

Other **IsBad**... functions

BOOL IsBadHugeWritePtr(void _huge *lpP, DWORD dwSize)

IsBadHugeWritePtr() returns non-zero if *lpP* points to non-writable memory (that is, the memory is "bad"). It returns zero if the memory is writable.
dwSize specifies the amount of memory to check.

RELATED FUNCTION

Other **IsBad**... functions

BOOL IsBadReadPtr(const void FAR *lpP, UINT dwSize)

IsBadReadPtr() returns non-zero if *lpP* points to non-readable memory (that is, the memory is "bad"). It returns zero if the memory is readable.
dwSize specifies the amount of memory to check.

RELATED FUNCTION

Other **IsBad**... functions

BOOL IsBadStringPtr(const void FAR *lpP, UINT dwSize)

IsBadStringPtr() returns non-zero if memory pointed to by *lpP* is not a valid string (that is, the string is "bad"). It returns zero if the memory contains a valid string.

dwSize specifies the amount of memory to check.

RELATED FUNCTION

Other **IsBad**... functions

BOOL IsBadWritePtr(void FAR *lpP, UINT dwSize)

IsBadWritePtr() returns non-zero if *lpP* points to non-writable memory (that is, the memory is "bad"). It returns zero if the memory is writable.

dwSize specifies the amount of memory to check.

RELATED FUNCTION

Other **IsBad**... functions

HLOCAL LocalAlloc(UINT How, UINT Size)

LocalAlloc() allocates memory from the local heap and returns a handle to it. It returns NULL if the allocation request cannot be granted.

The amount of memory to allocate is specified by *Size*.

Various attributes about the allocated memory are determined by the value of *How*. It may be any valid combination of the following values.

Value	Effect
LHND	Memory is moveable and initialized to zero.
LMEM_DISCARDABLE	Memory is discardable.
LMEM_FIXED	Memory is not moveable.
LMEM_MOVEABLE	Memory is moveable.
LMEM_NOCOMPACT	Memory may not be compacted or removed.
LMEM_NODISCARD	Memory may not be discarded.
LMEM_ZEROINIT	Memory is initialized to zero.
LPTR	Memory is not moveable and is initialized to zero.

USAGE

For Windows NT/Win32, there is no distinction between the local heap and the global heap.

RELATED FUNCTIONS

GlobalAlloc()
LocalFree()

UINT LocalCompact(UINT *dwSize)*

LocalCompact() defragments the local heap by compacting all moveable objects. It will also remove discardable objects, if necessary. The function attempts to create as much free memory as specified by *dwSize*. It returns the size of the largest object that can be allocated.

This function is not supported by Windows NT/Win32.

USAGE

To find out the size of the largest object that can be allocated if all discardable objects are removed and the heap is compacted, specify zero for *dwSize*.

If the requested amount of memory cannot be obtained, the function still compacts the heap.

RELATED FUNCTION

LocalFree()

HLOCAL LocalDiscard(HLOCAL *hMemory)*

LocalDiscard() discards the memory associated with the specified local memory handle. If successful, it returns the handle to the object that was discarded. If the function fails, NULL is returned.

USAGE

The memory being discarded must have been allocated using either **Local-Alloc()** or **LocalReAlloc()**. Further, the **LMEM_DISCARDABLE** attribute must have been specified when the memory was allocated.

A discarded object is different from a freed object. A discarded object's handle is still valid and may be used in a call to **LocalReAlloc()**.

RELATED FUNCTIONS

LocalFree()
LocalReAlloc()

UINT LocalFlags(HLOCAL *hObj*)

LocalFlags() returns various attributes associated with the specified local memory object.

The handle to the object is passed in *hObj*.

The return value is encoded as follows. The object's lock count is contained in the low-order byte. The high-order byte contains one or both of these values: **LMEM_DISCARDABLE** (object may be discarded) or **LMEM_DIS-CARDED** (object is discarded).

RELATED FUNCTIONS

GlobalFlags()
LocalAlloc()
LocalFree()
LocalLock()

HLOCAL LocalFree(HLOCAL *hObj*)

LocalFree() releases the memory associated with the specified object. It returns NULL if successful, or *hObj* if the object cannot be freed.

The handle of the object to free is passed in *hObj*.

USAGE

This function destroys the specified handle, and it cannot be used to reallocate memory. Also, once an object has been freed, do not try to free it again. A runtime error will almost certainly result.

RELATED FUNCTIONS

LocalAlloc()
LocalReAlloc()

HLOCAL LocalHandle(void NEAR *npMemory)

LocalHandle() returns the handle associated with the specified memory. It returns NULL on failure (for example, if the memory has no handle associated with it).

npMemory is a **NEAR** pointer to the memory that you want the handle to.

RELATED FUNCTIONS

GlobalHandle()
LocalAlloc()

void NEAR * LocalLock(HLOCAL hObj)

LocalLock() locks the specified object. If that object has already been locked, then its lock count is incremented. This function applies only to moveable objects.

The handle of the object to lock is passed in *hObj*.

LocalLock() returns the address of the start of the object if successful, and NULL on failure.

USAGE

A local memory object must be locked before it can be used by your program. Thus, **LocalLock()** is the way that your program obtains a pointer to a local memory object.

A locked object (even a discardable one) will not be removed or relocated until its lock count drops to zero.

This fragment allocates a moveable local object and then locks it:

```
HLOCAL hObj;
char *p;
hObj = LocalAlloc(LMEM_MOVEABLE, 100);
p = (char *) LocalLock(hObj);
```

RELATED FUNCTIONS

GlobalLock()
LocalUnlock()

HLOCAL LocalReAlloc(HLOCAL *hObj*, UINT *dwSize*, UINT *How*)

LocalReAlloc() reallocates (changes the size of) a piece of dynamically allocated memory. (This memory must have been allocated initially by calling **LocalAlloc()**.) The function returns a handle to the memory if successful, or NULL on failure.

The handle to the memory to reallocate is passed in *hObj*. Remember, the handle returned by **LocalReAlloc()** may be different from *hObj*.

The amount of memory that you want to allocate is passed in *dwSize*. This value may be larger or smaller than what is currently allocated.

How the memory is actually allocated is determined by *How*, which may be any valid combination of the following (or zero if none apply).

Value	Effect
LMEM_DISCARDABLE	Memory is discardable.
LMEM_MODIFY	Must be used with LMEM_DISCARDABLE.
LMEM_MOVEABLE	Memory is moveable.
LMEM_NOCOMPACT	Memory may not be compacted or removed.
LMEM_ZEROINIT	Memory is initialized to zero.

USAGE

The following fragment reallocates the memory associated with *hMem*.

```
hMem = LocalReAlloc(hMem, 100, LMEM_DISCARDABLE);
```

RELATED FUNCTION

LocalAlloc()

UINT LocalSize(HLOCAL *hObj*)

LocalSize() returns the size of the memory associated with the handle passed in *hObj*. It returns zero on error or if the memory has been discarded.

RELATED FUNCTION

LocalAlloc()

BOOL LocalUnlock(HLOCAL *hObj*)

LocalUnlock() decrements the lock count associated with the specified memory. It returns zero if, after decrementing, the lock count is zero (that is, the memory is fully unlocked). It returns non-zero otherwise.

The handle of the memory to unlock is passed in *hObj*.

USAGE

The following fragment fully unlocks the object associated with *hObj*. (This type of procedure could be used to fully unlock an object when the program is being reset, for example.)

```
while(LocalUnlock(hObj)) ;
```

RELATED FUNCTION

LocalLock()

LPVOID VirtualAlloc(LPVOID *lpRegion,*
DWORD *dwSize,*
DWORD *dwType,*
DWORD *dwAccess*)

VirtualAlloc() allocates virtual memory. It returns a pointer to the start of this memory, or NULL if the allocation request cannot be granted.

You may specify the starting address of the virtual memory that you want to allocate. This address is passed in *lpRegion* and must be on a 64K boundary if the memory is being reserved or on a page boundary if the memory is being committed. (In either case, if the specified address isn't on the proper boundary, the address will be rounded down, as needed.) If you don't care where the memory is allocated, you may specify this parameter as NULL.

The number of bytes that you want to allocate is passed in *dwSize.*

How the virtual memory is allocated is determined by the value of *dwType.* If it is **MEM_RESERVE**, the specified number of bytes is reserved in the virtual address space, but not actually allocated. If it is **MEM_COMMIT,** then the specified memory is actually allocated.

The access mode of the memory is determined by the value of *dwAccess.* If it is **PAGE_NOACCESS**, then no access is allowed. (This value is used only when reserving memory.) If it is **PAGE_READONLY**, the memory may be read but not written. If it is **PAGE_READWRITE**, read/write access is granted.

USAGE

Typically, you will first reserve a region of the virtual address space large enough to fill the needs of your application. Once this is done, your application then commits pages from this space as needed.

RELATED FUNCTIONS

GlobalAlloc()
LocalAlloc()
VirtualFree()

BOOL VirtualFree(LPVOID *lpRegion,* DWORD *dwSize,* DWORD *dwHow)*

VirtualFree() frees a region of virtual memory previously allocated using **VirtualAlloc()**. It returns non-zero if successful, and zero on failure.

The starting address of the memory to release is pointed to by *lpRegion.* The number of bytes to free is passed in *dwSize.*

The exact operation performed by **VirtualFree()** depends upon the value of *dwHow.* If it is **MEM_DECOMMIT**, then the region is decommitted but still held in reserve. If *dwHow* is **MEM_RELEASE**, the memory is freed.

USAGE

To release committed memory, first decommit it, then release it. Once memory has been decommitted, but is still reserved, no attempt should be made to access it (except to recommit it to another use). Doing so will cause an access fault.

RELATED FUNCTIONS

GlobalFree()
LocalFree()
VirtualAlloc()

BOOL VirtualLock(LPVOID *lpRegion,* DWORD *dwSize)*

VirtualLock() causes the specified region of virtual memory to remain in physical memory (that is, it "locks" the memory in place). This prevents the overhead that is incurred when a page fault occurs. The function returns non-zero if successful, and zero on failure.

The starting address of the region to lock is pointed to by *lpRegion.* (This address must have been obtained through a call to **VirtualAlloc()**.) The size of the region is passed in *dwSize.*

USAGE

The region that you attempt to lock must consist of committed pages.

To unlock a region, call **VirtualUnlock()**.

VirtualLock() replaces the 16-bit Windows function **GlobalPageLock()**, *which has this prototype:*

UINT GlobalPageLock(HGLOBAL hObj);

This function returns the current lock count, or zero if an error occurs. The use of this function is not recommended. If used, it must only be called from a DLL.

RELATED FUNCTION

VirtualUnlock()

BOOL VirtualProtect(LPVOID *lpRegion,*
DWORD *dwSize,*
DWORD *dwAccess,*
PDWORD *lpPrev)*

VirtualProtect() changes how the specified region of virtual memory may be accessed. It returns non-zero if successful, and zero otherwise.

The starting address of the region is pointed to by *lpRegion*. The size of the region is passed in *dwSize*. This memory must have been allocated originally using **VirtualAlloc()**, and it must consist entirely of committed pages.

The new access mode is passed in *dwAccess*. If it is **PAGE_NOACCESS**, then no access is allowed. If it is **PAGE_READONLY**, the memory may be read but not written. If it is **PAGE_READWRITE**, read/write access is granted.

The previous access mode is assigned to the variable pointed to by *lpPrev*. If you don't need this information, use NULL for this parameter.

RELATED FUNCTION

VirtualProtectEx()

BOOL VirtualProtectEx(HANDLE *hProcess,*
LPVOID *lpRegion,*
DWORD *dwSize,*
DWORD *dwAccess,*
PDWORD *lpPrev*)

VirtualProtectEx() changes how the specified region of virtual memory may be accessed for the specified process. It returns non-zero if successful, and zero otherwise.

The handle to the process that owns the virtual memory is passed in *hProcess.*

The starting address of the region is pointed to by *lpRegion.* The size of the region is passed in *dwSize.* This memory must have been allocated originally using **VirtualAlloc()**, and it must consist entirely of committed pages.

The new access mode is passed in *dwAccess.* If it is **PAGE_NOACCESS**, then no access is allowed. If it is **PAGE_READONLY**, the memory may be read but not written. If it is **PAGE_READWRITE**, read/write access is granted.

The previous access mode is assigned to the variable pointed to by *lpPrev.* If you don't need this information, use NULL for this parameter.

USAGE

The process being affected must have the **PROCESS_VM_OPERATION** flag set. If it does not, the function will fail.

RELATED FUNCTION

VirtualProtect()

DWORD VirtualQuery(LPVOID *lpRegion,*
PMEMORY_BASIC_INFORMATION *pInfo,*
DWORD *dwSize*)

VirtualQuery() obtains information about the specified virtual memory. It returns the number of bytes copied into the structure pointed to by *pInfo*.

The region of virtual memory in question is pointed to by *lpRegion*.

On return, the **MEMORY_BASIC_INFORMATION** structure pointed to by *pInfo* will contain information about the specified region. *dwSize* must contain the size of the **MEMORY_BASIC_INFORMATION** structure. The **MEMORY_BASIC_INFORMATION** structure is defined like this:

```
typedef struct _MEMORY_BASIC_INFORMATION {
  PVOID BaseAddress;
  PVOID AllocationBase;
  DWORD AllocationProtect;
  DWORD RegionSize;
  DWORD State;
  DWORD Protect;
  DWORD Type;
} MEMORY_BASIC_INFORMATION;
```

Here, **BaseAddress** is the starting address of the memory region specified by *lpRegion*. **AllocationBase** is the starting address of the virtual memory region allocated to the process.

AllocationProtect contains the access mode of the region when it was first allocated. If it is **PAGE_NOACCESS**, then no access is allowed. If it is **PAGE_READONLY**, the memory may be read but not written. If it is **PAGE_READWRITE**, read/write access is granted.

RegionSize is the size of the region. A region is defined by those continuous pages that have identical attributes.

The **State** member contains the status of the region. If it is **MEM_COMMIT**, the region is committed. If it is **MEM_RESERVE**, the memory is reserved. If it is **MEM_FREE**, the memory is not allocated to the calling application.

The current access mode of the region is contained in **Protect**. It will be one of the previously described access modes.

Type contains the **MEM_PRIVATE** value.

RELATED FUNCTION

VirtualQueryEx()

DWORD VirtualQueryEx(HANDLE *hProcess,*
LPVOID *lpRegion,*
PMEMORY_BASIC_INFORMATION *pInfo,*
DWORD *dwSize*)

VirtualQueryEx() obtains information about the specified virtual memory for the specified process. It returns the number of bytes copied into the structure pointed to by *pInfo.*

The handle to the process that owns the memory is passed in *hProcess.*

The region of virtual memory in question is pointed to by *lpRegion.*

On return, the **MEMORY_BASIC_INFORMATION** structure pointed to by *pInfo* will contain information about the specified region. *dwSize* must contain the size of the **MEMORY_BASIC_INFORMATION** structure. The **MEMORY_BASIC_INFORMATION** structure is defined like this:

```
typedef struct _MEMORY_BASIC_INFORMATION {
  PVOID BaseAddress;
  PVOID AllocationBase;
  DWORD AllocationProtect;
  DWORD RegionSize;
  DWORD State;
  DWORD Protect;
  DWORD Type;
} MEMORY_BASIC_INFORMATION;
```

Here, **BaseAddress** is the starting address of the memory region specified by *lpRegion.* **AllocationBase** is the starting address of the virtual memory region allocated to the process.

AllocationProtect contains the access mode of the region when it was first allocated. If it is **PAGE_NOACCESS**, then no access is allowed. If it is **PAGE_READONLY**, the memory may be read but not written. If it is **PAGE_READWRITE**, read/write access is granted.

RegionSize is the size of the region. A region is defined by those continuous pages that have identical attributes.

The **State** member contains the status of the region. If it is **MEM_COM-MIT**, the region is committed. If it is **MEM_RESERVE**, the memory is reserved. If it is **MEM_FREE**, the memory is not allocated to the calling application.

The current access mode of the region is contained in **Protect**. It will be one of the previously described access modes.

Type contains the **MEM_PRIVATE** value.

RELATED FUNCTION

VirtualQuery()

BOOL VirtualUnlock(LPVOID *lpRegion*,   DWORD *dwSize*)

VirtualUnlock() unlocks the specified region of virtual memory, which allows it to be removed from physical memory. It returns non-zero if successful, and zero on failure.

The starting address of the region to unlock is pointed to by *lpRegion*. (This address must have been locked previously through a call to **VirtualLock()**.) The size of the region is passed in *dwSize*.

USAGE

The region that you attempt to lock must consist of committed pages.

VirtualUnlock() *replaces the 16-bit Windows function* **GlobalPageUnlock()**, *which has this prototype:*

UINT GlobalPageUnlock(HGLOBAL hObj);

The function returns the current lock count, or zero if an error occurs. The use of this function is not recommended. If used it must only be called from a DLL.

RELATED FUNCTION

VirtualLock()

A Complete Programming Example

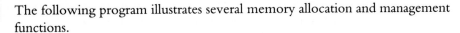 The following program illustrates several memory allocation and management functions.

```
/*
  Using Memory Allocation Functions.
*/

#include <windows.h>

LONG FAR PASCAL WndProc(HWND, UINT, WPARAM, LPARAM);

char szProgName[] = "ProgName"; /* name of window class */
HGLOBAL hMem;
char far *p;

int PASCAL WinMain(HINSTANCE hInst, HINSTANCE hPreInst,
                   LPSTR lpszCmdLine, int nCmdShow)
{
  MSG lpMsg;
  WNDCLASS wcApp;
  HWND hWnd;

  if (!hPreInst) { /* if no previous instance */
    wcApp.lpszClassName = szProgName; /* window class name */
    wcApp.hInstance     = hInst; /* handle to this instance */
    wcApp.lpfnWndProc   = WndProc; /* window function */
    wcApp.hCursor       = LoadCursor(NULL, IDC_ARROW);
    wcApp.hIcon         = LoadIcon(NULL, IDI_APPLICATION);
    wcApp.lpszMenuName  = NULL;

    /* make the background of window white */
    wcApp.hbrBackground = GetStockObject(WHITE_BRUSH);
    wcApp.style         = 0; /* use default window style */
    wcApp.cbClsExtra    = 0; /* no extra info */
    wcApp.cbWndExtra    = 0; /* no extra info */
```

```
      /* register the window class */
      if (!RegisterClass (&wcApp))
        return FALSE;
    }

    /* Now that window has been registered, a window
       can be created. */
    hWnd = CreateWindow(
      szProgName,
      "Demonstrate Allocation Functions",
      WS_OVERLAPPEDWINDOW,
      CW_USEDEFAULT,
      CW_USEDEFAULT,
      CW_USEDEFAULT,
      CW_USEDEFAULT,
      (HWND)NULL,
      (HMENU) NULL,
      (HANDLE)hInst,
      (LPSTR)NULL
    );

    /* Display the Window. */
    ShowWindow(hWnd, nCmdShow);
    UpdateWindow(hWnd);

    /* Create the message loop. */
    while (GetMessage(&lpMsg, NULL, 0, 0)) {
      TranslateMessage(&lpMsg); /* allow use of keyboard */
      DispatchMessage(&lpMsg); /* return control to Windows */
    }
    return(lpMsg.wParam);
}

/* Window Function. */
LONG FAR PASCAL WndProc(HWND hWnd, UINT messg,
                        WPARAM wParam, LPARAM lParam)
{
  HDC hdc;
  PAINTSTRUCT ps;

  switch (messg) {
    case WM_CREATE:
      hMem = GlobalAlloc(GHND, (DWORD) 100);
      if(!hMem) { /* check the pointer */
```

```
        MessageBox(hWnd, "Cannot Allocate", "Error", MB_OK);
        PostQuitMessage(0);
      }

      p = GlobalLock(hMem);
      if(!p) { /* check the pointer */
        MessageBox(hWnd, "Invalid Pointer", "Error", MB_OK);
        PostQuitMessage(0);
      }
      break;

    /* ... */

    case WM_DESTROY: /* terminate the program */
      GlobalUnlock(hMem);
      GlobalFree(hMem);
      PostQuitMessage(0);
      break;
    /* Let Windows process any messages not specified in
       the preceding cases. */
    default:
      return(DefWindowProc(hWnd, messg, wParam, lParam));
  }
  return(0L);
}
```

Chapter 17

Metafiles

T H I S chapter describes Windows metafile functions. These functions can be used to open, close, copy, create, delete, and enumerate both regular and enhanced metafiles. A *metafile* contains a visual image (somewhat similar to a bitmap) that is stored in a device-independent structure. There are two types of metafiles; regular and enhanced. Only regular metafiles are supported by 16-bit Windows. Windows NT/Win32 supports both regular and enhanced metafiles. However, for new Windows NT/Win32 programs, you should use only enhanced metafiles.

A complete programming example is presented at the end of this chapter that demonstrates metafiles.

HENHMETAFILE CloseEnhMetaFile(HDC *hdc*)

CloseEnhMetaFile() closes an enhanced metafile device context. *hdc* is the handle of the enhanced metafile device context. The function returns a handle to the enhanced metafile device context if successful, and NULL otherwise.

USAGE

Closing an enhanced metafile device context is not the same as deleting the device context (see **DeleteEnhMetaFile()**). The handle returned by **CloseEnhMetaFile()** is used by several of the other enhanced metafile functions.

Here is a small portion of code that illustrates the use of this function.

```
static HMETAFILE hMFile;
HDC hEMDC;
LPRECT lpRect;
    .
    .
```

```
        .
case WM_CREATE:
  hEMDC = CreateEnhMetaFile(hdc, NULL, &lpRect, NULL);
  if (hEMDC != NULL) {
    MoveToEx(hdc, 10, 10, NULL);
    LineTo(hdc, 300, 400);
    hEMFile = CloseEnhMetaFile(hEMDC);
  }
      .

      .

  break;

case WM_PAINT:
    .

    .

  PlayEnhMetaFile(hdc, hEMFile, &lpRect);
  break;


case WM_COMMAND:
    .

    .

  CopyEnhMetaFile(hEMFile, "mymeta.mf");
  break;

case WM_DESTROY:
  DeleteEnhMetaFile(hEMFile);
  PostQuitMessage(0);
  break;
```

RELATED FUNCTIONS

CopyEnhMetaFile()
CreateEnhMetaFile()
DeleteEnhMetaFile()
EnumEnhMetaFile()

HMETAFILE CloseMetaFile(HDC *hdc*)

CloseMetaFile() closes a metafile device context. *hdc* is the handle of the metafile device context. The function returns a handle to the metafile if successful, and NULL otherwise.

USAGE

Closing a metafile device context is not the same as deleting a device context (see **DeleteMetaFile()**). After a successful call, the handle returned by **CloseMetaFile()** can be used to display (or otherwise access) the metafile.

Here is a small portion of code that illustrates the use of this function.

```
static HMETAFILE hMFile;
HDC hMDC;
     .
     .
     .
case WM_CREATE:
  hMDC = CreateMetaFile(NULL);
  if (hMDC != NULL) {
    Rectangle(hdc, 10, 10, 100, 200);
    hMFile = CloseMetaFile(hMDC);
  }
     .
     .
     .
  break;

case WM_PAINT:
   .
   .
   .
  PlayMetaFile(hdc, hMFile);
  break;

case WM_COMMAND:
   .
   .
   .
  CopyMetaFile(hMFile, "mymeta.mf");
```

```
  break;

case WM_DESTROY:
  DeleteMetaFile(hMFile);
  PostQuitMessage(0);
  break;
```

RELATED FUNCTIONS

CreateMetaFile()
PlayMetaFile()

HENHMETAFILE CopyEnhMetaFile(HENHMETAFILE *hemf*, LPTSTR *lpszFileName*)

CopyEnhMetaFile() copies the contents of an enhanced metafile. *hemf* is a handle to an enhanced metafile. *lpszFileName* points to a string identifying the file about to receive the copy. The function returns a handle to the copy of the enhanced metafile if successful, and NULL otherwise.

USAGE

When *lpszFileName* is assigned NULL, **CopyEnhMetaFile()** copies the enhanced metafile into memory instead of to an external file. **CopyEnhMetaFile()** is capable of handling either ANSI or Unicode character sets.

Here is a small portion of code that illustrates the use of this function.

```
static HMETAFILE hMFile;
HDC hEMDC;
LPRECT lpRect;

   .

   .

   .
case WM_CREATE:
  hEMDC = CreateEnhMetaFile(hdc, NULL, &lpRect, NULL);
  if (hEMDC != NULL) {
    MoveToEx(hdc, 10, 10, NULL);
    LineTo(hdc, 300, 400);
```

```
        hEMFile = CloseEnhMetaFile(hEMDC);
    }
        .
        .
        .

    break;

case WM_PAINT:
    .

    .

    .
    PlayEnhMetaFile(hdc, hEMFile, &lpRect);
    break;


case WM_COMMAND:
    .

    .

    .
    CopyEnhMetaFile(hEMFile, "mymeta.mf");
    break;

case WM_DESTROY:
    DeleteEnhMetaFile(hEMFile);
    PostQuitMessage(0);
    break;
```

RELATED FUNCTION

DeleteEnhMetaFile()

HMETAFILE CopyMetaFile(HMETAFILE *hmfSource*, LPCSTR *lpszFileName*)

CopyMetaFile() copies a metafile. *hmfSource* is the handle to the metafile about to be copied. *lpszFileName* points to a string identifying the name of the file receiving the copy. The function returns the handle to the new metafile if successful, and NULL otherwise.

USAGE

When *lpszFileName* is assigned NULL, **CopyMetaFile()** copies the metafile directly into memory instead of a file on disk.

Here is a small portion of code that illustrates the use of this function.

```
static HMETAFILE hMFile;
HDC hMDC;
   .

   .

   .
case WM_CREATE:
  hMDC = CreateMetaFile(NULL);
  if (hMDC != NULL) {
    Rectangle(hdc, 10, 10, 100, 200);
    hMFile = CloseMetaFile(hMDC);
  }
     .

     .

     .
  break;

case WM_PAINT:
     .

     .

     .
  PlayMetaFile(hdc, hMFile);
  break;


case WM_COMMAND:
     .

     .

     .
  CopyMetaFile(hMFile, "mymeta.mf");
  break;

case WM_DESTROY:
  DeleteMetaFile(hMFile);
  PostQuitMessage(0);
  break;
```

RELATED FUNCTIONS

GetMetaFile()
PlayMetaFile()

HDC CreateEnhMetaFile(HDC *hdcDevCntxt,*
LPTSTR *lpszFileName,*
LPRECT *lpBoundRect,*
LPTSTR *lpOpDescrip*)

CreateEnhMetaFile() creates a device-independent context using an enhanced metafile device context and returns a handle to the device-independent context. *hdcDevCntxt* is the handle of the target device for the enhanced metafile. *lpszFileName* points to the name of the file that is being created.

lpBoundRect points to a **RECT** structure that contains the dimensions of the object being created. *lpOpDescrip* is an optional pointer to a string identifying the application that originally created the object and the object's title.

The function returns a valid handle to the device context for the enhanced metafile if successful, and NULL otherwise. The returned handle may be used by any GDI drawing function.

RECT is defined like this for Windows NT/Win32.

```
typedef struct tagRECT {
  LONG left;
  LONG top;
  LONG right;
  LONG bottom;
} RECT;
```

USAGE

CreateEnhMetaFile() uses the device context specified by *hdcDevCntxt* to record the resolution and color format of the device that originally created the object. *lpszFileName* may be assigned NULL, forcing **CreateEnhMetaFile()** to create the object in memory instead of being written to an external disk file.

lpOpDescrip is an optional parameter, which is ignored by **CreateEnhMeta-File()** if assigned NULL. When *lpOpDescrip* is used to specify the object's authoring application and title, the pointer must point to a string that separates the application's name from the object's title with a null terminator. The string must end with two nulls. An example string would look like this:

"Creating Application\0Picture Title\0\0"

Here is a small portion of code that illustrates the use of this function.

```
static HMETAFILE hMFile;
HDC hEMDC;
LPRECT lpRect;
    .

    .

    .

case WM_CREATE:
  hEMDC = CreateEnhMetaFile(hdc, NULL, &lpRect, NULL);
  if (hEMDC != NULL) {
    MoveToEx(hdc, 10, 10, NULL);
    LineTo(hdc, 300, 400);
    hEMFile = CloseEnhMetaFile(hEMDC);
  }
    .

    .

    .

  break;

case WM_PAINT:
    .

    .

    .

  PlayEnhMetaFile(hdc, hEMFile, &lpRect);
  break;

case WM_COMMAND:
    .

    .

    .

  CopyEnhMetaFile(hEMFile, "mymeta.mf");
  break;

case WM_DESTROY:
  DeleteEnhMetaFile(hEMFile);
```

```
PostQuitMessage(0);
break;
```

RELATED FUNCTIONS

CloseEnhMetaFile()
DeleteEnhMetaFile()

HDC CreateMetaFile(LPCSTR *lpszFileName*)

CreateMetaFile() creates a metafile device context and returns a handle to it. *lpszFileName* points to a string identifying the file about to receive the created metafile. The function returns a handle to the created metafile device context if successful, and NULL otherwise.

USAGE

lpszFileName may be assigned a NULL instructing **CreateMetaFile()** to store the created metafile device context in memory, instead of exporting the information to an external file.

Here is a small portion of code that illustrates the use of this function.

```
static HMETAFILE hMFile;
HDC hMDC;
    .
    .
    .
case WM_CREATE:
  hMDC = CreateMetaFile(NULL);
  if (hMDC != NULL) {
    Rectangle(hdc, 10, 10, 100, 200);
    hMFile = CloseMetaFile(hMDC);
  }
    .
    .
    .
  break;

case WM_PAINT:
    .
    .
    .
```

```
      PlayMetaFile(hdc, hMFile);
      break;

  case WM_COMMAND:
      .

      .

      .

      CopyMetaFile(hMFile, "mymeta.mf");
      break;

  case WM_DESTROY:
      DeleteMetaFile(hMFile);
      PostQuitMessage(0);
      break;
```

RELATED FUNCTION

DeleteMetaFile()

BOOL DeleteEnhMetaFile(HENHMETAFILE *hemf*)

DeleteEnhMetaFile() deletes the metafile specified by *hemf*. The function returns TRUE if successful, and FALSE otherwise.

USAGE

If the metafile is stored in memory, **DeleteEnhMetaFile()** deletes the metafile, returning the allocated memory to the available memory pool. If the metafile is stored on disk, **DeleteEnhMetafile()** deletes the handle to the metafile, but it does not actually erase the file from disk.

Here is a small portion of code that illustrates the use of this function.

```
static HMETAFILE hMFile;
HDC hEMDC;
LPRECT lpRect;
  .

  .

  .

case WM_CREATE:
    hEMDC = CreateEnhMetaFile(hdc, NULL, &lpRect, NULL);
```

```
    if (hEMDC != NULL) {
      MoveToEx(hdc, 10, 10, NULL);
      LineTo(hdc, 300, 400);
      hEMFile = CloseEnhMetaFile(hEMDC);
    }
        .
        .
        .

  break;

case WM_PAINT:
    .
    .

    .
  PlayEnhMetaFile(hdc, hEMFile, &lpRect);
  break;


case WM_COMMAND:
    .
    .

    .
  CopyEnhMetaFile(hEMFile, "mymeta.mf");
  break;

case WM_DESTROY:
  DeleteEnhMetaFile(hEMFile);
  PostQuitMessage(0);
  break;
```

RELATED FUNCTIONS

CopyEnhMetaFile()
CreateEnhMetaFile()
GetEnhMetaFile()

BOOL DeleteMetaFile(HMETAFILE *hmf*)

DeleteMetaFile() deletes the metafile identified by *hmf*. The function returns TRUE if successful, and FALSE otherwise.

USAGE

If the metafile is stored in memory, **DeleteMetaFile()** deletes the metafile, returning the allocated memory to the available memory pool. If the metafile is stored on disk, **DeleteMetafile()** deletes the handle to the metafile, but it does not actually erase the file from disk.

Here is a small portion of code that illustrates the use of this function.

```
static HMETAFILE hMFile;
HDC hMDC;
    .
    .
    .
case WM_CREATE:
  hMDC = CreateMetaFile(NULL);
  if (hMDC != NULL) {
    Rectangle(hdc, 10, 10, 100, 200);
    hMFile = CloseMetaFile(hMDC);
  }
    .
    .
    .
  break;

case WM_PAINT:
    .
    .
    .
  PlayMetaFile(hdc, hMFile);
  break;

case WM_COMMAND:
    .
    .
    .
  CopyMetaFile(hMFile, "mymeta.mf");
  break;

case WM_DESTROY:
  DeleteMetaFile(hMFile);
```

```
PostQuitMessage(0);
break;
```

RELATED FUNCTIONS

CopyMetaFile()
CreateMetaFile()
GetMetaFile()

BOOL EnumEnhMetaFile(HDC *hdc,*
HENHMETAFILE *hemf,*
ENHMFENUMPROC *lpCallBack,*
LPVOID *lpAppData,*
LPRECT *lpRect*)

EnumEnhMetaFile() successively returns each record from within the enhanced metafile, passing it to the specified callback function for processing. *hdc* gives the device context. *hemf* is the handle of the enhanced metafile. *lpCallBack* identifies the user-defined callback function used to process each record. *lpAppData* identifies optional, user-defined data passed to the callback function. *lpRect* points to a **RECT** structure specifying the enhanced metafile picture's upper-left and lower-right bounding coordinates.

The function returns TRUE if the callback function has enumerated all of the enhanced metafile's records, and FALSE otherwise.

USAGE

If *hdc* is NULL, **EnumEnhMetaFile()** ignores *lpRect*.

The callback function pointed to by *lpcallback* must have the following prototype. (Of course, the name of the function is arbitrary.)

```
int CALLBACK EnhMetaFileFunc(HDC hdc,
           HANDLETABLE FAR *lpHTable,
           ENHMETARECORD FAR *lpMetaRec,
           int iObjCount,
           LPARAM lpAppData)
```

This function successively processes enhanced metafile records. When called by Windows, *hdc* contains the device context. *lpHTable* points to the various handles associated with the object. *lpMetaRec* is passed one of the valid record pointers by **EnumEnhMetaFile()**. *iObjCount* identifies the number of entries in *lpHTable*. *lpAppData* points to user-defined data.

The function must return a non-zero return value if it wants **Enum-EnhMetaFile()** to continue processing enhanced metafile records; a zero return value terminates the enumeration process.

RELATED FUNCTIONS

PlayEnhMetaFile()
PlayEnhMetaFileRecord()

BOOL EnumMetaFile(HDC *hdc*, HLOCAL *hlmf*, MFENUMPROC *mprocCallBack*, LPARAM *lpAppData*)

EnumMetaFile() successively returns each record from within the metafile, passing it to the specified callback function for processing. *hdc* is the handle of the device context. *hlmf* is the handle of the metafile. *mprocCallBack* identifies the application-specific callback function used to process each record. *lpAppData* identifies optional user-defined information passed to the callback function.

The function returns TRUE if the callback function has enumerated all of the enhanced metafile's records, and FALSE otherwise.

USAGE

mprocCallBack points to the procedure-instance address of the user-defined callback function created by a call to **MakeProcInstance()**.

The callback function pointed to by *mprocCallBack* must have the following prototype. (Of course, the name of the function is arbitrary.)

RELATED FUNCTIONS

EnumMetaFileFunc()
PlayMetaFile()

```
int CALLBACK EnumMetaFileFunc(HDC hdc,
                    HANDLETABLE FAR *lpHTable,
                    METARECORD FAR *lpMetaRect,
                    int iObjCount,
                    PARAM lpAppData)
```

This function successively processes metafile records. When called by Windows, *hdc* contains the device context. *lpHTable* points to the various handles associated with the object. *lpMetaRect* is passed one of the valid record pointers by the **EnumMetaFile()** function. *iObjCount* identifies the number of entries in *lpHTable*. *lpAppData* points to user-defined data.

The function must return a non-zero value if it wants **EnumMetaFile()** to continue processing enhanced metafile records; a zero return value terminates the enumeration process.

The application's module definition file must use an **EXPORTS** statement to register the application-defined function name. (**EnumMetaFileFunc()** is used here only as an example.) Also, the callback function must be registered with **EnumMetaFile()** by passing the callback function's address to **Enum-MetaFile()**.

Here is a small portion of code that illustrates the use of this function.

```
static HMETAFILE hMFile;
HDC hMDC;
   .
   .
   .
```

```
case WM_CREATE:
  if(!hMFile) {
    hMFile = GetMetaFile("metafile.mf");
      .
      .
      .
   break;
case WM_PAINT:
    .
    .
    .
  PlayMetaFile(hdc, hMFile);
  break;


case WM_COMMAND:
    .
    .
    .
  fpEnumProc = MakeProcInstance(MF_Function, hInst);
  EnumMetaFile(hdc, hMFile, fpEnumProc, NULL)
  FreeProcInstance(fpEnumProc);
  ReleaseDC(hwnd, hdc);
  break;
```

RELATED FUNCTION

PlayMetaFile()

BOOL GdiComment(HDC *hdc*, UINT *uBuffSize*, LPBYTE *lpBuffAddress*)

GdiComment() copies the information pointed to by *lpBuffAddress* into the enhanced metafile identified by *hdc*. *uBuffSize* contains the size of the buffer, in bytes. The function returns TRUE if successful, and FALSE otherwise.

USAGE

You use **GdiComment()** to add clarifying comments to an enhanced metafile. Of course, such comments are optional.

RELATED FUNCTION

CreateEnhMetaFile()

HENHMETAFILE GetEnhMetaFile(LPTSTR *lpszFileName*)

GetEnhMetaFile() returns a handle to an enhanced metafile. *lpszFileName* is a pointer to the name of the source file for the enhanced metafile. The function returns a valid enhanced metafile handle if successful, and NULL otherwise.

USAGE

GetEnhMetaFile() is capable of handling either ANSI or Unicode character set filenames. **GetEnhMetaFile()** cannot process Windows 3.*x* metafile formats without first calling **SetWinMetaFileBits()** to convert it to the Windows NT enhanced metafile format.

Here is a small portion of code that illustrates the use of this function.

```
static HMETAFILE hEMFile;
    .
    .
    .
case WM_CREATE:
  if(!hEMFile) {
    hEMFile = GetEnhMetaFile("metafile.mf");
    .
    .
    .
  break;
```

RELATED FUNCTION

SetWinMetaFileBits()

UINT GetEnhMetaFileBits(HENHMETAFILE *hemf,*
UINT *uBufferSize,*
LPBYTE *lpBuffAddress)*

GetEnhMetaFileBits() obtains a copy of the specified enhanced metafile. *hemf* is the handle to the enhanced metafile about to be copied. *uBufferSize* contains the size of the buffer, in bytes. *lpBuffAddress* is a pointer to the buffer into which the metafile will be copied. The function returns the number of bytes copied if successful, and zero otherwise.

USAGE

If *lpBuffAddress* is assigned NULL, **GetEnhMetaFileBits()** returns the number of bytes necessary to hold the enhanced metafile. This information can then be used in a subsequent call to **GetEnhMetaFileBits()**, with the *uBufferSize* parameter set to the previous function call's return value.

RELATED FUNCTIONS

GetWinMetaFileBits()
SetEnhMetaFileBits()

UINT GetEnhMetaFileDescription(HENHMETAFILE *hemf,*
UINT *uBuffSize,*
LPTSTR *lpszBuffer)*

GetEnhMetaFileDescription() obtains a copy of the optional enhanced metafile description. *hemf* is the handle of the enhanced metafile. *uBuffSize* indicates the size of the buffer, in bytes. *lpszBuffer* is a pointer to the buffer receiving the copy of the enhanced metafile description. The function returns the number of characters copied into the buffer if successful, and NULL otherwise.

USAGE

Your application can determine if the enhanced metafile has an optional description by first making a call to **GetEnhMetaFileDescription()** with *lpszBuffer* being NULL. When *lpszBuffer* is NULL, the function returns the number of characters in the optional description if available (but does not copy the description). It returns NULL otherwise.

RELATED FUNCTION

CreateEnhMetaFile()

UINT GetEnhMetaFileHeader(HENHMETAFILE *hemf*,
UINT uBuffSize,
LPENHMETAHEADER lpemh)

GetEnhMetaFileHeader() obtains a copy of the enhanced metafile header. *hemf* gives the enhanced metafile. *uBuffSize* contains the size of the buffer, in bytes. *lpemh* is a pointer to the buffer receiving the copy of the enhanced metafile header. The function returns the number of bytes copied into the buffer if successful, and NULL otherwise.

USAGE

Your application can determine the size of the enhanced metafile header by first making a call to **GetEnhMetaFileHeader()** with *lpemh* being NULL. When *lpemh* is NULL, the function returns the number of characters in the header if available (but does not copy the header). It returns NULL otherwise.

RELATED FUNCTION

PlayEnhMetaFile()

UINT GetEnhMetaFilePaletteEntries
(HENHMETAFILE hemf,
UINT UEntryCount,
LPPALETTEENTRY lppe)

GetEnhMetaFilePaletteEntries() obtains a copy of the optional enhanced metafile color palette entries. *hemf* is the handle of the enhanced metafile.

uEntryCount contains the number of colors to obtain. *lppe* is a pointer to an array of **PALETTEENTRY** structures. The function returns the number of entries obtained if successful, and NULL otherwise.

The **PALETTEENTRY** structure is shown here.

```
typedef struct tagPALETTEENTRY {
  BYTE peRed;
  BYTE peGreen;
  BYTE peBlue;
  BYTE peFlags;
} PALETTEENTRY;
```

In this structure **peRed** gives a red intensity value, **peGreen** gives a green intensity value, and **peBlue** gives a blue intensity value. **peFlags** gives how the palette entry will be used and can be any of the following values: **PC_EX-PLICIT** (the low-order word of the logical palette entry designates a hardware palette index), **PC_NOCOLLAPSE** (the color will be placed in an unused entry in the palette instead of being matched to an existing color), and **PC_RESERVED** (the logical palette entry will be used for palette animation).

USAGE

Your application can determine if the enhanced metafile has any optional color palette entries by first making a call to **GetEnhMetaFilePaletteEntries()** with *lppe* being NULL. When *lppe* is NULL, the function returns the number of entries in the optional color palette if available (but does not copy the color palette entries). It returns NULL otherwise.

RELATED FUNCTION

PlayEnhMetaFile()

HMETAFILE GetMetaFile(LPCTSTR *lpszFileName*)

The **GetMetaFile()** function returns a handle to a metafile. *lpszFileName* is a pointer to the name of the source file containing the metafile. The function returns a valid metafile handle if successful, and NULL otherwise.

USAGE

Here is a small portion of code that illustrates the use of this function.

```
      static HMETAFILE hMFile;
      HDC hMDC;
                .
                .
                .

      case WM_CREATE:
        if(!hMFile) {
          hMFile = GetMetaFile("metafile.mf");
              .
              .
              .

         break;
      case WM_PAINT:
              .
              .
              .

         PlayMetaFile(hdc, hMFile);
         break;


      case WM_COMMAND:
              .
              .
              .

         fpEnumProc = MakeProcInstance(MF_Function, hInst);
         EnumMetaFile(hdc, hMFile, fpEnumProc, NULL)
         FreeProcInstance(fpEnumProc);
         ReleaseDC(hwnd, hdc);
         break;
```

RELATED FUNCTION

DeleteMetaFile()

HGLOBAL GetMetaFileBits(HMETAFILE *hmf*)

GetMetaFileBits() returns a handle to a metafile held in global memory. *hmf* is the handle of the global memory metafile. The function returns a valid handle if successful, and NULL otherwise.

USAGE

Your application must use the returned global memory handle to refer to the metafile after calling **GetMetaFileBits()**, since the function call invalidates *hmf*. Your application should call the **GlobalFree()** function to free the global memory metafile when it is no longer needed.

Here is a small portion of code that illustrates the use of this function.

```
static HMETAFILE hMFile;
HDC hMDC;
HGLOBAL hMem;
    .
    .
    .

case WM_COMMAND:
    .
    .
    .


    hMem = GetMetaFileBits(hMFile);
    break;
```

RELATED FUNCTION

GlobalFree()

UINT GetMetaFileBitsEx(HMETAFILE *hmf,*
UINT *uBuffSize,*
LPVOID *lpvMetaData*)

GetMetaFileBitsEx() copies a metafile. *hmf* is the handle of the metafile. *uBuffSize* contains the size of the buffer, in bytes, that receives the copied metafile. *lpvMetaData* points to the buffer receiving the copied metafile. The function returns the number of bytes copied into the buffer if successful, and NULL otherwise.

USAGE

When *lpvMetaData* is assigned NULL, the function returns the number of bytes needed to store the copied metafile, but does not make the copy.

RELATED FUNCTION

SetMetaFileBitsEx()

UINT GetWinMetaFileBits(HENHMETAFILE *hemf*,
UINT *uBuffSize*,
LPBYTE *lpBuffer*,
int *iMapMode*, HDC *hdc*)

GetWinMetaFileBits() converts enhanced metafile record formats into the 16-bit Windows metafile formats. *hemf* is the handle of the enhanced metafile. *uBuffSize* contains the size of the buffer, in bytes, that receives the converted records. *lpBuffer* is a pointer to the buffer receiving the converted records.

The mapping mode used to create the enhanced metafile is passed in *iMapMode*. *hdc* is the handle of the device context. The function returns the number of bytes copied into the buffer if successful, and NULL otherwise.

USAGE

lpBuffer may be assigned NULL, instructing **GetWinMetaFileBits()** to return the minimum size of the buffer pointed to by *lpBuffer*. (In this case, no conversion is performed.)

RELATED FUNCTION

DeleteEnhMetaFile()

BOOL PlayEnhMetaFile(HDC *hdc,*
HENHMETAFILE *hemf,*
LPRECT *lpRect*)

PlayEnhMetaFile() plays (displays) an enhanced metafile. *hdc* is the handle of the device context. *hemf* is the handle of the enhanced metafile. *lpRect* is a pointer to a **RECT** structure that contains the dimensions of the object. The function returns TRUE if successful, and FALSE otherwise.

USAGE

Here is a small portion of code that illustrates the use of this function.

```
 static HMETAFILE hMFile;
HDC hEMDC;
LPRECT lpRect;
  .
  .
  .
case WM_CREATE:
  hEMDC = CreateEnhMetaFile(hdc, NULL, &lpRect, NULL);
  if (hEMDC != NULL) {
    MoveToEx(hdc, 10, 10, NULL);
    LineTo(hdc, 300, 400);
    hEMFile = CloseEnhMetaFile(hEMDC);
  }
    .
    .
    .

  break;

case WM_PAINT:
  .
  .
```

```
        .
    PlayEnhMetaFile(hdc, hEMFile, &lpRect);
    break;


case WM_COMMAND:
    .

    .

    .
    CopyEnhMetaFile(hEMFile, "mymeta.mf");
    break;

case WM_DESTROY:
    DeleteEnhMetaFile(hEMFile);
    PostQuitMessage(0);
    break;
```

Any thread may make a call to **CancelDC()** to abort the **PlayEnhMeta-File()** function.

RELATED FUNCTION

CancelDC()

BOOL PlayEnhMetaFileRecord(HDC *hdc,*
LPHANDLETABLE *lpHTable,*
LPENHMETARECORD *lpemRec,*
UINT *uHandleCount*)

PlayEnhMetaFileRecord() plays (displays) an enhanced metafile, record-by-record. *hdc* is the handle of the device context. *lpHTable* is a pointer to the enhanced metafile handle table. *lpemRec* points to the enhanced metafile record about to be displayed. The number of entries in *lpHTable* is passed in *uHandle-Count.* The function returns TRUE if successful, and FALSE otherwise.

RELATED FUNCTIONS

EnumEnhMetaFile()
EnumEnhMetaFileFunc()

BOOL PlayMetaFile(HDC *hdc,* HMETAFILE *hmf*)

PlayMetaFile() plays (displays) a metafile. *hdc* is a handle of the device context. *hmf* is a handle to the metafile. The function returns TRUE if successful, and FALSE otherwise.

USAGE

Here is a small portion of code that illustrates the use of this function.

```
static HMETAFILE hMFile;
HDC hMDC;
  .
  .
  .
case WM_CREATE:
  hMDC = CreateMetaFile(NULL);
  if (hMDC != NULL) {
    Rectangle(hdc, 10, 10, 100, 200);
    hMFile = CloseMetaFile(hMDC);
  }
    .
    .
    .
  break;

case WM_PAINT:
  .
  .
  .
  PlayMetaFile(hdc, hMFile);
  break;


case WM_COMMAND:
  .
  .
  .
  CopyMetaFile(hMFile, "mymeta.mf");
  break;

case WM_DESTROY:
  DeleteMetaFile(hMFile);
```

```
PostQuitMessage(0);
break;
```

RELATED FUNCTION

PlayMetaFileRecord()

void PlayMetaFileRecord(HDC *hdc*, HANDLETABLE FAR★ *lpHTable*, METARECORD FAR★ *lpMetaRec*, UINT *uHandleCount*)

PlayMetaFileRecord() plays (displays) a metafile, record-by-record. *hdc* is the handle of the device context. *lpHTable* is a pointer to the metafile handle table. *lpMetaRec* points to the metafile record about to be played. The number of entries in *lpHTable* is passed in *uHandleCount*. The function returns TRUE if successful, and FALSE otherwise.

RELATED FUNCTIONS

EnumMetaFile()
EnumMetaFileFunc()

HENHMETAFILE SetEnhMetaFileBits(UINT *uBuffSize*, LPBYTE *lpMetaData*)

SetEnhMetaFileBits() creates an enhanced metafile that is stored in memory. *uBuffSize* contains the size of the *lpMetaData* buffer. *lpMetaData* points to the buffer containing the enhanced metafile. The function returns a valid enhanced metafile if successful, and NULL otherwise.

USAGE

The function cannot process 16-bit Windows-format metafiles without first making a translation to the enhanced metafile format using a call to **SetWin-MetaFileBits()**. *lpMetaData* obtains its metafile information with a call to

GetEnhMetaFileBits(). Calling **DeleteEnhMetaFile()** deletes the metafile when it is no longer needed.

RELATED FUNCTIONS

DeleteEnhMetaFile()
GetEnhMetaFileBits()
SetWinMetaFileBits()

HGLOBAL SetMetaFileBits(HMETAFILE *hmf*)

SetMetaFileBits() creates a metafile that is stored in memory. *hmf* is the handle of the metafile data being used to create the memory metafile. The function either returns a valid handle to a memory metafile if successful, or NULL otherwise.

USAGE

Since Windows reuses the *hmf* handle, your application must use the global handle returned by **SetMetaFileBits()**. A call to **DeleteMetaFile()** frees the handle.

Here is a small portion of code that illustrates the use of this function.

```
static HMETAFILE hMFile;
HDC hMDC;
HGLOBAL hMem;
   .
   .
   .
case WM_COMMAND:
   .
   .
   .

  hMFile = SetMetaFileBits(hMem);
  break;

case WM_DESTROY:
  DeleteMetaFile(hMFile);
  PostQuitMessage(0);
  break;
```

RELATED FUNCTIONS

DeleteMetaFile()
GetMetaFileBits()

HMETAFILE SetMetaFileBitsEx(UINT *uBuffSize,*
LPBYTE *lpMetaData*)

SetMetaFileBitsEx() creates a 16-bit Windows-format, memory-based metafile. *uBuffSize* contains the size of the *lpMetaData* buffer. *lpMetaData* points to the metafile data. The function returns a handle to the created metafile if successful, and NULL otherwise.

USAGE

lpMetaData obtains its information from a previous call to **GetMetaFileBits-Ex()**. Conversions from 16-bit Windows-format metafiles to enhanced-format metafiles are accomplished with calls to **SetWinMetaFileBits()**. A call to **DeleteMetaFile()** frees the handle when it is no longer needed.

RELATED FUNCTIONS

DeleteMetaFile()
GetMetaFileBitsEx()
SetWinMetaFileBits()

HENHMETAFILE SetWinMetaFileBits(UINT *uBuffSize,*
LPBYTE *lpMetaData,*
HDC *hdc,*
LPMETAFILEPICT *lpmfp*)

SetWinMetaFileBits() converts a 16-bit Windows-format metafile into an enhanced-format metafile. *uBuffSize* contains the size of the Windows-format metafile. *lpMetaData* points to the 16-bit Windows-format metafile. *hdc* gives the device context. *lpmfp* is a pointer to a **METAFILEPICT** structure identifying the desired size and mapping mode used to create the Windows-format metafile. The function returns a handle to the newly created memory-based enhanced metafile if successful, and NULL otherwise.

The **METAFILEPICT** structure is shown here. **mm** contains the mapping mode where the picture is drawn. **xExt** contains the size of the metafile picture (excluding **MM_ISOTROPIC** and **MM_ANISOTROPIC**). **yExt** gives the size of the metafile picture (excluding **MM_ISOTROPIC** and **MM_AN-ISOTROPIC**). **hMF** is the handle of the memory metafile.

```
typedef struct tagMETAFILEPICT {
   LONG mm;
   LONG xExt;
   LONG yExt;
   HMETAFILE hMF;
} METAFILEPICT;
```

USAGE

If *hdc* is assigned NULL, **SetWinMetaFileBits()** uses the current output device resolution. When *hdc* is not NULL, the function uses the resolution of the specified device. Assigning a NULL to *lpmfp* forces the function to use the default **MM_ANISOTROPIC** mapping mode. A call to **DeleteEnhMetaFile()** frees the enhanced metafile handle when it is no longer needed.

RELATED FUNCTIONS

DeleteEnhMetaFile()
GetWinMetaFileBits()

A Complete Programming Example

Here are two simple metafile example programs. The first program creates a metafile named METAFILE.WMF. This metafile contains the description for a rectangle. The second program plays the metafile created by the first program. Both programs can be compiled within the IDE of either the Borland or Microsoft compilers. If you are compiling from the command line, you will have to create a MAKE file, too.

Here is the code for the first program, called CREMETA.C.

```
/*

  Create a Metafile
```

```
*/

#include <windows.h>

int PASCAL WinMain(HANDLE hInstance, HANDLE hPreInstance,
                   LPSTR lpszCmdLine, int nCmdShow)
{
  HDC hMetaFile = CreateMetaFile("METAFILE.WMF");
  Rectangle (hMetaFile, 20, 20, 200, 200);
  DeleteMetaFile(CloseMetaFile (hMetaFile));
  return FALSE;
}
```

Here is the code for the second program, called PLAYMETA.C.

```
/*
   Plays a previously created metafile named METAFILE.WMF.
   This file was created by CREMETA.C program.
*/

#include <windows.h>

LONG FAR PASCAL WndProc(HWND, UINT, WPARAM, LPARAM);

char szProgName[] = "ProgName"; /* name of window class */

int PASCAL WinMain(HINSTANCE hInst, HINSTANCE hPreInst,
                   LPSTR lpszCmdLine, int nCmdShow)
{
  HWND hWnd;
  MSG lpMsg;
  WNDCLASS wcApp;

  if (!hPreInst) { /* if no previous instance */
    wcApp.lpszClassName = szProgName; /* window class name */
    wcApp.hInstance     = hInst; /* handle to this instance */
    wcApp.lpfnWndProc   = WndProc; /* window function */
    wcApp.hCursor       = LoadCursor(NULL, IDC_ARROW);
    wcApp.hIcon         = LoadIcon(NULL, IDI_APPLICATION);
    wcApp.lpszMenuName  = NULL;

    /* make the background of window gray */
```

```
    wcApp.hbrBackground = GetStockObject(GRAY_BRUSH);
    wcApp.style         = 0; /* use default window style */
    wcApp.cbClsExtra    = 0; /* no extra info */
    wcApp.cbWndExtra    = 0; /* no extra info */

    /* register the window class */
    if (!RegisterClass (&wcApp))
      return FALSE;
  }


  /* Now that window has been registered, a window
     can be created. */
  hWnd = CreateWindow(szProgName,
                      "Metafile Demonstration",
                      WS_OVERLAPPEDWINDOW,
                      CW_USEDEFAULT,
                      CW_USEDEFAULT,
                      CW_USEDEFAULT,
                      CW_USEDEFAULT,
                      (HWND)NULL,
                      (HMENU) NULL,
                      (HANDLE)hInst,
                      (LPSTR)NULL);

  /* Display the Window. */
  ShowWindow(hWnd, nCmdShow);
  UpdateWindow(hWnd);

  /* Create the message loop. */
  while (GetMessage(&lpMsg, NULL, 0, 0)) {
    TranslateMessage(&lpMsg); /* allow use of keyboard */
    DispatchMessage(&lpMsg); /* return control to Windows */
  }
  return(lpMsg.wParam);
}

LONG FAR PASCAL WndProc(HWND hWnd, UINT messg,
                        WPARAM wParam, LPARAM lParam)
{
  PAINTSTRUCT ps;
  HDC hdc;
  HANDLE hmf;
```

```
switch (messg) {
  case WM_PAINT:
    hdc = BeginPaint(hWnd, &ps);

    hmf = GetMetaFile("METAFILE.WMF");
    PlayMetaFile(hdc, hmf);

    DeleteMetaFile(hmf);
    EndPaint(hWnd, &ps);
    break;

  case WM_DESTROY: /* terminate the program */
    PostQuitMessage(0);
    break;

  default:
    return(DefWindowProc(hWnd, messg, wParam, lParam));
  }
  return(0L);
}
```

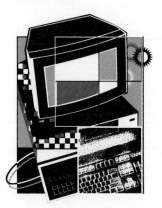

Chapter 18

MCI Functions

T H I S chapter describes Windows' high-level MCI (Media Control Interface) functions. The MCI functions are used to control various devices, such as tape recorders, video cassette players, and music sequencers.

The MCI functions communicate with a device by passing it messages. Along with each message is a structure and a set of flags related to that message. The MCI messages are described in Appendix A.

HANDLE mciGetCreatorTask(MCIDEVICEID *IDDevice*)

mciGetCreatorTask() returns the handle of the task that opened a device. *IDDevice* is the ID of the device whose creator task is to be obtained. When the function is successful, it returns the handle of the task that opened the device. When the device ID is not valid, the function returns NULL.

MCIDEVICEID mciGetDeviceID(LPCTSTR *lpszDevice*)

mciGetDeviceID() returns the device ID of the named device. *lpszDevice* is a pointer to the name of the device.

When the function is successful, it returns the device ID. On failure, it returns zero.

BOOL mciGetErrorString(DWORD *fdwError,*
LPTSTR *lpszErrorString,*
UINT *nSize*)

mciGetErrorString() obtains a string describing an MCI error code. *fdwError* contains the error code. This code is returned by either

mciSendCommand() or **mciSendString()**. *lpszErrorString* is a pointer to a character array that receives the error string. *nSize* contains the length of the buffer pointed to by *lpszErrorString* in characters.

USAGE

Here is a small piece of code that illustrates the use of this function.

```
DWORD dwmciError;

void MCIErrors(HWND hwnd, DWORD dwError)
{
  static char szErrorString[40];

  mciGetErrorString(dwmciError, szErrorString, 40);
  MessageBox(hwnd, szErrorString, szApplName,
             MB_ICONHAND | MB_OK);}
```

The function returns TRUE when successful, and FALSE otherwise.

YIELDPROC mciGetYieldProc(MCIDEVICEID *IDDevice*, LPDWORD *lpdwYieldData*)

mciGetYieldProc() returns the address of the callback function that is called by Windows when it is waiting for an MCI command to finish. This function is only called if the **MCI_WAIT** flag was specified when the command was executed.

IDDevice contains the MCI device being watched. Yield data that will be passed to the wait callback function is passed in the buffer pointed to by *lpdwYieldData*. (*lpdwYieldData* can be NULL when there is no yield data.)

When this function is successful, it returns the address of the yield callback function. When the device ID is not valid, the function returns NULL.

RELATED FUNCTION

mciSetYieldProc()

MCIERROR mciSendCommand (MCIDEVICEID *IDDevice*, UINT *uMsg*, DWORD *dwFlags*, DWORD *dwStruct*)

mciSendCommand() transmits a message (i.e., a command) to an MCI device.

IDDevice contains the device ID of the MCI device being sent the command. The command, itself, is passed in *uMsg*. *dwFlags* contains flags related to the command. *dwStruct* contains a pointer to a structure associated with the command. (The command messages and their related flags and structures are described in Appendix A.)

The function returns zero if successful, and an error code if unsuccessful. The error codes are shown here.

Value	Purpose
MCIERR_BAD_TIME_FORMAT	Illegal time format.
MCIERR_CANNOT_USE_ALL	"All" not allowed.
MCIERR_CREATEWINDOW	Window cannot be created or used.
MCIERR_DEVICE_LOCKED	Device locked until it closes.
MCIERR_DEVICE_NOT_READY	Device not ready.
MCIERR_DEVICE_TYPE_REQUIRED	Device name must be valid device type.
MCIERR_DRIVER	Unspecified device error.
MCIERR_DRIVER_INTERNAL	Internal driver error.
MCIERR_FILE_NOT_FOUND	File not found.
MCIERR_FILE_NOT_SAVED	File not saved.
MCIERR_FILE_READ	File read operation failed.
MCIERR_FILE_WRITE	File write operation failed.
MCIERR_FLAGS_NOT_COMPATIBLE	Incompatible parameter specification.
MCIERR_HARDWARE	Hardware error on the media device.
MCIERR_INTERNAL	Internal error.
MCIERR_INVALID_DEVICE_ID	Invalid device identifier.
MCIERR_INVALID_DEVICE_NAME	Device not open, or unknown.
MCIERR_INVALID_FILE	File format invalid.
MCIERR_MULTIPLE	Errors occurred in multiple devices.
MCIERR_NO_WINDOW	No display window.
MCIERR_NULL_PARAMETER_BLOCK	Pointer to structure was NULL.
MCIERR_OUT_OF_MEMORY	Not enough memory.

Value	Purpose
MCIERR_OUTOFRANGE	Value out of range.
MCIERR_UNNAMED_RESOURCE	File unnamed.
MCIERR_UNRECOGNIZED_COMMAND	Command unknown.
MCIERR_UNSUPPORTED_FUNCTION	Action unavailable.
MCIERR_SEQ_DIV_INCOMPATIBLE	Set song pointer incompatible.
MCIERR_SEQ_PORT_INUSE	Specified port in use.
MCIERR_SEQ_PORT_MAPNODEVICE	Current map to nonexistent device.
MCIERR_SEQ_PORT_MISCERROR	Miscellaneous error with port.
MCIERR_SEQ_PORT_NONEXISTENT	Port does not exist.
MCIERR_SEQ_PORTUNSPECIFIED	No MIDI port specified.
MCIERR_SEQ_NOMIDIPRESENT	No MIDI ports present.
MCIERR_SEQ_TIMER	Timer error.
MCIERR_WAVE_INPUTSINUSE	No waveform recording device free.
MCIERR_WAVE_INPUTSUNSUITABLE	No waveform recording device available.
MCIERR_WAVE_INPUTUNSPECIFIED	Any waveform recording device can be used.
MCIERR_WAVE_OUTPUTSINUSE	No waveform playback device free.
MCIERR_WAVE_OUTPUTSUNSUITABLE	No waveform playback device available.
MCIERR_WAVE_OUTPUTUNSPECIFIED	Any waveform playback device can be used.
MCIERR_WAVE_SETINPUTINUSE	Set waveform recording device in use.
MCIERR_WAVE_ SETINPUTUNSUITABLE	Set waveform recording device not compatible with set format.
MCIERR_WAVE_SETOUTPUTINUSE	Set waveform playback device in use.
MCIERR_WAVE_ SETOUTPUTUNSUITABLE	Set waveform playback device not compatible with set format.

USAGE

Here is a small piece of code that illustrates the use of this function.

```
DWORD dwmciError;
MCI_OPEN_PARAMS mciOpenParm;
    .
    .
    .
mciOpenParm.dwCallback = 0L;
mciOpenParm.wDeviceID = 0;
mciOpenParm.WReserved0 = 0;
mciOpenParm.lpstrDeviceType = NULL;
mciOpenParm.lpstrElementName = szFileName;
mciOpenParm.lpstrAlias = NULL;
```

```
              .
              .
              .
dwmciError = mciSendCommand(0, MCI_OPEN,
                    MCI_WAIT | MCI_OPEN_ELEMENT,
                    (DWORD) (LPMCI_OPEN_PARMS) &mciOpenParm);
              .
              .
              .
```

RELATED FUNCTIONS

mciGetErrorString()
mciSendString()

MCIERROR mciSendString(LPCTSTR *lpszCommand*,
LPTSTR *lpszRetInfo*,
UINT *nSize*,
HANDLE *hwndCallback*)

mciSendString() transmits a command string to the MCI device. The device affected is contained in the command string.

lpszCommand is a pointer to a null-terminated string that contains the MCI command. MCI command strings have the following general form.

[*command*] [*device*] [*parameters*]

lpszRetInfo is a pointer to a character array. On return, this array will contain information returned by the device. It can be NULL if no information is needed. *nSize* gives the size of the *lpszRetInfo* array. *hwndCallback* contains the handle of the callback window. This parameter is only meaningful when **"notify"** is included in the command string.

The function returns zero if successful, and an error code if unsuccessful. These error values can be any of those shown here. (The error return codes for **mciSendCommand()** also apply.)

Value	Purpose
MCIERR_BAD_CONSTANT	Value is unknown.
MCIERR_BAD_INTEGER	Integer in command is invalid or missing.

Value	Purpose
MCIERR_DUPLICATE_FLAGS	Flag/value given twice.
MCIERR_MISSING_COMMAND_STRING	No command given.
MCIERR_MISSING_DEVICE_NAME	No device name given.
MCIERR_MISSING_STRING_ARGUMENT	String value missing from command.
MCIERR_NEW_REQUIRES_ALIAS	Alias must be used with "new" device name.
MCIERR_NO_CLOSING_QUOTE	Closing quotation mark missing.
MCIERR_NOTIFY_ON_AUTO_OPEN	"Notify" flag illegal with auto-open.
MCIERR_PARAM_OVERFLOW	Output string not long enough.
MCIERR_PARSER_INTERNAL	Internal parser error.
MCIERR_UNRECOGNIZED_KEYWORD	Unknown command parameter specified.

RELATED FUNCTIONS

mciGetErrorString()
mciSendCommand()

BOOL mciSetYieldProc(MCIDEVICEID *IDDevice,*
YIELDPROC *YieldProc,*
DWORD *dwYieldData*)

mciSetYieldProc() registers the address of the callback function that is called by Windows when it is waiting for an MCI command to finish. This function is only called if the **MCI_WAIT** flag was specified when the command was executed.

IDDevice contains the ID of the device that the procedure will monitor. *YieldProc* contains the address of the procedure. This value can be NULL, in which case the function disables any existing yield procedure. *dwYieldData* contains user-defined data that is sent to the yield procedure.

The function returns TRUE when successful, and FALSE otherwise.

RELATED FUNCTION

mciGetYieldProc()

Chapter 19

Multimedia Timers

T H I S chapter describes Windows' multimedia timer and related functions. These functions can be used to start and stop system timers, get time values, and so on.

WORD timeBeginPeriod(WORD *wResolution*)

Your application or driver must call **timeBeginPeriod()** to set the minimum timer resolution before using any timer event services. *wResolution* specifies, in milliseconds, the timer resolution. The function returns zero if successful, or **TIMERR_NOCANDO** otherwise.

Under Windows NT, wResolution is of type **UINT** *and the function's return type is* **MMRESULT**.

USAGE

Your application should call **timeEndPeriod()** as soon as timer event services are no longer required.

This fragment illustrates **timeBeginPeriod()**.

```
#define RES 2        /* a 2 millisecond accuracy */

TIMECAPS tmcap;
UINT wTResol;

timeGetDevCaps(&tmcap, sizeof(TIMECAPS));
wTResol = min(max(tmcap.wPeriodMin, RES), tmcap.wPeriodMax);
timeBeginPeriod(wTResol);
```

RELATED FUNCTION

timeEndPeriod()

WORD timeEndPeriod(WORD *wResolution*)

timeEndPeriod() resets any timer resolutions set with **timeBeginPeriod()**.
wResolution must match the millisecond timer resolution specified in the
previous call to **timeBeginPeriod()**. The function returns zero if successful,
or **TIMERR_NOCANDO** otherwise.

NOTE

Under Windows NT, wResolution *is of type* **UINT** *and the function's return type is*
MMRESULT.

USAGE

Each call to **timeBeginPeriod()** must be matched with a call to **timeEnd-
Period()**, using the same *wResolution* value.

Your application should call **timeEndPeriod()** when timer event services
are no longer required.

This fragment illustrates **timeEndPeriod()**.

```
#define RES 2        /* a 2 millisecond accuracy */

TIMECAPS tmcap;
UINT wTResol;

timeGetDevCaps(&tmcap, sizeof(TIMECAPS));
wTResol = min(max(tmcap.wPeriodMin, RES), tmcap.wPeriodMax);
timeEndPeriod(wTResol);
```

RELATED FUNCTION

timeBeginPeriod()

MMRESULT timeGetDevCaps(LPTIMECAPS *lpTimeCaps,* UINT *uStrucSize*)

timeGetDevCaps() obtains the capabilities of a specific timer device. *lpTimeCaps* is a pointer to a **TIMECAPS** structure that, on return, will contain the timer capabilities. *uStrucSize* contains the size of the **TIMECAPS** structure, in bytes. The function returns zero if successful, or **TIMERR_NOCANDO** otherwise.

The **TIMECAPS** structure is shown here.

```
typedef struct timecaps_tag {
  UINT wPeriodMin;
  UINT wPeriodMax;
} TIMECAPS;
```

Here, **wPeriodMin** and **wPeriodMax** contain the minimum and the maximum period supported by the timer, respectively. Both of these values are in milliseconds.

USAGE

Here is a small portion of code that illustrates the use of this function.

```
LPTIMECAPS lpmytimecaps;
    .
    .
    .
timeGetDevCaps(lpmytimecaps, sizeof(LPTIMECAPS));
if (lpmytimecaps.wPeriodMax >= lpmytimecaps.wPeriodMin) {
    .
    .
    .
```

RELATED FUNCTION

GetDeviceCaps()

MMRESULT timeGetSystemTime
(LPMMTIME *lpMMTime,*
UINT *uStrucSize*)

timeGetSystemTime() obtains the elapsed time since Windows was started. *lpMMTime* points to an **MMTIME** structure and *uStrucSize* specifies the size, in bytes, of this structure. On return, the **MMTIME** structure will contain the elapsed time. The function returns zero if successful.

The **MMTIME** is shown here.

```
typedef struct mmtime_tag {
  WORD wType;
  union {
    DWORD ms;
    DWORD sample;
    DWORD cb;
    struct {
      BYTE hour;
      BYTE min;
      BYTE sec;
      BYTE frame;
      BYTE fps;
      BYTE dummy;
    } smpte;
    struct {
      DWORD songptrpos;
    } midi;
  } u;
} MMTIME;
```

Here, **wType** specifies the type of data stored in the union. It can be one of the following values: **TIME_MS** (union contains time in milliseconds), **TIME_SAMPLES** (union contains number of wave samples), **TIME_BYTES** (union contains byte offset), **TIME_SMPTE** (union contains

Society of Motion Picture and Television Engineers time), or **TIME_MIDI** (union contains Musical Instrument Digital Interface time).

The union members are **ms** (milliseconds), **sample** (number of samples), **cb** (byte count), **smpte** (SMPTE time), or **midi** (MIDI time). Of these, only **ms** is used by the **timeGetSystemTime()** functions.

The **smpte** structure uses the following members: **hour** (hours), **min** (minutes), **sec** (seconds), **frame** (frames), **fps** (frames per second), and **dummy** (for alignment).

The **midi** structure member is **songptrpos** and is used as a song pointer position counter.

USAGE

Upon returning from the call to **timeGetsystemTime()**, your application can examine the **ms** field of the **MMTIME** structure to find out the elapsed time in milliseconds.

Here is a small portion of code that illustrates the use of this function.

```
LPMMTIME lpmytime;
      .
      .
      .
timeGetSystemTime(lpmytime, sizeof(LPMMTIME));
if (lpmytime.ms > 1000 ) {
      .
      .
      .
```

RELATED FUNCTION

timeGetTime()

DWORD timeGetTime(void)

timeGetTime() returns the number of elapsed milliseconds since Windows was started.

USAGE

timeGetTime() does not use the multimedia **MMTIME** structure to return elapsed time.

Here is a small portion of code that illustrates the use of this function.

```
DWORD dwTotalElap;
    .
    .
    .
dwTotalElap = timeGetTime();
```

RELATED FUNCTION

timeGetSystemTime()

WORD timeKillEvent(WORD *wEventID*)

timeKillEvent() terminates a timer event. *wEventID* is the ID of the timer event. The function returns zero if successful, or **TIMERR_NOCANDO** otherwise.

 NOTE

Under Windows NT wEventID *is of type* **UINT** *and the function returns* **MMRESULT**.

USAGE

The *wEventID* used in the call to **timeKillEvent()** must have been obtained from a previous call to **timeSetEvent()**.

Here is a small portion of code that illustrates the use of this function.

```
NPSEQ npSeq;
WORD wTimerID;
    .
    .
    .
timeKillEvent(npSeq -> wTimerID);
```

RELATED FUNCTION

timeSetEvent()

UINT timeSetEvent(UINT *uEventDelay*,
UINT *uDelayAccuracy*,
LPTIMECALLBACK *lpSetEventFunc*,
DWORD *dwAppData*, UINT *uFlag*)

timeSetEvent() registers a timer callback event. *uEventDelay* specifies the delay for the event in milliseconds. *uDelayAccuracy* determines the accuracy of the event delay, in milliseconds. *lpSetEventFunc* is a pointer to a user-defined callback function automatically invoked after the specified *uEventPeriod*. *dwAppData* contains any application-specific data that is passed to the callback function. *uFlag* determines the type of the event. The function returns a valid event ID if successful, and NULL otherwise.

USAGE

Timer events may be one of two types, as specified by *uFlag*:

Constant	Description
TIME_ONESHOT	The timer event happens once.
TIME_PERIODIC	The event is triggered repeatedly, with a delay interval of *uEventDelay* milliseconds.

The callback function used by **timeSetEvent()** must have this prototype:

```
void CALLBACK setEventCBFunc(UINT uEventID,
                            UINT uNotUsed1,
                            DWORD dwAppData,
                            DWORD dwNotUsed2,
                            DWORD dwNotUsed3)
```

The name of this function is arbitrary. Your application may give this callback function any valid function name. This user-defined callback function is automatically invoked when its associated timer goes off. *uEventID* is the ID of the specific timer event invoking the callback function. *dwAppData* will contain the user-defined data specified when **timeSetEvent()** was invoked. The other three parameters, *uNotUsed1*, *uNotUsed2*, and *uNotUsed3*, are currently not used. The function has no return value.

The callback function must be exported in the application's module-definition file using the **EXPORTS** statement. (This does not apply to Windows NT.)

Here is a small portion of code that illustrates the use of this function.

```
wTimerID = timeSetEvent((UINT) 1000, (UINT) 2, CallbackFunction,
                         NULL, TIME_ONESHOT);
```

RELATED FUNCTIONS

setEventFunc()
timeBeginPeriod()
timeEndPeriod()
timeKillEvent()

A Complete Programming Example

Here is a complete Windows NT C++ programming example that illustrates how to use **timeGetSystemTime()** and how to access the **MMTIME** structure.

```
//
//   nttimer
//   A simple Windows NT application that demonstrates the use
//   of a multimedia timer function.
//

#include <windows.h>
#include <mmsystem.h>
#include <string.h>
#include <stdlib.h>

LRESULT CALLBACK WndProc(HWND, UINT, WPARAM, LPARAM);

char szProgName[] = "ProgName";

int WINAPI WinMain(HINSTANCE hInst, HINSTANCE hPreInst,
                   LPSTR lpszCmdLine, int nCmdShow)
{
  HWND hWnd;
  MSG lpMsg;
  WNDCLASS wcApp;
  if (!hPreInst) {
    wcApp.lpszClassName = szProgName;
```

```
        wcApp.hInstance    = hInst;
        wcApp.lpfnWndProc  = WndProc;
        wcApp.hCursor      = LoadCursor(NULL, IDC_ARROW);
        wcApp.hIcon        = NULL;
        wcApp.lpszMenuName = NULL;
        wcApp.hbrBackground = GetStockObject(LTGRAY_BRUSH);
        wcApp.style        = CS_HREDRAW | CS_VREDRAW;
        wcApp.cbClsExtra   = 0;
        wcApp.cbWndExtra   = 0;
        if (!RegisterClass (&wcApp))
          return FALSE;
    }
    hWnd = CreateWindow(szProgName,
                        "Multimedia Timer Information",
                        WS_OVERLAPPEDWINDOW, CW_USEDEFAULT,
                        CW_USEDEFAULT, CW_USEDEFAULT,
                        CW_USEDEFAULT, (HWND)NULL, (HMENU)NULL,
                        (HANDLE)hInst, (LPSTR)NULL);
    ShowWindow(hWnd, nCmdShow);
    UpdateWindow(hWnd);
    while (GetMessage(&lpMsg, NULL, 0, 0)) {
      TranslateMessage(&lpMsg);
      DispatchMessage(&lpMsg);
    }
    return(lpMsg.wParam);
}

LRESULT CALLBACK WndProc(HWND hWnd, UINT messg,
                         WPARAM wParam, LPARAM lParam)
{
  HDC hdc;
  PAINTSTRUCT ps;
  LPMMTIME pmytime;
  char buf[80];

  switch (messg)
  {
    case WM_PAINT:
      hdc = BeginPaint(hWnd, &ps);

      pmytime -> wType = (WORD) TIME_MS;
      timeGetSystemTime(pmytime, sizeof(MMTIME));

      TextOut(hdc, 10, 10,
```

```
                "Milliseconds since system was started:", 38);
        _itoa((int) pmytime -> u.ms, buf, 10);
        TextOut(hdc, 10, 40, buf, strlen(buf));

        ValidateRect(hWnd, NULL);
        EndPaint(hWnd, &ps);
        break;

    case WM_DESTROY:
      PostQuitMessage(0);
      break;

    default:
      return(DefWindowProc(hWnd, messg, wParam, lParam));
  }
  return(0L);
}
```

Chapter 20

MIDI Multimedia Functions

tHIS chapter describes Windows' MIDI functions, which can be used to open, close, create, delete, and otherwise handle MIDI devices. MIDI stands for Musical Instrument Digital Interface.

The MIDI functions require the header MMSYSTEM.H.

MMRESULT auxGetDevCaps(UINT *uDeviceID,*
LPAUXCAPS *lpacaps,*
UINT *uStrucSize)*

auxGetDevCaps() obtains the capabilities for the specified device. *uDeviceID* is the ID of the auxiliary output device in question. *lpacaps* is a pointer to an **AUXCAPS** structure, which the function fills with the specified device's capabilities. *uStrucSize* contains the size of the **AUXCAPS** structure. The function returns zero if successful, and one of two error constants if unsuccessful.

The **AUXCAPS** structure is defined like this:

```
typedef struct auxcaps_tag {
  WORD wMid;
  WORD wPid;
  MMVERSION vDriverVersion;
  TCHAR szPname[MAXPNAMELEN];
  WORD wTechnology;
  DWORD dwSupport;
} AUXCAPS;
```

In the structure, **wMid** is the identifier for the device driver of the audio device. **wPid** is the product ID code of the audio device. **vDriverVersion** gives the version number of the device driver. Here, the major version number is in the high-order byte, while the minor version number is in the low-order byte. **szPname** is a null-terminated string that holds the product name. **wTechnology** is the type of the audio output and is either **AUX-**

CAPS_AUXIN (for audio output from auxiliary input jacks) or **AUX-CAPS_CDAUDIO** (for audio output from an internal CD-ROM drive).

dwSupport can be **AUXCAPS_LRVOLUME** (for support of left and right volume control) and/or **AUXCAPS_VOLUME** (for a simple volume control).

USAGE

On error, **auxGetDevCaps()** returns one of these two constants: **MMSYSERR_BADDEVICEID** (illegal device driver ID) or **MMSYSERR_NODRIVER** (no device driver present).

uDeviceID may be assigned **AUX_MAPPER**, which instructs the function to automatically detect auxiliary devices.

RELATED FUNCTION

auxGetNumDevs()

UINT auxGetNumDevs(void)

auxGetNumDevs() determines how many auxiliary output devices are currently installed. The function returns the number of devices present in the system.

RELATED FUNCTION

auxDevCaps()

MMRESULT auxGetVolume(UINT *uDeviceID,* LPDWORD *lpdwVolSetting)*

auxGetVolume() obtains the volume setting for the specified auxiliary output device. *uDeviceID* is the auxiliary output device in question. *lpdwVolSetting* is a pointer to a memory location that, on return, will contain the volume setting. The function returns zero if successful, or one of two error conditions if unsuccessful.

USAGE

On error, **auxGetVolume()** may return one of these two constants: **MMSYSERR_BADDEVICEID** (illegal device driver ID) or **MMSYSERR_NODRIVER** (no device driver present).

Valid volume settings range from a minimum of 0 to 0xFFFF. The left channel volume is in the low-order word and the right channel volume is in the high-order word. Devices with one channel use only the low-order word.

RELATED FUNCTION

auxSetVolume()

MMRESULT auxOutMessage(UINT *uID*, UINT *uMsg*, DWORD *dwParm1*, DWORD *dwParm2*)

auxOutMessage() outputs a message to the auxiliary output device specified by *uID*. The function returns the value generated by the device as a response to the message.

uID is the device ID of the affected device. *uMsg* contains the message that will be sent. *dwParm1* and *dwParm2* contain values associated with the message.

RELATED FUNCTIONS

auxSetVolume()
auxGetDevCaps()

MMRESULT auxSetVolume(UINT *uDeviceID*, DWORD *dwVolSetting*)

auxSetVolume() sets the volume level for the specified auxiliary output device. *uDeviceID* contains the auxiliary output device. *dwVolSetting* contains the volume setting. The function returns zero if successful, or one of two error messages if unsuccessful.

USAGE

On error, **auxSetVolume()** may return one of these two constants: **MMSYSERR_BADDEVICEID** (illegal device driver ID) or **MMSY-SERR_NODRIVER** (no device driver present).

The volume range is 0 through 0xFFFF. However, many devices only use the high-nibble (4-bits) of each word. The left channel is in the low-order word and the right channel is in the high-order word.

RELATED FUNCTION

auxGetVolume()

BOOL MessageBeep(UINT *uSoundType*)

MessageBeep() plays the specified waveform sound. *uSoundType* selects the waveform sound. The function returns TRUE if successful, and FALSE otherwise.

USAGE

uSoundType may be one of the following values:

Value	Description
-1	Outputs a simple beep
MB_ICONASTERISK	Plays the wave file that is assigned to the SystemAsterisk entry in WIN.INI
MB_ICONEXCLAMATION	Plays the wave file that is assigned to the SystemExclamation entry in WIN.INI
MB_ICONHAND	Plays the wave file that is assigned to the SystemHand entry in WIN.INI
MB_ICONQUESTION	Plays the wave file that is assigned to the SystemQuestion entry in WIN.INI
MB_OK	Plays the wave file that is assigned to the SystemDefault entry in WIN.INI

The specified waveform sound is played asynchronously.

RELATED FUNCTION

MessageBox()

MMRESULT midiInAddBuffer(HMIDIIN *hMidiIn*, LPMIDIHDR *lpMidiHdr*, UINT *uStrucSize*)

midiInAddBuffer() is used for system-exclusive message processing. The function sends an input buffer to the specified MIDI device and returns when the buffer is filled.

hMidiIn is the handle of the MIDI input device. *lpMidiHdr* is a pointer to a **MIDIHDR** structure that is filled by the function. *uStrucSize* contains the size of the structure. The function returns zero if successful, or one of two error conditions if unsuccessful.

The **MIDIHDR** structure is shown here.

```
typedef struct midihdr_tag {
  LPSTR lpData;
  DWORD dwBufferLength;
  DWORD dwBytesRecorded;
  DWORD dwUser;
  DWORD dwFlags;
  struct midihdr_tag *lpNext;
  DWORD reserved;
} MIDIHDR;
```

In this structure **lpData** is a pointer to the system-exclusive data buffer. **dwBufferLength** contains the size, in bytes, of the data buffer. **dwBytesRecorded** contains the amount of data in the buffer. **dwUser** is user-defined data. **dwFlags** contains one or more flags that provide information about the data buffer. When set to **MHDR_DONE**, the device driver indicates when it is finished with the data buffer and is returning it. When set to **MHDR_PREPARED**, Windows indicates that the data buffer has been prepared with a call to **midiInPrepareHeader()** or **midiOutPrepareHeader()**. **lpNext** and **reserved** are reserved.

USAGE

On error, **midiInAddBuffer()** may return one of these two constants: **MMSYSERR_INVALHANDLE** (invalid device handle) or **MIDIERR_-UNPREPARED** (unprepared **MIDIHDR** structure).

A call to **midiInPrepareHeader()** is required to prepare the **MIDIHDR** structure. In addition, the **MIDIHDR** structure and the **lpData** field of the **MIDIHDR** structure must point to a memory buffer created with a call to **GlobalAlloc()**. **GlobalAlloc()** must use the **GMEM_SHARE** and **GMEM_MOVEABLE** flags.

Here is a small portion of code that illustrates the use of this function.

```
static HMIDIIN hmidiIn;
static MIDIHDR midiHdr;
HWND hwnd;
int iError;
       .
       .
       .
iError = midiInAddBuffer(hmidiIn, &midiHdr, sizeof(MIDIHDR));
```

RELATED FUNCTION

midiInPrepareHeader()

MMRESULT midiInClose(HMIDIIN *hMidiIn*)

midiInClose() closes a MIDI input device. *hMidiIn* is the handle to the MIDI input device about to be closed. The function returns zero if successful, or one of two error flags if unsuccessful.

USAGE

On error, **midiInClose()** returns one of these two constants: **MMSYSERR_INVALHANDLE** (invalid device handle) or **MIDIERR_-STILLPLAYING** (device not finished).

Here is a small portion of code that illustrates the use of this function.

```
static HMIDIIN hmidiIn;
HWND hwnd;
       .
       .
       .
midiInClose(hmidiIn);
```

RELATED FUNCTION

midiInOpen()

void CALLBACK midiInFunc(HMIDIIN *hMidiIn*,
UINT *uMsg*,
DWORD *dwAppData*,
DWORD *dwParam1*,
DWORD *dwParam2*)

midiInFunc() is a user-defined callback function used by **midiInOpen()**. The name of this function is arbitrary. However, the actual function name must be exported with an **EXPORTS** statement in the application's module definition file. (This is not necessary for Windows NT.) *hMidiIn* is the handle of the MIDI input device whose messages are being processed by the callback function. *uMsg* contains the particular MIDI input device message being processed. *dwAppData* contains any optional message-specific information. *dwParam1* and *dwParam2* contain message parameters. The function has no return value.

USAGE

The code segment for the callback function must be marked **FIXED** in the module definition file. (Not required for Windows NT.)

RELATED FUNCTIONS

midiInClose()
midiInOpen()

MMRESULT midiInGetDevCaps(UINT *uDeviceID*,
LPMIDIINCAPS *lpMidiICaps*,
UINT *uStrucSize*)

midiInGetDevCaps() obtains the capabilities for the specified input device. *uDeviceID* is the input device in question. *lpMidiICaps* is a pointer to a **MIDIINCAPS** structure, which the function fills with the specified device's capabilities. *uStrucSize* identifies the size of the **MIDIINCAPS** structure. The function returns zero if successful, or one of two error constants if unsuccessful.

The **MIDIINCAPS** structure is shown here.

```
typedef struct midiincaps_tag {
  WORD wMid;
  WORD wPid;
  MMVERSION vDriverVersion;
  TCHAR szPname[MAXPNAMELEN];
} MIDIINCAPS;
```

In this structure, **wMid** is the manufacturer ID for the device driver of the given MIDI input device. **wPid** is the product ID for the MIDI input device. **vDriverVersion** contains the version number of the device driver. Here, the major version number is in the high-order byte and the minor version number is in the low-order byte. **szPname** is a null-terminated string that holds the product name.

USAGE

On error, **midiInGetDevCaps()** returns one of these two constants: **MMSYSERR_BADDEVICEID** (illegal device driver ID) or **MMSY-SERR_NODRIVER** (no driver present).

Here is a small portion of code that illustrates the use of this function.

```
int i;
MIDIINCAPS midiIC;
short iNumDev;

iNumDev = midiInGetNumDevs();

for(i=0; i< iNumDev; i++) {

midiInGetDevCaps(i, &midiIC, sizeof(midiIC));
  .
  .
  .
}
```

RELATED FUNCTION

midiInGetNumDevs()

MMRESULT midiInGetErrorText(UINT *uErrorID*,
LPSTR *lpszTextDescrip*,
UINT *uBuffSize*)

midiInGetErrorText() obtains a string explaining the specified error. *uErrorID* identifies an error by number. *lpszTextDescrip* is a pointer to a buffer that will, on return, contain the textual clarification. *uBuffSize* tells the function the size, in bytes, of the array pointed to by *lpszTextDescrip*. The function returns zero if successful, or **MMSYSERR_BADERRNUM** if unsuccessful.

USAGE

The MMSYSTEM.H header file contains the **MAXERRORLENGTH** constant, which your application may use to dimension the array receiving the error string. Technically, all error descriptions should be shorter than **MAXERRORLENGTH**. However, **midiInGetErrorText()** will truncate any information beyond the specified buffer size. **midiInGetErrorText()** always creates a null-terminated string within the buffer pointed to by *lpszTextDescrip*.

RELATED FUNCTION

midiInGetDevCaps()

MMRESULT midiInGetID(HMIDIIN *hmidi*,
PUINT *lpdwDev*)

midiInGetID() obtains the ID associated with the specified device. It returns zero if successful and **MMSYSERR_INVALHANDLE** (invalid handle) on failure.

The handle of the device is passed in *hmidi*. On return, the device ID will be in the variable pointed to by *lpdwDev*.

RELATED FUNCTIONS

midiInGetNumDevs()
midiOutGetID()

UINT midiInGetNumDevs(void)

Your application uses **midiInGetNumDevs()** to determine how many MIDI input devices are currently in the system. The function returns the number of MIDI devices registered.

USAGE

Here is a small portion of code that illustrates the use of this function.

```
int i;
MIDIINCAPS midiIC;
short iNumDev;

iNumDev = midiInGetNumDevs();

for(i=0; i< iNumDev; i++) {

  midiInGetDevCaps(i, &midiIC, sizeof(midiIC));
  .
  .
  .

}
```

RELATED FUNCTION

midiInGetDevCaps()

MMRESULT midiInMessage(HMIDIIN *hmidi*, UINT *uMsg*, DWORD *dwParam1*, DWORD *dwParam2*)

midiInMessage() outputs a message to the MIDI input device specified by *hmidi*. It returns *uMsg*.

The handle of the affected device is passed in *hmidi*. The message is passed in *uMsg*. *dwParm1* and *dwParm2* contain user-defined values related to the message.

RELATED FUNCTIONS

midiInGetID()
midiOutGetID()

MMRESULT midiInOpen(LPHMIDIIN *lphMidiIn,*
UINT *uDeviceID,*
DWORD *dwCallBackFunc,*
DWORD *dwCallBackData,*
DWORD *dwOpenFlag*)

midiInOpen() opens a MIDI input device. *lphMidiIn* is a pointer to a handle that becomes the handle to the MIDI input device after it is opened. *uDeviceID* is the ID of the MIDI input device to open. *dwCallBackFunc* either points to a callback function or contains the handle of a window that processes the newly opened MIDI input device messages. (See **midiInFunc()**.)

dwCallBackData contains instance-specific data that will be passed to the callback function. *dwOpenFlag* determines what type of information is being represented by *dwCallBackFunc*. The function returns zero if successful, or one of three error constants if unsuccessful.

USAGE

If *dwOpenFlag* is assigned **CALLBACK_FUNCTION**, the following messages are sent to the callback function:

MIM_OPEN
MIM_CLOSE
MIM_DATA
MIM_LONGDATA
MIM_ERROR
MIM_LONGERROR

If *dwOpenFlag* is assigned **CALLBACK_WINDOW**, the following messages are sent to the callback window procedure:

MM_MIM_OPEN
MM_MIM_CLOSE
MM_MIM_DATA

MM_MIM_LONGDATA
MM_MIM_ERROR
MM_MIM_LONGERROR

dwOpenFlag may be assigned **CALLBACK_NULL** if no callback routine is necessary.

On error, **midiInOpen()** returns one of these three constants:

Constant	Description
MMSYSERR_ALLOCATED	Identifies the selected MIDI input device as already being opened
MMSYSERR_BADDEVICEID	Signals an illegal device ID
MMSYSERR_NOMEM	Indicates that the required memory allocation failed

Here is a small portion of code that illustrates the use of this function.

```
static HMIDIIN hmidiIn;
static WORD wDevID;
HWND hwnd;
   .
   .
   .
midiInOpen(&hmidiIn, wDevID, hwnd, 0L, CALLBACK_WINDOW);
```

RELATED FUNCTION

midiInClose()

MMRESULT midiInPrepareHeader(HMIDIIN *hMidiIn*, LPMIDIHDR *lpMidiInHdr*, UINT *uStrucSize*)

midiInPrepareHeader() prepares a buffer to be used by a MIDI input device. *hMidiIn* is a handle to a valid MIDI input device. *lpMidiInHdr* is a pointer to a **MIDIHDR** structure.

uStrucSize tells the function how many bytes are in the **MIDIHDR** structure. The function returns zero if successful, or one of two error constants if unsuccessful.

USAGE

On error, **midiInPrepareHeader()** may return one of these two constants: **MMSYSERR_INVALHANDLE** (invalid MIDI input device handle) or **MMSYSERR_NOMEM** (unsuccessful attempt to allocate the memory).

The functions **GlobalAlloc()** and **GlobalLock()** must be used to allocate and lock the **MIDIHDR** structure pointed to by *lpMidiInHdr* and the memory pointed to by **lpData**. The allocated memory must also have been marked **GMEM_MOVEABLE** and **GMEM_SHARE**.

Here is a small portion of code that illustrates the use of this function.

```
static HMIDIIN hmidiIn;
static LPMIDIHDR pmidiHdr;
HWND hwnd;    .
         .
         .
midiInPrepareHeader(hmidiIn, &pmidiHdr, sizeof(MIDIHDR));
```

RELATED FUNCTION

midiInUnprepareHeader()

MMRESULT midiInReset(HMIDIIN *hMidiIn*)

midiInReset() resets the specified device. Any further input from the specified MIDI input device is stopped. *hMidiIn* is the handle of the MIDI input device about to be reset. The function returns zero if successful, or **MMSYSERR_IN-VALHANDLE** if *hMidiIn* contained an invalid MIDI input device handle.

USAGE

Here is a small portion of code that illustrates the use of this function.

```
static HMIDIIN hmidiIn;
HWND hwnd;
        .
        .
        .
midiInReset(hmidiIn);
```

RELATED FUNCTIONS

midiInStart()
midiInStop()

MMRESULT midiInStart(HMIDIIN *hMidiIn*)

midiInStart() begins inputting from the selected MIDI input device. *hMidiIn* is the handle to the MIDI input device. The function returns zero if successful, or **MMSYSERR_INVALHANDLE** if unsuccessful.

USAGE

System messages are placed in the buffers created by the call to **midiIn-AddBuffer()**.

Here is a small portion of code that illustrates the use of this function.

```
static HMIDIIN hmidiIn;
HWND hwnd;
    .
    .
    .
midiInStart(hmidiIn);
```

RELATED FUNCTIONS

midiInReset()
midiInStop()

MMRESULT midiInStop(HMIDIIN *hMidiIn*)

midiInStop() stops any further MIDI input on the selected MIDI input device. *hMidiIn* is the handle of the MIDI input device about to be stopped. The function returns zero if successful, or **MMSYSERR_INVALHANDLE** if unsuccessful.

USAGE

A call to **midiInStop()** marks the current system-exclusive message buffer as completed.

Here is a small portion of code that illustrates the use of this function.

```
static HMIDIIN hmidiIn;
HWND hwnd;
    .
    .
    .
midiInStop(hmidiIn);
```

RELATED FUNCTIONS

midiInReset()
midiInStart()

MMRESULT midiInUnprepareHeader(HMIDIIN *hMidiIn,* LPMIDIHDR *lpMidiInHdr,* UINT *uStrucSize)*

Your application makes a call to **midiInUnprepareHeader()**, just before calling **GlobalFree()**, in order to clean up the **MIDIHDR** structure before being freed. *hMidiIn* is a handle to the MIDI input device. *lpMidiInHdr* is a pointer to the **MIDIHDR** structure about to be cleaned up.

uStrucSize tells the function how many bytes are in the **MIDIHDR** structure. The function returns zero if successful, or one of two error constants if unsuccessful.

USAGE

On error, **midiInUnprepareHeader()** returns either of these two constants: **MIDIERR_STILLPLAYING** (device is not finished) or **MMSYSERR_IN-VALHANDLE** (invalid MIDI input device handle).

Here is a small portion of code that illustrates the use of this function.

```
static HMIDIIN hmidiIn;
static LPMIDIHDR pMidiInHdr;
HWND hwnd;
    .
    .
    .
midiInUnprepareHeader(hmidiIn, &pMidiInHdr, sizeof(MIDIHDR));
```

RELATED FUNCTION

midiInPrepareHeader()

MMRESULT midiOutCacheDrumPatches
(HMIDIOUT *hMidiOut,*
UINT *uDrumPatch,*
LPWORD *lpKEYARRAY,*
UINT *uCacheFlag)*

Since certain synthesizers are unable to keep all required percussion patches loaded simultaneously, a call to **midiOutCacheDrumPatches()** can cache the patches. This guarantees that they are accessible when needed.

hMidiOut is a handle to an internal MIDI synthesizer. *uDrumPatch* selects which drum patch to cache. *lpKEYARRAY* is a pointer to a **KEYARRAY** array containing the key numbers of the selected percussion patches. *uCacheFlag* defines the caching operation. The function returns zero if successful, or one of three error constants if unsuccessful.

USAGE

uCacheFlag may be one of the following four constants:

Constant	Description
MIDI_CACHE_ALL	Caches all of the patches in the **KEYARRAY** array
MIDI_CACHE_BESTFIT	Caches as many patches as possible and flags any **KEYARRAY** entries as being cached
MIDI_CACHE_QUERY	Changes each **KEYARRAY** entry, flagging cached and uncached entries
MIDI_UNCACHE	Uncaches the specified patches and clears the **KEYARRAY** array

On error, **midiOutCacheDrumPatches()** returns one of these three error constants:

Constant	Description
MMSYSERR_INVALHANDLE	Signals the use of an invalid device handle
MMSYSERR_NOMEM	Indicates insufficient memory to perform the cache operation
MMSYSERR_NOTSUPPORTED	Indicates that the selected device does not support caching of percussion patches

To see if the internal MIDI synthesizer supports percussion patch caching, your application should make a call to **midiOutGetDevCaps()** and see if the **dwSupport** field of the **MIDIOUTCAPS** structure is set to **MIDI-CAPS_CACHE**.

RELATED FUNCTIONS

midiOutCachePatches()
midiOutGetDevCaps()

MMRESULT   midiOutCachePatches
(HMIDIOUT *hMidiOut,*
UINT *uPatchBank,*
LPWORD *lpPATCHARRAY,*
UINT *uCacheFlag*)

Since certain synthesizers are unable to keep all required settings (i.e., patches) loaded simultaneously, a call to **midiOutCachePatches()** can cache the patches. This guarantees that they are accessible when needed.

hMidiOut is a handle to an internal MIDI synthesizer. *uPatchBank* selects which bank of patches to cache. *lpPATCHARRAY* is a pointer to a **PATCHARRAY** array containing the key numbers of the selected patches. *uCacheFlag* defines the caching operation. The function returns zero if successful, or one of three error constants if unsuccessful.

USAGE

uCacheFlag may be one of the following four constants:

Constant	Description
MIDI_CACHE_ALL	Caches all of the patches in the **PATCHARRAY** array
MIDI_CACHE_BESTFIT	Caches as many patches as possible and flags any **PATCHARRAY** entries as being cached
MIDI_CACHE_QUERY	Changes each **PATCHARRAY** entry, flagging cached and uncached entries
MIDI_UNCACHE	Uncaches the specified patches and clears the **PATCHARRAY** array

On error, **midiOutCachePatches()** returns one of these three error constants:

Constant	Description
MMSYSERR_INVALHANDLE	Signals the use of an invalid device handle
MMSYSERR_NOMEM	Indicates insufficient memory to perform the cache operation
MMSYSERR_NOTSUPPORTED	Indicates that the selected device does not support caching of percussion patches

To see if the internal MIDI synthesizer supports percussion patching, your application should make a call to **midiOutGetDevCaps()** and see if the **dwSupport** field of the **MIDIOUTCAPS** structure is set to **MIDI-CAPS_CACHE**.

RELATED FUNCTIONS

midiOutCacheDrumPatches()
midiOutGetDevCaps()

MMRESULT midiOutClose(HMIDIOUT *hMidiOut*)

midiOutClose() closes a MIDI output device. *hMidiOut* is a handle to the MIDI output device being closed. The function returns zero if successful, or one of two error constants if unsuccessful.

USAGE

On error, **midiOutClose()** returns either of these two constants: **MMSYSERR_INVALHANDLE** (invalid MIDI device handle) or **MIDIERR_STILLPLAYING** (the specified MIDI output device still has buffers in the output queue).

A call to **midiOutClose()** fails while there are pending buffers in the output queue. The application can make a call to **midiOutReset()** to mark all output buffers as having been processed.

Here is a small portion of code that illustrates the use of this function.

```
static HMIDIOUT
hmidiOut;
HWND hwnd;
        .

        .

        .
midiOutClose(hmidiOut);
```

RELATED FUNCTION

midiOutOpen()

void CALLBACK midiOutFunc(HMIDIOUT *hMidiOut*,
UINT *uMsg*,
DWORD *dwAppData*,
DWORD *dwParam1*,
DWORD *dwParam2*)

midiOutFunc() is a user-defined callback function used by **midiOutOpen().** The name of the function is arbitrary. However, it must be exported with an **EXPORTS** statement in the application's module definition file. (This step is not required for Windows NT.)

hMidiOut identifies the MIDI output device whose messages are being processed by the callback function. *uMsg* contains the particular MIDI output device message being processed. *dwAppData* contains any optional user-defined information. *dwParam1* and *dwParam2* contain message parameters. The function has no return value.

USAGE

The code segment for the callback function must be marked **FIXED** in the module definition file. (This is not required by Windows NT.)

RELATED FUNCTIONS

midiOutClose()
midiOutOpen()

MMRESULT midiOutGetDevCaps(UINT *uDeviceID*, LPMIDIOUTCAPS *lpOutCaps*, UINT *uStrucSize*)

midiOutGetDevCaps() obtains the capabilities for the specified output device. *uDeviceID* is the ID of the output device in question. *lpOutCaps* is a pointer to a **MIDIOUTCAPS** structure, which the function fills with the specified device's capabilities. *uStrucSize* contains the size of the **MIDIOUTCAPS** structure. The function returns zero if successful, or one of two error constants if unsuccessful.

USAGE

The **MIDIOUTCAPS** structure is shown here.

```
typedef struct midioutcaps_tag {
  WORD wMid;
  WORD wPid;
  MMVERSION vDriverVersion;
  TCHAR szPname[MAXPNAMELEN];
  WORD wTechnology;
  WORD wVoices;
  WORD wNotes;
  WORD wChannelMask;
  DWORD dwSupport;
} MIDIOUTCAPS;
```

In this structure **wMid** is the manufacturer ID for the device driver. **wPid** is the product ID for the MIDI output device. **vDriverVersion** contains the version number of the device driver. Here, the major version number is in the high-order byte and the minor version number is in the low-order byte. **szPname** is a null-terminated string that holds the product name.

wTechnology contains the type of output device and can be **MOD_MIDIPORT** (a hardware port), **MOD_SQSYNTH** (a square wave synthesizer), **MOD_FMSYNTH** (a FM synthesizer), or **MOD_MAPPER** (a Microsoft MIDI Mapper). **wVoices** contains the number of voices supported via an internal synthesizer. **wNotes** contains the maximum number of notes that may be played simultaneously.

wChannelMask contains the channels that an internal synthesizer responds to. Here, the least significant bit is for channel 0 and the most significant bit is for channel 15. **dwSupport** contains optional features supported by the device and can be **MIDICAPS_VOLUME** (for support of a volume control), **MIDICAPS_LRVOLUME** (for support of a left and right volume control), or **MIDICAPS_CACHE** (for support of patch caching).

On error, **midiOutGetDevCaps()** returns one of these two constants: **MMSYSERR_BADDEVICEID** (illegal device driver ID), **MMSYSERR_NO-DRIVER** (no device driver present), or **MMSYSERR_NOMEM** (cannot allocate memory).

Here is a small portion of code that illustrates the use of this function.

```
int i;
MIDIOUTCAPS midiIC;
short iNumOutDevs;

iNumOutDevs = midiOutGetNumDevs();

for(i=0; i< iNumOutDevs; i++) {
  midiOutGetDevCaps(i, &midiIC, sizeof(midiIC));
  .
  .
  .
}
```

RELATED FUNCTION

midiOutGetNumDevs()

MMRESULT midiOutGetErrorText(UINT *uErrorID*, LPSTR *lpszTextDescrip*, UINT *uBuffSize*)

midiOutGetErrorText() obtains a string explaining the specified error. *uErrorID* identifies an error by number. *lpszTextDescrip* is a pointer to a character array that, on return, will contain the textual clarification. *uBuffSize* tells the function how big the buffer is. The function returns zero if successful, or **MMSYSERR_BADERRNUM** if unsuccessful.

USAGE

The MMSYSTEM.H header file contains the **MAXERRORLENGTH** constant that your application may use to dimension the buffer. Technically, all error descriptions should be less than **MAXERRORLENGTH**. However, **midiOutGetErrorText()** will truncate any information beyond the specified buffer size. **midiOutGetErrorText()** always creates a null-terminated string within the buffer pointed to by *lpsz TextDescrip*.

RELATED FUNCTION

midiOutGetDevCaps()

UINT midiOutGetNumDevs(VOID)

midiOutGetNumDevs() determines how many MIDI output devices are currently in the system. The function returns the number of MIDI devices registered.

USAGE

Here is a small portion of code that illustrates the use of this function.

```
int i;
MIDIOUTCAPS midiIC;
short iNumOutDevs;

iNumOutDevs = midiOutGetNumDevs();

for(i=0; i< iNumOutDevs; i++) {
   midiOutGetDevCaps(i, &midiIC, sizeof(midiIC));
   .
   .
   .
}
```

RELATED FUNCTION

midiOutGetDevCaps()

MMRESULT midiOutGetVolume(UINT *uDeviceID*, LPDWORD *lpdwVolSetting*)

midiOutGetVolume() obtains the volume setting for the specified output device. *uDeviceID* gives the output device in question. *lpdwVolSetting* is a pointer to a memory location that will, on return, contain the volume setting. The function returns zero if successful, or one of three error conditions if unsuccessful.

USAGE

On error, **midiOutGetVolume()** may return one of these three constants:

Constant	Description
MMSYSERR_INVALHANDLE	Flags the use of an invalid device handle
MMSYSERR_NODRIVER	Indicates that the specified device driver has not been installed
MMSYSERR_NOTSUPPORTED	Indicates that the specified device cannot return volume information

Valid volume settings range from a minimum of 0 to 0xFFFF. The left channel volume is in the low-order word and the right channel volume is in the high-order word. Devices with one channel use only the low-order word.

Your application can make a call to **midiOutGetDevCaps()** and check the **dwSupport** field of the **MIDIOUTCAPS** structure to see if the **MIDICAPS_VOLUME** flag is set, indicating that the device supports volume control.

RELATED FUNCTION

midiOutSetVolume()

MMRESULT midiOutLongMsg(HMIDIOUT *hMidiOut*, LPMIDIHDR *lpMidiOutHdr*, UINT *uStrucSize*)

midiOutLongMsg() sends a system-exclusive MIDI message to a MIDI output device. *hMidiOut* is the handle to a valid MIDI output device. *lpMidiOutHdr* is a pointer to a **MIDIHDR** structure. *uStrucSize* tells the function how many bytes are in the **MIDIHDR** structure. The function returns zero if successful, or one of three error constants if unsuccessful.

USAGE

On error, **midiOutLongMsg()** may return one of these three constants:

Constant	Description
MMSYSERR_INVALHANDLE	Signals an invalid MIDI input device handle
MIDIERR_UNPREPARED	Indicates that the **MIDIHDR** structure has not yet been prepared
MIDIERR_NOTREADY	Indicates a busy MIDI output device

The functions **GlobalAlloc()** and **GlobalLock()** must be used to allocate and lock the **MIDIHDR** structure pointed to by *lpMidiOutHdr*. The allocated memory must also have been marked **GMEM_MOVEABLE** and **GMEM_SHARE**.

RELATED FUNCTIONS

midiOutPrepareHeader()
midiOutShortMsg()

MMRESULT midiOutOpen(LPHMIDIOUT *lphMidiOut,*
UINT *uDeviceID,*
DWORD *dwCallBackFunc,*
DWORD *dwCallBackData,*
DWORD *dwOpenFlag)*

midiOutOpen() opens a MIDI output device. On return, the variable pointed to by *lphMidiOut* will contain the handle to the MIDI output device about to be opened. *uDeviceID* is the ID of the MIDI output device to open. *dwCallBackFunc* either points to a callback function or contains the handle of a window that processes the newly opened MIDI output device messages. (See **midiOutFunc()**.) *dwCallBackData* contains any user-defined callback function-specific data. *dwOpenFlag* instructs **midiOutOpen()** on the type of information being represented by *dwCallBackFunc*. The function returns zero if successful, or one of five error constants if unsuccessful.

USAGE

If *dwOpenFlag* is assigned **CALLBACK_FUNCTION**, the following messages are sent to the callback function:

```
MOM_OPEN
MOM_CLOSE
MOM_DONE
```

If *dwOpenFlag* is assigned **CALLBACK_WINDOW**, the following messages are sent to the callback window procedure:

```
MM_MOM_OPEN
MM_MOM_CLOSE
MM_MOM_DONE
```

dwOpenFlag may be assigned **CALLBACK_NULL** if no callback routine or window is necessary.

On error, **midiOutOpen()** returns one of these constants:

Constant	Description
MIDIERR_NODEVICE	Indicates that a port in the selected MIDI map doesn't exist (only happens when opening a MIDI output device)
MIDIERR_NOMAP	Indicates that there is currently no MIDI map (only happens when opening a MIDI output device)
MMSYSERR_ALLOCATED	Identifies the selected MIDI output device as already being opened
MMSYSERR_BADDEVICEID	Signals an illegal device ID
MMSYSERR_NOMEM	Indicates that the required memory allocation failed

Here is a small portion of code that illustrates the use of this function.

```
static HMIDIOUT
 hmidiOut;
static WORD wDevID;
HWND hwnd;
    .
    .
    .

midiOutOpen(hmidiOut, wDevID, hwnd, 0L, CALLBACK_WINDOW);
```

RELATED FUNCTION

midiOutClose()

MMRESULT midiOutPrepareHeader (HMIDIOUT *hMidiOut,* LPMIDIHDR *lpMidiOutHdr,* UINT *uStrucSize*)

midiOutPrepareHeader() prepares a buffer to be used by a MIDI output device. *hMidiOut* is the handle to a valid MIDI output device. *lpMidiOutHdr* is a pointer to a **MIDIHDR** structure. *uStrucSize* tells the function how many bytes are in the **MIDIHDR** structure. The function returns zero if successful, or one of two error constants if unsuccessful.

USAGE

On error, **midiOutPrepareHeader()** may return one of these two constants: **MMSYSERR_INVALHANDLE** (invalid MIDI output device handle) or **MMSYSERR_NOMEM** (unsuccessful attempt to allocate the memory).

The functions **GlobalAlloc()** and **GlobalLock()** must be used to allocate and lock the **MIDIHDR** structure pointed to by *lpMidiOutHdr*. The allocated memory must also have been marked **GMEM_MOVEABLE** and **GMEM_SHARE**.

Here is a small portion of code that illustrates the use of this function.

```
static HMIDIOUT hmidiOut;
static LPMIDIHDR pmidiHdr;
HWND hwnd;
   .
   .
   .

midiOutPrepareHeader(hmidiOut, &pmidiHdr, sizeof(MIDIHDR));
```

RELATED FUNCTION

midiOutUnprepareHeader()

MMRESULT midiOutReset(HMIDIOUT *hMidiOut*)

midiOutReset() resets the specified output device. That is, it cancels all notes currently playing and labels any pending output buffers as completed. *hMidiOut* is the handle of the MIDI output device to reset. The function returns zero if successful, or **MMSYSERR_INVALHANDLE** if passed an invalid MIDI output device handle.

USAGE

In addition to canceling all notes being played on all channels, **midiOutReset()** turns off any sustains.

Here is a small portion of code that illustrates the use of this function.

```
static HMIDIOUT hmidiOut;
HWND hwnd;
       .
       .
       .
midiOutReset(hmidiOut);
```

RELATED FUNCTION

midiOutClose()

MMRESULT midiOutSetVolume(UINT *uDeviceID*, DWORD *dwVolSetting*)

midiOutSetVolume() sets the volume for the specified output device. *uDeviceID* is the affected output device. *dwVolSetting* contains the volume. The function returns zero if successful, or one of three error conditions if unsuccessful.

USAGE

On error, **midiOutSetVolume()** may return one of these three constants:

Constant	Description
MMSYSERR_INVALHANDLE	Flags the use of an invalid device handle
MMSYSERR_NODRIVER	Indicates that the specified device driver has not been installed
MMSYSERR_NOTSUPPORTED	Indicates that the specified device does not allow volume settings

Valid volume settings range from a minimum of 0 to 0xFFFF. The left channel volume is in the low-order word and the right channel volume is in the high-order word. Devices with one channel use only the low-order word.

Your application can make a call to **midiOutGetDevCaps()** and check the **dwSupport** field of the **MIDIOUTCAPS** structure to see if the **MIDICAPS_VOLUME** flag is set, indicating that the device supports volume control.

RELATED FUNCTION

midiOutGetVolume()

MMRESULT midiOutShortMsg(HMIDIOUT *hMidiOut*, DWORD *dwMsg*)

midiOutShortMsg() posts a short message to a MIDI output device. *hMidiOut* is the handle of the MIDI output device. *dwMsg* contains the message. The function returns zero if successful, or one of two error constants if unsuccessful.

USAGE

On error, **midiOutShortMsg()** will return one of these two constants: **MMSYSERR_INVALHANDLE** (an invalid MIDI input device handle) or **MIDIERR_NOTREADY** (device is busy).

Do not use **midiOutShortMsg()** to post any system-exclusive messages (see **midiOutLongMsg()**).

RELATED FUNCTION

midiOutLongMsg()

MMRESULT midiOutUnprepareHeader (HMIDIOUT *hmidiOut*, LPMIDIHDR *lpMidiOutHdr*, UINT *uStrucSize*)

midiOutUnprepareHeader() "unprepares" a buffer used by a MIDI output device. (The buffer was "prepared" using **midiOutPrepareHeader()**.) *hmidiOut* is a handle to a valid MIDI output device. *lpMidiOutHdr* is a pointer to a **MIDIHDR** structure.

uStrucSize tells the function how many bytes are in the **MIDIHDR** structure. The function returns zero if successful, or one of two error constants if unsuccessful.

USAGE

On error, **midiOutUnprepareHeader()** may return one of these two constants: **MIDIERR_STILLPLAYING** (the **MIDIHDR** header pointed to by *lpMidiOutHdr* is still playing) or **MMSYSERR_INVALHANDLE** (invalid MIDI output device handle).

The application must call **midiOutUnprepareHeader()** after the *lpMidi-OutHdr* buffer has been passed to **midiOutLongMsg()** and prior to invoking **GlobalFree()** to return the unprepared buffer to the available memory pool.

Here is a small portion of code that illustrates the use of this function.

```
static HMIDIOUT hMidiOut;
static LPMIDIHDR pMidiOutHdr;
HWND hwnd;
        .
        .
        .
midiOutUnprepareHeader(hMidiZOut, &pMidiOutHdr,
                 sizeof(MIDIHDR);
```

RELATED FUNCTION

midiOutPrepareHeader()

A Complete Programming Example

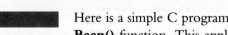

Here is a simple C program that demonstrates the flexibility of the **Message-Beep()** function. This application will work on a wide variety of computers with different sound boards installed. Remember: You must have a sound adapter installed in your system in order to use this program.

```
/*
  Demonstrate MIDI MessageBeep() function.
*/

#include <windows.h>
```

```c
#include <mmsystem.h>

LONG FAR PASCAL WndProc(HWND, UINT, WPARAM, LPARAM);

char szProgName[] = "ProgName"; /* name of window class */

int PASCAL WinMain(HINSTANCE hInst, HINSTANCE hPreInst,
                   LPSTR lpszCmdLine, int nCmdShow)
{
  HWND hWnd;
  MSG lpMsg;
  WNDCLASS wcApp;

  if (!hPreInst) { /* if no previous instance */
    wcApp.lpszClassName = szProgName; /* window class name */
    wcApp.hInstance     = hInst; /* handle to this instance */
    wcApp.lpfnWndProc   = WndProc; /* window function */
    wcApp.hCursor       = LoadCursor(NULL, IDC_ARROW);
    wcApp.hIcon         = LoadIcon(NULL, IDI_APPLICATION);
    wcApp.lpszMenuName  = NULL;

    /* make the background of window gray */
    wcApp.hbrBackground = GetStockObject(LTGRAY_BRUSH);
    wcApp.style         = 0; /* use default window style */
    wcApp.cbClsExtra    = 0; /* no extra info */
    wcApp.cbWndExtra    = 0; /* no extra info */

    /* register the window class */
    if (!RegisterClass (&wcApp))
      return FALSE;
  }

  /* Now that window has been registered, a window
     can be created. */
  hWnd = CreateWindow(szProgName,
                      "Demonstrate MessageBeep()",
                      WS_OVERLAPPEDWINDOW,
                      CW_USEDEFAULT,
                      CW_USEDEFAULT,
                      CW_USEDEFAULT,
                      CW_USEDEFAULT,
                      (HWND)NULL,
                      (HMENU) NULL,
                      (HANDLE)hInst,
```

```
                              (LPSTR)NULL);

    /* Display the Window. */
    ShowWindow(hWnd, nCmdShow);
    UpdateWindow(hWnd);

    /* Create the message loop. */
    while (GetMessage(&lpMsg, NULL, 0, 0)) {
      TranslateMessage(&lpMsg); /* allow use of keyboard */
      DispatchMessage(&lpMsg); /* return control to Windows */
    }
    return(lpMsg.wParam);
}

/* Window Function. */
LONG FAR PASCAL WndProc(HWND hWnd, UINT messg,
                        WPARAM wParam, LPARAM lParam)
{
  HDC hdc;
  PAINTSTRUCT ps;

  switch (messg) {
    case WM_PAINT:
      hdc = BeginPaint(hWnd, &ps);

      MessageBox(hWnd, "Play MB_ICONASTERISK",
                 "MessageBeep()", MB_OK);
      MessageBeep(MB_ICONASTERISK);

      MessageBox(hWnd, "Play MB_ICONEXCLAMATION",
                 "MessageBeep()", MB_OK);
      MessageBeep(MB_ICONEXCLAMATION);

      MessageBox(hWnd, "Play MB_ICONHAND",
                 "MessageBeep()", MB_OK);
      MessageBeep(MB_ICONHAND);

      MessageBox(hWnd, "Play MB_ICONQUESTION",
                 "MessageBeep()", MB_OK);
      MessageBeep(MB_ICONQUESTION);
      break;

    case WM_DESTROY: /* terminate the program */
      PostQuitMessage(0);
```

```
      break;

   default:
      return(DefWindowProc(hWnd, messg, wParam, lParam));
   }
   return(0L);
}
```

Chapter 21

Multimedia Wave Functions

T H I S chapter describes Windows' wave functions. These functions can be used to add, open, close, reset, read, and write multimedia waveform audio devices. To use these functions, you must include MMSYSTEM.H in your program.

MMRESULT waveInAddBuffer(HWAVEIN *hMMWaveIn,* LPWAVEHDR *lpWaveHdr,* UINT *uStrucSize*)

waveInAddBuffer() is passed a wave input buffer; it fills and then returns the buffer. *hMMWaveIn* is a handle to a wave input device. *lpWaveHdr* is a pointer to a **WAVEHDR** structure. *uStrucSize* identifies the size of the structure, in bytes.

The function returns zero if successful, or one of three error constants otherwise.

The **WAVEHDR** structure is shown here.

```
typedef struct wavehdr_tag {
  LPSTR lpData;
  DWORD dwBufferLength;
  DWORD dwBytesRecorded;
  DWORD dwUser;
  DWORD dwFlags;
  DWORD dwLoops;
  struct wavehdr_tag *lpNext;
  DWORD reserved;
} WAVEHDR;
```

Here, **lpData** is a pointer to a waveform data buffer. **dwBufferLength** contains the length of the data buffer. **dwBytesRecorded** contains the amount of input data that is currently in the buffer. **dwUser** contains user-defined data (32-bits).

dwFlags contains one or more flags. They can be **WHDR_DONE** (the device driver is finished with the buffer and returns it), **WHDR_BEGIN-**

LOOP (the buffer is the first in a loop), **WHDR_ENDLOOP** (the buffer is the last in a loop), or **WHDR_PREPARED** (the buffer is prepared with a call to **waveInPrepareHeader()** or **waveOutPrepareHeader()**).

dwLoops contains the number of times to play the loop. **lpNext** and **reserved** are reserved.

USAGE

On error **waveInAddBuffer()** returns one of these constants:

Constant	Description
MMSYSERR_HANDLEBUSY	Indicates that the specified wave input device is currently being used
MMSYSERR_INVALHANDLE	Indicates that the specified wave input device handle is invalid
WAVERR_UNPREPARED	Flags an unprepared wave input buffer

A call to **waveInPrepareHeader()** is required to prepare the **WAVEHDR** structure. In addition, the **lpData** field of the **WAVEHDR** structure must point to a memory buffer created with a call to **GlobalAlloc()**. **GlobalAlloc()** must use the **GMEM_SHARE** and **GMEM_MOVEABLE** flags. The buffer must also be locked, using a call to **GlobalLock()**.

Here is a small portion of code that illustrates the use of this function.

```
static HWAVEIN hMMWaveIn;
static LPWAVEHDR pMMWaveHdr;
HWND hwnd;
   .
   .
   .

waveInPrepareHeader(hMMWaveIn, pMMWaveHdr, sizeof(WAVEHDR));
waveInAddBuffer(hMMWaveIn, pMMWaveHdr, sizeof(WAVEHDR));
```

RELATED FUNCTION

waveInPrepareHeader()

MMRESULT waveInClose(HWAVEIN *hMMWaveIn*)

waveInClose() closes a waveform input device. *hMMWaveIn* is the handle to the waveform input device about to be closed.

The function returns zero if successful, or one of two error constants otherwise.

USAGE

On error **waveInClose()** returns one of these constants: **MMSY-SERR_INVALHANDLE** (invalid device handle) or **MIDIERR_STILL-PLAYING** (unfinished input buffers in the input queue).

Here is a small portion of code that illustrates the use of this function.

```
static HWAVEIN hMMWaveIn;
HWND hwnd;
    .
    .
    .
waveInClose(hMMWaveIn);
```

RELATED FUNCTIONS

waveInAddBuffer()
waveInOpen()
waveInReset()

MMRESULT waveInGetDevCaps(UINT *uDeviceID*, LPWAVEINCAPS *lpWaveCaps*, UINT *uStrucSize*)

waveInGetDevCaps() determines the capabilities for the specified waveform input device. *uDeviceID* is the ID of the waveform input device in question. *lpWaveCaps* is a pointer to a **LPWAVEINCAPS** structure that the function fills with the specified device's capabilities. *uStrucSize* contains the size of the **LPWAVEINCAPS** structure.

The function returns zero if successful, or one of two error constants if unsuccessful.

The **WAVEINCAPS** structure is shown here.

```
typedef struct waveincaps_tag {
  WORD wMid;
  WORD wPid;
  VERSION vDriverVersion;
```

```
TCHAR szPname[MAXPNAMELEN];
DWORD dwFormats;
WORD wChannels;
} WAVEINCAPS;
```

Here, **wMid** contains a manufacturer ID for the device driver. **wPid** contains a product ID for the waveform input device. **vDriverVersion** contains the version number, where the major version number is in the high-order byte and the minor version number is in the low-order byte.

szPname is a string that contains the product name. **dwFormats** describes the standard formats supported and can be one or more of the following macros:

WAVE_FORMAT_1M08 (11.025 kHz, monaural, 8-bit)
WAVE_FORMAT_1S08 (11.025 kHz, stereo, 8-bit)
WAVE_FORMAT_1M16 (11.025 kHz, monaural, 16-bit)
WAVE_FORMAT_1S16 (11.025 kHz, stereo, 16-bit)
WAVE_FORMAT_2M08 (22.05 kHz, monaural, 8-bit)
WAVE_FORMAT_2S08 (22.05 kHz, stereo, 8-bit)
WAVE_FORMAT_2M16 (22.05 kHz, monaural, 16-bit)
WAVE_FORMAT_2S16 (22.05 kHz, stereo, 16-bit)
WAVE_FORMAT_4M08 (44.1 kHz, monaural, 8-bit)
WAVE_FORMAT_4S08 (44.1 kHz, stereo, 8-bit)
WAVE_FORMAT_4M16 (44.1 kHz, monaural, 16-bit)
WAVE_FORMAT_4S16 (44.1 kHz stereo, 16-bit)

wChannels will be 1 for monaural input or 2 for stereo input.

USAGE

On error **waveInGetDevCaps()** returns one of these constants: **MMSYSERR_BADDEVICEID** (illegal device driver ID) or **MMSY-SERR_NODRIVER** (no device driver present).

uDeviceID may be assigned **WAVE_MAPPER**, which instructs the function to return the auxiliary wave mapper device ID.

RELATED FUNCTION

waveInGetNumDevs()

MMRESULT waveInGetErrorText(UINT *uErrorID*, LPSTR *lpszTextDescrip*, UINT *uBuffSize*)

waveInGetErrorText() obtains a string explaining the specified error. *uErrorID* identifies an error by number. *lpszTextDescrip* is a pointer to a character array that, on return, will contain the textual version of the error. The size of the array is passed in *uBuffSize*.

The function returns zero if successful, or **MMSYSERR_BADERRNUM** if unsuccessful.

USAGE

The MMSYSTEM.H header file contains the **MAXERRORLENGTH** constant, which your application may use to dimension the buffer. Technically, all error descriptions should be less than **MAXERRORLENGTH**. However, **waveInGetErrorText()** will truncate any information beyond the specified buffer size.

waveInGetErrorText() always creates a null-terminated string within the buffer pointed to by *lpszTextDescrip*.

RELATED FUNCTION

waveInGetDevCaps()

MMRESULT waveInGetID(HWAVEIN *hWave*, PUINT *lpID*)

Given a device handle, **waveInGetID()** obtains the corresponding device ID. *hWave* is the handle of the waveform input device in question. On return, the variable pointed to by *lpID* will contain the device ID.

The function returns either **MMSYSERR_INVALHANDLE** (invalid device handle) or **MMSYSERR_HANDLEBUSY** (handle being used by another thread).

RELATED FUNCTION

waveOutGetID()

MMRESULT waveInGetNumDevs(VOID)

waveInGetNumDevs() determines how many waveform input devices are currently installed. The function returns the number of devices present in the system.

RELATED FUNCTION

waveInGetDevCaps()

MMRESULT waveInGetPosition(HWAVEIN *hWave*, LPMMTIME *lpTime*, UINT *nSize*)

waveInGetPosition() obtains the input position (as specified by a time value) of the waveform device associated with *hWave*. *hWave* is the handle to the device. *lpTime* points to an **MMTIME** structure that will receive the current position. Before the call, the **wType** field of the structure must be set to a valid time format supported by the device. The size of the structure is passed in *nSize*.

The function returns **MMSYSERR_INVALHANDLE** (invalid device handle) on error or zero if successful.

RELATED FUNCTION

waveOutGetPosition()

MMRESULT waveInMessage(HWAVEIN *hWave*, UINT *uMsg*, DWORD *dwParm1*, DWORD *dwParm2*)

waveInMessage() sends a message to the waveform input device specified by *hWave*. *hWave* is the handle to the device being sent the message. *uMsg* contains the message. *dwParm1* and *dwParm2* contain additional data related to the message.

The function returns a value generated by the device driver controlling the device.

RELATED FUNCTION

waveOutMessage()

MMRESULT waveInOpen(LPHWAVEIN *lphMMWaveIn,*
UINT *uDeviceID,*
LPWAVEFORMAT *lpWavForm,*
DWORD *dwCallBackFunc,*
DWORD *dwCallBackData,*
DWORD *dwOpenFlag)*

waveInOpen() opens a MIDI waveform input device. *lphMMWaveIn* points to a variable that will become the handle to the MIDI waveform input device being opened. *uDeviceID* is the ID of the MIDI waveform input device to open. *lpWavForm* is a pointer to a **WAVEFORMAT** structure selecting the desired waveform recording format.

dwCallBackFunc either points to a callback function or contains the handle of a window that processes the newly opened MIDI input device messages. *dwCallBackData* contains user-specific data that will be passed to the callback function. *dwOpenFlag* specifies how the device is opened.

The function returns zero if successful, or one of three error constants if unsuccessful.

The **WAVEFORMAT** structure is shown here.

```
typedef struct waveformat_tag {
  WORD wFormatTag;
  WORD nChannels;
  DWORD nSamplesPerSec;
  DWORD nAvgBytesPerSec;
  WORD nBlockAlign;
} WAVEFORMAT;
```

Here, **wFormatTag** gives the format type, which is **WAVE_FORMAT_PCM** and states that the waveform data is pulse code modulated (PCM). **nChannels** contains the number of channels.

nSamplesPerSec contains the sample rate (samples/second). **nAvgBytesPerSec** contains the average data-transfer rate that is required in bytes/second. **nBlockAlign** contains the block alignment, in bytes.

USAGE

dwOpenFlag may be assigned one of the following four constants:

WAVE_ALLOWSYNC
WAVE_FORMAT_QUERY
CALLBACK_FUNCTION
CALLBACK_WINDOW

WAVE_ALLOWSYNC is required to open a synchronous waveform input device. The function fails if the mode is not supported. **WAVE_FORMAT_QUERY** queries the specified waveform input device to see if it supports the specified format.

If *dwOpenFlag* is assigned **CALLBACK_FUNCTION**, the following messages are sent to the callback function:

WIM_OPEN
WIM_CLOSE
WIM_DATA

If *dwOpenFlag* is assigned **CALLBACK_WINDOW**, the following messages are sent to the callback window procedure:

MM_WIM_OPEN
MM_WIM_CLOSE
MM_WIM_DATA

On error **waveInOpen()** returns one of these constants:

Constant	Description
MMSYSERR_ALLOCATED	Identifies the selected MIDI input device as already being opened
MMSYSERR_BADDEVICEID	Signals an illegal device ID
MMSYSERR_NOMEM	Indicates that the required memory allocation failed
WAVERR_BADFORMAT	Indicates that **waveInOpen()** failed due to the selection of an invalid format

The callback function pointed to by *dwCallBackFunc* must have this prototype:

```
void CALLBACK waveInFunc(HWAVEIN hMMWaveIn,
                         UINT uMsg,
                         DWORD dwAppData,
                         DWORD dwParam1,
                         DWORD dwParam2)
```

Of course, the name of the function is arbitrary. However, the function name must be exported with an **EXPORTS** statement in the application's module definition file. (This step is not necessary when using Windows NT.)

hMMWaveIn is the handle of the MIDI waveform input device whose messages are being processed by the callback function. *uMsg* contains the particular MIDI input device message being processed. *dwAppData* contains the data specified in the *dwCallBackData* parameter of **waveInOpen()**. *dwParam1* and *dwParam2* contain user-defined message parameters. The function has no return value.

The code segment for the callback function must be marked **FIXED** in the module definition file. (This does not apply to Windows NT.)

Here is a small portion of code that illustrates the use of this function.

```
static HWAVEIN hMMWaveIn;
static PCMWAVEFORMAT pcmWF;
HWND hwnd;
   .
   .
   .
waveInOpen(&hMMWaveIn, 0, &pcmWF.wf, hwnd, 0L,
          CALLBACK_WINDOW)
```

RELATED FUNCTION

waveInClose()

MMRESULT waveInPrepareHeader
(HWAVEIN *hMMWaveIn*,
LPWAVEHDR *lpWaveInHdr*,
UINT *uStrucSize*)

waveInPrepareHeader() prepares a buffer to be used by a MIDI waveform input device. *hMMWaveIn* is a handle to a valid MIDI waveform input device.

lpWaveInHdr is a pointer to a **WAVEHDR** structure. *uStrucSize* contains the size of the **WAVEHDR** structure.

The function returns zero if successful, or one of three error constants if unsuccessful.

USAGE

On error **waveInPrepareHeader()** may return one of these constants:

Constant	Description
MMSYSERR_HANDLEBUSY	Indicates that the handle is currently being used by some other thread
MMSYSERR_INVALHANDLE	Signals an invalid MIDI waveform input device handle
MMSYSERR_NOMEM	Flags an unsuccessful attempt to allocate the memory

The functions **GlobalAlloc()** and **GlobalLock()** are needed to allocate and lock the **WAVEHDR** structure pointed to by *lpWaveInHdr*. The allocated memory must also have been marked **GMEM_MOVEABLE** and **GMEM_-SHARE**. These requirements also apply to memory pointed to by the **lpData** member of **WAVEHDR**.

Here is a small portion of code that illustrates the use of this function.

```
static HWAVEIN hMMWaveIn;
static LPWAVEHDR pMMWaveHdr;
HWND hwnd;
   .
   .
   .
waveInPrepareHeader(hMMWaveIn, pMMWaveHdr, sizeof(WAVEHDR));
```

RELATED FUNCTION

waveInUnprepareHeader()

MMRESULT waveInReset(HWAVEIN *hMMWaveIn*)

waveInReset() resets (that is, stops any further input from) the specified MIDI waveform input device. *hMMWaveIn* is the handle of the MIDI waveform input device about to be reset.

The function returns zero if successful, or one of two error constants otherwise.

USAGE

On error **waveInReset()** returns one of these constants: **MMSY-SERR_INVALHANDLE** (invalid device handle) or **MMSYSERR_HAN-DLEBUSY** (handle being used by another thread).

waveInReset() flags all pending input buffers as completed.

Here is a small portion of code that illustrates the use of this function.

```
static HWAVEIN hMMWaveIn;
          .
          .
          .
waveInReset(hMMWaveIn)
```

RELATED FUNCTIONS

waveInStart()
waveInStop()

MMRESULT waveInStart(HWAVEIN *hMMWaveIn*)

waveInStart() begins inputting from the selected MIDI waveform input device. *hMMWaveIn* is the handle to the MIDI waveform input device.

The function returns zero if successful, or one of two error constants otherwise.

USAGE

On error **waveInStart()** returns one of these constants: **MMSYSERR_IN-VALHANDLE** (invalid device handle) or **MMSYSERR_HANDLEBUSY** (handle being used by another thread).

RELATED FUNCTIONS

waveInReset()
waveInStop()

MMRESULT waveInStop(HWAVEIN *hMMWaveIn*)

waveInStop() stops any further MIDI input from the specified MIDI waveform input device. *hMMWaveIn* is the handle of the MIDI waveform input device about to be stopped.

The function returns zero if successful, or one of two error constants otherwise.

USAGE

On error **waveInStop()** returns one of these constants: **MMSYSERR_IN-VALHANDLE** (invalid device handle) or **MMSYSERR_HANDLEBUSY** (handle being used by another thread).

A call to **waveInStop()** marks the current system-exclusive message buffer as completed.

RELATED FUNCTIONS

waveInReset()
waveInStart()

MMRESULT waveInUnprepareHeader
(HWAVEIN *hMMWaveIn,* LPWAVEHDR *lpWaveInHdr,* UINT *uStrucSize*)

Your application makes a call to **waveInUnprepareHeader()** just before calling **GlobalFree()** in order to "unprepare" the **WAVEHDR** structure before being freed. This structure was prepared using **waveInPrepareHeader()**.

hMMWaveIn is the handle to the MIDI waveform input device. *lpWaveInHdr* is a pointer to the **WAVEHDR** structure about to be "unprepared". *uStrucSize* tells the function how many bytes are in the **WAVEHDR** structure.

The function returns zero if successful, or one of three error constants if unsuccessful.

USAGE

On error **waveInUnprepareHeader()** returns one of these constants:

Constant	Description
MMSYSERR_HANDLEBUSY	*hMMWaveIn* handle identifies a handle being used by another thread
MMSYSERR_INVALHANDLE	Flags an invalid MIDI input device handle
WAVERR_STILLPLAYING	Tells **waveInUnprepareHeader()** that the buffer is still in the queue

Here is a small portion of code that illustrates the use of this function.

```
static HWAVEIN hMMWaveIn;
static LPWAVEHDR pMMWaveHdr;
HWND hwnd;
   .
   .
   .
waveInUnprepareHeader(hMMWaveIn, pMMWaveHdr, sizeof (WAVEHDR));
```

RELATED FUNCTION

waveInPrepareHeader()

MMRESULT waveOutBreakLoop(HWAVEOUT *hWave*)

waveOutBreakLoop() stops a loop and allows playback to resume after the loop. The handle to the waveform output device is passed in *hWave*. The function returns zero if successful. On error, it returns either **MMSYSERR_INVALHANDLE** (invalid device handle) or **MMSYSERR_HANDLEBUSY** (handle being used by another thread).

RELATED FUNCTIONS

waveOutPause()
waveOutWrite()

MMRESULT waveOutClose(HWAVEOUT *hWaveOut*)

waveOutClose() closes a MIDI waveform output device. *hWaveOut* is the handle to the MIDI waveform output device being closed.

The function returns zero if successful, or one of three error constants if unsuccessful.

USAGE

On error **waveOutClose()** returns one of these constants:

Constant	Description
MMSYSERR_HANDLEBUSY	*hMMWaveIn* handle identifies a handle being used by another thread
MMSYSERR_INVALHANDLE	Flags the use of an invalid MIDI device handle
WAVERR_STILLPLAYING	Indicates that the specified MIDI output device still has buffers in the output queue

A call to **waveOutClose()** fails while there are pending buffers in the output queue. The application can make a call to **waveOutReset()** to mark all output buffers as having been processed.

Here is a small portion of code that illustrates the use of this function.

```
static HWAVEOUT hMMWaveOut;
static LPWAVEHDR pMMWaveHdr;
HWND hwnd;
   .
   .
   .

waveOutUnprepareHeader(hMMWaveOut, pMMWaveHdr, sizeof(WAVEHDR));
waveOutClose(&hMMWaveOut)
```

RELATED FUNCTIONS

waveOutOpen()
waveOutReset()

MMRESULT waveOutGetDevCaps(UINT *uDeviceID*, LPWAVEOUTCAPS *lpOutCaps*, UINT *uStrucSize*)

waveOutGetDevCaps() determines the capabilities for the specified waveform output device. *uDeviceID* is the ID of the waveform output device in question. *lpOutCaps* is a pointer to a **WAVEOUTCAPS** structure that the function fills with the specified device's capabilities. *uStrucSize* contains the size of the **WAVEOUTCAPS** structure.

The function returns zero if successful, or one of two error constants if unsuccessful.

The **WAVEOUTCAPS** structure is shown here.

```
typedef struct waveoutcaps_tag {
  WORD wMid;
  WORD wPid;
  MMVERSION vDriverVersion;
  TCHAR szPname[MAXPNAMELEN];
  DWORD dwFormats;
  WORD wChannels;
  DWORD dwSupport;
} WAVEOUTCAPS;
```

Here, **wMid** is the manufacturer ID for the device driver. **wPid** contains the product ID for the output device. **vDriverVersion** contains the version number, where the major version number is in the high-order byte and the minor version number is in the low-order byte.

szPname is a string that contains the product name. **dwFormats** describes the standard formats supported and can be one or more of the following:

WAVE_FORMAT_1M08 (11.025 kHz, monaural, 8-bit)
WAVE_FORMAT_1S08 (11.025 kHz, stereo, 8-bit)
WAVE_FORMAT_1M16 (11.025 kHz, monaural, 16-bit)
WAVE_FORMAT_1S16 (11.025 kHz, stereo, 16-bit)
WAVE_FORMAT_2M08 (22.05 kHz, monaural, 8-bit)
WAVE_FORMAT_2S08 (22.05 kHz, stereo, 8-bit)
WAVE_FORMAT_2M16 (22.05 kHz, monaural, 16-bit)
WAVE_FORMAT_2S16 (22.05 kHz, stereo, 16-bit)
WAVE_FORMAT_4M08 (44.1 kHz, monaural, 8-bit)
WAVE_FORMAT_4S08 (44.1 kHz, stereo, 8-bit)

WAVE_FORMAT_4M16 (44.1 kHz, monaural, 16-bit)
WAVE_FORMAT_4S16 (44.1 kHz, stereo, 16-bit)

wChannels is either 1 for monaural or 2 for stereo. **dwSupport** describes optional features for the device and can be:

WAVECAPS_PITCH (pitch control)
WAVECAPS_PLAYBACKRATE (playback rate control)
WAVECAPS_VOLUME (volume control)
WAVECAPS_LRVOLUME (separate left and right volume controls)

USAGE

On error **waveOutGetDevCaps()** returns one of these constants: **MMSYSERR_BADDEVICEID** (illegal device driver ID) or **MMSYSERR_NODRIVER** (no device driver present).

RELATED FUNCTION

waveOutGetNumDevs()

MMRESULT waveOutGetErrorText(UINT *uErrorID,*
LPSTR *lpszTextDescrip,*
UINT *uBuffSize*)

waveOutGetErrorText() obtains a string explaining the specified error. *uErrorID* identifies an error by number. *lpszTextDescrip* is a pointer to a buffer that will contain the textual representation of the error. *uBuffSize* tells the function how big the buffer is.

The function returns zero if successful, or **MMSYSERR_BADERRNUM** if unsuccessful.

USAGE

The MMSYSTEM.H header file contains the **MAXERRORLENGTH** constant, which your application may use to dimension the buffer. Technically, all error descriptions should be less than **MAXERRORLENGTH**. However, **waveOutGetErrorText()** will truncate any information beyond the specified buffer size.

waveOutGetErrorText() always creates a null-terminated string within the buffer pointed to by *lpszTextDescrip*.

RELATED FUNCTION

waveOutGetDevCaps()

MMRESULT waveOutGetID(HWAVEOUT *hWave*, PUINT *lpID*)

Given a device handle, **waveOutGetID()** obtains the corresponding device ID. *hWave* is the handle of the waveform output device in question. On return, the variable pointed to by *lpID* will contain the device ID.

The function returns either **MMSYSERR_INVALHANDLE** (invalid device handle) or **MMSYSERR_HANDLEBUSY** (handle being used by another thread).

RELATED FUNCTION

waveInGetID()

MMRESULT waveOutGetNumDevs(void)

waveOutGetNumDevs() determines how many MIDI waveform output devices are currently in the system. The function returns the number of MIDI waveform output devices registered.

RELATED FUNCTION

waveOutGetDevCaps()

MMRESULT waveOutGetPitch(HWAVEOUT *hWaveOut*, LPDWORD *lpdwPitch*)

waveOutGetPitch() determines the current waveform output device pitch setting. *hWaveOut* is the handle to the waveform output device. *lpdwPitch* is a pointer to a memory location which the function fills with the current pitch setting.

The function returns zero if successful, or one of three error constants otherwise.

USAGE

On error **waveOutGetPitch()** returns one of these constants:

Constant	Description
MMSYSERR_HANDLEBUSY	Indicates that the specified wave input device is currently being used
MMSYSERR_INVALHANDLE	Indicates that the specified wave input device handle is invalid
MMSYSERR_NOTSUPPORTED	Indicates that the specified waveform output device cannot return a pitch setting

If successful **waveOutGetPitch()** will fill the memory location pointed to by *lpdwPitch* with a positive fixed-point value. The low-order word contains the fractional part, and the high-order word contains the signed integer part. The fractional part is represented in sixteenths. For example, a fractional value of 0x4000 represents 1/4 and 0x8000 represents 1/2. Thus, a value of 0x000E4000 designates a multiplier of 14.25.

RELATED FUNCTION

waveOutSetPitch()

MMRESULT waveOutGetPlaybackRate
(HWAVEOUT *hWaveOut,*
LPDWORD *lpdwPlayRate*)

waveOutGetPlaybackRate() obtains an output device's playback rate. *hWaveOut* identifies the waveform output device in question. The function returns the current playback rate in the memory location pointed to by the *lpdwPlayRate* pointer.

The function returns zero if successful, or one of three error constants otherwise.

USAGE

On error **waveOutGetPlaybackRate()** returns one of these constants:

Constant	Description
MMSYSERR_HANDLEBUSY	Indicates that the specified wave input device is currently being used
MMSYSERR_INVALHANDLE	Indicates that the specified wave input device handle is invalid
MMSYSERR_NOTSUPPORTED	Indicates that the specified waveform output device cannot return a pitch setting

If successful **waveOutGetPlaybackRate()** will fill the memory location pointed to by *lpdwPlayRate* with a positive fixed-point value. The low-order word contains the fractional part, and the high-order word contains the signed integer part. The fractional part is represented in sixteenths. For example, a fractional value of 0x4000 represents 1/4 and 0x8000 represents 1/2. Thus, a value of 0x000E4000 designates a multiplier of 14.25.

RELATED FUNCTION

waveOutSetPlaybackRate()

MMRESULT waveOutGetPosition(HWAVEOUT *hWave*, LPMMTIME *lpTime*, UINT *nSize*)

waveOutGetPosition() obtains the output position (as specified by a time value) of the waveform device associated with *hWave*. *hWave* is the handle to the device. *lpTime* points to an **MMTIME** structure that will receive the current position. Before the call, the **wType** field of the structure must be set to a valid time format supported by the device. The size of the structure is passed in *nSize*.

The function returns zero if successful. On failure, it returns either **MMSYSERR_INVALHANDLE** (invalid device handle) or **MMSYSERR_HANDLEBUSY** (handle being used by another thread).

RELATED FUNCTION

waveInGetPosition()

MMRESULT waveOutGetVolume(UINT *uDeviceID*, LPDWORD *pdwVolSetting*)

waveOutGetVolume() obtains the volume setting for the specified waveform output device. *uDeviceID* is the ID of the waveform output device in question. *lpdwVolSetting* is a pointer to a memory location that will contain the returned volume setting.

The function returns zero if successful, or one of three error conditions otherwise.

USAGE

On error **waveOutGetVolume()** may return one of these constants:

Constant	Description
MMSYSERR_INVALHANDLE	Flags the use of an invalid device handle
MMSYSERR_NODRIVER	Indicates that the specified device driver has not been installed
MMSYSERR_NOTSUPPORTED	Indicates the specified device cannot return volume information

Valid volume settings range from a minimum of 0 to 0xFFFF. The left channel volume is in the low-order word and right channel volume is in the high-order word. Devices with one channel use only the low-order word.

Your application can make a call to **waveOutGetDevCaps()** and check the **dwSupport** field of the **WAVEOUTCAPS** structure to see if the **WAVE-CAPS_VOLUME** flag is set, indicating that the device supports volume control.

RELATED FUNCTION

waveOutSetVolume()

MMRESULT waveOutMessage(HWAVEOUT *hWave*, UINT *uMsg*, DWORD *dwParm1*, DWORD *dwParm2*)

waveOutMessage() sends a message to the waveform output device specified by *hWave*. *hWave* is the handle to the device being sent the message. *uMsg* contains the message. *dwParm1* and *dwParm2* contain additional data related to the message.

The function returns a value generated by the device driver controling the device.

RELATED FUNCTION

waveInMessage()

MMRESULT waveOutOpen(LPHWAVEOUT *lphWaveOut,*
UINT *uDeviceID,*
LPWAVEFORMAT *lpWaveFormat,*
DWORD *dwCallBackFunc,*
DWORD *dwCallBackData,*
DWORD *dwOpenFlag*)

waveOutOpen() opens a MIDI waveform output device. *lphWaveOut* points to a variable that will become the handle to the MIDI waveform output device being opened. *uDeviceID* identifies the MIDI waveform output device to open. *lpWaveFormat* is a pointer to a **WAVEFORMAT** structure specifying the waveform output format.

dwCallBackFunc either points to the callback function or contains the handle of a window. In either case, *dwCallBackFunc* determines what object will process the newly opened MIDI waveform output device messages. *dwCallBackData* contains user-defined data that is passed to the callback function. *dwOpenFlag* determines how the device is opened.

The function returns zero if successful, or one of three error constants if unsuccessful.

USAGE

dwOpenFlag may be assigned one of the following four constants:

WAVE_ALLOWSYNC
WAVE_FORMAT_QUERY
CALLBACK_FUNCTION
CALLBACK_WINDOW

WAVE_ALLOWSYNC is required to open a synchronous waveform output device. The function fails if the mode is not supported. **WAVE_FOR-MAT_QUERY** queries the specified waveform output device to see if it supports the specified format.

If *dwOpenFlag* is assigned **CALLBACK_FUNCTION**, the following messages are sent to the callback function:

WOM_OPEN
WOM_CLOSE
WOM_DONE

If *dwOpenFlag* is assigned **CALLBACK_WINDOW**, the following messages are sent to the callback window procedure:

MM_WOM_OPEN
MM_WOM_CLOSE
MM_WOM_DONE

On error **waveOutOpen()** returns one of these constants:

Constant	Description
MMSYSERR_ALLOCATED	Identifies the selected MIDI output device as already being opened
MMSYSERR_BADDEVICEID	Signals an illegal device ID
MMSYSERR_NOMEM	Indicates that the required memory allocation failed
WAVERR_BADFORMAT	Indicates failure to open with an unavailable wave output format

The callback function pointed to by *dwCallBackFunc* must have this prototype:

```
void CALLBACK waveOutFunc(HWAVEOUT hMMWaveOut,
                    UINT uMsg,
                    DWORD dwAppData,
                    DWORD dwParam1,
                    DWORD dwParam2)
```

Of course, the name of the function is arbitrary. However, the function name must be exported with an **EXPORTS** statement in the application's module definition file. (This step is not necessary when using Windows NT.)

hMMWaveOut is the handle of the MIDI waveform output device whose messages are being processed by the callback function. *uMsg* contains the particular MIDI output device message being processed. *dwAppData* contains the data specified in the *dwCallBackData* parameter of **waveOutOpen()**.

dwParam1 and *dwParam2* contain user-defined message parameters. The function has no return value.

The code segment for the callback function must be marked **FIXED** in the module definition file. (This does not apply to Windows NT.)

Here is a small portion of code that illustrates the use of this function.

```
static HWAVEOUT hMMWaveOut;
static PCMWAVEFORMAT pcmWF;
HWND hwnd;
      .
      .
      .
waveOutOpen(&hMMWaveOut, 0, &pcmWF.wf, hwnd, OL,
          CALLBACK_WINDOW));
```

RELATED FUNCTION

waveOutClose()

MMRESULT waveOutPause(HWAVEOUT *hWave*)

waveOutPause() pauses playback on an output device. *hWave* is the handle of the affected waveform output device.

The function returns zero if successful. On failure it returns either **MMSYSERR_INVALHANDLE** (invalid device handle) or **MMSYSERR_HANDLEBUSY** (handle being used by another thread).

RELATED FUNCTION

waveOutRestart()

MMRESULT waveOutPrepareHeader
(HWAVEOUT *hWaveOut*, LPWAVEHDR *lpWaveOutHdr*, UINT *uStrucSize*)

waveOutPrepareHeader() prepares a buffer to be used by a MIDI waveform output device. *hWaveOut* is the handle to a valid MIDI waveform output device. *lpWaveOutHdr* is a pointer to a **WAVEHDR** structure. *uStrucSize* tells the function how many bytes are in the **WAVEHDR** structure.

The function returns zero if successful, or one of three error constants if unsuccessful.

USAGE

On error **waveOutPrepareHeader()** may return one of these constants:

Constant	Description
MMSYSERR_HANDLEBUSY	Indicates that the specified wave input device is currently being used
MMSYSERR_INVALHANDLE	Signals an invalid MIDI output device handle
MMSYSERR_NOMEM	Flags an unsuccessful attempt to allocate the memory

The functions **GlobalAlloc()** and **GlobalLock()** are needed to allocate and lock the **WAVEHDR** structure pointed to by *lpWaveOutHdr*. The allocated memory must also have been marked **GMEM_MOVEABLE** and **GMEM_-SHARE**. These requirements also apply to the memory pointed to by the **lpData** member of **WAVEHDR**.

Here is a small portion of code that illustrates the use of this function.

```
static HWAVEOUT hMMWaveOut;
static LPWAVEHDR pMMWaveHdr;
HWND hwnd;
     .
     .
     .

waveOutPrepareHeader(hMMWaveOut, pMMWaveHdr, sizeof(WAVEHDR));
waveOutWrite(hMMWaveOut, pMMWaveHdr, sizeof(WAVEHDR));
```

RELATED FUNCTION

waveOutUnprepareHeader()

MMRESULT waveOutReset(HWAVEOUT *hWaveOut*)

waveOutReset() resets the specified device and prepares it to accept new information. *hWaveOut* is the handle to the affected MIDI waveform output device. The function returns zero if successful.

USAGE

On error **waveOutReset()** will return one of the following error constants:

Constant	Description
MMSYSERR_HANDLEBUSY	Indicates that the specified wave device is currently being used
MMSYSERR_INVALHANDLE	Indicates that the specified wave device handle is invalid

Here is a small portion of code that illustrates the use of this function.

```
static HWAVEOUT hMMWaveOut;
   .
   .
   .
waveOutReset(hMMWaveOut)
```

MMRESULT waveOutRestart(HWAVEOUT *hWave*)

waveOutRestart() restarts an output device that was paused using a call to **waveOutPause()**. The handle of the waveform output device is passed in *hWave*.

The function returns zero if successful. On failure, it returns either **MMSYSERR_INVALHANDLE** (invalid device handle) or **MMSYSERR_HANDLEBUSY** (handle being used by another thread).

RELATED FUNCTION

waveOutPause()

MMRESULT waveOutSetPitch(HWAVEOUT *hWaveOut*, DWORD *dwPitch*)

waveOutSetPitch() sets the pitch for the specified device. *hWaveOut* is a handle to the waveform output device. *dwPitch* contains the pitch setting.

The function returns zero if successful, or one of three error constants otherwise.

USAGE

On error **waveOutSetPitch()** returns one of these constants:

Constant	Description
MMSYSERR_HANDLEBUSY	Indicates that the specified wave input device is currently being used
MMSYSERR_INVALHANDLE	Indicates that the specified wave input device handle is invalid
MMSYSERR_NOTSUPPORTED	Indicates that the specified waveform output device cannot return a pitch setting

dwPitch contains a positive fixed-point value. The low-order word contains the fractional part, and the high-order word contains the signed integer part. The fractional part is represented in sixteenths. For example, a fractional value of 0x4000 represents 1/4 and 0x8000 represents 1/2. Thus, a value of 0x000E4000 designates a multiplier of 14.25.

RELATED FUNCTION

waveOutGetPitch()

MMRESULT waveOutSetPlaybackRate (HWAVEOUT *hWaveOut*, DWORD *dwPlayRate*)

waveOutSetPlaybackRate() sets the specified waveform output device's playback rate. *hWaveOut* is the handle of the waveform output device in question. *dwPlayRate* contains the desired playback rate.

The function returns zero if successful, or one of three error constants otherwise.

USAGE

On error **waveOutSetPlaybackRate()** returns one of these constants:

Constant	Description
MMSYSERR_HANDLEBUSY	Indicates that the specified wave input device is currently being used
MMSYSERR_INVALHANDLE	Indicates that the specified wave input device handle is invalid
MMSYSERR_NOTSUPPORTED	Indicates that the specified waveform output device does not support payback rate changes

dwPlayRate contains a positive fixed-point value. The low-order word contains the fractional part, and the high-order word contains the signed integer part. The fractional part is represented in sixteenths. For example, a fractional value of 0x4000 represents 1/4 and 0x8000 represents 1/2. Thus, a value of 0x000E4000 designates a multiplier of 14.25.

RELATED FUNCTION

waveOutSetPlaybackRate()

MMRESULT waveOutSetVolume(UINT *uDeviceID*, DWORD *dwVolSetting*)

waveOutSetVolume() sets the volume for the specified waveform output device. *uDeviceID* is the ID of the output device. *dwVolSetting* contains the volume setting.

The function returns zero if successful, or one of three error conditions otherwise.

USAGE

On error **waveOutSetVolume()** may return one of these constants:

Constant	Description
MMSYSERR_INVALHANDLE	Flags the use of an invalid device handle
MMSYSERR_NODRIVER	Indicates that the specified device driver has not been installed
MMSYSERR_NOTSUPPORTED	Indicates the specified device does not allow volume settings

Valid volume settings range from a minimum of 0 to 0xFFFF. The left channel volume is in the low-order word and the right channel volume is in the high-order word. Devices with one channel use only the low-order word.

Your application can make a call to **waveOutGetDevCaps()** and check the **dwSupport** field of the **WAVEOUTCAPS** structure to see if the **WAVECAPS_VOLUME** flag is set, indicating that the device supports volume control.

RELATED FUNCTION

waveOutGetVolume()

MMRESULT waveOutUnprepareHeader (HWAVEOUT*hWaveOut,* LPWAVEHDR*lpWaveOutHdr,* UINT *uStrucSize*)

waveOutUnprepareHeader() "unprepares" a buffer used by a MIDI waveform output device. (This buffer was prepared using **waveOutPrepare-Header()**.) *hWaveOut* is the handle to a valid MIDI waveform output device. *lpWaveOutHdr* is a pointer to a **WAVEHDR** structure. *uStrucSize* contains the size of the **WAVEHDR** structure.

The function returns zero if successful, or one of three error constants if unsuccessful.

USAGE

On error **waveOutUnprepareHeader()** may return one of these constants:

Constant	Description
MMSYSERR_HANDLEBUSY	Indicates that the specified wave input device is currently being used
WAVERR_STILLPLAYING	Indicates that the **WAVEHDR** structure pointed to by *lpWaveOutHdr* is still playing
MMSYSERR_INVALHANDLE	Signals an invalid MIDI output device handle

The application must call **waveOutUnprepareHeader()** after the *lpWaveOutHdr* buffer has been passed to **waveOutWrite()**, and prior to invoking **GlobalFree()** to return the unprepared buffer to the available memory pool. You must wait until the buffer has been processed by the output device driver before you "unprepare" it.

Here is a small portion of code that illustrates the use of this function.

```
static HWAVEIN hMMWaveOut;
static LPWAVEHDR pMMWaveHdr;
HWND hwnd;
```

.
.
.

```
waveOutUnprepareHeader(hMMWaveOut, pMMWaveHdr, sizeof(WAVEHDR));
waveOutClose(&hMMWaveOut)
```

RELATED FUNCTION

waveOutPrepareHeader()

MMRESULT waveOutWrite(HWAVEOUT *hWaveOut,* LPWAVEHDR *lpWaveOutHdr,* UINT *uStrucSize*)

waveOutWrite() sends information to a MIDI waveform output device. *hWaveOut* is the handle to a valid MIDI output device. *lpWaveOutHdr* is a pointer to a **WAVEHDR** structure. *uStrucSize* tells the function how many bytes are in the **WAVEHDR** structure.

The function returns zero if successful, or one of three error constants if unsuccessful.

USAGE

On error **waveOutWrite()** may return one of these constants:

Constant	Description
MMSYSERR_HANDLEBUSY	Indicates that the specified wave input device is currently being used
MMSYSERR_INVALHANDLE	Signals an invalid MIDI input device handle
WAVERR_UNPREPARED	Indicates that the **WAVEHDR** structure has not yet been prepared

The functions **GlobalAlloc()** and **GlobalLock()** are needed to allocate and lock the **WAVEHDR** structure pointed to by *lpWaveOutHdr*. The allocated memory must also have been marked **GMEM_MOVEABLE** and **GMEM_-SHARE**. These requirements also apply to the memory pointed to by the **lpData** member of **WAVEHDR**.

Here is a small portion of code that illustrates the use of this function.

```
static HWAVEOUT hMMWaveOut;
static LPWAVEHDR pMMWaveHdr;
HWND hwnd;
    .
    .
    .

waveOutPrepareHeader(hMMWaveOut, pMMWaveHdr, sizeof(WAVEHDR));
waveOutWrite(hMMWaveOut, pMMWaveHdr, sizeof(WAVEHDR));
```

RELATED FUNCTION

waveOutPrepareHeader()

Chapter 22

Multimedia File I/O

HIS chapter describes Windows' multimedia file I/O functions. In addition to normal tasks, these functions can be used to open and close files in both normal and advanced modes of operation.

The multimedia file functions generally operate on RIFF files. RIFF is an acronym for Resource Interchange File Format. A RIFF file is composed of chunks. A *chunk* is a piece of a file beginning with a four-byte character code that identifies the chunk. Next is a **DWORD** value containing the size of the data that follows. The data completes the chunk. Generally, the first four bytes of the data are a type identifier that describes what type of data the chunk contains.

LONG FAR PASCAL IOProc(LPSTR *lpmmioInfo,*
UINT *uMsg,*
LONG *lAppData1,*
LONG *lAppData2*)

IOProc() is a user-defined callback function that processes multimedia I/O. Of course, the name of the function is arbitrary. However, whatever name you use, it must be included in the application's module-definition file using the **EXPORTS** statement. (This does not apply to Windows NT.) This function is registered using the **mmioInstallIOProc()** function.

lpmmioInfo is a pointer to a **MMIOINFO** structure. The value of *uMsg* determines what I/O operation to perform. It may be one of the following: **MMIOM_OPEN, MMIOM_CLOSE, MMIOM_READ, MMIOM_WRITE,** or **MMIOM_SEEK.** *lAppData1* and *lAppData2* contain any optional parameters used by the *uMsg.* The function should return zero upon error. Otherwise, it must return a value related to the operation it performs.

The **MMIOINFO** structure is shown here.

```
typedef struct _MMIOINFO {
  DWORD dwFlags;
  FOURCC fccIOProc;
  LPMMIOPROC pIOProc;
  UINT wErrorRet;
  HANDLE htask;
  LONG cchBuffer;
  LPSTR pchBuffer;
  LPSTR pchNext;
  LPSTR pchEndRead;
  LPSTR pchEndWrite;
  LONG lBufOffset;
  LONG lDiskOffset;
  DWORD adwInfo[3];
  DWORD dwReserved1;
  DWORD dwReserved2;
  HMMIO hmmio;
} MMIOINFO;
```

Here, **dwFlags** describes how a file was opened. This value can be **MMIO_READ** (file opened for reading only), **MMIO_WRITE** (file opened for writing only), **MMIO_READWRITE** (file opened for reading and writing), **MMIO_COMPAT** (file opened in compatibility mode), **MMIO_EXCLUSIVE** (file opened in exclusive mode with no read and write access by a process), **MMIO_DENYWRITE** (processes denied write access), **MMIO_DENYREAD** (processes denied read access), **MMIO_DENYNONE** (processes allowed read or write access), **MMIO_CRE-ATE** (**mmioOpen()** created or truncated the file), or **MMIO_ALLOCBUF** (file's I/O buffer was allocated by **mmioOpen()** or **mmioSetBuffer()**).

fccIOProc contains a four-character ID code. **pIOProc** is a pointer to the file's I/O procedure. **wErrorRet** holds the error code value returned by **mmioOpen()**. **htask** is the handle of the task.

cchBuffer contains the size of the file's I/O buffer. **pchBuffer** is a pointer to the file's I/O buffer. **pchNext** is a pointer to the next location in the buffer to be read/written. **pchEndRead** points to the end of the buffer at which point data may be read. **pchEndWrite** points to the end of the buffer at which point data may be written.

lBufOffset is reserved. **lDiskOffset** contains the file position. **adwInfo** holds state information. **dwReserved1** and **dwReserved2** are currently reserved. **hmmio** is the handle of the open file.

The **fccIOProc** field of the **MMIOINFO** structure pointed to by *lpmmioInfo* contains the uppercase four-character code that specifies the I/O procedure used by the file.

RELATED FUNCTION

mmioInstallIOProc()

MMRESULT mmioAdvance(HMMIO *hmmio*,   LPMMIOINFO *lpmmioInfo*,   UINT *uFlag*)

mmioAdvance() advances through a file's I/O buffer. Its exact operation varies depending on whether the file is opened for input or output. **mmioAdvance()** advances the I/O buffer of a file either by filling a buffer from disk for a file opened in input mode, or by writing the buffer for a file opened in output mode. The **pchNext, pchEndRead**, and **pchEndWrite** fields of the **MMIOINFO** structure are updated to reflect the new state of the I/O buffer.

For output files, the **dwFlags** field of the **MMIOINFO** structure must have been set to **MMIO_DIRTY** in order for data to physically be written to disk.

hmmio is a handle to a file opened with a call to **mmioOpen()**. *lpmmioInfo* is a pointer to a **MMIOINFO** structure. *uFlag* is either **MMIO_READ** or **MMIO_WRITE**.

The function returns zero if successful, or one of five error constants otherwise.

USAGE

The buffer operated on by **mmioAdvance()** must have been opened for direct access using a call to **mmioGetInfo()**. That is, the structure pointed to by *lpmmioInfo* must have been obtained from **mmioGetInfo()**.

On error **mmioAdvance()** returns one of the following constants:

Constant	Description
MMIOERR_CANNOTEXPAND	Indicates that the specified memory file cannot be expanded
MMIOERR_CANNOTREAD	Indicates that an error occurred while trying to fill the input buffer

Constant	Description
MMIOERR_CANNOTWRITE	Indicates that an error occurred while trying to write the buffer to disk
MMIOERR_OUTOFMEMORY	Indicates that there was not enough memory to expand the buffer as requested
MMIOERR_UNBUFFERED	Indicates that the specified file has not been opened for buffered I/O

The only way to check for EOF when using **mmioAdvance()** is to see if the **pchNext** and **pchEndRead** fields of the **MMIOINFO** structure are equal.

RELATED FUNCTION

mmioGetInfo()

MMRESULT mmioAscend(HMMIO *hmmio*, LPMMCKINFO *lpmmckInfo*, UINT *uUnusedFlag*)

mmioAscend() ascends out of a chunk. That is, the file position indicator is moved to the end of the chunk. The file must have been created with a call to **mmioCreateChunk()** or descended into with a call to **mmioDescend()**. *hmmio* is the handle to a file in RIFF format. *lpmmckInfo* is a pointer to an **MMCKINFO** structure. *uUnusedFlag* is not used and should be assigned a NULL. The function returns zero if successful, or **MMIOER_CANNOT-WRITE** or **MMIOERR_CANNOTSEEK** otherwise.

The **MMCKINFO** structure is shown here.

```
typedef struct _MMCKINFO {
  FOURCC ckid;
  DWORD cksize;
  FOURCC fccType;
  DWORD dwDataOffset;
  DWORD dwFlags;
} MMCKINFO;
```

Here, **ckid** contains the identifier of the chunk. **cksize** contains the size of the chunk's data. **fccType** contains the chunk's type. **dwDataOffset** contains the offset to the start of the chunk's data. This offset is relative to the start of the file. **dwFlags** contains flags providing additional information.

USAGE

The structure pointed to by *lpmmckInfo* must have valid field contents obtained from a previous call to either **mmioCreateChunk()** or **mmioDescend()**. The current file pointer is assumed to be at the end of the chunk if a call was made to **mmioCreateChunk()**, or the **MMIO_DIRTY** flag is set in the **dwFlags** field of the structure pointed to by *lpmmckInfo*. If the chunk size does not match the specification in the **cksize** field of the same structure, **mmioAscend()** adjusts the chunk size before ascending from the chunk. Odd chunk size specifications cause the function to place a null byte at the end of the chunk. **mmioAscend()** moves the file pointer to the end of the chunk if the function call was successful.

Here is a small piece of code that illustrates the use of this function.

```
WORD wErr1, wErr2, wErr3, wErrAll;
HMMIO hmmio;
MMCKINFO mmckinfo;
char szMusicID[] = "MUSIC";
char szDataID[]="ISCD";
    .
    .
    .
mmckinfo.ckid = mmioStringToFOURCC(szDataID, 0);
wErr1 = mmioCreateChunk(hmmio, &mmckinfo, 0);
wErr2 = (mmioWrite(hmmio, (LPSTR) pmusic,
          sizeof(MUSIC)) != sizeof(MUSIC));
wErr3 = mmioAscend(hmmio, &mmckinfo, 0);
wErrAll = wErr1 | wErr2 | wErr3;
```

RELATED FUNCTIONS

mmioCreateChunk()
mmioDescend()

MMRESULT mmioClose(HMMIO *hmmio*, UINT *uFlag*)

mmioClose() closes any file opened with a call to **mmioOpen()**. *hmmio* is the handle to the file about to be closed. *uFlag* defines file close options.

The function returns zero if successful, or **MMIOERR_CANNOTCLOSE** or **MMIOERR_CANNOTWRITE** otherwise.

USAGE

uFlag may be assigned **MMIO_FHOPEN** when *hmmio* contains the handle to a previously opened DOS/Windows file. In this case, **mmioClose**() closes the **MMIO** file handle, but not the DOS/Windows file handle. With **MMIO_FHOPEN** specified, the user-defined **IOProc()** callback function must close the actual DOS/Windows file.

Here is a small piece of code that illustrates the use of this function.

```
WORD wErr;
HMMIO hmmio;
    .
    .
    .
wErr = mmioClose(hmmio, 0);
```

RELATED FUNCTION

mmioOpen()

MMRESULT mmioCreateChunk(HMMIO *hmmio,*
LPMMCKINFO *lpmmckInfo,*
UINT *uFlag*)

mmioCreateChunk() creates a chunk in a RIFF file at the current file position. The file must have been previously opened with a call to **mmioOpen()**. *hmmio* is the handle to an opened RIFF file. *lpmmckInfo* is a pointer to an **MMCKINFO** structure. *uFlag* may be either **MMIO_CREATERIFF** or **MMIO_CREATEL-IST** and specifies the type of chunk being created.

The function returns zero if successful, or **MMIOERR_CANNOTSEEK** or **MMIOERR_CANNOTWRITE** otherwise.

USAGE

Chunks should only be added to the end of a file; otherwise, critical data will be overwritten. **mmioCreateChunk()** sets the **dwFlags** field of the **MMCKINFO** structure pointed to by *lpmmckInfo* to **MMIO_DIRTY**.

Here is a small piece of code that illustrates the use of this function.

```
WORD wErr1, wErr2, wErr3, wErrAll;
HMMIO hmmio;
MMCKINFO mmckinfo;
char szMusicID[] = "MUSIC";
char szDataID[]="ISCD";
    .
    .
    .

mmckinfo.ckid = mmioStringToFOURCC(szDataID, 0);
wErr1 = mmioCreateChunk(hmmio, &mmckinfo, 0);
wErr2 = (mmioWrite(hmmio, (LPSTR) pmusic,
            sizeof(MUSIC)) != sizeof(MUSIC));
wErr3 = mmioAscend(hmmio, &mmckinfo, 0);
wErrAll = wErr1 | wErr2 | wErr3;
```

RELATED FUNCTION

mmioOpen()

MMRESULT mmioDescend(HMMIO *hmmio*, LPMMCKINFO *lpmmckInfo*, LPMMCKINFO *lpOptmmckInfo*, UINT *uFlag*)

mmioDescend() descends into or searches for a specific chunk within the specified RIFF file. (Descending into a chunk causes the file position indicator to be set to the start of the chunk's data.) *hmmio* is the handle to a previously opened RIFF file. *lpmmckInfo* points to a **MMCKINFO** structure. On return, this structure contains updated information as described below. *lpOptmmckInfo* is a pointer to an optional parent **MMCKINFO** structure. *uFlag* selects the search options.

The function returns zero if successful, or **MMIOERR_CANNOTSEEK** or **MMIOERR_CHUNKNOTFOUND** otherwise.

USAGE

On return, the structure pointed to by *lpmmckInfo* will have the following fields updated. **ckid** will contain the chunk ID. **cksize** will contain the size of the chunk's data. **fccType** will hold the form type for a RIFF format, or list type for a LIST format. **dwDataOffset** will contain the offset from the beginning of the file of the chunk's data.

If *lpOptmmckInfo* is not NULL, it is assumed that the specified chunk is a parent chunk encapsulating the chunk being searched for. **mmioDescend()** will only descend into the encapsulating parent chunk if *lpOptmmckInfo* is not NULL.

Here is a small piece of code that illustrates the use of this function.

```
HMMIO hmmio;
MMCKINFO mmckinfo;
    .
    .
    .
if (mmioDescend(hmmio, &mmckinfo, NULL, MMIO_FINDRIFF))
{ ...
```

RELATED FUNCTION

mmioAscend()

MMRESULT mmioFlush(HMMIO *hmmio,*
UINT *uUnusedFlag*)

mmioFlush() flushes the file buffer to disk. *hmmio* is the handle to the file. *uUnusedFlag* should be set to NULL and is currently not used.

The function returns zero if successful, or **MMIOERR_CANNOT-WRITE** otherwise.

USAGE

mmioFlush() will only flush the buffer if it has been previously written to. Care should be taken when writing the overall output logic for your application since a call to **mmioWrite()** may succeed, while the call to **mmioFlush()** may fail if there is insufficient disk space to write the buffer.

RELATED FUNCTION

mmioWrite()

FOURCC mmioFOURCC(char *c1*, char *c2*, char *c3*, char *c4*)

mmioFOURCC() converts the four characters *c1, c2, c3,* and *c4* to a single **FOURCC** four-character code, which the function returns.

USAGE

You can use the character code returned by **mmioFOURCC()** in a call to **mmioInstallIOProc()**.

RELATED FUNCTION

mmioInstallIOProc()

MMRESULT mmioGetInfo(HMMIO *hmmio*, LPMMIOINFO *lpmmInfo*, UINT *uUnusedFlag*)

After using **mmioOpen()** to open a file for buffered I/O, you can use **mmioGetInfo()** to obtain information that lets you directly access the I/O buffer. *hmmio* is the handle to the opened file. *lpmmInfo* is a pointer to an **MMIOINFO** structure, which the function fills with the requested information. *uUnusedFlag* must be set to NULL and is currently unused. The function returns zero if successful.

RELATED FUNCTIONS

mmioAdvance()
mmioSetInfo()

LPMMIOPROC mmioInstallIOProc(FOURCC *fccIOCode*, LPMMIOPROC *lpIOProc*, DWORD *dwFlag*)

mmioInstallIOProc() installs or removes or finds a previously installed custom I/O procedure. *fccIOCode* is the four-character code ID of the I/O procedure to install, find, or remove. *lpIOProc* contains the address of the I/O procedure to install. *dwFlag* is one of four constants that determine whether to install, remove, or find the specified I/O procedure.

The function returns a handle to the I/O procedure installed, removed, or found if successful, and NULL otherwise.

USAGE

The characters in *fccIOCode* must all be uppercase.

The address associated with *lpIOProc* must have been obtained from a call to the **MakeProcInstance()** function. (This does not apply to Windows NT.) *dwFlag* may be one of the following four values:

Constant	Description
MMIO_FINDPROC	Instructs **mmioInstallIOProc()** to search for the specified I/O procedure
MMIO_GLOBALPROC	Instructs **mmioInstallIOProc()** to install the I/O procedure for global use
MMIO_INSTALLPROC	Instructs **mmioInstallIOProc()** to install the specified I/O procedure
MMIO_REMOVEPROC	Instructs **mmioInstallIOProc()** to remove the specified I/O procedure

Since **mmioInstallIOProc()** maintains a separate list of installed I/O procedures, multiple applications can use the same I/O procedure name for different I/O procedures without creating any conflicts. When searching for a specific I/O procedure, local procedures are searched first, followed by global procedures.

RELATED FUNCTIONS

IOProc()
mmioOpen()

HHMIO mmioOpen(LPSTR *lpszFileName*,
LPMMIOINFO *lpmmioInfo*,
DWORD *dwOpenFlags*)

mmioOpen() opens a file for either buffered or unbuffered I/O. *lpszFileName* is a pointer to name of the file about to be opened. *lpmmioInfo* is a pointer to a **MMIOINFO** structure containing any application-specific information pertaining to the opening of the file. *dwOpenFlags* defines how the file is to be opened.

The function returns a handle to the opened file if successful, and NULL otherwise.

USAGE

If *lpszFileName* does not contain a + symbol, **mmioOpen()** assumes *lpszFilename* points to the name of a DOS/Windows file. When the filename is in the form "filename.ext+cod", the file extension ".ext" identifies an installed I/O procedure that is called to perform I/O on the file. The filename, including the null-terminator, must not exceed 128 bytes.

lpmmioInfo should be NULL unless the application is using **mmioOpen()** either to open a memory file or to specify the size of a buffer for buffered I/O. When opening a memory file, *lpszFileName* is assigned NULL. When *lpmmioInfo* is not NULL, any unused fields within the **MMIOINFO** structure pointed to by *lpmmioInfo* must be assigned NULL.

To open a file that will be processed by an already installed custom I/O function, set the **fccIOProc** field of the **MMIOINFO** structure to the four-character code identifying the custom I/O callback function and assign NULL to the **pIOProc**.

To open a file that will be processed by a currently uninstalled custom I/O function, set the **pIOProc** field to point to the custom I/O callback function and set **fccIOProc** to NULL. This causes the custom I/O function to be installed.

To open an internally allocated memory file, **pchBuffer** must be NULL and **fccIOProc** must be set to **FOURCC_MEM**. The initial size of the buffer must be assigned to **cchBuffer**. The value of **adwInfo[0]** specifies the number of bytes by which the buffer will be expanded, when necessary.

To open a caller-supplied buffer, **pchBuffer** must point to the memory buffer and **fccIOProc** must be set to **FOURCC_MEM**. The size of the buffer is specified **cchBuffer**. The value of **adwInfo[0]** specifies the number of bytes by which the buffer will be expanded, when necessary.

When using an open DOS file handle with **MMIO**, set the **fccIOProc** field to **FOURCC_DOS**, **pchBuffer** to NULL, and **adwInfo[0]** to the DOS file handle.

dwOpenFlags defines the options used when opening the file:

Constant	Description
MMIO_ALLOCBUF	Opens a file for buffered I/O; to override the default 8K buffer size, the **cchBuffer** field of the **MMIOINFO** structure should be set to the desired size.
MMIO_COMPAT	Designates a file that can be simultaneously opened by any process on the target machine.
MMIO_CREATE	Creates a new file if none exists by the *lpszFileName,* or reinitializes an existing file's length to zero if one exists by the specified name.
MMIO_DELETE	Deletes the specified file.
MMIO_DENYNONE	Opens the file so that more than one process may read and/or write to it.
MMIO_DENYREAD	Opens the file and prevents any other process from reading the file.
MMIO_DENYWRITE	Opens the file and prevents any other process from writing to the file.
MMIO_EXCLUSIVE	Opens the file and prevents any other process from reading from or writing to the file.
MMIO_EXIST	Determines whether the file specified by *lpszFileName* exists or not.
MMIO_GETTEMP	Creates a temporary file by the filename pointed to by *lpszFileName.*
MMIO_PARSE	Generates a full, qualified filename from the path specified in *lpszFileName*; the null-terminated qualified name is placed back in the buffer pointed to by *lpszFileName.*
MMIO_READ	Opens a file in read mode only.
MMIO_READWRITE	Opens a file for both reading and writing.
MMIO_WRITE	Opens a file for output only.

MMIO_READ, MMIO_READWRITE, and **MMIO_WRITE** are mutually exclusive. Your application should therefore only select one of them.

For 16-bit Windows, the DOS SHARE command must be executed prior to calling **mmioOpen()** with any of the following file-sharing modes:

MMIO_COMPAT
MMIO_EXCLUSIVE
MMIO_DENYREAD
MMIO_DENYWRITE
MMIO_DENYNONE

Since the application will not automatically close the opened file upon termination, your program must make a call to **mmioClose()** and explicitly close any files opened with **mmioOpen()**.

Here is a small piece of code that illustrates the use of this function.

L 22.7

```
HMMIO hmmio;
char szFileName[]="MyFile";
            .
            .
            .
hmmio = mmioOpen(szFileName, NULL, MMIO_CREATE |
                 MMIO_READWRITE);
```

RELATED FUNCTION

mmioClose()

LRESULT mmioRead(HMMIO *hmmio*, LPSTR *lpstrBuffer*, LONG *lBuffSize*)

mmioRead() reads information from a file. *hmmio* is the handle to an input file opened by **mmioOpen()**. *lpstrBuffer* is a pointer to the buffer that is filled with information. *lBuffSize* contains the number of bytes to read.

The function returns the number of bytes read if successful, zero if there were no more bytes to read, or –1 if an input error occurred.

USAGE

NOTE

16-bit Windows applications use a huge pointer data type to represent lpstrBuffer.

Here is a small piece of code that illustrates the use of this function.

```
HMMIO hmmio;
char szMusicID[] = "MUSIC";
        .
        .
        .
if (mmioRead(hmmio, (LPSTR) &instrument,
    sizeof(MUSIC)) != sizeof(MUSIC))
```

```
{
    .
    .
    .
}
```

RELATED FUNCTION

mmioWrite()

MMRESULT mmioRename(LPCSTR *lpszOld,*
 LPCSTR *lpszNew,*
 LPMMIOINFO *lpInfo,*
 DWORD *dwNotUsed*)

mmioRename() changes the name of the file specified by *lpszOld* to that specified by *lpszNew*. The function returns zero if successful and non-zero on failure.

lpszOld points to the old name and *lpszNew* points to the new name. *lpInfo* points to an **MMIOINFO** structure that contains any additional information that you want to change. This parameter may be NULL if no other changes are required. If it is not, then any fields that are unused must be set to NULL. *dwNotUsed* must be zero.

RELATED FUNCTION

mmioOpen()

LRESULT mmioSeek(HMMIO *hmmio,*
 LONG *lFilePtrOffset,*
 int *iOriginFlag*)

mmioSeek() moves a file pointer. *hmmio* is the handle to the file that was opened by **mmioOpen()**. *lFilePtrOffset* specifies the number of bytes to move the file pointer. *iOriginFlag* is one of three constants identifying the type of file pointer movement.

The function returns the new file pointer position if successful, or -1 otherwise.

USAGE

Your application can either read or write information at the new file pointer position. *iOriginFlag* may be one of the following three constants:

Constant	Description
SEEK_CUR	Moves *lFilePtrOffset* bytes from the current file pointer position
SEEK_END	Moves *lFilePtrOffset* bytes from the end of the file
SEEK_SET	Moves *lFilePtrOffset* bytes from the beginning of the file

RELATED FUNCTION

mmioOpen()

LRESULT mmioSendMessage(HMMIO *hmmio*, UINT *uMsg*, LONG *lAppData1*, LONG *lAppData2*)

mmioSendMessage() sends a message to the specified file's I/O function. *hmmio* is the handle to the specified file. *uMsg* contains the specific I/O message. *lAppData1* and *lAppData2* contain any additional information associated with the specific I/O message.

The function returns zero if the I/O procedure does not recognize the message; otherwise, the function returns an application-specific value.

USAGE

This function should only be used to send user-defined messages that have values above or equal to the **MMIO_USER** constant. You should not use the function to send the following messages:

MMIOM_CLOSE
MMIOM_OPEN
MMIOM_READ
MMIOM_SEEK
MMIOM_WRITE
MMIOM_WRITEFLUSH

RELATED FUNCTION

mmioInstallIOProc()

MMRESULT mmioSetBuffer(HMMIO *hmmio,*
LPSTR *lpstrBuffer,*
LONG *lBuffSize,*
UINT *uUnusedFlag*)

mmioSetBuffer() turns buffered I/O on or off. *hmmio* is a handle to the file. *lpstrBuffer* is a pointer to the buffer to be used. *lBuffSize* contains the size of the buffer, in bytes. *uUnusedFlag* should be set to NULL and is currently unused.

The function returns zero if successful, or **MMIOERR_CANNOT-WRITE** or **MMIOERR_OUTOFMEMORY** otherwise.

USAGE

If *lpstrBuffer* is NULL, the function allocates its own internal buffer; otherwise, the pointer must point to a buffer previously allocated by the application. To turn file buffering off, set the *lpstrBuffer* parameter to NULL and *lBuffSize* to zero.

RELATED FUNCTION

mmioGetInfo()

MMRESULT mmioSetInfo(HMMIO *hmmio,*
LPMMIOINFO *lpmmioInfo,*
UINT *uUnusedFlag*)

Once a file has been opened with a call to **mmioOpen()** and **mmioGetInfo()** has been called, your application can make a call to **mmioSetInfo()** to change the file's status. *hmmio* is the handle to the file. *lpmmioInfo* is a pointer to a **MMIOINFO** structure containing the information obtained from the call to **mmioGetInfo()**.

uUnusedFlag should be set to NULL and is currently unused. The function returns zero if successful.

USAGE

You must set the **dwFlags** field of the **MMIOINFO** structure pointed to by *lpmmioInfo* to **MMIO_DIRTY** when the application has written to the I/O buffer. This will guarantee that the buffer is flushed before terminating direct buffer access.

RELATED FUNCTIONS

mmioGetInfo()
mmioOpen()

FOURCC mmioStringToFOURCC(LPCSTR *lpsz*, UINT *uFlag*)

mmioStringToFOURCC takes the four-character null-terminated string pointed to by *lpsz* and converts it to the four-character code used by **mmioInstallIOProc()**. *uFlag* may be set to **MMIO_TOUPPER** to convert the four characters to all uppercase. The function returns the converted character code.

USAGE

The function performs no error checking on the particular four characters passed in the string.

Here is a small piece of code that illustrates the use of this function.

```
WORD wErr1, wErr2, wErr3, wErrAll;
HMMIO hmmio;
MMCKINFO mmckinfo;
char szMusicID[] = "MUSIC";
char szDataID[]="ISCD";
    .
    .
    .
mmckinfo.ckid = mmioStringToFOURCC(szDataID, 0);
wErr1 = mmioCreateChunk(hmmio, &mmckinfo, 0);
wErr2 = (mmioWrite(hmmio, (LPSTR) pmusic,
         sizeof(MUSIC)) != sizeof(MUSIC));
wErr3 = mmioAscend(hmmio, &mmckinfo, 0);
wErrAll = wErr1 | wErr2 | wErr3;
```

RELATED FUNCTION

mmioInstallIOProc()

LRESULT mmioWrite(HMMIO *hmmio*, LPSTR *lpstr*, LONG *lBytesToWrite*)

mmioWrite() copies the information in the buffer pointed to by *lpstr* to a file. *hmmio* is the handle to the file. *lBytesToWrite* contains the number of bytes from the buffer to write.

The function returns the number of bytes written if successful, or –1 otherwise.

USAGE

The function automatically updates the file position pointer.

The file must have been opened by **mmioOpen()**.

Here is a small piece of code that illustrates the use of this function.

```
WORD wErr1, wErr2, wErr3, wErrAll;
HMMIO hmmio;
MMCKINFO mmckinfo;
char szMusicID[] = "MUSIC";
char szDataID[]="ISCD";
    .
    .
    .
mmckinfo.ckid = mmioStringToFOURCC(szDataID, 0);
wErr1 = mmioCreateChunk(hmmio, &mmckinfo, 0);
wErr2 = (mmioWrite(hmmio, (LPSTR) pmusic,
            sizeof(MUSIC)) != sizeof(MUSIC));
wErr3 = mmioAscend(hmmio, &mmckinfo, 0);
wErrAll = wErr1 | wErr2 | wErr3;
```

RELATED FUNCTION

mmioRead()

Chapter 23

Object Linking and

Embedding (OLE)

t H I S chapter describes Windows' Object Linking and Embedding functions. These functions can be used, among other things, to create, enumerate, and retrieve objects. Many function descriptions contain a small portion of code to help you understand how various parameters are used.

OLESTATUS OleActivate(LPOLEOBJECT *lpObj,*
UINT *iVerb,* BOOL *fShow,*
BOOL *fTakeFocus,* HWND *hwnd,*
const RECT FAR ⋆ *lpBounds)*

OleActivate() activates an object, usually to be edited or played. The function returns **OLE_OK** if the operation is successful. If the function fails, it returns **OLE_BUSY, OLE_ERROR_OBJECT,** or **OLE_WAIT_FOR_RELEASE**.

lpObj points to the object that is to be activated. *iVerb* contains the operation. If *fShow* is TRUE, the window will be displayed. If it is FALSE, the window is not displayed. If *fTakeFocus* is TRUE, the server will gain input focus. If FALSE, it does not gain input focus. (*fTakeFocus* is ignored unless *fShow* is TRUE.)

hwnd is the handle of the document window that contains the object. A NULL value is permitted.

lpBounds is a pointer to a **RECT** structure that contains the bounding rectangle's coordinates. The units depend upon the mapping mode. *lpBounds* can also be NULL.

The **RECT** structure is shown here.

```
typedef struct tagRECT {
    int left;
    int top;
    int right;
    int bottom;
} RECT;
```

NOTE

For Windows NT/Win32, the members of **RECT** *are of type* **LONG***.*

USAGE

Editing of objects usually occurs asynchronously. The server runs in one window and the client in another. Changes are posted through the callback function.

Here is a small portion of code illustrating how this function might be used.

```
LPOLEOBJECT lpObj;
RECT rc;
OLESTATUS olestatus;
HWND hwndPart;
    .
    .
    .

hwndPart = GetParent(hwnd);
    .
    .
    .

olestatus = OleActivate(lpObj, wParam,
                    TRUE, TRUE, hwndPart, &rc);
```

RELATED FUNCTIONS

OleQueryOpen()
OleSetData()

OLESTATUS OleBlockServer(LHSERVER *lhServ*)

OleBlockServer() queues incoming requests for the server until **OleUnBlockServer()** is called. These two functions allow the server to control the processing of client application requests. Client messages are blocked, but server messages continue to be sent.

The function returns **OLE_OK** if successful, and **OLE_ERROR_HANDLE** if unsuccessful.

lhServ is the handle of the server for which requests are being queued. When the operation is completed, **OleUnblockServer()** must be called.

RELATED FUNCTIONS

OleRegisterServer()
OleUnblockServer()

OLESTATUS OleClone(LPOLEOBJECT *lpObj,*
LPOLECLIENT *lpClnt,*
LHCLIENTDOC *lhClntDoc,*
LPSTR *lpszObjName,*
LPOLEOBJECT FAR ★ *lplpObj*)

OleClone() copies an object. The copy is independent of the server. The function returns **OLE_OK** if successful. If unsuccessful, it returns **OLE_BUSY, OLE_ERROR_HANDLE, OLE_ERROR_OBJECT,** or **OLE_ERROR_NAME.**

lpObj is a pointer to the object to be copied. *lpClnt* is a pointer to an **OLECLIENT** structure that is associated with the copied object. *lhClntDoc* is the handle of the client document where the new object is to be created.

lpszObjName is a pointer to a string that contains the client name for the object. *lplpObj* is a pointer to a variable in which the DLL will store a pointer to the cloned object.

The **OLECLIENT** structure is shown here.

```
typedef struct _OLECLIENT{
  LPOLECLIENTVTBL lpvtbl;
} OLECLIENT;
```

Here, **lpvtbl** is a pointer to a table of function pointers for the client application.

RELATED FUNCTION

OleEqual()

OLESTATUS OleClose(LPOLEOBJECT *lpObj*)

OleClose() closes an OLE object. This effectively ends the connection with the server. The function returns **OLE_OK** if successful. If unsuccessful, it returns **OLE_BUSY, OLE_ERROR_OBJECT,** or **OLE_WAIT_FOR_RELEASE.**

lpObj is a pointer to the object to be closed.

USAGE

Here is a small portion of code illustrating how this function might be used.

```
LPOLEOBJECT lpObj;
OLESTATUS olestatus;
     .
     .
     .
olestatus = OleClose(lpObj);
```

RELATED FUNCTIONS

OleActivate()
OleDelete()
OleReconnect()

OLESTATUS OleCopyFromLink(LPOLEOBJECT *lpObj,*
LPSTR *lpszProto,*
LPOLECLIENT *lpClnt,*
LHCLIENTDOC *lhClntDoc,*
LPSTR *lpszObjName,*
LPOLEOBJECT FAR * *lplpObj*)

OleCopyFromLink() makes an embedded copy of a linked object. The function returns **OLE_OK** if successful. If unsuccessful, it returns **OLE_BUSY**, **OLE_ERROR_HANDLE**, **OLE_ERROR_NAME**, **OLE_ERROR_OB-JECT**, **OLE_ERROR_PROTOCOL**, or **OLE_WAIT_FOR_RELEASE**.

lpObj is a pointer to the linked object. *lpszProto* is a pointer to a string that contains the name of the protocol for the newly embedded object. (At the time of this writing, this string must contain "StdFileEditing".)

lpClnt is a pointer to an **OLECLIENT** structure used by the new object. *lhClntDoc* is the handle of the client document where the object will be created. *lpszObjName* is a pointer to a string containing the object's name. *lplpObj* is a pointer to a variable in which the DLL will store a pointer to the object.

RELATED FUNCTION

OleObjectConvert()

OLESTATUS OleCopyToClipboard(LPOLEOBJECT *lpObj*)

OleCopyToClipboard() copies an object to the Clipboard. This function should be called when a user selects the Copy or Cut command from an Edit menu. The function returns **OLE_OK** if successful, and **OLE_ERROR_OBJECT** if unsuccessful.

The client application is responsible for opening and emptying the Clipboard. *lpObj* is a pointer to the object to be copied to the Clipboard.

USAGE

Here is a small portion of code illustrating how this function might be used.

```
LPOLEOBJECT lpObj;
    .
    .
    .
lpObj = (LPOLEOBJECT)SendMessage(hWndPrevActive,
        PM_GETOBJECT, 0, 0L);
if(OLE_OK == OleCopyToClipboard(lpObj))
    .
    .
    .
```

OLESTATUS OleCreate(LPSTR *lpszProto*,
        LPOLECLIENT *lpClnt*,
        LPSTR *lpszClass*,
        LHCLIENTDOC *lhClntDoc*,
        LPSTR *lpszObjName*,
        LPOLEOBJECT FAR ★ *lplpObj*,
        OLEOPT_RENDER *renderOpt*,
        OLECLIPFORMAT *cfFormat*)

OleCreate() creates an embedded OLE object.

The function returns **OLE_OK** if successful. If unsuccessful, it returns **OLE_ERROR_HANDLE, OLE_ERROR_NAME, OLE_ERROR_- PROTOCOL,** or **OLE_WAIT_FOR_RELEASE.**

lpszProto is a pointer to a string containing the name of the protocol for the newly embedded object. (At the time of this writing, this string must contain "StdFileEditing".) *lpClnt* is a pointer to an **OLECLIENT** structure associated with the newly embedded object. *lpszClass* is a pointer to a string that holds the class name of of the object. *lhClntDoc* is the handle of the client document where the object is created.

lpszObjName is a pointer to a string that contains the client name for the object. *lplpObj* is a pointer to a variable in which the DLL will store a pointer to the object. *renderOpt* determines how the object's presentation data is handled. Values for this parameter are shown in Table 23-1.

cfFormat gives the Clipboard format when *renderOpt* is **olerender_format**. This format is then used in a call to **OleGetData()**. The DLL handles the data and draws the object only when the specified format is **CF_METAFILEPICT, CF_ENHMETAFILE, CF_DIB,** or **CF_BITMAP**.

RELATED FUNCTIONS

OleCreateFromClip()
OleCreateFromTemplate()
OleDraw()
OleGetData()

Value	Purpose
olerender_none	No presentation data is obtained by the client DLL and, thus, it does not draw the object (frequently used for hyperlinks).
olerender_draw	**OleDraw()** is called by the client, and the DLL obtains the presentation data. This is the most frequently used option.
olerender_format	**OleGetData()** is called by the client to get data in a given format. The client DLL gets the data in the format specified by the *cfFormat* parameter.

Table 23-1
Purpose of renderOpt Values

OLESTATUS OleCreateFromClip(LPSTR *lpszProto*,
LPOLECLIENT *lpClnt*,
LHCLIENTDOC *lhClntDoc*,
LPSTR *lpszObjName*,
LPOLEOBJECT FAR ★ *lplpObj*,
OLEOPT_RENDER *renderOpt*,
OLECLIPFORMAT *cfFormat*)

OleCreateFromClip() creates an object from the Clipboard. The function returns **OLE_OK** if successful. If unsuccessful, it returns **OLE_ER-ROR_CLIP**, **OLE_ERROR_FORMAT**, **OLE_ERROR_HANDLE**, **OLE_ERROR_NAME**, **OLE_ERROR_OPTION**, **OLE_ERROR_-PROTOCOL**, or **OLE_WAIT_FOR_RELEASE**.

lpszProto is a pointer to a string containing the name of the protocol for the newly embedded object. At the time of this writing, this string must contain "StdFileEditing" or "Static" (if the picture cannot be edited).

lpClnt is a pointer to an **OLECLIENT** structure associated with the newly embedded object. *lhClntDoc* is the handle of the client document where the object is being created. *lpszObjName* is a pointer to a string that holds the client name for the object.

lplpObj is a pointer to a variable in which the DLL will store a pointer to the object. *renderOpt* determines how the object's presentation data is handled. Values for this parameter were shown previously in Table 23-1.

cfFormat contains the Clipboard format when *renderOpt* is **olerender_format**. This format is then used in a call to **OleGetData()**. The DLL handles the data and draws the object only when the specified format is **CF_METAFILEPICT**, **CF_ENHMETAFILE**, **CF_DIB**, or **CF_BITMAP**.

RELATED FUNCTIONS

OleCreate()
OleCreateFromTemplate()
OleDraw()
OleGetData()
OleQueryCreateFromClip()

OLESTATUS OleCreateFromFile(LPSTR *lpszProto,*
LPOLECLIENT *lpClnt,*
LPSTR *lpszClass,*
LPSTR *lpszFile,*
LHCLIENTDOC *lhClntDoc,*
LPSTR *lpszObjName,*
LPOLEOBJECT FAR * *lplpObj,*
OLEOPT_RENDER *renderOpt,*
OLECLIPFORMAT *cfFormat***)**

OleCreateFromFile() creates an embedded object from a file. The function returns **OLE_OK** if successful. If unsuccessful, it returns **OLE_ER-ROR_CLASS**, **OLE_ERROR_HANDLE**, **OLE_ERROR_MEMORY**, **OLE_-ERROR_NAME**, **OLE_ERROR_PROTOCOL**, or **OLE_WAIT_FOR_-RELEASE**.

lpszProto is a pointer to a string containing the name of the protocol for the newly embedded object. (At the time of this writing, this string must be "StdFileEditing".) *lpClnt* is a pointer to an **OLECLIENT** structure associated with the object. *lpszClass* is a pointer to a string that holds the class name of the object being created. *lpszFile* is a pointer to a string that contains the name of the file where the object will be found.

lhClntDoc is the handle of the client document where the object will be created. *lpszObjName* is a pointer to a string that holds the client name for the object. *lplpObj* is a pointer to a variable in which the DLL will store a pointer to the object. *renderOpt* determines how the object's presentation data is handled. Values for this parameter were shown previously in Table 23-1.

cfFormat contains the Clipboard format when *renderOpt* contains the value **olerender_format**. This format is then used in a call to **OleGetData()**. The DLL handles the data and draws the object only when the specified format is **CF_METAFILEPICT**, **CF_ENHMETAFILE**, **CF_DIB**, or **CF_BITMAP**.

RELATED FUNCTIONS

OleCreate()
OleCreateFromTemplate()
OleDraw()
OleGetData()

OLESTATUS OleCreateFromTemplate(LPSTR *lpszProto,*
LPOLECLIENT *lpClnt,*
LPSTR *lpszTemplate,*
LHCLIENTDOC *lhClntDoc,*
LPSTR *lpszObjName,*
LPOLEOBJECT FAR ★ *lplpObj,*
OLEOPT_RENDER *renderOpt,*
OLECLIPFORMAT *cfFormat*)

OleCreateFromTemplate() creates an object from a template. The template is actually another OLE object that serves as a model for the creation of the new object. The function will return **OLE_OK** if successful. If unsuccessful, it returns **OLE_ERROR_CLASS, OLE_ERROR_GENERIC, OLE_ERROR_HANDLE, OLE_ERROR_MEMORY, OLE_ERROR_NAME, OLE_ERROR_PROTOCOL,** or **OLE_WAIT_FOR_RELEASE**.

lpszProto is a pointer to a string giving the name of the protocol for the newly embedded object. (At the time of this writing, this value must be "StdFileEditing".) *lpClnt* is a pointer to an **OLECLIENT** structure associated with the newly embedded object. *lpszTemplate* is a pointer to a string that holds the path and filename of the template file for the new object. The new object is loaded from the template file by opening the server for editing.

lhClntDoc is the handle of the client document where the object will be created. *lpszObjName* is a pointer to a string that contains the client name for the object. *lplpObj* is a pointer to a variable in which the DLL will store the pointer to the object. *renderOpt* determines how the object's presentation data is handled. Values for this parameter were shown previously in Table 23-1.

cfFormat determines the Clipboard format when *renderOpt* contains the value **olerender_format**. This format is then used in a call to **OleGetData()**. The DLL handles the data and draws the object only when the specified format is **CF_METAFILEPICT, CF_ENHMETAFILE, CF_DIB,** or **CF_BITMAP**.

RELATED FUNCTIONS

OleCreate()
OleCreateFromClip()
OleDraw()
OleGetData()
OleObjectConvert()

OLESTATUS OleCreateInvisible(LPSTR *lpszProto,*
LPOLECLIENT *lpClnt,*
LPSTR *lpszClass,*
LHCLIENTDOC *lhClntDoc,*
LPSTR *lpszObjName,*
LPOLEOBJECT FAR ★ *lplpObj,*
OLEOPT_RENDER *renderOpt,*
OLECLIPFORMAT *cfFormat,*
BOOL *fActivate*)

OleCreateInvisible() creates an object but doesn't display the server application. The function can start the server and create the object, or it can create a blank object without having to start the server. The function returns **OLE_OK** if successful. If unsuccessful, it returns **OLE_ERROR_CLASS**, **OLE_ERROR_HANDLE**, **OLE_ERROR_NAME**, or **OLE_ERROR_PROTOCOL**.

lpszProto is a pointer to the name of the protocol for the object. (At the time of this writing, this string must hold the value "StdFileEditing".) *lpClnt* is a pointer to an **OLECLIENT** structure associated with the newly embedded object. *lpszClass* is a pointer to a string that contains the class name of the object that being created.

lhClntDoc is the handle of the client document where the object will be created. *lpszObjName* is a pointer to a string that holds the client name for the object. *lplpObj* is a pointer to a variable in which the DLL will store the pointer to the object. *renderOpt* determines how the object's presentation data is handled. Values for this parameter were shown previously in Table 23-1.

cfFormat determines the Clipboard format when *renderOpt* contains the value **olerender_format**. This format is then used in a call to **OleGetData()**. The DLL handles the data and draws the object only when the specified format is **CF_METAFILEPICT**, **CF_ENHMETAFILE**, **CF_DIB**, or **CF_BITMAP**.

If *fActivate* is TRUE, the server is started. If *fActivate* is false, the server is not started. In this case, a blank object is created.

RELATED FUNCTIONS

OleActivate()
OleClose()
OleSetBounds()
OleSetColorScheme()

OleSetTargetDevice()
OleUpdate()

OLESTATUS OleCreateLinkFromClip(LPSTR *lpszProto*, LPOLECLIENT *lpClnt*, LHCLIENTDOC *lhClntDoc*, LPSTR *lpszObjName*, LPOLEOBJECT FAR ★ *lplpObj*, OLEOPT_RENDER *renderOpt*, OLECLIPFORMAT *cfFormat*)

OleCreateLinkFromClip() creates a link to the object from the Clipboard. The function returns **OLE_OK** if successful. If unsuccessful, it returns **OLE_ERROR_CLIP**, **OLE_ERROR_FORMAT**, **OLE_ERROR_-HANDLE, OLE_ERROR_NAME, OLE_ERROR_OPTION, OLE_-ERROR_PROTOCOL**, or **OLE_WAIT_FOR_RELEASE**.

lpszProto is a pointer to the name of the protocol for the object. (At the time of this writing, this string must hold the value "StdFileEditing".) *lpClnt* is a pointer to an **OLECLIENT** structure associated with the newly embedded object.

lhClntDoc is the handle of the client document where the object will be created. *lpszObjName* is a pointer to a string that contains the client name for the object. *lplpObj* is a pointer to a variable in which the DLL will store the pointer to the object. *renderOpt* determines how the object's presentation data is handled. Values for this parameter were shown previously in Table 23-1.

cfFormat determines the Clipboard format when *renderOpt* contains the value **olerender_format**. This format is then used in a call to **OleGetData()**. The DLL handles the data and draws the object only when the specified format is **CF_METAFILEPICT, CF_ENHMETAFILE, CF_DIB**, or **CF_BITMAP**.

RELATED FUNCTIONS

OleCreate()
OleCreateFromTemplate()
OleDraw()
OleGetData()
OleQueryLinkFromClip()

OLESTATUS OleCreateLinkFromFile(LPSTR *lpszProto,*
                         LPOLECLIENT *lpClnt,*
                         LPSTR *lpszClass,*
                         LPSTR *lpszFile,*
                         LPSTR *lpszItem,*
                         LHCLIENTDOC *lhClntDoc,*
                         LPSTR *lpszObjName,*
                         LPOLEOBJECT FAR ★ *lplpObj,*
                         OLEOPT_RENDER *renderOpt,*
                         OLECLIPFORMAT *cfFormat*)

OleCreateLinkFromFile() creates a link to an object in a file. The client DLL can start the server to obtain the presentation data. However, the object is not visible for editing in the server. The function returns **OLE_OK** if successful. If unsuccessful, it returns **OLE_ERROR_CLASS**, **OLE_ERROR_HANDLE**, **OLE_ERROR_MEMORY**, **OLE_ERROR_NAME**, **OLE_ERROR_PROTOCOL**, or **OLE_WAIT_FOR_RELEASE**.

lpszProto is a pointer to the name of the protocol for the object. (At the time of this writing, this string must hold the value "StdFileEditing".) *lpClnt* is a pointer to an **OLECLIENT** structure associated with the newly embedded object.

lpszClass is a pointer to a string that contains the class name of the newly created object. When this value is NULL, the extension of the filename (pointed to by *lpszFile*) determines the class name for the object. The name of the file that contains the objects is pointed to by *lpszFile*.

The portion of the file to link is specified by the string pointed to by *lpszItem*. If NULL, the whole document is linked. *lhClntDoc* is the handle of the client document where the object will be created. *lpszObjName* is a pointer to a string that contains the client name for the object.

lplpObj is a pointer to a variable in which the DLL will store the pointer to the object. *renderOpt* determines how the object's presentation data is handled. Values for this parameter were shown previously in Table 23-1.

cfFormat determines the Clipboard format when *renderOpt* contains the value **olerender_format**. This format is then used in a call to **OleGetData()**. The DLL handles the data and draws the object only when the specified format is **CF_METAFILEPICT**, **CF_ENHMETAFILE**, **CF_DIB**, or **CF_BITMAP**.

RELATED FUNCTIONS

OleCreate()
OleCreateFromFile()
OleCreateFromTemplate()
OleDraw()
OleGetData()

OLESTATUS OleDelete(LPOLEOBJECT *lpObj*)

OleDelete() deletes (permanently removes) an object and frees its memory. The function returns **OLE_OK** if successful. If unsuccessful, it returns **OLE_BUSY**, **OLE_ERROR_OBJECT**, or **OLE_WAIT_FOR_RELEASE**.

lpObj is a pointer to the object that is to be deleted.

RELATED FUNCTIONS

OleClose()
OleRelease()

OLESTATUS OleDraw(LPOLEOBJECT *lpObj*, HDC *hdc*, const RECT FAR * *lprcBounds*, const RECT FAR * *lprcWBounds*, HDC *hdcFormat*)

OleDraw() draws an object into the specified rectangle. The function returns **OLE_OK** if successful. If unsuccessful, it returns **OLE_ERROR_ABORT**, **OLE_ERROR_BLANK, OLE_ERROR_DRAW, OLE_ERROR_HANDLE, OLE_ERROR_MEMORY,** or **OLE_ERROR_OBJECT.**

NOTE

OLE_ERROR_ABORT *is returned when the callback function returns FALSE while drawing.*

lpObj is a pointer to the object to be drawn. *hdc* is the handle of the device context. *lprcBounds* is a pointer to a **RECT** structure that contains the coordinates for the bounding rectangle in logical units. The object is drawn inside this rectangle.

lprcWBounds is used when *hdc* is a handle to a metafile. In this case, the parameter should be set to NULL. When *hdc* is a metafile, *lprcWBounds* points to a **RECT** structure defining the bounding rectangle of the window that will be drawn (the left and top members of the **RECT** structure specify the window origin, while the right and bottom members specify the window extents).

hdcFormat is the handle of the device context for the target device for determining the object's format.

RELATED FUNCTION

OleSetBounds()

OLECLIPFORMAT OleEnumFormats (LPOLEOBJECT *lpObj,* OLECLIPFORMAT *cfFormat*)

OleEnumFormats() enumerates data formats for an object. The function returns the next format. If there are no additional formats, NULL is returned.

lpObj is a pointer to the object. *cfFormat* must contain the format returned by the previous call to **OleEnumFormats()**. However, *cfFormat* is set to zero the first time this function is called.

RELATED FUNCTION

OleGetData()

OLESTATUS OleEnumObjects(LHCLIENTDOC *lhDoc,* LPOLEOBJECT FAR * *lplpObj*)

OleEnumObjects() enumerates objects in a document. The function returns **OLE_OK** if successful. If unsuccessful, it returns **OLE_ERROR_HANDLE** or **OLE_ERROR_OBJECT**.

lhDoc is the handle to the document that contains the objects. *lplpObj* is a pointer to an object pointer. On return, *lplpObj* will point to the object returned by the function. This parameter should point to NULL when the function is first called. Objects are returned in sequence until no additional objects are available. A NULL object is then returned when this occurs.

RELATED FUNCTIONS

OleDelete()
OleRelease()

OLESTATUS OleEqual(LPOLEOBJECT *lpObj1*, LPOLEOBJECT *lpObj2*)

OleEqual() compares two objects and determines if they are equal. The function returns **OLE_OK** when the objects are equal. If the objects are not equal, it returns **OLE_ERROR_OBJECT** or **OLE_ERROR_NOT_EQUAL.**

The objects are pointed to by *lpObj1* and *lpObj2*. Embedded objects are considered equal when their item, class, and native data are similar. Linked objects are considered equal when their item, class, and document are similar.

RELATED FUNCTIONS

OleClone()
OleQueryOutOfDate()

OLESTATUS OleExecute(LPOLEOBJECT *lpObj*, HGLOBAL *hCommands*, UINT *wReserved*)

OleExecute() sends DDE execute commands to a server. The function returns **OLE_OK** if successful. If unsuccessful, it returns **OLE_BUSY**, **OLE_ERROR_COMMAND**, **OLE_ERROR_MEMORY**, **OLE_ERROR_NOT_OPEN**, **OLE_ERROR_OBJECT**, **OLE_ERROR_PROTOCOL**, **OLE_ERROR_STATIC**, or **OLE_WAIT_FOR_RELEASE**.

The execute commands are sent to the server pointed to by *lpObj*. *hCommands* is the handle to the memory that contains the DDE commands. *wReserved* is reserved and must be set to zero.

RELATED FUNCTION

OleQueryProtocol()

OLESTATUS OleGetData(LPOLEOBJECT *lpObj,*
OLECLIPFORMAT *cfFormat,*
HANDLE FAR * *phData*)

OleGetData() retrieves data from an object in a given format. The function returns **OLE_OK** if successful. If unsuccessful, it returns **OLE_BUSY**, **OLE_ERROR_BLANK**, **OLE_ERROR_FORMAT**, **OLE_WARN_DE-LETE_DATA**, or **OLE_WAIT_FOR_RELEASE**.

The object that contains the data is pointed to by *lpObj*. cfFormat determines the format for which data will be returned.

NOTE

The format can be a predefined Clipboard format or a value returned by **RegisterClipboardFormat()**.

On return, *phData* will point to the handle of the data requested.

USAGE

When **OLE_WARN_DELETE_DATA** is returned by the function because the client DLL cannot interpret it, the memory associated with the data should be released. If the *cfFormat* parameter uses a **CF_METAFILE** or **CF_BITMAP** value, the *phData* parameter will point to a GDI object when the function returns.

RELATED FUNCTIONS

OleEnumFormats()
OleSetData()
RegisterClipboardFormat()

OLESTATUS OleGetLinkUpdateOptions
(LPOLEOBJECT *lpObj,*
OLEOPT_UPDATE FAR * *lpUpdateOpt*)

OleGetLinkUpdateOptions() retrieves update options for an object. The function returns **OLE_OK** if successful, and **OLE_ERROR_OBJECT** if unsuccessful.

lpObj is a pointer to the object. On return, *lpUpdateOpt* will point to a variable that contains the value of the link update option for the object. The link update option can be selected from those shown here:

Option	Purpose
oleupdate_always	Update the link object when possible. (Support is provided for the automatic link update option button in the Links dialog box.)
oleupdate_onsave	Update the link object when the source document is saved.
oleupdate_oncall	Update the link object when requested by the client application. (Support is provided for the manual link update option button in the Links dialog box.)

RELATED FUNCTION

OleSetLinkUpdateOptions()

BOOL OleIsDcMeta(HDC *hdc*)

OleIsDcMeta() determines if a device context is a metafile device context. *hdc* is the handle to the device context. The function returns a positive value if *hdc* is a metafile DC, and NULL if it isn't.

OLESTATUS OleLoadFromStream
(LPOLESTREAM *lpStream,*
LPSTR *lpszProto,*
LPOLECLIENT *lpClnt,*
LHCLIENTDOC *lhClntDoc,*
LPSTR *lpszObjName,*
LPOLEOBJECT FAR * *lplpObj*)

OleLoadFromStream() loads an object from a document. The function returns **OLE_OK** if successful. If unsuccessful, it returns **OLE_ERROR_HANDLE, OLE_ERROR_NAME, OLE_ERROR_PROTOCOL, OLE_ERROR_-STATIC_FROM_OTHER_OS, OLE_ERROR_STREAM,** or **OLE_-WAIT_FOR_RELEASE**.

lpStream is a pointer to an **OLESTREAM** structure. The client application allocates and initializes this structure.

The **OLESTREAM** structure is shown here. In it, *lpvtbl* is a pointer to a table of function pointers for the client application.

```
typedef struct _OLESTREAM{
  LPOLESTREAMVTBL lpvtbl;
} OLESTREAM;
```

The **OLESTREAMVTBL** structure is shown here.

```
typedef struct _OLESTREAMVTBL
{
  DWORD (CALLBACK* Get)(LPOLESTREAM, void FAR*, DWORD);
  DWORD (CALLBACK* Put)(LPOLESTREAM, OLE_CONST void FAR*, DWORD);
} OLESTREAMVTBL;
```

Here, **Get()** obtains data from the stream, and **Put()** puts data into the stream. Therefore, data is obtained by the client DLL by calling the **Get()** function in the **OLESTREAMVTBL** structure.

lpszProto is a pointer to a string that contains the name of the protocol to be used. It must be either "StdFileEditing" or "Static". *lpClnt* is a pointer to an **OLECLIENT** structure associated with the object.

lhClntDoc is the handle of the client document where the object is being built. *lpszObjName* is a pointer to the client name for the object. *lplpObj* is a pointer to a variable in which the client DLL places a pointer to the recently loaded object.

USAGE

The DLL automatically links the client and server when the application calls **OleLoadFromStream()**, if the object is linked and both server and document are open.

RELATED FUNCTIONS

OleSaveToStream()
OleQuerySize()

OLESTATUS OleLockServer(LPOLEOBJECT *lpObj*, LHSERVER FAR * *lphSrvr*)

OleLockServer() locks the server in memory. This function is called by the client and it causes the the server to remain in memory. The function returns **OLE_OK** if successful. If unsuccessful, it returns **OLE_ERROR_COMM**, OLE_ER-

ROR_LAUNCH , **OLE_ERROR_OBJECT**, **OLE_ERROR_MEMORY**, or **OLE_ERROR_STATIC**.

lpObj is a pointer to an object that will be retained in memory. The handle pointed to by *lphSrvr* will be the handle to the server application after the function returns.

This function allows an application to rapidly open objects.

OleLockServer() increases the lock count associated with the server and **OleUnlockServer()** decreases the lock count. The lock count must be zero before your program terminates to release the server from memory.

RELATED FUNCTION

OleUnlockServer()

OLESTATUS OleObjectConvert(LPOLEOBJECT *lpObj*,
LPSTR *lpszProto*,
LPOLECLIENT *lpClnt*,
LHCLIENTDOC *lhClntDoc*,
LPSTR *lpszObjName*,
LPOLEOBJECT FAR ★ *lplpObj*)

OleObjectConvert() creates a new object from an existing object using the given protocol. The function returns **OLE_OK** if successful. If unsuccessful, it returns **OLE_BUSY**, **OLE_ERROR_HANDLE**, **OLE_ERROR_MEMORY**, **OLE_ERROR_NAME**, **OLE_ERROR_OBJECT**, **OLE_ERROR_PROTOCOL**, or **OLE_ERROR_STATIC**.

lpObj is a pointer to the object that is to be converted. *lpszProto* is a pointer to a the protocol to be used. This string must be either "StdFileEditing" or "Static". *lpClnt* is a pointer to an **OLECLIENT** structure associated with the object. The client application allocates and initializes this structure.

lhClntDoc is the handle of the client document where the object is being built. *lpszObjName* is a pointer to the client name for the object. *lplpObj* is a pointer to a variable in which the client DLL places a pointer to the recently loaded object.

Currently, only linked or embedded objects can be changed to static objects.

RELATED FUNCTION

OleClone()

OLESTATUS OleQueryBounds(LPOLEOBJECT *lpObj,* RECT FAR * *lpBounds*)

OleQueryBounds() obtains the dimensions of an object's bounding rectangle. The function returns **OLE_OK** if successful. If unsuccessful, it returns **OLE_ER-ROR_BLANK**, **OLE_ERROR_GENERIC**, **OLE_ERROR_MEMORY**, or **OLE_ERROR_OBJECT**.

lpObj is a pointer to the object under query, and *lpBounds* is a pointer to a **RECT** structure that recieves the dimensions. Specifically, **rect.left** is 0, **rect.top** is 0, **rect.right** is the X extent, and **rect.bottom** is the Y extent.

DWORD OleQueryClientVersion(void)

OleQueryClientVersion() gets the version number for the client DLL.

This function returns a double word. The major version number is in the low byte of the low word. The minor version number is in the high byte of the low word. The high word is currently reserved.

RELATED FUNCTION

OleQueryServerVersion()

OLESTATUS OleQueryCreateFromClip(LPSTR *lpszProto,* OLEOPT_RENDER *renderOpt,* OLECLIPFORMAT *cfFormat*)

OleQueryCreateFromClip() determines if the Clipboard object supports the given protocol and rendering options. The function returns **OLE_OK** if successful. If unsuccessful, it returns **OLE_ERROR_FORMAT** or **OLE_ERROR_PROTOCOL**.

lpszProto is a pointer to the name of the protocol for use by the client. This value is either "StdFileEditing" or "Static". *renderOpt* determines how the object's presentation data is handled. This parameter can be one of the values shown earlier in Table 23-1.

cfFormat determines the Clipboard format when *renderOpt* is **olerender_format**. If **CF_METAFILEPICT**, **CF_ENHMETAFILE**, **CF_DIB**, or **CF_BITMAP** is used for the format, the DLL obtains the data and draws the object. This function is usually used to enable a Paste operation.

The **olerender_draw** option is the most frequently used option.

USAGE

Here is a small portion of code illustrating how this function might be used.

```
OleQueryCreateFromClip("Static", olerender_draw, 0)
```

RELATED FUNCTIONS

OleCreateFromClip()
OleDraw()
OleGetData()

OLESTATUS OleQueryLinkFromClip(LPSTR *lpszProto,*
OLEOPT_RENDER *renderOpt,*
OLECLIPFORMAT *cfFormat*)

OleQueryLinkFromClip() checks to see if a client application can use Clipboard data to create a linked object with the given protocol and rendering. The function returns **OLE_OK** if successful. If unsuccessful, it returns **OLE_ERROR_FORMAT** or **OLE_ERROR_PROTOCOL**.

lpszProto is a pointer to the protocol for the newly embedded object. (At the time of this writing, this string must be "StdFileEditing".) *renderOpt* determines how the object's presentation data is handled. Values for this parameter were shown previously in Table 23-1.

cfFormat determines the Clipboard format when *renderOpt* is **olerender_format**. This format is then used in a call to **OleGetData()**. The DLL handles the data and draws the object only when the specified format is **CF_METAFILEPICT**, **CF_ENHMETAFILE**, **CF_DIB**, or **CF_BITMAP**.

This function is often used to determine if a Paste Link command is possible. The **olerender_none** value is supplied when hyperlinks support is desired. **olerender_draw** is the value most frequently used.

USAGE

Here is a small portion of code illustrating how this function might be used.

```
if(OLE_OK == OleQueryLinkFromClip("StdFileEditing",
                                  olerender_draw, 0) {
    .
    .
    .
```

RELATED FUNCTIONS

OleCreateLinkFromClip()
OleDraw()
OleGetData()

OLESTATUS OleQueryName(LPOLEOBJECT *lpObj,*
LPSTR *lpszObject,*
UINT FAR * *lpwBuffSize*)

OleQueryName() obtains the name of an object. The function returns **OLE_OK** if successful. If unsuccessful, it returns **OLE_ERROR_OBJECT** or **OLE_ERROR_SIZE**.

lpObj is a pointer to the object in question. *lpszObject* is a pointer to a character array that will, on return, contain the name of the object.

lpwBuffSize is the size of the buffer pointed to by *lpszObject*. The buffer is measured in bytes. The variable pointed to by *lpwBuffSiz* contains the number of bytes actually copied to the buffer when the function returns.

RELATED FUNCTION

OleRename()

OLESTATUS OleQueryOpen(LPOLEOBJECT *lpObj*)

OleQueryOpen() determines if the given object is open. The function returns **OLE_OK** if the object is open. If the object is not open, it returns **OLE_ERROR_OBJECT** or **OLE_ERROR_NOT_OPEN**.

lpObj is a pointer to the object.

RELATED FUNCTION

OleActivate()

OLESTATUS OleQueryOutOfDate(LPOLEOBJECT *lpObj*)

OleQueryOutOfDate() determines if an object is out of date. The function returns **OLE_OK** if the object is current, and **OLE_ERROR_OBJECT** if not current.

lpObj is a pointer to the object.

RELATED FUNCTIONS

OleEqual()
OleUpdate()

LPVOID OleQueryProtocol(LPOLEOBJECT *lpObj*, LPSTR *lpszProto*)

OleQueryProtocol() determines if an object supports a given protocol. If the protocol is supported, the function returns a pointer to an OLEOBJECT. If the protocol is not supported, it returns NULL.

lpObj is a pointer to the object. *lpszProto* is a pointer to the protocol. This value can currently be "StdFileEditing" or "StdExecute". Other protocols may be supported.

RELATED FUNCTION

OleExecute()

OLESTATUS OleQueryReleaseError(LPOLEOBJECT *lpObj*)

OleQueryReleaseError() obtains the error value for an object acted upon by an asynchronous operation. The function returns **OLE_OK** if the operation is successful, and **OLE_ERROR_OBJECT** if unsuccessful.

lpObj is a pointer to an object whose error value is queried.

An **OLE_RELEASE** notification is received by the client when an asynchronous operation has ended. The client then calls **OleQueryReleaseError()**

to determine if the operation was terminated with or without an error. Error values are reset upon a return from the callback function.

RELATED FUNCTIONS

OleQueryReleaseMethod()
OleQueryReleaseStatus()

OLE_RELEASE_METHOD OleQueryReleaseMethod (LPOLEOBJECT *lpObj*)

OleQueryReleaseMethod() determines what operation has just completed for the specified object.

lpObj is a pointer to an object.

The function returns a value that indicates the type of operation that has just completed. It will be one of these values.

Return Value	Operation
OLE_NONE	No operation active
OLE_DELETE	ObjectDelete
OLE_LNKPASTE	PasteLink (auto reconnect)
OLE_EMBPASTE	PasteandUpdate
OLE_SHOW	Show
OLE_RUN	Run
OLE_ACTIVATE	Activate
OLE_UPDATE	Update
OLE_CLOSE	Close
OLE_RECONNECT	Reconnect
OLE_SETUPDATEOPTIONS	Setting update options
OLE_SERVERUNLAUNCH	Server is stopping
OLE_LOADFROMSTREAM	LoadFromStream (auto reconnect)
OLE_SETDATA	OleSetData
OLE_REQUESTDATA	OleRequestData
OLE_OTHER	Other miscellaneous asynchronous operations
OLE_CREATE	Create
OLE_CREATEFROMTEMPLATE	CreateFromTemplate
OLE_CREATELINKFROMFILE	CreateLinkFromFile
OLE_COPYFROMLNK	CopyFromLink (auto reconnect)
OLE_CREATEFROMFILE	CreateFromFile

The function returns **OLE_ERROR_OBJECT** if the *lpObj* parameter is not valid.

RELATED FUNCTIONS

OleQueryReleaseError()
OleQueryReleaseStatus()

OLESTATUS OleQueryReleaseStatus
(LPOLEOBJECT *lpObj*)

OleQueryReleaseStatus() determines if an operation has completed. If the function is successful, it returns **OLE_OK**. If unsuccessful, it returns **OLE_BUSY** or **OLE_ERROR_OBJECT**.

lpObj is a pointer to an object where the operation is being queried.

USAGE

Here is a small portion of code illustrating how this function might be used.

```
LPOLEOBJECT lpObjWindow;
OLESTATUS olestatus;
    .
    .
    .
olestatus = OleQueryReleaseStatus(lpObjWindow);
    .
    .
    .
```

RELATED FUNCTIONS

OleQueryReleaseError()
OleQueryReleaseMethod()

DWORD OleQueryServerVersion(void)

OleQueryServerVersion() returns the version number of the server DLL.

The version is contained in a double word. The major version number can be found in the low byte of the low word, while the minor version number is in the high byte of the low word. At this time, the high word is not used and is reserved.

RELATED FUNCTION

OleQueryClientVersion()

OLESTATUS OleQuerySize(LPOLEOBJECT *lpObj,* DWORD FAR * *pdwSize)*

OleQuerySize() determines the size of an object. The function returns **OLE_OK** if successful, and **OLE_ERROR_OBJECT** if unsuccessful.

lpObj is a pointer to the object. *pdwSize* is a pointer to a variable that, on return, will contain the size of the object.

RELATED FUNCTION

OleLoadFromStream()

OLESTATUS OleQueryType(LPOLEOBJECT *lpObj,* LONG FAR * *lpType)*

OleQueryType() determines if a given object is embedded, lined, or static in nature. This functions returns **OLE_OK** if successful, and **OLE_ERROR_OB-JECT** if unsuccessful.

lpObj is a pointer to the object. *lpType* is a pointer to a variable that will, on return, contain the object type when the function returns. This value will be either **OT_EMBEDDED** (object is embedded), **OT_LINK** (object is a link) or **OT_STATIC** (object is a static picture).

RELATED FUNCTION

OleEnumFormats()

OLESTATUS OleReconnect(LPOLEOBJECT *lpObj)*

OleReconnect() reconnects a link to an open linked object. This function returns **OLE_OK** if successful. If unsuccessful, it returns **OLE_BUSY**, **OLE_ER-ROR_OBJECT**, **OLE_ERROR_NOT_LINK**, or **OLE_WAIT_FOR_-RELEASE**.

lpObj is a pointer to the object that is to be reconnected.

USAGE

Here is a small portion of code illustrating how this function might be used.

```
LPOLEOBJECT lpObj;
OLESTATUS olestatus;
        .
        .
        .
if(OLE_OK != olestatus)
  olestatus = OleReconnect(lpObj);
```

RELATED FUNCTIONS

OleActivate()
OleClose()
OleQueryOpen()

OLESTATUS OleRegisterClientDoc(LPSTR *lpszClass,*
LPSTR *lpszDoc,*
LONG *reserved,*
LHCLIENTDOC FAR ★ *lplhDoc*)

OleRegisterClientDoc() registers a client document with the appropriate client DLL. This function returns **OLE_OK** if successful. If unsuccessful, it returns **OLE_ERROR_NAME** or **OLE_ERROR_MEMORY**.

lpszClass is a pointer to the name of the class for the client document. *lpszDoc* is a pointer to the location of the client document. This is the path and filename of the document. The *reserved* parameter is zero. *lplhDoc* is a pointer to a handle that will, on return, contain the client document's handle.

USAGE

Here is a small portion of code illustrating how this function might be used.

```
olestatus = OleRegisterClientDoc("ClntDoc", (LPSTR) szFile,
                                 0, &lpDoc);
```

RELATED FUNCTION

OleRevokeClientDoc()

OLESTATUS OleRegisterServer(LPSTR *lpszClass,*
LPOLESERVER *lpServ,*
LHSERVER FAR ★ *lplhserver,*
HINSTANCE *hInst,*
OLE_SERVER_USE *srvruse*)

OleRegisterServer() registers a server. This function returns **OLE_OK** if successful. If unsuccessful, it returns **OLE_ERROR_PROTECT_ONLY, OLE_ERROR_CLASS**, or **OLE_ERROR_MEMORY**.

lpszClass is a pointer to the name of the class that is being registered. *lpServ* is a pointer to an **OLESERVER** structure. This structure is allocated and initialized by the server application. *lplhserver* is a pointer to a variable of type **LHSERVER** in which the handle of the server is stored.

hInst is the instance handle of the server. *srvruse* determines if the server uses single or multiple instances to support multiple objects. This parameter is set to **OLE_SERVER_SINGLE** or **OLE_SERVER_MULTI**.

USAGE

The **OLESERVER** structure is shown here.

```
typedef struct _OLESERVER
{
  LPOLESERVERVTBL lpvtbl;
} OLESERVER;
```

Here, **lpvtbl** is a pointer to a table of function pointers for the server application.

RELATED FUNCTIONS

OleRegisterServerDoc()
OleRevokeServer()

OLESTATUS OleRegisterServerDoc(LHSERVER *lhServ,*
LPSTR *lpszDocName,*
LPOLESERVERDOC *lpDoc,*
LHSERVERDOC FAR ★ *lplhDoc)*

OleRegisterServerDoc() registers a document with the server DLL. Registration is necessary when other client applications have also established links to the document. This function returns **OLE_OK** if successful. If unsuccessful, it returns **OLE_ER-ROR_HANDLE, OLE_ERROR_MEMORY,** or **OLE_ERROR_TERMI-NATE**.

lhServ is the handle of the server. The handle is obtained via **OleRegister-Server()**. *lpszDocName* is a pointer to the name assigned to the document. *lpDoc* is a pointer to an **OLESERVERDOC** structure associated with the document.

The **OLESERVERDOC** is shown here.

```
typedef struct _OLESERVERDOC{
  LPOLESERVERDOCVTBL lpvtbl;
} OLESERVERDOC;
```

Here, **lpvtbl** is a pointer to a table of function pointers for a document. The server application is responsible for the allocation and initialization of the structure's values.

lplhDoc is a pointer to a handle that, on return, will be associated with the document.

RELATED FUNCTIONS

OleRegisterServer()
OleRevokeServerDoc()

OLESTATUS OleRelease(LPOLEOBJECT *lpObj)*

OleRelease() releases an object from memory. If the object was open, it will be closed. This function returns **OLE_OK** if successful. If unsuccessful, it returns **OLE_BUSY, OLE_ERROR_OBJECT,** or **OLE_WAIT_FOR_RELEASE**.

lpObj is a pointer to the object. This function should be used for all open objects when closing the client document.

RELATED FUNCTION

OleDelete()

OLESTATUS OleRename(LPOLEOBJECT *lpObj*, LPSTR *lpszNewName*)

OleRename() changes the name of an object. This function returns **OLE_OK** if successful. If unsuccessful, it returns **OLE_ERROR_OBJECT** or **OLE_ERROR_NAME**.

lpObj is a pointer to the object that is to be renamed. *lpszNewName* is a pointer to the new name for the object.

RELATED FUNCTION

OleQueryName()

OLESTATUS OleRenameClientDoc (LHCLIENTDOC *lhClntDoc*, LPSTR *lpszNewDocName*)

OleRenameClientDoc() alerts the client application library that the name of a document has changed. This function returns an **OLE_OK** if successful, and **OLE_ERROR_HANDLE** if unsuccessful.

lhClntDoc is the handle of the document that has been renamed. *lpszNew-DocName* is a pointer to the document's new name. Client applications typically use this function when a File menu item, such as Save or Save As, is selected.

USAGE

Here is a small portion of code illustrating how this function might be used.

```
LHCLIENTDOC lhClnt;
LPSTR lpszNewDocName;
OLESTATUS olestatus;
    .
    .
    .

olestatus = OleRenameClientDoc(lhClnt, lpszNewDocName);
    .
    .
    .
```

RELATED FUNCTIONS

OleRegisterClientDoc()
OleRevokeClientDoc()
OleRevertClientDoc()
OleSavedClientDoc()

OLESTATUS OleRenameServerDoc
(LHSERVERDOC *lhDoc,*
LPSTR *lpszDocName*)

OleRenameServerDoc() notifies the server DLL that the name of a document has changed. This function returns **OLE_OK** if successful. If unsuccessful, it returns **OLE_ERROR_HANDLE** or **OLE_ERROR_MEMORY**.

lhDoc is the handle of the document that has been renamed. *lpszDocName* is a pointer to the document's new name.

RELATED FUNCTIONS

OleRegisterServerDoc()
OleRevokeServerDoc()
OleSavedServerDoc()

OLESTATUS OleRequestData(LPOLEOBJECT *lpObj,*
OLECLIPFORMAT *cfFormat*)

OleRequestData() initiates a request for data from the server by specifying the format of the data desired. This function returns **OLE_OK** if successful. If unsuccessful, it returns **OLE_BUSY, OLE_ERROR_FORMAT, OLE_-ERROR_GENERIC, OLE_ERROR_NOT_OPEN, OLE_ERROR_OB-JECT**, or **OLE_WAIT_FOR_RELEASE**.

lpObj is a pointer to the object that contains the desired data. (This object is associated with the server.) *cfFormat* gives the format in which data will be returned and can be a predefined or custom Clipboard format.

Data is obtained from the object by using **OleGetData()** or by the use of functions such as **OleQueryBounds()** or **OleQuerySize()**.

RELATED FUNCTIONS

OleEnumFormats()
OleGetData()
OleSetData()

OLESTATUS OleRevertClientDoc(LHCLIENTDOC *lhDoc*)

OleRevertClientDoc() notifies the client DLL that the state of the specified document has been returned to a previously saved state. The function returns **OLE_OK** if successful.

lhDoc is the handle of the document.

RELATED FUNCTION

OleSavedClientDoc()

OLESTATUS OleRevertServerDoc(LHSERVERDOC *lhDoc*)

OleRevertServerDoc() notifies the server DLL that the state of the specified document has been returned to a previously saved state. The function returns **OLE_OK** if successful.

lhDoc is the handle of the document.

RELATED FUNCTION

OleSavedServerDoc()

OLESTATUS OleRevokeClientDoc (LHCLIENTDOC *lhClntDoc*)

OleRevokeClientDoc() notifies the client DLL that a document has been closed. This function returns **OLE_OK** if successful. If unsuccessful, it returns **OLE_ERROR_HANDLE** or **OLE_ERROR_NOT_EMPTY**.

lhClntDoc is a handle of the document that has been closed.

USAGE

Here is a small portion of code illustrating how this function might be used.

```
LHCLIENTDOC lhClnt;
OLESTATUS olestatus;
        .
        .
        .
olestatus = OleRevokeClientDoc(lhClnt);
        .
        .
        .
```

RELATED FUNCTION
────────────────────

OleRegisterClientDoc()

OLESTATUS OleRevokeObject(LPOLECLIENT *lpClnt*)

OleRevokeObject() prevents access to an object. This function is used by server applications when the user deletes an object. This function returns **OLE_OK** if successful.

lpClnt is a pointer to an **OLECLIENT** structure. This structure is associated with the object.

RELATED FUNCTION
────────────────────

OleRevokeServer()

OLESTATUS OleRevokeServer(LHSERVER *lhServer*)

OleRevokeServer() closes registered documents. It is called by the server. This function returns **OLE_OK** if successful. If unsuccessful, it returns **OLE_ERROR_HANDLE** or **OLE_WAIT_FOR_RELEASE**.

lhServer is the handle of the server that is to be revoked. This handle is obtained via **OleRegisterServer()**.

RELATED FUNCTIONS
─────────────────────

OleRegisterServer()
OleRevokeServerDoc()
OleRevokeObject()

OLESTATUS OleRevokeServerDoc
(LHSERVERDOC *lhDoc*)

OleRevokeServerDoc() revokes the given document. Server applications use this function when a document is closed.

lhDoc is a handle used to indicate the document to revoke. This handle can be obtained via **OleRegisterServerDoc()**.

This function returns **OLE_OK** if successful. If unsuccessful, it returns **OLE_ERROR_HANDLE** or **OLE_WAIT_FOR_RELEASE**.

RELATED FUNCTIONS

OleRegisterServerDoc()
OleRevokeObject()
OleRevokeServer()

OLESTATUS OleSavedClientDoc
(LHCLIENTDOC *lhClntDoc*)

OleSavedClientDoc() notifies the client application library that the specified document has been saved. This function returns **OLE_OK** if successful, and **OLE_ERROR_HANDLE** if unsuccessful.

lhClntDoc is the handle of the document that was saved.

USAGE

Here is a small portion of code illustrating how this function might be used.

```
LHCLIENTDOC lhClnt;
OLESTATUS olestatus;
    .
    .
    .
if(!fSaveAs)
  olestatus = OleSavedClientDoc(lhClnt);
    .
    .
    .
```

RELATED FUNCTIONS

OleRegisterClientDoc()
OleRevokeClientDoc()
OleRenameClientDoc()

OLESTATUS OleSavedServerDoc
(LHSERVERDOC *lhDoc*)

OleSavedServerDoc() notifies the server DLL that the specified document has been saved. This function returns **OLE_OK** if successful. If unsuccessful, it returns **OLE_ERROR_CANT_UPDATE_CLIENT** or **OLE_ERROR_HANDLE**.

lhDoc is the handle of the document that has been saved.

If an **OLE_ERROR_CANT_UPDATE_CLIENT** error value is received, the server application must indicate that the user cannot update the document until the server terminates or closes the application.

RELATED FUNCTIONS

OleRegisterServerDoc()
OleRevokeServerDoc()
OleRenameServerDoc()

OLESTATUS OleSaveToStream(LPOLEOBJECT *lpObj*,
LPOLESTREAM *lpStream*)

OleSaveToStream() saves the specified object to the specified stream. This functions returns **OLE_OK** if successful. If unsuccessful, it returns **OLE_ERROR_BLANK, OLE_ERROR_MEMORY, OLE_ERROR_OBJECT,** or **OLE_ERROR_STREAM**.

lpObj is a pointer to the object. *lpStream* is a pointer to an **OLESTREAM** structure that will receive the object information. **OleQuerySize()** can be used to determine the number of bytes to set aside for the object.

USAGE

Here is a small portion of code illustrating how this function might be used.

```
LPOLEOBJECT lpObj;
LPOLESTREAM lpStream;
OLESTATUS olestatus;
        .

        .

        .

if(OLE_OK != olestatus)
        .

        .

        .

  olestatus = OleSaveToStream(lpObj,lpStream);
        .

        .

        .
```

RELATED FUNCTIONS

OleLoadFromStream()
OleQuerySize()

OLESTATUS OleSetBounds(LPOLEOBJECT *lpObj*, const RECT FAR ★ *lpBounds*)

OleSetBounds() specifies the dimensions of the bounding rectangle for the given object. This function returns **OLE_OK** if successful. If unsuccessful, it returns **OLE_BUSY**, **OLE_ERROR_MEMORY**, **OLE_ERROR_OB-JECT**, or **OLE_WAIT_FOR_RELEASE**.

lpObj is a pointer to the object. *lpBounds* is a pointer to a **RECT** structure that contains the coordinates of the bounding rectangle in **MM_HIMETRIC** units.

USAGE

Here is a small portion of code illustrating how this function might be used.

```
LPOLEOBJECT lpObj;
RECT rc;
OLESTATUS olestatus;
        .

        .

        .

olestatus = OleSetBounds(lpObj, &rc);
        .
```

.
.

RELATED FUNCTIONS

OleDraw()
OleQueryBounds()
SetMapMode()

OLESTATUS OleSetColorScheme(LPOLEOBJECT *lpObj*, const LOGPALETTE FAR * *lpPalette*)

OleSetColorScheme() allows a client application to request that a specific palette be assigned a server application when a given object is edited. The server can ignore the recommendation.

This function returns **OLE_OK** if successful. If unsuccessful, it returns **OLE_BUSY, OLE_ERROR_MEMORY, OLE_ERROR_OBJECT, OLE_-ERROR_PALETTE**, or **OLE_WAIT_FOR_RELEASE**.

lpObj is a pointer to an **OLEOBJECT** structure associated with the object for which the palette is to be used. *lpPalette* is a pointer to a **LOGPALETTE** structure. This structure describes the requested palette.

The **LOGPALETTE** structure is shown here.

```
typedef struct tagLOGPALETTE {
  WORD palVersion;
  WORD palNumEntries;
  PALETTEENTRY palPalEntry[1];
} LOGPALETTE;
```

Here, **palVersion** gives the Windows version number for the structure (at this time it is still 0x300). **palNumEntries** gives the number of entries in the logical color palette. **palPalEntry** gives an array of **PALETTEENTRY** structures used to define the color and usage of each entry in the logical palette.

The first value in the **palPalEntry** array gives the foreground color. The second value gives the background color. Of the remaining structure entries, the first half are fill colors and the second half are line and text colors.

The **PALETTEENTRY** structure is shown here.

```
typedef struct tagPALETTEENTRY {
  BYTE peRed;
```

```
    BYTE peGreen;
    BYTE peBlue;
    BYTE peFlags;
} PALETTEENTRY;
```

Here, **peRed** gives a red intensity value, **peGreen** a green intensity value, and **peBlue** a blue intensity value. **peFlags** gives an indication of how the palette entry is to be used and can be **PC_EXPLICIT** (the low-order word indicates a hardware palette index), **PC_NOCOLLAPSE** (the color is in an unused entry in the system palette not matched to an existing color in the system palette), or **PC_RESERVED** (the logical palette entry is for palette animation).

OLESTATUS OleSetData(LPOLEOBJECT *lpObject* OLECLIPFORMAT *cfFormat,* HANDLE *hData*)

OleSetData() sends data to a server. This server must be associated with a given object. If the function is successful, it returns **OLE_OK**. If unsuccessful, it returns **OLE_BUSY, OLE_ERROR_BLANK, OLE_ERROR_COMM, OLE_ERROR_MEMORY, OLE_ERROR_NOT_OPEN, OLE_ERROR_OBJECT**, or **OLE_WAIT_FOR_RELEASE**.

lpObj is a pointer to an object that is associated with the server that will receive the data. *cfFormat* indicates the format of the data being sent, and *hData* is the handle of a memory object that contains the data.

RELATED FUNCTIONS

OleGetData()
OleRequestData()

OLESTATUS OleSetHostNames(LPOLEOBJECT *lpObj,* LPSTR *lpszClient,* LPSTR *lpszClientObj*)

OleSetHostNames() sets the name of the client application and the name of the object. The function returns **OLE_OK** if successful. If unsuccessful, it returns **OLE_BUSY, OLE_ERROR_MEMORY, OLE_ERROR_OBJECT**, or **OLE_WAIT_FOR_RELEASE**.

lpObj is a pointer to the object in question. *lpszClient* is a pointer to a string that will become the name of the client application. *lpszClientObj* is a pointer to a string that contains the name of the object.

This function will return an **OLE_ERROR_OBJECT** if the object is linked.

This function is used by the client to set the name of the object the first time the object is actived.

USAGE

Here is a small portion of code illustrating how this function might be used.

```
LPOLEOBJECT lpObj;
OLESTATUS olestatus;
        .
        .
        .
olestatus = OleSetHostNames(lpObj, (LPSTR) lpszClnt,
                        (LPSTR) lpszClntObj);
        .
        .
        .
```

OLESTATUS OleSetLinkUpdateOptions
(LPOLEOBJECT *lpObj,*
OLEOPT_UPDATE *UpdateOpt*)

OleSetLinkUpdateOptions() sets link-update options for an object. The function returns **OLE_OK** if successful. If unsuccessful, it returns **OR_OPTION, OLE_ERROR_STATIC**, or **OLE_WAIT_FOR_RELEASE**.

lpObj is a pointer to the object. *UpdateOpt* contains the link-update option. It can be one of the following.

Option	Purpose
oleupdate_always	Update the object when possible. (Support for automatic link update radio buttons is provided for the Links dialog box.)
oleupdate_onsave	Update the object when the server saves the source document.
oleupdate_oncall	Update the object when requested by the client. (Support for manual link update radio buttons is provided for the Links dialog box.)

USAGE

Here is a small portion of code illustrating how this function might be used.

```
LPOLEOBJECT lpObj;
OLEOPT_UPDATE UpdateOpt
OLESTATUS olestatus;
    .
    .
    .
olestatus = OleSetLinkUpdateOptions(lpObj,
                                UpdateOpt);
    .
    .
    .
```

RELATED FUNCTION

OleGetLinkUpdateOptions()

OLESTATUS OleSetTargetDevice(LPOLEOBJECT *lpObj*, HGLOBAL *hTargetDevice*)

OleSetTargetDevice() sets the target device for an object. The function returns **OLE_OK** if successful. If unsuccessful, it returns **OLE_BUSY**, **OLE_ERROR_MEMORY**, **OLE_ERROR_OBJECT**, or **OLE_WAIT_FOR_- RELEASE**.

lpObj is a pointer to the object.

hTargetDevice is the handle of an **OLETARGETDEVICE** structure. This structure provides a description of the target device for the object. Its template is shown here.

```
typedef struct _OLETARGETDEVICE {
  UINT otdDeviceNameOffset;
  UINT otdDriverNameOffset;
  UINT otdPortNameOffset;
  UINT otdExtDevModeOffset;
  UINT otdExtDevModeSize;
  UINT otdEnvironmentOffset;
  UINT otdEnvironmentSize;
  BYTE otdData[];
} OLETARGETDEVICE;
```

The structure's members **otdDeviceNameOffset, otdDriverNameOffset**, and **otdPortNameOffset** refer to null-terminated strings. **otdExtDevMode-Offset** and **otdExtDevModeSize** specify the start and size of a **DEVMODE** structure. **otdEnvironmentOffset** and **otdEnvironmentSize** specify the start of the environment array and its size.

OleSetTargetDevice() will then permit a linked or embedded object to be properly formatted for a given target device. Clients must call this function when the target device changes. Clients must call the DLL, for a redraw of the object, if the client is notified via the server that the object has changed.

OLESTATUS OleUnblockServer(LHSERVER *lhServ,* BOOL FAR * *lpfRequest*)

OleUnblockServer() processes a request from the queue. (This function is only used after blocking a queue using **OleBlockServer()**.) The function returns **OLE_OK** if successful. If unsuccessful, it returns **OLE_ERROR_-HANDLE** or **OLE_ERROR_MEMORY**.

lhServ is the handle of the server where requests are queued. *lpfRequest* is a pointer to a flag that, on return, specified if there are additional requests present in the queue. The flag will be TRUE for additional requests and FALSE if there are no additional requests.

USAGE

Here is a small portion of code illustrating how this function might be used.

```
LHSERVER lhServ;
BOOL FAR * lpfRequest;
OLESTATUS olestatus;
    .
    .
    .

olestatus = OleUnblockServer(lhServ, lpfRequest);
    .
    .
    .
```

RELATED FUNCTION

OleBlockServer()

OLESTATUS OleUnlockServer(LHSERVER *hServer*)

OleUnlockServer() releases the server that is locked via the **OleLockServer()** function. The function returns **OLE_OK** if successful. If unsuccessful, it returns **OLE_ERROR_HANDLE** or **OLE_WAIT_FOR_RELEASE**.

hServer is the handle of the server to be released from memory. The handle can be obtained with a call to **OleLockServer()**.

OleLockSever() increases the lock count associated with the server and **OleUnlockServer()** decreases the lock count. The lock count must be zero before your program terminates to release the server from memory.

If an **OLE_WAIT_FOR_RELEASE** value is returned, a call to **OleQueryReleaseStatus()** will determine if the unlocking process is complete. The server is unlocked when a call to the **OleQueryReleaseStatus()** function does not return an **OLE_BUSY**.

RELATED FUNCTIONS

OleLockServer()
OleQueryReleaseStatus()

OLESTATUS OleUpdate(LPOLEOBJECT *lpObj*)

OleUpdate() updates an object. The function returns **OLE_OK** if successful. If unsuccessful, it returns **OLE_BUSY**, **OLE_ERROR_GENERIC**, **OLE_-ERROR_OBJECT**, or **OLE_WAIT_FOR_RELEASE**.

lpObj is a pointer to the object to be updated.

This function is used to update objects with respect to any linked objects it contains.

USAGE

Here is a small portion of code illustrating how this function might be used.

```
LPOLEOBJECT lpObj;
OLESTATUS olestatus;
     .
     .
     .
olestatus = OleUpdate(lpObj);
     .
```

RELATED FUNCTION

OleQueryOutOfDate()

Chapter 24

Paths

T H I S chapter describes Windows' path functions. In this context, a *path* is a logical representation of a shape that is associated with a device context. (As used in this chapter, the term *path* does not refer to files, directories, etc.) Once selected into a device context, a path can be filled, outlined, or otherwise manipulated. Therefore, like the pen or the brush, a path is another type of object that can be selected into and used by a device context.

A path is defined using the following sequence:

1. Call **BeginPath()**

2. Define how the shape is drawn

3. Dall **EndPath()**

This sequence is referred to as a *path bracket*.

A complete programming example at the end of this chapter illustrates several of these easy-to-use path functions.

The path functions apply only to Windows NT/Win32.

BOOL AbortPath(HDC *hdc*)

AbortPath() closes and removes any paths in the device context. The function returns TRUE if successful, and FALSE if unsuccessful.

hdc is the handle of the device context.

RELATED FUNCTIONS

BeginPath()
EndPath()

BOOL BeginPath(HDC *hdc*)

BeginPath() opens a path bracket. That is, it begins the path bracket sequence. Once the object has been defined, the path bracket sequence is closed with a call to **EndPath()**.

The function returns TRUE if successful, and FALSE if unsuccessful.

hdc is the handle of the device context. All previous paths will be discarded.

Most all GDI graphics primitives can be used to define points in a path, including **LineTo()**, **Pie()**, **Ellipse()**, and **TextOut()**.

RELATED FUNCTIONS

EndPath()
FillPath()
PathToRegion()
SelectClipPath()
StrokeAndFillPath()
StrokePath()
WidenPath()

BOOL CloseFigure(HDC *hdc*)

CloseFigure() closes an open figure. The function returns TRUE if successful, and FALSE if unsuccessful.

hdc is the handle of the device context. A figure is closed by drawing a line from the current position to the first point of the figure. A figure is considered open until it is closed with a call to this function.

RELATED FUNCTIONS
_____

BeginPath()
EndPath()
ExtCreatePen()

BOOL EndPath(HDC *hdc*)

EndPath() closes a path bracket. That is, it terminates the path bracket sequence that was begun with a call to **BeginPath()**. The function also selects the path into the device context. The function returns TRUE if successful, and FALSE if unsuccessful.

hdc is the handle of the device context.

RELATED FUNCTION
_____

BeginPath()

BOOL FillPath(HDC *hdc*)

FillPath() fills the interior of the path using the currently selected brush and fill. If necessary, an open figure will be closed. The function returns TRUE if successful, and FALSE if unsuccessful.

hdc is the handle of a device context affected.

The path can be removed from the device context once the interior has been filled.

RELATED FUNCTIONS
_____

BeginPath()
SetPolyFillMode()
StrokeAndFillPath()
StrokePath()

BOOL FlattenPath(HDC *hdc*)

FlattenPath() transforms curves in the selected device context into a series of lines. The function returns TRUE if successful, and FALSE if unsuccessful.

hdc is the handle of a device context.

RELATED FUNCTION

WidenPath()

BOOL GetMiterLimit(HDC *hdc*, PFLOAT *lpLim*)

GetMiterLimit() obtains the miter limit associated with a device context. The function returns TRUE if successful, and FALSE if unsuccessful.

hdc is the handle of the device context. *lpLim* is a pointer to a variable that, on return, will contain the miter limit.

RELATED FUNCTIONS

ExtCreatePen()
SetMiterLimit()

int GetPath(HDC *hdc*, LPPOINT *lpPts*, LPBYTE *lpTypes*, int *nSize*)

GetPath() obtains the coordinates that describe the currently selected path. This function will return the number of points obtained if the *nSize* parameter is non-zero. If *nSize* is 0, the function will return the total number of points in the path. When *nSize* is not zero and is less than the number of points in the path, the function will return a -1.

hdc is the handle of the a device context. *lpPts* is a pointer to an array of **POINT** structures. On return, this array will contain the line endpoints and curve control points of the path.

The **POINT** structure is shown here.

```
typedef struct tagPOINT {
  LONG x;
  LONG y;
} POINT;
```

lpTypes is a pointer to an array of bytes containing the vertex types. The point types can be any of those shown here.

Type	Purpose
PT_BEZIERTO	The related point in *lpPts* is a control point or ending point for a Bézier curve. **PT_BEZIERTO** types must occur in sets of three. The point preceding this group gives the starting point for the Bézier curve. The first two **PT_BEZIERTO** types act as control points, while the third point is the ending point.
PT_LINETO	The previous point and the related point in *lpPts* are endpoints for a line.
PT_MOVETO	The related point in *lpPts* starts a disjoint figure.

NOTE

PT_LINETO *or* **PT_BEZIERTO** *can also be ORed with* **PT_CLOSEFIGURE** *for the last point in the object. This causes the figure to be closed after the line or curve is drawn.*

The size of the array pointed to by *lpPts* array is passed in *nSize*. This number must match the size of the *lpTypes* array.

RELATED FUNCTIONS

FlattenPath()
PolyDraw()
WidenPath()

HRGN PathToRegion(HDC *hdc*)

PathToRegion() converts a path into a region. If the function is successful, it returns the handle to the valid region. If the function is not successful, it returns FALSE.

hdc is the handle of a device context containing a closed path. (The path must be closed.)

RELATED FUNCTIONS

BeginPath()
EndPath()
SetPolyFillMode()

BOOL SelectClipPath(HDC *hdc,* int *iMode*)

SelectClipPath() causes the current path to become the current clipping region. The function returns TRUE if successful, and FALSE if unsuccessful.

hdc is the handle of the device context. *iMode* determines how the path is combined with any preexisting clipping region. It can be one of the following.

Value	Purpose
RGN_AND	The resulting clipping region consists of the intersection of the old clipping region and the path.
RGN_COPY	The old clipping region is replaced by the current path.
RGN_DIFF	The resulting clipping region is that part of the old clipping region that is not part of the path.
RGN_OR	The resulting clipping region is the union of the old clipping region and the path.
RGN_XOR	The resulting clipping region includes the union of the old clipping region and the path with intersecting areas excluded.

USAGE

The path is combined with any preexisting clipping region to produce the new region.

RELATED FUNCTIONS

BeginPath()
EndPath()

BOOL SetMiterLimit(HDC *hdc*, FLOAT *eNLimit*, PFLOAT *peOLimit*)

SetMiterLimit() sets the limit on the length of miter joins. The function returns TRUE if successful, and FALSE if unsuccessful.

hdc is the handle of the device context. The miter limit is passed in *eNLimit*. *peOLimit* is a pointer to a variable that, on return, will contain the previous miter limit. If NULL, the previous miter limit is not returned.

USAGE

By default, miter length is 10.0. The miter limit is defined as the maximum permitted ratio of the miter length to the line width. The miter length is specified as the distance from the intersection of line walls on the inside of a miter join to the intersection of the line walls on the outside of a miter join.

RELATED FUNCTION

ExtCreatePen()

BOOL StrokeAndFillPath(HDC *hdc*)

StrokeAndFillPath() closes all open figures in a path. It also strokes the outline of the path using the selected pen and fills the interior using the selected brush. The function returns TRUE if successful, and FALSE if unsuccessful.

hdc is the handle of the device context.

This function will stroke and fill but not overlap the stroked region, even for wide pens.

RELATED FUNCTIONS

BeginPath()
FillPath()SetPolyFillMode()
StrokePath()

BOOL StrokePath(HDC *hdc*)

StrokePath() draws the path using the current pen. The path must be closed. The function returns TRUE if successful, and FALSE if unsuccessful.

hdc is the handle of the device context containing the path.

RELATED FUNCTIONS

BeginPath()
EndPath()
ExtCreatePen()

BOOL WidenPath(HDC *hdc*)

WidenPath() redefines the path as the area to be painted when the path is stroked with the selected pen. The function returns TRUE if successful, and FALSE if unsuccessful.

hdc is the handle of the device context containing the closed path.

The pen must be a geometric pen or a cosmetic pen created with a width greater than one.

If the path contains Bézier curves, they are converted to a series of straight lines.

RELATED FUNCTIONS

BeginPath()
EndPath()
SetMiterLimit()

A Complete Programming Example

Here is a complete Windows NT programming example that illustrates several Win32 path functions. In this example, three line segments are drawn within a path. The figure is closed with a call to the **CloseFigure()** function. The figure is then drawn and filled with a call to **StrokeAndFillPath()**.

```
/*
 *  ntpaths
 *  A simple Windows NT application that demonstrates
 *  the use of several path functions.
 */

#include <windows.h>

LRESULT CALLBACK WndProc(HWND, UINT, WPARAM, LPARAM);

char szProgName[] = "ProgName";

int WINAPI WinMain(HINSTANCE hInst, HINSTANCE hPreInst,
                   LPSTR lpszCmdLine, int nCmdShow)
{
  HWND hWnd;
  MSG lpMsg;
  WNDCLASS wcApp;
  if (!hPreInst) {
    wcApp.lpszClassName = szProgName;
    wcApp.hInstance     = hInst;
    wcApp.lpfnWndProc   = WndProc;
    wcApp.hCursor       = LoadCursor(NULL, IDC_ARROW);
    wcApp.hIcon         = NULL;
    wcApp.lpszMenuName  = NULL;
    wcApp.hbrBackground = GetStockObject(WHITE_BRUSH);
    wcApp.style         = CS_HREDRAW | CS_VREDRAW;
    wcApp.cbClsExtra    = 0;
    wcApp.cbWndExtra    = 0;
    if (!RegisterClass (&wcApp))
      return FALSE;
  }
  hWnd = CreateWindow(szProgName,
                      "Using Path Functions Under Windows NT",
                      WS_OVERLAPPEDWINDOW, CW_USEDEFAULT,
```

```
                              CW_USEDEFAULT, CW_USEDEFAULT,
                              CW_USEDEFAULT, (HWND)NULL, (HMENU)NULL,
                              (HANDLE)hInst, (LPSTR)NULL);
    ShowWindow(hWnd, nCmdShow);
    UpdateWindow(hWnd);
    while (GetMessage(&lpMsg, NULL, 0, 0)) {
      TranslateMessage(&lpMsg);
      DispatchMessage(&lpMsg);
    }
    return(lpMsg.wParam);
}

LRESULT CALLBACK WndProc(HWND hWnd, UINT messg,
                         WPARAM wParam, LPARAM lParam)
{
    HDC hdc;
    PAINTSTRUCT ps;
    HPEN hNPen;
    HBRUSH hNBrush;

    switch (messg)
    {

      case WM_PAINT:
        hdc = BeginPaint(hWnd, &ps);

        hNPen = CreatePen(PS_SOLID, 4, RGB(255, 0, 0));
        hNBrush = CreateSolidBrush(RGB(0, 0, 255));
        SelectObject(hdc, hNPen);
        SelectObject(hdc, hNBrush);

        /* define three sides of a rectangle */
        BeginPath(hdc);
        MoveToEx(hdc, 100, 100, NULL);
        LineTo(hdc, 300, 100);
        LineTo(hdc, 300, 200);
        LineTo(hdc, 100, 200);
        CloseFigure(hdc);
        EndPath(hdc);

        StrokeAndFillPath(hdc);

        DeleteObject(hNPen);
        DeleteObject(hNBrush);
```

```
            ValidateRect(hWnd, NULL);
            EndPaint(hWnd, &ps);
            break;

        case WM_DESTROY:
          PostQuitMessage(0);
          break;

        default:
          return(DefWindowProc(hWnd, messg, wParam, lParam));
    }
    return(0L);
}
```

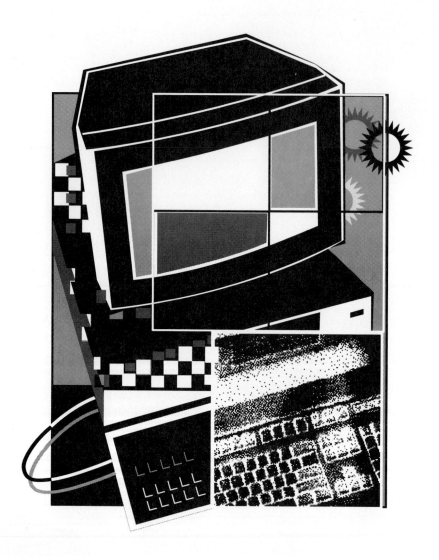

Chapter 25

Pipes

T H I S chapter describes Windows' pipe functions. These functions can be used to call, create, connect or disconnect pipes, and perform transactions.

BOOL CallNamedPipe(LPCTSTR *lpszPipeName*,
LPVOID *lpvWrtBuf*,
DWORD *cbWrtBuf*,
LPVOID *lpvRdBuf*,
DWORD *cbRdBuf*,
LPDWORD *lpcbRd*,
DWORD *dwTimeInt*)

CallNamedPipe() connects to a message-style pipe. Once connected, the function can write to and read from the pipe. When completed, it closes the pipe. The function returns TRUE if successful, and FALSE if unsuccessful.

lpszPipeName is a pointer to the name of the pipe. *lpvWrtBuf* is a pointer to a buffer that contains the information written to the pipe. *cbWrtBuf* contains the size of *lpvWrtBuf*.

lpvRdBuf is a pointer to the buffer that contains data input from the pipe. *cbRdBuf* gives the size of *lpvRdBuf*. On return, *lpcbRd* points to a 32-bit variable that will contain the number of bytes read from the pipe. The function returns FALSE when the message written to the pipe by the server is longer than *cbRdBuf*. In this case, the remainder of the message will be lost.

dwTimeInt contains the time to wait for the pipe to become available, in milliseconds. This parameter may also contain one of these values: **NMPWAIT_NOWAIT** (the pipe is not to be waited for), **NMPWAIT_WAIT_-FOREVER** (wait forever), and **NMPWAIT_USE_DEFAULT_WAIT** (use the default timeout).

USAGE

Here is a small portion of code that illustrates the use of this function.

```
#define WRITE_BUFFER 2000
#define READ_BUFFER  2000
#define TIME_INT      200
       .
       .
       .
char WrtBuf[WRITE_BUFFER];
char RdBuf[READ_BUFFER];
DWORD ByteRd;
       .
       .
       .
CallNamedPipe("mypipe",
              WrtBuf,
              WRITE_BUFFER,
              RdBuf,
              READ_BUFFER,
              &ByteRd,
              TIME_INT);
```

RELATED FUNCTIONS

CloseHandle()
CreateFile()
CreateNamedPipe()
TransactNamedPipe()
WaitNamedPipe()

BOOL ConnectNamedPipe(HANDLE *hNamedPipe,* LPOVERLAPPED *lpOl*)

ConnectNamedPipe() connects to a named pipe. The function returns TRUE if successful. If the function is not successful, it returns FALSE.

hNamedPipe is the handle of the server end of a named pipe's instance. (This handle is obtained by calling **CreateNamedPipe()**.) *lpOl* is a pointer to an

OVERLAPPED structure. *lpOl* can be set to NULL when an overlapped I/O is not required.

The **OVERLAPPED** structure is shown here.

```
typedef struct _OVERLAPPED {
  DWORD Internal;
  DWORD InternalHigh;
  DWORD Offset;
  DWORD OffsetHigh;
  HANDLE hEvent;
} OVERLAPPED;
```

Here, **Internal** is reserved for operating system use. **InternalHigh** is also reserved for operating system use. **Offset** contains the low-order word of the position at which a file transfer will start. **OffsetHigh** contains the high-order word of the offset at which a transfer begins. (That is, the starting point for the transfer is a four-byte quantity contained in **Offset** and **OffsetHigh**.) **hEvent** is the handle of an event that is set to a signaled state after transfer has finished.

USAGE

The pipe handle's wait mode can be set to blocking or nonblocking. The wait mode can be specified by **CreateNamedPipe()** and changed in **SetNamedPipeHandleState()**.

The function can then be set to execute synchronously or in overlapped mode. The function will execute in overlapped mode if **FILE_-FLAG_OVERLAPPED** was set when the pipe handle was created and *lpOl* is not NULL. With this mode, the **OVERLAPPED** structure must hold a handle to a manual reset event object. The function executes synchronously if the overlapped conditions are not met or *lpOl* is NULL.

When operating in nonblocking mode, this function returns TRUE the first time it is called for a pipe instance that has just been disconnected from a previous client. This means the pipe is available for connection to a new client. Otherwise, FALSE is returned. In both cases, the function will not wait. Instead, it returns immediately.

USAGE

The following portion of code shows how this function might be used.

```
HANDLE hPipe;

    .

    .

    .

ConnectNamedPipe(hPipe, NULL);
```

RELATED FUNCTIONS

CreateFile()
CallNamedPipe()
CreateEvent()
CreateNamedPipe()
DisconnectNamedPipe()
GetOverlappedResult()
SetNamedPipeHandleState()
SleepEx()
WaitForSingleObjectEx()
WaitForMultipleObjectsEx()

HANDLE CreateNamedPipe(LPCTSTR *lpName,*
DWORD *dwOpenMode,*
DWORD *dwPipeMode,*
DWORD *nMaxInstances,*
DWORD *nOutBufSize,*
DWORD *nInBufSize,*
DWORD *nDefTimeInt,*
LPSECURITY_ATTRIBUTES *lpSecurityAtt***)**

CreateNamedPipe() creates an instance of a named pipe and returns a handle to it. This function has two uses. First, a server may use it to create the first instance of a specific named pipe. Second, a sever may obtain a new instance handle to an existing named pipe. If the function is successful, it returns the handle to the server end of a named pipe instance. If the function is unsuccessful, it returns **INVALID_HANDLE_VALUE**.

lpName is a pointer to the pipe and has this general form:

\\.*pipe**pipename*

The *pipename* can be up to 256 characters in length and is not case sensitive.

dwOpenMode determines how the pipe is opened. This parameter consists of a direction flag combined with one or more options. The pipe direction flags are shown here.

Flag	Direction
PIPE_ACCESS_DUPLEX	The pipe is bidirectional.
PIPE_ACCESS_INBOUND	The pipe flows from the client to the server.
PIPE_ACCESS_OUTBOUND	The pipe flows from the server to the client.

The option flags are shown here.

Flags	Option
FILE_FLAG_WRITE_THROUGH	Only write-through mode is enabled. When enabled, the functions writing to a named pipe do not return until the data is transmitted and is in the pipe's buffer on the connected computer. When not enabled, the system buffers data until a minimum number of bytes accumulate. This mode is only useful for write operations on byte-type pipes where the client and server processes are on different systems.
FILE_FLAG_OVERLAPPED	Overlapped (asynchronous) mode is enabled and those functions doing read, write, and connect operations can return immediately. If the operations are time-consuming, they are performed in the background. If this mode is not enabled, the read, write, and connect operations do not return until the operation has completed.

dwOpenMode can also include any combination of the security access mode flags shown here, if applicable to your application.

Flag	Security
ACCESS_SYSTEM_SECURITY	Write access is granted to the pipe's system ACL.
WRITE_DAC	Write access is granted to the pipe's discretionary ACL.
WRITE_OWNER	Write access is granted to the named pipe's owner.

dwPipeMode determines the pipe handle's type, read mode, and wait mode. It consists of one value from each of the next three tables.

Here are the type flags.

Flag	Type
PIPE_TYPE_BYTE	Data is written as a stream of bytes.
PIPE_TYPE_MESSAGE	Data is written as a stream of messages.

Here are the read mode flags.

Flag	Read Mode
PIPE_READMODE_BYTE	Data is read as a stream of bytes.
PIPE_READMODE_MESSAGE	Data is read as a stream of messages. This flag may not be used with PIPE_TYPE_BYTE.

Here are the wait mode flags.

Flag	Wait Mode
PIPE_WAIT	Blocking
PIPE_NOWAIT	Nonblocking

nMaxInstances contains the maximum number of instances that can be created for this pipe.

NOTE

The number in nMaxInstances *must be used for all instances of the pipe. Values can range from 1 to* **PIPE_UNLIMITED_INSTANCES**.

The number of bytes to reserve to the output buffer is passed in *nOutBufSize*. The number of bytes to reserve for the input buffer is passed in *nInBufSize*.

nDefTimeInt contains the default timeout value, in milliseconds. *lpSecurityAtt* is a pointer to a **SECURITY_ATTRIBUTES** structure. This structure contains the security attributes for the pipe. If *lpSecurityAtt* is NULL, default security is assumed. (Use NULL if security does not apply to your application.) The **SECURITY_ATTRIBUTES** structure is shown here.

```
typedef struct _SECURITY_ATTRIBUTES {
  DWORD  nLength;
  LPVOID lpSecurityDescriptor;
```

```
   BOOL    bInheritHandle;
} SECURITY_ATTRIBUTES;
```

Here, **nLength** contains the size of the structure. **lpSecurityDescriptor** is a pointer to a security descriptor; when NULL, the object can be assigned the default security descriptor. If **bInheritHandle** is TRUE, a new process inherits the handle associated with this structure. If **bInheritHandle** is FALSE, a new process will not inherit the handle.

USAGE

The following portion of code illustrates how this function might be used.

```
#define IN_BUFFER_SIZE    1500
#define OUT_BUFFER_SIZE   1500
#define TIME_OUT           100
     .
     .
     .

SECURITY_ATTRIBUTES   secatt;
     .
     .
     .
hPipe = CreateNamedPipe ("\\\\.\\PIPE\\mypipe",
                         PIPE_ACCESS_DUPLEX
                         FILE_FLAG_OVERLAPPED,
                         PIPE_WAIT | PIPE_READMODE_MESSAGE
                         | PIPE_TYPE_MESSAGE,
                         MAX_PIPE_INSTANCES,
                         OUT_BUFFER_SIZE,
                         IN_BUFFER_SIZE,
                         TIME_OUT,
                         &secatt);
```

Here, the first parameter names the pipe "mypipe". The second parameter creates a two-way pipe using an overlapped structure. The third parameter waits for messages with the specified mode and type. The fourth parameter sets the maximum instance limit. The fifth and sixth parameters set the buffer size, the seventh parameter defines the timeout interval, and the last parameter gives the security attributes.

RELATED FUNCTIONS

ConnectNamedPipe()
ReadFileEx()
TransactNamedPipe()
WaitNamedPipe()
WriteFileEx()

BOOL DisconnectNamedPipe(HANDLE *hNamedPipe*)

DisconnectNamedPipe() disconnects the server end of a named pipe. The function returns TRUE if successful, and FALSE if unsuccessful.

hNamedPipe is the handle to an instance of a named pipe. This handle is returned by a call to **CreateNamedPipe()**.

USAGE

Keep in mind that pipes have two ends. **DisconnectNamedPipe()** will always close the server end of a named pipe even if the client end is open. If this occurs, the client receives an error message when an attempt is made to access the pipe. The client is still, however, obligated to use **CloseHandle()** to close its end of the pipe.

It is the server's responsibility to disconnect a pipe handle from a previous client before attempting to connect the handle to another client.

Here is a small portion of code that illustrates the use of this function.

```
HANDLE hPipe;
    .
    .
    .
DisconnectNamedPipe (hPipe);
```

RELATED FUNCTIONS

CloseHandle()
ConnectNamedPipe()
CreateNamedPipe()
FlushFileBuffers()

BOOL GetNamedPipeHandleState(HANDLE *hNamedPipe,*
LPDWORD *lpdwState,*
LPDWORD *lpdwCurInst,*
LPDWORD *lpcbMaxCollect,*
LPDWORD *lpdwCollectTimeInt,*
LPTSTR *lpszUser,*
DWORD *cchMaxUser)*

GetNamedPipeHandleState() obtains the state of a named pipe. This may change over the pipe's lifetime. The function returns TRUE if successful, and FALSE if unsuccessful.

hNamedPipe is the handle for the named pipe for which information is to be obtained. This handle must have a **GENERIC_READ** access.

lpdwState is a pointer to a variable that, on return, contains flags describing the present state of the handle. This value can be NULL, if no state information is required. The flags can be either or both of these values: **PIPE_NOWAIT** or **PIPE_READMODE_MESSAGE**. If neither flag is present, the pipe handle is in blocking, byte-read mode. If **PIPE_NOWAIT** is present, the pipe is in nonblocking mode. If **PIPE_READMODE_MESSAGE** is present, the pipe reads messages.

lpdwCurInst is a pointer to a variable that, on return, will contain the number of current pipe instances. If this value is NULL, the information is not returned. *lpcbMaxCollect* is a pointer to a variable that, on return, will contain the maximum number of bytes to be collected on the client computer before transmission is made to the server. This parameter may be NULL if this information is not needed.

lpdwCollectTimeInt is a pointer to a variable that, on return, will contain the timeout (in milliseconds) before a remote named pipe transfers information. This parameter is set to NULL when the timeout interval is not required.

On return, the string pointed to by *lpszUser* will contain the user name of the client application. This parameter is set to NULL when the name is not needed. *cchMaxUser* contains the size of the *lpszUser* buffer. If *lpszUser* is NULL, *cchMaxUser* is ignored.

RELATED FUNCTION

SetNamedPipeHandleState()

BOOL GetNamedPipeInfo(HANDLE *hNamedPipe,*
LPDWORD *lpdwType,*
LPDWORD *lpcbOutBuf,*
LPDWORD *lpcbInBuf,*
LPDWORD *lpcMaxInst*)

GetNamedPipeInfo() obtains information about the named pipe. The function returns TRUE if successful, and FALSE if unsuccessful.

hNamedPipe is the handle of the named pipe instance. This handle must have **GENERIC_READ** access to the named pipe. *lpdwType* is a pointer to a variable that will, on return, contain flags that describe the type of the named pipe and whether the handle belongs to the server or client. If information is not required, this value may be set to NULL. *lpdwType* may contain either or both **PIPE_SERVER_END** or **PIPE_TYPE_MESSAGE**. If neither flag is present, then the pipe handle is for the client end of a byte-based pipe. If **PIPE_SERVER_END** is set, then the handle references the server end of the named pipe instance. If **PIPE_TYPE_MESSAGE**, then the named pipe is message-based.

lpcbOutBuf is a pointer to a variable that, on return, contains the size of the output buffer. If this value is zero, the buffer size is allocated as needed. If the output buffer size is not needed, set *lpcbOutBuf* to NULL. *lpcbInBuf* is a pointer to a variable that, on return, contains the size of the input buffer. If this value is zero, the buffer size is allocated as needed. If the input buffer size is not needed, set *lpcbInBuf* to NULL.

lpcMaxInst is a pointer to a variable that, on return, contains the maximum number of pipe instances that can be created. When the variable is set to **PIPE_UNLIMITED_INSTANCES**, the number of pipe instances is governed by the system's resources. Set *lpcMaxInst* to NULL if the number of pipe instances is not desired.

RELATED FUNCTIONS

CreateNamedPipe()
GetNamedPipeHandleState()

BOOL ImpersonateNamedPipeClient
(HANDLE *hNamedPipe*)

ImpersonateNamedPipeClient() allows a named pipe's server to impersonate a client process. Impersonation allows the server to take on the security attributes of the client. When impersonation is finished, the **RevertToSelf()** function should be called. The function returns TRUE if successful, and FALSE if unsuccessful.

hNamedPipe is the handle of the named pipe.

USAGE

This function only applies when security is used.
Here is a small portion of code that illustrates the use of this function.

```
HANDLE hPipe;
    .
    .
    .
ImpersonateNamedPipeClient(hPipe);
    .
    .
    .
RevertToSelf(void);
```

RELATED FUNCTIONS

DdeImpersonateClient()
RevertToSelf()

BOOL PeekNamedPipe(HANDLE *hPipe,*
LPVOID *lpvBuffer,*
DWORD *cbBuffer,*
LPDWORD *lpcbRd,*
LPDWORD *lpcbAvail,*
LPDWORD *lpcbMsg***)**

PeekNamedPipe() copies data from a named or anonymous pipe, but does not remove it. The function returns TRUE if successful, and FALSE if unsuccessful.

hPipe is the handle, with **GENERIC_READ** access, to identify the pipe. This handle can be obtained by calling **CreateNamedPipe()** or **CreateFile()**, or from the read end of an anonymous pipe as returned by **CreatePipe()**.

Data from the pipe is put into the buffer pointed to by *lpvBuffer*. This pointer can be NULL when no data is required. *cbBuffer* contains the size of the *lpvBuffer* buffer. When *lpvBuffer* is NULL, this parameter is ignored. *lpcbRd* is a pointer to a variable that, on return, contains the number of bytes read from the pipe. This parameter can be NULL if no data is read.

The total number of bytes that can be read from the pipe are stored in the variable pointed to by *lpcbAvail*. When this value is NULL, the information is not obtained. *lpcbMsg* is a pointer to a variable that, on return, contains the number of bytes remaining in the message. This value is zero for either byte-type named pipes or anonymous pipes. *lpcbMsg* is NULL if the number of bytes remaining is not desired.

USAGE

When the handle is a named pipe handle, operating in byte-read mode, the function will read data up to the size given in *cbBuffer*. When operating in message-read mode, the function will read the next message. When the message is larger than *cbBuffer*, the function fills the buffer and puts the number of unread bytes left in the message into the variable pointed to by *lpcbMsg*. This is still considered a successful outcome and the function returns TRUE.

RELATED FUNCTIONS

CreateFile()
CreateNamedPipe()
CreatePipe()
ReadFile()
WriteFile()

BOOL RevertToSelf(void)

RevertToSelf() cancels the impersonation of a client application. This function should be used after finishing any impersonation started with **DdeImpersonate-Client()**, **ImpersonateNamedPipeClient()**, or **ImpersonateSelf()**. The function returns TRUE if successful, and FALSE if unsuccessful.

USAGE

Here is a small portion of code that illustrates the use of this function.

```
HANDLE hPipe;
   .
   .
   .

ImpersonateNamedPipeClient(hPipe);
   .
   .
   .

RevertToSelf(void);
```

RELATED FUNCTIONS

DdeImpersonateClient()
ImpersonateNamedPipeClient()
ImpersonateSelf()

BOOL SetNamedPipeHandleState(HANDLE *hNamedPipe,*
LPDWORD *lpdwMode,*
LPDWORD *lpcbMaxCollect,*
LPDWORD *lpdwCollectDataTimeInt*)

SetNamedPipeHandleState() sets the state of the named pipe. The function returns TRUE if successful, and FALSE if unsuccessful.

If the handle is to the client end of a named pipe, with the named pipe server process on a remote computer, the function can be used to control local buffering.

hNamedPipe is the handle, with **GENERIC_WRITE** access, to the named pipe instance. This handle is to the server end of the pipe when returned by **CreateNamedPipe()**, or to the client end of the pipe when returned by **CreateFile()**.

lpdwMode is a pointer to a variable that specifies the pipe's mode. This mode is a combination of a read mode flag and wait mode flag. (If neither is needed, then this parameter may be NULL.) The read mode flag may be either **PIPE_READMODE_BYTE** (data is read as a string of bytes) or **PIPE_READMODE_MESSAGE** (data is read as a stream of messages). The wait mode flags may be either **PIPE_WAIT** (blocking mode) or **PIPE_NOWAIT** (nonblocking mode).

lpcbMaxCollect is a pointer to a variable that contains the maximum number of bytes that may be collected by the client before transmission to the server. NULL is used when the pipe handle is to the server end of a named pipe or when the client and server are on the same computer. If the client process uses **FILE_FLAG_WRITE_THROUGH** in **CreateFile()** when creating the handle, this will be ignored. When this value is NULL, this parameter is ignored.

lpdwCollectDataTimeInt is a variable that contains the length of the timeout (specified in milliseconds) that can elapse before a remote named pipe transfers data. NULL should be used when the given pipe handle is to the server end of a named pipe or if client and server processes are on the same computer. If

FILE_FLAG_WRITE_THROUGH is used with **CreateFile()**, this parameter will be ignored. Also, if *lpcbMaxCollect* is NULL, then *lpdwCollectDataTimeInt* must also be NULL.

RELATED FUNCTIONS

ConnectNamedPipe()
CreateFile()
CreateNamedPipe()
GetNamedPipeHandleState()
ReadFile()
WriteFile()

BOOL TransactNamedPipe(HANDLE *hNamedPipe,*
LPVOID *lpvWrtBuf,*
DWORD *cbWrtBuf,*
LPVOID *lpvRdBuf,*
DWORD *cbRdBuf,*
LPDWORD *lpcbRd,*
LPOVERLAPPED *lpOl*)

TransactNamedPipe() both writes and reads a message to and from the named pipe using a single network operation. The function returns TRUE if successful, and FALSE if unsuccessful. A return of FALSE can mean that the message to be read is longer than *cbRdBuf*.

hNamedPipe is the handle of the named pipe. It will have been obtained from either **CreateNamedPipe()** or **CreateFile()**.) *lpvWrtBuf* is a pointer to a buffer that contains the information written to the pipe. The size of the output buffer pointed to by *lpvWrtBuf* is passed *cbWrtBuf*.

lpvRdBuf is a pointer to the buffer that obtains the data from the pipe. The size of the input buffer pointed to by *lpvRdBuf* is passed in *cbRdBuf*. On return, *lpcbRd* will point to a variable that contains the number of bytes actually read from the pipe.

lpOl is a pointer to an **OVERLAPPED** structure or it may be NULL. If NULL—or **FILE_FLAG_OVERLAPPED** is not used with **CreateNamed-Pipe()** or **CreateFile()** when the handle was created—this function will not return until the operation is completed. (That is, the operation will be performed synchronously.) When the above conditions are not satisfied, the function is executed as an overlapped operation. (That is, the operation will be performed asynchronously.) In this case, the **OVERLAPPED** structure must contain a manual reset event object. When the operation is not completed immediately, the function returns FALSE.

USAGE

This function can fail when the pipe is not a message-type pipe or when the pipe handle is not in message-read mode.

Here is a small portion of code that illustrates the use of this function.

```
#define WRITE_BUFFER 1500
#define READ_BUFFER  1500
    .
    .
    .
char WrtBuf[WRITE_BUFFER];
char RdBuf[READ_BUFFER];
unsigned long ByteRd;
    .
    .
    .
TransactNamedPipe("mypipe",
            WrtBuf,
            WRITE_BUFFER,
            RdBuf,
            READ_BUFFER,
            &ByteRd,
            NULL);
```

RELATED FUNCTIONS

CreateEvent()
CreateFile()
CreateNamedPipe()
PeekNamedPipe()
ReadFileEx()
SetNamedPipeHandleState()

BOOL WaitNamedPipe(LPCSTR *lpszPipeName,* DWORD *dwTimeInt*)

WaitNamedPipe() waits for an instance of the named pipe to become available. This function returns TRUE if an instance of the pipe is available before the timeout interval elapses; otherwise, it returns FALSE.

lpszPipeName is a pointer to the name of the named pipe and includes the name assigned to the computer where the server process is running.

A period (.) may be used for the server name when the pipe is local.

dwTimeInt specifies the length of time, in milliseconds, that the function will wait. If *dwTimeInt* is specified as **NMPWAIT_USE_DEFAULT_WAIT**, the timeout interval is the default given by the server process when **CreateNamedPipe()** was called. If *dwTimeInt* is **NMPWAIT_WAIT_FOREVER**, the function never returns until an instance of the named pipe is available.

USAGE

When the function call is successful, the **CreateFile()** function can be used to open a handle to the named pipe.

Here is a small portion of code that illustrates the use of this function.

```
#define TIME_INT   100

     .
     .

WaitNamedPipe("\\\\.\\pipe\\mypipe", TIME_INT);
```

RELATED FUNCTIONS

CallNamedPipe()
ConnectNamedPipe()
CreateFile()
CreateNamedPipe()

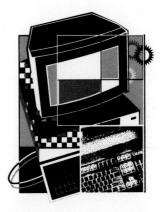

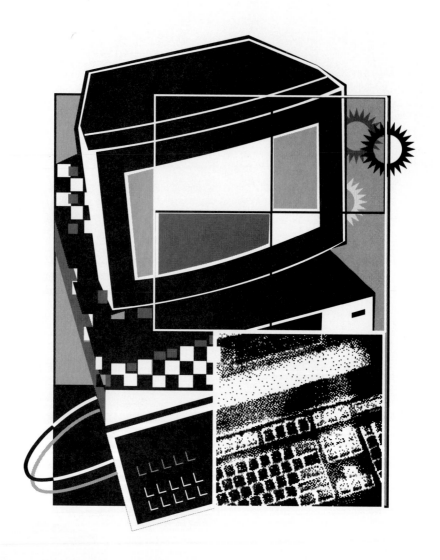

Chapter 26

Printing

T H I S chapter describes Windows' printing functions. These functions can be used to control print jobs, initialize the printer, or cancel printing.

int AbortDoc(HDC *hdc*)

AbortDoc() halts the current print job. The function returns an integer value greater than zero if successful, and negative if unsuccessful.

hdc is the handle of the device context for the print job.

USAGE

Applications call the **EndDoc()** function when ending successful print jobs. Applications call the **AbortDoc()** function in order to stop a print job. Print jobs are halted when an error occurs or when the user wishes to cancel the job.

Print jobs started via the Print Manager and canceled by the **AbortDoc()** function will have the entire spool job cleared. In this case, the printer receives no data. When a cancellation occurs without the involvement of the Print Manager, any data sent to the printer may be printed. An attempt is made to reset the printer and end the job.

RELATED FUNCTIONS

EndDoc()
SetAbortProc()
StartDoc()

BOOL AbortPrinter(HANDLE *hPrt*)

AbortPrinter() erases the spool file of the printer. This function is only used if print spooling is used. The function returns TRUE if successful, and FALSE if unsuccessful.

hPrt is the handle of the printer whose spooling file will be erased.

USAGE

Here is a small portion of code to illustrate the use of this function.

```
HANDLE hPrt;
   .
   .
   .
OpenPrinter("Laser_Jet", &hPrt, NULL);
   .
   .
   .
AbortPrinter(hPrt);
```

RELATED FUNCTION

OpenPrinter()

BOOL AddForm(HANDLE *hPrt*, DWORD *cLevel*, LPBYTE *pForm*)

AddForm() adds a form to the list of forms recognized by the printer. The function returns TRUE if successful, and FALSE if unsuccessful.

hPrt is the handle of the printer. *cLevel* contains the version of the structure pointed to by *pForm* and must be 1. (Other values may be allowed by future releases of Windows.) *pForm* is a pointer to a **FORM_INFO_1** structure, which is shown here.

```
typedef struct _FORM_INFO_1 {
  LPTSTR pName;
  SIZEL Size;
  RECTL ImageableArea;
} FORM_INFO_1;
```

Here, **pName** is a pointer to the name of the form. **Size** contains the width and height of the form, in steps of .001 millimeters. **ImageableArea** contains the width and height of the printable portion of the form in steps of .001 millimeters.

RELATED FUNCTIONS

EnumForms()
OpenPrinter()

BOOL AddJob(HANDLE *hPrt,* DWORD *cLevel,* LPBYTE *pData,* DWORD *cbBuff,* LPDWORD *pcbNumCopied*)

AddJob() obtains the path and filename of a file that can be used to store a print job. The function returns TRUE if successful, and FALSE if unsuccessful.

hPrt is the handle of the printer. *cLevel* contains the version of the structure pointed to by *pData* and must be 1. (Other values may be allowed by future releases of Windows.) *pData* is a pointer to an **ADDJOB_INFO_1** structure, that will, on return, contain the path and filename information. **ADDJOB_INFO_1** is shown here.

```
typedef struct _ADDJOB_INFO_1 {
  LPTSTR Path;
  DWORD  JobId;
} ADDJOB_INFO_1;
```

Here, **Path** is a pointer to the path and filename for the print job's storage. **JobId** is the ID of the print job.

In the function, *cbBuff* contains the size of the buffer pointed to by *pData*. *pcbNumCopied* is a pointer to a variable that, on return, will contain the number of bytes copied into the structure pointed to by *pData*.

USAGE

If the size of the buffer pointed to by *pData* is too small, then, on return, *pcbNumCopied* will contain the required size of the buffer.

The path and filename returned in **ADDJOB_INFO_1** can be opened with **CreateFile()**. The job identification returned in the structure can be passed to **SetJob()** and **ScheduleJob()** to control the print job.

RELATED FUNCTIONS

OpenPrinter()
ScheduleJob()
SetJob()

HANDLE AddPrinter(LPTSTR *lpszName*, DWORD *dwLevel*, LPBYTE *lpbPrt*)

AddPrinter() adds a printer to the list of supported printers. The function returns the handle of the new printer object if successful, and NULL if unsuccessful.

lpszName is a pointer to the name of the server. When set to NULL, the print processor is locally installed. *dwLevel* gives the version of the structure pointed to by *lpbPrt* and must be 2. *lpbPrt* is a pointer to a **PRINTER_INFO_2** structure, shown here.

```
typedef struct _PRINTER_INFO_2 {
  LPTSTR pServerName;
  LPTSTR pPrinterName;
  LPTSTR pShareName;
  LPTSTR pPortName;
  LPTSTR pDriverName;
  LPTSTR pComment;
  LPTSTR pLocation;
  LPDEVMODE pDevMode;
```

```
     LPTSTR pSepFile;
     LPTSTR pPrintProcessor;
     LPTSTR pDatatype;
     LPTSTR pParameters;
     PSECURITY_DESCRIPTOR pSecurityDescriptor;
     DWORD Attributes;
     DWORD Priority;
     DWORD DefaultPriority;
     DWORD StartTime;
     DWORD UntilTime;
     DWORD Status;
     DWORD cJobs;
     DWORD AveragePPM;
} PRINTER_INFO_2;
```

The following structure members must be set before calling **AddPrinter()**: **pServerName, pPrinterName, pPortName**, and **pDriverName**. The following structure members may be set before the function is called: **Attributes, DefaultPriority, pComment, pDatatype, pDevMode, pLocation, pParameters, pPrintProcessor, Priority, pSecurityDescriptor, pSepFile, pShareName, StartTime,** and **UntilTime**. These structure members are reserved: **Status, cJobs,** and **AveragePPM**. Their values must not be altered.

In the structure, **pServerName** is a pointer to the name of the server that controls the printer. If this name is NULL, the printer is controlled locally. **pPrinterName** is a pointer to the name of the printer.

pShareName is a pointer to the name of the sharepoint for the printer. (This name is only relevant if the printer is shared.) **pPortName** is a pointer to the name or names of the ports connected to the printer.

pDriverName is a pointer to the name of the printer driver. **pComment** is a pointer to a string that contains a comment about the printer.

pLocation is a pointer to a description of the physical location for the printer. **pDevMode** is a pointer to a **DEVMODE** structure that defines default printer settings.

pSepFile is a pointer to the name of the file that contains the output used for the page that separates multiple print jobs. **pPrintProcessor** is a pointer to the name of the print processor.

pDatatype is a pointer to the name of the data type used to record the print job. **pParameters** is a pointer to the default print processor parameters.

pSecurityDescriptor is a pointer to a **SECURITY_DESCRIPTOR** structure for the printer and can be set to NULL if security is not applicable.

Attributes contains printer attributes and can be **PRINTER_ATTRIB-
UTE_QUEUED**, **PRINTER_ATTRIBUTE_DIRECT**, **PRINTER_AT-
TRIBUTE_DEFAULT**, or **PRINTER_ATTRIBUTE_SHARED**.

Priority contains the print job's spooler priority. **DefaultPriority** contains
the default spooling priority value that is assigned to print jobs.

StartTime contains the earliest time that a printer will print a job. **UntilTime** contains the latest time a printer will print a job.

Status contains the printer's status and can be **PRINTER_STATUS_PAUSED**
or **PRINTER_STATUS_PENDING_DELETION**.

cJobs contains the number of print jobs in the print queue. **AveragePPM**
contains the average number of pages printed per minute.

RELATED FUNCTIONS

DeletePrinter()
GetPrinter()
PrinterProperties()
SetPrinter()

BOOL AddPrinterDriver(LPTSTR *lpszName,*
DWORD *dwLevel,*
LPBYTE *lpbDrvInfo*)

AddPrinterDriver() installs (adds) a local or remote printer driver. The
function returns TRUE if successful, and FALSE if unsuccessful.

lpszName is a pointer to the name of the server where the driver is to be
installed. To install the driver locally, use NULL for this parameter.

dwLevel contains the version number of the structure that the *lpbDrvInfo*
points to. Currently, this version number is 2. (However, later releases of Windows
may allow other versions.) *lpbDrvInfo* is a pointer to a **DRIVER_INFO_2**
structure, which is shown here.

```
typedef struct _DRIVER_INFO_2 {
  DWORD   cVersion;
  LPTSTR  pName;
  LPTSTR  pEnvironment;
  LPTSTR  pDriverPath;
```

```
    LPTSTR pDataFile;
    LPTSTR pConfigFile;
} DRIVER_INFO_2;
```

Here, **cVersion** holds a version number for the printer driver. **pName** is a pointer to the name of the driver. **pEnvironment** is a pointer to a string that describes the environment for which the driver was written. If a NULL, the environment of the calling process is used.

pDriverPath is a pointer to the path and/or filename for the file containing the device driver. **pDataFile** is a pointer to the path and/or filename for the driver's data file.

pConfigFile is a pointer to the path and/or filename for the device driver's configuration DLL.

USAGE

AddPrinterDriver() requires that all files used by the driver be in the printer driver directory of the system. This directory can be located with the use of the **GetPrinterDriverDirectory()** function. The currently installed printer drivers can then be found with a call to the **EnumPrinterDrivers()** function.

RELATED FUNCTIONS

EnumPrinterDrivers()
GetPrinterDriverDirectory()

BOOL AddPrintProcessor(LPTSTR *lpszServer,*
LPTSTR *lpszEnv,*
LPTSTR *lpszPath,*
LPTSTR *lpszName)*

AddPrintProcessor() installs a print processor and then adds the print processor name to the list of supported print processors. The function returns TRUE if successful, and FALSE if unsuccessful.

lpszServer is a pointer to the name of the server where the print processor is to be installed. When this value is set to NULL, the print processor is installed on the local computer.

lpszEnv is a pointer to the environment string. If this parameter is NULL, the calling process's environment is used.

lpszPath is a pointer to the name of the file containing the print processor, which must be located in the system print processor directory. *lpszName* is a pointer to the name of the print processor.

RELATED FUNCTIONS

EnumPrintProcessors()
GetPrintProcessorDirectory()

LONG AdvancedDocumentProperties(HWND *hWnd,*
HANDLE *hPrt,*
LPTSTR *lpszDevName,*
PDEVMODE *pdmOutput,*
PDEVMODE *pdmInput)*

AdvancedDocumentProperties() displays the printer configuration dialog box. This dialog box lets the user change attributes associated with the printer. The function returns TRUE if successful, and FALSE if unsuccessful.

hWnd is the handle of the parent window that owns the printer configuration dialog box. *hPrt* is the handle of a printer.

lpszDevName is a pointer to the name of the device. *pdmOutput* is a pointer to a **DEVMODE** structure that will be filled by the dialog box. (That is, on return, it will contain the user's configuration choices.)

The Windows NT/Win32 version of the **DEVMODE** structure is shown here.

```
typedef struct _devicemode {
  TCHAR   dmDeviceName[32];
  WORD    dmSpecVersion;
  WORD    dmDriverVersion;
```

```
    WORD     dmSize;
    WORD     dmDriverExtra;
    DWORD    dmFields;
    short    dmOrientation;
    short    dmPaperSize;
    short    dmPaperLength;
    short    dmPaperWidth;
    short    dmScale;
    short    dmCopies;
    short    dmDefaultSource;
    short    dmPrintQuality;
    short    dmColor;
    short    dmDuplex;
    short    dmYResolution;
    short    dmTTOption;
    short    dmCollate;
    TCHAR    dmFormName[32];
    WORD     dmUnusedPadding;
    USHORT   dmBitsPerPel;
    DWORD    dmPelsWidth;
    DWORD    dmPelsHeight;
    DWORD    dmDisplayFlags;
    DWORD    dmDisplayFrequency;
} DEVMODE;
```

While most of the members of this structure are self-explanatory, here is a brief description.

dmDeviceName contains the name of the device. **dmSpecVersion** contains the Windows version number. (This structure may vary between different versions of Windows.) **dmDriverVersion** contains the device driver's printer number. **dmSize** must contain the size, in bytes, of the **DEVMODE** structure.

dmDriverExtra specifies the number of bytes that follow the **DEVMODE** structure that contain information used by the driver. If none are used (as is typical), then this member must be zero.

dmFields specifies which of the other members of the **DEVMODE** structure contain valid initialization values. (Not all devices support all fields.) It can be any combination of the following values:

```
DM_ORIENTATION
DM_PAPERSIZE
DM_PAPERLENGTH
DM_PAPERWIDTH
```

DM_SCALE
DM_COPI ES
DM_DEFAULTSOURCE
DM_PRINTQUALITY
DM_COLOR
DM_DUPLEX
DM_YRESOLUTION
DM_TTOPTION

Another way to set the **dmFields** member is to compute its value using the fact that **DM_ORIENTATION** is defined as the value 1, **DM_PAPERSIZE** as the value 2, **DM_PAPERLENGTH** as the value 4, and so on.

dmOrientation determines whether the paper in the printer is longer than wide (use **DMORIENT_PORTRAIT**) or wider than it is long (use **DMORIENT_LANDSCAPE**).

dmPaperSize contains the size of the paper used by a printer. It may be one of the following values.

Macro	Size
DMPAPER_LETTER	8 1/2 × 11 (inches)
DMPAPER_LETTERSMALL	8 1/2 × 11 (inches)
DMPAPER_TABLOID	11 × 17 (inches)
DMPAPER_LEDGER	17 × 11 (inches)
DMPAPER_LEGAL	8 1/2 × 14 (inches)
DMPAPER_STATEMENT	5 1/2 × 8 1/2 (inches)
DMPAPER_EXECUTIVE	7 1/4 × 10 1/2 (inches)
DMPAPER_A3	297 × 420 (mm)
DMPAPER_A4	210 × 297 (mm)
DMPAPER_A4SMALL	210 × 297 (mm)
DMPAPER_A5	148 × 210 (mm)
DMPAPER_B4	250 × 354 (mm)
DMPAPER_B5	182 × 257 (mm)
DMPAPER_FOLIO	8 1/2 × 13 (inches)
DMPAPER_QUARTO	215 × 275 (mm)
DMPAPER_10X14	10 × 14 (inches)
DMPAPER_11X17	11 × 17 (inches)
DMPAPER_NOTE	8 1/2 × 11 (inches)
DMPAPER_ENV_9	3 7/8 × 8 7/8 (inches)
DMPAPER_ENV_10	4 1/8 × 9 1/2 (inches)
DMPAPER_ENV_11	4 1/2 × 10 3/8 (inches)
DMPAPER_ENV_12	4 3/4 × 11 (inches)

Macro	Size
DMPAPER_ENV_14	5 × 11 1/2 (inches)
DMPAPER_CSHEET	C size sheet
DMPAPER_DSHEET	D size sheet
DMPAPER_ESHEET	E size sheet
DMPAPER_ENV_DL	110 × 220 (mm)
DMPAPER_ENV_C5	162 × 229 (mm)
DMPAPER_ENV_C3	324 × 458 (mm)
DMPAPER_ENV_C4	229 × 324 (mm)
DMPAPER_ENV_C6	114 × 162 (mm)
DMPAPER_ENV_C65	114 × 229 (mm)
DMPAPER_ENV_B4	250 × 353 (mm)
DMPAPER_ENV_B5	176 × 250 (mm)
DMPAPER_ENV_B6	176 × 125 (mm)
DMPAPER_ENV_ITALY	110 × 230 (mm)
DMPAPER_ENV_MONARCH	3.875 × 7.5 (inches)
DMPAPER_ENV_PERSONAL	3 5/8 × 6 1/2 (inches)
DMPAPER_FANFOLD_US	14 7/8 × 11 (inches)
DMPAPER_FANFOLD_STD_GERMAN	8 1/2 × 12 (inches)
DMPAPER_FANFOLD_LGL_GERMAN	8 1/2 × 13 (inches)

dmPaperSize may be set to zero if the paper size is specified in **dmPaper-Length** and **dmPaperWidth** instead.

dmPaperLength contains the length of the paper. **dmPaperWidth** contains the width of the paper.

dmScale contains a scaling factor. This value sizes the output. The value specifies a percentage. That is, a **dmScale** value of 20 means that output will be scaled by 20 percent.

dmCopies contains the number of copies to be printed.

dmDefaultSource is not used and must be set to zero.

dmPrintQuality determines the printer resolution. It must be one of these values: **DMRES_HIGH, DMRES_MEDIUM, DMRES_LOW**, or **DMRES_DRAFT**. If it contains another positive integer value, then this value specifies the number of horizontal dots-per-inch used by the device.

The value of **dmColor** determines whether a color printer actually prints in color or in monochrome. It must be one of these values: **DMCOLOR_COLOR** or **DMCOLOR_MONOCHROME**.

For printers capable of printing on both sides of the paper, the **dmDuplex** member specifies how this will take place. It must be one of these values: **DMDUP_SIMPLEX, DMDUP_HORIZONTAL**, or **DMDUP_VERTICAL**.

dmYResolution contains the number of vertical dots-per-inch.

dmTTOption governs how TrueType fonts are printed. It will be one of the following values. **DMTT_BITMAP** (TrueType fonts printed as graphics), **DMTT_DOWNLOAD** (download TrueType fonts), or **DMTT_SUBDEV** (use device fonts rather than TrueType fonts).

dmUnusedPadding is used to align this structure on a **DWORD** boundary. **dmCollate** determines if collation will be used when printing multiple copies and can be set to **DMCOLLATE_TRUE** (collates multiple copies) or **DMCOLLATE_FALSE** (does not collate). **dmFormName** contains the name of the form to use. These names are available via a call to **EnumForms()**.

dmBitsPerPel contains the color resolution of the display device (bits per pixel). **dmPelsWidth** contains the width of a video device (in pixels). **dmPelsHeight** contains the height of a video device (in pixels).

dmDisplayFlags contains the display mode and can be set to **DM_GRAYSCALE** (a non-color device) or **DM_INTERLACED** (display mode is interlaced). **dmDisplayFrequency** contains the frequency of the display device in a specific mode (in Hertz).

In the function, *pdmInput* is also a pointer to a **DEVMODE** structure. This structure holds the configuration data used to initialize the controls of the dialog box.

RELATED FUNCTION

GetPrinter()

BOOL ClosePrinter(HANDLE *hPrt*)

ClosePrinter() closes a printer handle. The function returns TRUE if successful, and FALSE if unsuccessful.

hPrt is the handle of the printer object that is to be closed.

USAGE

Here is a small portion of code to illustrate the use of this function.

```
HANDLE hPrt;
char pEnv[BuffSize]="";
DWORD dwCpyNeed;
LPBYTE pDrvInfo2;
    .
```

```
      .
      .
      .
GetPrinterDriver(hPrt, pEnv, 2, NULL, 0, &dwCpyNeed);
pDriverInfo2 = (LPBYTE) LocalAlloc (LPTR, dwCpyNeed);
GetPrinterDriver(hPrt, pEnv, 2, pDrvInfo2,
                 dwCpyNeed, &dwCpyNeed);
      .
      .
      .
ClosePrinter(hPrt);
```

RELATED FUNCTIONS

AddPrinter()
OpenPrinter()

BOOL DeleteForm(HANDLE *hPrt,* LPTSTR *lpszFmName*)

DeleteForm() deletes a form name from the list of forms available to the specified printer. The function returns TRUE if successful, and FALSE if unsuccessful.

hPrt is a handle to the printer. *lpszFmName* is a pointer to the form name that is to be removed.

RELATED FUNCTION

AddForm()

BOOL DeletePrinter(HANDLE *hPrt*)

DeletePrinter() deletes a printer handle. The function returns TRUE if successful, and FALSE if unsuccessful.

hPrt is the handle of the printer object to be deleted.

RELATED FUNCTIONS

AddPrinter()
EnumPrinters()

BOOL DeletePrinterDriver(LPTSTR *lpszName*,
LPTSTR *lpszEnv*,
LPTSTR *lpszDrvName*)

DeletePrinterDriver() deletes the printer driver name from the list of supported drivers. (It does not actually remove the driver from disk, however.) The function returns TRUE if successful, and FALSE if unsuccessful.

lpszName is a pointer to the name of the server where the driver will be deleted. When set to NULL, the driver will be removed locally.

lpszEnv is a pointer to the environment string that describes where the driver will be deleted. If NULL, the environment of the calling process is used. *lpszDrvName* is a pointer to the name of the driver being deleted.

RELATED FUNCTION

EnumPrinterDrivers()

BOOL DeletePrintProcessor(LPTSTR *lpszServer*,
LPTSTR *lpszEnv*,
LPTSTR *lpszName*)

DeletePrintProcessor() deletes a print processor from the list of supported print processors. The function returns non-zero if successful, and zero on failure.

The name of the server where the print processor will be deleted is pointed to by *lpszServer*. When this value is set to NULL, the print processor is deleted from the local computer. *lpszEnv* is a pointer to the environment string. If this parameter is NULL, the calling process's environment is used. *lpszName* is a pointer to the name of the print processor.

RELATED FUNCTIONS

AddPrintProcessor()
EnumPrintProcessors()
GetPrintProcessorDirectory()

LONG DocumentProperties(HWND *hWnd*,
HANDLE *hPrt*,
LPTSTR *pDeviceName*,
PDEVMODE *pdmOutput*,
PDEVMODE *pdmInput*,
DWORD *fMode*)

DocumentProperties() activates a printer configuration dialog box. This allows the user to change how a document is printed.

hWnd is the handle of the parent window of the printer configuration dialog box. *hPrt* is the handle of the printer object. *pDeviceName* is a pointer to the name of a device being configured.

pdmOutput is a pointer to a **DEVMODE** structure. On return, this structure will contain the printer configuration data. *pdmInput* is also a pointer to a **DEVMODE** structure. The contents of this structure are used to initialize the dialog box.

fMode determines the operation of the function. When set to zero, the function returns the number of bytes required by the **DEVMODE** structure. If not zero, then it must be one or more of these values.

Value	Meaning
DM_IN_BUFFER	(Input) The function combines the printer driver's print settings with those in the **DEVMODE** structure. The function updates the structure members given by the **DEVMODE** structure's *dmFields* member. The settings in the **DEVMODE** structure override the printer driver's print settings.
DM_IN_PROMPT	(Input) The function shows the printer driver's "Print Setup" dialog box. Then any changes via the **DEVMODE** data structure are made.
DM_OUT_BUFFER	(Output) The function writes the printer driver's print settings to the **DEVMODE** data structure given by *pdmOutput*. A sufficiently large buffer must be given to hold the information.

The function's return value is the size of the buffer needed to hold the printer driver initialization data when the *fMode* parameter is set to 0. Otherwise, if successful, the return value will be **IDOK** or **IDCANCEL**. If the function fails, the return value will be negative.

RELATED FUNCTIONS

AdvancedDocumentProperties()
CreateDC()
GetPrinter()
OpenPrinter()

int EndDoc(HDC *hdc*)

EndDoc() terminates a print job. The function returns an integer value greater than zero if successful, and a negative value if unsuccessful.

hdc is the handle of the device context. This function should be called when a print job has completed.

USAGE

Here is a small portion of code to illustrate the use of this function.

```
StartDoc(hdc, lpdi);
   .
   .
   .
EndDoc(hdc);
```

RELATED FUNCTION

StartDoc()

BOOL EndDocPrinter(HANDLE *hPrt*)

EndDocPrinter() terminates a print job for a specific printer. The function returns TRUE if successful, and FALSE if unsuccessful.

hPrt is the handle of a printer for which the print job will be ended.

RELATED FUNCTION

EndDoc()

int EndPage(HDC *hdc*)

EndPage() notifies the device that the application has completed writing to a page. Use this function to request a new page advance from the device driver. The function returns an integer greater than zero if successful, and a negative value if unsuccessful.

hdc is the handle of the device context for the print job.

RELATED FUNCTIONS

ResetDC()
StartPage()

BOOL EndPagePrinter(HANDLE *hPrt*)

EndPagePrinter() ends one page and starts the next. The function returns TRUE if successful, and FALSE if unsuccessful.

hPrt is the handle of the affected printer.

USAGE

To print pages, first call **StartPagePrinter()**. To stop printing, call **End-PagePrinter()**. Pages are sent to the print file using **WritePrinter()**.

RELATED FUNCTIONS

OpenPrinter()
StartPagePrinter()
WritePrinter()

BOOL EnumForms(HANDLE *hPrt*, DWORD *dwLevel*, LPBYTE *lpbForm*, DWORD *dwBuf*, LPDWORD *lpdwCpyNeed*, LPDWORD *lpdwRet*)

EnumForms() enumerates the forms supported by a printer. The function returns TRUE if successful, and FALSE if unsuccessful.

hPrt is the handle of the printer. *dwLevel* gives the version of the structure pointed to by *lpbForm* points and must be 1. (Other values may be supported by new releases of Windows.) *lpbForm* is a pointer to an array of **FORM_INFO_1** structures (see **AddForm()**).*dwBuf* contains the number of elements in this array.

lpdwCpyNeed is a pointer to a variable that will, on return, contain the number of bytes copied to the array pointed to by *lpbForm* or the required size of this array.

On return, *lpdwRet* is a pointer to a variable that contains the number of **FORM_INFO_1** structures copied into the array.

RELATED FUNCTIONS

AddPrinter()
OpenPrinter()

BOOL EnumJobs(HANDLE *hPrt*, DWORD *dwFirstJob*, DWORD *dwNoJobs*, DWORD *dwLevel*, LPBYTE *lpbJob*, DWORD *dwBuf*, LPDWORD *lpdwCpyNeed*, LPDWORD *lpdwRet*)

EnumJobs() fills **JOB_INFO_1** or **JOB_INFO_2** structures with information about the print jobs for a printer. The function returns TRUE if successful, and FALSE if unsuccessful.

The **JOB_INFO_1** structure is shown here.

```
typedef struct _JOB_INFO_1 {
  DWORD JobId;
  LPTSTR pPrinterName;
  LPTSTR pMachineName;
  LPTSTR pUserName;
  LPTSTR pDocument;
  LPTSTR pDatatype;
  LPTSTR pStatus;
  DWORD Status;
  DWORD Priority;
  DWORD Position;
  DWORD TotalPages;
  DWORD PagesPrinted;
```

```
    SYSTEMTIME Submitted;
} JOB_INFO_1;
```

Here, **JobId** contains a job ID. **pPrinterName** is a pointer to the name of
the printer where the job is spooled. **pMachineName** is a pointer to the name
of the machine that created the print job. **pUserName** is a pointer to the name
of the user that owns the print job.

pDocument is a pointer to the name of the print job. **pDatatype** is a pointer
to the type of data in the print job. **pStatus** is a pointer to the status of the print
job. **Status** contains the job status and can be set to one or more of these values:

JOB_STATUS_DELETING
JOB_STATUS_ERROR
JOB_STATUS_OFFLINE
JOB_STATUS_PAPEROUT
JOB_STATUS_PAUSED
JOB_STATUS_PRINTED
JOB_STATUS_PRINTING
JOB_STATUS_SPOOLING.

Priority contains the job priority. **Position** contains the position of the job
in the print queue. **TotalPages** contains the number of pages in the document.
PagesPrinted contains the number of pages printed. **Submitted** contains the
time the document entered the print queue.

The **JOB_INFO_2** structure is shown here.

```
typedef struct _JOB_INFO_2 {
  DWORD JobId;
  LPTSTR pPrinterName;
  LPTSTR pMachineName;
  LPTSTR pUserName;
  LPTSTR pDocument;
  LPTSTR pNotifyName;
  LPTSTR pDatatype;
  LPTSTR pPrintProcessor;
  LPTSTR pParameters;
  LPTSTR pDriverName;
  LPDEVMODE pDevMode;
  LPTSTR pStatus;
  PSECURITY_DESCRIPTOR pSecurityDescriptor;
  DWORD Status;
```

```
    DWORD Priority;
    DWORD Position;
    DWORD StartTime;
    DWORD UntilTime;
    DWORD TotalPages;
    DWORD Size;
    SYSTEMTIME Submitted;
    DWORD Time;
    DWORD PagesPrinted ;
} JOB_INFO_2;
```

Here, **JobId** contains the job ID. **pPrinterName** is a pointer to the name of the printer where the job is spooled. **pMachineName** is a pointer to the name of the machine that created the print job. **pUserName** is a pointer to the name of the user that owns the print job.

pDocument is a pointer to the name of the print job. **pNotifyName** is a pointer to the name of the user to be notified when the job is complete or an error has occurred. **pDatatype** is a pointer to the type of data in the print job. **pPrintProcessor** is a pointer to the name of the print processor.

pParameters is a pointer to the print processor parameters. **pDriverName** is a pointer to the name of the printer driver. **pDevMode** is a pointer to a **DEVMODE** structure for the printer driver. **pStatus** is a pointer to the print job status. **pSecurityDescriptor** is set to NULL. **Status** contains the job status and can be one or more of these values:

```
JOB_STATUS_PAUSED
JOB_STATUS_ERROR
JOB_STATUS_DELETING
JOB_STATUS_SPOOLING
JOB_STATUS_PRINTING
JOB_STATUS_OFFLINE
JOB_STATUS_PAPEROUT
JOB_STATUS_PRINTED
```

Priority contains the priority of the job. **Position** contains the position of the job in the queue. **StartTime** contains the earliest time that a job can be printed. **UntilTime** contains the latest time that the job can be printed. **TotalPages** contains the number of pages in the job.

Size contains the number of bytes in the print job. The time the job was sent to the print drive is contained in **Submitted**. The number of seconds since the job began printing is contained in **Time**. **PagesPrinted** contains the number of pages printed so far.

In the function, *hPrt* is the handle of the printer object. *dwFirstJob* contains the job number of the first enumerated job. (This is its location in the print queue.) The number of jobs that you want to enumerate is passed in *dwNoJobs*. *dwLevel* determines if the function uses **JOB_INFO_1** (*dwLevel* is 1) or **JOB_INFO_2** (*dwLevel* is 2) structures.

lpbJob is a pointer to an array of **JOB_INFO_1** or **JOB_INFO_2** structures. *dwBuf* gives the size of the array *lpbJob* in bytes. *lpdwCpyNeed* is a pointer to a variable that will, on return, contain the number of bytes copied when the function succeeds, or the minimum size (in bytes) required for the *lpbJob* array if the function does not succeed. *lpdwRet* is a pointer to a variable that, on return, contains the number of **JOB_INFO_1** or **JOB_INFO_2** structures assigned information.

RELATED FUNCTIONS

GetJob()
OpenPrinter()
SetJob()

BOOL EnumPorts(LPTSTR *lpszName*, DWORD *dwLevel*, LPBYTE *lpbPorts*, DWORD *cbBuff*, LPDWORD *lpdwCpyNeed*, LPDWORD *lpdwRet*)

EnumPorts() enumerates the server-side ports that are available for printing. The function returns TRUE if successful, and FALSE if unsuccessful.

lpszName is a pointer to the name of the server where the ports are to be enumerated. When set to NULL, local (rather than server) ports are obtained. *dwLevel* contains the version of the structure where *lpbPorts* points and must be 1. (Other values may be allowed by later releases of Windows.) *lpbPorts* is a pointer to an array of **PORT_INFO_1** structures that will receive the enumerated ports.

PORT_INFO_1 is shown here.

```
typedef struct _PORT_INFO_1 {
  LPSTR pName;
} PORT_INFO_1;
```

Here, **pName** is a pointer to the name of the printer port.

cbBuff contains the size of the *lpbPorts* array. (This value is in bytes.) *lpdwCpyNeed* is a pointer to a variable that, on return, will contain the number of bytes actually written to the *lpbPorts* array. (If the array is too small, then *lpdwCpyNeed* will contain the minimum number of bytes required to hold the information.)

On return, the variable pointed to by *lpdwRet* will contain the number of ports enumerated. (This is the number of structures that will actually contain port data as returned by the function.)

RELATED FUNCTIONS

AddPort()
DeletePort()

BOOL EnumPrinterDrivers(LPTSTR *lpszName,*
LPTSTR *lpszEnv,*
DWORD *dwLevel,*
LPBYTE *lpbDrvInfo,*
DWORD *cbBuff,*
LPDWORD *lpdwCpyNeed,*
LPDWORD *lpdwRet)*

EnumPrinterDrivers() enumerates the printer drivers installed on a printer server. The function returns TRUE if successful, and FALSE if unsuccessful.

lpszName is a pointer to the name of the server where the drivers will be obtained. When set to NULL, local drivers will be enumerated. *lpszEnv* is a pointer to the environment string. When set to NULL, the calling process's environment is used.

dwLevel contains the version of the structure pointed to by *lpbDrvInfo* and must be 1 to 2. *lpbDrvInfo* is a pointer to an array of **DRIVER_INFO_1** or **DRIVER_INFO_2** structures.

The **DRIVER_INFO_1** structure is shown here.

```
typedef struct _DRIVER_INFO_1 {
  LPTSTR pName;
} DRIVER_INFO_1;
```

Here, **pName** is a pointer to the name of a printer driver.
The **DRIVER_INFO_2** structure is shown here.

```
typedef struct _DRIVER_INFO_2 {
  DWORD cVersion;
  LPTSTR pName;
  LPTSTR pEnvironment;
  LPTSTR pDriverPath;
  LPTSTR pDataFile;
  LPTSTR pConfigFile;
} DRIVER_INFO_2;
```

The members of the **DRIVER_INFO_2** structure were described under **AddPrinterDriver()**, earlier in this chapter.

In the function, the size, in bytes, of the array pointed to by *lpbDrvInfo* is passed in *cbBuf*. *lpdwCpyNeed* is a pointer to a variable that, on return, contains the number of bytes copied when the function is successful, or the minimum size of the *lpbDrvInfo* array (in bytes) if *cbBuff* specifies too small an array.

On return, the variable pointed to by *lpdwRet* will contain the number of drivers enumerated. (This is the number of structures that will actually contain driver data as returned by the function.)

RELATED FUNCTIONS

AddPrinterDriver()
GetPrinterDriver()

BOOL EnumPrinters(DWORD *dwType,*
  LPTSTR *lpszName,*
  DWORD *dwLevel,*
  LPBYTE *lpbPrinters,*
  DWORD *cbBuff,*
  LPDWORD *lpdwCpyNeed,*
  LPDWORD *lpdwReturned***)**

EnumPrinters() enumerates printers. The function returns TRUE if successful, and FALSE if unsuccessful.

dwType gives the type of printer objects the function will enumerate. This can be one or more of the following values.

Value	Meaning
PRINTER_ENUM_CONNECTIONS	Enumerates printers the user has previously made connections to.
PRINTER_ENUM_LOCAL	Enumerates only locally installed printers.
PRINTER_ENUM_NAME	Enumerates the printer specified by *lpszName*. When NULL, the available print providers are enumerated.
PRINTER_ENUM_NETWORK	Enumerates known network printers for the local server. *dwLevel* must be 1.
PRINTER_ENUM_REMOTE	Enumerates network printers. *dwLevel* must be 1.
PRINTER_ENUM_SHARED	Enumerates printers with the shared attribute.

The name of the server from which the printers are being enumerated is pointed to by *lpszName*.

dwLevel determines which type of the structures are pointed to by *lpbPrinters*. Its value must be 1 or 2. *lpbPrinters* is a pointer to an array of **PRINTER_INFO_1** (when *dwLevel* is 1) or **PRINTER_INFO_2** (when *dwLevel* is 2) structures. *cbBuff* contains the size of the array, in bytes.

lpdwCpyNeed is a pointer to a variable that, on return, contains the number of bytes copied when the function is successful, or the number of bytes needed when *cbBuff* is too small. *lpdwCpyNeed* is a pointer to a variable that, on return, contains the number of bytes copied when the function is successful, or the minimum size of the *lpbPrinters* array (in bytes) if *cbBuff* specifies too small an array.

The **PRINTER_INFO_1** structure is shown here.

```
typedef struct _PRINTER_INFO_1 {
  DWORD Flags;
  LPTSTR pDescription;
  LPTSTR pName;
  LPTSTR pComment;
} PRINTER_INFO_1;
```

Here, **Flags** can be set to **PRINTER_ENUM_EXPAND** (signal calling application to enumerate object), **PRINTER_ENUM_CONTAINER** (printer object might contain enumerable objects), **PRINTER_ENUM_ICON1** (application should show a top-level network name icon), **PRINTER_ENUM_ICON2** (application should show an icon to identify the object as a network domain),

PRINTER_ENUM_ICON3 (application should show an icon to identify the object as a print server), **PRINTER_ENUM_ICON4** to **PRINTER_ENUM_ICON7** (reserved for future use), **PRINTER_ENUM_ICON8** (application should show an icon that identifies the object as a printer).

pDescription is a pointer to a description of the contents of the structure. **pName** is a pointer to the name of the contents. **pComment** is a pointer to an optional description of the structure.

The **PRINTER_INFO_2** structure is described under **AddPrinter()**.

USAGE

Here is a small portion of code to illustrate the use of this function.

```
DWORD   dwCpyNeed;
DWORD   dwPrtRet2;
DWORD   dwMaxPrt;
LPTSTR  lpName = gszEnumName;

LPPRINTER_INFO_2 pPrtInfo2;

EnumPrinters(gdwEnumFlags, lpName, 2, NULL, 0, &dwCpyNeed,
          &dwPrtRet2);

pPrtInfo2 = (LPPRINTER_INFO_2) LocalAlloc (LPTR, dwCpyNeed);

EnumPrinters(gdwEnumFlags, lpName, 2, (LPBYTE) pPrtInfo2,
          dwCpyNeed, &dwCpyNeed, &dwPrtRet2);
```

RELATED FUNCTIONS

AddPrinter()
DeletePrinter()
GetPrinter()
SetPrinter()

BOOL EnumPrintProcessors(LPSTR *lpszName,*
LPSTR *lpszEnv,*
DWORD *dwLevel,*
LPBYTE *lpbProcinfo,*
DWORD *cbBuff,*
LPDWORD *lpdwCpyNeed,*
LPDWORD *lpdwRet*)

EnumPrintProcessors() enumerates a server's print processors. The function returns TRUE if successful, and FALSE if unsuccessful.

lpszName is a pointer to a the name of the server where the processors will be obtained. When set to NULL, print processors on the local computer are enumerated. *lpszEnv* is a pointer to the environment string. When set to NULL, the calling process's environment is used.

The version of the structures pointed to by *lpbProcInfo* is determined by the value of *dwLevel*, which must be 1. (Other values may be allowed by future releases of Windows.) *lpbprocInfo* is a pointer to an array of **PRINTPROCES-SOR_INFO_1** structures.

The **PRINTPROCESSOR_INFO_1** structure is shown here.

```
typedef struct _PRINTPROCESSOR_INFO_1 {
  LPSTR pName;
} PRINTPROCESSOR_INFO_1;
```

Here, **pName** is a pointer to the name of a print processor.

In the function, the size, in bytes, of the array pointed to by *lpbProcInfo* is passed in *cbBuf*. *lpdwCpyNeed* is a pointer to a variable that, on return, contains the number of bytes copied when the function is successful, or the minimum size of the *lpbProcInfo* array (in bytes) if *cbBuff* specifies too small an array.

On return, the variable pointed to by *lpdwRet* will contain the number of print processors enumerated. (This is the number of structures that will actually contain print processor data as returned by the function.)

RELATED FUNCTIONS

AddPrintProcessor()
EnumPrinters()

BOOL GetForm(HANDLE *hPrt*, LPTSTR *lpszForm*, DWORD *dwLevel*, LPBYTE *lpbForm*, DWORD *cbBuff*, LPDWORD *lpdwCpyNeed*)

GetForm() obtains a form specification. The function returns TRUE if successful, and FALSE if unsuccessful.

hPrt is the handle of the printer. *lpszForm* is a pointer to the name of the form. The version of the structure pointed to by *lpbForm* is passed in *dwLevel* and must be 1. (Other values may be allowed by future releases of Windows.) *lpbForm* is a pointer to an array containing the initialized **FORM_INFO_1** structure. (See **AddForm()** for a description of **FORM_INFO_1**.) On return, this array will contain the desired form specification.

The size of the array, in bytes, pointed to by *lpbForm* is passed in *cbBuff*. *lpdwCpyNeed* is a pointer to a variable that, on return, contains the number of bytes copied when the function is successful, or the minimum size of the *lpbForm* array (in bytes) if *cbBuff* specifies too small an array.

RELATED FUNCTIONS

AddForm()
DeleteForm()

BOOL GetJob(HANDLE *hPrt*, DWORD *dwJobId*, DWORD *dwLevel*, LPBYTE *lpbJob*, DWORD *cbBuff*, LPDWORD *lpdwCpyNeed*)

GetJob() obtains information about a print job. The function returns TRUE if successful, and FALSE if unsuccessful.

hPrt is the handle of the printer that is processing the job. *dwJobId* is the ID of the print job.

The version number of the structure pointed to by *lpbJob* is passed in *dwLevel* and must be either 1 or 2. (Other values may be allowed by future releases of Windows.) *lpbJob* is a pointer to an array that holds a **JOB_INFO_1** or **JOB_INFO_2** structure (see **EnumJobs()**). When *dwLevel* is set to 1, a **JOB_INFO_1** structure is used. When *dwLevel* is set to 2, a **JOB_INFO_2** structure is used.

The size, in bytes, of the array pointed to by *lpbJob* is passed in *cbBuff*. *lpdwCpyNeed* is a pointer to a variable that, on return, contains the number of bytes copied when the function is successful, or the minimum size of the *lpbJob* array (in bytes) if *cbBuff* specifies too small an array.

RELATED FUNCTIONS

AddJob()
ScheduleJob()
SetJob()

BOOL GetPrinter(HANDLE *hPrt,* DWORD *dwLevel,* LPBYTE *lpbPrt,* DWORD *cbBuff,* LPDWORD *lpdwCpyNeed*)

GetPrinter() obtains information about a printer. The function returns TRUE if successful, and FALSE if unsuccessful.

hPrt is the handle of the printer.

The version number of the structure pointed to by *lpbPrt* is passed in *dwLevel* and must be 1, 2, or 3. *lpbPrt* is a pointer to an array that holds a **PRINTER_INFO_1**, **PRINTER_INFO_2**, or **PRINTER_INFO_3** structure as determined by *dwLevel*.

The **PRINTER_INFO_1** structure is shown here.

```
typedef struct _PRINTER_INFO_1 {
  DWORD Flags;
  LPTSTR pDescription;
  LPTSTR pName;
  LPTSTR pComment;
} PRINTER_INFO_1;
```

This structure's members were described earlier in this chapter, under **EnumPrinters()**.

The **PRINTER_INFO_2** structure is shown here.

```
typedef struct _PRINTER_INFO_2 {
  LPTSTR pServerName;
  LPTSTR pPrinterName;
  LPTSTR pShareName;
  LPTSTR pPortName;
  LPTSTR pDriverName;
  LPTSTR pComment;
  LPTSTR pLocation;
  LPDEVMODE pDevMode;
  LPTSTR pSepFile;
  LPTSTR pPrintProcessor;
  LPTSTR pDatatype;
  LPTSTR pParameters;
  PSECURITY_DESCRIPTOR pSecurityDescriptor;
  DWORD Attributes;
  DWORD Priority;
  DWORD DefaultPriority;
  DWORD StartTime;
  DWORD UntilTime;
  DWORD Status;
  DWORD cJobs;
  DWORD AveragePPM;
} PRINTER_INFO_2;
```

This structure's members were described earlier in this chapter, under **AddPrinter()**.

The **PRINTER_INFO_3** structure is shown here.

```
typedef struct _PRINTER_INFO_3 {
  PSECURITY_DESCRIPTOR pSecurityDescriptor;
} PRINTER_INFO_3;
```

Here, **pSecurityDescriptor** is a pointer to a **SECURITY_DESCRIPTOR** structure that contains a printer's security information.

The size, in bytes, of the array pointed to by *lpbPrt* is passed in *cbBuff*. *lpdwCpyNeed* is a pointer to a variable that, on return, contains the number of bytes copied when the function is successful, or the minimum size of the *lpbPrt* array (in bytes) if *cbBuff* specifies too small an array.

USAGE

If the structure contains a pointer to a security descriptor, just the components of the security descriptor that the caller is allowed access to will be available. Likewise, an access permission of **READ_CONTROL** allows access by the owner, primary group, and discretionary **ACL**. **ACCESS_SYSTEM_SECURITY** allows access by the system **ACL**.

RELATED FUNCTIONS

AbortPrinter()
AddPrinter()
ClosePrinter()
DeletePrinter()
EnumPrinters()
OpenPrinter()
SetPrinter()

DWORD GetPrinterData(HANDLE *hPrt,*
LPTSTR *pValueName,*
LPDWORD *pType,*
LPBYTE *pData,*
DWORD *cbBuff,*
LPDWORD *lpdwCpyNeed*)

GetPrinterData() obtains printer configuration data for a printer. The function returns TRUE if successful, and FALSE if unsuccessful.

hPrt is the handle of the printer. *pValueName* is a pointer to the name of the type of data to obtain. *pType* is a pointer to a variable that, on return, contains the data type stored by **SetPrinterData()**. *pType* may be set to NULL if this information is not needed.

pData is a pointer to an array of bytes. On return, this array contains the configuration data. The size of the *pData* array is passed in *cbBuff*. *lpdwCpyNeed* is a pointer to a variable that, on return, contains the number of bytes copied when the function is successful, or the minimum size of the *pData* array if *cbBuff* specifies too small an array.

RELATED FUNCTIONS

OpenPrinter()
SetPrinter()

BOOL GetPrinterDriver(HANDLE *hPrt,*
LPTSTR *lpszEnv,*
DWORD *dwLevel,*
LPBYTE *lpbDrvInfo,*
DWORD *cbBuff,*
LPDWORD *lpdwCpyNeed*)

GetPrinterDriver() obtains driver data for a printer. The function returns
TRUE if successful, and FALSE if unsuccessful.

hPrt is the handle of the printer for which the driver data will be obtained.
lpszEnv is a pointer to the environment string. If set to NULL, the calling
process's environment is used.

The version number of the structure pointed to by *lpbDrvInfo* is passed in
dwLevel and must be 1 or 2. (Other values may be supported by future releases
of Windows.)

lpbDrvInfo is a pointer to a **DRIVER_INFO_1** or **DRIVER_INFO_2**
structure (see **EnumPrinterDrivers()**) as determined by the value of *dwLevel*.
When *dwLevel* is set to 1, a **DRIVER_INFO_1** structure is used. When it is
set to 2, a **DRIVER_INFO_2** structure is used.

The size, in bytes, of the array pointed to by *lpbDrvInfo* is passed in *cbBuff*.
lpdwCpyNeed is a pointer to a variable that, on return, contains the number of
bytes copied when the function is successful, or the minimum size of the
lpbDrvInfo array (in bytes) if *cbBuff* specifies too small an array.

USAGE

Here is a small portion of code to illustrate the use of this function.

```
HANDLE hPrt;
char pEnv[BuffSize]="";
DWORD dwCpyNeed;
LPBYTE pDrvInfo2;
```

```
        .
        .
        .
GetPrinterDriver(hPrt, pEnv, 2, NULL, 0, &dwCpyNeed);
pDriverInfo2 = (LPBYTE) LocalAlloc (LPTR, dwCpyNeed);
GetPrinterDriver(hPrt, pEnv, 2, pDrvInfo2,
                 dwCpyNeed, &dwCpyNeed);
        .
        .
        .
ClosePrinter(hPrt);
```

RELATED FUNCTIONS

AddPrinterDriver()
EnumPrinterDrivers()
LoadLibrary()
OpenPrinter()

BOOL GetPrinterDriverDirectory(LPTSTR *lpszName*,
LPTSTR *lpszEnv*,
DWORD *dwLevel*,
LPBYTE *lpbDir*,
DWORD *cbBuff*,
LPDWORD *lpdwCpyNeed*)

GetPrinterDriverDirectory() obtains the path to the printer driver directory. The function returns TRUE if successful, and FALSE if unsuccessful.

lpszName is a pointer to the name of the server where the printer driver exists. If this value is set to NULL, the local driver directory path is obtained. *lpszEnv* is a pointer to the environment string. If this value is set to NULL, the environment of the calling process is used.

dwLevel determines what type of structure is stored in the array pointed to by *lpbDir*. At the time of this writing, this value must be 1. *lpbDir* is a pointer to an array of bytes that, on return, will contain the path.

The size, in bytes, of the array pointed to by *lpbDir* is passed in *cbBuff*. *lpdwCpyNeed* is a pointer to a variable that, on return, contains the number of bytes copied when the function is successful, or the minimum size of the *lpbDir* array (in bytes) if *cbBuff* specifies too small an array.

RELATED FUNCTION

AddPrinterDriver()

BOOL GetPrintProcessorDirectory(LPTSTR *lpszName,*
LPTSTR *lpszEnv,*
DWORD *dwLevel,*
LPBYTE *lpbProcDir,*
DWORD *cbBuff,*
LPDWORD *lpdwCpyNeed***)**

GetPrintProcessorDirectory() obtains the path to the print processor on the server. The function returns TRUE if successful, and FALSE if unsuccessful.

lpszName is a pointer to the name of the server. If set to NULL, the local path is returned. *lpszEnv* is a pointer to the environment string. If set to NULL, the calling process's environment is used.

dwLevel determines what type of structure is stored in the array pointed to by *lpbProcDir*. At the time of this writing, this value must be 1. *lpbProcDir* is a pointer to an array of bytes that, on return, will contain the path.

The size, in bytes, of the array pointed to by *lpbProcDir* is passed in *cbBuff*. *lpdwCpyNeed* is a pointer to a variable that, on return, contains the number of bytes copied when the function is successful. If the size specified by *cbBuff* is too small, then the minimum size of the *lpbProcDir* array (in bytes) is assigned to the variable pointed to by *lpdwCpyNeed*.

RELATED FUNCTION

AddPrintProcessor()

BOOL OpenPrinter(LPTSTR *pPrnName,*
LPHANDLE *phPrt,*
LPPRINTER_DEFAULTS *pDefault*)

OpenPrinter() opens a printer or print server. The function returns TRUE if successful, and FALSE if unsuccessful.

pPrnName is a pointer to the name of the printer or print server being opened. *phPrt* is a pointer to a variable that, on return, contains the handle of the printer or print server object. *pDefault* is a pointer to a **PRINTER_DEFAULTS** structure. (This value can also be set to NULL if no defaults are required.)

The **PRINTER_DEFAULTS** structure is shown here.

```
typedef struct _PRINTER_DEFAULTS {
  LPTSTR pDatatype;
  LPDEVMODE pDevMode;
  ACCESS_MASK DesiredAccess;
} PRINTER_DEFAULTS;
```

Here, **pDatatype** is a pointer to the printer's default data type. **pDevMode** is a pointer to a **DEVMODE** structure that contains initialization information. **DesiredAccess** contains the printer's access rights.

USAGE

Here is a small portion of code to illustrate the use of this function.

```
HANDLE hPrt;
  .
  .
  .
OpenPrinter("Laser_Jet", &hPrt, NULL);
```

RELATED FUNCTIONS

ClosePrinter()
WaitForPrinterChange()

BOOL PrinterProperties(hwnd *hWnd*, HANDLE *hPrt*)

PrinterProperties() activates a printer properties dialog box. The function returns TRUE if successful, and FALSE if unsuccessful.

hWnd is the handle of the parent window. *hPrt* is the handle of the printer object.

RELATED FUNCTION

OpenPrinter()

BOOL ReadPrinter(HANDLE *hPrt*, LPVOID *lpBuf*, DWORD *cbBuff*, LPDWORD *lpdwBytes*)

ReadPrinter() reads data from the bidirectional printer. The function returns TRUE if successful, and FALSE if unsuccessful.

hPrt is the handle of the printer. *lpBuf* is a pointer to an array that will receive the data. The size of this array, in bytes, is passed in *cbBuff*. *lpdwBytes* is a pointer to a variable that, on return, will contain the number of bytes received.

RELATED FUNCTION

OpenPrinter()

BOOL ScheduleJob(HANDLE *hPrt*, DWORD *dwJobID*)

ScheduleJob() notifies the print spooler that a job can be scheduled for printing. The function returns TRUE if successful, and FALSE if unsuccessful.

hPrt is the handle of the printer. The ID of the print job is passed in *dwJobID*.

RELATED FUNCTIONS

AddJob()
OpenPrinter()

int SetAbortProc(HDC *hdc,* ABORTPROC *lpAbortProc*)

SetAbortProc() registers a user-defined function that is used to terminate a print job. The function returns an integer value greater than zero if successful, and **SP_ERROR** if unsuccessful.

hdc is the handle of the device context. *lpAbortProc* is a pointer to the user-defined abort function.

USAGE

The function pointed to by *lpAbortProc* must have this prototype:

BOOL CALLBACK *AbortFunc*(HDC *hdc,* int *err*);

Of course, the name of the function is arbitrary. When called, *hdc* contains the device context. *err* will be either zero, which means that no error has occurred, or non-zero otherwise.

This function must return non-zero if you want the print job to continue, or zero to abort the job.

RELATED FUNCTIONS

AbortDoc()
AbortProc()

BOOL SetForm(HANDLE *hPrt,* LPTSTR *lpszForm,* DWORD *dwLevel,* LPBYTE *lpbForm*)

SetForm() initializes a printer to accept a form. The function returns TRUE if successful, and FALSE if unsuccessful.

hPrt is the handle of the printer that will print the form. *lpszForm* is a pointer to the name of the form.

The version of the structure pointed to by *lpbForm* is determined by the value of *dwLevel*. At the time of this writing, *dwLevel* must be 1. *lpbForm* is a pointer to a **FORM_INFO_1** structure (see **AddForm()** for a description).

RELATED FUNCTION

OpenPrinter()

BOOL SetJob(HANDLE *hPrt*, DWORD *dwJobID*, DWORD *dwLevel*, LPBYTE *lpbJob*, DWORD *dwCommd*)

SetJob() controls the printing of a job or sets a print job's attributes. The function returns TRUE if successful, and FALSE if unsuccessful.

hPrt is the handle of the printer. *dwJobID* is the ID of the print job.

The version of the structure pointed to by *lpbJob* is determined by the value of *dwLevel*. It must be 0, 1, or 2. *lpbJob* is a pointer to a structure that describes the print job and must be of either type **JOB_INFO_1** or **JOB_INFO_2**. (See **EnumJobs()** for a description of these structures.) *lpbJob* must be NULL when *dwLevel* is set to 0. Otherwise, if a **JOB_INFO_1** structure is used, then *dwLevel* must be 1. If a **JOB_INFO_2** structure is used, then *dwLevel* must be 2.

dwCommd determines what action the function takes. It must be one of these values.

Value	Action
JOB_CONTROL_CANCEL	The print job is deleted.
JOB_CONTROL_PAUSE	The print job is paused.
JOB_CONTROL_RESTART	The print job is restarted.
JOB_CONTROL_RESUME	The print job is resumed.

Clients are required to have **PRINTER_ACCESS_ADMINISTER** access permission to change the job order on the printer.

RELATED FUNCTIONS

OpenPrinter()
SetJob()
SetPrinter()

BOOL SetPrinter(HANDLE *hPrt*, DWORD *dwLevel*, LPBYTE *lpbPrt*, DWORD *dwCommd*)

SetPrinter() controls the printer. The function returns TRUE if successful, and FALSE if unsuccessful.

hPrt is the handle of the printer. The version of the structure pointed to by *lpbPrt* is determined by the value of *dwLevel*. It must be 0, 1, or 2. *lpbPrt* is a pointer to a structure that describes the printer and must be of either type **PRINTER_INFO_1** or **PRINTER_INFO_2**. (See **GetPrinter()** for a description of these structures.) *lpbPrt* must be NULL when *dwLevel* is set to 0. Otherwise, if a **PRINTER_INFO_1** structure is used, then *dwLevel* must be 1. If a **PRINTER_INFO_2** structure is used, then *dwLevel* must be 2.

dwCommd determines the printer's new state and can be one of these values.

Value	State
PRINTER_CONTROL_PAUSE	The printer pauses.
PRINTER_CONTROL_PURGE	All print jobs in the printer are deleted.
PRINTER_CONTROL_RESUME	The printer resumes.

dwCommd may also be zero, in which case the printer's state is unchanged.

Scheduling of all print jobs is suspended for a paused printer. When a printer is cleared, so are all scheduled print jobs for that printer.

RELATED FUNCTIONS

AddPrinter()
GetPrinter()
OpenPrinter()

DWORD SetPrinterData(HANDLE *hPrt,*
       LPTSTR *lpszType,*
       DWORD *dwType,*
       LPBYTE *lpbData,*
       DWORD *cbData*)

SetPrinterData() configures a printer. The function returns non-zero if successful, and zero on failure.

hPrt is the handle of the printer being configured. *lpszType* is a pointer to the name of the configuration data to set. *dwType* contains the type of configuration data and can be one of these values.

Value	Type
REG_BINARY	Any form of binary data is acceptable.
REG_DWORD	A 32-bit value.
REG_DWORD_BIG_ENDIAN	A 32-bit value in *big-endian* format (the most significant byte of a word is the low-order word).
REG_DWORD_LITTLE_ENDIAN	A 32-bit value using *little-endian* format (the most significant byte of a word is the high-order word).
REG_EXPAND_SZ	A null-terminated Unicode or ANSI string with unexpanded references to environment variables.
REG_LINK	A Unicode symbolic link.
REG_MULTI_SZ	An array of null-terminated strings. These strings are terminated by two null characters.
REG_NONE	Value type not defined.
REG_RESOURCE_LIST	A resource list for device drivers.
REG_SZ	A null-terminated Unicode or ANSI string.

lpbData is a pointer to an array of bytes. This array holds the printer configuration data. *cbData* contains the size of the array.

RELATED FUNCTIONS

GetPrinter()
OpenPrinter()

---

int StartDoc(HDC *hdc*, LPDOCINFO *lpDi*)

StartDoc() starts a document print job. The function returns an integer value greater than zero if successful, and **SP_ERROR** if unsuccessful. The value returned is the ID of the print job.

hdc is a handle to the device context. *lpDi* is a pointer to a **DOCINFO** structure that has this general form.

```
typedef struct {
  int cbSize;
  LPCSTR lpszDocName;
  LPCSTR lpszOutput;
} DOCINFO;
```

Here, **cbSize** contains the size of the **DOCINFO** structure. **lpszDoc-Name** and **lpszOutput** point to the names of the document and the output file, respectively.

USAGE

This function is called just before a print job is started. This will prevent multipage documents from being mixed with other print jobs. The function's return value can also be used to obtain or set the priority of a job.

Here is a small portion of code to illustrate the use of this function.

```
HDC hdc;
LPDOCINFO lpdi;
     .
     .
     .
int StartDoc(hdc, lpdi);
```

RELATED FUNCTIONS

EndDoc()
GetJob()
SetJob()

DWORD StartDocPrinter(HANDLE *hPrint,* DWORD *dwLevel,* LPBYTE *lpbDoc*)

StartDocPrinter() spools a document. It returns the print job's ID value if successful, and zero on failure.

hPrint is the handle of the printer.

The version of the structure pointed to by *lpbDoc* is determined by the value of *dwLevel*. At the time of this writing, this value must be 1. *lpbDoc* is a pointer to a **DOC_INFO_1** structure that describes the document being spooled. It has this general form.

```
typedef struct _DOC_INFO_1 {
    LPSTR pDocName;
    LPSTR pOutputFile;
```

```
   LPSTR pDatatype;
} DOC_INFO_1;
```

Here, **pDocName**, **pOutputFile**, and **pDatatype** point to the name of the document, the name of the output file, and the name of the data type, respectively.

RELATED FUNCTIONS

EndDocPrinter()
StartDoc()
StartPagePrinter()

int StartPage(HDC *hdc*)

StartPage() initializes the printer driver. The function returns an integer value greater than zero if successful, and a negative value if unsuccessful.

hdc is a handle to the device context.

RELATED FUNCTIONS

EndPage()
ResetDC()

BOOL StartPagePrinter(HANDLE *hPrint*)

StartpagePrinter() notifies the spooler that a page will be printed. The function returns non-zero if successful, and zero on failure.

The handle of the printer is passed in *hPrint*.

USAGE

Once the page has been printed, your application should make a call to **EndPagePrinter()**.

RELATED FUNCTIONS

EndPagePrinter()
StartPage()

BOOL WritePrinter(HANDLE *hPrt,* LPVOID *pBuf,*
DWORD *cbBuff,*
LPDWORD *lpdwWrtn*)

WritePrinter() signals the print spooler that the data can be written to the printer. The function returns TRUE if successful, and FALSE if unsuccessful.

hPrt is the handle of the printer. *pBuf* is a pointer to the data to send to the printer. *cbBuff* contains the size of the data, in bytes. *lpdwWrtn* is a pointer to a variable that, on return, will contain the number of bytes actually written to the printer.

RELATED FUNCTION

OpenPrinter()

Chapter 27

Processes and Threads

T H I S chapter describes the Windows functions used to manipulate processes and threads. Since multithreaded programs are not allowed in 16-bit Windows, most of the functions in this chapter apply only to Windows NT/Win32.

BOOL CreateProcess(LPCTSTR *lpszImgName,*
LPCTSTR *lpszCommLine,*
LPSECURITY_ATTRIBUTES *lpSaProcess,*
LPSECURITY_ATTRIBUTES *lpSaThread,*
BOOL *fInhHnd,* DWORD *fdwCreate,*
LPVOID *lpvEnv,* LPCTSTR *lpszCurDir,*
LPSTARTUPINFO *lpsiStartInfo,*
LPPROCESS_INFORMATION *lppiProcInfo)*

CreateProcess() creates a new process. It also creates the main thread for the process and begins its execution.

lpszImgName is a pointer to the path and filename of the program which is to be executed. The current drive and/or current directory are used if the drive and/or path is not provided. If this parameter is NULL, the program name is the first token in the string pointed to by *lpszCommLine*.

lpszCommLine is a pointer to the command line for the application about to be executed. When this value is NULL, the string pointed to by *lpszImgName* is used as the command line. When *lpszImgName* and *lpszCommLine* are not NULL, *lpszImgName* points to the name of the program to execute and *lpszCommLine* points to the command line. When the filename does not contain a file extension, an executable file (EXE) is the default.

lpSaProcess is a pointer to a **SECURITY_ATTRIBUTES** structure. This structure is used to specify the security attributes for the process and should not be directly modified. If NULL, the process will be created with a default security descriptor and a non-inheritable handle is created.

lpSaThread is a pointer to a **SECURITY_ATTRIBUTES** structure. This structure gives the security attributes for the primary thread of the process. If *lpSaThread* is NULL, the process is created with a default security descriptor and a non-inheritable handle is created.

fInhHnd determines whether handles are inherited from the calling process. If it is TRUE, each open handle in the calling process is inherited by the new process. These inherited handles have the same values and access privileges as the original handles. If FALSE, no handles are inherited.

fdwCreate contains flags that determine how the process is created. There are two types of flags: creation and priority. You may choose one flag from each category. The creation flags are shown here.

Value	Effect
DEBUG_PROCESS	The calling process is a debugger that debugs the new process. Further child processes will also be debugged.
DEBUG_ONLY_THIS_PROCESS	The calling process is a debugger that debugs the new process. When the new process creates additional processes, they are not debugged.
CREATE_SUSPENDED	The new process's main thread is initially suspended.
DETACHED_PROCESS	The new process cannot access the console of the parent. The new process, however, uses **AllocConsole()** when a new console is desired. This cannot be used with **CREATE_NEW_CONSOLE**.
CREATE_NEW_CONSOLE	The new process receives a new console. This cannot be used with **DETACHED_PROCESS**.
CREATE_NEW_PROCESS_GROUP	The new process becomes the root of a new process group. The group includes all of the descendants of the root process. The ID of the new group is identical to the process ID. This can be obtained from the **PROCESS_INFORMATION** structure pointed to by *lppiProcInfo*.

The priority flags are shown next. When none of the priority class flags are specified the priority class usually defaults to **NORMAL_PRIORITY_CLASS**. The exception is when the creating process is **IDLE_PRIORITY_CLASS**; then the default priority class becomes **IDLE_PRIORITY_CLASS** for the child class.

Flag	Effect
IDLE_PRIORITY_CLASS	A process whose threads execute only when the system is idle. These threads are preempted by the threads of any process running in a higher priority class. The idle priority class is inherited by child processes of the parent.
NORMAL_PRIORITY_CLASS	A normal process.
HIGH_PRIORITY_CLASS	A process performing time-critical tasks. It must be executed immediately for correct execution. This class of threads preempts the threads of normal or idle priority class processes.
REALTIME_PRIORITY_CLASS	A process given the highest priority level possible. Real-time priority class threads preempt all the threads of all other processes.

lpvEnv is a pointer to an environment block for the new process. When this value is set to NULL, the new process uses the calling process's environment. The block is composed of null-terminated strings. The block ends with two nulls. Each string takes on the following form:

name=value

lpszCurDir points to a string that contains the current directory and drive for the new process. If *lpszCurDir* is NULL, the directory and drive used by the calling process is assumed.

lpsiStartInfo is a pointer to a **STARTUPINFO** structure. This structure indicates how the main window should appear for the new process. The **STARTUPINFO** structure is shown here.

```
typedef struct _STARTUPINFO {
  DWORD cb;
  LPTSTR lpReserved;
  LPTSTR lpDesktop;
  LPTSTR lpTitle;
  DWORD dwX;
  DWORD dwY;
  DWORD dwXSize;
  DWORD dwYSize;
  DWORD dwXCountChars;
  DWORD dwYCountChars;
  DWORD dwFillAttribute;
  DWORD dwFlags;
  WORD  wShowWindow;
  WORD  cbReserved2;
```

```
      LPBYTE lpReserved2;
      HANDLE hStdInput;
      HANDLE hStdOutput;
      HANDLE hStdError;
} STARTUPINFO;
```

Here, **cb** contains the size of the structure. **lpReserved** is reserved. **lpDesktop** is a pointer to the name of a desktop to start the process in, unless set to NULL. **lpTitle** is a pointer to the title displayed in the title bar for console processes. When set to NULL, the name of the executable file is used as the title.

dwX and **dwY** contain the x and y coordinates of the upper-left corner of a window (in pixels). This value is ignored unless **dwFlags** uses **STARTF_USEPOSITION**. **dwXSize** and **dwYSize** contain the width and height of the window (in pixels). This value is ignored unless **dwFlags** uses **STARTF_USESIZE**. **dwXCountChars** and **dwYCountChars** contain the screen buffer width and height in character columns and rows. This value is ignored unless **dwFlags** gives **STARTF_USECOUNTCHARS**.

dwFillAttribute contains the initial text and background colors for a console process. This value is ignored unless **dwFlags** gives **STARTF_-USEFILLATTRIBUTE**.

dwFlags enables several **STARTUPINFO** members. It may be any valid combination of the following.

Value	Purpose
STARTF_USESHOWWINDOW	Enables wShowWindow
STARTF_USEPOSITION	Enables dwX and dwY
STARTF_USESIZE	Enables dwXSize and dwYSize
STARTF_USECOUNTCHARS	Enables dwXCountChars and dwYCountChars
STARTF_USEFILLATTRIBUTE	Enables dwFillAttribute
STARTF_USESTDHANDLES	Enable standard handles
STARTF_FORCEONFEEDBACK	Cursor is in feedback mode for two seconds after a call to **CreateProcess()**
STARTF_FORCEOFFFEEDBACK	Feedback cursor is forced off as process starts
STARTF_SCREENSAVER	When present, system will handle application as a screen saver

wShowWindow contains the default value for **ShowWindow()** if the visibility parameter of **ShowWindow()** is set to **SW_SHOWDEFAULT**. **cbReserved2** (set to 0) and **lpReserved2** (set to NULL) are reserved.

hStdInput contains the process's standard input handle. **hStdOutput** contains the process's standard output handle. Both handles only apply if **STARTF_USESTDHANDLES** is specified in **dwFlags**.

hStdError contains the process's standard error handle when **STARTF_-USESTDHANDLES** is specified in **dwFlags**.

In the **CreateProcess()** function *lppiProcInfo* is a pointer to a **PROCESS_INFORMATION** structure. This structure obtains identification information for the new process. **PROCESS_INFORMATION** is shown here.

```
typedef struct _PROCESS_INFORMATION {
  HANDLE hProcess;
  HANDLE hThread;
  DWORD dwProcessId;
  DWORD dwThreadId;
} PROCESS_INFORMATION;
```

Here, **hProcess** is a handle to the new process. **hThread** is a handle to the main thread. **dwProcessId** is the global process ID of the process. **dwThreadId** is the global thread ID of the thread.

The function returns TRUE if successful, and FALSE if unsuccessful.

USAGE

The **ExitProcess()** function is the best way to terminate the newly created process.

The process will remain active in the system until all threads within the process have been terminated and all handles to the process (*and any related threads*) have been closed.

Here is a small portion of code that illustrates how this function might be used.

```
STARTUPINFO          si;
PROCESS_INFORMATION  pi;
    .
    .
    .

/* STARTUPINFO structure */
si.cb              = sizeof (STARTUPINFO);
si.lpReserved      = 0;
si.lpDesktop       = NULL;
si.lpTitle         = NULL;
si.dwX             = 0;
si.dwY             = 0;
si.dwXSize         = 0;
```

```
si.dwYSize          = 0;
si.dwXCountChars    = 0;
si.dwYCountChars    = 0;
si.dwFillAttribute  = 0;
si.dwFlags          = 0;
si.wShowWindow      = 0;
si.cbReserved2      = 0;
si.lpReserved2      = 0;

ret = CreateProcess (NULL, "TEST.EXE", NULL, NULL,
                     FALSE, DETACHED_PROCESS,
                     NULL, NULL, &si, &pi );
```

RELATED FUNCTIONS

CloseHandle()
CreateRemoteThread()
CreateThread()
ExitProcess()
ExitThread()
GetExitCodeProcess()
OpenProcess()
ResumeThread()
TerminateProcess()

HANDLE CreateRemoteThread(HANDLE *hProcess,*
      LPSECURITY_ATTRIBUTES *lpSa,*
      DWORD *cbStack,*
      LPTHREAD_START_ROUTINE *lpStartAddr,*
      LPVOID *lpvThreadParm,*
      DWORD *fdwCreate,*
      LPDWORD *lpIDThread***)**

CreateRemoteThread() creates a thread that executes in another process'
address space. The function returns the handle to the new thread if successful,
and NULL if unsuccessful.

hProcess is the handle of the process in which the thread is created. It must
have **PROCESS_CREATE_THREAD** access rights.

lpSa is a pointer to a **SECURITY_ATTRIBUTES** structure. It contains the security attributes for the thread. When set to NULL, the thread is created with a default security descriptor and a non-inheritable handle is created.

The size of the new thread's stack is passed in *cbStack*. To obtain the same stack size as used by the main thread of the process, pass zero in this parameter. The stack is automatically allocated in the process's memory space and freed when the thread is terminated.

lpStartAddr is a pointer to the starting address of the new thread. That is, this address is the entry point for the thread and the place at which execution begins. *lpvThreadParm* is a pointer to a user-defined 32-bit value that is passed to the thread. *fdwCreate* contains flags that affect the creation of the thread. When the **CREATE_SUSPENDED** flag is used, the thread is initially suspended. A zero value causes the thread to run immediately after being created.

lpIDThread is a pointer to a variable that will, on return, contain the thread ID.

USAGE

Once started, the new thread can access all the objects opened by its host process. The new thread is created with a **THREAD_PRIORITY_NORMAL** thread priority. The priority value of a thread can be obtained or set with calls to **GetThreadPriority()** and **SetThreadPriority()**.

When terminated, the thread is in a signaled state. Thus, any other threads that were waiting on the object may proceed. The thread remains in the system until is has terminated and all handles to it have closed.

RELATED FUNCTIONS

CloseHandle()
CreateProcess()
CreateThread()
ExitProcess()
ExitThread()
ResumeThread()

HANDLE CreateThread(LPSECURITY_ATTRIBUTES *lpSa,*
DWORD *cbStack,*
LPTHREAD_START_ROUTINE *lpStartAddr,*
LPVOID *lpvThreadParm,*
DWORD *fdwCreate,*
LPDWORD *lpIDThread)*

CreateThread() creates a thread that becomes part of the calling process. The function returns the handle to the new thread if successful, and NULL if unsuccessful.

lpSa is a pointer to a **SECURITY_ATTRIBUTES** structure. This structure contains the security attributes for the thread. When set to NULL, the thread is created with a default security descriptor and a non-inheritable handle is created.

The size of the new thread's stack is passed in *cbStack*. To obtain the same stack size as used by the main thread of the process, pass zero in this parameter. The stack is automatically allocated in the process's memory space and freed when the thread is terminated.

lpStartAddr is a pointer to the starting address of the new thread. That is, this address is the entry point for the thread and the place at which execution begins.

lpvThreadParm is a pointer to a user-defined 32-bit value that is passed to the thread. *fdwCreate* contains flags that affect the creation of the thread. When the **CREATE_SUSPENDED** flag is used, the thread is initially suspended. A zero value causes the thread to run immediately after being created.

lpIDThread is a pointer to a variable that will, on return, contain the thread ID.

USAGE

Once started, the new thread can access all the objects opened by its host process. The new thread is created with a **THREAD_PRIORITY_NOR-MAL** thread priority. The priority value of a thread can be obtained or set with calls to **GetThreadPriority()** and **SetThreadPriority()**.

When terminated, the thread is in a signaled state. Thus, any other threads that were waiting on the object may proceed. The thread remains in the system until is has terminated and all handles to it have closed.

Here is a small portion of code that illustrates the use of this function.

```
DWORD   ThreadID;
static DWORD *pNewColor;

case WM_CREATE:

  pNewColor = malloc(sizeof(DWORD));
  *pNewColor = ORANGE;
  hNewThread = CreateThread (NULL, 0,
                             (LPTHREAD_START_ROUTINE)ThreadProc,
                             (LPVOID)pNewColor, 0,
                             (LPDWORD)&ThreadID);

  if (hNewThread)
    MessageBox(hWnd, "Orange thread was created",
              "Thread?", MB_OK);
    else
      MessageBox(hWnd, "Orange thread was not created",
                "Thread?", MB_ICONEXCLAMATION | MB_OK);
```

RELATED FUNCTIONS

CloseHandle()
CreateProcess()
CreateRemoteThread()
ExitProcess()
ExitThread()
ResumeThread()

void ExitProcess(UINT *uExitCode*)

ExitProcess() terminates a process. *uExitCode* contains the exit code for the process. This same exit code is used by all threads terminated as a result of this function call.

ExitProcess() provides an orderly termination of the process. It calls the entry function of all attached DLLs and states that the process is about to detach from the DLL. Once the DLLs have executed their process termination code, the function ends the current process.

USAGE

When a process is terminated, all of its threads are also stopped.

RELATED FUNCTIONS

CreateProcess()
CreateRemoteThread()
CreateThread()
ExitThread()
GetExitCodeProcess()
GetExitCodeThread()
OpenProcess()
TerminateProcess()

void ExitThread(DWORD *dwExitCode*)

ExitThread() terminates execution of a thread. *dwExitCode* contains the exit code for the calling thread.

This function provides an orderly termination of a thread. Specifically, the thread's stack is deallocated and the entry function of all attached DLLs is called. This indicates that the thread is being detached from the DLL. If this is the last thread in a process, the process is also terminated.

Upon calling this function, the state of the thread object becomes signaled. This allows any other threads that were waiting for the given thread to be released. Also, the termination status of the thread goes from **STILL_ACTIVE** to the value passed in *dwExitCode*.

RELATED FUNCTIONS

CreateProcess()
CreateRemoteThread()
CreateThread()
ExitProcess()
GetExitCodeThread()
TerminateThread()

HANDLE GetCurrentProcess(void)

GetCurrentProcess() returns a pseudohandle for the calling process. A pseudohandle is a constant that is used as the current process handle whenever a process requires a handle to itself. This pseudohandle is granted the maximum allowed access rights.

USAGE

CloseHandle() has no effect on pseudohandles since they do not have to be explicitly closed.

Here is a small portion of code that illustrates the use of this function.

```
HANDLE PseudoHandle;

PseudoHandle = GetCurrentProcess();
```

RELATED FUNCTIONS

GetCurrentProcessId()
GetCurrentThread()
OpenProcess()

DWORD GetCurrentProcessId(void)

GetCurrentProcessId() returns the process's ID. This function cannot fail.

USAGE

Here is a small portion of code that illustrates the use of this function.

```
DWORD ProcessID;

ProcessID = GetCurrentProcessId();
```

RELATED FUNCTIONS

GetCurrentProcess()
OpenProcess()

HANDLE GetCurrentThread(void)

GetCurrentThread() returns a pseudohandle to the thread that calls this function. The pseudohandle is a constant that is used as the current thread handle whenever a thread requires a handle to itself.

This pseudohandle is granted the maximum allowed access rights.

USAGE

CloseHandle() has no effect on pseudohandles since they do not have to be explicitly closed.

Here is a small portion of code that illustrates the use of this function.

```
HANDLE PseudoHandle;

PseudoHandle = GetCurrentThread();
```

RELATED FUNCTIONS

GetCurrentProcess()
GetCurrentThreadId()

DWORD GetCurrentThreadId(void)

GetCurrentThreadId() returns the thread's ID. This function cannot fail.

USAGE

Here is a small portion of code that illustrates the use of this function.

```
DWORD ThreadID;

ThreadID = GetCurrentThreadId();
```

RELATED FUNCTIONS

GetCurrentThread()
OpenThread()

DWORD GetCurrentTime(void)

GetCurrentTime() returns the time that has elapsed since Windows began running. The elapsed time is represented in milliseconds.

USAGE

Here is a small portion of code that illustrates the use of this function.

```
DWORD TimeValue;

TimeValue = GetCurrentTime(VOID);
```

RELATED FUNCTIONS

GetMessageTime()
GetSystemTime()
GetTickCount()
SetSystemTime()

BOOL GetExitCodeProcess(HANDLE *hProcess*, LPDWORD *lpdwExitCode*)

GetExitCodeProcess() obtains a process' termination status. *hProcess* is the handle of the process in question. (It must have **PROCESS_QUERY_IN-FORMATION** access rights.) *lpdwExitCode* is a pointer to a variable that, on return, contains the process's termination status value.

An executing process has a **STILL_ACTIVE** status. A terminated process will have an exit value that is either its return value from **WinMain()** (or **main()** if applicable) or the value specified in a call to either **ExitProcess()** or **Termi-nate-Process()**. However, if the process terminated because of an unhandled exception, then that exception code will be its termination status value.

The function returns TRUE if successful, and FALSE if unsuccessful.

USAGE

Here is a small portion of code that illustrates the use of this function.

```
HANDLE hProcess;
DWORD lpdwExitCode;

GetExitCodeProcess(hProcess, &lpdwExitCode);
```

RELATED FUNCTIONS

ExitProcess()
ExitThread()
TerminateProcess()

BOOL GetExitCodeThread(HANDLE *hThread,*
LPDWORD *lpdwExitCode*)

GetExitCodeThread() obtains the termination status of the given thread. *hThread* is the handle of the thread. (It must have **THREAD_QUERY_IN-FORMATION** access rights.) *lpdwExitCode* is a pointer to a variable that, on return, contains the thread's termination status value.

An executing thread has a **STILL_ACTIVE** status. A terminated thread will have an exit value that is either the value return by the thread entry function or the value specified in a call to either **ExitThread()** or **TerminateThread()**. If the entire process has terminated, then the value will be that specified by the process that owned the thread.

The function returns TRUE if successful, and FALSE if unsuccessful.

USAGE

Here is a small portion of code that illustrates the use of this function.

```
HANDLE hThread;
DWORD lpdwExitCode;

GetExitCodeThread(hThread, &lpdwExitCode);
```

RELATED FUNCTIONS

GetExitCodeProcess()
ExitThread()
TerminateThread()

DWORD GetPriorityClass(HANDLE *hProcess*)

GetPriorityClass() returns a process's priority class. *hProcess* is the handle of the process. (It must have **PROCESS_QUERY_INFORMATION** access rights.)

The function returns the priority class of the specified process if successful, and zero if unsuccessful. The priority class value will be one of the values shown here.

Value	Priority
IDLE_PRIORITY_CLASS	A process whose threads execute only when the system is idle. These threads are preempted by the threads of any process running in a higher priority class. The idle priority class is inherited by child processes of the parent.
NORMAL_PRIORITY_CLASS	A normal process.
HIGH_PRIORITY_CLASS	A process performing time-critical tasks. It must be executed immediately for correct execution. This class of threads preempts the threads of normal or idle priority class processes.
REALTIME_PRIORITY_CLASS	A process given the highest priority level possible. Real-time priority class threads preempt all the threads of all other processes.

USAGE

The thread's base priority level is a combination of its priority class combined with the priority value of each thread in the process.

Here is a small portion of code that illustrates the use of this function.

```
HANDLE hProcess;
DWORD PriorityClass;

PriorityClass = GetPriorityClass(hProcess);
```

RELATED FUNCTIONS

SetPriorityClass()
GetThreadPriority()
SetThreadPriority()

BOOL GetProcessShutdownParameters
(LPDWORD *lpdwLevel,*
LPDWORD *lpdwHow)*

GetProcessShutdownParameters() obtains a process's termination level (i.e., its order in the shutdown process) and flag settings describing the exact nature of the termination. It returns non-zero if successful, and zero on failure.

The process's termination level is put into the variable pointed to by *lpdwLevel*. It will be in the range 0x100 through 0x4FF. The larger the value, the higher the process is in the termination list. (Higher values are shut down before lower ones.) The variable pointed to by *lpdwHow* will contain the value **SHUTDOWN_NORETRY** (no retry dialog box is displayed) or zero.

RELATED FUNCTION

SetProcessShutdownParameters()

int GetThreadPriority(HANDLE *hThread)*

GetThreadPriority() returns a thread's priority setting. *hThread* is the handle of the thread in question and it must have **THREAD_QUERY_INFOR-MATION** access rights.

The function returns the thread's priority level if successful, or **THREAD_PRIORITY_ERROR_RETURN** if unsuccessful. The thread's priority level will be one of the values shown here.

Value	Priority
THREAD_PRIORITY_IDLE	A base priority level of 1 is assigned to **IDLE_PRIORITY_CLASS**, **NORMAL_PRIORITY_CLASS**, or **HIGH_PRIORITY_CLASS** processes. A base priority level of 16 is assigned to **REALTIME_PRIORITY_CLASS** processes.
THREAD_PRIORITY_LOWEST	2 points below normal priority relative to the priority class.
THREAD_PRIORITY_BELOW_NORMAL	1 point below normal priority relative to the priority class.
THREAD_PRIORITY_NORMAL	Normal priority for the priority class.
THREAD_PRIORITY_ABOVE_NORMAL	1 point above normal priority relative to the priority class.
THREAD_PRIORITY_HIGHEST	2 points above normal priority relative to the priority class.
THREAD_PRIORITY_TIME_CRITICAL	A base priority level of 15 is assigned to **IDLE_PRIORITY_CLASS**, **NORMAL_PRIORITY_CLASS**, or **HIGH_PRIORITY_CLASS** processes. A base priority level of 31 is assigned to **REALTIME_PRIORITY_CLASS** processes.

USAGE

The thread priority value and the priority class of the thread's process are used to obtain the base priority level of the thread.

Here is a small portion of code that illustrates the use of this function.

```
HANDLE hThread;
int PriorityLevel;

PriorityLevel = GetThreadPriority(hThread);
```

RELATED FUNCTIONS

SetThreadPriority()
GetPriorityClass()
SetPriorityClass()

BOOL GetThreadSelectorEntry(HANDLE *hThread,*
DWORD *dwSlct,*
LPLDT_ENTRY *lpSlctEntry*)

GetThreadSelectorEntry() obtains a descriptor table entry. *hThread* is the handle of the thread in question and it must have **THREAD_QUERY_IN-FORMATION** access rights.

dwSlct contains the global or local selector value to find in the thread's descriptor tables. *lpSlctEntry* is a pointer to a structure. This structure obtains a copy of the descriptor table entry when the given selector has an entry in the thread's descriptor table.

If successful, the function returns TRUE, and the structure pointed to by the *lpSlctEntry* parameter contains a copy of the given descriptor table entry. If unsuccessful, the function returns FALSE.

GetThreadSelectorEntry() applies only to systems based on the Intel x86 family of processors.

USAGE

This function can be used to convert segment-relative addresses to linear virtual addresses for debugging.

HANDLE OpenProcess(DWORD *fdwAccess,* BOOL *fInh,*
DWORD *IDProcess*)

OpenProcess() returns a handle to a process. *fdwAccess* contains the access rights the handle will have to the process. If security is supported (as in Windows NT) the access is compared with the security descriptor for the target process.

The valid security flags that can be used by this function are shown here. These values can be combined with **STANDARD_RIGHTS_REQUIRED**.

Flag	Access
PROCESS_CREATE_PROCESS	Reserved for internal use.
PROCESS_CREATE_THREAD	Allows the process handle from **CreateRemoteThread()** to create a new thread in the process.
PROCESS_DUP_HANDLE	Allows the process handle to function as the source or target process when using **DuplicateHandle()** to replicate a handle.
PROCESS_QUERY_INFORMATION	Allows using the process handle in **GetExitCodeProcess()** and **GetPriorityClass()** for obtaining information from the process object.
PROCESS_SET_INFORMATION	Allows using the process handle in **SetPriorityClass**() to set the priority class of the process.
PROCESS_TERMINATE	Allows the process handle to terminate the process by using **TerminateProcess().**
PROCESS_VM_OPERATION	Allows the process handle in **VirtualProtectEx()** and **WriteProcessMemory()** to change the virtual memory of the process.
PROCESS_VM_READ	Allows the process handle in **ReadProcessMemory()** to read the process's virtual memory.
PROCESS_VM_WRITE	Allows the process handle in **WriteProcessMemory()** to write to the process's virtual memory.
SYNCHRONIZE	Allows the process handle to wait for the process to terminate when using any wait function.
PROCESS_ALL_ACCESS	Allows all access flags for the process object.

fInh determines if the handle, returned by the function, can be inherited by a new process. If TRUE, the handle can be inherited. If FALSE, the handle cannot be inherited.

IDProcess gives the process ID of the process to be opened.

The function returns the value of the handle of the given process if successful, or NULL if unsuccessful.

RELATED FUNCTIONS

CreateProcess()
GetCurrentProcess()
GetCurrentProcessId()

DWORD ResumeThread(HANDLE *hThread*)

ResumeThread() decrements the specified thread's suspension count. Once the count reaches zero, the execution of the thread is continued. It returns the thread's suspension count prior to being decremented.

hThread is the handle of the thread to be continued and it must have **THREAD_SUSPEND_RESUME** access rights.

USAGE

If the function is successful, a value of 1 indicates that the thread was suspended and has now resumed execution. A return value of 0 indicates that the thread was not suspended. For return values greater than 1, the thread is still suspended.

Here is a small portion of code that illustrates how this function might be used.

```
case IDM_RESUMEORANGE:

    OrangeSuspendCnt=ResumeThread (hNewThread);
    wsprintf(Buf, "The orange thread suspension count is %d",
            OrangeSuspendCnt);
    MessageBox(hWnd, Buf, "Orange Suspension Count", MB_OK);
    return (0);
```

RELATED FUNCTION

SuspendThread()

BOOL SetPriorityClass(HANDLE *hProcess*, DWORD *fdwPrty*)

SetPriorityClass() sets a process's priority class. The function returns TRUE if successful, or FALSE if unsuccessful.

hProcess is the handle of the process and it must have **PROCESS_SET_IN-FORMATION** access rights. *fdwPrty* gives the priority class for the process and can be selected from those values shown here.

Value	Priority
IDLE_PRIORITY_CLASS	A process whose threads execute only when the system is idle. These threads are preempted by the threads of any process running in a higher priority class. The idle priority class is inherited by child processes of the parent.
NORMAL_PRIORITY_CLASS	A normal process.
HIGH_PRIORITY_CLASS	A process performing time-critical tasks. It must be executed immediately for correct execution. This class of threads preempts the threads of normal or idle priority class processes.
REALTIME_PRIORITY_CLASS	A process given the highest priority level possible. Real-time priority class threads preempt all the threads of all other processes.

Each thread is assigned a base priority level determined by the priority value of the thread and the priority class of the thread's process. This priority level is used when assigning CPU time. A thread's base priority level ranges from 1 to 31. The normal base priority level for **IDLE_PRIORITY_CLASS** is 4; for **NORMAL_PRIORITY_CLASS**, 9 (if the window is in *foreground*) or 7 (if the window is in *background*); for **HIGH_PRIORITY_CLASS**, 13; and for **REALTIME_PRIORITY_CLASS**, 24.

The initial priority class of a process can be set in **CreateProcess()**. When the priority class is not given, a default of **NORMAL_PRIORITY_CLASS** is assumed unless the creating process uses **IDLE_PRIORITY_CLASS**. For this situation, **IDLE_PRIORITY_CLASS** is used.

NOTE

Threads with a base priority level greater than 11 interfere with the operation of the operating system.

The following table shows the base priority setting associated with various combinations of thread priority and priority classes values.

Thread Priority	Priority Class	Base
THREAD_PRIORITY_IDLE	Idle, normal, or high	1
THREAD_PRIORITY_LOWEST	Idle	2
THREAD_PRIORITY_BELOW_NORMAL	Idle	3
THREAD_PRIORITY_NORMAL	Idle	4
THREAD_PRIORITY_LOWEST	Background normal	5
THREAD_PRIORITY_ABOVE_NORMAL	Idle	5
THREAD_PRIORITY_BELOW_NORMAL	Background normal	6
THREAD_PRIORITY_HIGHEST	Idle	6
THREAD_PRIORITY_LOWEST	Foreground normal	7
THREAD_PRIORITY_NORMAL	Background normal	7
THREAD_PRIORITY_BELOW_NORMAL	Foreground normal	8
THREAD_PRIORITY_ABOVE_NORMAL	Background normal	8
THREAD_PRIORITY_NORMAL	Foreground normal	9
THREAD_PRIORITY_HIGHEST	Background normal	9
THREAD_PRIORITY_ABOVE_NORMAL	Foreground normal	10
THREAD_PRIORITY_LOWEST	High	11
THREAD_PRIORITY_HIGHEST	Foreground normal	11
THREAD_PRIORITY_BELOW_NORMAL	High	12
THREAD_PRIORITY_NORMAL	High	13
THREAD_PRIORITY_ABOVE_NORMAL	High	14
THREAD_PRIORITY_TIME_CRITICAL	Idle, normal, or high	15
THREAD_PRIORITY_HIGHEST	High	15
THREAD_PRIORITY_IDLE	Real-time	16
THREAD_PRIORITY_LOWEST	Real-time	22
THREAD_PRIORITY_BELOW_NORMAL	Real-time	23
THREAD_PRIORITY_NORMAL	Real-time	24
THREAD_PRIORITY_ABOVE_NORMAL	Real-time	25
THREAD_PRIORITY_HIGHEST	Real-time	26
THREAD_PRIORITY_TIME_CRITICAL	Real-time	31

USAGE

The base priority of each thread in the process is a combination of the priority set by the function and the priority value of each thread in the process.

Here is a small portion of code that illustrates the use of this function.

```
HANDLE hProcess;

SetPriorityClass(hProcess, NORMAL_PRIORITY_CLASS);
```

RELATED FUNCTIONS

CreateProcess()
CreateThread()
GetPriorityClass()
GetThreadPriority()
SetThreadPriority()

BOOL SetProcessShutdownParameters(DWORD *dwLevel*, DWORD *dwHow*)

SetProcessShutdownParameters() sets a process's termination level (i.e., its order in the shutdown process) and determines exactly how the termination will occur. It returns non-zero if successful, and zero on failure.

The process's termination level is passed in *dwLevel*. It must be in the range 0x100 through 0x4FF. The larger the value, the higher the process is in the termination list. (Higher values are shut down before lower ones.) *dwHow* contains either **SHUTDOWN_NORETRY** (no retry dialog box is displayed) or zero.

RELATED FUNCTION

GetProcessShutdownParameters()

BOOL SetThreadPriority(HANDLE *hThread*, int *nPriority*)

SetThreadPriority() sets a thread's priority. The function returns TRUE if successful, or FALSE if unsuccessful.

hThread is the handle of the thread and must have **THREAD_SET_IN-FORMATION** access. *nPriority* gives the priority value for the thread and can be selected from the values shown here.

Value	Priority
THREAD_PRIORITY_IDLE	A base priority level of 1 is assigned to **IDLE_PRIORITY_CLASS**, **NORMAL_PRIORITY_CLASS**, or **HIGH_PRIORITY_CLASS** processes. A base priority level of 16 is assigned to **REALTIME_PRIOR-ITY_CLASS** processes.
THREAD_PRIORITY_LOWEST	2 points below normal priority relative to the priority class.
THREAD_PRIORITY_BELOW_NORMAL	1 point below normal priority relative to the priority class.
THREAD_PRIORITY_NORMAL	Normal priority for the priority class.
THREAD_PRIORITY_ABOVE_NORMAL	1 point above normal priority relative to the priority class.
THREAD_PRIORITY_HIGHEST	2 points above normal priority relative to the priority class.
THREAD_PRIORITY_TIME_CRITICAL	A base priority level of 15 is assigned to **IDLE_PRIORITY_CLASS**, **NORMAL_PRIORITY_CLASS**, or **HIGH_PRIORITY_CLASS** processes. A base priority level of 31 is assigned to **REALTIME_PRIOR-ITY_CLASS** processes.

Each thread is assigned a base priority level that is a combination of the priority value of the thread and the priority class of the thread's process. This priority level is used when assigning CPU time.

RELATED FUNCTIONS

GetThreadPriority()
GetPriorityClass()
SetPriorityClass()

HINSTANCE ShellExecute(HWND *hwnd,*
LPCTSTR *lpszOp,*
LPCTSTR *lpszFile,*
LPTSTR *lpszParam,*
LPCTSTR *lpszDir,*
INT *wShowCmd*)

ShellExecute() opens or prints a file. *hwnd* is the handle of the parent window. *lpszOp* is a pointer to a the name of the operation to perform. This string must contain either "open" or "print". If set to NULL, then "open" is assummed.

lpszFile is a pointer to the name of the file. *lpszParam* is a pointer to a string containing the parameters passed to the application when the *lpszFile* uses an EXE file. *lpszParam* is NULL when *lpszFile* describes a document file.

lpszDir is a pointer to a string containing the name of the default directory. *wShowCmd* determines how the application is shown once it is opened. When *lpszFile* describes a document file, *wShowCmd* is zero.

The function opens executable files regardless of the *lpszOp* value.

In order for a document file to be printed, an application that can print it must be associated with the file. If this is not the case, an error will result.

If the function is successful, an instance handle of the application that was run will be returned. If the function is not successful, the return value will be less than or equal to 32.

RELATED FUNCTION

FindExecutable()

void Sleep(DWORD *cTimeInt*)

DWORD SleepEx(DWORD *cTimeInt,* BOOL *fAlert*)

Sleep() suspends the execution of the current thread for the specified delay. **SleepEx()** suspends the execution of the current thread for a specified delay or until an I/O completion callback function is executed.

cTimeInt contains a time period for the suspended execution, in milliseconds. If a zero is used, the thread will give up the remainder of the time slice to another thread of equal priority that is ready to execute. If no other threads with the same priority are ready, the function returns and the thread continues execution. If **INFINITE** is specified, an infinite delay occurs. The **Sleep()** function does not return a value.

In **SleepEx()**, if *fAlert* is TRUE, the function will return if the timeout period has completed or an I/O completion callback function is executed. The functions that generate calls to the I/O completion callback function are **ReadFileEx()** and **WriteFileEx()**.

SleepEx() returns a zero when the given time interval has expired. The return value is **WAIT_IO_COMPLETION** when the function returns because of an I/O completion callback when *fAlert* is TRUE.

USAGE

Here is a small portion of code that illustrates the use of this function.

```
Sleep(500); // A .5 second delay
```

RELATED FUNCTIONS

ReadFileEx()
WaitForMultipleObjectsEx()
WaitForSingleObjectEx()
WriteFileEx()

DWORD SuspendThread(HANDLE *hThread*)

SuspendThread() suspends a thread. *hThread* is the handle of the thread and it must have **THREAD_SUSPEND_RESUME** access rights.

Every thread is assigned a suspension count. When this count is greater than zero, the thread is suspended. If the count is zero, the thread is not suspended and can be executed when it next receives a time slice. The target thread's suspension count can be incremented with a call to **SuspendThread()**. The maximum suspend count is **MAXIMUM_SUSPEND_COUNT**. The suspend count can be decremented with a call to **ResumeThread()**.

The function returns the thread's previous suspend count if successful, or 4294967295 (0xFFFFFFFF) on failure.

USAGE

Here is a portion of code that illustrates the use of this function.

```
case IDM_SUSPENDORANGE:

    SuspendThread(hNewThread);
    OrangeSuspendCnt += 1;
    wsprintf(Buf, "The orange thread suspension count is %d",
             OrangeSuspendCnt);
    MessageBox(hWnd, Buf, "Orange Suspension Count", MB_OK);
    return (0);
```

RELATED FUNCTION

ResumeThread()

BOOL TerminateProcess(HANDLE *hProcess,*
UINT *uExitCode*)

TerminateProcess() terminates a process and all associated threads. *hProcess* is the handle to the process to be terminated. (It must have **PROCESS_TER-MINATE** access rights.)

uExitCode contains the exit code for the process. This code will also apply to threads associated with the process.

NOTE

GetExitCodeProcess() *can be used to obtain the process exit code, and* **GetExitCode-Thread()** *can be used to obtain the thread exit code.*

Terminating a process causes all open object handles to be closed and all threads in the process to be terminated. The state of the process object becomes signaled, and any threads waiting for the process to terminate are satisfied. The states of all threads of the process become signaled and satisfy any threads waiting for the threads to terminate. The termination status changes from **STILL_ACTIVE** to *uExitCode*.

TerminateProcess() causes a process to exit in a somewhat "unclean" manner, however, because global data used by a DLL may be corrupted.

Terminating a process does not mean the process object has been removed from the system or that child processes are terminated.

The function returns TRUE if successful, or FALSE if unsuccessful.

USAGE

Here is a small portion of code that illustrates the use of this function.

```
ret = TerminateProcess (hProcess, 0);
if  (ret == TRUE)
  MessageBox (hWnd, "Process Terminated",
              "Process", ID_OK);
```

RELATED FUNCTIONS

ExitProcess()
OpenProcess()

BOOL TerminateThread(HANDLE *hThread,*
DWORD *dwExitCode*)

TerminateThread() terminates a thread. (That is, the thread's execution is stopped.) *hThread* is the handle of the thread that is to be terminated and it must have **THREAD_TERMINATE** access rights. *dwExitCode* contains the exit code for the thread. The exit code can be obtained with a call to **GetExitCodeThread()**.

When this function is called and the target thread is the last thread of a process, the thread's process is also terminated.

When a thread is terminated, it enters a signaled state and any other threads that had been waiting for the thread to terminate are released. Also, the thread's termination status changes from **STILL_ACTIVE** to the value provided by *dwExitCode*.

Terminating a thread does not mean the thread object has been removed from the system. Thread objects are only deleted when the final thread handle is closed.

The function returns TRUE if successful, or FALSE if unsuccessful.

USAGE

Here is a small portion of code that illustrates the use of this function.

```
case WM_DESTROY:

    TerminateThread(hNewThread, 0);
    free (pNewColor);
    PostQuitMessage (0);
    return (0);
```

RELATED FUNCTION

ExitThread()

DWORD WaitForInputIdle(HANDLE *hProcess,* DWORD *dwTimeInt*)

WaitForInputIdle() pauses execution until a process is waiting for input from the user. This function applies only to GUI programs, not to console applications.

hProcess is the handle of the process. *dwTimeInt* contains the number of milliseconds that the function should wait for the program to wait for input. That is, if the program does not wait for input within the specified number of milliseconds, **WaitforInputIdle()** returns anyway. If **INFINITE** is used for this value, the function does not return until the process is idle.

WaitForInputIdle() returns zero if the process has become idle; **WAIT_TIMEOUT** if the function timed out; or 0xFFFFFFFF if an error occurs.

RELATED FUNCTION

CreateProcess()

UINT WinExec(LPCSTR *lpszCmdLine,* UINT *fuCmdShow*)

WinExec() executes an application. This function is primarily for 16-bit Windows. Windows NT/Win32 applications should use **CreateProcess()**.

lpszCmdLine is a pointer to a string that holds the command line to be executed. *fuCmdShow* states how the Windows application window is to be shown.

If the function is successful, a value greater than 31 will be returned. If the function is not successful, various values may be returned: Zero means the system has expended memory or resources. **ERROR_FILE_NOT_FOUND** means the file was not found. **ERROR_PATH_NOT_FOUND** means the path was not found, and **ERROR_BAD_FORMAT** signals an invalid executable (EXE) file.

RELATED FUNCTION

CreateProcess()

A Complete Programming Example

The following Windows NT/Win32 program creates both processes and threads. A new process is created each time Execute Process is selected from the menu. You can kill a process by selecting Kill Process from the menu.

A thread is created each time the Execute Thread menu option is selected. The thread beeps 10 times and displays the number of each beep along with its thread ID on the screen. Another thread can be started before the first is finished.

For additional examples and extended coverage of processes and threads, refer to Chapter 14 in Volume 1 of this series.

```c
/* A simple multithreaded program. */

#define PROCMAX 5 /* maximum number of processes */

#include <windows.h>
#include <string.h>
#include <stdio.h>
#include "proc.h"

LRESULT CALLBACK WindowFunc(HWND, UINT, WPARAM, LPARAM);
DWORD MyThread(LPVOID param);

char szWinName[] = "MyWin"; /* name of window class */

char str[255]; /* holds output strings */

int X=0, Y=0; /* current output location */
int maxX, maxY; /* screen dimensions */

int procnum = 0; /* number of active processes */

DWORD Tid; /* thread ID */

HDC memdc;
HBITMAP hbit;
HBRUSH hbrush;

PROCESS_INFORMATION pinfo[PROCMAX];

int WINAPI WinMain(HINSTANCE hInst, HINSTANCE hPreInst,
                   LPSTR lpszCmdLine, int nCmdShow)
{
  HWND hWnd;
  MSG lpMsg;
  WNDCLASS wcApp;
  HANDLE hAccel;

  /* Define a window class. */
```

```c
wcApp.hInstance = hInst; /* handle to this instance */
wcApp.lpszClassName = szWinName; /* window class name */
wcApp.lpfnWndProc = WindowFunc; /* window function */
wcApp.style = 0; /* default style */

wcApp.hIcon = LoadIcon(NULL, IDI_APPLICATION); /* icon style */
wcApp.hCursor = LoadCursor(NULL, IDC_ARROW); /* cursor style */

/* specify name of menu resource */
wcApp.lpszMenuName = "MYMENU"; /* main menu */

wcApp.cbClsExtra = 0; /* no extra */
wcApp.cbWndExtra = 0; /* information needed */

/* Make the window light gray. */
wcApp.hbrBackground = GetStockObject(WHITE_BRUSH);

/* Register the window class. */
if(!RegisterClass (&wcApp)) return 0;

/* Now that a window class has been registered, a window
   can be created. */
hWnd = CreateWindow(
  szWinName, /* name of window class */
  "Demonstrate Threads and Processes", /* title */
  WS_OVERLAPPEDWINDOW, /* window style - normal */
  CW_USEDEFAULT, /* X coordinate - let Windows decide */
  CW_USEDEFAULT, /* Y coordinate - let Windows decide */
  CW_USEDEFAULT, /* width - let Windows decide */
  CW_USEDEFAULT, /* height - let Windows decide */
  HWND_DESKTOP, /* handle of parent window - there isn't one */
  NULL, /* no menu */
  hInst, /* handle of this instance of the program */
  NULL /* no additional arguments */
);

/* load accelerators */
hAccel = LoadAccelerators(hInst, "MYMENU");

/* Display the window. */
ShowWindow(hWnd, nCmdShow);
UpdateWindow(hWnd);

/* Create the message loop. */
```

```
      while(GetMessage(&lpMsg, NULL, 0, 0))
      {
        if(!TranslateAccelerator(hWnd, hAccel, &lpMsg)) {
          TranslateMessage(&lpMsg); /* allow use of keyboard */
          DispatchMessage(&lpMsg); /* return control to Windows */
        }
      }
      return lpMsg.wParam;
    }


    /* This function is called by Windows NT and is passed
       messages from the message queue.
    */
    LRESULT CALLBACK WindowFunc(HWND hWnd, UINT messg, WPARAM wParam,
                    LPARAM lParam)
    {
      HDC hdc;
      PAINTSTRUCT paintstruct;
      TEXTMETRIC tm;
      STARTUPINFO startin;

      switch(messg) {
        case WM_CREATE:
          /* get screen coordinates */
          maxX = GetSystemMetrics(SM_CXSCREEN);
          maxY = GetSystemMetrics(SM_CYSCREEN);

          /* make a compatible memory image device */
          hdc = GetDC(hWnd);
          memdc = CreateCompatibleDC(hdc);
          hbit = CreateCompatibleBitmap(hdc, maxX, maxY);
          SelectObject(memdc, hbit);
          hbrush = GetStockObject(WHITE_BRUSH);
          SelectObject(memdc, hbrush);
          PatBlt(memdc, 0, 0, maxX, maxY, PATCOPY);
          ReleaseDC(hWnd, hdc);
          break;
        case WM_COMMAND:
          switch(LOWORD(wParam)) {
            case ID_PROCESS:
              if(procnum==PROCMAX) {
                MessageBox(hWnd, "Can't Create", "", MB_OK);
                break; /* no more than PROCMAX */
```

```
  }

  /* get text metrics */
  GetTextMetrics(memdc, &tm);

  sprintf(str, "Execute Process %d.", procnum);
  TextOut(memdc, X, Y, str, strlen(str)); /* output string */
  Y = Y + tm.tmHeight + tm.tmExternalLeading; /* next line */
  InvalidateRect(hWnd, NULL, 1);

  /* Start a new process */
  startin.cb = sizeof(STARTUPINFO);
  startin.lpReserved = NULL;
  startin.lpDesktop = NULL;
  startin.lpTitle = NULL;
  startin.dwFlags = STARTF_USESHOWWINDOW;
  startin.cbReserved2 = 0;
  startin.lpReserved2 = NULL;
  startin.wShowWindow = SW_SHOWMINIMIZED;

  CreateProcess(NULL, "test.exe",
                NULL, NULL, FALSE, 0,
                NULL, NULL, &startin, &pinfo[procnum]);
  procnum++;
  break;
case ID_KILLPROC:
  if(procnum) procnum--;
  else {
    MessageBox(hWnd, "No process to terminate.",
               "", MB_OK);
    break;
  }
  TerminateProcess(pinfo[procnum].hProcess, 0);
  sprintf(str, "Terminate Process %d.", procnum);
  TextOut(memdc, X, Y, str, strlen(str)); /* output string */
  Y = Y + tm.tmHeight + tm.tmExternalLeading; /* next line */
  InvalidateRect(hWnd, NULL, 1);
  break;
case ID_THREAD:
  CreateThread(NULL, 0, (LPTHREAD_START_ROUTINE)MyThread,
               (LPVOID) NULL, 0, &Tid);
  InvalidateRect(hWnd, NULL, 1);
  break;
```

```
            case ID_HELP:
              MessageBox(hWnd,
                         "F2: Start Process\nF3: Kill Process\n"
                         "F4: Start Thread",
                         "Help", MB_OK);
              break;
          }
          break;
        case WM_PAINT: /* process a repaint request */
          hdc = BeginPaint(hWnd, &paintstruct); /* get DC */

          /* now, copy memory image onto screen */
          BitBlt(hdc, 0, 0, maxX, maxY, memdc, 0, 0, SRCCOPY);
          EndPaint(hWnd, &paintstruct); /* release DC */
          break;
        case WM_LBUTTONDOWN: /* process left button */
          X = LOWORD(lParam); /* set X,Y to */
          Y = HIWORD(lParam); /* mouse location */
          break;
        case WM_DESTROY: /* terminate the program */
          DeleteDC(memdc); /* delete the memory device */
          PostQuitMessage(0);
          break;
        default:
          /* Let Windows NT process any messages not specified in
          the preceding switch statement. */
          return DefWindowProc(hWnd, messg, wParam, lParam);
      }
      return 0;
    }


/* A thread of execution within the process. */
DWORD MyThread(LPVOID param)
{
  int i;
  DWORD curTid = Tid;
  TEXTMETRIC tm;

  /* get text metrics */
  GetTextMetrics(memdc, &tm);
```

```
  for(i=0; i<10; i++) {
    Sleep(500);
    sprintf(str, "Thread ID #%d, beep #%d",
            curTid, i);
    TextOut(memdc, X, Y, str, strlen(str)); /* output string */
    Y = Y + tm.tmHeight + tm.tmExternalLeading; /* next line */
    InvalidateRect((HWND) param, NULL, 1);
    MessageBeep(-1);
  }
}
```

This program uses the PROC.H file, which is shown here.

```
#define ID_PROCESS 100
#define ID_KILLPROC 101
#define ID_THREAD 102
#define ID_HELP 103
```

This program requires the following resource file.

```
#include <windows.h>
#include "proc.h"

MYMENU MENU
{
  MENUITEM "&Execute Process", ID_PROCESS
  MENUITEM "&Kill Process", ID_KILLPROC
  MENUITEM "Execute &Thread", ID_THREAD
  MENUITEM "&Help", ID_HELP
}

MYMENU ACCELERATORS
{
  VK_F2, ID_PROCESS, VIRTKEY
  VK_F3, ID_KILLPROC, VIRTKEY
  VK_F4, ID_THREAD, VIRTKEY
  VK_F1, ID_HELP, VIRTKEY
}
```

Chapter 28

Regions

T H I S chapter describes Windows' region functions. These functions can be used to create, combine, fill, frame, offset, and paint regions. A complete programming example at the end of this chapter illustrates several of these region functions.

int CombineRgn(HRGN *hrgnDest,* HRGN *hrgnSrc1,* HRGN *hrgnSrc2,* int *fnCombMode*)

CombineRgn() combines two regions.

hrgnDest is the handle of the new region. The new region has dimensions specified by the combination of the original two regions. *hrgnSrc1* is the handle of the first region. *hrgnSrc2* is the handle of the second region. *fnCombMode* determines how the regions are to be combined. This value can be selected from those shown here.

Value	Purpose
RGN_AND	The combined region is the intersection of the two regions.
RGN_COPY	The combined region is formed by making a copy of the region specified by *hrgnSrc1*.
RGN_DIFF	The combined region uses parts of *hrgnSrc1* that are not also part of *hrgnSrc2*.
RGN_OR	The combined region is the union of two regions.
RGN_XOR	The combined region is created from the union of two combined regions less overlapping areas.

The return value gives the type of region that was formed. It will be one of these values.

Value	Type of Region
NULLREGION	An empty region.
SIMPLEREGION	A single rectangle defines the region.
COMPLEXREGION	Multiple rectangles define the region.
ERROR	No region created.

USAGE

Here is a small portion of code that illustrates the use of this function.

```
static HRGN hRgnClip;
static HRGN hRgn1, hRgn2;
    .
    .
    .

hRgn1 = CreateEllipticRgn(25, 100, 225, 200);
hRgn2 = CreateEllipticRgn(175, 100, 375, 200);
hRgnClip = CreateRectRgn(0, 0, 1, 1);
CombineRgn(hRgnClip, hRgn1, hRgn2, RGN_XOR);
SelectClipRgn(hdc, hRgnClip);
```

RELATED FUNCTIONS

CreateEllipticRgn()
CreateEllipticRgnIndirect()
CreatePolygonRgn()
CreatePolyPolygonRgn()
CreateRectRgn()
CreateRectRgnIndirect()
CreateRoundRectRgn()

HRGN CreateEllipticRgn(int *nLRect,* int *nTRect,* int *nRRect,* int *nBRect*)

CreateEllipticRgn() creates an elliptical region. It returns a handle to the region if successful, and NULL on failure. All parameters refer to the coordinates of the bounding rectangle in which the ellipse is defined.

nLRect is the x coordinate of the upper-left corner. *nTRect* is the y coordinate of the upper-left corner. *nRRect* is the x coordinate of the lower-right corner. *nBRect* is the y coordinate of the lower-right corner.

USAGE

Here is a small portion of code that illustrates the use of this function.

```
static HRGN hRgn1;
  .
  .
  .
hRgn1 = CreateEllipticRgn(25, 100, 225, 200);
```

RELATED FUNCTIONS

CreateEllipticRgnIndirect()
DeleteObject()
SelectObject()

HRGN CreateEllipticRgnIndirect(CONST RECT ⋆ *lpRc*)

CreateEllipticRgnIndirect() creates an elliptical region indirectly. The function returns a handle to the region if successful, and NULL on failure.

lpRc is a pointer to a **RECT** structure that defines the bounding rectangle that contains the ellipse.

The **RECT** structure is shown here.

```
typedef struct tagRECT }
  int left;
  int top;
  int right;
  int bottom;
} RECT;
```

For Windows NT/Win32, the members of **RECT** *are of type* **LONG**.

As related to **CreateEllipticRgnIndirect()**, **left** and **top** specify the coordinate of upper-left corner. **right** and **bottom** specify the coordinate of the lower-right corner.

RELATED FUNCTIONS

CreateEllipticRgn()
DeleteObject()
SelectObject()

HRGN CreatePolygonRgn(CONST POINT * *lpPnt*,
int *cPnt*,
int *fnPolyFillMode*)

CreatePolygonRgn() creates a polygonal region. The function returns the handle of the region if successful, and NULL if unsuccessful.

lpPnt is a pointer to an array of **POINT** structures. These **POINT** structures define the vertices of the polygon, which must be a closed figure.

The **POINT** structure is shown here.

```
typedef struct tagPOINT { /* pt */
  int x;
  int y;
} POINT;
```

For Windows NT/Win32, the members of **POINT** *are of type* **LONG**.

In the function, *cPnt* contains the number of array points.

fnPolyFillMode determines the fill mode used to find which pixels are in the region; it can be either **ALTERNATE** or **WINDING**. Experimentation is the easiest way to decide which mode is best for your application.

RELATED FUNCTIONS

CreatePolyPolygonRgn()
DeleteObject()
SelectObject()
SetPolyFillMode()

HRGN CreatePolyPolygonRgn(CONST POINT * *lpPnt*, CONST INT * *lpPolyCounts*, int *nCount*, int *fnPolyFillMode*)

CreatePolyPolygonRgn() creates a region made up of a series of polygons. Overlapping is permitted. Also, the polygons must all be closed. The function returns the handle of the region if successful, and NULL if unsuccessful.

lpPnt is a pointer to an array of **POINT** structures that hold the vertices of consecutive closed polygons. *lpPolyCounts* is a pointer to an array of integers. Each integer in the array contains the number of endpoints in the corresponding polygon in the *lpPnt* array. *nCount* contains the number of elements contained in the *lpPnt* array. (This is also the number of elements in the *lpPolyCounts* array.)

fnPolyFillMode determines the fill mode used to find which pixels are in the region; it can be either **ALTERNATE** or **WINDING**. Experimentation is the easiest way to decide which mode is best for your application.

RELATED FUNCTIONS

CreatePolygonRgn()
DeleteObject()
SelectObject()
SetPolyFillMode()

HRGN CreateRectRgn(int *nLRect*, int *nTRect*, int *nRRect*, int *nBRect*)

CreateRectRgn() creates a rectangular region as defined by its parameters. The function returns the handle of the region if successful, and NULL if unsuccessful.

The rectangle is defined like this. *nLRect,nTRect* is the coordinate of the upper-left corner. *nRRect,nBRect* is the coordinate of the lower-right corner.

USAGE

Here is a small portion of code that illustrates the use of this function.

```
static HRGN hRgnClip;
   .
   .
   .
hRgnClip = CreateRectRgn(10, 50, 100, 150);
```

RELATED FUNCTIONS

CreateRectRgnIndirect()
CreateRoundRectRgn()
DeleteObject()
SelectObject()

HRGN CreateRectRgnIndirect(CONST RECT ★ *lpRc*)

CreateRectRgnIndirect() indirectly creates a rectangular region. The function returns the handle of the region if successful, and NULL if unsuccessful.

lpRc is a pointer to a **RECT** structure that defines the region. The **RECT** structure is shown here.

```
typedef struct tagRECT {
   int left;
   int top;
   int right;
   int bottom;
} RECT;
```

NOTE

For Windows NT/Win32, the members of **RECT** *are of type* **LONG**.

RELATED FUNCTIONS

CreateRectRgn()
CreateRoundRectRgn()
DeleteObject()
SelectObject()

HRGN CreateRoundRectRgn(int *nLRect,* int *nTRect,* int *nRRect,* int *nBRect,* int *nWidthEllp,* int *nHeightEllp*)

CreateRoundRectRgn() creates a rectangular region with rounded corners, as defined by its parameters. The function returns the handle of the region if successful, and NULL if unsuccessful.

The rectangle is defined like this. *nLRect,nTRect* is the coordinate of the upper-left corner. *nRRect,nBRect* is the coordinate of the lower-right corner.

The way the rectangle's corners are rounded (i.e., their "roundness") is determined by the width and height of an ellipse. *nWidthEllp* defines the width of the ellipse. *nHeightEllp* defines the height of the ellipse.

RELATED FUNCTIONS

CreateRectRgn()
CreateRectRgnIndirect()
DeleteObject()
SelectObject()

BOOL EqualRgn(HRGN *hrgnSrc1,* HRGN *hrgnSrc2*)

EqualRgn() compares two regions for equality. The function returns TRUE when both regions are identical, FALSE if they differ, or ERROR if one or both of the region handles is not valid. (The regions are equal if they are of the same size and shape.)

hrgnSrc1 is the handle of the first region. *hrgnSrc2* is the handle of the second region.

RELATED FUNCTIONS

CreateRectRgn()
CreateRectRgnIndirect()

HRGN ExtCreateRegion(CONST XFORM *lpXform, DWORD nCount, CONST RGNDATA *lpRgnData)

ExtCreateRegion() creates a new region by transforming an existing region. The function returns the handle of the region if successful, and NULL if unsuccessful. This is a very useful function if your program must translate or rotate a region.

lpXform is a pointer to an **XFORM** structure that contains transformation data that will be applied. When NULL, no transformation occurs.

The **XFORM** structure is shown here.

```
typedef struct tagXFORM {
  FLOAT eM11;
  FLOAT eM12;
  FLOAT eM21;
  FLOAT eM22;
  FLOAT eDx;
  FLOAT eDy;
} XFORM;
```

Here, **eM11** gives scaling (horizontal scaling component), rotation (cosine of rotation angle), and reflection (horizontal component). **eM12** gives shear (horizontal proportionality constant) or rotation (sine of rotation angle).

eM21 gives shear (vertical proportionality constant) or rotation (negative sine of the rotation angle). **eM22** gives scaling (vertical scaling component), rotation (cosine of rotation angle), or reflection (vertical reflection component).

eDx gives the horizontal translation component and **eDy** gives the vertical translation component.

In the function, *nCount* is the size of the data (in bytes) pointed to by *lpRgnData*. *lpRgnData* is a pointer to a **RGNDATA** structure that defines the region.

The **RGNDATA** structure is shown here.

```
typedef struct _RGNDATA {
  RGNDATAHEADER rdh;
  char Buffer[1];
} RGNDATA;
```

Here, **rdh** is a **RGNDATAHEADER** structure. **Buffer** is a buffer containing the **RECT** structures that define the region. (The dimension of **Buffer** is shown as 1, but in actuality, this array will be as large as necessary to hold the points that define the region.)

The **RGNDATAHEADER** structure is shown here.

```
typedef struct _RGNDATAHEADER {
  DWORD dwSize;
  DWORD iType;
  DWORD nCount;
  DWORD nRgnSize;
  RECT rcBound;
} RGNDATAHEADER;
```

Here, **dwSize** is the header size in bytes. **iType** describes the type of region and must be **RDH_RECTANGLES**. **nCount** is the number of rectangles in the region. **nRgnSize** is the size of the buffer needed for the **RECT** structures that define the region. **rcBound** defines the region's bounding rectangle.

RELATED FUNCTION

GetRegionData()

BOOL FillRgn(HDC *hdc*, HRGN *hrgn*, HBRUSH *hbr*)

FillRgn() fills a region. The function returns TRUE if successful, and FALSE if unsuccessful.

hdc is the handle of the device context. *hrgn* is the handle of the region. *hbr* is the handle of the brush that fills the region.

RELATED FUNCTIONS

CreateBrushIndirect()
CreateDIBPatternBrush()
CreateHatchBrush()
CreatePatternBrush()

CreateSolidBrush()
PaintRgn()

BOOL FrameRgn(HDC *hdc*, HRGN *hrgn*, HBRUSH *hbr*, int *nWidth*, int *nHeight*)

FrameRgn() draws a border around (i.e., "frames") a region. The function returns TRUE if successful, and FALSE if unsuccessful.

hdc is the handle of the device context. *hrgn* is the handle of the region. *hbr* is the handle of the brush used to draw the border. (Notice that the current brush, *not* the current pen is used to frame the region.)

nWidth gives the width of vertical brush strokes and *nHeight* gives the height of horizontal brush strokes.

All dimensions are specified in logical units.

RELATED FUNCTIONS

FillRgn()
PaintRgn()

int GetPolyFillMode(HDC *hdc*)

GetPolyFillMode() returns the current polygon fill mode.

hdc is the handle of the device context.

When the function is successful, the fill mode is returned. It will be either **ALTERNATE** or **WINDING**. If the function is not successful, a zero is returned.

RELATED FUNCTION

SetPolyFillMode()

DWORD GetRegionData(HRGN *hrgn*, DWORD *dwCount*, LPRGNDATA *lpRgnData*)

GetRegionData() obtains information about a region.

hrgn is the handle of the region. *dwCount* contains the number of bytes in the data pointed to by *lpRgnData*. *lpRgnData* is a pointer to a **RGNDATA** structure. On return, this structure will contain the information about the region.

Generally, the function returns 1 if successful. However two special conditions may affect the return value. If the size of the buffer pointed to by *lpRgnData* is too small or if *lpRgnData* is NULL, the value returned is the minimum size of the buffer that can hold the information. If the function is not successful, the return value is zero.

RELATED FUNCTION

ExtCreateRegion()

---

int GetRgnBox(HRGN *hrgn*, LPRECT *lpRc*)

GetRgnBox() obtains the bounding rectangle of the given region.

hrgn is the handle of the region. *lpRc* is a pointer to a **RECT** structure. On return, this structure will contain the coordinates of the bounding rectangle.

The return value describes the region's complexity and can be one of these values.

Value	Type of Region
NULLREGION	The region is empty.
SIMPLEREGION	The region is a single rectangle.
COMPLEXREGION	The region is formed by multiple rectangles.

If the function is not successful, a zero is returned.

RELATED FUNCTION

FrameRgn()

BOOL InvertRgn(HDC *hdc*, HRGN *hrgn*)

InvertRgn() is used to invert the colors in a region. The function returns TRUE if successful, and FALSE if unsuccessful.

hdc is the handle of the device context. *hrgn* is the handle of the region.

RELATED FUNCTIONS

FillRgn()
PaintRgn()

int OffsetRgn(HRGN *hrgn,* int *nXOffset,*
int *nYOffset*)

OffsetRgn() moves a region.

hrgn is the handle of the region. *nXOffset* contains the number of horizontal units to move and *nYOffset* contains the number of vertical units to move. All offsets are specified in logical units and may be either positive or negative.

The return value gives the region's complexity and will be one of these values.

Value	Type of Region
NULLREGION	The region is empty.
SIMPLEREGION	The region is a single rectangle.
COMPLEXREGION	The region is formed by multiple rectangles.
ERROR	The region is unaffected.

RELATED FUNCTIONS

FrameRgn()
GetRgnBox()

BOOL PaintRgn(HDC *hdc,* HRGN *hrgn*)

PaintRgn() paints a region using the currently selected brush. The function returns TRUE if successful, and FALSE if unsuccessful.

hdc is the handle of the device context. *hrgn* is the handle of the region that is to be filled.

RELATED FUNCTION

FillRgn()

BOOL PtInRegion(HRGN *hrgn*, int *X*, int *Y*)

PtInRegion() determines whether a point is inside a region. If the point is in the region, the function returns TRUE. If the point is not in the region, the function returns a FALSE.

hrgn is the handle of the region. *X, Y* are the coordinates of the point.

RELATED FUNCTION

RectInRegion()

BOOL RectInRegion(HRGN *hrgn*, CONST RECT **lpRc*)

RectInRegion() returns TRUE if any part of the given rectangle is within the given region's boundaries. It returns FALSE if the rectangle and region do not overlap.

hrgn is the handle of the region. *lpRc* is a pointer to a **RECT** structure. This structure holds the coordinates of the rectangle.

RELATED FUNCTION

PtInRegion()

int SelectClipRgn(HDC *hdc*, HRGN *hrgn*)

SelectClipRgn() uses the specified region as the current clipping region for the specified device context.

hdc is a handle to the device context. *hrgn* is the handle of a copy of the region that is to be selected. Since a copy is used, the region can be selected repeatedly for numerous device contexts.

If the function is successful, a value giving the region's complexity is returned. This value can be any one of these values.

Value	Type of Region
NULLREGION	The region is empty.
SIMPLEREGION	The region is a single rectangle.
COMPLEXREGION	The region is formed by multiple rectangles.
ERROR	The region is unaffected.

USAGE

Here is a small portion of code that illustrates the use of this function.

```
HDC hdc;
static HRGN hRgnClip;
    .
    .
    .

SelectClipRgn(hdc, hRgnClip);
```

RELATED FUNCTION

ExtSelectClipRgn()

int SetPolyFillMode(HDC *hdc*, int *iPolyFillMode*)

SetPolyFillMode() sets the polygon fill mode for the functions used to fill polygons. The function returns the previous fill mode if successful, and zero if unsuccessful.

hdc is the handle of the device context. *iPolyFillMode* gives the new fill mode, which may be **ALTERNATE** or **WINDING**. Experimentation is the easiest way to determine which fill mode works best for your application.

RELATED FUNCTION

GetPolyFillMode()

A Complete Programming Example

The following program illustrates several region functions and can be compiled for use under Windows NT. With slight modifications to the supporting code, this application can also be used with Windows under DOS.

This program creates two overlapping elliptical regions in the window. Horizontal and vertical lines are produced with the use of two **for** loops, but they only fill the specified regions. The areas where the regions overlap are not filled because **RGN_XOR** is specified.

```
//
//  ntregions
//  A simple Windows NT application that demonstrates the use
//  of functions that manipulate regions.
//  Two regions are created.  Pattern fill occurs only within
//  the two regions.  Portions that overlap are not filled (XOR).
//

#include <windows.h>

LRESULT CALLBACK WndProc(HWND, UINT, WPARAM, LPARAM);

char szProgName[] = "ProgName";

int WINAPI WinMain(HINSTANCE hInst, HINSTANCE hPreInst,
                   LPSTR lpszCmdLine, int nCmdShow)
{
  HWND hWnd;
  MSG lpMsg;
  WNDCLASS wcApp;
  if (!hPreInst) {
    wcApp.lpszClassName = szProgName;
    wcApp.hInstance     = hInst;
    wcApp.lpfnWndProc   = WndProc;
    wcApp.hCursor       = LoadCursor(NULL, IDC_ARROW);
    wcApp.hIcon         = NULL;
    wcApp.lpszMenuName  = NULL;
    wcApp.hbrBackground = GetStockObject(WHITE_BRUSH);
    wcApp.style         = CS_HREDRAW | CS_VREDRAW;
    wcApp.cbClsExtra    = 0;
    wcApp.cbWndExtra    = 0;
    if (!RegisterClass (&wcApp))
```

```
        return FALSE;
    }
    hWnd = CreateWindow(szProgName, "Regions Under Windows NT",
                        WS_OVERLAPPEDWINDOW, CW_USEDEFAULT,
                        CW_USEDEFAULT, CW_USEDEFAULT,
                        CW_USEDEFAULT, (HWND)NULL, (HMENU)NULL,
                        (HANDLE)hInst, (LPSTR)NULL);
    ShowWindow(hWnd, nCmdShow);
    UpdateWindow(hWnd);
    while (GetMessage(&lpMsg, NULL, 0, 0)) {
        TranslateMessage(&lpMsg);
        DispatchMessage(&lpMsg);
    }
    return(lpMsg.wParam);
}


LRESULT CALLBACK WndProc(HWND hWnd, UINT messg,
                         WPARAM wParam, LPARAM lParam)
{
    HDC hdc;
    PAINTSTRUCT ps;
    static HRGN hRgnClip;
    static HRGN hRgn1, hRgn2;
    int i;

    switch (messg)
    {
        case WM_PAINT:
            hdc = BeginPaint(hWnd, &ps);

            hRgn1 = CreateEllipticRgn(25, 100, 225, 200);
            hRgn2 = CreateEllipticRgn(175, 100, 375, 200);
            hRgnClip = CreateRectRgn(0, 0, 1, 1);
            CombineRgn(hRgnClip, hRgn1, hRgn2, RGN_XOR);
            SelectClipRgn(hdc, hRgnClip);

            // vertical grid lines
            for (i = 0; i < 400; i += 5) {
                MoveToEx(hdc, i, 0, NULL);
                LineTo(hdc, i, 300);
            }

            // horizontal grid lines
            for (i = 0; i < 300; i += 5) {
```

```
        MoveToEx(hdc, 0, i, NULL);
        LineTo(hdc, 400, i);
      }

      ValidateRect(hWnd, NULL);
      EndPaint(hWnd, &ps);
      break;

  case WM_DESTROY:
    DeleteObject(hRgn1);
    DeleteObject(hRgn2);
    DeleteObject(hRgnClip);
    PostQuitMessage(0);
    break;

  default:
    return(DefWindowProc(hWnd, messg, wParam, lParam));
}
return(0L);}
```

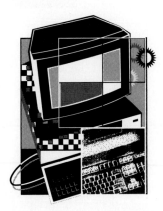

Chapter 29

Registration

H I S chapter describes Windows' registration functions. Registration (and the Windows registry) is designed to replace old-stye initialization files, such as WIN.INI. The registry provides several improvements over .INI files, especially in the areas of security and maintainability. Although 16-bit Windows supports the registry, Windows NT/Win32 has greatly expanded its capabilities.

LONG RegCloseKey(HKEY *hKey*)

RegCloseKey() releases the handle of the key. If the function is successful, a value of **ERROR_SUCCESS** is returned. If the function is not successful, an error value is returned.

hKey is the handle of the key to be closed.

USAGE

Key handles should be closed when they are no longer necessary.
Here is a small portion of code that illustrates the use of this function.

```
HKEY hKey;
LONG RetValue;

RetValue = RegCloseKey (hKey);
```

RELATED FUNCTIONS

RegCreateKey()
RegCreateKeyEx()
RegDeleteKey()
RegFlushKey()
RegOpenKey()
RegOpenKeyEx()

RegSetValue()
RegSetValueEx()

LONG RegCreateKey(HKEY *hKey,* LPCSTR *lpszSubKey,* PHKEY *lphkResult*)

RegCreateKey() creates a registration key, or if it already exists in the registry, the function will open it. If the function is successful, a value of **ER-ROR_SUCCESS** is returned. If the function is not successful, an error value is returned.

hKey is the handle of an open key or one of these predefined handles:

HKEY_CLASSES_ROOT
HKEY_CURRENT_USER
HKEY_LOCAL_MACHINE
HKEY_USERS

The key that is opened or created is a subkey of *hKey* and must be opened with **KEY_CREATE_SUB_KEY**.

lpszSubKey is a pointer to the name of the key or keys to open or create. When *hKey* is a predefined value, *lpszSubKey* can be set to NULL. *lphkResult* is a pointer to a variable that, on return, contains the handle of the newly created or opened key.

USAGE

NOTE

New applications should use **RegCreateKeyEx()** *in place of this function.*

This function can create several keys at the same time. For example, the *lpszSubKey* string can contain *subkey1\subkey2\subkey3.*

RELATED FUNCTIONS

RegCloseKey()
RegCreateKeyEx()
RegDeleteKey()
RegOpenKey()

RegOpenKeyEx()
RegSetValue()

LONG RegCreateKeyEx(HKEY *hKey*, LPCTSTR *lpszSubKey*, DWORD *dwReserved*, LPTSTR *lpszClass*, DWORD *fdwOpt*, REGSAM *samDesired*, LPSECURITY_ATTRIBUTES *lpSecurityAtt*, PHKEY *phkResult*, LPDWORD *lpdwDisp*)

RegCreateKeyEx() creates a registration key, or if it already exists in the registry, the function will open it. If the function is successful, a value of **ERROR_SUCCESS** is returned. If the function is not successful, an error value is returned.

hKey is the handle of an open key or one of these predefined handles:

HKEY_CLASSES_ROOT
HKEY_CURRENT_USER
HKEY_LOCAL_MACHINE
HKEY_USERS

The key that is opened or created is a subkey of *hKey* and must be opened with **KEY_CREATE_SUB_KEY**.

lpszSubKey is a pointer to the name of the key or keys to open or create. *dwReserved* is reserved and must be zero. *lpszClass* is a pointer to the class or object type for the key, which is ignored if the key presently exists. *fdwOpt* contains any options for the key. This value can be either of those shown here.

Value	Purpose
REG_OPTION_NON_VOLATILE	The key is not volatile and its information is saved to a file (which is not lost if the system is restarted). Note: **RegSaveKey()** does not save volatile key information.
REG_OPTION_VOLATILE	The key is volatile and its information resides only in memory (which is lost if the system is restarted). Note: **RegSaveKey()** does not save volatile key information.

samDesired contains the security access attributes for the key. This value can be any valid combination of the values shown here

Value	Purpose
KEY_ALL_ACCESS	A predefined combination that includes **KEY_QUERY_VALUE, KEY_ENUMERATE_SUB_KEYS, KEY_NOTIFY, KEY_CREATE_SUB_KEY, KEY_CREATE_LINK**, and **KEY_SET_VALUE**
KEY_CREATE_LINK	Allows the creation of a symbolic link
KEY_CREATE_SUB_KEY	Allows the creation of subkeys
KEY_ENUMERATE_SUB_KEYS	Allows the enumeration of subkeys
KEY_EXECUTE	Allows a read access
KEY_NOTIFY	Allows a notification change
KEY_QUERY_VALUE	Allows a query of subkey data
KEY_READ	A predefined combination that includes **KEY_QUERY_VALUE, KEY_ENUMERATE_SUB_KEYS**, and **KEY_NOTIFY**
KEY_SET_VALUE	Allows subkey data to be set
KEY_WRITE	Predefined combination that includes **KEY_SET_VALUE** and **KEY_CREATE_SUB_KEY**

lpSecurityAtt is a pointer to a **SECURITY_ATTRIBUTES** structure. This structure gives the security attributes of the key but should not be directly altered by the user. When this value is NULL, the default security descriptor is used. Security is ignored when the operating system does not provide security support.

phkResult is a pointer to a variable that, on return, will contain the handle of the key that has just been created or opened. *lpdwDisp* is a pointer to a variable that, on return, describes which action took place. It will either be **REG_CRE-ATED_NEW_KEY**, if a new key was created, or **REG_OPENED_EXIST-ING_KEY**, if an already existing key was opened.

USAGE

RegCreateKeyEx() can create several keys at the same time. For example, the *lpszSubKey* string can contain *subkey1\subkey2\subkey3*.

RELATED FUNCTIONS

RegCreateKey()
RegDeleteKey()

RegOpenKey()
RegOpenKeyEx()
RegSaveKey()

LONG RegDeleteKey(HKEY *hKey,*
LPCTSTR *lpszSubKey*)

RegDeleteKey() deletes the given key if that key does not have subkeys. When the function is successful, **RegDeleteKey()** deletes the key from the registration database and returns a value of **ERROR_SUCCESS**. The entire key and all its values are removed. If the function is not successful, an error value is returned.

hKey is the handle of an open key or one of these predefined handles:

  HKEY_CLASSES_ROOT
  HKEY_CURRENT_USER
  HKEY_LOCAL_MACHINE
  HKEY_USERS

lpszSubKey is a pointer to the name of the key to remove.

RELATED FUNCTIONS

RegCloseKey()
RegCreateKeyEx()
RegOpenKeyEx()

LONG RegDeleteValue(HKEY *hKey,*
LPTSTR *lpszValue*)

RegDeleteValue() removes a value from the registry key. If the function is successful, a value of **ERROR_SUCCESS** is returned. If the function is not successful, an error value is returned.

hKey is the handle of an open key or one of these predefined handles:

HKEY_CLASSES_ROOT
HKEY_CURRENT_USER
HKEY_LOCAL_MACHINE
HKEY_USERS

This key must have been opened with **KEY_SET_VALUE** access privileges.

lpszValue is a pointer to the name of the value to remove.

USAGE

If you wish to remove the value that has been previously specified using **RegSetValue()**, specify *lpszValue* as NULL (or make it point to a null string).

RELATED FUNCTIONS

RegSetValue()
RegSetValueEx()

LONG RegEnumKey(HKEY *hKey,* DWORD *iSubKey,* LPSTR *lpszName,* DWORD *nSize)*

RegEnumKey() enumerates subkeys of an open registry key. **RegEnumKeyEx()** should be used by new applications. If the function is successful (that is, it has obtained a subkey), a value of **ERROR_SUCCESS** is returned. If the function is not successful (that is, there are no more subkeys to enumerate), an error value is returned.

hKey is the handle of an open key or one of these predefined handles:

HKEY_CLASSES_ROOT
HKEY_CURRENT_USER
HKEY_LOCAL_MACHINE
HKEY_USERS

hKey must have been opened with **KEY_ENUMERATE_SUB_KEYS** access rights.

iSubKey is the index of the subkey to obtain and should be zero for the first call. Increment this value for each subsequent call. The function does not return subkeys in any specific order.

lpszName is a pointer to an array that, on return, will contain the name of the subkey. *nSize* is the size of the *lpszName* array.

USAGE

The minimum size of the array pointed to by *lpszName* can be determined with the use of **RegQueryInfoKey()** to find the largest subkey size for the key. In no case will a subkey require more than **MAX_PATH** + 1 characters, however.

Here is a small portion of code that illustrates the use of this function.

```
HKEY hKey;
CHAR Key_Name[MAX_PATH+1];
DWORD retVal;
    .
    .
    .

for (i=0, retVal = ERROR_SUCCESS; retVal ==
    ERROR_SUCCESS; i++) {
  retVal = RegEnumKey(hKey, i, Key_Name, MAX_PATH);
    .
    .
    .
```

RELATED FUNCTIONS

RegCloseKey()
RegCreateKeyEx()
RegDeleteKey()
RegEnumKeyEx()
RegOpenKeyEx()
RegQueryInfoKey()
RegQueryValue()

LONG RegEnumKeyEx(HKEY *hKey,* **DWORD** *iSubkey,*
                           LPTSTR *lpszName,*
                           LPDWORD *lpNameSize,*
                           LPDWORD *lpdwReserved,*
                           LPTSTR *lpszClass,*
                           LPDWORD *lpClassSize,*
                           PFILETIME *lpftLastWrite***)**

RegEnumKeyEx() enumerates subkeys of an open registry key. It also obtains the subkey's class name and the time when it was last modified. If the function is successful (that is, it has obtained a subkey), a value of **ERROR_SUCCESS** is returned. If the function is not successful (that is, there are no more subkeys to enumerate), an error value is returned.

hKey is the handle of an open key or one of these predefined handles:

HKEY_CLASSES_ROOT
HKEY_CURRENT_USER
HKEY_LOCAL_MACHINE
HKEY_USERS

hKey must have been opened with **KEY_ENUMERATE_SUB_KEYS** access privileges.

iSubKey is the index of the subkey to obtain and should be zero for the first call. Increment this value for each subsequent call. The function does not return subkeys in any specific order.

lpszName is a pointer to an array that, on return, will contain the name of the subkey. *lpNameSize* is a pointer to a variable that contains the size of the *lpszName* array. On return, this variable will contain the number of characters copied into the *lpszName* array.

lpdwReserved is a pointer that is currently reserved and should be set to NULL.

lpszClass is a pointer to an array that, on return, contains the class of the subkey. If the subkey's class is not needed, then use NULL for this parameter. *lpClassSize* is a pointer to a variable that contains the size of the array pointed to by *lpszClass*. On return, this variable will contain the number of characters copied into the *lpszClass* array.

lpftLastWrite is a pointer to a variable that, on return, contains the time when the subkey was last modified.

USAGE

The minimum size of the array pointed to by *lpszName* can be determined with the use of **RegQueryInfoKey()** to find the largest subkey size for the key. In no case will a subkey require more than **MAX_PATH** + 1 characters, however.

See **RegEnumKey()** for a small code example.

RELATED FUNCTIONS

RegDeleteKey()
RegEnumKey()

LONG RegEnumValue(HKEY *hKey*, **DWORD** *iValue*,
                     LPTSTR *lpszValue*,
                     LPDWORD *lpValueSize*,
                     LPDWORD *lpdwReserved*,
                     LPDWORD *lpdwType*,
                     LPBYTE *lpDataSize*,
                     LPDWORD *lpcbData***)**

RegEnumValue() enumerates the values associated with a registry key. If the function is successful (that is, it has obtained a value), a value of **ERROR_SUC-CESS** is returned. If the function is not successful (that is, there are no more values associated with the key to enumerate), an error value is returned.

hKey is the handle of an open key or one of these predefined handles:

HKEY_CLASSES_ROOT
HKEY_CURRENT_USER

HKEY_LOCAL_MACHINE
HKEY_USERS

hKey must have been opened with **KEY_QUERY_VALUE** access rights. The values obtained are associated with this key.

iValue is the index of the value to obtain and should be zero for the first call. Increment this value for each subsequent call. The function does not return values in any specific order.

lpszValue is a pointer to an array that, on return, contains the value obtained by the function. *lpValueSize* is a pointer to a variable that contains the size of the *lpszValue* array. On return, this variable will contain the number of characters copied into the *lpszValue* array.

lpdwReserved is reserved and must be NULL. *lpdwType* is a pointer to a variable that, on return, contains the type of the value obtained by the function. *lpdwType* may be NULL if the type is not need. Otherwise, it will be one of these values.

Value	Type
REG_BINARY	Data in any binary form
REG_DWORD	Data as a 32-bit number
REG_DWORD_LITTLE_ENDIAN	Data as a 32-bit number in little-endian format (**LSB** in low-memory, **MSB** in high-memory—common to Intel design)
REG_DWORD_BIG_ENDIAN	Data as a 32-bit number in big-endian format (**LSB** in high-memory, **MSB** in low-memory)
REG_EXPAND_SZ	Data as a null-terminated string containing unexpanded references to environment variables
REG_LINK	Data as a Unicode symbolic link
REG_MULTI_SZ	Data as an array of null-terminated strings, terminate with two null characters
REG_NONE	Data with no defined value type
REG_RESOURCE_LIST	Data as a device-driver resource list
REG_SZ	Data as a null-terminated string, Unicode or ANSI

lpbData is a pointer to an array that, on return, contains the data associated with the value. If this data is not needed, pass NULL for *lpbData*.

lpDataSize is a pointer to a variable that contains the size of the *lpbData* array. (This parameter can be NULL if it is not required.) On return, this variable will hold the number of bytes stored in the *lpbData* array.

USAGE

Here is a small portion of code that illustrates the use of this function.

```
DWORD retVal;
DWORD dwValName = MAX_VALUE_NAME;
CHAR ValName[MAX_VALUE_NAME];
     .
     .
     .
for (i = 0, retVal = ERROR_SUCCESS; i < dwVal; i++) {
  dwValName = MAX_VALUE_NAME;
  ValName[0] = '\0';
  retVal = RegEnumValue(hKey, i, ValName, &dwValName,
                        NULL, NULL, NULL, NULL);
     .
     .
     .
}
```

RELATED FUNCTIONS

RegCreateKeyEx()
RegEnumKey()
RegEnumKeyEx()
RegOpenKeyEx()
RegQueryInfoKey()

LONG RegFlushKey(HKEY *hKey*)

RegFlushKey() saves all of the attributes for a key in the registry. If the function is successful, a value of **ERROR_SUCCESS** is returned. If the function is not successful, an error value is returned.

hKey is the handle of an open key or one of these predefined handles:

HKEY_CLASSES_ROOT
HKEY_CURRENT_USER
HKEY_LOCAL_MACHINE
HKEY_USERS

RELATED FUNCTIONS

RegCloseKey()
RegDeleteKey()

LONG RegNotifyChangeKeyValue(HKEY *hKey,*
        BOOL *fSubTree,*
        DWORD *fdwNfyFilter,*
        HANDLE *hEvent,*
        BOOL *fAsync***)**

RegNotifyChangeKeyValue() determines when a key has changed. If the function is successful, a value of **ERROR_SUCCESS** is returned. If the function is not successful, an error value is returned.

 hKey is the handle of an open key or one of these predefined handles:

  HKEY_CLASSES_ROOT
  HKEY_CURRENT_USER
  HKEY_LOCAL_MACHINE
  HKEY_USERS

 When *fSubTree* is TRUE, changes in the key and its subkeys are monitored. When FALSE, only changes in the key, itself, will be monitored.

 fdwNfyFilter determines what types of changes in the key (or keys) will be reported. This value can be any valid combination of those shown here.

Flag	Type of Change
REG_NOTIFY_CHANGE_NAME	Changes to key names for the key or subkeys.
REG_NOTIFY_CHANGE_ATTRIBUTES	Changes in a key's or subkey's attributes.
REG_NOTIFY_CHANGE_LAST_SET	Changes to the write time for the key or subkeys.
REG_NOTIFY_CHANGE_SECURITY	Changes to the security descriptor for the key or subkeys.

hEvent is the handle of an event that is signalled when one of the monitored changes takes place. When *fAsync* is TRUE, the function returns immediately, and changes are reported by signaling this event. When FALSE, *hEvent* is ignored and the function waits until the specified key or subkeys have changed.

RELATED FUNCTIONS

RegDeleteKey()
RegEnumKey()
RegEnumKeyEx()
RegEnumValue()
RegQueryInfoKey()
RegQueryValue()
RegQueryValueEx()

LONG RegOpenKey(HKEY *hKey,*
LPCSTR *lpszSubKey,*
PHKEY *phkResult*)

RegOpenKey() opens a subkey. **RegOpenKeyEx()** should be used by new applications. If the function is successful, a value of **ERROR_SUCCESS** is returned. If the function is not successful, an error value is returned.

hKey is the handle of an open key or one of these predefined handles:

HKEY_CLASSES_ROOT
HKEY_CURRENT_USER
HKEY_LOCAL_MACHINE
HKEY_USERS

The key being opened will be a subkey of *hKey*.
lpszSubKey is a pointer to the name of the subkey to open. *phkResult* is a pointer to a variable that, on return, contains the handle of the subkey.

RELATED FUNCTIONS

RegCreateKey()
RegCreateKeyEx()
RegDeleteKey()
RegOpenKeyEx()

LONG RegOpenKeyEx(HKEY *hKey,*
LPCTSTR *lpszSubKey,*
DWORD *dwReserved,*
REGSAM *samDesired,*
PHKEY *phkResult*)

RegOpenKeyEx() opens a subkey. It is an extended version of **Reg-OpenKey()**. If the function is successful, a value of **ERROR_SUCCESS** is returned. If the function is not successful, an error value is returned.

hKey is the handle of an open key or one of these predefined handles:

HKEY_CLASSES_ROOT
HKEY_CURRENT_USER
HKEY_LOCAL_MACHINE
HKEY_USERS

The key being opened will be a subkey of *hKey*.

lpszSubKey is a pointer to the name of the subkey to open. (If *lpszSubKey* is NULL, a handle to *hKey* is opened.)

dwReserved is reserved and must be zero. *samDesired* determines the security access for the subkey handle. This value can be any combination of the values shown here.

Value	Purpose
KEY_ALL_ACCESS	A predefined combination that includes **KEY_QUERY_VALUE, KEY_ENUMERATE_SUB_KEYS, KEY_NOTIFY, KEY_CREATE_SUB_KEY, KEY_CREATE_LINK,** and **KEY_SET_VALUE**
KEY_CREATE_LINK	Allows the creation of a symbolic link
KEY_CREATE_SUB_KEY	Allows the creation of subkeys
KEY_ENUMERATE_SUB_KEYS	Allows the enumeration of subkeys
KEY_EXECUTE	Allows a read access
KEY_NOTIFY	Allows a notification change
KEY_QUERY_VALUE	Allows a query of subkey data
KEY_READ	A predefined combination that includes **KEY_QUERY_VALUE, KEY_ENUMERATE_SUB_KEYS,** and **KEY_NOTIFY**

Value	Purpose
KEY_SET_VALUE	Allows subkey data to be set
KEY_WRITE	Predefined combination that includes **KEY_SET_VALUE** and **KEY_CREATE_SUB_KEY**

phkResult is a pointer to a variable that, on return, contains the handle of the subkey. **RegOpenKeyEx()** does not create the key if it does not already exist in the registry.

USAGE

Here is a small portion of code that illustrates the use of this function.

```
HKEY hKeyRoot;
HKEY hKey;
CHAR RegPath[MAX_PATH];
DWORD retCode;
CHAR MyBuffer[80];
  .
  .
  .

retCode = RegOpenKeyEx(hKeyRoot,    // Root Key handle
                       RegPath,     // Child key path name
                       0,
                       KEY_EXECUTE, // Read access request
                       &hKey);      // Returned key's address

if (retCode) {
  wsprintf (MyBuffer, "RegOpenKeyEx = %d", retCode);
  MessageBox (hWnd, MyBuffer, "KeyData", MB_OK);
}
```

RELATED FUNCTIONS

RegCreateKeyEx()
RegDeleteKey()
RegOpenKey()

LONG RegQueryInfoKey(HKEY *hKey,*
LPTSTR *lpszClass,*
LPDWORD *lpClassSize,*
LPDWORD *lpdwReserved,*
LPDWORD *lpcSubKeys,*
LPDWORD *lpcchMaxSubkey,*
LPDWORD *lpcchMaxClass,*
LPDWORD *lpcValues,*
LPDWORD *lpcchMaxValName,*
LPDWORD *lpcbMaxValueData,*
LPDWORD *lpcbSecurityDesc,*
PFILETIME *lpftLastWriteTime***)**

RegQueryInfoKey() obtains information on a registry key. If the function is successful, a value of **ERROR_SUCCESS** is returned. If the function is not successful, an error value is returned.

hKey is the handle of an open key or one of these predefined handles:

HKEY_CLASSES_ROOT
HKEY_CURRENT_USER
HKEY_LOCAL_MACHINE
HKEY_USERS

hKey must have **KEY_QUERY_VALUE** access privileges.

lpszClass is a pointer to an array that, on return, contains the class name for the key. *lpClassSize* points to a variable that contains the length of the array pointed to by *lpszClass*. On return, this variable will contain the number of characters copied to the array.

lpdwReserved is a pointer that is currently reserved and should be set to NULL.

lpcSubKeys is a pointer to a variable that, on return, contains the number of subkeys associated with the key. *lpcchMaxSubkey* is a pointer to a variable that, on return, contains the length of the longest subkey name. *lpcchMaxClass* is a pointer to a variable that, on return, contains the length of the longest subkey class name.

On return, the following variables will be set: *lpcValues* is a pointer to a variable that will contain the number of values associated with the key.

lpcchMaxValName is a pointer to a variable that will contain the length of the name of the longest value associated with the key. *lpcbMaxValueData* is a pointer to a variable that will contain the length of the longest data associated with the key.

lpcbSecurityDesc is a pointer to a variable that, on return, contains the length of the security descriptor for the key. *lpftLastWriteTime* is a pointer to a variable that, on return, contains a **FILETIME** structure that holds the last time the key or its related elements were changed.

USAGE

The **FILETIME** structure is shown here.

```
typedef struct _FILETIME {
  DWORD dwLowDateTime;
  DWORD dwHighDateTime;
} FILETIME;
```

Here, **dwLowDateTime** holds the low-order 32 bits and **dwHighDateTime** holds the high-order 32 bits of the time.

Here is a small portion of code that illustrates the use of this function.

```
CHAR      ClassName[MAX_PATH] = "";
DWORD     dwcClassLen = MAX_PATH;
DWORD     dwcSubKeys;
DWORD     dwcMaxSubKey;
DWORD     dwcMaxClass;
DWORD     dwcValues;
DWORD     dwcMaxValueName;
DWORD     dwcMaxValueData;
DWORD     dwcSecDesc;
FILETIME  ftLastWriteTime;
        .
        .
        .

RegQueryInfoKey(hKey,          // handle for key
            ClassName,         // class name buffer
            &dwcClassLen,      // class string length
            NULL,
            &dwcSubKeys,       // number of sub keys
            &dwcMaxSubKey,     // sub key (max) size
            &dwcMaxClass,      // class string (max) length
            &dwcValues,        // Number of values for key
```

```
          &dwcMaxValueName,   // value name (max) length
          &dwcMaxValueData,   // value data (max)
          &dwcSecDesc,        // security descriptor
          &ftLastWriteTime);  // time of last write
```

RELATED FUNCTIONS

RegDeleteKey()
RegEnumKey()
RegEnumKeyEx()
RegEnumValue()
RegQueryValue()
RegQueryValueEx()

LONG RegQueryValue(HKEY *hKey,*
LPCSTR *lpszSubKey,*
LPSTR *lpszValue,*
LONG FAR **lpValueSize*)

RegQueryValue() obtains the value associated with the unnamed value for a key in the registry. If the function is successful, a value of **ERROR_SUCCESS** is returned. If the function is not successful, an error value is returned. **RegQueryValueEx()** should be used for new applications.

 hKey is the handle of an open key or one of these predefined handles:

HKEY_CLASSES_ROOT
HKEY_CURRENT_USER
HKEY_LOCAL_MACHINE
HKEY_USERS

 hKey must have **KEY_QUERY_VALUE** access rights.

 lpszSubKey is a pointer to the name of the subkey from which to obtain the value. If *lpszSubKey* is NULL, then the value is obtained from the key specified in *hKey*.

 lpszValue is a pointer to an array that, on return, will contain the value associated with the specified key. This parameter may be NULL, in which case the value is not obtained.

lpValueSize is a pointer to a variable that contains the size of the *lpszValue* array. On return, this variable will contain the number of characters copied to the array.

USAGE

If the array pointed to by *lpszValue* is not large enough, the function returns the value **ERROR_MORE_DATA** and saves the required buffer size in the variable pointed to by *lpValueSize*.

RELATED FUNCTIONS

RegEnumKey()
RegEnumKeyEx()
RegEnumValue()
RegQueryInfoKey()
RegQueryValueEx()
RegSetValue()
RegSetValueEx()

LONG RegQueryValueEx(HKEY *hKey,*
        LPTSTR *lpszValueName,*
        LPDWORD *lpdwReserved,*
        LPDWORD *lpdwType,*
        LPBYTE *lpbData,*
        LPDWORD *lpDataSize)*

RegQueryValueEx() obtains extended value information associated with a registry key. If the function is successful, a value of **ERROR_SUCCESS** is returned. If the function is not successful, an error value is returned.

hKey is the handle of an open key or one of these predefined handles:

HKEY_CLASSES_ROOT
HKEY_CURRENT_USER
HKEY_LOCAL_MACHINE
HKEY_USERS

The key must have **KEY_QUERY_VALUE** access privileges.

lpszValueName is a pointer to the name of the value desired. *lpdwReserved* is currently reserved and must be set to NULL.

lpdwType is a pointer to a variable that, on return, contains the type of the value. Valid types are shown here. (When the type is not required, set this parameter to NULL.)

Value	Type
REG_BINARY	Data in any binary form
REG_DWORD	Data as a 32-bit number
REG_DWORD_LITTLE_ENDIAN	Data as a 32-bit number in little-endian format (**LSB** in low-memory, **MSB** in high-memory—common to Intel design)
REG_DWORD_BIG_ENDIAN	Data as a 32-bit number in big-endian format (**LSB** in high-memory, **MSB** in low-memory)
REG_EXPAND_SZ	Data as a null-terminated string containing unexpanded references to environment variables
REG_LINK	Data as a Unicode symbolic link
REG_MULTI_SZ	Data as an array of null-terminated strings, terminate with two null characters
REG_NONE	Data with no defined value type
REG_RESOURCE_LIST	Data as a device-driver resource list
REG_SZ	Data as a null-terminated string, Unicode or ANSI

lpbData is a pointer to a buffer that, on return, contains the data for the value. It can be NULL if the data is not needed. *lpDataSize* is a pointer to a variable that contains the size of the buffer in bytes. On return, *lpDataSize* will point to the number of bytes stored in the buffer.

RELATED FUNCTIONS

ExpandEnvironmentStrings()
RegEnumKey()
RegEnumKeyEx()
RegEnumValue()
RegQueryInfoKey()
RegQueryValue()

LONG RegReplaceKey(HKEY *hKey,*
LPCTSTR *lpszSubKey,*
LPCTSTR *lpszNewFile,*
LPCTSTR *lpszBackupFile*)

RegReplaceKey() changes the file associated with a key. When the system is restarted, the values stored in the new file will be used by the key and its subkeys. If the function is successful, a value of **ERROR_SUCCESS** is returned. If the function is not successful, an error value is returned.

hKey is the handle of an open key or one of these predefined handles:

> HKEY_CLASSES_ROOT
> HKEY_CURRENT_USER
> HKEY_LOCAL_MACHINE
> HKEY_USERS

lpszSubKey is a pointer to the name of the key or subkeys whose file is being changed. (It must be a subkey of *hKey*.) When *hKey* is a predefined value, *lpszSubKey* can be set to NULL. Otherwise, the key must descend directly from **HKEY_LOCAL_MACHINE** or **HKEY_USERS**.

lpszNewFile is a pointer to the filename of the new file. The function copies the old registration file (that is, the one being replaced) to the file whose name is pointed to by *lpszBackupFile*. (When the FAT file system is used, these filenames must not include an extension.)

USAGE

The replacement file is generally created using **RegSaveKey()**.

RELATED FUNCTIONS

RegDeleteKey()
RegLoadKey()
RegRestoreKey()

LONG RegRestoreKey(HKEY *hKey*,
LPCTSTR *lpszFile*,
DWORD *dwVolatile*)

RegRestoreKey() obtains the registry information in a file. If the function is successful, a value of **ERROR_SUCCESS** is returned. If the function is not successful, an error value is returned.

hKey is the handle of an open key or one of these predefined handles:

    HKEY_CLASSES_ROOT
    HKEY_CURRENT_USER
    HKEY_LOCAL_MACHINE
    HKEY_USERS

lpszFile is a pointer to the registry file. The information contained in this file will replace any information associated with the open key. (When the FAT file system is used, this filename must not include an extension.)

dwVolatile is used to create a volatile key. If a key is volatile, it will exist only until Windows is reloaded. It a key is not volatile, it will maintain its value. To create a volatile key, pass **REG_WHOLE_HIVE_VOLATILE** in the *dwVolatile* parameter. For a non-volatile key, specify zero. Volatile keys only apply if *hKey* is either **HKEY_USERS** or **HKEY_LOCAL_MACHINE**.

RELATED FUNCTIONS

RegDeleteKey()
RegLoadKey()
RegReplaceKey()
RegSaveKey()

LONG RegSaveKey(HKEY *hKey*, LPCTSTR *lpszFile*,
LPSECURITY_ATTRIBUTES *lpsa*)

RegSaveKey() saves a key, its subkeys, and associated values in a file. The user must have a *SeBackupPrivilege* security privilege. If the function is successful, a value of **ERROR_SUCCESS** is returned. If the function is not successful, an error value is returned.

hKey is the handle of an open key or one of these predefined handles:

HKEY_CLASSES_ROOT
HKEY_CURRENT_USER
HKEY_LOCAL_MACHINE
HKEY_USERS

The information about the key is saved into the file whose name is pointed to by *lpszFile*. This file must not preexist. (If the file system is FAT, then the name may not include an extension.)

lpsa is a pointer to a **SECURITY_ATTRIBUTES** structure. If NULL, the default security descriptor is used.

RELATED FUNCTIONS

RegCreateKeyEx()
RegDeleteKey()
RegLoadKey()
RegReplaceKey()
RegRestoreKey()

LONG RegSetKeySecurity(HKEY *hKey,*
SECURITY_INFORMATION *Si,*
PSECURITY_DESCRIPTOR *pSd*)

RegSetKeySecurity() sets the security attributes associated with a key. If the function is successful, a value of **ERROR_SUCCESS** is returned. If the function is not successful, an error value is returned.

hKey is the handle of an open key or predefined handle for which the security descriptor is set. Predefined handles are shown here.

HKEY_CLASSES_ROOT
HKEY_CURRENT_USER
HKEY_LOCAL_MACHINE
HKEY_USERS

Si contains the **SECURITY_INFORMATION** structure.

pSd is a pointer to a **SECURITY_DESCRIPTOR** structure that contains the new security attributes.

USAGE

The calling function must have one of the following:

WRITE_OWNER	permission
SE_TAKE_OWNERSHIP_NAME	privilege
WRITE_DAC	permission
SE_SECURITY_NAME	privilege

RELATED FUNCTIONS

RegDeleteKey()
RegGetKeySecurity()

LONG RegSetValue(HKEY *hKey,*
LPCSTR *lpszSubKey,*
DWORD *dwType,*
LPCSTR *lpszString,*
DWORD *dwStringSize*)

RegSetValue() associates a string with a key. **RegSetValueEx()** should be used for new applications. If the function is successful, a value of **ERROR_SUCCESS** is returned. If the function is not successful, an error value is returned.

hKey is the handle of an open key or one of these predefined handles:

HKEY_CLASSES_ROOT
HKEY_CURRENT_USER
HKEY_LOCAL_MACHINE
HKEY_USERS

hKey must have **KEY_SET_VALUE** access privileges.

lpszSubKey is a pointer to the name of the subkey that will be associated with the specified string. *lpszSubKey* can be set to NULL, in which case *hKey* will be used. If the subkey does not exist, this function will create it.

dwType contains the type of the string being associated with the key. This value must be **REG_SZ**, although other values may be supported by future releases of Windows.

lpszString is a pointer to the string to link with the key. *dwStringSize* is the length of the string less the terminating null character.

RELATED FUNCTIONS

RegFlushKey()
RegQueryValue()
RegQueryValueEx()
RegSetValueEx()

LONG RegSetValueEx(HKEY *hKey,*
LPCTSTR *lpszValueName,*
DWORD *dwReserved,*
DWORD *dwType,*
CONST LPBYTE *lpbData,*
DWORD *dwDataSize*)

RegSetValueEx() saves data, along with value and type information, in the value field of a registry key. If the function is successful, a value of **ERROR_SUCCESS** is returned. If the function is not successful, an error value is returned.

hKey is the handle of an open key or one of these predefined handles:

HKEY_CLASSES_ROOT
HKEY_CURRENT_USER
HKEY_LOCAL_MACHINE
HKEY_USERS

The key must be opened with **KEY_SET_VALUE** access rights.

lpszValueName is a pointer to the name of the value being changed. *dwReserved* is currently reserved and must be set to NULL. *dwType* gives the type of information to be stored as the value's data. Values that can be used for this parameter are shown here.

Value	Type
REG_BINARY	Data in any binary form
REG_DWORD	Data as a 32-bit number
REG_DWORD_LITTLE_ENDIAN	Data as a 32-bit number in little-endian format (**LSB** in low-memory, **MSB** in high-memory—common to Intel design)
REG_DWORD_BIG_ENDIAN	Data as a 32-bit number in big-endian format (**LSB** in high-memory, **MSB** in low-memory)
REG_EXPAND_SZ	Data as a null-terminated string containing unexpanded references to environment variables
REG_LINK	Data as a Unicode symbolic link
REG_MULTI_SZ	Data as an array of null-terminated strings, terminate with two null characters
REG_NONE	Data with no defined value type
REG_RESOURCE_LIST	Data as a device-driver resource list
REG_SZ	Data as a null-terminated string, Unicode or ANSI

lpbData is a pointer to a buffer. This buffer holds the data to be linked with the value. *dwDataSize* gives the size of this data (in bytes). For string data, the null-terminator must also be counted.

RELATED FUNCTIONS

RegFlushKey()
RegQueryValue()
RegQueryValueEx()
RegSetValue()

A Complete Programming Example

Here is a complete C program that illustrates several functions described in this chapter. This program displays registration information in a window with a gray background.

```c
/*
  Demonstrate registration functions.
*/

#include <windows.h>
#include <shellapi.h>

LONG FAR PASCAL WndProc(HWND, UINT, WPARAM, LPARAM);

char szProgName[] = "ProgName"; /* name of window class */

int PASCAL WinMain(HINSTANCE hInst, HINSTANCE hPreInst,
                   LPSTR lpszCmdLine, int nCmdShow)
{
  HWND hWnd;
  MSG lpMsg;
  WNDCLASS wcApp;

  if (!hPreInst) { /* if no previous instance */
    wcApp.lpszClassName = szProgName; /* window class name */
    wcApp.hInstance     = hInst; /* handle to this instance */
    wcApp.lpfnWndProc   = WndProc; /* window function */
    wcApp.hCursor       = LoadCursor(NULL, IDC_ARROW);
    wcApp.hIcon         = LoadIcon(NULL, IDI_APPLICATION);
    wcApp.lpszMenuName  = NULL;

    /* make the background of window gray */
    wcApp.hbrBackground = GetStockObject(GRAY_BRUSH);
    wcApp.style         = 0; /* use default window style */
    wcApp.cbClsExtra    = 0; /* no extra info */
    wcApp.cbWndExtra    = 0; /* no extra info */

    /* register the window class */
    if (!RegisterClass (&wcApp))
      return FALSE;
  }

  /* Now that window has been registered, a window
          can be created. */
  hWnd = CreateWindow(szProgName,
                      "Demonstrate Registration Functions",
                      WS_OVERLAPPEDWINDOW,
                      CW_USEDEFAULT,
                      CW_USEDEFAULT,
```

```
                           CW_USEDEFAULT,
                           CW_USEDEFAULT,
                           (HWND)NULL,
                           (HMENU) NULL,
                           (HANDLE)hInst,
                           (LPSTR)NULL);

   /* Display the Window. */
   ShowWindow(hWnd, nCmdShow);
   UpdateWindow(hWnd);

   /* Create the message loop. */
   while (GetMessage(&lpMsg, NULL, 0, 0)) {
     TranslateMessage(&lpMsg); /* allow use of keyboard */
     DispatchMessage(&lpMsg); /* return control to Windows */
   }
   return(lpMsg.wParam);
}


/* Window Function. */
LONG FAR PASCAL WndProc(HWND hWnd, UINT messg,
                        WPARAM wParam, LPARAM lParam)
{
   HKEY hkProtocol;

   switch (messg) {
     case WM_CREATE:
       if (RegCreateKey(HKEY_CLASSES_ROOT,
                        "MyDocument\\protocol\\StdFileEditing",
                        &hkProtocol)== ERROR_SUCCESS)
         MessageBox(hWnd, "Created a key", "Registration", MB_OK);
       else
         MessageBox(hWnd, "No key created", "Registration", MB_OK);

       if (RegSetValue(hkProtocol, "language\\0",
                       REG_SZ, "COPY", 4)== ERROR_SUCCESS)
         MessageBox(hWnd, "Created a sub-key", "Registration", MB_OK);
       else
         MessageBox(hWnd, "No sub-key created", "Registration", MB_OK);

       RegCloseKey(hkProtocol);
       break;

     case WM_DESTROY: /* terminate the program */
```

```
        PostQuitMessage(0);
        break;

    default:
        return(DefWindowProc(hWnd, messg, wParam, lParam));
    }
    return(0L);
}
```

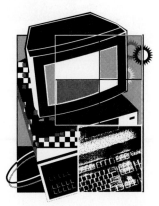

Chapter 30

Resource Management

H I S chapter describes Windows' resource management functions. These functions can be used to enumerate, find, load, and lock resources. A complete programming example at the end of this chapter illustrates several of these resource management functions.

Win32 only

BOOL EnumResourceLanguages(HINSTANCE *hModule*,
LPCTSTR *lpszType*,
LPCTSTR *lpszResName*,
ENUMRESLANGPROC *lpEnumFunc*,
LONG *lParm*)

EnumResourceLanguages() searches a module for the given type and name of resource. Each time one is found, its language is reported to a user-defined callback function. **EnumResourceLanguages()** function returns TRUE if successful (that is, a name is enumerated), and FALSE if unsuccessful.

hModule is the module handle of the executable file that holds the resources. When set to NULL, resource names in the calling process's executable file will be enumerated.

lpszType is a pointer to the type name of the resources being enumerated. It can be any value selected from Table 30-1.

lpszResName is a pointer to the name of the resource.

lpEnumFunc is a pointer to a user-defined callback function. This function is called each time a resource is found. *lParm* contains a value to be passed to the callback function from the application. (This value may be used for any purpose you like.)

Name	Name type
RT_ACCELERATOR	Keyboard accelerator table
RT_BITMAP	Bitmap resources
RT_DIALOG	Dialog box resources
RT_FONT	Font resources
RT_FONTDIR	Font directory resources
RT_MENU	Menu resources
RT_RCDATA	Raw data resources
RT_STRING	String table resources
RT_MESSAGETABLE	Message table resources
RT_CURSOR	Cursor resources
RT_GROUP_CURSOR	Cursor resources (non-hardware dependent)
RT_ICON	Icon resources
RT_GROUP_ICON	Icon resources (non-hardware dependent)
RT_VERSION	Version resources

Table 30-1
Resource Names

USAGE

The callback function pointed to by *lpEnumFunc* must have this prototype.

```
BOOL CALLBACK EnumResourceFunc(HANDLE hMod,
                    LPCTSTR lpszType,
                    LPCTSTR lpszResName,
                    WORD wLang,
                    LONG lParam);
```

Of course, the name of this function is arbitrary. The function parameters receive the module handle of the file being searched (*hMod*), a pointer to the type of resources being searched for (*lpszType*), a pointer to the name of the resource being enumerated (*lpszResName*), the resource's language ID (*wLang*), and a user-defined value specified by **EnumResourceLanguages()** (*lParam*). To continue enumerating languages, the function must return TRUE. To stop, it must return FALSE.

Resources are enumerated until FALSE is returned by the callback function or all resources have been found.

BOOL EnumResourceNames(HINSTANCE *hModule,*
LPCTSTR *lpszType,*
ENUMRESNAMEPROC *lpEnumFunc,*
LONG *lParm*)

EnumResourceNames() searches a module for the given type of resource. Each time one is found, it's name is reported to a user-defined callback function. **EnumResourceNames()** returns TRUE if successful (that is, a name is enumerated), and FALSE if unsuccessful.

hModule is the module handle of the executable file that holds the resources. When set to NULL, resource names in the calling process's executable file will be enumerated.

lpszType is a pointer to the type name of the resources being enumerated. It can be any value selected from Table 30-1.

lpEnumFunc is a pointer to a user-defined callback function. This function is called each time a resource name is found. *lParm* contains a value to be passed to the callback function from the application. (This value may be used for any purpose you like.)

USAGE

The callback function pointed to by *lpEnumFunc* must have this prototype.

```
BOOL CALLBACK EnumResourceFunc(HANDLE hMod,
                               LPCTSTR lpszType,
                               LPTSTR lpszResName,
                               LONG lParam);
```

Of course, the name of this function is arbitrary. The function parameters receive the module handle of the file being searched (*hMod*), a pointer to the type of names being searched for (*lpszType*), a pointer to the name of the resource being enumerated (*lpszResName*), and a user-defined value specified by **EnumResourceNames()** (*lParam*). To continue enumerating names, the function must return TRUE. To stop, it must return FALSE.

Resources are enumerated until FALSE is returned by the callback function or all resources have been found.

RELATED FUNCTIONS

EnumResourceLanguages()
EnumResourceTypes()

BOOL EnumResourceTypes(HINSTANCE *hModule,* ENUMRESTYPEPROC *lpEnumFunc,* LONG *lParm*)

EnumResourceTypes() examines a module for resources. When it finds a resource, it passes its type to a callback function defined by the application. **EnumResourceTypes()** returns TRUE if successful, and FALSE if unsuccessful.

hModule is the module handle of the executable file that holds the resources. When set to NULL, resource names in the calling process's executable file will be enumerated.

lpEnumFunc is a pointer to the callback function which is called each time a resource is enumerated. *lParm* contains a value to be passed to the callback function from the application. (This value may be used for any purpose you like.)

USAGE

The callback function pointed to by *lpEnumFunc* must have this prototype.

```
BOOL CALLBACK EnumResourceFunc(HANDLE hMod,
                               LPTSTR lpszType,
                               LONG lParam);
```

Of course, the name of this function is arbitrary. The function parameters receive the module handle of the file being searched (*hMod*), a pointer to the resource type (*lpszType*), and a user-defined value specified by **EnumResourceTypes()** (*lParam*). To continue enumerating types, the function must return TRUE. To stop, it must return FALSE.

The type names are shown in Table 30-1.

Resource types are enumerated until FALSE is returned by the callback function or all resources have been found.

RELATED FUNCTIONS

EnumResourceLanguages()
EnumResourceNames()

HRSRC FindResource(HINSTANCE *hModule,*
LPCTSTR *lpszName,*
LPCTSTR *lpszType)*

FindResource() finds where a resource is located within a module. If the function is successful, a handle to a resource information block is returned. If the function is not successful, a NULL is returned.

hModule is the module handle of the executable file that holds the resources. *lpszName* is a pointer to the name of the resource. *lpszType* is a pointer to the resource type (shown in Table 30-1).

USAGE

The amount of memory that resources require can be reduced by referencing them by their ID value instead of directly by their name.

lpszName or *lpszType* can be viewed as being made up of a high- and low-order word. If either parameter's high-order word is zero, its corresponding low-order word gives the ID value of the name or type of resource. If the high-order word for either parameter is non-zero, the parameter is a long pointer to a null-terminated string. If a # is the first character in this string, the string is interpreted as being a number that gives the ID of the name or type for the resource.

The handle returned by **FindResource()** can be use by **LoadResource()** to load the resource. Remember, the easiest way to load standard resources, such as bitmaps, icons, and the like, is to use functions such as **LoadBitmap()**, **LoadIcon()**, and so on.

Here is a small portion of code that illustrates the use of this function.

```
static HANDLE hRes;
static HRSRC hStrRes;
char szMyStr[12];
    .
    .
    .

LoadString(hInstance, IDS_STR, szMyStr, sizeof szMyStr);
hStrRes = FindResource(hInstance, szMyStr, "TEXT");
```

RELATED FUNCTIONS

FindResourceEx()
FormatMessage()
LoadAccelerators()
LoadBitmap()
LoadCursor()
LoadIcon()
LoadMenu()
LoadResource()
LoadString()
LockResource()
SizeofResource()

HRSRC FindResourceEx(HINSTANCE *hModule,*
LPCTSTR *lpszType,*
LPCTSTR *lpszName,*
WORD *wLang*)

FindResourceEx() finds where a resource is located within a module. It is an expanded form of **FindResource()**. If the function is successful, a handle to a resource information block is returned. If the function is not successful, a NULL is returned.

hModule is the module handle of the executable file that holds the resource. When set to NULL, the calling process's executable file will be searched.

lpszType is a pointer to the resource type and can be any of the types shown earlier in Table 30-1. *lpszName* is a pointer to the name of the resource.

wLang is the language of the resource. When this value is **MAKELANGID (LANG_NEUTRAL, SUBLANG_NEUTRAL)**, the language is the one currently associated with the calling thread. The **MAKELANGID** macro can be used to create this value if the above default is not desired.

USAGE

The amount of memory that resources require can be reduced by referencing them by their ID value instead of directly by their name.

lpszName or *lpszType* can be viewed as being made up of a high- and low-order word. If either parameter's high-order word is zero, its corresponding low-order word gives the ID value of the name or type of resource. If the high-order word for either parameter is non-zero, the parameter is a long pointer to a null-terminated string. If a # is the first character in this string, the string is interpreted as being a number that gives the ID of the name or type for the resource.

The handle returned by **FindResourceEx()** can be use by **LoadResource()** to load the resource. Remember, the easiest way to load standard resources, such as bitmaps, icons, and the like, is to use functions such as **LoadBitmap()**, **LoadIcon()**, and so on.

RELATED FUNCTIONS

FindResource()
LoadResource()

BOOL FreeResource(HGLOBAL *hglbResource*)

FreeResource() releases a resource. Resources are not freed until there are no longer any active references to them. The **FreeResource()** function operates by decrementing the reference count associated with a loaded resource. When this count becomes zero, the resource is freed. The function returns zero if successful, and non-zero if unsuccessful.

NOTE

This function is now obsolete under Win32.

hglbResource is the handle of the global data used by the resource. The handle is created with **LoadResource()**. Remember, **LoadResource()** increments the resource's reference count and **FreeResource()** decrements it. Not until the reference count is zero does the resource actually get released.

USAGE

Here is a small portion of code that illustrates the use of this function.

```
static HANDLE hRes;
    .
    .
    .
FreeResource(hRes);
```

RELATED FUNCTIONS

LoadResource()
LockResource()

HGLOBAL LoadResource(HINSTANCE *hModule*, HRSRC *hResInfo*)

LoadResource() loads a resource. If successful, the function returns a handle to the global memory block holding the data for the resource; if unsuccessful, it returns NULL.

hModule is the handle of the module containing the executable file holding the resource. When set to NULL, the calling process's executable file will be searched. *hResInfo* is the handle of the resource itself. The resource's handle is generally obtained by calling **FindResource()** or **FindResourceEx()**.

USAGE

Here is a small portion of code that illustrates the use of this function.

```
static HANDLE hRes;
static HRSRC hStrRes;
       .
       .
       .
hRes = LoadResource(hInstance, hStrRes);
```

RELATED FUNCTIONS

FindResource()
LoadLibrary()
LoadModule()
LockResource()

LPVOID LockResource(HGLOBAL *hglb*)

LockResource() locks a resource in system memory. If the function is successful and the loaded resource is locked, a pointer to the first byte of the resource is returned. If the function is not successful, a NULL is returned.

hglb is a handle for the resource to be locked, which is obtained by **LoadResource()**.

USAGE

A locked resource must be unlocked by calling **UnlockResource()**. However, for Windows NT/Win32 applications this is no longer necessary.

Here is a small portion of code that illustrates the use of this function.

```
static HANDLE hRes;
char far *lpString;
       .
       .
       .
lpString = LockResource(hRes);
```

RELATED FUNCTIONS

FindResource()
FindResourceEx()
LoadResource()

DWORD SizeofResource(HINSTANCE *hModule,* HRSRC *hrsrc*)

SizeofResource() returns the approximate size of a resource. It returns zero on failure.

hModule is the module handle of the executable file holding the resource. *hrsrc* is the handle of the resource. This handle is obtained from either **FindResource()** or **FindResourceEx()**.

USAGE

Caution should be used, since the return value might not be the actual size of the resource due to alignment problems.

RELATED FUNCTIONS

FindResource()
FindResourceEx()
LoadResource()
LockResource()

BOOL UnlockResource(HGLOBAL *hglblResData*)

UnlockResource() unlocks the resource specified by *hglblResData* and decrements the reference count of the resource by one. (This macro is now obsolete under Windows NT/Win32.) The call returns zero if successful, and non-zero if unsuccessful.

hglblResData is the handle of the global memory object that is to be unlocked.

RELATED FUNCTIONS

GlobalUnlock()
LoadResource()
LockResource()

A Complete Programming Example

Here is a complete Windows NT program that illustrates the use of several resource functions. This application consists of the following files:

NTRES.H, a header file
NTRES.RC, a resource file
NTRES.C, the source code
NTRES.ASC, an ASCII text file

Here is the code for the header file:

```
#define IDS_STR 0
```

The resource file code is shown here.

```
#include "ntres.h"

MyStr TEXT c:\msvcnt\ntres.asc

STRINGTABLE
{
   IDS_STR, "MyStr"
}
```

The Windows NT source code is straightforward. Here is the complete listing.

```
//
//  ntres
//  A simple Windows NT application that demonstrates the use
//  of resource functions.
//  This program will find, load, unlock, lock and free a
//  string table resource.
```

```
//

#include <windows.h>
#include "ntres.h"

LRESULT CALLBACK WndProc(HWND, UINT, WPARAM, LPARAM);

char szProgName[] = "ProgName";
HINSTANCE hInstance;

int WINAPI WinMain(HINSTANCE hInst, HINSTANCE hPreInst,
                   LPSTR lpszCmdLine, int nCmdShow)
{
  HWND hWnd;
  MSG lpMsg;
  WNDCLASS wcApp;
  if (!hPreInst) {
    wcApp.lpszClassName = szProgName;
    wcApp.hInstance     = hInst;
    wcApp.lpfnWndProc   = WndProc;
    wcApp.hCursor       = LoadCursor(NULL, IDC_ARROW);
    wcApp.hIcon         = NULL;
    wcApp.lpszMenuName  = NULL;
    wcApp.hbrBackground = GetStockObject(WHITE_BRUSH);
    wcApp.style         = CS_HREDRAW | CS_VREDRAW;
    wcApp.cbClsExtra    = 0;
    wcApp.cbWndExtra    = 0;
    if (!RegisterClass (&wcApp))
      return FALSE;
  }
  hWnd = CreateWindow(szProgName, "Using Resources Under Windows NT",
                      WS_OVERLAPPEDWINDOW, CW_USEDEFAULT,
                      CW_USEDEFAULT, CW_USEDEFAULT,
                      CW_USEDEFAULT, (HWND)NULL, (HMENU)NULL,
                      (HANDLE)hInst, (LPSTR)NULL);
  ShowWindow(hWnd, nCmdShow);
  UpdateWindow(hWnd);
  while (GetMessage(&lpMsg, NULL, 0, 0)) {
    TranslateMessage(&lpMsg);
    DispatchMessage(&lpMsg);
  }
  return(lpMsg.wParam);
}
```

```
LRESULT CALLBACK WndProc(HWND hWnd, UINT messg,
                         WPARAM wParam, LPARAM lParam)
{
  HDC hdc;
  PAINTSTRUCT ps;
  static HANDLE hRes;
  static HRSRC hStrRes;
  char szMyStr[12];
  char far *lpString;
  RECT rect;

  switch (messg)
  {
    case WM_CREATE:
      LoadString(hInstance, IDS_STR, szMyStr, sizeof szMyStr);
      hStrRes = FindResource(hInstance, szMyStr, "TEXT");
      hRes = LoadResource(hInstance, hStrRes);
      lpString = LockResource(hRes);
      GlobalUnlock(hRes);
      return(0);

    case WM_PAINT:
      hdc = BeginPaint(hWnd, &ps);

      lpString = LockResource(hRes);
      GetClientRect(hWnd, &rect);
      rect.left += 10;
      rect.top += 12;
      DrawText(hdc, lpString, -1, &rect, DT_LEFT);

      GlobalUnlock(hRes);

      ValidateRect(hWnd, NULL);
      EndPaint(hWnd, &ps);
      break;

    case WM_DESTROY:
      FreeResource(hRes);
      PostQuitMessage(0);
      break;

    default:
      return(DefWindowProc(hWnd, messg, wParam, lParam));
  }
```

```
   return(0L);
}
```

This application loads a string resource, which can be as simple as a few lines of text, as shown in the file NTRES.ASC.

```
This is just a simple line of text.
There is nothing fancy here.
What do you think of this example?
```

Chapter 31

Security

T H I S chapter describes Windows' security functions. These functions are used with Windows NT/Win32 applications to manage security privileges for files and file I/O. These functions are only valid when applied to the NTFS file system.

BOOL AccessCheck
(PSECURITY_DESCRIPTOR *psdDescriptor,*
HANDLE *hClientToken,*
DWORD *dwAccessSelect,*
PGENERIC_MAPPING *pGMappina,*
PPRIVILEGE_SET *pPSet,*
LPDWORD *lpdwpPSetLength,*
LPDWORD *lpdwGrantedAccess,*
LPBOOL *lpbStatus*)

AccessCheck() checks the calling application's requested access of a particular object against the object's assigned access privilege level. *psdDescriptor* is a pointer to the object's assigned access privilege level. *hClientToken* is the handle to the object in question. *dwAccessSelect* is set by the calling application and specifies the type of access desired of the object.

pGMappina is a pointer to the mapping associated with the particular type of object in question. *pPSet* is a pointer to the buffer used by **AccessCheck()** to return the privileges used to perform the access validation. *lpdwpPSetLength* defines the length of the buffer pointed to by *pPSet,* in bytes.

lpdwGrantedAccess is a pointer to a double-word buffer that **AccessCheck()** will use to return the access mask indicating which accesses were granted. *lpbStatus* contains a returned TRUE or FALSE indicating the success or failure of the access check.

The function returns TRUE if successful, and FALSE otherwise.

USAGE

If **AccessCheck()** returns TRUE, the *lpdwGrantedAccess* access mask matches the *dwAccessSelect* access mask.

RELATED FUNCTIONS

AreAllAccessesGranted()
AreAnyAccessesGranted()
PrivilegeCheck()

BOOL AccessCheckAndAuditAlarm
(LPTSTR *lptstrSubSysName,*
LPVOID *hObject,*
LPTSTR *lptstrObjType,*
LPTSTR *lptstrObjName,*
PSECURITY_DESCRIPTOR *psdDescriptor,*
DWORD *dwAccessSelect,*
PGENERIC_MAPPING *pGMappina,*
BOOL *bCreateFlag,*
LPDWORD *lpdwGrantedAccess,*
LPBOOL *lpbStatus,*
LPBOOL *lpbAuditFlag***)**

Use **AccessCheckAndAuditAlarm()** to verify the access privilege and generate any appropriate audit and alarm messages. *lptstrSubSysName* points to the name of the calling subsystem function. *hObject* is a handle to the client object being checked.

lptstrObjType is a string pointer to the type of object being accessed or created. *lptstrObjName* is a string pointer to the name of the object being accessed or created. *psdDescriptor* is a pointer to the security descriptor defining the access privileges of the object.

dwAccessSelect contains the requested access privilege mask. *pGMappina* is a pointer to the generic mapping associated with the object in question. *bCreateFlag* returns TRUE if a new object was created, or FALSE if an existing object is opened with the requested access privileges.

lpdwGrantedAccess contains the actual access mask granted if the function was successful. *lpbStatus* returns either **STATUS_SUCCESS**, **STATUS_AC-CESS_DENIED**, or **STATUS_OBJECT_NOT_FOUND**. *lpbAuditFlag* is used by **ObjectCloseAuditAlarm()** when the object handle is closed.

USAGE

AccessCheckAndAuditAlarm() requires the calling procedure to have the **seSecurityPrivilege** access privilege.

RELATED FUNCTIONS

AccessCheck()
AreAllAccessesGranted()
AreAnyAccessesGranted()
ObjectCloseAuditAlarm()

BOOL AddAccessAllowedAce(PACL *pacl,*
DWORD *dwAccessRevision,*
DWORD *dwAccessMask,*
PSID *psid)*

AddAccessAllowedAce() adds access to a specific security identifier's access control list. *pacl* is a pointer to an **ACL** structure. (See **AddAce()**.) *dwAccessRevision* specifies the revision level of the access allowed or access control list being added.

dwAccessMask contains the access mask identifying the particular access being granted to the security identifier. *psid* is a pointer to a **SID** structure, identifying the security identifier being granted access. (*SID* structures are internal and must not be modified directly.)

The function returns TRUE if successful, and FALSE otherwise.

USAGE

AddAccessAllowedAce() adds the **ACCESS_ALLOWED** access privilege to an **ACE** header in an **ACL** control list.

RELATED FUNCTIONS

AddAce()
DeleteAce()
GetAce()

BOOL AddAce(PACL *pacl*, DWORD *dwAceRevision*,
DWORD *dwStartIndex*,
LPVOID *lpvAceList*,
DWORD *dwListLength*)

AddAce() adds one or more access control entries to an access control list. *pacl* is a pointer to the **ACL** structure containing an existing access control list description. *dwAceRevision* defines the revision level of the access control entry being added.

dwStartIndex defines the position within the access control list where the new access control entry or entries will be inserted. *lpvAceList* is a pointer to the access control entry or entries being added. *dwListLength* defines the size of the list, in bytes, pointed to by *lpvAceList*.

The function returns TRUE if successful, and FALSE otherwise.

USAGE

The **ACL** structure looks like this:

```
struct _ACL {
  BYTE AclRevision;
  BYTE Sbz1;
  WORD AclSize;
  WORD AceCount;
  WORD Sbz2;
} ACL;
```

The **ACL** structure is the header for an access control list, followed by one or more access control entries or **ACE**s. **AclRevision** is usually set to

ACL_REVISION. Sbz1 defines the amount of byte padding (1-zero byte, or 16-bit alignment) applied to the **ACL_REVISION** member.

AclSize defines the size of the access control list, including the number of bytes needed by the **ACL** header and all of its associated **ACE** entries. **AceCount** identifies the number of **ACE** entries in the access control list. **Sbz2** defines the alignment, in bytes, for the **ACL** list (2-zero bytes, or 32-bit boundary).

A call to **GetLastError()** will return more detailed information about the error generated when **AddAce()** returns FALSE.

RELATED FUNCTIONS

DeleteAce()
GetAce()

BOOL AdjustTokenGroups(HANDLE *hToken*,
BOOL *bResetFlag*,
PTOKEN_GROUPS *pNewTGroups*,
DWORD *dwBuffSize*,
PTOKEN_GROUPS *pOldTGroups*,
PDWORD *pdwOldGroupSize*)

AdjustTokenGroups() enables or disables token groups. *hToken* is a handle to the token group being enabled or disabled. *bResetFlag* returns TRUE if the token group was reset to the initial default enabled or disabled state, or FALSE if the token group was set according to *pNewTGroups*. *pNewTGroups* is an optional pointer to a **TOKEN_GROUPS** structure containing the groups whose states are about to be enabled or disabled.

dwBuffSize is optional and defines the number of bytes in the buffer pointed to by *pOldTGroups* if present. *pOldTGroups* is a pointer to a **TOKEN_GROUPS** structure that will return with the previous state of any token groups being modified. *pdwOldGroupSize* defines the number of bytes needed to hold the previous token group information.

The function returns TRUE if successful, and FALSE otherwise.

USAGE

The **TOKEN_GROUPS** structure looks like this:

```
struct _TOKEN_GROUPS {
DWORD GroupCount;
SID_AND_ATTRIBUTES Groups[ANYSIZE_ARRAY];
} TOKEN_GROUPS;
```

The **TOKEN_GROUPS** structure defines a set of groups in an access token. **GroupCount** identifies the number of groups in the access token. **Groups** is an array of **SID_AND_ATTRIBUTES** structures identifying the security identifiers and attributes. The following attributes are legal:

Attribute	Description
SE_GROUP_ENABLED_BY_DEFAULT	Group is enabled by default
SE_GROUP_ENABLED	Group is enabled
SE_GROUP_LOGON_ID	Group is a logon identifier
SE_GROUP_MANDATORY	Group cannot be disabled
SE_GROUP_OWNER	User is the owner of the group, or the SID can be assigned as the owner of the token or objects

The **SID_AND_ATTRIBUTES** structure looks like this:

```
struct _SID_AND_ATTRIBUTES {
  PSID Sid;
  DWORD Attributes;
} SID_AND_ATTRIBUTES ;
```

Sid is a pointer to a **SID** structure. **Attributes** is a **SID**-specific 32-bit flag. No token groups are changed if the buffer pointed to by *pOldTGroups* is too small.

RELATED FUNCTIONS

AdjustTokenPrivileges()
GetTokenInformation()

BOOL AdjustTokenPrivileges(HANDLE *hToken,*
BOOL *bDisableFlag,*
PTOKEN_PRIVILEGES *pNewTPrivileges,*
DWORD *dwBuffSize,*
PTOKEN_PRIVILEGES *pOldTPrivileges,*
PDWORD *pdwOldPrivilegeSize*)

AdjustTokenPrivileges() enables or disables token privileges. *hToken* is a handle to the token being enabled or disabled. *bDisableFlag* returns TRUE if the token was disabled, or FALSE if the token group was set according to *pNewTPrivileges*. *pNewTPrivileges* is an optional pointer to a **TOKEN_PRIVILEGES** structure containing the tokens whose states are about to be enabled or disabled.

dwBuffSize is optional and defines the number of bytes in the buffer pointed to by *pOldTPrivileges* if present. *pOldTPrivileges* is a pointer to a **TOKEN_PRIVILEGES** structure that will return with the previous state of any token being modified. *pdwOldPrivilegeSize* defines the number of bytes needed to hold the previous token information.

The function returns TRUE if successful, and FALSE otherwise.

USAGE

The **TOKEN_PRIVILEGES** structure looks like this:

```
struct _TOKEN_PRIVILEGES {
  DWORD PrivilegeCount;
  LUID_AND_ATTRIBUTES Privileges[ANYSIZE_ARRAY];
} TOKEN_PRIVILEGES;
```

The **TOKEN_PRIVILEGES** structure defines the set of privileges for an access token. **PrivilegeCount** defines the number of privileges applied. **Privileges** may be one of the following values:

SE_PRIVILEGE_ENABLED_BY_DEFAULT
SE_PRIVILEGE_ENABLED
SE_PRIVILEGE_USED_FOR_ACCESS

No tokens are changed if the buffer pointed to by *pOldTPrivileges* is too small. Here is a small portion of code that illustrates the use of this function.

```
HANDLE hAccToken;
TOKEN_PRIVILEGES tpTokenPriv;
    .
    .
    .

AdjustTokenPrivileges(hAccToken,
                      FALSE,
                      &tpTokenPriv,
                      sizeof(TOKEN_PRIVILEGES),
                      NULL, NULL);
```

RELATED FUNCTIONS

AdjustTokenGroups()
GetTokenInformation()

BOOL AreAllAccessesGranted (DWORD *dwAccessGranted,* DWORD *dwAccessRequested*)

AreAllAccessesGranted() returns TRUE if all of the *dwAccessRequested* flags match those of *dwAccessGranted*. *dwAccessGranted* contains the granted access mask, and *dwAccessRequested* contains the requested access mask.

The function returns FALSE if there is no match.

USAGE

AreAllAccessesGranted() is used when dereferencing an object handle.

RELATED FUNCTION

AreAnyAccessesGranted()

BOOL AreAnyAccessesGranted (DWORD *dwAccessGranted,* DWORD *dwAccessRequested*)

AreAnyAccessesGranted() returns TRUE if any of the *dwAccessRequested* flags match those of *dwAccessGranted*. *dwAccessGranted* contains the granted access mask. *dwAccessRequested* contains the requested access mask.

The function returns FALSE if none of the requested flags match.

USAGE

AreAnyAccessesGranted() is used to check access mask subsets.

RELATED FUNCTION

AreAllAccessesGranted()

BOOL CopySid(DWORD *dwDestinationSidSize,* PSID *psidDestination,* PSID *psidSource*)

CopySid() copies the source **SID** security identifier into the destination **SID**. *dwDestinationSidSize* specifies the number of bytes in the destination **SID** buffer. *psidDestination* is a pointer to the buffer receiving the **SID** copy. *psidSource* is a pointer to the **SID** being copied.

The function returns TRUE if successful, and FALSE otherwise.

USAGE

Use **GetLastError()** to obtain a detailed description of any errors generated when **CopySid()** returns FALSE.

RELATED FUNCTIONS

EqualSid()
GetLengthSid()
InitializeSid()
IsValidSid()

BOOL DeleteAce(PACL *pacl*, DWORD *dwIndex*)

DeleteAce() deletes an access control entry or **ACE** from an access control list, or **ACL**. *pacl* is a pointer to the access control structure (**ACL**). *dwIndex* selects which of the **ACE** structures within the **ACL** to delete.

The function returns TRUE if successful, and FALSE otherwise.

USAGE

The *dwIndex* starts at an offset of zero into the access control list.

RELATED FUNCTIONS

AddAce()
GetAce()

BOOL EqualSid(PSID *psid1*, PSID *psid2*)

EqualSid() returns TRUE if the two security identifier values pointed to by *psid1* and *psid2* are equal. The function returns FALSE otherwise.

USAGE

The value returned by **EqualSid()** is undefined if either of the **SID**s pointed to are invalid.

Here is a small portion of code that illustrates the use of this function.

```
PSID psidSid;
PSID psidLogonSid;

    .
    .
    .


if (EqualSid(psidSid, psidLogonSid))
{
    .
    .
    .

}
```

RELATED FUNCTIONS

CopySid()
IsValidSid()

BOOL GetAce(PACL *pacl,* DWORD *dwACLIndex,* LPVOID *★lpvACE*)

GetAce() returns a pointer to the specified **ACE** structure within an **ACL** access control list. *pacl* is a pointer to an access control list or **ACL**. *dwACLIndex* selects which of the **ACE** structures to return the pointer of. *lpvACE* contains the returned **ACE** pointer.

The function returns TRUE if successful, and FALSE otherwise.

USAGE

dwACLIndex is zero-based.

Here is a small portion of code that illustrates the use of this function.

```
PACL paclACL;
DWORD dwAcl;
ACCESS_ALLOWED_ACE *paaAlldAce;
    .
    .
    .

if (!GetAce(paclACL, dwAcl,(LPVOID *) &paaAlldAce))
{
    .
    .
    .

}
```

RELATED FUNCTIONS

AddAce()
DeleteAce()

BOOL GetAclInformation(PACL *pacl,*
LPVOID *lpvAclInfo,*
DWORD *dwBuffSize,*
ACL_INFORMATION_CLASS *aclInfoClass*)

GetAclInformation() returns the information for a specific access control list. *pacl* is a pointer to an existing **ACL** (access control list) structure. *lpvAclInfo* is a pointer to a buffer that the function uses to return the requested statistics.

dwBuffSize defines the size of the buffer pointed to by *lpvAclInfo,* in bytes. *aclInfoClass* determines the type of statistics reported.

The function returns TRUE if successful, and FALSE otherwise.

USAGE

aclInfoClass may be one of two values:

Constant	Description
AclRevisionInformation	Causes *lpvAclInfo* to return with an **ACL_REVISION_INFORMATION** data structure filled with the specified **ACL**'s information
AclsizeInformation	Causes *lpvAclInfo* to return with an **ACL_SIZE_INFORMATION** data structure filled with the specified **ACL**'s information

Here is a small portion of code that illustrates the use of this function.

```
PACL paclACL;
ACL_SIZE_INFORMATION asiAclSize;
ACL_INFORMATION_CLASS AclSizeInfo;
DWORD dwBuffLength;
    .
    .
    .

dwBuffLength = sizeof(asiAclSize);

if (!GetAclInformation(paclACL,
                    (LPVOID) &asiAclSize,
                    (DWORD) dwBuffLength,
                    (ACL_INFORMATION_CLASS) AclSizeInfo))
    {
```

.
.
.

}

RELATED FUNCTIONS

AddAce()
DeleteAce()
GetAce()

BOOL GetFileSecurity(LPTSTR *lpszFileName,*
         SECURITY_INFORMATION *siRequestedSecurity,*
         PSECURITY_DESCRIPTOR *psdDescriptor,*
         DWORD *dwBuffSize,*
         LPDWORD *lpdwBytesNeeded***)**

Your application uses **GetFileSecurity()** to return a **SECURITY_DE-SCRIPTOR** structure filled with the specified file or directory's security status. *lpszFileName* is a pointer to a NULL-terminated string representing the file or directory in question.

siRequestedSecurity is a **SECURITY_INFORMATION** data structure containing the security information being requested. *psdDescriptor* is a pointer to a **SECURITY_DESCRIPTOR** that the function will fill with the requested file or subdirectory's security status.

dwBuffSize defines the number of bytes required by the buffer pointed to by *psdDescriptor*. *lpdwBytesNeeded* is filled and returned by **GetFileSecurity()**, representing the number of bytes required to store a complete security descriptor.

The function returns TRUE if successful, and FALSE otherwise.

USAGE

GetFileSecurity() can handle file and directory names stored either in ASCII or Unicode (wide-character) format. In order for an application to make a legal call to **GetFileSecurity()**, the application must have a **READ_CONTROL** access or be the actual owner of the file or directory in question.

Here is a small portion of code that illustrates the use of this function.

```
LPTSTR lpszFullName;
DWORD dwSDLength;
DWORD dwSDLenReq;
PSECURITY_DESCRIPTOR psdSecDes;
    .
    .
    .
if (!GetFileSecurity(lpszFullName,
    (SECURITY_INFORMATION)( OWNER_SECURITY_INFORMATION
                          | GROUP_SECURITY_INFORMATION
                          | DACL_SECURITY_INFORMATION
                          | SACL_SECURITY_INFORMATION),
    psdSecDes,
    dwSDLength,
    (LPDWORD)&dwSDLenReq))
{
    .
    .
    .
}
```

RELATED FUNCTION

SetFileSecurity()

DWORD GetLengthSid(PSID *psid*)

Use **GetLengthSid()** to return the number of bytes in a valid **SID**. *psid* is a pointer to a valid **SID**. The function returns the length of the valid **SID** in bytes if successful.

USAGE

The value returned by **GetLengthSid()** is undefined when passed an illegal **SID**.

RELATED FUNCTIONS

CopySid()
EqualSid()

HWINSTA GetProcessWindowStation(VOID)

GetProcessWindowStation() returns the handle to a window station. The function returns a valid handle if successful, and NULL otherwise.

USAGE

The function will return NULL if the owning process is not a Win32 application. Here is a small portion of code that illustrates the use of this function.

```
HANDLE hWinStation;
    .
    .
    .
hWinStation = GetProcessWindowStation();
```

BOOL GetSecurityDescriptorControl
(PSECURITY_DESCRIPTOR *psdDescriptor*,
PSECURITY_DESCRIPTOR_CONTROL *psdcControl*,
LPDWORD *lpdwRvision*)

GetSecurityDescriptorControl() returns the specified security descriptor and control information. *psdDescriptor* is a pointer to a **SECURITY_DE-SCRIPTOR** structure whose control and revision information the function returns.

psdcControl is a pointer to a **SECURITY_DESCRIPTOR_CONTROL** structure that **GetSecurityDescriptorControl()** will fill with the security descriptor's control information. *lpdwRevision* is a pointer to a double-word that the function will use to assign and return the security descriptor's revision value.

The function returns TRUE if successful, and FALSE otherwise.

USAGE

The **SECURITY_DESCRIPTOR_CONTROL** structure may be one or more of the following values:

SE_DACL_DEFAULTED
SE_DACL_PRESENT
SE_GROUP_DEFAULTED
SE_OWNER_DEFAULTED
SE_SACL_DEFAULTED
SE_SACL_PRESENT
SE_SELF_RELATIVE

GetSecurityDescriptorControl() always sets the *lpdwRevision,* even when the function call returns an error.

Here is a small portion of code that illustrates the use of this function.

```
PSECURITY_DESCRIPTOR psdSecDes;
SECURITY_DESCRIPTOR_CONTROL sdcSDControl;
DWORD dwSDRev;

    .
    .
    .


if (!GetSecurityDescriptorControl(psdSecDes,
    (PSECURITY_DESCRIPTOR_CONTROL) &sdcSDControl,
    (LPDWORD) &dwSDRev))
{
    .
    .
    .

}
```

RELATED FUNCTIONS

GetSecurityDescriptorGroup()
GetSecurityDescriptorLength()
GetSecurityDescriptorOwner()
InitializeSecurityDescriptor()

BOOL GetSecurityDescriptorDacL (PSECURITY_DESCRIPTOR *psdDescriptor,* LPBOOL *lpbIsDaclPresent,* PACL *pDacl,* LPBOOL *lpfSetDaclDefaulted*)

Your application can use **GetSecurityDescriptorDacl()** to return an object's discretionary access control list. *psdDescriptor* is a pointer to a **SECURITY_DESCRIPTOR** data structure identifying which object's discretionary **ACL** information the function is to retrieve.

lpbIsDaclPresent is a pointer to a Boolean variable that the function fills. *pDacl* is a pointer to an **ACL** structure that the function fills if the object has a previously defined discretionary **ACL**. *lpfSetDaclDefaulted* is a pointer to a flag, **SE_DACL_DEFAULTED**.

When present, the function returns the discretionary **ACL** using a default mechanism. If not present, the discretionary **ACL** was directly specified by the user. The function returns TRUE if successful, and FALSE otherwise.

USAGE

The **SECURITY_DESCRIPTOR** structure contains the following set of bit flags:

SE_OWNER_DEFAULTED
SE_GROUP_DEFAULTED
SE_DACL_PRESENT
SE_DACL_DEFAULTED
SE_SACL_PRESENT
SE_SACL_DEFAULTED
SE_SELF_RELATIVE

Discretionary **ACL**s detail an object's security privileges on a per-group or per-user basis. If **GetSecurityDescriptorDacl()** returns *lpbIsDaclPresent,* with a TRUE, the remaining parameters are returned with valid information.

Here is a small portion of code that illustrates the use of this function.

```
PSECURITY_DESCRIPTOR psdSecDes;
BOOL bHasDACL;
BOOL bDaclDefaulted;
PACL paclDACL;
    .
    .
    .

if (!GetSecurityDescriptorDacl(psdSecDes,
                          (LPBOOL)&bHasDACL,
                          (PACL *)&paclDACL,
                          (LPBOOL)&bDaclDefaulted))
{
    .
    .
    .

}
```

RELATED FUNCTIONS

GetSecurityDescriptorGroup()
GetSecurityDescriptorLength()
GetSecurityDescriptorOwner()
IsValidSecurityDescriptor()

BOOL GetSecurityDescriptorGroup (PSECURITY_DESCRIPTOR *psdDescriptor*, PSID *pSID*, LPBOOL *lpbSetGroupDefaulted*)

You use **GetSecurityDescriptorGroup()** to return a security descriptor's primary group. *psdDescriptor* is a pointer to a **SECURITY_DESCRIPTOR** structure identifying which object's group information is being returned.

pSID is a pointer to a pointer to an **SID** structure that the function will set to a valid group **SID** if a group is present. *lpbSetGroupDefaulted* is set to NULL if no group **SID** is present, or it is set to the object's security descriptor **SE_GROUP_DEFAULTED** control flag.

The function returns TRUE if successful, and FALSE otherwise.

USAGE

Discretionary **ACL**s detail an object's security privileges on a per-group or per-user basis.

Here is a small portion of code that illustrates the use of this function.

```
PSECURITY_DESCRIPTOR psdSecDes;
BOOL bGroupDefaulted;
PSID psidGroup;
        .
        .
        .
if (!GetSecurityDescriptorGroup(psdSecDes,
                          (PSID *) &psidGroup,
                          (LPBOOL) &bGroupDefaulted))
{
        .
        .
        .
}
```

RELATED FUNCTIONS

GetSecurityDescriptorControl()
InitializeSecurityDescriptor()
IsValidSecurityDescriptor()

DWORD GetSecurityDescriptorLength
(PSECURITY_DESCRIPTOR *psdDescriptor*)

GetSecurityDescriptorLength() returns the number of bytes required by an object's **SECURITY_DESCRIPTOR** structure, including all **SID**s and **ACL**s. *psdDescriptor* is a pointer to the object's security descriptor, which the function calculates the size of, in bytes.

The function returns the number of bytes required by the security descriptor if successful, or an undefined value if unsuccessful.

USAGE

The WINNT.H header file currently defines **SECURITY_DESCRIP-TOR_MIN_LENGTH** to be 20 bytes. If **GetSecurityDescriptorLength()**

returns **SECURITY_DESCRIPTOR_MIN_LENGTH**, then the security
descriptor pointed to by *psdDescriptor* contains no associated **SID**s or **ACL**s.

Here is a small portion of code that illustrates the use of this function.

```
PSECURITY_DESCRIPTOR psdSecDes;
DWORD dwSDLength;
     .
     .
     .

dwSDLength = GetSecurityDescriptorLength(psdSecDes);
     .
     .
     .
```

RELATED FUNCTIONS

GetSecurityDescriptorControl()
GetSecurityDescriptorOwner()
InitializeSecurityDescriptor()
IsValidSecurityDescriptor()

BOOL GetSecurityDescriptorOwner
(PSECURITY_DESCRIPTOR *psdDescriptor*,
PSID **pSIDOwner*,
LPBOOL *lpfOwnerDefaulted*)

An application uses **GetSecurityDescriptorOwner()** to return the owner of
the **PSECURITY_DESCRIPTOR** pointed to by *psdDescriptor*. If an owner
is present, **GetSecurityDescriptorOwner()** assigns the pointer pointed to by
pSIDOwner to the address of the security descriptor's owner **SID**; otherwise it
is set to NULL.

lpfOwnerDefaulted is set to NULL if there is no security descriptor owner;
otherwise the function sets *lpfOwnerDefaulted* to the security descriptor's
SE_OWNER_DEFAULTED control flag. The function returns TRUE if
successful, and FALSE otherwise.

USAGE

A call to **GetLastError()** returns extended error information if the function
returns FALSE.

RELATED FUNCTIONS

GetSecurityDescriptorGroup()
GetSecurityDescriptorControl()
GetSecurityDescriptorLength()
IsValidSecurityDescriptor

BOOL GetSecurityDescriptorSacl
(PSECURITY_DESCRIPTOR *psdDescriptor,*
LPBOOL *lpbIsSaclPresent,*
PACL *pSacl,*
LPBOOL *lpfSetSaclDefaulted*)

Use **GetSecurityDescriptorSacl()** to return an object's system access control list. *psdDescriptor* is a pointer to a **SECURITY_DESCRIPTOR** data structure identifying which object's system **ACL** information the function is to retrieve.

lpbIsSaclPresent is a pointer to a Boolean variable that the function fills. *pSacl* is a pointer to an **ACL** structure that the function fills if the object has a previously defined system **ACL**.

lpfSetSaclDefaulted is a pointer to a flag, **SE_SACL_DEFAULTED**. When present, the function returns the system **ACL** using a default mechanism. If not present, the system **ACL** was directly specified by the user.

The function returns TRUE if successful, and FALSE otherwise.

USAGE

System **ACL**s detail an object's security privileges on a per-group or per-user basis. If **GetSecurityDescriptorSacl()** returns *lpbIsSaclPresent,* with a TRUE, the remaining parameters are returned with valid information.

Here is a small portion of code that illustrates the use of this function.

```
PSECURITY_DESCRIPTOR psdSecDes;
BOOL bSaclDefaulted;
BOOL bHasSACL;
PACL paclSACL;
    .
    .
    .
if (!GetSecurityDescriptorSacl(psdSecDes,
```

```
                                   (LPBOOL) &bHasSACL,
                                   (PACL *) &paclSACL,
                                   (LPBOOL) &bSaclDefaulted))
{
            .
            .
            .
}
```

RELATED FUNCTIONS

GetSecurityDescriptorGroup()
GetSecurityDescriptorLength()
GetSecurityDescriptorOwner()
IsValidSecurityDescriptor()

PSID_IDENTIFIER_AUTHORITY
GetSidIdentifierAuthority(PSID *pSID*)

GetSidIdentifierAuthority() retrieves the address of a **SID**'s identifier authority field if successful. *pSID* points to a valid **SID** whose identifier authority address the function returns.

USAGE

The value returned by **GetSidIdentifierAuthority()** is undefined when passed an invalid *pSID*.

Here is a small portion of code that illustrates the use of this function.

```
PSID psidSid;
SID_IDENTIFIER_AUTHORITY siaSidAuthority;
       .
       .
       .
siaSidAuthority = *(GetSidIdentifierAuthority(psidSid));
```

RELATED FUNCTIONS

CopySid()
GetLengthSid()

InitializeSid()
IsValidSid(

DWORD GetSidLengthRequired
(UCHAR *ucSubAuthorityCount*)

GetSidLengthRequired() returns the number of bytes required to store an **SID** with the specified number of subauthorities. *ucSubAuthorityCount* identifies the number of subauthorities being stored in the **SID**. The function returns the number of bytes necessary to store the **SID** if successful; otherwise the return value is undefined.

USAGE

Here is a small portion of code that illustrates the use of this function.

```
DWORD dwSidWith1SubAuthorities;
DWORD dwSidWith2SubAuthorities;
     .
     .
     .
dwSidWith1SubAuthorities = GetSidLengthRequired(1);
dwSidWith2SubAuthorities = GetSidLengthRequired(2);
```

RELATED FUNCTIONS

CopySid()
GetLengthSid()
InitializeSid()
IsValidSid()

PDWORD GetSidSubAuthority(PSID *pSID*,
DWORD *dwIndex*)

GetSidSubAuthority() retrieves the address of a specific subauthority. *pSID* is a pointer to an **SID** structure. *dwIndex* is an index into the array selecting which subauthority element address the function will return if successful. The return value is undefined otherwise.

Here is a small portion of code that illustrates the use of this function.

```
psidNULLSid = (PSID)LocalAlloc(LPTR, dwSidWith1SubAuthority);
psidWorldSid = (PSID)LocalAlloc(LPTR, dwSidWith1SubAuthority);
    .
    .
    .
InitializeSid(psidNULLSid, &siaNULLSidAuthority, 1);
InitializeSid(psidWorldSid, &siaWorldSidAuthority, 1);
    .
    .
    .
*(GetSidSubAuthority(psidNULLSid, 0)) = SECURITY_NULL_RID;
*(GetSidSubAuthority(psidWorldSid, 0)) = SECURITY_WORLD_RID;
```

USAGE

dwIndex is a zero-based index, with the first array element at an offset of zero.

RELATED FUNCTIONS

CopySid()
GetLengthSid()
InitializeSid()
IsValidSid()

PUCHAR GetSidSubAuthorityCount(PSID *pSID*)

GetSidSubAuthorityCount() returns the address for the subauthority count field of the **SID** security identifier pointed to by *pSID*.

USAGE

The return value for **GetSidSubAuthorityCount()** is undefined if passed an invalid *pSID*.

Here is a small portion of code that illustrates the use of this function.

```
PSID psidSid;
DWORD dwNumSubAuthorities;
           .
           .
           .
dwNumSubAuthorities = (DWORD)( *(GetSidSubAuthorityCount(psidSid)));
```

RELATED FUNCTIONS

CopySid()
EqualSid()
GetLengthSid()
InitializeSid()
IsValidSid()

BOOL GetTokenInformation(HANDLE *hToken,*
TOKEN_INFORMATION_CLASS *ticClass,*
LPVOID *lpvTokenInfo,*
DWORD *dwBuffSize,*
PDWORD *pdwActualSize*)

Your application uses **GetTokenInformation()** to find out more information
about a specific token. *hToken* is a handle to the token in question. *ticClass* selects
the type of token information requested by the caller. *lpvTokenInfo* is a pointer
to a buffer that the function will fill with the requested token information.

dwBuffSize defines the size of the buffer. *pdwActualSize* is calculated and filled
by the function and indicates the actual number of bytes required by the
information placed into the buffer pointed to by *lpvTokenInfo*.

The function returns TRUE if successful, and FALSE otherwise.

USAGE

GetTokenInformation() can return information for the following:

TOKEN_INFORMATION_CLASSes
TOKEN_USER

TOKEN_GROUPS
TOKEN_PRIVILEGES
TOKEN_OWNER
TOKEN_PRIMARY_GROUP
TOKEN_DEFAULT_DACL
TOKEN_SOURCE
TOKEN_TYPE
SECURITY_IMPERSONATION_LEVEL
TOKEN_STATISTICS

Here is a small portion of code that illustrates the use of this function.

```
#define TOK_INFO_BUF   100(
DWORD dwTokInfBufSz;

UCHAR ucTokInfBuf [TOK_INFO_BUF] = "";
ticInfoClass = TokenUser;
dwTokInfBufSz = TOK_INFO_BUF;

if (!GetTokenInformation(hAccToken,
                    ticInfoClass,
                    ucTokInfBuf,
                    (DWORD) TOK_INFO_BUF,
                    &dwTokInfBufSz))
{
    .
    .
    .
}
```

RELATED FUNCTIONS

AdjustTokenGroups()
AdjustTokenPrivileges()
SetTokenInformation()

BOOL GetUserObjectSecurity(HANDLE *hObject,*
PSECURITY_INFORMATION *psiSecurityInfo,*
PSECURITY_DESCRIPTOR *psdReturnedDescriptor,*
DWORD *dwBuffSize,*
LPDWORD *lpdwActualSize*)

You use **GetUserObjectSecurity()** to obtain an object's security information. *hObject* identifies the object in question. *psiSecurityInfo* is a pointer to a **SECURITY_INFORMATION** structure whose security information is about to be returned.

psdReturnedDescriptor is a pointer to a buffer that the function fills with the requested security information. *dwBuffSize* identifies the size of the buffer, in bytes. *lpdwActualSize* returns the actual number of bytes of information placed in the buffer pointed to by *psdReturnedDescriptor*.

The function returns TRUE if successful, and FALSE otherwise.

USAGE

The **SECURITY_INFORMATION** structure is typedefed as:

DWORD SECURITY_INFORMATION

The SECURITY_INFORMATION structure identifies the object-related security information being set or queried, including the object owner, primary group, discretionary access control list, and system **ACL** designated by a bit flag:

DACL_SECURITY_INFORMATION
GROUP_SECURITY_INFORMATION
OWNER_SECURITY_INFORMATION
SACL_SECURITY_INFORMATION

lpdwActualSize returns a **STATUS_BUFFER_TOO_SMALL** value when the requested information is too large to fit in the buffer.

Here is a small portion of code that illustrates the use of this function.

```
#define SD_BUF 8096
HANDLE hWinStation;
SECURITY_INFORMATION siSInfo;
PSECURITY_DESCRIPTOR psdSecDes;
DWORD dwSDLength = SD_BUF;
DWORD dwSDLenReq;
    .
    .
    .

if (!GetUserObjectSecurity(hWinStation,
                           &siSInfo,
                           psdSecDes,
                           dwSDLength,
                           (LPDWORD) &dwSDLenReq))
{
    .
    .
    .
}
```

RELATED FUNCTION

SetUserObjectSecurity()

BOOL ImpersonateNamedPipeClient (HANDLE *hNamedPipe*)

Your application uses **ImpersonateNamedPipeClient()** to impersonate the pipe identified by *hNamedPipe*.

The function returns TRUE if successful, and FALSE otherwise.

USAGE

The function can only be called by local named pipes, and it allows the server end of the pipe to impersonate the client end.

RELATED FUNCTIONS

DdeImpersonateClient()
DeRevertToSelf()

BOOL InitializeAcl(PACL *pAcl*, DWORD *dwBuffSize*, DWORD *dwRevisionLevel*)

Use **InitializeAcl()** to create a new access control structure, or **ACL**. *pAcl* is a pointer to a buffer that the function will fill with the new **ACL** structure. *dwBuffSize* specifies the size of the buffer, in bytes. *dwRevisionLevel* must be set to **ACL_REVISION2**.

The function returns TRUE if successful, and FALSE otherwise.

USAGE

The newly created **ACL** contains no entries.

RELATED FUNCTIONS

AddAccessAllowedAce()
DeleteAce()
GetAce()
IsValidAcl()
SetAclInformation()

BOOL InitializeSecurityDescriptor (PSECURITY_DESCRIPTOR *psdDescriptor*, DWORD *dwRevisionLevel*)

You use **InitializeSecurityDescriptor()** to initialize the new security descriptor pointed to by *psdDescriptor*. *dwRevisionLevel* must be set to **SECURITY_DESCRIPTOR_REVISION**.

The function returns TRUE if successful, and FALSE otherwise.

USAGE

An initialized security descriptor has no system or discretionary **ACL** and no owner or primary group. It has all control flags initialized to NULL, and the security descriptor contains only the revision level.

RELATED FUNCTIONS

GetSecurityDescriptorGroup()
GetSecurityDescriptorControl()
GetSecurityDescriptorOwner()
IsValidSecurityDescriptor()

BOOL InitializeSid(PSID *pSid,*
SID_IDENTIFIER_AUTHORITY *psiaIdentAuthority,*
BYTE *bSubAuthorityCount)*

InitializeSid() initializes the **SID** security identifier pointed to by *pSid.*
psiaIdentAuthority points to an **SID_IDENTIFIER_AUTHORITY** structure
being placed into the **SID**. *bSubAuthorityCount* sets the number of subauthorities
for the **SID**.

USAGE

The **SID_IDENTIFIER_AUTHORITY** structure looks like this:

```
struct _SID_IDENTIFIER_AUTHORITY {
  BYTE Value[6];
} SID_IDENTIFIER_AUTHORITY ;
```

The **SID_IDENTIFIER_AUTHORITY** structure contains the top-level
authority of an **SID** security identifier. **Value** is an array of six bytes defining
the **SID**'s authority and may be combinations of the following values:

SECURITY_NULL_SID_AUTHORITY
SECURITY_WORLD_SID_AUTHORITY
SECURITY_LOCAL_SID_AUTHORITY
SECURITY_CREATOR_SID_AUTHORITY
SECURITY_NT_AUTHORITY

InitializeSid() does not set the subauthority values. This is done with
additional function calls, for example, to **GetSidSubAuthority()**.
Here is a small portion of code that illustrates the use of this function.

```
psidNULLSid = (PSID)LocalAlloc(LPTR, dwSidWith1SubAuthority);
psidWorldSid = (PSID)LocalAlloc(LPTR, dwSidWith1SubAuthority);
    .
    .
    .
InitializeSid(psidNULLSid, &siaNULLSidAuthority, 1);
InitializeSid(psidWorldSid, &siaWorldSidAuthority, 1);
    .
    .
    .
*(GetSidSubAuthority(psidNULLSid, 0)) = SECURITY_NULL_RID;
*(GetSidSubAuthority(psidWorldSid, 0)) = SECURITY_WORLD_RID;
```

RELATED FUNCTIONS

CopySid()
EqualSid()
IsValidSid()
GetSidSubAuthority()

BOOL IsValidAcl(PACL *pAcl*)

Your application uses **IsValidAcl()** to determine if the **ACL** pointed to by *pAcl* is valid or not.

The function returns TRUE for a valid access control list, and FALSE otherwise.

USAGE

IsValidAcl() checks both the **ACL** revision level and the number of **ACEs** specified by the **AceCount** field.

Here is a small portion of code that illustrates the use of this function.

```
PACL paclACL;
    .
    .
    .
if (!IsValidAcl(paclACL))
{
    .
    .
```

.

}

RELATED FUNCTIONS

AddAce()
DeleteAce()
GetAce()
InitializeAcl()
SetAclInformation()

BOOL IsValidSecurityDescriptor (PSECURITY_DESCRIPTOR *psdDescriptor*)

IsValidSecurityDescriptor() verifies the security descriptor pointed to by
psdDescriptor.

The function returns TRUE for a valid security descriptor, and FALSE otherwise.

USAGE

IsValidSecurityDescriptor() checks and validates each component of the
security descriptor by evaluating the revision level.

Here is a small portion of code used to illustrate the use of this function.

```
PSECURITY_DESCRIPTOR psdSecDes;
    .
    .
    .

if (!IsValidSecurityDescriptor(psdSecDes))
{
    .
    .
    .

}
```

RELATED FUNCTIONS

GetSecurityDescriptorControl()
GetSecurityDescriptorOwner()
InitializeSecurityDescriptor()

BOOL IsValidSid(PSID *pSid*)

IsValidSid() validates the **SID** structure pointed to by *pSid*.

The function returns TRUE for a valid **SID**, and FALSE otherwise.

USAGE

IsValidSid() checks for a valid revision number and that the number of subauthorities is less than or equal to the maximum.

Here is a small portion of code used to illustrate this function.

```
PSID psidSid;
    .
    .
    .
if (!IsValidSid(psidSid))
{
    .
    .
    .
}
```

RELATED FUNCTIONS

EqualSid()
GetLengthSid()
InitializeSid()
GetSidSubAuthority()
GetSidSubAuthorityCount()

VOID MapGenericMask(PDWORD *pdwAccessMask,* PGENERIC_MAPPING *pgmMapping*)

Use **MapGenericMask()** to map all generic accesses within an access mask. *pdwAccessMask* is a pointer to an access mask into which the function will map the accesses defined by the **GENERIC_MAPPING** structure pointed to by *pgmMapping*. The function has no return value.

USAGE

The **GENERIC_MAPPING** structure looks like this:

```
struct _GENERIC_MAPPING {
  ACCESS_MASK GenericRead;
  ACCESS_MASK GenericWrite;
  ACCESS_MASK GenericExecute;
  ACCESS_MASK GenericAll;
} GENERIC_MAPPING;
```

The **GENERIC_MAPPING** structure details an object's mapping of generic to specific and standard access rights. **GenericRead** defines a read access mask. **GenericWrite** defines a write access mask. **GenericExecute** defines an execute access mask. **GenericAll** defines a mask representing all access types.

The function does not set the **GenericAll**, **GenericRead**, or **GenericWrite** generic bits.

RELATED FUNCTIONS

AreAllAccessesGranted()
AreAnyAccessesGranted()

BOOL ObjectCloseAuditAlarm
(LPTSTR *lpszSubSystemName*,
LPVOID *lpvObjectHandle*,
BOOL *bGenerateOnClose*)

Windows NT can generate audit and alarm messages. **ObjectCloseAudit-Alarm()** turns this feature on for the object identified by *lpvObjectHandle*.

lpszSubSystemName is a pointer to a NULL-terminated string identifying the subsystem making the function call. *bGenerateOnClose* is a Boolean flag returned from a call to either **ObjectOpenAuditAlarm()** or **AccessCheckAndAudit-Alarm()**.

USAGE

Note that a call to **ObjectCloseAuditAlarm()** can generate a high volume of messages, causing overall system performance to deteriorate.

RELATED FUNCTIONS

AccessCheckAndAuditAlarm()
AreAllAccessesGranted()
AreAnyAccessesGranted()
PrivilegeCheck()

BOOL ObjectOpenAuditAlarm
         (LPTSTR *lpszSubsystemName,*
         LPVOID *lpvObjectHandle,*
         LPTSTR *lpszObjectType,*
         LPTSTR *lpszObjectName,*
         PSECURITY_DESCRIPTOR *psidDescriptor,*
         HANDLE *hToken,*
         DWORD *dwDesiredAccess,*
         DWORD *dwGrantedAccess,*
         PPRIVILEGE_SET *pPS,*
         BOOL *bObjectCreation,*
         BOOL *bAccessGranted,*
         LPBOOL *lpbGenerateOnClose)*

When an application attempts to access or create a new server object, **Object-OpenAuditAlarm()** generates audit and alarm messages.

lpszSubsystemName is a pointer to a NULL-terminated string identifying the calling subsystem. *lpvObjectHandle* is a handle to the object in question. *lpszObjectType* is a pointer to a NULL-terminated string identifying the object's type.

lpszObjectName is a pointer to a NULL-terminated string identifying the object's name. *psidDescriptor* is a pointer to the object's security descriptor. *hToken* is a handle to the token object of the client calling the function.

dwDesiredAccess contains the desired access mask. *dwGrantedAccess* is filled by the function call and returns the granted access mask. *pPS* is a pointer to a **PRIVILEGE_SET** structure specifying the privileges needed for the access attempt.

bObjectCreation is TRUE if the function will create a new object if access is granted, or FALSE if opening an existing object. *bAccessGranted* is TRUE if access was granted, and FALSE otherwise. *lpbGenerateOnClose* is set by the audit generation function.

The function returns TRUE if successful, and FALSE otherwise.

USAGE

The **PRIVILEGE_SET** structure looks like this:

```
struct _PRIVILEGE_SET {
  DWORD PrivilegeCount;
  DWORD Control;
  LUID_AND_ATTRIBUTES Privilege[ANYSIZE_ARRAY];
} PRIVILEGE_SET;
```

You set the **PRIVILEGE_SET** structure to define a set of privileges. **PrivilegeCount** defines the number of privileges in the set. **Control** defines a privilege control flag (only **PRIVILEGE_SET_ALL_NECESSARY** is currently defined). **Privilege[]** defines an array of **LUID_AND_ATTRIBUTES**:

SE_PRIVILEGE_ENABLED_BY_DEFAULT
SE_PRIVILEGE_ENABLED
SE_PRIVILEGE_USED_FOR_ACCESS

hToken must be open for **TOKEN_QUERY** access and must be obtained by a token thread that is impersonating the client. *dwGrantedAccess* should contain the same access mask values set by one of the **AccessCheck...()** functions.

RELATED FUNCTIONS

AccessCheck()
AccessCheckAndAuditAlarm()
AreAllAccessesGranted()
AreAnyAccessesGranted()
MapGenericMask()

BOOL ObjectPrivilegeAuditAlarm

(LPTSTR *lpszSubsystemName,*
LPVOID *lpvObjectHandle*
HANDLE *hToken,*
DWORD *dwDesiredAccess*
PPRIVILEGE_SET *pPS,*
BOOL *bAccessGranted***)**

ObjectPrivilegeAuditAlarm() generates an audit and alarm message whenever an attempt is made to perform a privileged operation on the object identified by *lpvObjectHandle.*

lpszSubsystemName is a pointer to a NULL-terminated string identifying the subsystem making the function call. *hToken* is a handle to the token object representing the client making the function call.

dwDesiredAccess contains the privileged access type mask. *pPS* is a pointer to a **PRIVILEGE_SET** structure containing the privileges required for the requested operation. **ObjectPrivilegeAuditAlarm()** assigns *bAccessGranted* TRUE if access was granted, and FALSE otherwise.

The function returns TRUE if successful, and FALSE otherwise.

USAGE

Note that a call to **ObjectPrivilegeAuditAlarm()** can generate a high volume of messages, causing overall system performance to deteriorate.

RELATED FUNCTIONS

AccessCheck()
AccessCheckAndAuditAlarm()
AreAllAccessesGranted()
AreAnyAccessesGranted()
MapGenericMask()
PrivilegeCheck()

BOOL OpenProcessToken(HANDLE *hProcess,*
DWORD *dwDesiredAccess,*
PHANDLE *phToken)*

Use **OpenProcessToken()** to open the token object pointed to by *phToken* under the process identified by *hProcess. dwDesiredAccess* is an access mask selecting the desired type of token access.

The function returns TRUE if successful, and FALSE otherwise.

USAGE

OpenProcessToken() compares the *dwDesiredAccess* requested against the token's discretionary access control list.

RELATED FUNCTIONS

AdjustTokenPrivileges()
GetTokenInformation()
SetTokenInformation()

BOOL OpenThreadToken(HANDLE *hThread,*
DWORD *dwDesiredAccess,*
BOOL *bOpenAsSelf,*
PHANDLE *phToken)*

Use **OpenThreadToken()** to open the token owned by the thread pointed to by *hThread. dwDesiredAccess* is an access mask selecting the desired type of token access.

bOpenAsSelf is TRUE if the access should be made using the calling thread's process-level security context, or FALSE when using the unmodified current security context. *phToken* returns with the handle to the newly-opened token.

The function returns TRUE if successful, and FALSE otherwise.

USAGE

OpenThreadToken() compares the *dwDesiredAccess* requested against the token's discretionary access control list.

RELATED FUNCTIONS

AdjustTokenGroups()
AdjustTokenPrivileges()
GetTokenInformation()
SetTokenInformation()

BOOL PrivilegeCheck(HANDLE *hClientToken,* PPRIVILEGE_SET *pPS,* LPBOOL *lpbHasFullPrivilege*)

PrivilegeCheck() returns TRUE if the caller's client's security context has the selected privileges. *hClientToken* is a handle to a token object of a client attempting access.

pPS is a pointer to a **PRIVILEGE_SET** structure containing the privileges in question. *lpbHasFullPrivilege* is set to TRUE if the client has all selected privileges, and FALSE otherwise.

The function returns TRUE if successful, and FALSE otherwise.

USAGE

hToken must be open for **TOKEN_QUERY** access and must be obtained by a token thread that is impersonating the client.

RELATED FUNCTIONS

AccessCheck()
AccessCheckAndAuditAlarm()
AreAllAccessesGranted()
AreAnyAccessesGranted()

MapGenericMask()
ObjectPrivilegeAuditAlarm()

BOOL PrivilegedServiceAuditAlarm
(LPTSTR *lpszSubSystemName,*
LPTSTR *lpszServiceName,*
HANDLE *hToken,*
PPRIVILEGE_SET *pPS,*
BOOL *bAccessGranted*)

Use the **PrivilegedServiceAuditAlarm()** to activate the audit and alarm messages for any attempts to execute privileged system services. *lpszSubSystemName* is a pointer to a string identifying the subsystem calling **PrivilegedServiceAuditAlarm()**. *lpszServiceName* is a pointer to a string containing the name of the privileged subsystem service.

hToken is a handle to the client object requesting the privileged system operation. *pPS* is a pointer to a **PRIVILEGE_SET** structure identifying the privileges needed to perform the requested operation. *bAccessGranted* is a pointer to a Boolean TRUE if access was granted, or FALSE if access was denied.

The function returns TRUE if successful, and FALSE otherwise.

USAGE

The calling procedure to **PrivilegedServiceAuditAlarm()** must have *SeSecurityPrivilege* (See **SetFileSecurity()**). Note, however, that a call to **PrivilegedServiceAuditAlarm()** can generate a high volume of messages, causing overall system performance to deteriorate.

RELATED FUNCTIONS

AccessCheck()
AccessCheckAndAuditAlarm()
AreAllAccessesGranted()
AreAnyAccessesGranted()
PrivilegeCheck()

BOOL SetAclInformation(PACL *pAcl*,
LPVOID *lpvAclInfo*,
DWORD *dwAclInfoLength*,
ACL_INFORMATION_CLASS *AclClassInfo*)

Applications use **SetAclInformation()** to detail the specifics of a security access control list or **ACL**. *pAcl* is a pointer to an **ACL** structure that the function will use to set the specifics for the **ACL**. *lpvAclInfo* is a pointer to a buffer containing the information defining the security access control list.

dwAclInfoLength identifies the size, in bytes, of the *lpvAclInfo* buffer. *AclClassInfo* identifies the class of information being used.

The function returns TRUE if successful, and FALSE otherwise.

USAGE

AclClassInfo may be set to **AclRevisionInformation**. This means that the *lpvAclInfo* buffer points to an **ACL_REVISION_INFORMATION** structure. This structure contains one **DWORD** member, called **AclRevision**, that holds the revision number.

RELATED FUNCTIONS

AddAccessAllowedAce()
AddAce()
DeleteAce()
GetAce()
GetAclInformation()
InitializeAce()
IsValidAcl()

BOOL SetFileSecurity(LPTSTR *lpszFileName*,
SECURITY_INFORMATION *siSecurityInformation*,
PSECURITY_DESCRIPTOR *psdDescriptor*)

You use **SetFileSecurity()** to set the security level for a file or directory. *lpszFileName* is a pointer to a NULL-terminated string identifying either a file or subdirectory.

siSecurityInformation is a **SECURITY_INFORMATION** structure containing the specifics for the **SECURITY_INFORMATION** structure pointed to by *psdDescriptor*.

The function returns TRUE if successful, and FALSE otherwise.

USAGE

SetFileSecurity() will only be successful under the following circumstances:

Caller's Status	To Set the Object's
SeSecurityPrivilege	SACL
WRITE_DAC permission	DACL
WRITE_OWNER permission	owner

RELATED FUNCTION

GetFileSecurity()

BOOL SetPrivateObjectSecurity (SECURITY_INFORMATION *siSecurityInformation*, PSECURITY_DESCRIPTOR *psiModificationDescriptor*, PSECURITY_DESCRIPTOR *psiObjectSecurityInformation*, PGENERIC_MAPPING **ppgmSecurityDescriptor*, HANDLE *hToken*)

Use **SetPrivateObjectSecurity()** to change an object's security descriptor. *siSecurityInformation* is a **SECURITY_INFORMATION** structure defining the security information about to be applied to the object.

psiModificationDescriptor is a pointer to a **SECURITY_DESCRIPTOR** structure containing the security descriptor being applied to the object. *psiObjectSecurityInformation* is a pointer to the **SECURITY_DESCRIPTOR** structure being changed.

ppgmSecurityDescriptor is a pointer to a **GENERIC_MAPPING** structure defining the object's mapping of generic to specific access types. *hToken* identifies the client token whose security is being changed.

The function returns TRUE if successful, and FALSE otherwise.

USAGE

SetPrivateObjectSecurity() will allocate additional memory to create a larger security descriptor, if necessary.

RELATED FUNCTION

SetUserObjectSecurity()

BOOL SetSecurityDescriptorDacl
(PSECURITY_DESCRIPTOR *psdSecurityDescriptor,*
BOOL *bIsDaclPresent,*
PACL *pACL,* BOOL *bDefaultDacl)*

SetSecurityDescriptorDacl() sets or replaces a discretionary access control list. *psdSecurityDescriptor* is a pointer to a **SECURITY_DESCRIPTOR** structure being added to the **ACL**.

When *bIsDaclPresent* is TRUE, the function uses the *pACL* and *bDefaultDacl* parameters. If FALSE, *pACL* and *bDefaultDacl* are ignored. (If *bIsDaclPresent* is FALSE, then there is no DACL in the security descriptor.)

pACL is a pointer to an **ACL** structure. If *bDefaultDacl* is TRUE, the *Dacl* came from a default mechanism; otherwise it was explicitly defined by the user.

The function returns TRUE if successful, and FALSE otherwise.

USAGE

SetSecurityDescriptorDacl() will set or clear the *DaclPresent* and *DaclDefaulted* fields in the **SECURITY_DESCRIPTOR** structure to match *bIsDaclPresent* and *bDefaultDacl,* respectively.

RELATED FUNCTIONS

GetSecurityDescriptorGroup()
GetSecurityDescriptorControl()
GetSecurityDescriptorDacl()
IsValidSecurityDescriptor()

BOOL SetSecurityDescriptorGroup
(PSECURITY_DESCRIPTOR *psdSecurityDescriptor,*
PSID *psidGroup,*
BOOL *bDefaultedGroup*)

Your application uses **SetSecurityDescriptorGroup()** to set or replace a primary group within a security descriptor. *psdSecurityDescriptor* is a pointer to a **SECURITY_DESCRIPTOR** structure whose primary group is being set or replaced.

psidGroup is a pointer to an **SID** structure that the function uses to reference, not copy, the **SID**. If TRUE, *bDefaultedGroup* indicates that the group was derived from a default mechanism; if FALSE, it indicates that the group was defined by the user.

The function returns TRUE if successful, and FALSE otherwise.

USAGE

psidGroup may be NULL, in which case **SetSecurityDescriptorGroup()** will reset the primary group information within the security descriptor.

RELATED FUNCTIONS

GetSecurityDescriptorGroup()
GetSecurityDescriptorLength()
InitializeSecurityDescriptor()

BOOL SetSecurityDescriptorOwner
(PSECURITY_DESCRIPTOR *psdSecurityDescriptor,*
PSID *psidOwner,*
BOOL *bDefaultOwner*)

SetSecurityDescriptorOwner() sets or replaces a security descriptor's owner. *psdSecurityDescriptor* is a pointer to a **SECURITY_DESCRIPTOR** structure whose owner is about to be set or replaced. *psidOwner* is a pointer to an **SID** structure identifying the new owner.

If TRUE, *bDefaultOwner* indicates that the owner was obtained from the default procedure; if FALSE, the owner was declared by the user.

The function returns TRUE if successful, and FALSE otherwise.

USAGE

psidOwner may be NULL, in which case **SetSecurityDescriptorOwner()** will reset the owner, indicating that the security descriptor no longer has an owner. The function sets the security descriptor's *OwnerDefaulted* flag to match the *bDefaultOwner* parameter.

RELATED FUNCTIONS

GetSecurityDescriptorOwner()
IsValidSecurityDescriptor()

BOOL SetSecurityDescriptorSacl
(PSECURITY_DESCRIPTOR *psdSecurityDescriptor,*
BOOL *bIsSaclPresent,*
PACL *pACL,* BOOL *bDefaultSacl*)

SetSecurityDescriptorSacl() sets or replaces a system access control list. *psdSecurityDescriptor* is a pointer to a **SECURITY_DESCRIPTOR** structure being added to the **ACL**.

When *bIsSaclPresent* is TRUE, the function uses the *pACL* and *bDefaultSacl* parameters. If FALSE, *pACL,* and *bDefaultSacl* are ignored. (If *bIsSaclPresent* is FALSE, then there is no SACL in the security descriptor.)

pACL is a pointer to an **ACL** structure. If *bDefaultSacl* is TRUE, the *Sacl* came from a default mechanism; otherwise it was explicitly defined by the user.

The function returns TRUE if successful, and FALSE otherwise.

USAGE

SetSecurityDescriptorSacl() will set or clear the *SaclPresent* and *SaclDefaulted* fields in the **SECURITY_DESCRIPTOR** structure to match *bIsSaclPresent* and *bDefaultSacl,* respectively.

RELATED FUNCTIONS

GetSecurityDescriptorSacl()
IsValidSecurityDescriptor()
SetSecurityDescriptorGroup()
SetSecurityDescriptorOwner()

BOOL SetTokenInformation(HANDLE *hToken*,
TOKEN_INFORMATION_CLASS *tifClass*,
LPVOID *lpvTokenInfo*,
DWORD *dwTokenInfoLength*)

Use **SetTokenInformation()** to detail the types of information used by a token. *hToken* is a handle to the token in question. *tifClass* defines the type of token information being set, enumerated within the discussion of *lpvTokenInfo*.

lpvTokenInfo is a pointer to the buffer containing the information being set. *dwTokenInfoLength* defines the size of the buffer pointed to by *lpvTokenInfo*, in bytes.

The function returns TRUE if successful, and FALSE otherwise.

USAGE

lpvTokenInfo may be one of the following token information classes:

TOKEN_INFORMATION_CLASS	lpvTokenInfo Points to
TokendefaultDacl	**TOKEN_DEFAULT_DACL** structure
TokenGroups	Illegal
TokenImpersonationLevel	Illegal
TokenOwner	**TOKEN_OWNER** structure
TokenPrimaryGroup	**TOKEN_PRIMARY_GROUP** structure
TokenPrivileges	Illegal
TokenSource	Illegal
TokenType	Illegal
TokenUser	Illegal

RELATED FUNCTIONS

AdjustTokenGroups()
AdjustTokenPrivileges()

GetTokenInformation()
OpenProcessToken()

BOOL SetUserObjectSecurity(HANDLE *hToken,* PSECURITY_INFORMATION *psiSecurityInformation,* PSECURITY_DESCRIPTOR *psdSecurityDescriptor*)

SetUserObjectSecurity() sets an object's security descriptor values. *hToken* is a handle to the object in question. *psiSecurityInformation* is a pointer to a **SECURITY_INFORMATION** structure describing the security information values being set. *psdSecurityDescriptor* is a pointer to a **SECURITY_DE-SCRIPTOR** structure containing the security descriptor values being set.

The function returns TRUE if successful, and FALSE otherwise.

USAGE

If *hToken* is assigned a NULL, **SetUserObjectSecurity()** assumes that the caller is impersonating a client, therefore an impersonation token is used.

RELATED FUNCTION

GetUserObjectSecurity()

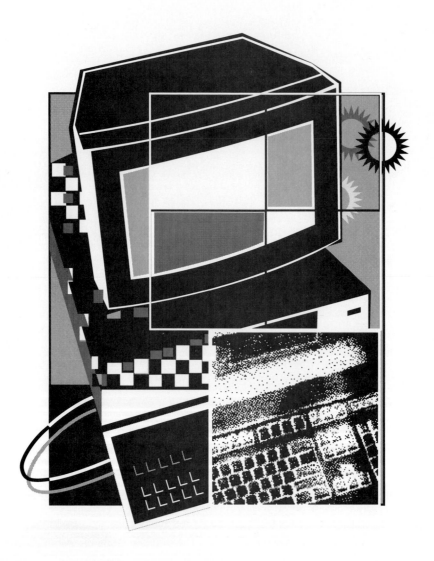

Chapter 32

Synchronization

T H I S chapter describes Windows' synchronization functions. These functions can be used to control access to critical sections. This synchronization is achieved using semaphores, critical sections, and event objects. A complete programming example is shown at the end of this chapter.

For an overview of synchronization and several additional program examples, refer to Chapter 14 in Volume 1 of this series.

HANDLE CreateEvent(LPSECURITY_ATTRIBUTES *lpSa,* BOOL *fManReset,* BOOL *fInitState,* LPCTSTR *lpszEventName*)

CreateEvent() creates an event object, either named or not named. The returned handle will have **EVENT_ALL_ACCESS** access to the new event object.

lpSa is a pointer to a **SECURITY_ATTRIBUTES** structure. This structure is used to provide the security attributes for the event object. If NULL, the event object will be created with a default security descriptor and the handle that will not be inherited.

fManReset indicates whether a manual-reset or auto-reset event object is created. When this value is TRUE, **ResetEvent()** will manually reset the state (non-signaled). If this value is FALSE, it will be reset automatically to non-signaled once a waiting thread is released.

fInitState gives the initial state of the event object. The state will be non-signaled unless this value is TRUE. *lpszEventName* is a pointer to a null-terminated string. This string gives the name of the event object and can be up to **MAX_PATH** characters in length. If this parameter matches the name of a named event object, the function obtains **EVENT_ALL_ACCESS** access to the object. If NULL, the event object is created without a name.

The handle can be closed with a call to **CloseHandle()** or automatically when the process terminates.

The function returns a handle to the event object if successful. If the function is unsuccessful because *lpszEventName* matches the name of an existing semaphore, mutex, or file-mapping object, the function returns NULL.

USAGE

Here is a small portion of code that illustrates the use of this function.

```
SECURITY_ATTRIBUTES SecurityAttrib;
  .
  .
  .

SecurityAttrib.bInheritHandle = TRUE;
SecurityAttrib.lpSecurityDescriptor = NULL;
SecurityAttrib.nLength = sizeof (SECURITY_ATTRIBUTES);
hEventObj = CreateEvent(&SecurityAttrib,
                    FALSE, FALSE, NULL);
```

When called, **CreateEvent()** sets the event object for auto-reset, non-signaled, and no name.

RELATED FUNCTIONS

CloseHandle()
OpenEvent()
ResetEvent()
SetEvent()
WaitForMultipleObjects()
WaitForMultipleObjectsEx()
WaitForSingleObject()
WaitForSingleObjectEx()

HANDLE CreateMutex(LPSECURITY_ATTRIBUTES *lpSa*, BOOL *fInitOwner*, LPCTSTR *lpszMutexName*)

CreateMutex() creates a mutex object that can be named or not named. The returned handle has **MUTEX_ALL_ACCESS** access to the new mutex object.

lpSa is a pointer to a **SECURITY_ATTRIBUTES** structure (discussed more fully in the previous chapter). This structure gives the mutex object's security attributes. If NULL, the object will be given the default security descriptor with a non-inheritable handle.

fInitOwner gives the mutex object's initial owner. This value must be TRUE in order to establish ownership.

lpszMutexName is a pointer to a null-terminated string. This string gives the name of the mutex object, which can be up to **MAX_PATH** characters in length. If this parameter matches the name of a named mutex object, the function obtains **MUTEX_ALL_ACCESS** access to the object. If NULL, the event object is created without a name.

Single-object wait functions return when the state of the object is signaled and release the waiting thread. Multiple-object wait functions can return when any of the objects are signaled and release the waiting thread.

Handles of the same mutex object can be shared by multiple processes, allowing the object's use for interprocess synchronization.

The handle can be closed by either **CloseHandle()** or by the system when the process terminates.

The function returns a handle to the mutex object if successful. If the function is unsuccessful because *lpszEventName* matches the name of an existing event, semaphore, or file-mapping object, the function returns NULL.

USAGE

Here is a small portion of code that illustrates the use of this function.

```
HANDLE hMutex;

hMutex = CreateMutex(NULL, FALSE, "MutexObjectName");
```

Here, a mutex object is created without a security descriptor. The mutex is not owned.

RELATED FUNCTIONS

CloseHandle()
MsgWaitForMultipleObjects()
OpenMutex()
ReleaseMutex()
WaitForMultipleObjects()
WaitForMultipleObjectsEx()
WaitForSingleObject()
WaitForSingleObjectEx()

HANDLE CreateSemaphore
(LPSECURITY_ATTRIBUTES *lpSa,*
LONG *cSemInitial,*
LONG *cSemMax,*
LPCTSTR *lpszSemName*)

CreateSemaphore() creates a semaphore object that can be named or not named. The handle has **SEMAPHORE_ALL_ACCESS** access to the new semaphore object.

lpSa is a pointer to a **SECURITY_ATTRIBUTES** structure. This structure gives the security attributes for the semaphore object. If NULL, the semaphore object is created with a default security descriptor and a non-inheritable handle.

cSemInitial gives an initial count for the semaphore object. (*cSemInitial* >= 0 and <= *cSemMax*). The count is decremented when a wait function releases a thread that was waiting for the semaphore and incremented by calling **Release-Semaphore()**. A count greater than zero places a semaphore in a signaled state, while a count of zero places a semaphore in a non-signaled state.

cSemMax gives the maximum count for the semaphore object. *lpszSemName* is a pointer to a null-terminated string. This string gives the name of the semaphore object and can be up to **MAX_PATH** characters in length. If this value is NULL, the object is created without a name. If this value matches the name of an existing named semaphore object, a **SEMAPHORE_ALL_AC-CESS** access will be made to the existing object. When *lpSa* is not NULL, the handle can be inherited but its security-descriptor is not considered.

Handles of the same mutex object can be shared by multiple processes, allowing the object's use for interprocess synchronization.

The handle can be closed by either **CloseHandle()** or by the system when the process terminates.

The function returns a handle to the mutex object if successful. If the function is unsuccessful because *lpszSemName* matches the name of an existing event, mutex, or file-mapping object, the function returns NULL.

USAGE

Here is a small portion of code that illustrates the use of this function.

```
HANDLE hSemaphore;

// semaphore with initial and maximum counts of 20

hSemaphore = CreateSemaphore(NULL, 20L, 20L, NULL);
```

RELATED FUNCTIONS

CloseHandle()
OpenSemaphore()
ReleaseSemaphore()
WaitForMultipleObjects()
WaitForMultipleObjectsEx()
WaitForSingleObject()
WaitForSingleObjectEx()

VOID DeleteCriticalSection
(LPCRITICAL_SECTION *lpcsCritSec*)

DeleteCriticalSection() removes a critical section object.

lpcsCritSec is a pointer to the critical section object.

When a critical section object is deleted, all system resources used by the object are freed.

No value is returned by this function.

USAGE

Here is a small portion of code that illustrates the use of this function.

```
// Call this function once all threads are stopped and all
// thread handles are closed.

DeleteCriticalSection(&TheQueue -> CritSect);
```

RELATED FUNCTIONS

EnterCriticalSection()
InitializeCriticalSection()
LeaveCriticalSection()

VOID EnterCriticalSection
(LPCRITICAL_SECTION *lpcsCritSec*)

EnterCriticalSection() waits for ownership of the critical section object and returns when the calling thread is given ownership.

lpcsCritSec is a pointer to the critical section object.

A critical section object can be used for mutual-exclusion synchronization by the threads of a single process. In this situation, the process allocates memory for use by the critical section object with a variable declared as type **CRITICAL_SECTION**. Objects must be initialized by **InitializeCriticalSection()**.

For synchronization between the threads of different processes a mutex object should be used.

This function does not return a value.

USAGE

Here is a small portion of code that illustrates the use of this function.

```
CRITICAL_SECTION GlobCritSect;
    .
    .
    .
```

```
EnterCriticalSection(&GlobCritSect);
```

RELATED FUNCTIONS

CreateMutex()
DeleteCriticalSection()
InitializeCriticalSection()
LeaveCriticalSection()

VOID InitializeCriticalSection
(LPCRITICAL_SECTION *lpcsCritSec*)

InitializeCriticalSection() initializes a critical section object.

lpcsCritSec is a pointer to the critical section object.

Mutual-exclusion synchronization can be achieved by allowing the threads of a single process to use a critical section object. The process manages the memory for the critical section object by declaring a variable of type **CRITICAL_SECTION**. A thread of the process must call **InitializeCriticalSection()** to initialize the object.

For synchronization between the threads of different processes a mutex object should be used. Critical section objects cannot be moved or copied.

This function does not return a value.

USAGE

Here is a small portion of code that illustrates the use of this function.

```
CRITICAL_SECTION GlobCritSect;
        .
        .
        .
InitializeCriticalSection(&GlobCritSect);
```

RELATED FUNCTIONS

CreateMutex()
DeleteCriticalSection()
EnterCriticalSection()
LeaveCriticalSection()

LONG InterlockedDecrement(LPLONG *lplVal*)

InterlockedDecrement() decrements the value of the variable and simultaneously checks the resulting value. This prevents multiple threads from using **InterlockedDecrement()** or **InterlockedIncrement()** to access the same variable at the same time.

lplVal is a pointer to a 32-bit variable to decrement. This function provides a technique for synchronizing access to a variable shared by multiple threads. The variable must be aligned on a 32-bit boundary.

If the decrement results in a zero value, the function also returns a zero. When the decrement is less than zero, the function returns a value less than zero. When the decrement results in a number greater than zero, the function returns a value greater than zero.

RELATED FUNCTION

InterlockedIncrement()

LONG InterlockedIncrement(LPLONG *lplVal*)

InterlockedIncrement() increments the value of the variable and simultaneously checks the resulting value. This prevents multiple threads from using **InterlockedDecrement()** or **InterlockedIncrement()** to access the same variable at the same time.

lplVal is a pointer to a 32-bit variable to increment.

If the increment results in a zero value, the function also returns zero. When the increment is less than zero, the function returns a value less than zero. When the increment results in a number greater than zero, the function returns a value greater than zero.

RELATED FUNCTION

InterlockedDecrement()

VOID LeaveCriticalSection (LPCRITICAL_SECTION *lpcsCritSec*)

LeaveCriticalSection() gives up ownership of the critical section object.

lpcsCritSec is a pointer to the critical section object.

Once a thread owns a critical section object it can make repeated calls to **EnterCriticalSection()** without blocking its execution. To release ownership, the thread calls **LeaveCriticalSection()**. It must make this call for each entrance to the critical section.

Mutually exclusive access to a shared resource can be provided by using the threads of a single process and a critical section object.

For synchronization between the threads of different processes a mutex object should be used.

This function does not return a value.

USAGE

Here is a small portion of code that illustrates the use of this function.

```
CRITICAL_SECTION GlobCritSect;
     .
     .
     .
LeaveCriticalSection(&GlobCritSect);
```

RELATED FUNCTIONS

CreateMutex()
DeleteCriticalSection()
EnterCriticalSection()
InitializeCriticalSection()

DWORD MsgWaitForMultipleObjects
(DWORD *cObjects,*
LPHANDLE *lphObjects,*
BOOL *fWaitAll,*
DWORD *dwTimeInt,*
DWORD *fdwWakeMask*)

MsgWaitForMultipleObjects() waits on multiple objects. It returns when one of three events occurs: any of the objects are in the signaled state, a type of input is available in the thread's input queue, or the timeout interval elapses. No return will occur if there was previously unread input of the given type in the queue.

cObjects gives the number of object handles in the array. *lphObjects* is a pointer to this array. The array can hold a maximum of **MAXIMUM_WAIT_OB-JECTS** object handles. *lphObjects* is a pointer used to point to an array of object handles with **SYNCHRONIZE** access.

fWaitAll gives the wait type, and when TRUE, will only return when all objects in the array are signaled. If FALSE, only one of the objects is signaled. *dwTimeInt* gives the timeout in milliseconds. When zero, the states of the objects are tested and the function returns immediately. When this value is set to **INFINITE**, the timeout interval never ends.

fdwWakeMask gives the possible types of input and can be selected from those types shown here:

Value	Purpose
QS_ALLINPUT	Messages are in queue
QS_HOTKEY	**WM_HOTKEY** message in queue
QS_INPUT	Input message in queue
QS_KEY	**WM_KEYUP, WM_KEYDOWN, WM_SYSKEYUP, or WM_SYSKEYDOWN** message in queue
QS_MOUSE	**WM_MOUSEMOVE, WM_LBUTTONUP, WM_RBUTTONDOWN,** and so on, in queue
QS_MOUSEBUTTON	**WM_LBUTTONUP, WM_RBUTTONDOWN,** and so on, mouse button message in queue
QS_MOUSEMOVE	**WM_MOUSEMOVE** message in queue
QS_PAINT	**WM_PAINT** message in queue
QS_POSTMESSAGE	Posted message in queue
QS_SENDMESSAGE	Message from another thread or application in queue
QS_TIMER	**WM_TIMER** message in queue

MsgWaitForMultipleObjects() is used to find whether conditions will satisfy the wait. When the wait is not satisfied, the thread enters a wait state.

The function returns 0xFFFFFFFF if unsuccessful. When successful, the returned value gives the event that caused the function to return, and can be any of the next four conditions:

◆ **WAIT_TIMEOUT**   The timeout interval has ended and the conditions given by *fWaitAll* and *fdwWakeMask* were not satisfied.

◆ **WAIT_OBJECT_0** to (**WAIT_OBJECT_0** + *cObjects* − *1*)   When *fWaitAll* is TRUE, the return value gives the state of all objects as signaled; when FALSE, the return value gives the *lphObjects* array index of the object that satisfied the wait.

◆ **WAIT_OBJECT_0** + *cObjects*   The input is the type given in *fdwWakeMask* and is available in the input queue.

◆ **WAIT_ABANDONED_0** to (**WAIT_ABANDONED_0** + *cObjects* − *1*)   When *fWaitAll* is TRUE, the return value gives the state of all objects as signaled. In this case, one of the objects is an abandoned mutex object. When *fWaitAll* is FALSE, the return value gives the *lphObjects* array index of an abandoned mutex object satisfying the wait.

RELATED FUNCTIONS

Sleep()
WaitForMultipleObjects()
WaitForMultipleObjectsEx()
WaitForSingleObject()

HANDLE OpenEvent(DWORD *fdwAccess,*
BOOL *fInherit,* LPCTSTR *lpszEventName*)

OpenEvent() obtains a handle on an existing named event object. This function requires that the event has been created by some process using **CreateEvent()**. The function returns the handle of the event object if successful, and NULL if unsuccessful.

fdwAccess gives access to the event object. If object security is in effect, the function fails when the security descriptor does not allow the given access for the calling process. Here are the values that can be used for this parameter:

Value	Purpose
EVENT_MODIFY_STATE	Permits the event handle to be used by **SetEvent()** and **ResetEvent()** for altering the event's state
SYNCHRONIZE	Permits the event handle to be used by any wait function to wait for the event state to be signaled
EVENT_ALL_ACCESS	Permits all access flags for the event object

fInherit determines whether the returned handle can be inherited. A process can inherit the handle when this is TRUE. *lpszEventName* is a pointer to a null-terminated string. This string identifies the event to be opened.

The handle is closed automatically by the system when the process terminates.

USAGE

Here is a small portion of code that illustrates the use of this function.

```
HANDLE hWrtEvnt;
   .
   .
   .
hWrtEvnt = OpenEvent(EVENT_ALL_ACCESS, FALSE, "WriteEvent");
```

RELATED FUNCTIONS

CloseHandle()
CreateEvent()
DuplicateHandle()
MsgWaitForMultipleObjects()
PulseEvent()
ResetEvent()
SetEvent()
WaitForMultipleObjects()
WaitForMultipleObjectsEx()
WaitForSingleObject()
WaitForSingleObjectEx()

HANDLE OpenMutex(DWORD *fdwAccess*, BOOL *fInherit*, LPCTSTR *lpszMutexName*)

OpenMutex() obtains a handle of an existing mutex object.

fdwAccess provides the access requested to the mutex object. When object security is supported, the function fails if the security descriptor does not permit the requested access. *fdwAccess* can be one or both of these values:

Value	Purpose
SYNCHRONIZE	Allows the mutex handle to be used in any wait function in order to obtain ownership of the mutex
MUTEX_ALL_ACCESS	Allows all access flags for the mutex object

fInherit states whether the handle is inheritable. This value must be TRUE in order for a process to inherit the handle. *lpszMutexName* is a pointer to a null-terminated string. This string gives the name of the mutex to open.

Handles of the same mutex object can be shared by multiple processes, allowing the object's use for interprocess synchronization.

The handle can be closed by either **CloseHandle()** or by the system when the process terminates.

The function returns a handle of the mutex object if successful, and NULL if unsuccessful.

USAGE

Here is a small portion of code that illustrates the use of this function.

```
HANDLE hMutex;

hMutex = OpenMutex(MUTEX_ALL_ACCESS, FALSE, "MutexObjectName");
```

Here, the mutex object is synchronized. The handle is not inherited.

RELATED FUNCTIONS

CloseHandle()
CreateMutex()
DuplicateHandle()
MsgWaitForMultipleObjects()
ReleaseMutex()
WaitForMultipleObjects()
WaitForMultipleObjectsEx()
WaitForSingleObject()
WaitForSingleObjectEx()

HANDLE OpenSemaphore(DWORD *fdwAccess,* BOOL *fInherit,* LPCTSTR *lpszSemName)*

OpenSemaphore() obtains a handle of an existing named semaphore object. The function returns the handle of the semaphore object if successful, and NULL if unsuccessful.

fdwAccess gives access to the semaphore object. If object security is enabled, the function fails when the security descriptor of the object does not allow this access for the calling process. The value used here can be selected from those shown below:

Value	Purpose
SEMAPHORE_MODIFY_STATE	Uses the semaphore handle to modify the count with the use of **ReleaseSemaphore()**.
SYNCHRONIZE	Uses the semaphore handle in wait functions to wait for a signaled state.
SEMAPHORE_ALL_ACCESS	Uses all access flags for the semaphore object.

When *fInherit* is TRUE, the returned handle is inheritable. When *fInherit* is FALSE, the handle may not be inherited.

lpszSemName is a pointer to a null-terminated string. This string provides the name(s) of the semaphore to be opened.

RELATED FUNCTIONS

CloseHandle()
CreateSemaphore()
DuplicateHandle()
MsgWaitForMultipleObjects()
ReleaseSemaphore()
WaitForMultipleObjects()
WaitForMultipleObjectsEx()
WaitForSingleObject()
WaitForSingleObjectEx()

BOOL PulseEvent(HANDLE *hEvent*)

PulseEvent() achieves, in a single operation, a method of setting the state of the specified event object (signaled) and then resetting it (non-signaled) once the correct number of waiting threads has been released. The handle can be returned by either **CreateEvent()** or **OpenEvent()** and must have **EVENT_MODIFY_STATE** access.

The function returns TRUE if successful, and FALSE otherwise.

hEvent is a handle used to identify the event object.

All waiting threads are released for manual-reset event objects, and the event object's state is reset to non-signaled. A single waiting thread is released for auto-reset event objects, and the event object's state is reset to non-signaled. When no threads are waiting or cannot be released immediately, the function sets the event object's state to non-signaled.

RELATED FUNCTIONS

CreateEvent()
MsgWaitForMultipleObjects()
OpenEvent()
ResetEvent()
SetEvent()
WaitForMultipleObjects()
WaitForMultipleObjectsEx()
WaitForSingleObject()
WaitForSingleObjectEx()

BOOL ReleaseMutex(HANDLE *hMutex*)

ReleaseMutex() releases ownership of the mutex object. **CreateMutex()** or **OpenMutex()** obtains this handle. The function returns TRUE if successful, and FALSE otherwise.

hMutex is a handle used to identify the mutex object.

If the handle of a mutex is given in a wait function, a thread can obtain ownership of a mutex. When ownership is no longer needed it can be released with a call to **ReleaseMutex()**.

USAGE

Here is a small portion of code that illustrates how this function might be used.

```
HANDLE hFileMutex;
    .
    .
    .
ReleaseMutex(hFileMutex);
```

RELATED FUNCTIONS

CreateMutex()
WaitForMultipleObjects()
WaitForMultipleObjectsEx()
WaitForSingleObject()
WaitForSingleObjectEx()

BOOL ReleaseSemaphore(HANDLE *hSemaphore*,
LONG *cReleaseCount*,
LPLONG *lplPrevCount*)

ReleaseSemaphore() increases the count of the semaphore object by the given amount. The function returns TRUE if successful, and FALSE otherwise.

hSemaphore is a handle used to identify the semaphore object. Use **Create-Semaphore()** or **OpenSemaphore()** to obtain the required handle with **SEMAPHORE_MODIFY_STATE** access.

cReleaseCount gives the increase in the semaphore object's current count, which must be greater than zero. *lplPrevCount* is a pointer to a 32-bit variable. This variable obtains the previous count for the semaphore and can be NULL if the previous information is not needed.

If the count is zero, the state of the semaphore object is non-signaled. If the count is greater than zero, the state of the semaphore object is signaled. The count of the semaphore is decreased by one for each time a waiting thread is released.

USAGE

Here is a small portion of code that illustrates the use of this function.

```
HANDLE hSemaphore;
LONG PrevCount;

// semaphore with initial and maximum counts of 20

hSemaphore = CreateSemaphore(NULL, 20L, 20L, NULL);
    .
    .
    .
ReleaseSemaphore(hSemaphore, 1, &PrevCount);
```

RELATED FUNCTIONS

CreateSemaphore()
MsgWaitForMultipleObjects()
OpenSemaphore()
WaitForMultipleObjects()
WaitForMultipleObjectsEx()
WaitForSingleObject()
WaitForSingleObjectEx()

BOOL ResetEvent(HANDLE *hEvent*)

ResetEvent() sets the state of the event object to non-signaled. The function returns TRUE if successful, and FALSE otherwise.

hEvent is a handle used to identify the event object. This handle is obtained from **CreateEvent()** or **OpenEvent()** and must have **EVENT_MOD-IFY_STATE** access.

SetEvent() or **PulseEvent()** can be used to change the state of an event object from non-signaled to signaled.

RELATED FUNCTIONS

CreateEvent()
OpenEvent()
PulseEvent()
SetEvent()

BOOL SetEvent(HANDLE *hEvent*)

SetEvent() sets the state of the event object to signaled. The function returns TRUE if successful, and FALSE otherwise.

hEvent is a handle used to identify the event object. This handle is obtained from **CreateEvent()** or **OpenEvent()** and must have **EVENT_MOD-IFY_STATE** access.

An auto-reset event object stays in a signaled state until a waiting thread is released. The state will then automatically change to non-signaled.

A manual-reset event object stays in a signaled state until it is set to non-signaled by **ResetEvent()**. During the period that the object's state is signaled, multiple waiting threads can be released.

USAGE

Here is a small portion of code that illustrates the use of this function.

```
HANDLE hRdEvnt;
    .
    .
    .

hRdEvnt = OpenEvent(EVENT_ALL_ACCESS, FALSE, "ReadEvent");

// hRdEvnt set to signaled state in order to release
// master process. hRdEvnt is reset automatically after
// release of master process.

if (!SetEvent(hRdEvnt)) {
    // error exit
```

RELATED FUNCTIONS

CreateEvent()
MsgWaitForMultipleObjects()
OpenEvent()
PulseEvent()
ResetEvent()
WaitForMultipleObjects()
WaitForMultipleObjectsEx()
WaitForSingleObject()
WaitForSingleObjectEx()

DWORD WaitForMultipleObjects(DWORD *cObjects*,
CONST HANDLE * *lphObjects*,
BOOL *fWaitAll*,
DWORD *dwTimeInt*)

WaitForMultipleObjects() returns when any of the objects are in the signaled state or when the timeout interval elapses.

cObjects gives the number of object handles in the array. *lphObjects* is a pointer to this array. The array can hold a maximum of **MAXIMUM_WAIT_OBJECTS** object handles. *lphObjects* is a pointer used to point to an array of object handles with **SYNCHRONIZE** access.

fWaitAll gives the wait type, and when TRUE, will return when all objects in the array are signaled. A FALSE is returned when only one of the objects is signaled. *dwTimeInt* gives the timeout in milliseconds. When zero, the states of the objects are tested and the function returns immediately. When this value is set to **INFINITE,** the timeout interval never ends.

This function is used to find whether conditions will satisfy the wait. When the wait is not satisfied, the thread enters a wait state.

The function returns 0xFFFFFFFF if unsuccessful. When the function is successful, the returned value gives the event that caused the function to return, and can be any of the next three conditions:

◆ **WAIT_TIMEOUT** The timeout interval has ended and the conditions given by *fWaitAll* were not satisfied.

◆ **WAIT_OBJECT_0** to (**WAIT_OBJECT_0** + *cObjects* − 1) When *fWaitAll* is TRUE, the return value gives the state of all objects as signaled; when FALSE, the return value gives the *lphObjects* array index of the object that satisfied the wait.

◆ **WAIT_ABANDONED_0** to (**WAIT_ABANDONED_0** + *cObjects* − 1) When *fWaitAll* is TRUE, the return value gives the state of all objects as signaled. In this case, one of the objects is an abandoned mutex object. When *fWaitAll* is FALSE, the return value gives the *lphObjects* array index of an abandoned mutex object satisfying the wait.

USAGE

Here is a small portion of code that illustrates the use of this function.

```
HANDLE hEvntObj[10];
   .
   .
   .
while (TRUE) {
  AnEvent = WaitForMultipleObjects(10, hEvntObj, FALSE, 250L);
```

Here, **WaitForMultipleObjects()** will wait for any of 10 objects. The time is set to 1/4 second.

RELATED FUNCTIONS

MsgWaitForMultipleObjects()
Sleep()
WaitForMultipleObjectsEx()
WaitForSingleObject()

DWORD WaitForMultipleObjectsEx(DWORD *cObjects*
CONST HANDLE * *lphObjects,*
BOOL *fWaitAll,*
DWORD *dwTimeInt,*
BOOL *fAlert)*

WaitForMultipleObjectsEx(), a Windows NT function, provides an extended wait, and it can be used to achieve an alertable wait. The function can return when: the system queues an input and output completion routine that is to be executed by the calling thread, when any of the objects are in the signaled state, or when the timeout interval elapses.

cObjects gives the number of object handles in the array. *lphObjects* is a pointer to this array. The array can hold a maximum of **MAXIMUM_WAIT_OBJECTS** object handles. *lphObjects* is a pointer used to point to an array of object handles with **SYNCHRONIZE** access.

fWaitAll gives the wait type, and when TRUE, will return when all objects in the array are signaled. A FALSE is returned when only one of the objects is signaled. *dwTimeInt* gives the timeout in milliseconds. When zero, the states of the objects are tested and the function returns immediately. When this value is set to **INFINITE**, the timeout interval never ends.

fAlert is used when the system queues an I/O routine for execution. When TRUE, the I/O completion routine is executed and the function returns. When FALSE, the I/O completion routine is not executed and the function does not return.

The function returns 0xFFFFFFFF if unsuccessful. When the function is successful, the returned value gives the event that caused the function to return, and can be any of the next five conditions:

◆   **WAIT_TIMEOUT**   The timeout interval has ended and the conditions given by *fWaitAll* and *fdwWakeMask* were not satisfied.

♦ **WAIT_OBJECT_0** to (**WAIT_OBJECT_0** + *cObjects* − *1*)   When *fWaitAll* is TRUE, the return value gives the state of all objects as signaled; when FALSE, the return value gives the *lphObjects* array index of the object that satisfied the wait.

♦ **WAIT_OBJECT_0** + *cObjects*   The input is the type given in *fdwWakeMask* and is available in the input queue.

♦ **WAIT_ABANDONED_0** to (**WAIT_ABANDONED_0** + *cObjects* − *1*)   When *fWaitAll* is TRUE, the return value gives the state of all objects as signaled. In this case, one of the objects is an abandoned mutex object. When *fWaitAll* is FALSE, the return value gives the *lphObjects* array index of an abandoned mutex object satisfying the wait.

♦ **WAIT_IO_COMPLETION**   I/O completion routines will be queued for execution.

RELATED FUNCTIONS

MsgWaitForMultipleObjects()
ReadFileEx()
SleepEx()
WaitForMultipleObjects()
WaitForSingleObjectEx()
WriteFileEx()

DWORD WaitForSingleObject(HANDLE *hObject*, DWORD *dwTimeInt*)

WaitForSingleObject() returns when the object is in the signaled state or when the timeout interval elapses.

hObject is a handle used to identify the object with **SYNCHRONIZE** access. *dwTimeInt* gives the timeout in milliseconds. When zero, the states of the objects are tested and the function returns immediately. When this value is set to **INFINITE**, the timeout interval never ends.

The function returns **WAIT_FAILED** if unsuccessful. When the function is successful, the returned value gives the event that caused the function to return, and can be any of the next three conditions:

♦ **WAIT_TIMEOUT** The timeout interval has ended with the object's state non-signaled.

♦ **WAIT_OBJECT_0** The state of the object is signaled.

♦ **WAIT_ABANDONED** The state of the object is signaled, it is a mutex object, and the thread owning the object ended without releasing ownership.

USAGE

Here is a small portion of code that illustrates the use of this function.

```
PROCESS_INFORMATION process_info;
    .
    .
    .
dwResult = WaitForSingleObject(process_info.hProcess, (DWORD) -1);
CloseHandle(process_info.hProcess);
```

RELATED FUNCTIONS

Sleep()
WaitForMultipleObjects()
WaitForSingleObjectsEx()

DWORD WaitForSingleObjectEx(HANDLE *hObject*
 DWORD *dwTimeInt,*
 BOOL *fAlert*)

WaitForSingleObjectEx() provides an extended wait, and it can be used to achieve an alertable wait. The function can return when the system queues an input and output completion routine that is to be executed by the calling thread, when any of the objects are in the signaled state, or when the timeout interval elapses.

hObject is a handle used to identify the object with **SYNCHRONIZE** access. *dwTimeInt* gives the timeout in milliseconds. When zero, the states of the objects are tested and the function returns immediately. When this value is set to **INFINITE**, the timeout interval never ends.

fAlert is used when the system queues an I/O routine for execution. When TRUE, the I/O completion routine is executed and the function returns. When FALSE, the I/O completion routine is not executed and the function does not return.

The function returns 0xFFFFFFFF if unsuccessful. When the function is successful, the returned value gives the event that caused the function to return, and can be any of the next four conditions:

◆ **WAIT_TIMEOUT** The timeout interval has ended with the object's state non-signaled.

◆ **WAIT_OBJECT_0** The state of the object is signaled.

◆ **WAIT_ABANDONED** The state of the object is signaled, it is a mutex object, and the thread owning the object ended without releasing ownership.

◆ **WAIT_IO_COMPLETION** I/O completion routines will be queued for execution.

RELATED FUNCTIONS

ReadFileEx()
SleepEx()
WaitForMultipleObjectsEx()
WaitForSingleObject()
WriteFileEx()

A Complete Programming Example

The following Windows NT/Win32 program creates both processes and threads and demonstrates synchronization using a semaphore to prevent two threads from executing concurrently.

```
/* A multithreaded program that illustrates synchronization
   using a standard semaphore. */

#define PROCMAX 5 /* maximum number of processes */

#include <windows.h>
#include <string.h>
#include <stdio.h>
#include "proc.h"

LRESULT CALLBACK WindowFunc(HWND, UINT, WPARAM, LPARAM);
DWORD MyThread1(LPVOID param);
DWORD MyThread2(LPVOID param);

char szWinName[] = "MyWin"; /* name of window class */

char str[255]; /* holds output strings */

int X=0, Y=0; /* current output location */
int maxX, maxY; /* screen dimensions */

int procnum = 0;

DWORD Tid1, Tid2; /* thread IDs */

HDC memdc;
HBITMAP hbit;
HBRUSH hbrush;

PROCESS_INFORMATION pinfo[PROCMAX];

HANDLE hSema; /* handle to semaphore */

TEXTMETRIC tm;

int WINAPI WinMain(HINSTANCE hInst, HINSTANCE hPreInst,
                   LPSTR lpszCmdLine, int nCmdShow)
{
```

```
HWND hWnd;
MSG lpMsg;
WNDCLASS wcApp;
HANDLE hAccel;

/* Define a window class. */
wcApp.hInstance = hInst; /* handle to this instance */
wcApp.lpszClassName = szWinName; /* window class name */
wcApp.lpfnWndProc = WindowFunc; /* window function */
wcApp.style = 0; /* default style */

wcApp.hIcon = LoadIcon(NULL, IDI_APPLICATION); /* icon style */
wcApp.hCursor = LoadCursor(NULL, IDC_ARROW); /* cursor style */

/* specify name of menu resource */
wcApp.lpszMenuName = "MYMENU"; /* main menu */

wcApp.cbClsExtra = 0; /* no extra */
wcApp.cbWndExtra = 0; /* information needed */

/* Make the window light gray. */
wcApp.hbrBackground = GetStockObject(WHITE_BRUSH);

/* Register the window class. */
if(!RegisterClass (&wcApp)) return 0;

/* Now that a window class has been registered, a window
   can be created. */
hWnd = CreateWindow(
  szWinName, /* name of window class */
  "Demonstrate Semaphore Synchronization", /* title */
  WS_OVERLAPPEDWINDOW, /* window style - normal */
  CW_USEDEFAULT, /* X coordinate - let Windows decide */
  CW_USEDEFAULT, /* Y coordinate - let Windows decide */
  CW_USEDEFAULT, /* width - let Windows decide */
  CW_USEDEFAULT, /* height - let Windows decide */
  HWND_DESKTOP, /* handle of parent window - there isn't one */
  NULL, /* no menu */
  hInst, /* handle of this instance of the program */
  NULL /* no additional arguments */
);

/* load accelerators */
hAccel = LoadAccelerators(hInst, "MYMENU");
```

```
/* Display the window. */
ShowWindow(hWnd, nCmdShow);
UpdateWindow(hWnd);

/* Create the message loop. */
while(GetMessage(&lpMsg, NULL, 0, 0))
{
  if(!TranslateAccelerator(hWnd, hAccel, &lpMsg)) {
    TranslateMessage(&lpMsg); /* allow use of keyboard */
    DispatchMessage(&lpMsg); /* return control to Windows */
  }
}
return lpMsg.wParam;
}


/* This function is called by Windows NT and is passed
   messages from the message queue.
*/
LRESULT CALLBACK WindowFunc(HWND hWnd, UINT messg, WPARAM wParam,
                LPARAM lParam)
{
  HDC hdc;
  PAINTSTRUCT paintstruct;
  STARTUPINFO startin;

  switch(messg) {
    case WM_CREATE:
      hSema = CreateSemaphore(NULL, 1, 1, "mysem");

      /* get screen coordinates */
      maxX = GetSystemMetrics(SM_CXSCREEN);
      maxY = GetSystemMetrics(SM_CYSCREEN);

      /* make a compatible memory image device */
      hdc = GetDC(hWnd);
      memdc = CreateCompatibleDC(hdc);
      hbit = CreateCompatibleBitmap(hdc, maxX, maxY);
      SelectObject(memdc, hbit);
      hbrush = GetStockObject(WHITE_BRUSH);
      SelectObject(memdc, hbrush);
      PatBlt(memdc, 0, 0, maxX, maxY, PATCOPY);
      ReleaseDC(hWnd, hdc);
      break;
```

```
case WM_COMMAND:
  switch(LOWORD(wParam)) {
    case ID_PROCESS:
      if(procnum==PROCMAX) {
        MessageBox(hWnd, "Can't Create", "", MB_OK);
        break; /* no more than PROCMAX */
      }

      /* get text metrics */
      GetTextMetrics(memdc, &tm);

      sprintf(str, "Execute Process %d.", procnum);
      TextOut(memdc, X, Y, str, strlen(str)); /* output string */
      Y = Y + tm.tmHeight + tm.tmExternalLeading; /* next line */
      InvalidateRect(hWnd, NULL, 1);

      /* Start a new process */
      startin.cb = sizeof(STARTUPINFO);
      startin.lpReserved = NULL;
      startin.lpDesktop = NULL;
      startin.lpTitle = NULL;
      startin.dwFlags = STARTF_USESHOWWINDOW;
      startin.cbReserved2 = 0;
      startin.lpReserved2 = NULL;
      startin.wShowWindow = SW_SHOWMINIMIZED;

      CreateProcess(NULL, "test.exe",
                    NULL, NULL, FALSE, 0,
                    NULL, NULL, &startin, &pinfo[procnum]);
      procnum++;
      break;
    case ID_KILLPROC:
      if(procnum) procnum--;
      else MessageBox(hWnd, "No process to terminate.",
                      "", MB_OK);
      TerminateProcess(pinfo[procnum].hProcess, 0);
      sprintf(str, "Terminate Process %d.", procnum);
      TextOut(memdc, X, Y, str, strlen(str)); /* output string */
      Y = Y + tm.tmHeight + tm.tmExternalLeading; /* next line */
      InvalidateRect(hWnd, NULL, 1);
      break;
    case ID_THREAD:
      CreateThread(NULL, 0, (LPTHREAD_START_ROUTINE)MyThread1,
                   (LPVOID) hWnd, 0, &Tid1);
```

```
        CreateThread(NULL, 0, (LPTHREAD_START_ROUTINE)MyThread2,
                    (LPVOID) hWnd, 0, &Tid2);
        break;
      case ID_HELP:
        MessageBox(hWnd, "F2: Start Process\nF3: Start Thread",
                  "Help", MB_OK);
        break;
    }
    break;
  case WM_PAINT: /* process a repaint request */
    hdc = BeginPaint(hWnd, &paintstruct); /* get DC */

    /* now, copy memory image onto screen */
    BitBlt(hdc, 0, 0, maxX, maxY, memdc, 0, 0, SRCCOPY);
    EndPaint(hWnd, &paintstruct); /* release DC */
    break;
  case WM_LBUTTONDOWN: /* process left button */
    X = LOWORD(lParam); /* set X,Y to */
    Y = HIWORD(lParam); /* mouse location */
    break;
  case WM_DESTROY: /* terminate the program */
    DeleteDC(memdc); /* delete the memory device */
    PostQuitMessage(0);
    break;
  default:
    /* Let Windows NT process any messages not specified in
    the preceding switch statement. */
    return DefWindowProc(hWnd, messg, wParam, lParam);
  }
  return 0;
}

/* First thread of execution. */
DWORD MyThread1(LPVOID param)
{
  int i;
  DWORD curTid = Tid1;

  /* get text metrics */
  GetTextMetrics(memdc, &tm);
```

```
  /* wait for access to be granted */
  if(WaitForSingleObject(hSema, 10000)==WAIT_TIMEOUT)
          MessageBox((HWND)param, "Time Out Thread 1",
                      "Semaphore Error", MB_OK);

  for(i=0; i<10; i++) {
    Sleep(500);
    sprintf(str, "Thread 1, ID #%d, beep #%d",
            curTid, i);
    TextOut(memdc, X, Y, str, strlen(str)); /* output string */
    Y = Y + tm.tmHeight + tm.tmExternalLeading; /* next line */
    InvalidateRect((HWND) param, NULL, 1);
    MessageBeep(-1);
  }
  ReleaseSemaphore(hSema, 1, NULL);
}

/* Second thread of execution. */
DWORD MyThread2(LPVOID param)
{
  int i;
  DWORD curTid = Tid2;

  /* get text metrics */
  GetTextMetrics(memdc, &tm);

  /* wait for access to be granted */
  if(WaitForSingleObject(hSema, 10000)==WAIT_TIMEOUT)
          MessageBox((HWND)param, "Time Out Thread 2",
                      "Semaphore Error", MB_OK);

  for(i=0; i<10; i++) {
    Sleep(200);
    sprintf(str, "Thread 2");
    TextOut(memdc, X, Y, str, strlen(str)); /* output string */
    Y = Y + tm.tmHeight + tm.tmExternalLeading; /* next line */
    InvalidateRect((HWND) param, NULL, 1);
  }
  ReleaseSemaphore(hSema, 1, NULL);
}
```

This program uses the PROC.H file, which is shown here.

```
#define ID_PROCESS 100
#define ID_KILLPROC 101
#define ID_THREAD 102
#define ID_HELP 103
```

This program requires the following resource file.

```
#include <windows.h>
#include "proc.h"

MYMENU MENU
{
  MENUITEM "&Execute Process", ID_PROCESS
  MENUITEM "&Kill Process", ID_KILLPROC
  MENUITEM "Execute &Thread", ID_THREAD
  MENUITEM "&Help", ID_HELP
}

MYMENU ACCELERATORS
{
  VK_F2, ID_PROCESS, VIRTKEY
  VK_F3, ID_KILLPROC, VIRTKEY
  VK_F4, ID_THREAD, VIRTKEY
  VK_F1, ID_HELP, VIRTKEY
}
```

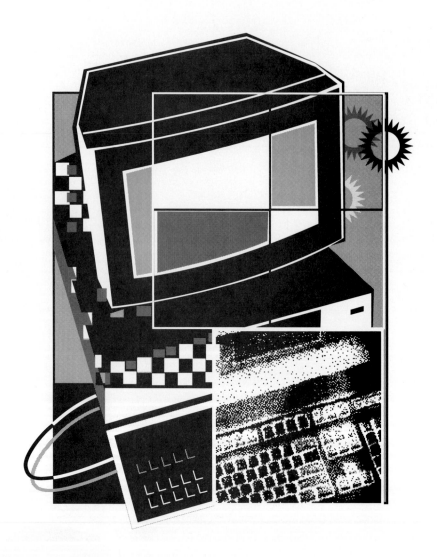

Chapter 33

Thread-Local Storage

THIS chapter describes Windows thread–local storage functions. These functions can be used to allocate, free, set, and get values pertaining to thread–local storage. (*Thread–local storage* refers to memory that is local to a thread.) Thread–local storage is frequently referred to by its acronym: TLS. A small portion of code at the end of this chapter illustrates the use of these four functions.

DWORD TlsAlloc(void)

TlsAlloc() returns an index to thread local storage. Once allocated, a thread uses the index to retrieve or store values local to the thread. If the function is successful, the return value will be the TLS index. If the function is not successful, –1 is returned.

USAGE

Once TLS indexes are allocated, each thread of the process can use the index to access its own TLS storage location. Values are then stored in this location by having the thread give the index value when calling **TlsSetValue()**. Values can be retrieved, in a similar manner, by having the thread give the same index value when calling **TlsGetValue()**.

The amount of thread-local storage indexes is finite and is specified by the value **TLS_MINIMUM_AVAILABLE**. (This value will never be less than 64, however.)

RELATED FUNCTIONS

TlsFree()
TlsGetValue()
TlsSetValue()

BOOL TlsFree(DWORD *dwTlsIndex*)

TlsFree() frees a thread-local storage index, thus allowing it to be reused. If the function is successful, a **TRUE** will be returned. If the function is not successful, a **FALSE** will be returned.

dwTlsIndex contains the TLS index to free. This index must have been previously obtained by calling **TlsAlloc()**.

RELATED FUNCTIONS

TlsAlloc()
TlsGetValue()
TlsSetValue()

LPVOID TlsGetValue(DWORD *dwTlsIndex*)

TlsGetValue() obtains the value associated with a given TLS index. If the function is successful, the return value will be the value found at the specified index. If the function is not successful, a zero will be returned.

dwTlsIndex contains a TLS index previously allocated by **TlsAlloc()**.

USAGE

Since zero is a valid value to store in thread-local storage, you will want to call **GetLastError()** if **TlsGetValue()** returns a zero value. If the value returned by **GetLastError()** is **NO_ERROR**, then zero was, in fact, stored at the specified index.

RELATED FUNCTIONS

TlsAlloc()
TlsSetValue()
TlsFree()

BOOL TlsSetValue(DWORD *dwTlsIndex,* LPVOID *lpvTlsValue*)

TlsSetValue() stores the value specified by *lpvTlsValue* into the thread-local storage location specified by *dwTlsIndex*. If the function is successful, a **TRUE** will be returned. If the function is not successful, a **FALSE** will be returned.

dwTlsIndex is the TLS index at which the value will be stored. This index must have been previously obtained by calling **TlsAlloc()**. *lpvTlsValue* is the value to be stored. Typically, *lpvTlsValue* is a pointer to data.

RELATED FUNCTIONS

TlsAlloc()
TlsGetValue()
TlsFree()

Using the Thread-Local Storage Functions

Here is a small portion of code that illustrates how these four thread-local storage functions might be used in an application.

```
DWORD TlsIdx;
    .
    .
    .
TlsIdx = TlsAlloc();
TlsSetValue(TlsIdx, malloc(200));
    .
    .
    .
free(TlsGetValue(TlsIdx));
TlsFree(TlsIdx))
    .
    .
    .
```

Appendix A

Windows Messages

Quick Reference

T H I S is an alphabetical listing of the Windows messages. Included is a short description of when or why a message is sent, what its *wParam* and *lParam* parameters contain, and the return value it must generate.

BM_GETCHECK

When sent To retrieve the check state of a check box or radio button.

wParam Not used, must be 0.

lParam Not used, must be 0.

Returns 0 if unchecked, 1 if checked, or 2 if undetermined.

BM_GETSTATE

When sent To retrieve the state of a check box or radio button.

wParam Not used, must be 0.

lParam Not used, must be 0.

Returns 0x0003 if checked, 0x0004 if highlight state, 0x0008 if focus state.

BM_SETCHECK

When sent Sets or removes a radio button or check box check mark.

wParam Sets state — 0 to uncheck, 1 to check, 2 to gray.

lParam Not used, must be 0.

Returns 0 always.

BM_SETSTATE

When sent Sets the highlighting state of a button.

wParam Defines the highlight state—!0 highlights, 0 turns off any highlighting.

lParam Not used, must be 0.

Returns 0 always.

BM_SETSTYLE

When sent To define the style of a button.

wParam Defines the button style.

lParam !0 redraws the button, 0 does not redraw button.

Returns 0 always.

BN_CLICKED

When sent When the user clicks a mouse button.

wParam Identifier of button.

lParam Button handle.

BN_DISABLE

When sent When a button is disabled.

BN_DOUBLECLICKED

When sent When the user double-clicks a mouse button.

BN_HILITE

When sent When the user highlights a button.

BN_PAINT

When sent When a button needs painting.

BN_UNHILITE

When sent When a button's highlight should be removed.

CB_ADDSTRING

When sent When a string is being added to the list box of a combo box. If combo box does not have CBS_SORT style, the string is added at the end of the list; otherwise it is added and the list is sorted.

wParam Not used, must be 0.

lParam Null-terminated string pointer to the string being added.

Returns The zero-based index of the added string if successful, CB_ERR on error, CB_ERRSPACE if no space was available.

CB_DELETESTRING

When sent When a string is to be deleted from the list box of a combo box.

wParam Zero-based index of string being deleted.

lParam Not used, must be 0.

Returns A count indicating the number of strings remaining in the list box.

CB_DIR

When sent When a list of filenames is being added to the list box of a combo box.

wParam Defines the files' attributes and may be combinations of the following:

DDL_ARCHIVE, DDL_DIRECTORY, DDL_DRIVES,
DDL_EXCLUSIVE, DDL_HIDDEN, DDL_READONLY,
DDL_READWRITE, DDL_SYSTEM

lParam A null-terminated string pointer specifying the file or files (if wild cards are present) to be added.

Returns A zero-based index of the last filename added to the list if successful, CB_ERR on error, or CB_ERRSPACE if no space was available.

CB_FINDSTRING

When sent To search a list box for the specified string prefix.

wParam −1 to start the search from the beginning of the list, or any other index position used as the starting search point. Any non −1 value starts the search one position after the index specified and then cycles back to the beginning of the list if necessary.

lParam A null-terminated string pointer to the search prefix. The search is not case-sensitive.

Returns The index of the matching item if found, or CB_ERR.

CB_FINDSTRINGEXACT

When sent To search a list box for the specified string.

wParam −1 to start the search from the beginning of the list, or any other index position used as the starting search point. Any non −1 value starts the search one position after the index specified and then cycles back to the beginning of the list if no match was found.

lParam A null-terminated string pointer to the search string. The search is not case-sensitive.

Returns The index of the matching item if found, or CB_ERR.

CB_GETCOUNT

When sent To determine the number of items in a list box.

wParam Not used, must be 0.

lParam Not used, must be 0.

Returns The number of items in the list if successful, CB_ERR otherwise.

CB_GETCURSEL

When sent To retrieve the index position of the currently selected item in a list box.

wParam Not used, must be 0.

lParam Not used, must be 0.

Returns The zero-based index of the selected item if successful, CB_ERR otherwise.

CB_GETDROPPEDCONTROLRECT

When sent When an application wants to know the screen coordinates of a drop-down list box of a combo box.

wParam Not used, must be 0.

lParam Points to a **RECT** structure being filled with the returned coordinates.

Returns CB_OKAY always.

CB_GETDROPPEDSTATE

When sent When an application wants to see if the list box of a combo box is dropped down.

wParam Not used, must be 0.

lParam Not used, must be 0.

Returns TRUE if dropped down, FALSE otherwise.

CB_GETEDITSEL

When Sent To determine the starting and ending character positions of the selection in an edit control of a combo box.

wParam Returns the starting position of the selection. (Not used by 16-bit Windows.)

lParam Returns the ending position of the selection. (Not used by 16-bit Windows.)

Returns Starting position in low word and ending position in high word.

CB_GETEXTENDEDUI

When sent To see if a combo box has the extended interface.

wParam Not used, must be 0.

lParam Not used, must be 0.

Returns TRUE if the combo box has the extended user interface, FALSE otherwise.

CB_GETITEMDATA

When sent Is sent to a combo box to retrieve the 32-bit value associated with an item.

wParam Is the index of the item in question.

lParam Not used, must be 0.

Returns The 32-bit value associated with the item if successful, CB_ERR otherwise.

CB_GETITEMHEIGHT

When sent To determine the height of items in a combo box.

wParam Specifies the component of the combo box whose height will be returned. −1 for the selection field, 0 for list items, or the index to a specific list box item.

lParam Not used, must be 0.

Returns The height in pixels if successful, CB_ERR otherwise.

CB_GETLBTEXT

When sent To return a string from the list box of a combo box.

wParam Specifies the index to the string being returned.

lParam Is a pointer to a buffer which receives a copy of the string in question.

Returns The length, in bytes, of the string (minus the null-string terminator) placed in the buffer if successful; CB_ERR otherwise.

CB_GETLBTEXTLEN

When sent To determine the length of a list-box string in a combo box.

wParam Is the index to the string in question.

lParam Not used, must be 0.

Returns The string length, in bytes, excluding the null-string terminator, if successful; CB_ERR otherwise.

CB_GETLOCALE

When sent To retrieve the current combo box locale, used in the sorting of list box entries. Locale identifiers represent country codes and language identifiers used by the Windows national language support routines.

wParam Not used, must be 0.

lParam Not used, must be 0.

Returns A 32-bit locale value.

CB_INSERTSTRING

When sent When an application wishes to insert a string into the list box of a combo box.

wParam Defines the position within the list where the new item is to be inserted. A value of −1 inserts the item at the end of the list.

lParam Is a pointer to a null-terminated string representing the item being inserted.

Returns The index position of the inserted string if successful, CB_ERR or CB_ERRSPACE otherwise.

CB_LIMITTEXT

When sent To limit the amount of text that can be added to the edit-control in a combo box.

wParam Contains the maximum number of characters allowed.

lParam Not used, must be 0.

Returns TRUE, always.

CB_RESETCONTENT

When sent Applications send this message whenever they want to remove all items from the list box of a combo box.

wParam Not used, must be 0.

lParam Not used, must be 0.

Returns CB_OKAY, always.

CB_SELECTSTRING

When sent To search a list box for the specified string and selects it, if found.

wParam −1 to start the search from the beginning of the list, or any other index position used as the starting search point. Any non −1 value starts the search one position after the index specified and then cycles back to the beginning of the list if no match was found.

lParam A null-terminated string pointer to the search prefix. The search is not case-sensitive.

Returns The index of the matching item if found, or CB_ERR.

CB_SETCURSEL

When sent To select a string in the list box of a combo box.

wParam Contains the index to the item being selected.

lParam Not used, must be 0.

Returns The index of the selected item if successful, CB_ERR otherwise.

CB_SETEDITSEL

When sent To select a set of characters from the edit-control of a combo box.

wParam Not used, must be 0.

lParam Low-order word — starting position, high-order word — ending position, of the characters being selected. If the low-order word is set to −1, the selection is removed. If the high-order word is set to −1, all characters from the starting character to the ending characters in the edit control of the combo box are selected.

Returns TRUE if successful, CB_ERR if the combo box has the CBS_DROPDOWNLIST style.

CB_SETEXTENDEDUI

When sent Selects the default or extended user interface.

wParam TRUE selects the extended user interface, FALSE selects the standard user interface.

lParam Not used, must be 0.

Returns CB_OKAY if successful, CB_ERR otherwise.

CB_SETITEMDATA

When sent Assigns a 32-bit value to a specific combo box item.

wParam Is the index to the item in question.

lParam Contains the new 32-bit value being associated.

Returns CB_ERR on error.

CB_SETITEMHEIGHT

When sent When an application wishes to set the height of a list box item or the selection field in a combo box.

wParam Selects which component of the combo box is having its height set. −1 targets the selection field, a value of 0 sets an item's height. If the combo box has the CBS_OWNERDRAWVARIABLE style, *wParam* identifies the individual item's index position.

lParam Contains the specified height, in pixels.

Returns CB_ERR when using an invalid height.

CB_SETLOCALE

When sent Applications send this message when wishing to set the current locale of a combo box. Locale identifiers represent country codes, and language identifiers used by the Windows national language support routines.

wParam Specifies the locale identifier for the combo box.

lParam Not used, must be 0.

Returns The previous locale if successful, CB_ERR otherwise.

CB_SHOWDROPDOWN

When sent Applications send this message whenever they wish to show or hide the list box of a combo box.

wParam   TRUE shows the list, FALSE hides the list.

lParam   Not used, must be 0.

Returns   TRUE, always.

CBN_CLOSEUP

When sent   When the list box of a combo box has closed.

wParam   Contains the identifier of the combo box.

lParam   Contains the handle of the combo box.

CBN_DBLCLK

When sent   When the user double-clicks a string within the list box of a combo box.

wParam   Contains the identifier of the combo box.

lParam   Contains the handle of the combo box.

CBN_DROPDOWN

When sent   When the list box of a combo box is about to be dropped down.

wParam   Contains the identifier of the combo box.

lParam   Contains the handle of the combo box.

CBN_EDITCHANGE

When sent When the user has made an editing change within the edit control of a combo box.

wParam Contains the identifier of the combo box.

lParam Contains the handle of the combo box.

CBN_EDITUPDATE

When sent When an edit control is about to display altered text.

wParam Contains the identifier of the combo box.

lParam Contains the handle of the combo box.

CBN_ERRSPACE

When sent When a combo box is unable to allocate sufficient memory for the requested operation.

wParam Contains the identifier of the combo box.

lParam Contains the handle of the combo box.

CBN_KILLFOCUS

When sent When a combo box has lost input focus.

wParam Contains the identifier of the combo box.

lParam Contains the handle of the combo box.

CBN_SELCHANGE

When sent When the user has made a new selection within the list box of a combo box.

wParam Contains the identifier of the combo box.

lParam Contains the handle of the combo box.

CBN_SELENDCANCEL

When sent When the user immediately makes a second selection after choosing an item within a list box, or closes the dialog box.

wParam Contains the identifier of the combo box.

lParam Contains the handle of the combo box.

CBN_SELENDOK

When sent When the user clicks on a valid selection within a list box and then closes the dialog box.

wParam Contains the identifier of the combo box.

lParam Contains the handle of the combo box.

CBN_SETFOCUS

When sent When a combo box receives the input focus.

wParam Contains the identifier of the combo box.

lParam Contains the handle of the combo box.

CPL_DBLCLK

When sent When the user double-clicks on a Control Panel application icon.

wParam Specifies the application number.

lParam Specifies the value returned by the control panel in the *lData* member of the **CPLINFO** or **NEWCPLINFO** structure.

Returns 0 if successful, !0 otherwise.

CPL_EXIT

When sent When an application supported by the Control Panel is about to exit.

Returns 0 if successful, !0 otherwise.

CPL_GETCOUNT

When sent When an application wishes to know how many applications are supported by the Control Panel.

Returns The number of applications available.

CPL_INIT

When sent When initializing a Control Panel DLL.

Returns !0 if successful, otherwise 0.

CPL_INQUIRE

When sent When requesting information about a Control Panel application.

wParam Contains the application number.

lParam Points to a **CPLINFO** structure used to return the requested information.

Returns 0 if successful.

CPL_NEWINQUIRE

When sent When requesting information about a Control Panel application.

wParam Contains the application number.

lParam Points to a **NEWCPLINFO** structure used to return the requested information.

Returns 0 if successful.

CPL_SELECT

When sent When the user selects a Control Panel application icon.

wParam Contains the application number.

lParam Specifies the value returned by the Control Panel in the *lData* member of the **CPLINFO** or **NEWCPLINFO** structure.

Returns 0 if successful, !0 otherwise.

CPL_STOP

When sent Sent for each closing application within the Control Panel.

wParam Contains the application number.

lParam Specifies the value returned by the Control Panel in the *lData* member of the **CPLINFO** or **NEWCPLINFO** structure.

Returns 0 if successful, !0 otherwise.

DM_GETDEFID

When sent When an application wishes to retrieve the identifier for a dialog box default push button.

Returns High-word, DC_HASDEFID; low-word, default push button identifier.

DM_SETDEFID

When sent When an application wishes to set the default push button in a dialog box.

wParam Contains the identifier for the new default push button.

Returns Always TRUE.

EM_CANUNDO

When sent When an application wishes to determine if an edit-control operation can be undone.

wParam Not used, must be 0.

lParam Not used, must be 0.

Returns TRUE if the operation can be undone, FALSE otherwise.

EM_EMPTYUNDOBUFFER

When sent When an application wishes to reset the edit-control undo flag.

wParam Not used, must be 0.

lParam Not used, must be 0.

EM_FMTLINES

When sent When an application wishes to turn soft line break characters on or off.

wParam TRUE inserts line break characters, FALSE removes line break characters.

lParam Not used, must be 0.

Returns The same value in *wParam*.

EM_GETFIRSTVISIBLELINE

When sent When an application wants the index to the top line in an edit control.

wParam Not used, must be 0.

lParam Not used, must be 0.

Returns The index to the uppermost visible line in an edit control.

EM_GETHANDLE

When sent When an application wants the handle to the memory allocated for an edit control's text.

wParam Not used, must be 0.

lParam Not used, must be 0.

Returns The memory handle if successful, 0 otherwise.

EM_GETLINE

When sent When an application wants a copy of a line of text from an edit control.

wParam Contains the line number being copied.

lParam Points to the buffer receiving the copied text.

Returns The number of characters copied into the buffer if successful, 0 otherwise.

EM_GETLINECOUNT

When sent When an application wishes to know the number of lines in an edit control.

wParam Not used, must be 0.

lParam Not used, must be 0.

Returns The number of lines or 1 if none exist.

EM_GETMODIFY

When sent When an application wants to know if an edit control's contents were changed.

wParam Not used, must be 0.

lParam Not used, must be 0.

Returns TRUE if the contents were modified, FALSE otherwise.

EM_GETPASSWORDCHAR

When sent To retrieve an edit-control's password character.

wParam Not used, must be 0.

lParam Not used, must be 0.

Returns The character to be displayed instead of the character being entered, NULL if no password character substitute exists.

EM_GETRECT

When sent To obtain the coordinates of an edit-control rectangle.

wParam Not used, must be 0.

lParam Points to a **RECT** structure returning the requested coordinates.

Returns A meaningless value.

EM_GETSEL

When sent To obtain the position of the current edit-control selection.

wParam Receives the starting position of the selection. (May be NULL.)

lParam Receives the ending position of the selection. (May be NULL.)

Returns Low-order word starting position, high-order word first character after the last selected character.

EM_GETWORDBREAKPROC

When sent When an application wants the address of the edit-control word-wrap function.

wParam Not used, must be 0.

lParam Not used, must be 0.

Returns The word-wrap function address if successful, NULL otherwise.

EM_LIMITTEXT

When sent To limit the amount of text allowed in an edit control.

wParam The maximum number of characters allowed.

lParam Not used, must be 0.

EM_LINEFROMCHAR

When sent To retrieve the line number of the line in an edit control that contains the specified character index.

wParam Contains the character index of the character in the line whose number is being retrieved.

lParam Not used, must be 0.

Returns The line number of the line in the multi-line edit control containing the character indexed.

EM_LINEINDEX

When sent To retrieve number of characters from the beginning of an edit control character to the specified line.

wParam Specifies the line number.

lParam Not used, must be 0.

Returns The character index of the line specified if successful, −1 otherwise.

EM_LINELENGTH

When sent To obtain the length of the line in an edit control that contains the character indexed.

wParam Contains the character index. A value of −1 returns the number of unselected characters on lines containing selected characters.

lParam Not used, must be 0.

Returns The length of the line in number-of-characters.

EM_LINESCROLL

When sent To scroll an edit control's text either vertically or horizontally.

wParam Contains the number of characters to scroll horizontally.

lParam Contains the number of characters to scroll vertically.

Returns TRUE if the message was sent to a multi-line edit control, FALSE if sent to a single-line edit control.

EM_REPLACESEL

When sent To replace the current selection in an edit control.

wParam Not used, must be 0.

lParam Pointer to a null-terminated string containing the replacement selection.

EM_SCROLL

When sent To vertically scroll an edit control's text.

wParam May be one of the following:

SB_LINEDOWN, SB_LINEUP, SB_PAGEDOWN, SB_PAGEUP

lParam Not used, must be 0.

Returns High-order word TRUE and low-order word containing the number of lines scrolled if successful. High-order word FALSE otherwise.

EM_SCROLLCARET

When sent To scroll the caret of an edit control into view.

wParam Not used, must be 0.

lParam Not used, must be 0.

Returns !0 if the message is sent to an edit control.

EM_SETHANDLE

When sent To set the handle to the memory section being used by an edit control.

wParam Contains the handle to the memory buffer.

lParam Not used, must be 0.

EM_SETMODIFY

When sent Used to set or clear an edit-control's modification flag.

wParam TRUE to set the modification flag, FALSE to reset or clear the modification flag.

EM_SETPASSWORDCHAR

When sent Used to set or remove an edit-control's password substitution character.

wParam Contains the substitution character. If 0, the user's entries are echo printed to the display.

lParam Not used, must be 0.

EM_SETREADONLY

When sent Used to set or clear the read-only style of an edit control.

wParam TRUE sets the read-only style, FALSE removes the read-only style.

Returns !0 if successful, 0 otherwise.

EM_SETRECT

When sent When an application wishes to set the formatting rectangle of an edit control.

wParam Not used, must be 0.

lParam Points to a **RECT** structure containing the bounding rectangle's coordinates.

EM_SETRECTNP

When sent When an application wishes to set the formatting rectangle of an edit control. This message is similar to **EM-SETRECT** except that the edit box is not redrawn.

wParam Not used, must be 0.

lParam Points to a **RECT** structure containing the bounding rectangle's coordinates.

EM_SETSEL

When sent Used by an application to select text within an edit control.

wParam Starting character position for the selection.

lParam Ending character position for the selection.

EM_SETTABSTOPS

When sent To set the tab stops within an edit control.

wParam The number of tab stops in the tab stop array pointed to by *lParam*. If 0, a default of 32 dialog box units per tab stop is used. If 1, *lParam* contains a value that specifies the distance between all tabs.

lParam Pointer to an array of unsigned integers specifying the tab stops in dialog units. If *wParam* is 1, then *lParam* contains a single value that is the standard tab spacing.

Returns TRUE if the tab stops were set, FALSE otherwise.

EM_SETWORDBREAK Obsolete

(*see* EM_SETWORDBREAKPROC.)

EM_SETWORDBREAKPROC

When sent To replace the default word-wrap function used to process edit control text.

wParam Not used, must be 0.

lParam Contains the address of the new word-wrap function.

EM_UNDO

When sent When an application wishes to undo the last operation in an edit control.

wParam Not used, must be 0.

lParam Not used, must be 0.

Returns TRUE, always for single-line edit controls. TRUE if the undo operation was successful for a multi-line edit control, or FALSE if unsuccessful.

EN_CHANGE

When sent When the user has made a change to the contents of an edit control.

wParam Identifier of the edit control.

lParam Handle of edit control.

EN_ERRSPACE

When sent When the edit control cannot allocate enough memory for the requested operation.

wParam Identifier of the edit control.

lParam Handle of the edit control.

EN_HSCROLL

When sent   When the user has clicked on the edit control's horizontal scroll bar.

wParam   Identifier of the edit control.

lParam   Handle of the edit control.

EN_KILLFOCUS

When sent   When the edit control is about to lose the input focus.

wParam   Low-word identifier of the edit control, high-word notification code.

lParam   Handle of the edit control.

EN_MAXTEXT

When sent   When an attempt is made to insert more characters into the edit control than allowed.

wParam   Identifier of the edit control.

lParam   Handle of the edit control.

EN_SETFOCUS

When sent   When an edit control is about to receive the input focus.

wParam Low-word identifier of the edit control, high-word notification code.

lParam Handle of the edit control.

EN_UPDATE

When sent When an edit control is about to display modified text.

wParam Identifier of the edit control.

lParam Handle of the edit control.

EN_VSCROLL

When sent When the user has clicked on an edit control's vertical scroll bar.

wParam Identifier of the edit control.

lParam Handle of the edit control.

FM_GETDRIVEINFO

When sent When an application wishes to know about the currently selected active drive from the File Manager window.

wParam Not used, must be 0.

lParam Pointer to the **FMS_GETDRIVEINFO** structure being filled with the requested information.

Returns !0 always.

FM_GETFILESEL

When sent When an application wishes to know about the currently selected file from the File Manager.

wParam Contains the index of the selected file.

lParam Pointer to the **FMS_GETFILESEL** structure being filled with the requested information.

Returns The index of the selected file.

FM_GETFILESELLFN

When sent When an application wishes to know about the currently selected file from the File Manager. The file can have a long filename.

wParam Contains the index of the selected file.

lParam Pointer to the **FMS_GETFILESEL** structure being filled with the requested information.

Returns The index of the selected file.

FM_GETFOCUS

When sent When an application wishes to know the type of the File Manager input focus window.

wParam Not used, must be 0.

lParam Not used, must be 0.

Returns The type of File Manager window that has the focus:

FMFOCUS_DIR, FMFOCUS_TREE, FMFOCUS_DRIVES, or
FMFOCUS_SEARCH

FM_GETSELCOUNT

When sent When an application wants to know the count of selected files in the active File Manager window.

wParam Not used, must be 0.

lParam Not used, must be 0.

Returns The number of selected files.

FM_GETSELCOUNTLFN

When sent When an application wants to know the count of selected files in the active File Manager window. The files can have long filenames.

wParam Not used, must be 0.

lParam Not used, must be 0.

Returns The number of selected files.

FM_REFRESH_WINDOWS

When sent When an application wants to repaint the File Manager's active window or all of its windows.

wParam TRUE repaints all windows, FALSE repaints only the active window.

lParam Not used, must be 0.

FM_RELOAD_EXTENSIONS

When sent When a File Manager extension or any other application wishes to reload all extension DLLs.

wParam Not used, must be 0.

lParam Not used, must be 0.

FMEVENT_INITMENU

When sent When the user selects the extension menu from the File Manager.

lParam Handle for the File Manager menu bar.

Returns 0 if successful.

FMEVENT_LOAD

When sent When the File Manager is loading an extension DLL.

lParam Pointer to an **FMS_LOAD** structure specifying the menu item's delta value.

Returns An extension DLL must continue to return TRUE while loading the DLL. When the extension DLL returns FALSE, communication with the extension DLL is terminated.

FMEVENT_SELCHANGE

When sent When the user has selected a filename within the File Manager.

Returns 0 if successful.

FMEVENT_TOOLBARLOAD

When sent When the File Manager is loading its toolbar.

lParam Pointer to **FMS_TOOLBARLOAD** structure containing the information about the button being added to the toolbar.

Returns TRUE if the DLL is loading the button, FALSE otherwise.

FMEVENT_UNLOAD

When sent When an extension DLL is being unloaded.

Returns 0 if successful.

FMEVENT_USER_REFRESH

When sent When the user has invoked the File Manager's Refresh command.

Returns 0 if successful.

LB_ADDFILE

When sent When an application wishes to add a filename to a directory listing in a list box.

wParam Not used, must be 0.

lParam Is a pointer to the filename being added.

Returns The index position of the inserted item if successful, LB_ERR otherwise.

LB_ADDSTRING

When sent When an application wants to add a string to a list box.

wParam Not used, must be 0.

lParam Is a pointer to the string being added.

Returns The index position of the inserted item if successful, LB_ERR or LB_ERRSPACE otherwise.

LB_DELETESTRING

When sent When an application wishes to delete a string from a list box.

wParam Contains the index to the item being deleted.

lParam Not used, must be 0.

Returns The number of strings remaining if successful, LB_ERR otherwise.

LB_DIR

When sent When an application wishes to add filenames to a list box.

wParam May be combinations of the following values:

DDL_ARCHIVE, DDL_DIRECTORY, DDL_DRIVES,
DDL_EXCLUSIVE, DDL_HIDDEN, DDL_READONLY,
DDL_READWRITE, DDL_SYSTEM

lParam A null-terminated string pointer specifying the file or files (if wild cards are present) to be added.

Returns A zero-based index of the last filename added to the list if successful, LB_ERR on error, or LB_ERRSPACE if no space was available.

LB_FINDSTRING

When sent To search a list box for the specified string.

wParam −1 to start the search from the beginning of the list, or any other index position used as the starting search point. Any non −1 value starts the search one position after the index specified and then cycles back to the beginning of the list if no match was found.

lParam A null-terminated string pointer to the search prefix. The search is not case-sensitive.

Returns The index of the matching item if found, or LB_ERR.

LB_FINDSTRINGEXACT

When sent To search a list box for the specific string.

wParam −1 to start the search from the beginning of the list, or any other index position used as the starting search point. Any non −1 value starts the search one position after the index specified and then cycles back to the beginning of the list if no match was found.

lParam A null-terminated string pointer to the search string. The search is not case-sensitive.

Returns The index of the matching item if found, or LB_ERR.

LB_GETANCHORINDEX

When sent Returns the index to a list box anchor item.

wParam Not used, must be 0.

lParam Not used, must be 0.

Returns The index to the anchor item, which is the last item selected by the user.

LB_GETCARETINDEX

When sent When an application wants to know which item in a list box has the highlighted focus rectangle.

wParam Not used, must be 0.

lParam Not used, must be 0.

Returns The index to the item with the focus rectangle.

LB_GETCOUNT

When sent When an application wants to know the number of items in a list box.

wParam Not used, must be 0.

lParam Not used, must be 0.

Returns The number of items in the list box if successful, LB_ERR otherwise.

LB_GETCURSEL

When sent When an application wants to know the index of the selected item in a list box.

wParam Not used, must be 0.

lParam Not used, must be 0.

Returns The index of the selected item if successful, LB_ERR otherwise.

LB_GETHORIZONTALEXTENT

When sent When an application wants to know how far the list in a list box can be scrolled horizontally.

wParam Not used, must be 0.

lParam Not used, must be 0.

Returns The number of pixels the list can be scrolled horizontally.

LB_GETITEMDATA

When sent To return the value associated with a list-box item.

wParam Contains the index to the item in question.

lParam Not used, must be 0.

Returns The 32-bit value associated with the item.

LB_GETITEMHEIGHT

When sent When an application wants to know the height of an item in a list box.

wParam Contains the index to the item in question.

lParam Not used, must be 0.

Returns The pixel height of the list box item if successful, LB_ERR otherwise.

LB_GETITEMRECT

When sent When the application wants to retrieve the bounding rectangle for a list box item.

wParam Contains the index of the item in question.

lParam Is a pointer to a **RECT** structure which receives the specified item's rectangular coordinates.

Returns LB_ERR on error.

LB_GETLOCALE

When sent To obtain the current list box locale. Locale identifiers represent country codes, and language identifiers used by the Windows national language support routines.

wParam Not used, must be 0.

lParam Not used, must be 0.

Returns A 32-bit value with the high-order word containing the country code, and the low-order word containing the language identifier.

LB_GETSEL

When sent When an application wants to know the selection status of a particular list box item.

wParam Contains the index of the item in question.

lParam Not used, must be 0.

Returns 0 if the item is not selected, !0 if selected, or LB_ERR on error.

LB_GETSELCOUNT

When sent When the application wants to know how many items in a multiple-selection list box were selected.

wParam Not used, must be 0.

lParam Not used, must be 0.

Returns The number of items selected for a multiple selection list box. LB_ERR for a single-selection list box.

LB_GETSELITEMS

When sent To obtain the indices of the selected items in a multiple selection list box.

wParam Contains the maximum number of items that can be placed into the buffer pointed to by *lParam.*

lParam Is a pointer to a buffer large enough to hold the maximum number of indices associated with the selected items.

Returns The number of indices placed into the buffer for a multiple selection list box. LB_ERR for a single-selection list box.

LB_GETTEXT

When sent When the application wants to retrieve a string from a list box.

wParam Contains the index to the text string being retrieved.

lParam Is a pointer to the buffer receiving the copied text.

Returns The number of characters in the string, not including the null-string terminator if successful, LB_ERR otherwise.

LB_GETTEXTLEN

When sent When the application wants to know the length of a list box string.

wParam Contains the index of the item in question.

lParam Not used, must be 0.

Returns The number of characters in the string, excluding the null-string terminator if successful, LB_ERR otherwise.

LB_GETTOPINDEX

When sent When the application wants to know the index for the first visible list-box item.

wParam Not used, must be 0.

lParam Not used, must be 0.

Returns The index to the first visible list box item.

LB_INSERTSTRING

When sent When an application wishes to insert a string into the list of a list box.

wParam Defines the position within the list where the new item is to be inserted. A value of −1 inserts the item at the end of the list.

lParam Is a pointer to a null-terminated string representing the item being inserted.

Returns The index position of the inserted string if successful, LB_ERR or LB_ERRSPACE otherwise.

LB_RESETCONTENT

When sent Applications send this message whenever they wish to remove all items from the list of a list box.

wParam Not used, must be 0.

lParam Not used, must be 0.

LB_SELECTSTRING

When sent To search a list box for the specified string prefix.

wParam −1 to start the search from the beginning of the list, or any other index position used as the starting search point. Any non −1 value starts the search one position after the index specified and then cycles back to the beginning of the list if no match was found.

lParam A null-terminated string pointer to the search prefix. The search is not case-sensitive.

Returns The index of the matching item if found, or LB_ERR.

LB_SELITEMRANGE

When sent When the application wishes to force or remove the selection of a single or consecutive items in a list box. Up to 65,536 items may be selected.

wParam If TRUE the specified item(s) is (are) selected. If FALSE the specified item(s) is(are) deselected.

lParam Low-order word contains the index of the first item being selected. High-order word contains the index of the last item being selected.

Returns LB_ERR on error.

LB_SELITEMRANGEEX (New Windows NT message)

When sent When the application wishes to force the selection of a single or consecutive items in a list box. Up to 65,536 items may be selected.

wParam Contains the index of the first item being selected.

lParam Contains the index of the last item being selected.

Returns LB_ERR on error.

LB_SETANCHORINDEX

When sent When an application wants to set the position for the anchor item.

wParam Contains the index of the item in the list of a list box being used as the anchor item.

lParam Not used, must be 0.

Returns 0 always.

LB_SETCARETINDEX

When sent When the application wants to set the focus rectangle in a list box.

wParam Contains the index of the item receiving the focus rectangle.

lParam If FALSE, the item is scrolled until it is completely visible. If TRUE, the item is scrolled until it is partially visible.

Returns LB_ERR on error.

LB_SETCOLUMNWIDTH

When sent When the application wants to set the width of columns in a list box.

wParam Contains the new column width, in pixels.

lParam Not used, must be 0.

LB_SETCOUNT

When sent When an application wishes to set the count of items in a no-data list box. This message is only valid for list boxes created with the LBS_NO-DATA style.

wParam Contains the new count of items in the list box.

lParam Not used, must be 0.

Returns LB_ERR or LB_ERRSPACE, on error.

LB_SETCURSEL

When sent When the application selects a string from a list box.

wParam Contains the index of the string being selected. If −1, no list box item is selected.

lParam Not used, must be 0.

Returns LB_ERR on error, or when *wParam* contains −1.

LB_SETHORIZONTALEXTENT

When sent When an application wishes to set the horizontal extent of a list box.

wParam Contains the number of pixels the list box can be horizontally scrolled.

lParam Not used, must be 0.

LB_SETITEMDATA

When sent When an application wants to associate a specific value with a list-box item.

wParam Contains the index of the item having its value set.

lParam Contains the 32-bit value being associated.

Returns LB_ERR on error.

LB_SETITEMHEIGHT

When sent When the application wants to set the height of an item or all items in a list box.

wParam Contains the index of the item whose height is being set (if the list box has the LBS_OWNERDRAWVARIABLE style), 0 otherwise (to set the height of all items).

lParam Contains the height, in pixels, of the item(s).

Returns LB_ERR on error.

LB_SETLOCALE

When sent When an application wishes to set the current list box locale. Locale identifiers represent country codes, and language identifiers used by the Windows national language support routines.

wParam Contains the locale identifier the list box will use for sorting when adding items.

lParam Not used, must be 0.

Returns The previous locale identifier if successful, LB_ERR otherwise.

LB_SETSEL

When sent When the application selects a string in a multi-selection list box.

wParam If TRUE, highlights the selected item. If FALSE, removes the highlight from the specified item.

lParam Contains the index of the string being selected. If −1, all items are highlighted or unhighlighted, based on *wParam*.

Returns LB_ERR on error.

LB_SETTABSTOPS

When sent To set the tab stops within an list box.

wParam The number of tab stops in the tab stop array pointed to by *lParam*.

lParam Pointer to an array of unsigned integers specifying the tab stops in dialog units.

Returns TRUE if the tab stops were set, FALSE otherwise.

LB_SETTOPINDEX

When sent When an application wants to guarantee that a list-box item is visible.

wParam Contains the index to the item in question.

lParam Not used, must be 0.

Returns LB_ERR on error.

LBN_DBLCLK

When sent When the user double-clicks on a list box string.

wParam Contains the list box identifier.

lParam Contains the list box handle.

LBN_ERRSPACE

When sent When there isn't enough memory for the list box to complete the requested operation.

wParam Contains the list box identifier.

lParam Contains the list box handle.

LBN_KILLFOCUS

When sent When a list box is about to lose the input focus.

wParam Contains the list box identifier.

lParam Contains the list box handle.

LBN_SELCANCEL

When sent When the user cancels the list box selection.

wParam Contains the list box identifier.

lParam Contains the list box handle.

LBN_SELCHANGE

When sent When the selection in a list box is about to change.

wParam Contains the list box identifier.

lParam Contains the list box handle.

LBN_SETFOCUS

When sent When a list box receives the input focus.

wParam Contains the list box identifier.

lParam Contains the list box handle.

MCI_BREAK

When sent An MCI message that sets the break key.

DWORD May be one of the following values:

MCI_NOTIFY, MCI_WAIT, MCI_BREAK_KEY,
MCI_BREAK_HWND, MCI_BREAK_OFF

LPMCI_BREAK_PARMS Points to an **MCI_BREAK_PARMS** structure.

Returns 0 if successful, MCI error code otherwise.

MCI_CLOSE

When sent An MCI message that terminates access to a device.

DWORD May be one of the following values:

MCI_NOTIFY, MCI_WAIT

LPMCI_GENERIC_PARMS Points to an **MCI_GENERIC_PARMS** structure.

Returns 0 if successful, MCI error code otherwise.

MCI_COPY

When sent An MCI message that copies data to the Clipboard. Flags and parameters are device specific.

DWORD May be:

MCI_NOTIFY, MCI_WAIT

LPMCI_GENERIC_PARMS Points to an **MCI_GENERIC_PARMS** structure.

Returns 0 if successful, MCI error code otherwise.

MCI_CUE

When sent An MCI message that cues a device for playback or recording.

DWORD May be:

MCI_NOTIFY, MCI_WAIT

For wave audio devices:

MCI_WAVE_INPUT, MCI_WAVE_OUTPUT

LPMCI_GENERIC_PARMS Points to an **MCI_GENERIC_PARMS** structure.

Returns 0 if successful, MCI error code otherwise.

MCI_CUT

When sent An MCI message that deletes data from an element and copies the item to the Clipboard.

DWORD May be:

MCI_NOTIFY, MCI_WAIT

LPMCI_GENERIC_PARMS Points to an **MCI_GENERIC_PARMS** structure.

Returns 0 if successful, MCI error code otherwise.

MCI_DELETE

When sent An MCI message that deletes data from an element.

DWORD May be:

MCI_NOTIFY, MCI_WAIT

For wave audio devices:

MCI_FROM, MCI_TO

LPMCI_GENERIC_PARMS Points to an **MCI_GENERIC_PARMS** structure.

LPMCI_WAVE_DELETE_PARMS Points to an **MCI_WAVE_DELETE_-PARMS** structure (for wave audio devices).

Returns 0 if successful, MCI error code otherwise.

MCI_FREEZE

When sent An MCI message that freezes the motion of the video display.

DWORD May be:

  MCI_NOTIFY, MCI_WAIT, MCI_OVLY_RECT

LPMCI_OVLY_RECT_PARMS Points to an **MCI_OVLY_RECT_PARMS** structure.

Returns 0 if successful, MCI error code otherwise.

MCI_GETDEVCAPS

When sent An MCI message that returns information about a device.

DWORD May be combinations of the following.
  For all devices:

  MCI_NOTIFY, MCI_WAIT, MCI_GETDEVCAPS_ITEM,
  MCI_GETDEVCAPS_CAN_EJECT,
  MCI_GETDEVCAPS_CAN_PLAY,
  MCI_GETDEVCAPS_CAN_RECORD,
  MCI_GETDEVCAPS_CAN_SAVE,
  MCI_GETDEVCAPS_COMPOUND_DEVICE,
  MCI_GETDEVCAPS_DEVICE_TYPE,
  MCI_GETDEVCAPS_HAS_AUDIO,
  MCI_GETDEVCAPS_HAS_VIDEO,
  MCI_GETDEVCAPS_USES_FILES

For animation devices:

MCI_GETDEVCAPS_ITEM,
MCI_ANIM_GETDEVCAPS_CAN_REVERSE,
MCI_ANIM_GETDEVCAPS_CAN_STRETCH,
MCI_ANIM_GETDEVCAPS_FAST_RATE,
MCI_ANIM_GETDEVCAPS_MAX_WINDOWS,
MCI_ANIM_GETDEVCAPS_NORMAL_RATE,
MCI_ANIM_GETDEVCAPS_PALETTES,
MCI_ANIM_GETDEVCAPS_SLOW_RATE

For videodisc devices:

MCI_GETDEVCAPS_ITEM,
MCI_VD_GETDEVCAPS_CAN_REVERSE,
MCI_VD_GETDEVCAPS_FAST_RATE,
MCI_VD_GETDEVCAPS_NORMAL_RATE,
MCI_VD_GETDEVCAPS_SLOW_RATE,
MCI_VD_GETDEVCAPS_CLV, MCI_VD_GETDEVCAPS_CAV

For video overlay devices:

MCI_GETDEVCAPS_ITEM,
MCI_OVLY_GETDEVCAPS_CAN_FREEZE,
MCI_OVLY_GETDEVCAPS_CAN_STRETCH,
MCI_OVLY_GETDEVCAPS_MAX_WINDOWS

For waveform audio devices:

MCI_GETDEVCAPS_ITEM, MCI_WAVE_GETDEVCAPS_INPUT,
MCI_WAVE_GETDEVCAPS_OUTPUT

LPMCI_GETDEVCAPS_PARMS Is a pointer to an **MCI_GETDEV-CAPS_PARMS** structure.

MCI_INFO

When sent An MCI message that returns string information from a device.

DWORD For all devices:

MCI_NOTIFY, MCI_WAIT, MCI_INFO_PRODUCT

For animation devices:

MCI_INFO_FILE, MCI_ANIM_INFO_TEXT

For video overlay devices:

MCI_INFO_FILE, MCI_OVLY_INFO_TEXT

For waveform audio devices:

MCI_INFO_FILE, MCI_WAVE_INPUT, MCI_WAVE_OUTPUT

LPMCI_INFO_PARMS Is a pointer to an **MCI_INFO_PARMS** structure.

Returns 0 if successful, MCI error code otherwise.

MCI_LOAD

When sent An MCI message that loads a file.

DWORD May be:

MCI_NOTIFY, MCI_WAIT, MCI_LOAD_FILE,
MCI_OVLY_RECT (for video overlay devices)

LPMCI_LOAD_PARMS Is a pointer to an **MCI_LOAD_PARMS** structure.

LPMCI_OVLY_LOAD_PARMS Is a pointer to an **MCI_OVLY_LOAD_-PARMS** structure (for video overlay devices).

Returns 0 if successful, MCI error code otherwise.

MCI_OPEN

When sent An MCI message that opens a device.

DWORD For all devices:

MCI_NOTIFY, MCI_WAIT, MCI_OPEN_ALIAS,
MCI_OPEN_SHAREABLE, MCI_OPEN_TYPE,
MCI_OPEN_TYPE_ID

For compound devices:

MCI_OPEN_ELEMENT, MCI_OPEN_ELEMENT_ID

For animation devices:

MCI_ANIM_OPEN_NOSTATIC, MCI_ANIM_OPEN_PARENT,
MCI_ANIM_OPEN_WS

For video overlay devices:

MCI_OVLY_OPEN_PARENT, MCI_OVLY_OPEN_WS

For audio waveform devices:

MCI_WAVE_OPEN_BUFFER

LPMCI_OPEN_PARMS Points to an **MCI_OPEN_PARMS** structure for all devices and compound devices.

LPMCI_ANIM_OPEN_PARMS Points to an **MCI_ANIM_OPEN_PARMS** structure, for animation devices.

LPMCI_OVLY_OPEN_PARMS Points to an **MCI_OVLY_OPEN_PARMS** structure, for video overlay devices.

LPMCI_WAVE_OPEN_PARMS Points to an **MCI_WAVE_OPEN_PARMS** structure, for audio waveform devices.

Returns 0 if successful, otherwise one of the following:

MCIERR_CANNOT_LOAD_DRIVER,
MCIERR_DEVICE_OPEN, MCIERR_DUPLICATE_ALIAS,
MCIERR_EXTENSION_NOT_FOUND,
MCIERR_FILENAME_REQUIRED,
MCIERR_MISSING_PARAMETER,
MCIERR_MUST_USE_SHAREABLE,
MCIERR_NO_ELEMENT_ALLOWED

MCI_PASTE

When sent An MCI message that pastes data from the Clipboard.

DWORD MCI_NOTIFY, MCI_WAIT

LPMCI_GENERIC_PARMS Is a pointer to an **MCI_GENERIC_PARMS** structure.

Returns 0 if successful, MCI error code otherwise.

MCI_PAUSE

When sent An MCI message that pauses the current operation.

DWORD MCI_NOTIFY, MCI_WAIT

LPMCI_GENERIC_PARMS Is a pointer to an **MCI_GENERIC_PARMS** structure.

Returns 0 if successful, MCI error code otherwise.

MCI_PLAY

When sent An MCI message that commences data output.

DWORD For all devices:

MCI_NOTIFY, MCI_WAIT, MCI_FROM, MCI_TO

For animation devices:

MCI_ANIM_PLAY_FAST, MCI_ANIM_PLAY_REVERSE, MCI_ANIM_PLAY_SCAN, MCI_ANIM_PLAY_SLOW, MCI_ANIM_PLAY_SPEED

For videodisc devices:

MCI_VD_PLAY_FAST, MCI_VD_PLAY_REVERSE, MCI_VD_PLAY_SCAN, MCI_VD_PLAY_SLOW, MCI_VD_PLAY_SPEED

LPMCI_PLAY_PARMS Is a pointer to an **MCI_PLAY_PARMS** structure.

LPMCI_ANIM_PLAY_PARMS Is a pointer to an **MCI_ANIM_PLAY_-PARMS** structure, for animation devices.

LPMCI_VD_PLAY_PARMS Is a pointer to an **MCI_VD_PLAY_PARMS** structure, for videodisc devices.

Returns 0 is successful, MCI error code otherwise.

MCI_PUT

When sent An MCI message that sets source, destination, and frame rectangles.

DWORD For all devices:

MCI_NOTIFY, MCI_WAIT

For animation devices

MCI_ANIM_RECT, MCI_ANIM_PUT_DESTINATION, MCI_ANIM_PUT_SOURCE

For video overlay devices:

MCI_OVLY_RECT, MCI_OVLY_PUT_DESTINATION, MCI_OVLY_PUT_FRAME, MCI_OVLY_PUT_SOURCE, MCI_OVLY_PUT_VIDEO

LPMCI_GENERIC_PARMS Is a pointer to an **MCI_GENERIC_-PARMS** structure.

LPMCI_ANIM_RECT_PARMS Is a pointer to an **MCI_ANIM_RECT_-PARMS** structure, for animation devices.

LPMCI_OVLY_RECT_PARMS Is a pointer to an **MCI_OVLY_RECT_-PARMS** structure, for video overlay devices.

Returns 0 if successful, MCI error code otherwise.

MCI_RECORD

When sent An MCI message that begins recording.

DWORD May be from the following values:

MCI_NOTIFY, MCI_WAIT, MCI_RECORD_INSERT,
MCI_FROM, MCI_RECORD_OVERWRITE, MCI_TO

LPMCI_RECORD_PARMS Is a pointer to an **MCI_RECORD_PARMS** structure.

Returns 0 if successful, MCI error code otherwise.

MCI_RESUME

When sent An MCI message that resumes a paused operation.

DWORD May be MCI_NOTIFY or MCI_WAIT.

LPMCI_GENERIC_PARMS Points to an **MCI_GENERIC_PARMS** structure.

Returns 0 if successful, MCI error code otherwise.

MCI_SAVE

When sent An MCI message to save a file.

DWORD For all devices:

MCI_NOTIFY, MCI_WAIT, MCI_SAVE_FILE

For video overlay devices:

MCI_OVLY_RECT

LPMCI_SAVE_PARMS Points to an **MCI_SAVE_PARMS** structure.

LPMCI_OVLY_SAVE_PARMS Is a pointer to an **MCI_OVLY_SAVE_-PARMS** structure, for video overlay devices.

Returns 0 if successful, MCI error code otherwise.

MCI_SEEK

When sent An MCI message that updates the current media position.

DWORD May be:

MCI_NOTIFY, MCI_WAIT, MCI_SEEK_TO_END,
MCI_SEEK_TO_START, MCI_TO, MCI_VD_SEEK_REVERSE (for
videodisc devices).

LPMCI_SEEK_PARMS Is a pointer to an **LPMCI_SEEK_PARMS** structure.

Returns 0 if successful, MCI error code otherwise.

MCI_SET

When sent An MCI message to set specific device information.

DWORD For all devices:

MCI_NOTIFY, MCI_WAIT, MCI_SET_AUDIO,
MCI_SET_DOOR_CLOSED, MCI_SET_DOOR_OPEN,
MCI_SET_TIME_FORMAT, MCI_SET_VIDEO, MCI_SET_ON,
MCI_SET_OFF

For animation devices:

MCI_SET_TIME_FORMAT, MCI_FORMAT_MILLISECONDS,
MCI_FORMAT_FRAMES

For CD audio devices:

MCI_SET_TIME_FORMAT, MCI_FORMAT_MILLISECONDS,
MCI_FORMAT_MSF, MCI_FORMAT_TMSF

For MIDI sequencer devices:

MCI_SEQ_SET_MASTER, MCI_SEQ_SET_OFFSET,
MCI_SEQ_SET_PORT, MCI_SEQ_NONE, MIDI_MAPPER,
MCI_SEQ_SET_SLAVE, MCI_SEQ_SET_TEMPO,
MCI_SET_TIME_FORMAT

For videodisc devices:

MCI_SET_TIME_FORMAT

For waveform audio devices:

MCI_WAVE_INPUT, MCI_WAVE_OUTPUT,
MCI_WAVE_SET_ANYINPUT, MCI_WAVE_SET_ANYOUTPUT,
MCI_WAVE_SET_AVGBYTESPERSEC,

MCI_WAVE_SET_BITSPERSAMPLE,
MCI_WAVE_SET_BLOCKALIGN, MCI_WAVE_SET_CHANNELS,
MCI_WAVE_SET_FORMATTAG,
MCI_WAVE_SET_SAMPLESPERSEC, MCI_SET_TIME_FORMAT

LPMCI_SET_PARMS Is a pointer to an **MCI_SET_PARMS** structure.

LPMCI_SEQ_SET_PARMS Is a pointer to an **MCI_SEQ_SET_PARMS** structure, for MIDI sequencer devices.

LPMCI_VD_SET_PARMS Is a pointer to an **MCI_VD_SET_PARMS** structure, for videodisc devices.

LPMCI_WAVE_SET_PARMS Is a pointer to an **MCI_WAVE_SET_-PARMS** data structure, for waveform audio devices.

Returns 0 if successful, MCI error code otherwise.

MCI_SOUND

When sent An MCI message that plays a registered system sound.

DWORD May be MCI_NOTIFY, MCI_WAIT, or MCI_SOUND_NAME.

LPMCI_SOUND_PARMS Is a pointer to an **MCI_SOUND_PARMS** structure.

Returns 0 if successful, MCI error code otherwise.

MCI_STATUS

When sent An MCI message that obtains specific device information.

DWORD   For all devices:

MCI_NOTIFY, MCI_WAIT, MCI_STATUS_ITEM

For animation devices:

MCI_STATUS_ITEM, MCI_ANIM_STATUS_FORWARD,
MCI_ANIM_STATUS_HPAL, MCI_ANIM_STATUS_HWND,
MCI_ANIM_STATUS_SPEED, MCI_STATUS_MEDIA_PRESENT

For CD audio devices:

MCI_STATUS_ITEM, MCI_STATUS_MEDIA_PRESENT

For MIDI sequencer devices:

MCI_STATUS_ITEM, MCI_SEQ_STATUS_DIVTYPE,
MCI_SEQ_STATUS_MASTER, MCI_SEQ_STATUS_OFFSET,
MCI_SEQ_STATUS_PORT, MCI_SEQ_STATUS_SLAVE,
MCI_SEQ_STATUS_TEMPO, MCI_STATUS_MEDIA_PRESENT

For videodisc devices:

MCI_STATUS_ITEM, MCI_STATUS_MEDIA_PRESENT,
MCI_VD_STATUS_DISC_SIZE, MCI_VD_STATUS_FORWARD,
MCI_VD_STATUS_MEDIA_TYPE, MCI_STATUS_MODE,
MCI_VD_STATUS_SIDE, MCI_VD_STATUS_SPEED

For waveform devices:

MCI_STATUS_ITEM, MCI_STATUS_MEDIA_PRESENT,
MCI_WAVE_INPUT, MCI_WAVE_OUTPUT,
MCI_WAVE_STATUS_AVGBYTESPERSEC,
MCI_WAVE_STATUS_BITSPERSAMPLE,
MCI_WAVE_STATUS_BLOCKALIGN,
MCI_WAVE_STATUS_CHANNELS, MCI_WAVE_FORMATTAG,
MCI_WAVE_STATUS_LEVEL,
MCI_WAVE_STATUS_SAMPLESPERSEC

For video overlay devices:

MCI_OVLY_STATUS_HWND, MCI_STATUS_ITEM,
MCI_STATUS_MEDIA_PRESENT

LPMCI_STATUS_PARMS: Is a pointer to an **MCI_STATUS_PARMS**
structure.

Returns 0 if successful, MCI error code otherwise.

MCI_STEP

When sent An MCI message that steps a player frame by frame.

DWORD

For all devices:

MCI_NOTIFY, MCI_WAIT

For animation devices:

MCI_ANIM_STEP_FRAMES, MCI_ANIM_STEP_REVERSE

For videodisc devices:

MCI_VD_STEP_FRAMES, MCI_VD_STEP_REVERSE

LPMCI_ANIM_STEP_PARMS Is a pointer to an **MCI_ANIM_STEP_-
PARMS** structure.

LPMCI_VD_STEP_PARMS Is a pointer to an **MCI_VD_STEP_PARMS**
structure, for videodisc devices.

Returns 0 if successful, MCI error code otherwise.

MCI_STOP

When sent An MCI message that stops all recording and playing operations.

DWORD May be:

MCI_NOTIFY, MCI_WAIT

LPMCI_GENERIC_PARMS Is a pointer to an **MCI_GENERIC_PARMS** structure.

Returns 0 if successful, MCI error code otherwise.

MCI_SYSINFO

When sent An MCI message that returns specific device information.

DWORD May be:

MCI_SYSINFO_INSTALLNAME, MCI_SYSINFO_NAME, MCI_SYSINFO_OPEN, MCI_SYSINFO_QUANTITY

LPMCI_SYSINFO_PARMS Is a pointer to an **MCI_SYSINFO_ PARMS** structure.

Returns 0 if successful, MCI error code otherwise.

MCI_UNFREEZE

When sent An MCI message that unfreezes the video image.

DWORD May be:

MCI_NOTIFY, MCI_WAIT, MCI_OVLY_RECT

LPMCI_OVLY_RECT_PARMS Points to an **MCI_OVLY_RECT_-PARMS** structure.

Returns 0 if successful, MCI error code otherwise.

MCI_WHERE

When sent An MCI message that returns the video clipping rectangle.

DWORD

For both animation and video overlay devices:

MCI_NOTIFY, MCI_WAIT

For animation devices:

MCI_ANIM_WHERE_DESTINATION,
MCI_ANIM_WHERE_SOURCE

For video overlay devices:

MCI_OVLY_WHERE_DESTINATION,
MCI_OVLY_WHERE_FRAME, MCI_OVLY_WHERE_SOURCE,
MCI_OVLY_WHERE_VIDEO

LPMCI_ANIM_RECT_PARMS Is a pointer to an **MCI_ANIM_RECT_-PARMS** structure, for animation devices.

LPMCI_OVLY_RECT_PARMS Is a pointer to an **MCI_OVLY_RECT_-PARMS** structure, for video overlay devices.

Returns 0 if successful, MCI error otherwise.

MCI_WINDOW

When sent An MCI message to set graphic window characteristics.

DWORD

For both animation and video overlay devices:

MCI_NOTIFY, MCI_WAIT

For animation devices:

MCI_ANIM_WINDOW_HWND, MCI_ANIM_WINDOW_STATE, MCI_ANIM_WINDOW_TEXT

For video overlay devices:

MCI_OVLY_WINDOW_HWND, MCI_OVLY_WINDOW_STATE, MCI_OVLY_WINDOW_TEXT

LPMCI_ANIM_WINDOW_PARMS Is a pointer to an **MCI_ANIM_-WINDOW_PARMS** structure, for animation devices.

LPMCI_OVLY_WINDOW_PARMS Is a pointer to an **MCI_OVLY_-WINDOW_PARMS** structure, for video overlay devices.

Returns 0 if successful, MCI error otherwise.

MIM_CLOSE

When sent To a MIDI input callback function when the input device is closed.

dwParam1 Unused.

dwParam2 Unused.

MIM_DATA

When sent To a MIDI input callback function when a MIDI message is received by the device.

dwParam1 The specific MIDI message received.

dwParam2 The time, in milliseconds, the message was received.

MIM_ERROR

When sent To a MIDI callback function when an invalid message is received by an input device.

dwParam1 The specific MIDI message received.

dwParam2 The time, in milliseconds, the message was received.

MIM_LONGDATA

When sent To a MIDI input callback function when an input buffer is returning filled with MIDI system-exclusive data.

dwParam1 Is a pointer to a **MIDIHDR** structure.

dwParam2 The time, in milliseconds, the message was received.

MIM_LONGERROR

When sent To a MIDI input callback function when an invalid system-exclusive message is received by a MIDI input device.

dwParam1 Is a pointer to a **MIDIHDR** structure.

dwParam2 The time, in milliseconds, the message was received.

MIM_OPEN

When sent To a MIDI callback function whenever a MIDI input device is opened.

dwParam1 Unused.

dwParam2 Unused.

MM_JOY1BUTTONDOWN

When sent To the window capturing joystick one when a button is pressed.

wParam Identifies which button was pressed and may be:

JOY_BUTTON1CHG, JOY_BUTTON2CHG,
JOY_BUTTON3CHG, JOY_BUTTON4CHG

combined with any of the flags in **MM_JOY1MOVE**.

lParam High-order word contains the joystick's current y-position, low-order word contains the current x-position.

MM_JOY1BUTTONUP

When sent To the window capturing joystick one when a button is released.

wParam Identifies which button was released and may be:

JOY_BUTTON1CHG, JOY_BUTTON2CHG,
JOY_BUTTON3CHG, JOY_BUTTON4CHG

combined with any of the flags in **MM_JOY1MOVE**.

lParam High-order word contains the joystick's current y-position, low-order word contains the current x-position.

MM_JOY1MOVE

When sent To the window capturing joystick one when the joystick position changes.

wParam Identifies which buttons are pressed and may be combinations of:

JOY_BUTTON1, JOY_BUTTON2, JOY_BUTTON3,
JOY_BUTTON4

lParam High-order word contains the joystick's current y-position, low-order word contains the current x-position.

MM_JOY1ZMOVE

When sent To the window capturing joystick one when the joystick z-position changes.

wParam Identifies which buttons are pressed and may be combinations of:

JOY_BUTTON1, JOY_BUTTON2, JOY_BUTTON3,
JOY_BUTTON4

lParam Low-order word contains the joystick's current z-position.

MM_JOY2BUTTONDOWN

When sent To the window capturing joystick two when a button is pressed.

wParam Identifies which button was pressed and may be:

JOY_BUTTON1CHG, JOY_BUTTON2CHG,
JOY_BUTTON3CHG, JOY_BUTTON4CHG

combined with any flags in **MM_JOY2MOVE**.

lParam High-order word contains the joystick's current y-position, low-order word contains the current x-position.

MM_JOY2BUTTONUP

When sent To the window capturing joystick two when a button is released.

wParam Identifies which button was released and may be:

JOY_BUTTON1CHG, JOY_BUTTON2CHG,
JOY_BUTTON3CHG, JOY_BUTTON4CHG

combined with any flags in **MM_JOY2MOVE**.

lParam High-order word contains the joystick's current y-position, low-order word contains the current x-position.

MM_JOY2MOVE

When sent To the window capturing joystick two when the joystick position changes.

wParam Identifies which buttons are pressed and may be combinations of:

JOY_BUTTON1, JOY_BUTTON2, JOY_BUTTON3, JOY_BUTTON4

lParam High-order word contains the joystick's current y-position, low-order word contains the current x-position.

MM_JOY2ZMOVE

When sent To the window capturing joystick two when the joystick z-position changes.

wParam Identifies which buttons are pressed and may be combinations of:

JOY_BUTTON1, JOY_BUTTON2, JOY_BUTTON3, JOY_BUTTON4

lParam Low-order word contains the joystick's current z-position.

MM_MCINOTIFY

When sent To a window whenever an MCI device has completed an operation.

wParam May be one of the following values:

MCI_NOTIFY_ABORTED, MCI_NOTIFY_SUCCESSFUL, MCI_NOTIFY_SUPERSEDED, MCI_NOTIFY_FAILURE

lParam The ID of the device initiating the callback.

Returns 0 if successful, MCI error code otherwise.

MM_MIM_CLOSE

When sent Whenever an MIDI input device is closing.

wParam The handle of the MIDI input device that was closed.

lParam Unused.

MM_MIM_DATA

When sent Whenever a MIDI message is received by a MIDI input device.

wParam The handle of the MIDI input device receiving the message.

lParam The specific MIDI message received.

MM_MIM_ERROR

When sent Whenever an invalid MIDI message is received.

wParam The handle of the MIDI input device receiving the message.

lParam The invalid MIDI message received.

MM_MIM_LONGDATA

When sent When a MIDI input buffer filled with system-exclusive data is returning.

dwParam1 The handle of the MIDI input device receiving the data.

dwParam2 Is a pointer to a **MIDIHDR** structure.

MM_MIM_LONGERROR

When sent When an invalid system-exclusive message is received.

dwParam1 The handle of the MIDI input device receiving the invalid message.

dwParam2 Is a pointer to a **MIDIHDR** structure.

MM_MIM_OPEN

When sent When a MIDI input device is opened.

wParam The handle of the opened MIDI input device.

lParam Unused.

MM_MOM_CLOSE

When sent When a MIDI output device is closed.

wParam The handle of the closed MIDI output device.

lParam Unused.

MM_MOM_DONE

When sent When a system exclusive buffer has been played and is being returned to the application.

wParam Contains the handle of the MIDI output device that played the buffer.

lParam Is a pointer to the **MIDIHDR** structure.

MM_MOM_OPEN

When sent When a MIDI output device is opened.

wParam The handle of the opened MIDI output device.

lParam Unused.

MM_WIM_CLOSE

When sent When a MIDI waveform input device is closed.

wParam Unused.

lParam Unused.

MM_WIM_DATA

When sent When a MIDI waveform input data is ready and the buffer is being returned to the application.

wParam Is a pointer to a **WAVEHDR** structure.

lParam Unused.

MM_WIM_OPEN

When sent When a MIDI waveform input device is opened.

wParam Unused.

lParam Unused.

MM_WOM_CLOSE

When sent When a MIDI waveform output device is closed.

wParam Unused.

lParam Unused.

MM_WOM_DONE

When sent When a MIDI waveform output buffer has been played or reset.

wParam Is a pointer to a **WAVEHDR** structure.

lParam Unused.

MM_WOM_OPEN

When sent When a MIDI waveform output device is opened.

wParam Unused.

lParam Unused.

MMIOM_CLOSE

When sent To an I/O procedure requesting that a file be closed.

lParam1 **mmioClose()** flags.

lParam2 Unused.

Returns 0 if successful, error code otherwise.

MMIOM_OPEN

When sent To an I/O procedure requesting that a file be opened or deleted.

lParam1 Is a pointer to a null-terminated string identifying the file in question.

lParam2 Not used, must be 0.

Returns 0 if successful, MMIOM_CANNOTOPEN or MMIOM_OUTOF-MEMORY is returned on error.

MMIOM_READ

When sent To an I/O procedure requesting that a file be read.

lParam1 Points to the buffer used to hold the input data.

lParam2 Identifies the number of bytes to read into the buffer.

Returns The number of bytes read, 0 if no more bytes are available, or −1 on error.

MMIOM_SEEK

When sent To an I/O procedure requesting that a file's current position be moved.

lParam1 The current position to move to based on *lParam2*.

lParam2 May be one of the following values:

SEEK_SET, SEEK_CUR, SEEK_END

Returns The new file position if successful, −1 otherwise.

MMIOM_WRITE

When sent To an I/O procedure requesting that a file be written.

lParam1 Points to the buffer containing the data being written.

lParam2 Contains the number of bytes to write.

Returns The number of bytes written if successful, −1 otherwise.

MMIOM_WRITEFLUSH

When sent To an I/O procedure requesting that data be written to a file and that data stored in any internal buffers be flushed.

lParam1 Points to the buffer containing the data being written.

lParam2 Contains the number of bytes in the buffer to write.

Returns The number of bytes written if successful, −1 otherwise.

MOM_CLOSE

When sent To a MIDI output callback function whenever a MIDI output device is closed.

dwParam1 Not used, must be 0.

dwParam2 Not used, must be 0.

MOM_DONE

When sent To a MIDI output callback function whenever a MIDI buffer has been played.

dwParam1 Is a pointer to a **MIDIHDR** structure.

dwParam2 Not used, must be 0.

MOM_OPEN

When sent To a MIDI output callback function whenever a MIDI output device is opened.

dwParam1 Not used, must be 0.

dwParam2 Not used, must be 0.

SBM_ENABLE_ARROWS (Windows NT)

When sent By the application to enable or disable scroll-bar arrows.

wParam May be one of the following:

   ESB_ENABLE_BOTH, ESB_DISABLE_LTUP,
   ESB_DISABLE_RTDN, ESB_DISABLE_BOTH

lParam Not used, must be 0.

Returns TRUE if successful, FALSE otherwise.

SBM_GETPOS

When sent Whenever the application wants to know the current position of the scroll bar thumb.

wParam Not used, must be 0.

lParam Not used, must be 0.

Returns The current position of the thumb.

SBM_GETRANGE

When sent Whenever an application wants to know the range of a scroll bar.

wParam Contains the minimum position.

lParam Contains the maximum position.

SBM_SETPOS

When sent Whenever an application wishes to set the position of a scroll bar thumb.

wParam Contains the new thumb position.

lParam Is TRUE if the new thumb position is to be redrawn, FALSE otherwise.

Returns If successful, the previous thumb position, 0 otherwise.

SBM_SETRANGE

When sent Whenever an application wishes to set the range of a scroll bar.

wParam Contains the minimum position.

lParam Contains the maximum position.

Returns 0 always.

SBM_SETRANGEREDRAW

When sent Whenever an application wishes to set the scroll range and redraw the scroll bar.

wParam Contains the minimum position.

lParam Contains the maximum position.

Returns If successful, the previous thumb position, 0 otherwise.

STM_GETICON

When sent When the application wants to retrieve the handle associated with an icon.

wParam Not used, must be 0.

lParam Not used, must be 0.

Returns The icon's handle if successful, 0 otherwise.

STM_SETICON

When sent When the application wishes to set the icon's handle.

wParam Contains the handle about to be associated with the icon.

lParam Not used, must be 0.

Returns The handle previously associated with the icon if successful, 0 otherwise.

WIM_CLOSE

When sent To a waveform input callback function when the waveform input device is closed.

dwParam1 Unused.

dwParam2 Unused.

WIM_DATA

When sent To a waveform input callback function whenever waveform input data is ready and the buffer is being returned to the application.

wParam Is a pointer to a **WAVEHDR** structure.

lParam Unused.

WIM_OPEN

When sent To a waveform callback function whenever a waveform input device is opened.

dwParam1 Unused.

dwParam2 Unused.

WM_ACTIVATE

When sent Used to note changes in the activation state of a window.

wParam LOWORD(wParam) is WA_ACTIVE, WA_CLICKACTIVE, or WA_INACTIVE. HIWORD(wParam) gives the window's minimized state.

lParam The window's handle.

Returns When processed by an application, a zero is returned.

WM_ACTIVATEAPP

When sent The application(s) is informed when a new task activates.

wParam TRUE if the window is being activated, FALSE otherwise.

lParam Gives the thread identifier when wParam is true.

Returns When processed by an application, a zero is returned.

WM_ASKCBFORMATNAME

When sent Obtains the name of a CF_OWNERDISPLAY Clipboard format.

wParam Gives the size of the buffer pointed to by *lParam*.

lParam A pointer to the buffer to receive the format name of the Clipboard.

Returns When processed by an application, a zero is returned.

WM_CANCELJOURNAL

When sent The journalling mode is cancelled by the user.

wParam Not used, must be zero.

lParam Not used, must be zero.

Returns This messages does not return a value.

WM_CANCELMODE

When sent Informs the window to cancel internal modes.

Returns When processed by an application, a zero is returned.

WM_CHANGECBCHAIN

When sent Informs the Clipboard viewer of the removal of a window from the chain.

wParam The handle for the window being removed from the Clipboard viewer chain.

lParam The handle of the next window in the chain.

Returns When processed by an application, a zero is returned.

WM_CHAR

When sent Signals that the user has pressed a character key.

wParam Gives the character code of the key.

lParam Gives the following information 0–15 for the repeat count (the number of times the keystroke is repeated). 16–23 gives the scan code. 24 indicates if the key is an extended key (function key, etc.) (for extended, 0 otherwise.) 25–28 reserved. 29 gives the context code (1 if ALT is also depressed, 0 otherwise). 30 gives the previous key state (1 if the key is down before the message is sent, or 0 if it is up). 31 gives the transition state (1 if the key is being released, or 0 if it is being pressed).

Returns When processed by an application, a zero is returned.

WM_CHARTOITEM

When sent The owner window is supplied list-box keystrokes.

wParam LOWORD returns value of key being pressed. HIWORD returns position of caret.

lParam Gives the handle of the list box.

Returns The action performed by the application in response to the message. A value of −1 or −2 means the application handled all aspects of selecting the item. No further action is required by the list box. A value of 0 or greater will be equal to the zero-based index of an item in the list box and asserts that the list box must perform the default action for the keystroke.

WM_CHILDACTIVATE

When sent Signals the activation of a child window.

Returns When processed by the application, a zero is returned.

WM_CHOOSEFONT_GETLOGFONT

When sent Obtains the **LOGFONT** structure for the Font dialog box.

wParam Not used, must be zero.

lParam A pointer to a **LOGFONT** structure.

Returns No return value.

WM_CLEAR

When sent To clear the current selection from an edit control.

wParam Not used, must be zero.

lParam Not used, must be zero.

Returns No value returned.

WM_CLOSE

When sent The system's Close menu command was selected.

Returns When processed by an application, a zero is returned.

WM_COMMAND

When sent When a command message is generated.

wParam LOWORD gives the ID of the menu item, control or accelerator. HIWORD gives the notification code if from a control, 1 when it is from an accelerator, 0 when from a menu.

lParam A handle for the control sending the message, NULL if message is from an accelerator or menu.

Returns When processed by an application, a zero is returned.

WM_COMPACTING

When sent A low memory condition is indicated.

wParam Compacting ratio. 0x8000 means a 50% ratio.

lParam Not used.

Returns When processed by an application, a zero is returned.

WM_COMPAREITEM

When sent To determine where a list or combo box item is located.

wParam Gives the ID of the control sending the message.

lParam A pointer to a **COMPAREITEMSTRUCT** structure.

Returns The relative position of the two items being compared. (−1 means item 1 precedes item 2, 0 means item 1 and 2 are equivalent, 1 means item 1 follows item 2 in the sorted order.)

WM_COPY

When sent The selected item is copied to the Clipboard from an edit control or combo box.

wParam Not used, must be 0.

lParam Not used, must be 0.

Returns No value returned.

WM_COPYDATA

When sent Data is passed to another application.

wParam The handle for the window that passes the data.

lParam A pointer to a **COPYDATASTRUCT** structure which contains the data.

Returns TRUE when the message is processed, otherwise FALSE.

WM_CPL_LAUNCH

When sent To start a control panel application.

wParam The handle of the window sending the message.

lParam A pointer to a string holding the name of the control panel application to be opened.

Returns If the application starts, TRUE is returned; otherwise FALSE is returned.

WM_CPL_LAUNCHED

When sent Signals the end of a control panel application.

wParam If the application was started, this value is TRUE, otherwise FALSE.

lParam Not used.

Returns The value returned by the application is ignored by this message.

WM_CREATE

When sent Signals the creation of a window.

wParam Not used.

lParam A pointer to a **CREATESTRUCT** structure. This stucture holds information about the window being created.

Returns Application returns a 0 to continue or a −1 to stop creation and destroy the window.

WM_CTLCOLORBTN

When sent Indicates that a button will be drawn.

wParam The handle to the display context for the button.

lParam The handle for the button.

Returns When processed, the handle to a brush used to fill the button will be returned.

WM_CTLCOLORDLG

When sent Indicates that a dialog box will be drawn.

wParam A handle to the device context for the dialog box.

lParam A handle to the dialog box.

Returns When processed, the handle to a brush used to fill the dialog box is returned.

WM_CTLCOLOREDIT

When sent Indicates that an edit control will be drawn.

wParam A handle for the device context of the edit control window.

lParam A handle for the edit control.

Returns When processed, the handle for a brush used to fill the edit control is returned.

WM_CTLCOLORLISTBOX

When sent Indicates that a list box will be drawn.

wParam A handle for the device context of the list box.

lParam A handle for the list box.

Returns When processed, a handle for a brush used to fill the list box is returned.

WM_CTLCOLORMSGBOX

When sent Indicates that a message box will be drawn.

wParam A handle for the device context of the message box.

lParam A handle for the message box.

Returns When processed, a handle for a brush will be returned. This brush paints the background of the message box.

WM_CTLCOLORSCROLLBAR

When sent Indicates that a scroll bar will be drawn.

wParam A handle for the display context of the scroll bar.

lParam A handle for the scroll bar.

Returns When processed, the handle for a brush used to fill the scroll bar is returned.

WM_CTLCOLORSTATIC

When sent Indicates that a static control will be drawn.

wParam A handle for the device context of the static control window.

lParam A handle for the static control.

Returns When processed, the handle for a brush used to fill the control is returned.

WM_CUT

When sent A selection is deleted from an edit control or combo box and copied to the Clipboard.

wParam Not used, must be 0.

lParam Not used, must be 0.

Returns No value returned.

WM_DDE_ACK

When sent Indicates that a DDE message has been received.

wParam A handle to the posting application.

lParam Holds packed parameters. These are unpacked using **UnpackDDE-lParam()**.

Returns No value returned.

WM_DDE_ADVISE

When sent To issue a request for a DDE data change update.

wParam A handle to the client window posting the message.

lParam Holds packed parameters. These are unpacked using **UnpackDDE-lParam()**.

Returns No value returned.

WM_DDE_DATA

When sent Data or notification of the availability of data is sent to a DDE client.

wParam A handle to the server window posting the message.

lParam Contains packed parameters that can be unpacked using **Unpack-DDElParam()**.

Returns No value returned.

WM_DDE_EXECUTE

When sent A command string is sent to a DDE server.

wParam A handle for the client window posting the message.

lParam A global memory object referencing a command string dependent on the window type involved in the conversation.

Returns No value returned.

WM_DDE_INITIATE

When sent To initiate a conversation with a DDE server application.

wParam A handle for the client window sending the message.

lParam LOWORD that identifies the application. The HIWORD that identifies the topic for the conversation.

Returns No value returned.

WM_DDE_POKE

When sent Unrequested data has been sent to a server.

wParam A handle that identifies the client window posting the message.

lParam Contains packed components unpacked using **UnpackDDElParam( )**.

Returns No value returned.

WM_DDE_REQUEST

When sent Data is requested from a DDE server.

wParam A handle identifing the client window sending the message.

lParam LOWORD contains a standard or registered clipboard format. HI-WORD contains an atom used to identify the requested data item.

Returns No value returned.

WM_DDE_TERMINATE

When sent Signals the end of a DDE conversation.

wParam A handle identifying the posting window.

lParam Not used, must be 0.

Returns No value returned.

WM_DDE_UNADVISE

When sent A DDE link is terminated.

wParam A handle used to identify the posting application.

lParam LOWORD holds the clipboard format for the item. HIWORD holds a global atom used to identify the item. If NULL, all WM_DDE_ADVISE links are terminated.

Returns No value returned.

WM_DEADCHAR

When sent Signals that a dead key was pressed by the user.

wParam Contains the character code of the dead key.

lParam Gives the following information: 0-15 for the repeat count (the number of times the keystroke is repeated). 16-23 gives the scan code. 24 indicates if the key is an extended key (function key, etc). Use 1 for extended, 0 otherwise. 25-28 reserved. 29 gives the context code (1 if ALT is also depressed, 0 otherwise). 30 gives the previous key state (1 if the key is pressed before the message is sent, or 0 if it is not). 31 gives the transition state (1 if the key is being released, or 0 if it is being pressed).

Returns When processed, a zero will be returned.

WM_DELETEITEM

When sent Signals that an owner-draw item or control was altered.

wParam Contains the ID of the control sending the WM_DELETEITEM message.

lParam A pointer to a **DELETEITEMSTRUCT** structure that holds information about the item deleted from the list box.

Returns When processed, a TRUE will be returned, otherwise FALSE.

WM_DESTROY

When sent Signals that the window is to be destroyed.

Returns When processed, a zero will be returned.

WM_DESTROYCLIPBOARD

When sent The owner is notified that the clipboard was emptied.

Returns When processed, a zero will be returned.

WM_DEVMODECHANGE

When sent Signals that the device-mode settings have changed.

wParam Not used, must be zero.

lParam A pointer to the device name.

Returns When processed, a zero will be returned.

WM_DRAWCLIPBOARD

When sent Signals that the clipboard contents have been changed.

Returns No value returned.

WM_DRAWITEM

When sent Signals that the owner-draw control/menu needs to be redrawn.

wParam Gives the ID of the control sending the WM_DRAWITEM message. (0 is sent if the message was generated by a menu.)

lParam A pointer to a **DRAWITEMSTRUCT** structure. This structure contains information about the item and the type of drawing to be done.

Returns When processed, a TRUE will be returned, otherwise FALSE.

WM_DROPFILES

When sent Signals that a file has been dropped.

wParam The handle of an internal structure that describes the dropped files.

lParam Not used, must be 0.

Returns When processed, a zero is returned.

WM_ENABLE

When sent Signals a changing enable state for a window.

wParam Use TRUE if a window is enabled and FALSE when the window is disabled.

lParam Not used, must be zero.

Returns When processed, a zero will be returned.

WM_ENDSESSION

When sent Signals if the Windows session is ending.

wParam TRUE when session is ended. Otherwise, FALSE.

lParam Not used, must be zero.

Returns When processed, a zero is returned.

WM_ENTERIDLE

When sent Signals an idle menu or modal dialog box.

wParam When MSGF_DIALOGBOX, a dialog box is idle. When MSGF_MENU, a menu is idle.

lParam A handle of the dialog or menu.

Returns When processed, a zero will be returned.

WM_ENTERMENULOOP

When sent Signals the entrance of a menu modal loop.

wParam TRUE if the menu is a popup menu and FALSE otherwise.

lParam Not used, must be zero.

Returns When processed, a zero will be returned.

WM_ERASEBKGND

When sent Signals the need to erase a window's background.

wParam A handle used to identify the device context.

lParam Not used, must be zero.

Returns When the background is erased, a non-zero value is returned. Otherwise, a zero is returned.

WM_EXITMENULOOP

When sent Signals the exit of a menu modal loop.

wParam TRUE if the menu is a popup and FALSE otherwise.

lParam Not used, must be 0.

Returns When processed, a zero will be returned.

WM_FONTCHANGE

When sent Signals a change in the font-resource pool.

wParam Not used, must be zero.

lParam Not used, must be zero.

Returns No value returned.

WM_GETDLGCODE

When sent Permits a dialog procedure to process control input.

Returns The following represent various return values:

DLGC_BUTTON for a button
DLGC_DEFPUSHBUTTON for a default push button
DLGC_HASSETSEL for EM_SETSEL messages
DLGC_RADIOBUTTON for a radio button
DLGC_STATIC for a static control
DLGC_UNDEFPUSHBUTTON for a non-default push button
DLGC_WANTALLKEYS for all keyboard input
DLGC_WANTARROWS for direction keys
DLGC_WANTCHARS for WM_CHAR messages
DLGC_WANTMESSAGE for all keyboard input
DLGC_WANTTAB for the TAB key

WM_GETFONT

When sent Obtains the font being used by a control.

wParam Not used, must be 0.

lParam Not used, must be 0.

Returns The handle for the font used by the control. If NULL, a system font is in use.

WM_GETHOTKEY

When sent Obtains the hot key's virtual key code.

wParam Not used, must be 0.

lParam Not used, must be 0.

Returns The virtual-key code of the hot key is returned. If NULL, no hot key is currently associated with the window.

WM_GETMINMAXINFO

When sent When a window changes its size or position.

wParam Not used.

lParam A pointer to a **MINMAXINFO** structure containing size or position information.

Returns When processed, a zero will be returned.

WM_GETTEXT

When sent To obtain the text that corresponds to a window.

wParam The number of characters to be copied plus the null character.

lParam A pointer to a buffer that holds the copied text.

Returns The number of characters actually copied.

WM_GETTEXTLENGTH

When sent Obtains the length of the text associated with a window.

wParam Not used, must be 0.

lParam Not used, must be 0.

Returns The length of the text, measured in characters.

WM_HOTKEY

When sent Signals that a hot key has been detected.

wParam Gives the ID of the hot key that generated the message.

lParam Not used.

Returns No value returned.

WM_HSCROLL

When sent Signals a click on a horizontal scroll bar.

wParam LOWORD gives a scroll bar value indicating the user's scrolling request. It will be one of the following. SB_BOTTOM means scroll toward lower right, SB_ENDSCROLL means end the scroll, SB_LINEDOWN means to scroll down one line, SB_LINEUP means to scroll up one line, SB_PAGE-DOWN means to scroll down one page, SB_PAGEUP means to scroll up one page, SB_THUMBPOSITION means to scroll to an absolute position, SB_THUMBTRACK means to drag the thumb to a given position, and SB_TOP means to scroll toward the upper left. HIWORD gives the current position of the thumb when LOWORD is SB_THUMBPOSITION or SB_THUMBTRACK.

lParam The handle of the scroll bar.

Returns When processed, a zero will be returned.

WM_HSCROLLCLIPBOARD

When sent Signals owner to scroll the contents of the Clipboard.

wParam A handle used to identify the Clipboard viewer window.

lParam LOWORD gives a scroll bar value indicating the user's scrolling request. SB_BOTTOM means scroll toward lower right, SB_ENDSCROLL means end the scroll, SB_LINEDOWN means to scroll down one line, SB_LINEUP means to scroll up one line, SB_PAGEDOWN means to scroll down one page, SB_PAGEUP means to scroll up one page, SB_THUMBPO-SITION means to scroll to an absolute position, and SB_TOP means to scroll toward the upper left. HIWORD gives the current position of the thumb if LOWORD is SB_THUMBPOSITION.

Returns When processed, a zero is returned.

WM_ICONERASEBKGND

When sent The minimized window is directed to fill the icon background.

wParam A handle indicating the icon's device context.

lParam Not used.

Returns When processed, a zero will be returned.

WM_INITDIALOG

When sent Initializes a dialog box.

wParam A handle used to identify the control about to receive the default keyboard focus.

lParam Initialization data obtained from **CreateDialogIndirectParam()**, **CreateDialogParam()**, **DialogBoxIndirectParam()**, or **DialogBox-Param()**.

Returns TRUE to set the keyboard focus to the control specified with *wParam*, otherwise FALSE.

WM_INITMENU

When sent Signals that a menu is to become active.

wParam A handle used to identify the menu.

lParam Not used.

Returns When processed, a zero will be returned.

WM_INITMENUPOPUP

When sent Signals that a pop-up menu is going to be displayed.

wParam A handle used to identify the pop-up menu.

lParam LOWORD gives the relative position of the menu item that activated the pop-up menu. HIWORD is TRUE if the menu is a System menu, FALSE otherwise.

Returns When processed, a zero will be returned.

WM_KEYDOWN

When sent Signals that a nonsystem key was pressed.

wParam The nonsystem key's virtual key code.

lParam Gives the following information. 0–15 for the repeat count (the number of times the keystroke is repeated). 16–23 gives the scan code. 24 indicates if the key is an extended key (1 for extended, 0 otherwise). 25–28 reserved. 29 gives the context code (0 always for this message). 30 gives the previous key state (1 if the key is down before the message is sent, or 0 if it is up). 31 gives the transition state (always 0 for this message).

Returns When processed, a zero will be returned.

WM_KEYUP

When sent Signals that a nonsystem key was released.

wParam The nonsystem key's virtual key code.

lParam A value from 0-15 holds the repeat count (ie. the number of times the keystroke is repeated). This count is 1 for a WM_KEYUP message. 16-23 gives the scan code. 24 tells if the key is an extended key (1 for an extended key, 0 otherwise). 25-28 are reserved. 29 gives the context code, always 0 for a WM_KEYUP message. 30 gives the previous key state, always 1 for a WM_KEYUP message. 31 gives the transition state, always 1 for a WM_KEYUP message.

Returns When processed, a zero will be returned.

WM_KILLFOCUS

When sent Signals that the keyboard focus is being lost by the window.

wParam A handle used to identify the window that has the keyboard focus.

lParam Not used.

Returns When processed, a zero will be returned.

WM_LBUTTONDBLCLK

When sent Signals that the left mouse button has been double-clicked.

wParam The following values are used for this parameter:

MK_CONTROL is set when the CTRL key is depressed
MK_MBUTTON is set when the middle mouse button is depressed
MK_RBUTTON is set when the right mouse button is depressed
MK_SHIFT is set when the SHIFT key is depressed

lParam LOWORD gives the x-coordinate of the cursor relative to the upper-left corner of the client area. HIWORD gives the y-coordinate of the cursor relative to the upper-left corner of the client area.

Returns When processed, a zero will be returned.

WM_LBUTTONDOWN

When sent Signals when the left mouse button is pressed.

wParam The following values are used for this parameter:

MK_CONTROL is set when the CTRL key is depressed
MK_MBUTTON is set when the middle mouse button is depressed
MK_RBUTTON is set when the right mouse button is depressed
MK_SHIFT is set when the SHIFT key is depressed

lParam LOWORD gives the x-coordinate of the cursor relative to the upper-left corner of the client area. HIWORD gives the y-coordinate of the cursor relative to the upper-left corner of the client area.

Returns When processed, a zero will be returned.

WM_LBUTTONUP

When sent Signals when the left mouse button is released.

wParam The following values are used for this parameter:

MK_CONTROL is set when the CTRL key is depressed
MK_LBUTTON is set when the left mouse button is depressed
MK_MBUTTON is set when the middle mouse button is depressed
MK_RBUTTON is set when the right mouse button is depressed
MK_SHIFT is set when the SHIFT key is depressed

lParam LOWORD gives the x-coordinate of the cursor relative to the upper-left corner of the client area. HIWORD gives the y-coordinate of the cursor relative to the upper-left corner of the client area.

Returns When processed, a zero will be returned.

WM_MBUTTONDBLCLK

When sent Signals that the middle mouse button has been double-clicked.

wParam The following values are used for this parameter:

MK_CONTROL is set when the CTRL key is depressed
MK_LBUTTON is set when the left mouse button is depressed
MK_MBUTTON is set when the middle mouse button is depressed
MK_RBUTTON is set when the right mouse button is depressed
MK_SHIFT is set when the SHIFT key is depressed

lParam LOWORD gives the x-coordinate of the cursor relative to the upper-left corner of the client area. HIWORD gives the y-coordinate of the cursor relative to the upper-left corner of the client area.

Returns When processed, a zero will be returned.

WM_MBUTTONDOWN

When sent Signals when the middle mouse button is pressed.

wParam The following values are used for this parameter:

MK_CONTROL is set when the CTRL key is depressed
MK_LBUTTON is set when the left mouse button is depressed
MK_RBUTTON is set when the right mouse button is depressed
MK_SHIFT is set when the SHIFT key is depressed

lParam LOWORD gives the x-coordinate of the cursor relative to the upper-left corner of the client area. HIWORD gives the y-coordinate of the cursor relative to the upper-left corner of the client area.

Returns When processed, a zero will be returned.

WM_MBUTTONUP

When sent Signals when the middle mouse button is released.

wParam The following values are used for this parameter:

MK_CONTROL is set when the CTRL key is depressed
MK_LBUTTON is set when the left mouse button is depressed
MK_RBUTTON is set when the right mouse button is depressed
MK_SHIFT is set when the SHIFT key is depressed

lParam LOWORD gives the x-coordinate of the cursor relative to the upper-left corner of the client area. HIWORD gives the y-coordinate of the cursor relative to the upper-left corner of the client area.

Returns When processed, a zero will be returned.

WM_MDIACTIVATE

When sent Signals when a MDI child window is activated.

wParam A handle for the child to activate (sending) or deactivate (receiving).

lParam Not used when sending message to MDI client and must be 0. When receiving a message from an MDI client this is the handle of the child to activate.

Returns When processed, a zero will be returned.

WM_MDICASCADE

When sent MDI child windows are arranged in a cascade format.

wParam The cascade flag (MDITILE_SKIPDISABLED), which prevents a MDI child window which has been disabled from being cascaded.

lParam Not used, must be 0.

Returns A TRUE is returned when successful, FALSE otherwise.

WM_MDICREATE

When sent Requests an MDI client to create a child window.

wParam Not used, must be 0.

lParam A pointer to an **MDICREATESTRUCT** structure.

Returns The handle to the new child window. If not successful, a NULL is returned.

WM_MDIDESTROY

When sent Closes an MDI child window.

wParam A handle to the child window to close.

lParam Not used, must be 0.

Returns A zero.

WM_MDIGETACTIVE

When sent Obtains the handle of the MDI child window that is active.

wParam Not used, must be 0.

lParam (Optional) A pointer to the maximized state flag variable.

Returns The handle of the active MDI child window.

WM_MDIICONARRANGE

When sent Minimized MDI child windows are arranged.

wParam Not used, must be zero.

lParam Not used, must be zero.

Returns No value returned.

WM_MDIMAXIMIZE

When sent A MDI child window is maximized.

wParam A handle to the child to maximize.

lParam Not used, must be zero.

Returns A zero.

WM_MDINEXT

When sent The next MDI child window is activated.

wParam A handle to the MDI child.

lParam When 0, the next child window is activated. If non-zero, the previous child window is activated.

Returns A zero.

WM_MDIREFRESHMENU

When sent A MDI frame window's menu is updated.

wParam Not used, must be zero.

lParam Not used, must be 0.

Returns The handle to the frame window menu when successful, NULL otherwise.

WM_MDIRESTORE

When sent Requests the MDI client to restore a child window.

wParam The handle used to identify the MDI child window.

lParam Not used, must be 0.

Returns A zero.

WM_MDISETMENU

When sent The MDI frame window's menu is replaced.

wParam A handle used to identify the new frame window menu, or NULL when this menu is not changed.

lParam A handle used to identify the new Window menu, or NULL when this menu is not changed.

Returns When successful, the handle to the old frame window menu is returned. Otherwise, a zero is returned.

WM_MDITILE

When sent MDI child windows are arranged in tiled format.

wParam Determines how windows are tiled. If MDITILE_HORIZONTAL, the windows are wide instead of tall. MDITILE_SKIPDISABLED does not allow disabled MDI child windows to be tiled. MDITILE_VERTICAL makes windows tall instead of wide.

lParam Not used, must be 0.

Returns TRUE when successful, FALSE when not successful.

WM_MEASUREITEM

When sent An owner-drawn control or item is being created.

wParam The value is 0 when the message is sent by a menu, non-zero when sent by a combo or list box.

lParam Points to a **MEASUREITEMSTRUCT** structure containing the dimensions of the object.

Returns True if the message is processed.

WM_MENUCHAR

When sent Signals the pressing of an unknown menu mnemonic.

wParam Low-order word corresponds to the ASCII value of the key pressed. High-order word is either MF_POPUP or MF_SYSMENU.

lParam Handle to the active menu.

Returns High-order word return value is either 0 — to signal need to discard character and beep, 1— signals to close the active menu, or 2 — signals the low-order word of the return value that contains the index of a menu item.

WM_MENUSELECT

When sent Signals the selection of a menu item by the user.

wParam Low-order word contains the identifier of the command menu item, or the menu-index if the item is a pop-up menu. The high-order word may be combinations of the following:

MF_BITMAP, MF_CHECKED, MF_DISABLED, MF_GRAYED, MF_MOUSESELECT, MF_OWNERDRAW, MF_POPUP, MF_SYSMEMU

lParam Identifies the menu selected by the user.

Returns 0 if the message was processed.

WM_MOUSEACTIVATE

When sent Signals a mouse click in an inactive window.

wParam Identifies the parent window of the selected window.

lParam Low-order word contains the hit-test value returned by the **DefWindowProc()** function. High-order word contains the identifier for the mouse message posted when the user clicked the mouse button.

Returns The function returns one of four values:

MA_ACTIVATE — activates the window and does not discard
the message
MA_NOACTIVATE — does not activate the window and does not
discard the message
MA_ACTIVATEANDEAT — activates the window and discards
the message
MA_NOACTIVATEANDEAT — does not activate the window but
does discard the message

WM_MOUSEMOVE

When sent Signals the movement of the mouse cursor.

wParam Any combination of:

MK_CONTROL, MK_LBUTTON,MK_MBUTTON,
MK_RBUTTON, MK_SHIFT

indicating which virtual keys are down.

lParam Low-order word contains the x-coordinate of of the cursor, high-order
word contains the y-coordinate of the cursor.

WM_MOVE

When sent Signals that the position of the window has changed.

lParam Low-order word contains the x-coordinate of the upper-left corner of
client area. High-order word contains the y-coordinate of the client area's
upper-left corner.

Returns 0 if the message is processed.

WM_NCACTIVATE

When sent The active state of the nonclient area is changed.

wParam TRUE to draw an active title bar or icon, FALSE draws an inactive title bar or icon.

Returns Ignored when *wParam* is TRUE, otherwise a return of TRUE instructs Windows to execute the requested draw, FALSE to ignore the requested change.

WM_NCCALCSIZE

When sent Determines the client area size and position of a window.

wParam If TRUE the application specifies the size of the client area, otherwise FALSE instructs Windows to determine the size.

lParam Points to an **NCCALCSIZE_PARAMS** structure containing the co-ordinates needed for the application to calculate the size and position of the client area.

Returns If *wParam* is FALSE, the return value should be 0. When *wParam* is TRUE, the return value may be 0 or any combination of:

WVR_ALIGNTOP, WVR_ALIGNLEFT, WVR_ALIGNBOTTOM, WVR_ALIGNRIGHT, WVR_HREDRAW, WVR_VREDRAW, WVR_REDRAW, WVR_VALIDRECTS

When *wParam* is TRUE and the return value is 0, the original client area is updated to the coordinates of the upper-left corner of the new client area.

WM_NCCREATE

When sent Signals a window is being created.

lParam Points to a **CREATESTRUCT** structure.

Returns TRUE to continue the creation of the window, FALSE signals **CreateWindow()** or **CreateWindowEx()**, to return a NULL handle.

WM_NCDESTROY

When sent Signals that the nonclient area of a window is being destroyed.

Returns 0 if the message was processed.

WM_NCHITTEST

When sent Signals a mouse action.

lParam Low-order word contains the x cursor coordinate relative to the upper-left corner of the screen, high-order word contains the y-coordinate.

Returns One of the following values:

HTBORDER, HTBOTTOM, HTBOTTOMLEFT,
HTBOTTOMRIGHT, HTCAPTION, HTCLIENT, HTERROR,
HTGROWBOX, HTHSCROLL, HTLEFT, HTMENU,
HTNOWHERE, HTREDUCE, HTRIGHT, HTSIZE,
HTSYSMENU, HTTOP, HTTOPLEFT, HTTOPRIGHT,
HTTRANSPARENT, HTVSCROLL, HTZOOM

WM_NCLBUTTONDBLCLK

When sent Signals the double-click of the left button on a nonclient portion of the window.

wParam Contains the hit-test code returned by **DefWindowProc()** after processing a **WM_NCHITTEST** message.

lParam Points to a **POINTS** structure containing the cursor's x- and y-coordinates relative to the upper-left corner of the display.

Returns 0 if the message is processed.

WM_NCLBUTTONDOWN

When sent Signals a left button press in the nonclient area.

wParam Contains the hit-test code returned by **DefWindowProc()** after processing a **WM_NCHITTEST** message.

lParam Points to a **POINTS** structure containing the cursor's x- and y-coordinates relative to the upper-left corner of the display.

Returns 0 if the message is processed.

WM_NCLBUTTONUP

When sent Signals the release of the left button in the nonclient area.

wParam Contains the hit-test code returned by **DefWindowProc()** after processing a **WM_NCHITTEST** message.

lParam Points to a **POINTS** structure containing the cursor's x- and y-coordinates relative to the upper-left corner of the display.

Returns 0 if the message is processed.

WM_NCMBUTTONDBLCLK

When sent Signals the double-click of the middle button on a nonclient portion of a window.

wParam Contains the hit-test code returned by **DefWindowProc()** after processing a **WM_NCHITTEST** message.

lParam Points to a **POINTS** structure containing the cursor's x- and y-coordinates relative to the upper-left corner of the display.

Returns 0 if the message is processed.

WM_NCMBUTTONDOWN

When sent Signals the press of the middle button in the nonclient area.

wParam Contains the hit-test code returned by **DefWindowProc()** after processing a **WM_NCHITTEST** message.

lParam Points to a **POINTS** structure containing the cursor's x- and y-coordinates relative to the upper-left corner of the display.

Returns 0 if the message is processed.

WM_NCMBUTTONUP

When sent Signals the release of the middle button in the nonclient area.

wParam Contains the hit-test code returned by **DefWindowProc()** after processing a **WM_NCHITTEST** message.

lParam Points to a **POINTS** structure containing the cursor's x- and y-coordinates relative to the upper-left corner of the display.

Returns 0 if the message is processed.

WM_NCMOUSEMOVE

When sent Signals mouse cursor movement in the nonclient area.

wParam Contains the hit-test code returned by **DefWindowProc()** after processing a **WM_NCHITTEST** message.

lParam Points to a **POINTS** structure containing the cursor's x- and y-coordinates relative to the upper-left corner of the display.

Returns 0 if the message is processed.

WM_NCPAINT

When sent Signals that a window's frame needs painting.

wParam Contains the handle to the update region.

Returns 0 if the message is processed.

WM_NCRBUTTONDBLCLK

When sent Signals the double-click of a right button on the nonclient portion of a window.

wParam Contains the hit-test code returned by **DefWindowProc()** after processing a **WM_NCHITTEST** message.

lParam Points to a **POINTS** structure containing the cursor's x- and y-coordinates relative to the upper-left corner of the display.

Returns 0 if the message is processed.

WM_NCRBUTTONDOWN

When sent Signals a right button press in a nonclient area.

wParam Contains the hit-test code returned by **DefWindowProc()** after processing a **WM_NCHITTEST** message.

lParam Points to a **POINTS** structure containing the cursor's x- and y-coordinates relative to the upper-left corner of the display.

Returns 0 if the message is processed.

WM_NCRBUTTONUP

When sent Signals a right button release in a nonclient area.

wParam Contains the hit-test code returned by **DefWindowProc()** after processing a **WM_NCHITTEST** message.

lParam Points to a **POINTS** structure containing the cursor's x- and y-coordinates relative to the upper-left corner of the display.

Returns 0 if the message is processed.

WM_NEXTDLGCTL

When sent The focus is changed to a different dialog box control.

wParam If *lParam* is TRUE, *wParam* identifies the control receiving the focus. If *lParam* is FALSE, *wParam* contains a flag indicating whether or not the previous or next control receives the input focus, 0 indicating that next control receives the focus, any other value giving the input focus to the previous control.

lParam TRUE or FALSE, see *wParam* description above.

Returns 0 if the message is processed.

WM_PAINT

When sent Signals that a window's client area needs painting.

wParam Not used.

lParam Not used.

Returns 0 if the message is processed.

WM_PAINTCLIPBOARD

When sent Requests that the owner redisplay the Clipboard contents.

wParam Specifies the clipboard viewer window.

lParam Pointer to a **PAINTSTRUCT** structure containing the coordinates of the client area to paint.

Returns 0 if the message is processed.

WM_PAINTICON

When sent Signals that the icon is to be painted.

wParam Not used.

lParam Not used.

Returns 0 if the message is processed.

WM_PALETTECHANGED

When sent Signals that the focus-window realized its palette.

wParam Is a handle to the window that changed the system palette.

lParam Not used.

WM_PALETTEISCHANGING

When sent A signal to Windows that the palette is changing.

wParam A handle to the window whose logical palette is being realized.

lParam Not used.

Returns 0 if the message is processed.

WM_PARENTNOTIFY

When sent Parent is notified of child-window activity.

wParam Low-order word may be one of the following:

  WM_CREATE, WM_DESTROY, WM_LBUTTONDOWN,
  WM_MBUTTONDOWN, WM_RBUTTONDOWN

The high-order word contains the child window identifier if the low-order word selects WM_CREATE or WM_DESTROY, otherwise the high-order word is undefined.

lParam Handle to the child window if the low-order word of *wParam* selects WM_CREATE or WM_DESTROY. Otherwise, it contains the x (low-order word) and y (high-order word) cursor coordinates.

Returns 0 if the message is processed.

WM_PASTE

When sent Clipboard data is inserted into an edit control.

wParam Not used.

lParam Not used.

Returns Does not return a value.

WM_POWER

When sent Signals that the system is entering suspended mode.

wParam May be one of the following values:

    PWR_SUSPENDREQUEST, PWR_SUSPENDRESUME,
    PWR_CRITICALRESUME

lParam Not used.

Returns Returns 0 for PWR_SUSPENDRESUME or PWR_CRITICAL-
RESUME. Otherwise, the return value is PWR_FAIL.

WM_QUERYDRAGICON

When sent A cursor handle is requested for a minimized window.

wParam Not used.

lParam Not used.

Returns Returns the handle to either the cursor or the icon to be displayed during the drag process.

WM_QUERYENDSESSION

When sent Requests the end of the Windows session.

wParam Is 0 if the user clicked on the Shutdown or Logoff options, !0 if the user selected the End Task option.

lParam Not used.

Returns TRUE if the request can be processed, FALSE otherwise.

WM_QUERYNEWPALETTE

When sent Permits a window to realize its logical palette.

wParam Not used.

lParam Not used.

Returns TRUE if successful, FALSE otherwise.

WM_QUERYOPEN

When sent Indicates that a minimized window should be restored.

wParam Not used.

lParam Not used.

Returns TRUE if successful, FALSE otherwise.

WM_QUEUESYNC

When sent CBT messages are delimited.

wParam Not used.

lParam Not used.

Returns 0 if the message is processed.

WM_QUIT

When sent Asks for permission to terminate an application.

wParam Contains the exit code passed to the **PostQuitMessage()** function.

lParam Not used.

Returns Does not have a return value.

WM_RBUTTONDBLCLK

When sent Signals the double-click of the right mouse button.

wParam Identifies which virtual keys are pressed; may be combinations of:

MK_CONTROL, MK_LBUTTON, MK_MBUTTON,
MK_RBUTTON, MK_SHIFT

lParam Low-order word contains the x cursor coordinate, high-order word contains the y cursor coordinate.

Returns 0 if the message is processed.

WM_RBUTTONDOWN

When sent Signals a press of the right mouse button.

wParam Identifies which virtual keys are pressed, may be combinations of:

MK_CONTROL, MK_LBUTTON, MK_MBUTTON, MK_SHIFT

lParam Low-order word contains the x cursor coordinate, high-order word contains the y cursor coordinate.

Returns 0 if the message is processed.

WM_RBUTTONUP

When sent Signals the release of the right mouse button.

wParam Identifies which virtual keys are pressed; may be combinations of:

MK_CONTROL, MK_LBUTTON, MK_MBUTTON, MK_SHIFT

lParam Low-order word contains the x cursor coordinate, high-order word contains the y cursor coordinate.

Returns 0 if the message is processed.

WM_RENDERALLFORMATS

When sent All clipboard formats are to be rendered by the owner.

wParam Not used.

lParam Not used.

Returns 0 if the message is processed.

WM_RENDERFORMAT

When sent Clipboard data to be rendered in specified format.

wParam Format to be used.

lParam Not used.

Returns 0 if the message is processed.

WM_SETCURSOR

When sent Signals a window to set the cursor shape.

wParam Handle of the window containing the cursor.

lParam High-order word identifies the mouse message, low-order word contains the hit-test code.

WM_SETFOCUS

When sent Keyboard focus has been obtained by the window.

wParam Contains the handle to the window losing the focus.

lParam Not used.

Returns 0 if the message is processed.

WM_SETFONT

When sent The font has been set for a control.

wParam Contains the handle of the font. NULL triggers the use of the system default font.

lParam If TRUE immediately redraws the control using the specified font.

Returns Does not return a value.

WM_SETHOTKEY

When sent A hot key is associated with a window.

wParam Contains the virtual key code of the new hot key or 0 which removes any previously set hot key.

lParam Must be 0.

Returns −1 — unsuccessful/invalid hot key, 0 — unsuccessful/invalid window, 1 — successful/ no other window has same hot key, 2 — successful/but another window has the same hot key.

WM_SETREDRAW

When sent Grants or restricts redrawing in a window.

wParam TRUE — sets the redraw flag, FALSE — resets the flag.

lParam Must be 0.

Returns 0 if the message is processed.

WM_SETTEXT

When sent Sets the text in a window.

wParam Must be 0.

lParam Null-terminated string pointer to the window text.

Returns TRUE if successful. LB_ERRSPACE or CB_ERRSPACE if there is insufficient memory to set the list or combo box text. CB_ERR if the combo box contained no edit control.

WM_SHOWWINDOW

When sent Signals if a window is to be hidden or shown.

wParam TRUE to show the window, FALSE to hide it.

lParam Identifies the status of the window in question. May be one of the following: SW_PARENTCLOSING, SW_PARENTOPENING. Contains a 0 if the message was sent as a result of a function call to **ShowWindow()**.

Returns 0 if the message is processed.

WM_SIZE

When sent Signals a size change in a window.

wParam Indicates the resizing option. May be one of the following:

SIZE_MAXIMIZED, SIZE_MINIMIZED, SIZE_RESTORED,
SIZE_MAXHIDE, SIZE_MAXSHOW

lParam High-order word contains the new client area's height, low-order word contains the new width.

Returns 0 if the message is processed.

WM_SIZECLIPBOARD

When sent Signals a change in the Clipboard size.

wParam Handle of the Clipboard viewer.

lParam Pointer to a **RECT** object containing the new Clipboard viewer client dimensions.

Returns 0 if the message is processed.

WM_SPOOLERSTATUS

When sent Signals when a print job is added or removed.

wParam Is SP_JOBSTATUS.

lParam Low-order word contains the number of jobs in the print queue.

Returns 0 if the message is processed.

WM_SYSCHAR

When sent Signals the press of a system-menu key.

wParam Contains the character code for the System-menu key.

lParam Bits 0-15 — contain the repeat count, bits 16-23 — contain the scan code, bit 24 is 1 if the key is an extended key, bits 25-28 — reserved, bit 29 is 1 if the ALT key is pressed, bit 30 contains the state of the key prior to the message, 1 if key was down, 0 if key was up, bit 31 contains the transition state, 1 if the key is being released, 0 if the key is being depressed.

Returns 0 if the message is processed.

WM_SYSCOLORCHANGE

When sent Signals the change in a system color value.

wParam Not used.

lParam Not used.

Returns None.

WM_SYSCOMMAND

When sent Signals the request of a system command.

wParam Identifies which type of system operation is being requested. May be one of the following:

   SC_CLOSE, SC_HOTKEY, SC_HSCROLL, SC_ICON,
   SC_KEYMENU, SC_MAXIMIZE, SC_MINIMIZE,
   SC_MOUSEMENU, SC_MOVE, SC_NEXTWINDOW,
   SC_PREVWINDOW, SC_RESTORE, SC_SCREENSAVE,
   SC_SIZE, SC_TASKLIST, SC_VSCROLL, SC_ZOOM

lParam If the system command was selected using the mouse, then *lParam* contains the x (low-order word) and y (high-order word) screen coordinates for the mouse cursor.

Returns 0 if the message is processed.

WM_SYSDEADCHAR

When sent Signals the press of a system dead key.

wParam Contains the character code of the system dead key.

lParam Bits 0-15 — contain the repeat count, bits 16-23 — contain the scan code, bit 24 is 1 if the key is an extended key, bits 25-28 — reserved, bit 29 is 1 if the ALT key is pressed, bit 30 contains the state of the key prior to the message, 1 if key was down, 0 if key was up, bit 31 contains the transition state, 1 if the key is being released, 0 if the key is being depressed.

Returns 0 if the message is processed.

WM_SYSKEYDOWN

When sent Signals the press of the ALT key in combination with another key.

wParam Contains the virtual-key code for the key being pressed simultaneously with the ALT key.

lParam Bits 0-15 — contain the repeat count, bits 16-23 — contain the scan code, bit 24 is 1 if the key is an extended key, bits 25-28 — reserved, bit 29 is 1 if the ALT key is pressed, bit 30 contains the state of the key prior to the message, 1 if key was down, 0 if key was up, bit 31 contains the transition state, 1 if the key is being released, 0 if the key is being depressed.

Returns 0 if the message is processed.

WM_SYSKEYUP

When sent Signals the release of a key that was pressed in combination with the ALT key.

wParam Contains the virtual-key code for the key being released while the ALT key is depressed.

lParam Bits 0-15 — contain the repeat count, bits 16-23 — contain the scan code, bit 24 is 1 if the key is an extended key, bits 25-28 — reserved, bit 29 is 1 if the ALT key is pressed, bit 30 contains the state of the key prior to the message, 1 if key was down, 0 if key was up, bit 31 scontains the transition state, 1 if the key is being released, 0 if the key is being depressed.

Returns 0 if the message is processed.

WM_TIMECHANGE

When sent Signals the setting of the system time.

wParam Must be 0.

lParam Must be 0.

Returns 0 if the message is processed.

WM_TIMER

When sent Signals the elapse of a time-out interval for a timer.

wParam Contains the timer ID.

lParam Either points to an application-specific callback function, or NULL if the message is to be posted in the application's message queue.

Returns 0 if the message is processed.

WM_UNDO

When sent The last operation in an edit control is undone.

wParam Not used.

lParam Not used.

Returns TRUE if successful, FALSE otherwise.

WM_USER

When sent Signals a range of message values. A value between 0 and (WM_USER −1) signals a Windows' message, WM_USER to 0x7FF signals private window class messages, 0x8000 through 0xBFFF are reserved for future Windows' messages, 0xC000 through 0xFFFF signals application-specific string messages, and values greater than 0xFFFF are reserved.

wParam Not used.

lParam Not used.

Returns None.

WM_VKEYTOITEM

When sent Supplies the list-box keystrokes to an owner window.

wParam High-order word contains the position of the caret. Low-order word contains the virtual key code for the key.

lParam Is the list-box identifier.

Returns A return value >= 0 indicates the index of a list box item and that the list box should perform the default action. A return value of −1 indicates that the list box should carry out the default action. A return value of −2 indicates that the application processed the list box item selection itself.

WM_VSCROLL

When sent Signals a click in a vertical scroll bar.

wParam Low-order word contains the user's scroll bar request, may be one of the following values:

SB_BOTTOM, SB_ENDSCROLL, SB_LINEDOWN, SB_LINEUP, SB_PAGEDOWN, SB_PAGEUP, SB_THUMBPOSITION, SB_TOP

The high-order word contains the current position for the thumb if the low-order word contains SB_THUMBPOSITION or SB_THUMBTRACK, otherwise the high-order word is unused.

lParam Identifies the control only if the message is sent by a scroll bar control. Otherwise, the parameter is unused.

Returns 0 if the message is processed.

WM_VSCROLLCLIPBOARD

When sent Signals the owner to scroll the contents of the clipboard.

wParam Contains the handle to the clipboard viewer.

lParam Low-order word may be one of the following scroll bar events:

SB_BOTTOM, SB_ENDSCROLL, SB_LINEDOWN, SB_LINEUP, SB_PAGEDOWN, SB_PAGEUP, SB_THUMBPOSITION, SB_TOP

The high-order word contains the current thumb position if the low-order word specifies the SB_THUMBPOSITION, otherwise the high-order word is unused.

Returns 0 if the message is processed.

WM_WINDOWPOSCHANGED

When sent Indicates that the size or position of a window has changed.

wParam Not used.

lParam Pointer to a **WINDOWPOS** structure containing the window's size and position.

Returns 0 if the message is processed.

WM_WINDOWPOSCHANGING

When sent Signals the new size or position of a window that is in the process of changing.

wParam Not used.

lParam Pointer to a **WINDOWPOS** structure containing the window's size and position.

Returns 0 if the message is processed.

WM_WININICHANGE

When sent Application(s) are signaled that the WIN.INI file has changed.

wParam Must be 0.

lParam Pointer to the null-terminated string representing the section of the WIN.INI file which has changed.

Returns 0 if the message is processed.

WOM_CLOSE

When sent The waveform output device is closed.

wParam Not used.

lParam Not used.

Returns None.

WOM_DONE

When sent The waveform output buffer has been played or reset.

wParam Pointer to the **WAVEHDR** structure identifying the buffer that has just be played or reset.

lParam Not used.

Returns None.

WOM_OPEN

When sent The waveform output device is open.

wParam Not used.

lParam Not used.

Returns None.

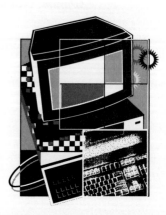

Index

868